THE OXFORD HANDBOOK OF

BUSINESS AND THE NATURAL ENVIRONMENT

THE OXFORD HANDBOOK OF

BUSINESS AND THE NATURAL ENVIRONMENT

Edited by

PRATIMA BANSAL

and

ANDREW J. HOFFMAN

OXFORD
UNIVERSITY PRESS

OXFORD
UNIVERSITY PRESS

Great Clarendon Street, Oxford OX2 6DP

Oxford University Press is a department of the University of Oxford.
It furthers the University's objective of excellence in research, scholarship,
and education by publishing worldwide in

Oxford New York

Auckland Cape Town Dar es Salaam Hong Kong Karachi
Kuala Lumpur Madrid Melbourne Mexico City Nairobi
New Delhi Shanghai Taipei Toronto

With offices in

Argentina Austria Brazil Chile Czech Republic France Greece
Guatemala Hungary Italy Japan Poland Portugal Singapore
South Korea Switzerland Thailand Turkey Ukraine Vietnam

Oxford is a registered trade mark of Oxford University Press
in the UK and in certain other countries

Published in the United States by Oxford University Press Inc., New York

British Library Cataloging in Publication Data
Data available

Library of Congress Cataloging in Publication Data
Data available

Typeset by SPI Publisher Services, Pondicherry, India
Printed in Great Britain
on acid-free paper by
MPG Books Group, Bodmin and King's Lynn

ISBN 978-0-19-958445-1

1 3 5 7 9 10 8 6 4 2

Contents

PART I: INTRODUCTION

PART II: BUSINESS STRATEGY

PART III: POLICY AND NON-MARKET
STRATEGIES

PART VI: MARKETING

PART VII: ACCOUNTING AND FINANCE

PART VIII: EMERGENT AND ASSOCIATED PERSPECTIVES

PART IX: FUTURE PERSPECTIVES

List of Figures

List of Tables

List of Abbreviations

....

AI	Appreciative inquiry
B2B	Business-to-business
BACT	Best available control technology
B&NE	Business and the natural environment
CAFE	Corporate average fuel economy
CAPT	Capital asset pricing model
CAR	Community action research
CBA	Cost benefit analysis
CDP	Carbon disclosure project
CITES	Convention on international trade in endangered species
CLSC	Closed–loop supply chain
CMS	Carbon management system
CSR	Corporate social responsibility
EPA	Environmental protection agency
EPR	Extended producer responsibility
EU	European Union
FDI	Foreign direct investment
FSC	Forest stewardship council
GDL	Goods-dominant logic
GHGs	Greenhouse gases
GIN	Greening of industry network
GSS	General social survey
IA	Integrated assessment
IB	International business
IS	Information systems
ISO	International organization of standardization
ISR	Industry self-regulation
LCA	Life cycle assessment
LEED	Leadership in energy and environmental design
LOOPE	Learning organizations with operational performance excellence
MEA	Millenium ecosystems assessment
MFA	Material flow analysis
MSI	Marketing science institute
NCE	New corporate environmentalism

NGO	Non-governmental organization
OECD	Organization for economic cooperation and development
OEM	Original equipment manufacturer
ONE	Organizations and the natural environment
POS	Positive organizational scholarship
PrAM	Product acquisition management
R&D	Research and development
REACH	Registration, evaluation and authorization of chemicals
RPS	Renewable portfolio standard
SD	Sustainable development
SDL	Service dominant logic
SFI	Sustainable forestry initiative
TCA	Transaction cost analysis
TRI	Toxics release industry
UNCED	United Nations conference on environment and development
UNPRI	United Nations principles for responsible investment
WEEE	Waste electrical and electronics equipment
WHO	World health organization

List of Contributors

Editors

Pratima Bansal Professor in the Ivey School of Business, University of Western Ontario. She also directs Ivey's Centre for Building Sustainable Value and is the Executive Director of the Network for Business Sustainability.

Andrew J. Hoffman Holcim (US) Professor of Sustainable Enterprise with joint appointments in the Ross School of Business and the School of Natural Resources & Environment, University of Michigan. He also serves as Director of the Erb Institute for Global Sustainable Enterprise.

Contributing Authors

James D. Abbey Doctoral Candidate in Supply Chain and Information Systems, Smeal College of Business, Pennsylvania State University.

Ryan Anderson Associate at Winston & Strawn LLP.

Subhabrata Bobby Banerjee Professor of Management and Associate Dean of Research, College of Business, University of Western Sydney.

David P. Baron David S. and Ann M. Barlow Professor of Political Economy and Strategy, Emeritus, Graduate School of Business, Stanford University.

Rob Bauer Professor of Finance, Maastricht University and Director of the European Centre for Corporate Engagement (ECCE), Netherlands.

Max H. Bazerman Jesse Isidor Straus Professor of Business Administration, Harvard Business School, Harvard University.

Stephanie Bertels Assistant Professor, Beedie School of Business, Simon Fraser University.

Jean-Louis Bertrand Associate Professor of Finance, and Banking and Risk Management Chairholder, ESSCA Ecole de Management, LUNAM University.

Krista Bondy Assistant Professor in Corporate Social Responsibility and Environmental Management, University of Bath.

Frank Boons Associate Professor, Public Administration Department, Erasmus University Rotterdam, Netherlands.

Nola Buhr Professor of Accounting, Edwards School of Business, University of Saskatchewan.

Charles H. Cho Associate Professor of Accounting at ESSEC Business School.

Petra Christmann Associate Professor of Management and Global Business, Rutgers Business School, Rutgers University.

Cary Coglianese Edward B. Shils Professor of Law, Professor of Political Science, and Director of the Penn Program on Regulation, Law School, University of Pennsylvania.

Magali A. Delmas Professor of Management, Anderson School of Management and the Institute of the Environment and Sustainability, University of California, Los Angeles.

Jeroen Derwall Assistant Professor of Finance, Maastricht University, European Centre for Corporate Engagement (ECCE), and Assistant Professor, Tilburg Sustainability Center (TSC), Tilburg University, Netherlands.

Timothy M. Devinney Professor of Strategy, Faculty of Business, University of Technology, Sydney, Australia.

John R. Ehrenfeld retired Director of the Program on Technology, Business, and Environment, MIT, retired Executive Director of the International Society for Industrial Ecology, and now on the adjunct faculty, Marlboro College Graduate Center.

John Elkington Co-Founder and Executive Chairman, Volans Ventures, and Co-Founder and Non-Executive Director, Sustainability.

Samantha Fairclough Assistant Professor of strategic Management and Enterpreneurship, School of Business Administration University of Mississippi.

Linda C. Forbes Associate Professor of Organization Studies, Ancell School of Business, Western Connecticut State University.

Andrew D. Gershoff Associate Professor of Marketing, McCombs School of Business, University of Texas, Austin.

Thomas N. Gladwin Max McGraw Professor of Sustainable Enterprise, with joint appointments in the Ross School of Business and the School of Natural Resources & Environment, University of Michigan. He also serves as Associate Director of the Erb Institute for Global Sustainable Enterprise.

Rob Gray Professor of Social and Environmental Accounting, Director of the Centre for Social and Environmental Accounting Research, School of Management, University of St Andrews, Scotland.

V. Daniel R. Guide, Jr. Professor of Operations & Supply Chain Management, Smeal College of Business, Pennsylvania State University.

Stuart L. Hart Samuel C. Johnson Chair in Sustainable Global Enterprise and Professor of Management, Cornell University's Johnson School of Management.

Irene M. Herremans CMA-Alberta Faculty Fellow, Haskayne School of Business, and adjunct Professor in Environmental Design, University of Calgary, Calgary, Alberta, Canada.

Jennifer Howard-Grenville Associate Professor of Management, Lundquist College of Business, University of Oregon.

Julie R. Irwin Professor of Marketing and Business, Government, and Society, McCombs School of Business, University of Texas, Austin.

John M. Jermier Exide Distinguished Professor of Sustainable Enterprise Research, College of Business, University of South Florida.

George Kassinis Associate Professor of Strategy, Department of Public and Business Administration, University of Cyprus, Cyprus.

Andrew King Professor, Tuck School of Business, Dartmouth College.

Robert D. Klassen Professor of Operations Management and Magna International Inc. Chair in Business Administration, Ivey Business School, University of Western Ontario.

Min-Dong Paul Lee Assistant Professor, Department of Management & Organization, College of Business Administration, University of South Florida.

Michael Lenox Samuel L. Slover Professor of Business, Darden School of Business, University of Virginia.

David L. Levy Chair of the Department of Management and Marketing, College of Management, University of Massachusetts, Boston, and Director of the Center for Sustainable Enterprise and Regional Competitiveness.

Benyamin B. Lichtenstein Associate Professor of Management and Entrepreneurship, College of Management, University of Massachusetts, Boston.

Reid Lifset Resident Scholar in Industrial Ecology, and Associate Director of the Industrial Environmental Management Program, Yale School of Forestry & Environmental Studies, and Editor-in-Chief of the *Journal of Industrial Ecology*.

Michael Lounsbury Alex Hamilton Professor, School of Business and the National Institute for Nanotechnology, University of Alberta.

Charmian Love Chief Executive, Volans Ventures.

Thomas P. Lyon Dow Professor of Sustainable Science, Technology and Commerce, with joint appointments in the Ross School of Business and the School of Natural Resources & Environment, University of Michigan. He also serves as Director of the Erb Institute for Global Sustainable Enterprise.

Dirk Matten Hewlett-Packard Chair in Corporate Social Responsibility, and Professor of Strategy, Schulich School of Business, York University, Toronto.

Nigel P. Melville Assistant Professor of Information Systems, Ross School of Business, University of Michigan.

Amy Minto Doctoral Candidate in Management, Lundquist College of Business, University of Oregon.

Jenny Mish Assistant Professor of Marketing, Mendoza College of Business, University of Notre Dame.

Dennis M. Patten Professor of Accounting, College of Business, Illinois State University.

James E. Post John F. Smith, Jr. Professor of Management, School of Management, Boston University.

Andrea M. Prado Assistant Professor, INCAE Business School.

Jorge Rivera Associate Professor of Strategic Management and Public Policy, School of Business, George Washington University.

Robin W. Roberts Al and Nancy Burnett Eminent Scholar, Kenneth G. Dixon School of Accounting, University of Central Florida.

Nigel Roome Professor of Governance, Corporate Responsibility and Sustainable Development, Vlerick Leuven Ghent Management School, Belgium.

Bryan R. Routledge Associate Professor of Finance, Tepper School of Business, Carnegie Mellon University.

Michael V. Russo Lundquist Professor of Sustainable Management, Lundquist College of Business, University of Oregon.

Debra L. Scammon Emma Eccles Jones Professor of Marketing, David Eccles School of Business, University of Utah.

Paul Shrivastava David O'Brien Distinguished Professor of Sustainable Enterprise, and Director of the David O'Brien Centre for Sustainable Enterprise, John Molson School of Business, Concordia University.

Lisa L. Shu Doctoral Candidate in Organizational Behavior and Psychology, Harvard Business School, Harvard University.

Bernard Sinclair-Desgagné International Economics and Governance Chair, and Chairman, International Business Department, HEC Montréal.

Sara B. Soderstrom Post Doctoral Fellow, Erb Institute for Global Sustainable Enterprise, University of Michigan.

Glen Taylor Associate Professor of Strategy and International Business, College of Business and Economics, California State University, East Bay.

Michael W. Toffel Associate Professor of Business Administration, Technology and Operations Management Unit, Harvard Business School, Harvard University.

Leigh Plunkett Tost Post-Doctoral Associate, Center for Leadership and Strategic Thinking, Foster School of Business, University of Washington.

Stephan Vachon Assistant Professor, Ivey Business School, University of Western Ontario.

Kimberly A. Wade-Benzoni Associate Professor of Management, and Center of Leadership and Ethics Scholar, Fuqua School of Business, Duke University.

Klaus Weber Associate Professor of Management & Organizations, Kellogg School of Management, Northwestern University.

Jeffrey G. York Assistant Professor of Management and Entrepreneurship, Leeds School of Business, University of Colorado.

PART I

INTRODUCTION

CHAPTER 1

RETROSPECTIVE, PERSPECTIVE, AND PROSPECTIVE: INTRODUCTION TO THE OXFORD HANDBOOK ON BUSINESS AND THE NATURAL ENVIRONMENT

ANDREW J. HOFFMAN
AND PRATIMA BANSAL

THE twentieth century witnessed unprecedented economic growth and human prosperity. World population increased by a factor of four, the world economy increased by a factor of fourteen (Thomas 2002), and average life expectancy increased by almost two-thirds (World Resources Institute 1994). In the US alone, life expectancy rose from 47.3 to 77.3 between the years 1900 and 2002 (National Center For Health Statistics 2004). But, this progress has been accompanied by unintended and, at times, extreme damage to the natural environment on which it was based.

By 2005, the Millennium Ecosystem Assessment, a study commissioned by the United Nations and involving more than 1,360 experts worldwide, concluded that humans have changed the Earth's ecosystems in the second half of the twentieth century "more rapidly and extensively than in any comparable period of time in human history" (2005: 1). Of the twenty-four global ecosystem services that were analyzed, 60 percent were found to be degraded or used unsustainably. Since the 1960s, the "modern environmental movement" had been calling attention to this outcome with an ever-growing list of environmental problems and crises. What began as a media focus on water and air issues, expanded into areas of toxic substances, hazardous waste sites, ozone depletion, acid rain, solid waste disposal, endocrine disruption, environmental racism, climate change and others.

And with this growing list of concerns, the corporate sector became increasingly seen not only as the cause of the environmental problems but also as the source of the solutions. And with this shift in emphasis, the concept of corporate environmentalism was born. Over the second half of the twentieth century, this concept was redefined through multiple iterations with ever-increasing complexity of the understanding of the intersection of business activity and environmental protection. As a result, conceptions of corporate environmentalism as simply regulatory compliance in the 1970s gave way to newer management conceptions of pollution prevention, total quality environmental management, industrial ecology, life-cycle analysis, environmental strategy, carbon footprinting, and sustainable development. By 2010, the empirical domain of business and the natural environment (B&NE) had become an established domain of management practice.

Concurrent with this evolution in corporate practice has been the emergence of academic research focused on business decision-making, firm behavior, and the protection of the natural environment. What began as a modest offshoot of management research in the late 1980s has grown into a maturing area of study within the management sciences, encompassing a wide range of disciplines. And now, with the established body of literature that has been built, it is possible to step back and view the state of this field in terms of where it has been and where it is going.

This chapter serves as an introduction to *The Oxford Handbook on Business and the Natural Environment*, whose purpose is to consider what is distinct about existing B&NE research and present the multiple directions in which the field is going. While an expanding number of books on the topic are also evidence of the growth of interest in this field, this Handbook stands out for its encompassing goal of comprehensively surveying the field of B&NE from a multi-disciplinary perspective, targeting an academic audience. Our objective is for the contents of this volume to serve as a definitive compendium of the past, present, and future work in this growing field.

In the following pages of this introduction, we provide a three-part treatment of the themes and focus of the chapters in this Handbook. The first is a *retrospective*, discussing in broad terms the history of B&NE. The second is a *perspective*, considering the central themes in the field as they exist today. The third is a *prospective*, presenting what we find to be common and overarching themes and, therefore, fruitful areas of future research.

Retrospective

In considering how the B&NE field arrived at its present state, it is useful to consider its trajectory both as an empirical phenomenon and as the academic endeavor that seeks to understand it.

Environmental issues within business management

The history of business and the natural environment can be traced back more than 500 years.[1] However, the issues of relevance to the research in this Handbook more commonly locate on events and issues that date from the mid twentieth century. The decade of the 1960s marks the beginning of concerted and sustained critical analysis of B&NE, marking the dawn of the "modern" environmental movement.[2]

With this as a starting point, the history of B&NE has evolved through periods of rapid and dramatic changes in values, beliefs, and norms: what organizational scholars refer to as a process of punctuated equilibrium (Kuhn 1970; Gersick 1991). While periods of elevated attention are finite in duration, the worldviews (including market, social, technical, and political arrangements) that precede and follow them are fundamentally different in nature. Since 1960, there have been three such periods of dramatic changes in the salience and values related to corporate environmental practice, what can be described as three "waves" of environmental management, shown in Figure 1.1 (Hoffman 2001; Elkington 2005).

Wave 1: *Corporate environmentalism as regulatory compliance*

The first wave of corporate environmentalism occurred in the late 1960s and early 1970s with the recognition that corporate environmental issues were a problem necessitating regulatory controls. It began with the publication of *Silent Spring* (Carson 1962), a book that challenged what Samuel Florman called the "golden age of engineering" (Florman

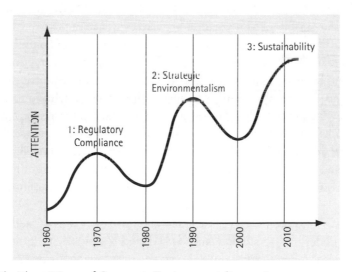

FIGURE 1.1 The Three Waves of Corporate Environmentalism, 1960–2010

[1] Post, Chapter 29.   [2] Weber & Soderstrom, Chapter 14.

1976) and helped bring about a growing awareness that chemicals were damaging the environment and ultimately ourselves. Other events that followed built on the concerns raised in this book and created support for environmental regulations as a correction and control on corporate activity. These included the initiation of the International Biological Program to analyze environmental damage and the biological and ecological mechanisms through which it occurs (1963); the formation of the Club of Rome by thirty-six European economists and scientists to analyze the dynamic interactions between industrial production, population, environmental damage, food consumption, and natural resource usage (1968); the decision by the UN General Assembly to authorize the Human Environment Conference in 1972 (1968); the Santa Barbara oil spill (1969); and the first Earth Day (1970) in which nearly 20 million people participated in a "National Teach-in on the Crisis of the Environment." The culmination of these events successfully captured and motivated a growing awareness of environmental issues in politics and, more importantly, in the press, which introduced the public to issues of population growth, air and water pollution, pesticide use, and the need for regulatory agencies.

In the wake of such events, newly formed regulatory agencies quickly became the arbiter of environmental rules and norms, negotiating on the one side with industry, and on the other with environmental activists. Although industry looked to the government for the definition of their environmental responsibilities as the general structure of environmental regulations became established in countries around the world, it also became increasingly defensive as it perceived government regulation becoming a restraint on economic activity. Within the corporate structure, environmental management was treated as externally directed "technical compliance." Although elevated to a separate corporate department, it remained an ancillary role with low organizational power, and focused strictly on legal requirements (Hoffman 2001).

Wave 2: Corporate environmentalism as strategic management

The second wave occurred in the late 1980s and early 1990s as industry moved to a proactive stance on environmental protection, treating it as a strategic concern. This shift was precipitated, in part, by two highly visible events that created public fear and distrust of corporate activities. First, in 1976, an explosion at Hoffmann-LaRoche's Icmesa chemical plant released a toxic cloud of dioxin over the town of Seveso in the Brianza district of Lombardy, one of the wealthiest and most industrialized regions of Italy. This prompted the European Community to establish the Seveso Directive, a new system for regulating industrial safety, emergency preparedness, and the disclosure of public information.

This event was followed by the 1984 accidental release of 45 tons of methyl isocyanate gas from two underground storage tanks at a Union Carbide (UC) pesticide plant in Bhopal, India resulting in the death of 3,500 people in the neighboring slums and injury to another 300,000. For the first time, a large multinational company (and importantly, its shareholders and insurers) found themselves vulnerable to massive civil penalties (the government of India issued an arrest warrant for the UC CEO and won a mediated settlement of $470 million) and a hostile takeover bid from GAF Corporation (after UC stock dropped from a pre-disaster price of between $50 and $58 to between $32 and $40 per share). The event forced companies and local citizenry to consider the risks that pollution creates as regulations for community "right-to-know" were established and lawsuits became more common to resolve liability concerns. Further, Bhopal altered the structure of overseas and pollution insurance liability, making coverage more difficult and more expensive to acquire.

These events were followed by several more that elevated attention to environmental issues into the second wave. For example, the Arctic ozone hole was discovered (1985); an accident at the Chernobyl nuclear reactor in Russia released a radioactive cloud over Eastern Europe (1986); the Brundtland Commission report *Our Common Future* was published, popularizing the term "sustainable development" (1987); the Montreal Protocol to phase out ozone-depleting substances was signed (1987); the Intergovernmental Panel on Climate Change was formed by the United Nations (1988); the oil tanker *Exxon Valdez* ran aground in Price William Sound causing unprecedented damage to a fragile ecosystem (1989); and the UN Conference on Environment and Development (UNCED) was held in Rio de Janeiro (1992).

For the firm, the elevated attention to environmental issues induced by these events ushered in a new focus on B&NE as a strategic issue. Environmental management became redefined as "pro-active management." The environmental department enjoyed new levels of organizational power, and environmental considerations began to be pushed into the line operations, integrating them into both processes and product decisions. Concepts like waste minimization, pollution prevention, and product stewardship entered the corporate lexicon.

Wave 3: Corporate environmentalism as sustainability

The third wave began in the latter part of the first decade of the twenty-first century and is focused on the merger of environmental and social issues with the global economy. This shift is driven by a series of events and issues that have forced an expansion of the scope of corporate environmentalism to include considerations for a restructuring of global economies. As a result, environmental issues are merging with broader concerns that, in sum, represent a growing awareness of our vulnerabilities and collective impact on the global environment. These concerns include:

Climate change and natural events. No single environmental issue dominates the field of B&NE more than climate change. The growing scientific consensus that humans have been altering the global climate through the release of greenhouse gas emissions since the Industrial Revolution has focused attention on the need to move the economy away from its foundations on fossil-fuel use and material consumption. Events that have galvanized public concern for climate change include the flooding of New Orleans by Hurricane Katrina, the melting of the polar ice cap and the opening of the Northwest Passage for the first time in human history, increasingly severe droughts in sub-Saharan Africa and floods in Southeast Asia.

Information technology. The spread and power of information technology (IT) has increased the pace at which concerns for sustainability have become visible throughout the world. IT makes global corporate activity more transparent, and brings issues like environmental degradation and income inequality into vivid relief. Further, IT alters power relationships, as non-governmental organizations can organize and mobilize powerful demonstrations that can force companies to alter practices (such as the Killer Coke campaign, or the Anti-WTO riots).

National security and global terrorism. As issues like climate change, drought and food scarcity force the migration of refugees and destabilize governments, many are beginning to connect environmental issues with national security. For example, disruptions in food production have led to civil unrest in many developing countries that are net food importers. A 2007 report by the US Military Advisory Board warns that "projected climate change poses a serious threat to America's national security... climate change acts as a threat multiplier for instability in some of the most volatile regions of the world" (CNA Corp 2007). Further, some have begun to connect sustainability with global terrorism, arguing that markets and economic connectivity of the world's poor is the only way to reduce the global threat of terrorism and extremism (Barnett 2003).

Economic competitiveness. Many analysts are calling for nations to maintain their economic competitiveness by developing the next generation of technologies for creating and conserving energy, food, and water (Friedman 2007). US Energy Secretary Chu, for example, equated China's research, development, and deployment efforts into renewable and alternative forms of energy and mobility as a threat to the competitiveness of the United States akin to the modern-day equivalent of the 1960s "sputnik moment" (Chu 2010).

Religious morality. Many of the world's religions have begun to re-examine their core values and scriptures in light of modern-day environmental issues. In 2006, more than 100 prominent pastors, theologians, and college presidents signed an "Evangelical Climate Initiative" calling for action on climate change. In 2007, the Vatican hosted a conference on climate change that acknowledged the seriousness of the issue, which was already causing suffering to the poor, and announced plans to install solar cells on the roofs of Vatican buildings and work toward carbon neutrality.

Resource and pollution prices. The increased demand for resources is affecting previously "free" ecosystem services. The Millennium Ecosystem Assessment warns that "higher operating costs or reduced operating flexibility should be expected due to diminished or degraded resources (such as fresh water) or increased regulation" (MEA 2005). Further, an October 2010 report commissioned by the United Nations Principles for Responsible Investment found that the top 3,000 publicly traded companies in the world produced over US $2.15 trillion worth of environmental damage in 2008, the equivalent of one-third of all global environmental costs. The report argues that as governments adopt "polluter pays" principles, "companies will have to meet the costs of reducing pollution and waste or pay compensation for the damage they cause" (UNPRI 2010).

The third wave of corporate environmentalism is still in progress. But, while the seeds of the social and market shift that will result are emerging, clarity on what will ultimately transpire has yet to unfold.

Environmental issues within business research

While the topic of the environment within business schools had originally begun as a domain of "corporate social responsibility," scholars within management schools more centrally entered the B&NE research domain in the second wave of corporate environmentalism of the late 1980s and early 1990s when business began to see environmental issues as strategic in nature. One of the first formal structures for research in this area was an international interest group of scholars, the Greening of Industry Network (GIN), which was formed in 1989. In producing one of the first collections of research in environmental management, GIN participants argued that "most regulation has not been based on a solid understanding of how industrial firms operated" and that future advances in environmental policy required an appreciation for the "intradynamic and interdynamic processes" of organizational learning that incorporate an awareness for how "various groups both inside and outside the firm conjointly shape its behavior and strategy" (Fischer & Schott 1993: 372).

This initiative to build a research community among management scholars was followed by the formation of the Management Institute for Environment and Business in 1990 (later to become a division of the World Resources Institute) and establishment of the Organizations and the Natural Environment (ONE) special interest group of the Academy of Management in 1994 (which later became a division in 2007).

Some of the research activity that these groups spawned paralleled developments in environmental sociology, such as a recognition of the differences between an anthropocentric and ecocentric perspective, as embodied in the Dominant Social Paradigm and New Ecological Paradigm (Gladwin, Kennelly, & Krause 1995; Starik & Rands 1995; Shrivastava 1995). But more commonly, B&NE research focused on variants of the question, "does it pay to be green?" and considered how to merge existing concerns for economic competitiveness with environmental demands to gain market advantage (Schmidheiny 1992; Smart 1992; Hart 1995; Porter & Van Der Linde 1995; Stead & Stead 1996; Roome 1998; Sexton et al. 1998). Much of the focus of this research was normative in nature, focusing on understanding and predicting why and how corporations "can take steps forward toward [being] environmentally more sustainable" (Starik & Marcus 2000: 542).

With this linkage more centrally relevant to the purpose and goals of the business school, B&NE began to generate its own identity within the various business school disciplines beginning in the mid 1990s. Business strategy was one of the first to enter the domain, with organizational theory following closely behind. B&NE has since permeated other business-school disciplines, such as marketing, accounting, operations, and finance, where each is forming their own formal institutions around the area.

Special issues on B&NE have helped to spur research in this area, such as those appearing in *Psychology & Marketing* (1994), *Journal of Advertising* (1995), *Academy of Management Review* (1995), *British Journal of Management* (1996), *American Behavioral Scientist* (1999), *Business History Review* (1999), *Academy of Management Journal* (2000), *Production and Operations Management* (2001), and others. Further, academic journals dedicated to the interface between managerial action and environmental protection also began to emerge, including *Organization & Environment* (started as *Industrial and Environmental Crisis Quarterly* in 1987 and changed to *O&E* in 1997), *Business Strategy & the Environment* (started in 1992) and the *Journal of Industrial Ecology* (started in 1997). The culmination of this legacy of work has created a rich portfolio of literature to understand the B&NE interface. This Handbook is a compendium and survey of this portfolio, documenting where the field has been, where it is, and where it is going.

As many scholars in this Handbook effectively point out (see chapters in 'Future Perspectives' [Part IX] this volume), more recent developments in B&NE research, concurrent with the third wave of corporate environmentalism, have been an expansion of the research domain to include considerations for social issues in the Triple Bottom Line, the Base of the Pyramid, global sourcing protocols, living wages, income inequality, social justice, and others. These social issues are often incorporated with the environmental and economic agenda under the rubric of sustainable development.

However, it is important to note that this Handbook is not centered on the field of sustainable development, which we see as still relatively nascent, but rather on the field of corporate environmentalism which has matured sufficiently to warrant a Handbook. This volume has come at a point where there is a need to review the substantial volume of past work in order to help shape the future of the field.

PERSECTIVE

The chapters in this Handbook are divided along fields of inquiry, with six sections representing groupings of disciplines in contemporary business schools: business strategy, policy and non-market strategies, organizational behavior and theory, operations and technology, marketing, and accounting and finance. Two additional sections offer chapters on emergent and associated perspectives of B&NE and summary remarks by leaders of the field on its accomplishments and future.

We chose a disciplinary structure for several reasons. First, it is the way in which business schools are generally organized. Researchers build identities within these disciplinary domains, and their research is positioned within the journals that serve them. Within each disciplinary tradition there exist distinct language, constructs, methods, and research tracks that build on prior work. Second, although we are adhering to convention, we hope that scholars can begin their inquiry in disciplines that represent familiar terrain but will then explore other traditions for fresh and new ideas to both invigorate their field and find opportunities for cross-disciplinary linkages. Ultimately, the key to fully addressing issues of B&NE lies in treating its extant questions holistically.[3] In this way, while we have structured this Handbook based on existing conventions, we hope that it will serve as a catalyst to help revolutionize both management research and the nature of the business school itself. What follows is a brief synopsis of the key questions and issues that guide each of the sections of this Handbook.

Business strategy

The chapters in this section make the economic case for environmental stewardship, but recognize that firms often go beyond what makes purely conventional economic sense to satisfy other strategic considerations. The contributing chapters isolate multiple mechanisms that result in a competitive advantage or higher profits for the firm, such as their resources, capabilities, and structure, and how they manage their stakeholders. The level of analysis is primarily focused on the organization, although some attention to the context, such as the international context, is also addressed.

Public policy and non-market strategies

This collection of chapters elevates the level of analysis from the firm to the macro environment, and addresses the question of what happens to the natural environment when markets fail. They recognize the importance of cooperative relationships among firms, certification agencies, non-governmental organizations (NGOs), and government regulations in addressing market failure. This work relies heavily on the fields of economics and political science to guide its analysis.

Organizational behavior and theory

The chapters that comprise this section span a range of levels of analysis and theories. At the individual level, researchers emphasize the constraints to individual cognition

---

[3] Banerjee, Chapter 31; Shrivastava, Chapter 35.

which shape individual behavior through biases such as discounting the future, posi-tive illusions of the state of the world, and self-serving behavior, which are shown to harm the environment. At the organizational level of analysis, researchers emphasize attributes such as organizational culture, structure, and symbols that influence organi-zational behavior. The analysis is raised to the institutional level by recognizing the importance of social movements as well as the institutional environment (regulative, normative, and cognitive-cultural) in shaping organizational actions. Although the level of analysis shifts among the chapters, each chapter acknowledges the role of psy-chology and sociology in understanding the interactions of individuals and organiza-tions in explaining the impact of organizational actions on the natural environment.

Operations and technology

These chapters adopt a technology-based posture towards the natural environment. The operations chapters analyze the environmental impact of the flow of goods and services within the firm and throughout the supply chain. The firm is seen as a production sys-tem, where the boundaries can span either a single firm or an entire supply chain. These chapters reconsider the conventional forward-flowing supply chains with a growing emphasis on reverse and closed loop supply chains. Also, they introduce the notion of industrial symbiosis, where geographic proximity enables the waste products of one firm to serve as valuable inputs for another. This set of chapters also highlights the value of information, both across firms by building supply chains, as well as within firms through information management.

Marketing

The three marketing chapters shift focus to the consumer, either from the perspective of the corporation, where the central question is how firms can target green consumers, or from the perspective of the consumer, where the central question is if consumers value environmental attributes in products. These chapters rely heavily on psychology and economics to unpack consumer-buying behavior and segmentation, with the ultimate goal of shifting markets to capitalize on green attributes.

Accounting and finance

The accounting and finance chapters focus on the firm and its relationship with its finan-cial stakeholders. These chapters emphasize the role of information, which can be used to guide managerial control functions and communicate the firm's commitment to the natural environment. The chapters also take the perspective of the investors, recogniz-ing that there is still a great deal of reticence by most investors towards behaviors that attend to the natural environment, but also an acknowledged growing interest. Investors, therefore, are looking both for firms to report their environmental impacts and for new instruments, such as weather derivatives, to hedge their risk.

Associated perspectives

The five chapters in this section offer alternative views of B&NE that do not neatly fit within a single theoretical tradition or discipline, although the perspectives they offer are growing in prominence. Three strong themes emerge in this section, each pertaining to the role of the social environment in understanding the natural environment. The first is an acknowledgement of the role of responsibility and morality in environmental decisions. The overlap between corporate social responsibility, stakeholder theory, and the natural environment is becoming increasingly evident, especially as the discourse moves towards sustainability and the triple bottom line. Another theme in this section acknowledges that our perspectives on the natural environment are socially constructed, and often by individuals and organizations with an economic interest in the final outcome. These chapters challenge us to take a more "critical" perspective and redefine the role of corporations in society. A final theme also recommends that the social and natural environments be integrated, applying systems theory to acknowledge the complex relationships among actors and elements within the system.

Future perspectives

The final section of this Handbook offers views of the future of the B&NE field from six individuals who have watched the field grow from its infancy. We selected contributors for this section from a broad range of perspectives, including academia and practice. These people took risks early in their careers, and in doing so, legitimized B&NE research and practice. Each contributor, in his own way, asks that we move the needle forward either by reinventing the field of B&NE or, in some cases, returning to its original root foundations. They argue that the position in which both society and the B&NE field currently sits is not "sustainable", and they implore researchers to find new ways of looking at the business enterprise.

PROSPECTIVE

Several themes emerge within the chapters of this Handbook: themes that transcend any individual discipline and offer directions for future inquiry within the B&NE field. This section delineates those themes along three dimensions: theoretical themes and opportunities, paradigmatic choices, and methodological themes and opportunities.

Theoretical themes and opportunities

B&NE research borrows heavily from existing theory within each of the business disciplines, allowing it to both build upon and expand prior research streams and create powerful linkages with tested insights that have accrued elsewhere. Chapters in this Handbook move beyond treatment of the natural environment as simply another empirical context with few distinctive elements. Instead, they identify themes that create opportunities for building the research domain through the identification of theoretical themes that are both unique to the field and are synergistic in spanning disciplines. In the section that follows, these themes allow us to map some future directions in which B&NE work may be extended.

Does it pay to be green? Or, should it even matter?

The question "does it pay" is worked into many chapters. Grounded primarily in the discourse of strategy, finance, and accounting,[4] the question draws a clear link between actions that are good for the environment and good for the firm. At the heart of this question is the assumption that there exists a win-win relationship between the interests of business and the environment, not a trade-off.[5]

While the question of whether it pays to be green has probably generated more research pages than any other single question, the answer remains unresolved. The meta-analyses point to either a small net positive or neutral relationship.[6] And ongoing studies on variants of this question seem to merely contribute to the growing cacophony of results. But, chapter authors point towards an increasing discomfort with this question and a recognition that increasingly more research is asking when, where, and how corporate activity can simultaneously promote economic and environmental growth.

It is clear from the chapters in this Handbook that the question of whether greening pays is highly contingent on the context and the approach. For example, resources and capabilities that can build competitive advantage or the way in which a firm markets its products can explain 'how',[7] and the international context can explain 'when' and even 'where'.[8] Also, researchers are trying to disentangle how environmental performance affects not just financial performance, but also the reactions of key stakeholders,[9] such as investors[10] and consumers,[11] who may influence and be influenced by the extent to which the firm benefits financially from greening activities.

[4] Bauer & Derwall, Chapter 25; Bondy & Matten, Chapter 28; Cho, Patten, & Roberts, Chapter 24; Russo & Minto, Chapter 2.
[5] Banerjee, Chapter 31; Buhr & Gray, Chapter 23; Hart, Chapter 29.
[6] Russo & Minto, Chapter 2.
[7] Scammon & Mish, Chapter 19.
[8] Christmann & Taylor, Chapter 3.
[9] Kassinis, Chapter 5; Delmas & Toffel, Chapter 13.
[10] Bauer & Derwall, Chapter 25; Cho, Patten, & Roberts, Chapter 24; Routledge, Chapter 27.
[11] Devinney, Chapter 21; Gershoff & Irwin, Chapter 20.

Whereas the bulk of work continues to be rooted in the question of whether, when and how greening pays, an increasing number of scholars argue that this is not even the right question to be asking. Some suggest that economic growth and corporate competitiveness may not be the real motivation for environmentally responsible managerial actions. Rather, they suggest that beliefs, values, and preferences shape individual and corporate actions.[12] Others suggest that this question taps into organizational actions that do not need to elicit substantive, deep-rooted change within organizations, but rather are based on the objective of greenwashing or astroturfing.[13] In fact, organizations will often use self-regulations (i.e. voluntary agreements among organizations to go beyond compliance) in an effort to deflect regulations or public pressures and stall substantive changes.[14]

Some scholars go beyond mere disenchantment with the question of whether greening pays, and argue that this question is distracting us from more important, relevant, and urgent questions. The question privileges the firm, rather than society or the environment, so that the environment serves the firm, rather than the firm being dependent on the environment.[15] Searching for the "holy grail" or win-win, they argue, dupes us into believing that there is no need to make difficult trade-offs when the integrity of the environment is at stake.[16]

The notion of trade-offs between business and the environment and society is peppered throughout the chapters, and nowhere more than in the section on Future Perspectives. Several authors in this section suggest that practitioners and researchers have not been willing to make the tough decisions necessary to foster environmental protection when the economic imperative may be threatened.[17] They argue that strategy scholars continue to advocate for growth, marketing scholars for selling, operations scholars for efficiencies, and finance and accounting scholars for control and valuation and that, taken together, the business disciplines are the ingredients of a recipe destined for collapse.[18]

The role of biases, passion and emotions in environmental decision-making

Most chapters assume that decisions are rational. In other words, actors act consistently, according to a set of ordered preferences to achieve a clear objective. Rational decision-making models are used to explain green behavior, where consumers, investors, and

---

[12] Buhr & Gray, Chapter 2; Lenox & York, Chapter 4.
[13] Lounsbury, Fairclough, & Lee, Chapter 12; Melville, Chapter 18; Forbes & Jermier, Chapter 30.
[14] King, Prado, & Rivera, Chapter 6.
[15] Banerjee, Chapter 31.
[16] Forbes & Jermier, Chapter 30.
[17] Banerjee, Chapter 31; Ehrenfeld, Chapter 33; Gladwin, Chapter 38.
[18] Roome, Chapter 34.

managers value the environment and it is integral to their preferences. If we can model preferences, we can predict individual behaviors.[19]

But several authors point out that, although actors may value the environment, they often act contrary to their interests. There is ample evidence that shows that consumers do not buy green[20] and that the majority of investors still do not invest in it.[21] Research in the area of cognitive barriers explores the biases that impede rationality and explain sub-optimal decision-making.[22] For example, evidence shows that consumers and investors generally prefer immediate certain rewards over future uncertain ones.

In addition to these alternatives to the rational decision-making model, there are two additional areas that provide opportunities for further research. First, most decision-making models privilege profit-seeking or self-interested values.[23] Valuing the natural environment is often seen as an aberration of, or departure from, self-interest. But there is a small but growing community of scholars who suggest that strict, economic self-interest is not always the norm. Positive Organizational Scholarship (POS) and Appreciative Inquiry (AI) are two such emergent areas that offer interesting avenues into the ways that individuals deviate positively to foster greater environmental progress.

The second avenue for further inquiry lies in the exploration of the role of emotion, art, and esthetic.[24] For example, entrepreneurs act on emotion,[25] and managers attempt to reduce their footprint even when it doesn't pay.[26] There is an opportunity then, for future researchers to consider decision-making models that do not assume rationality (as presently defined) and seek to develop more complex models of human behavior and the environment that are based on an expanded set of assumptions.

New actors, new organizations, new partnerships

Business makes money through markets, governments regulate market externalities, and NGOs protect the interests of civil society. This model of the economy and its constituent actors has historically been relatively clear and stable.

But environmental issues demonstrate that markets often fail, that prices do not reflect social interests, and that goods are not allocated efficiently or effectively.[27] Such failures can arise when property is shared,[28] which permits free riding and undermines environ-

---

[19] Devinney, Chapter 21; Routledge, Chapter 27.
[20] Devinney, Chapter 21; Gershoff & Irwin, Chapter 20.
[21] Bauer & Derwall, Chapter 25; Bertrand & Sinclair-Desgagné, Chapter 26.
[22] Shu & Bazerman, Chapter 9; Tost & Wade-Benzoni, Chapter 10.
[23] Bauer & Derwall, Chapter 25.
[24] Shrivastava, Chapter 35.
[25] Lenox & York, Chapter 4.
[26] Buhr & Gray, Chapter 23.
[27] Baron & Lyon, Chapter 7; Coglianese & Anderson, Chapter 8; King, Prado, & Rivera, Chapter 6.
[28] Routledge, Chapter 27.

mental justice.[29] Recent scholarship has stepped up to recognize important new developments in organizations and organizing.

There are new actors, and they span different levels of analysis. At the institutional or societal level, greater attention is being directed to social movements[30] and institutional entrepreneurs.[31] Social movements are taking on the many roles of "adversary, collaborator, monitor of soft regulation, ally in influencing governments or service provider".[32] NGOs are also playing a more active role in stepping in where governments fail, prodding firms to act responsibly.[33] The license to operate is shifting to stakeholders, so even fringe stakeholders or communities, who have never before had power, voice, or justice, are recognized as being increasingly influential.[34] Finally, organizational members are also acting as agents of change. The C-Suite is now welcoming chief environmental or sustainability officers,[35] and tempered radicals are being noticed throughout the organization (Meyerson 2003).

We are also seeing new organizational forms emerge. The lines between business, government, and NGOs have begun to blur to reveal new hybrid forms of organizing. Unbridled self-interest is yielding to organizations that balance self and society, sometimes referred to as social entrepreneurs, social enterprise,[36] B corporations, or hybrid organizations. These hybrids capitalize on market failures to expose an opportunity to repurpose the organization towards using the market to improve the natural environment. In addition, there are a new breed of organizations whose sole mission is to monitor, audit, and certify the reporting, management, and environmental performance of corporate practices, effectively acting as new forms of regulation and governance.[37]

The chapters in this Handbook also call attention to new and strange partnerships that form among organizations. Industry coalitions are emerging, through industry self-regulation, aimed not at pushing only their own self-interests but also the public interest.[38] Supply chains are becoming relevant units of analysis, as products are being pushed forward, backwards and even connecting front to back to form closed loops.[39] Industrial ecology is opening up unlikely partnerships, such as between a fish farm and a power plant.[40] These networks of organizations raise new questions, such as how do we measure a firm's environmental footprint, as what one firm does cascades through the network? At

[29] Bondy & Matten, Chapter 28; Weber & Soderstrom, Chapter 14.

[30] Weber & Soderstrom, Chapter 14.

[31] Lounsbury, Fairclough, & Lee, Chapter 12; Lenox & York, Chapter 4.

[32] Weber & Soderstrom, Chapter 14.

[33] Baron & Lyon, Chapter 7.

[34] Lounsbury, Fairclough, & Lee, Chapter 12; Kassinis, Chapter 5.

[35] Elkington & Love, Chapter 36.

[36] Lenox & York, Chapter 4.

[37] Baron & Lyon, Chapter 7; Delmas & Toffel, Chapter 13; Gray & Herremans, Chapter 22; King, Prado, & Rivera, Chapter 6; Lounsbury, Fairclough, & Lee, Chapter 12.

[38] King, Prado, & Rivera, Chapter 6.

[39] Abbey & Guide, Chapter 16; Klassen & Vachon, Chapter 15.

[40] Lifset & Boons, Chapter 17.

what level do we optimize the environmental footprint—the firm or the network? And, how can we reduce the environmental footprint, given the complexity of the system? The global/local tension is becoming more acute, as more micro enterprises are emerging, and forming collectives to manage local energy and water resources.

No longer does business represent a single-minded, profit-seeking monolith. Instead, there is more color and texture to organizations, replete with examples of businesses that mobilize against other businesses, NGOs that seek profit to further environmental goals, and networks of organizations that form strange bedfellows. Such organizational forms are revealing the value of "institutional pluralism" and organizational diversity,[41] which is a clear departure from the set of actors that once graced the business-school stage.

Bridging and blending the social and the natural environments

B&NE research, unlike research in most other business fields, touches both the social and natural environments. Although most prior B&NE research has focused on management and the goals of the corporation, efforts are increasing to see research opportunities at the interface.

For example, most chapters in this Handbook are firmly entrenched in the social environment and its many facets. They acknowledge the importance of socially constructed symbols that shape organizational actions, such as reporting, auditing, management systems, certifications, and technology.[42] Information becomes a critical medium for firms to measure, control, and communicate their environmental impacts.[43] They also recognize that socially constructed symbols are particularly open to manipulation and can be easily disconnected from substantive actions, resulting in greenwashing.[44] This leads some scholars to become preoccupied with the truthfulness of corporate claims on the environment and apply an ethical lens to corporate behavior, a theme that has been only marginal within the B&NE domain. But some argue that questions of morality and what individuals or firms 'should' do is the hallmark of discriminating sustainability from responsibility.[45] By bringing morality back into the fold of B&NE research, we bring greater attention to the individuals within the organization.[46] Some scholars criticize B&NE research for studying organizations whose humanity has been silenced. Instead they call for a focus on more embodied

---

[41] Delmas & Toffel, Chapter 13; Lounsbury, Fairclough, & Lee, Chapter 12.
[42] Buhr & Gray, Chapter 23; Forbes & Jermier, Chapter 30; Gray & Herremans, Chapter 22; King, Prado, & Rivera, Chapter 6.
[43] Melville, Chapter 18; Cho, Patten, & Roberts, Chapter 24.
[44] Forbes & Jermier, Chapter 30.
[45] Bondy & Matten, Chapter 28; Post, Chapter 29.
[46] Banerjee, Chapter 31; Gladwin, Chapter 38; Shrivastava, Chapter 35.

organizations with human-nature relationships that involve mind, emotions, sensory awareness, and esthetic.

But going further, many researchers are seeking to explore links between the social environment, and the natural or physical world, shifting their focus from the financial outcomes of environmental actions to the material or substantive impacts of firm actions on the natural environment. For example, several authors focus on the interaction between the social and material worlds and advocate for a systems view of material and energy flows.[47] Such systems acknowledge the complexity of the B&NE relationship, explicitly introducing multiple levels of analysis that incorporate the social and natural environments, and appreciating small adaptive changes that alter the system with both positive and negative feedback loops. Quick wins through technology, for example, can unlock solutions to environmental challenges (such as providing clean energy, developing new forms of energy storage, reusing material resources, and cleaning carbon sinks), but also expose new and unintended consequences that lead to new environmental problems (such as end-of-life treatment of rare earth metals in batteries and computer equipment).[48] A shift to a systems view of the B&NE relationship offers greater opportunities for optimizing social and environmental systems, but also greater complexities and challenges in managing them to predictable ends.

Paradigmatic choices

The chapters in this Handbook speak to one of two dominant paradigms, each representing distinctly different approaches to addressing environmental issues within the business school. The first thread involves a focus on environmental issues within the existing models, theories, and paradigms. The second pushes the literature to ask the "big" questions and push beyond the existing paradigm. The first is built on a model of "normal" science (Kuhn 1970), where existing theories are applicable to current dilemmas and problems. It generally assumes positivism, where business performance is the dependent variable and decision makers are rational. The second is built on a model of "revolutionary" science (Kuhn 1970), where the problem domain represents an anomaly such that existing theories no longer work, and new models and theories are necessary. This approach laments the natural environment's decline, questions the centrality of humankind, and believes that business studies need to be reoriented so that business no longer seeks to force the environment to serve the economy, but rather seeks economic activity to fit within environmental parameters.

The central argument of revolutionary science in B&NE is that business and business research cannot continue as is, if we are to tackle the arguably incommensurable assumptions of business and the natural environment. For example, scholars in the

---

[47] Levy & Lichenstein, Chapter 32; Lifset & Boons, Chapter 17; Ehrenfeld, Chapter 33; Gladwin, Chapter 38; Roome, Chapter 34.

[48] Ehrenfeld, Chapter 33; Gladwin, Chapter 38; Post, Chapter 29.

camp of revolutionary science advocate for "strong sustainability", and for researchers and managers to stop dabbling in "weak sustainability".[49] These proponents apply
concepts rare in the business lexicon such as flourishing,[50] morality,[51] citizenship,[52]
and esthetic and passion.[53] Ehrenfeld challenges us to reconfigure our approach,[54]
recognizing that "reducing unsustainability" is not the same as "creating sustainability" and that "virtually everything that business has done in the name of environmental management, greening, eco-efficiency, sustainable development, or, as it is
mistakenly used, sustainability fits only under the first rubric—reducing unsustainability." Gladwin goes further to excoriate the field for its failure "to substantively
acknowledge the magnitude, severity, persistence, complexity, exponential acceleration or the transformational urgency of the global environmental crisis."[55] He asks "Is
the field disconnected from environmental science? Is it addicted to reductionism,
positivism, empiricism, relativism, rationalism, and objectivism as the only basis of
knowledge generation?"

Whereas some might argue that the normal and revolutionary threads are orthogo-
nal, we see both themes emerging within the chapters of this Handbook to various
degrees and that they feed each other towards stronger and more fruitful research.
Normal science helps to build upon models and theories with rigorous analysis; revolutionary science pushes for an examination of those theories for possible alteration
and adjustment. Normal science patiently fits within existing paradigms for research,
while revolutionary science impatiently calls for more rapid change to address the
pace at which environmental systems threaten collapse. For example, much fruitful
research work on environmental management measurement controls is documented
in chapters in this book, but questions emerge as to whether they will have the impact
we need and at the pace with which we need it.[56] Or, research within the systems view[57]
is starting to shape a different paradigm—one in which business and humankind are
not necessarily the focal point of study, but embedded within a complex system, which
privileges elements based on their centrality and importance to the sustainability of
the network. In the end, research in normal science anchors B&NE research as a legitimate domain of empirical study within the structure of business-school research,
while revolutionary science becomes a force for rejuvenation and reorientation of that
research tradition, seeking to bring it more in line with the critical empirical issues on
which it must focus.

[49] Roome, Chapter 34.
[50] Ehrenfeld, Chapter 33.
[51] Gladwin, Chapter 38.
[52] Banerjee, Chapter 31.
[53] Shrivastava, Chapter 35.
[54] Ehrenfeld, Chapter 33.
[55] Gladwin, Chapter 38.
[56] Buhr & Gray, Chapter 23.
[57] Ehrenfeld, Chapter 33; Levy & Lichtenstein, Chapter 32; Roome, Chapter 34.

Methodological themes and opportunities

The methods used in B&NE research reflect disciplinary preferences and rely on a broad range that demonstrate particular benefits from the strengths of methodological diversity and plurality. But with each method comes weaknesses. For example, B&NE research grounded in economics tends to rely on large volumes of archival, quantitative data focused on large corporations. Insights from such datasets allow us to see the existence and persistence of predicted relationships. However, such approaches also rely on past trends, observable and accessible data, and stable relationships, which may not apply to a natural environment that we are only beginning to understand and is undergoing rapid and, at times, non-linear, changes. Institutional/macro level research grounded in sociology, relies heavily on archival longitudinal data and qualitative data which bring us closer to the richness of phenomena but limit the possibilities for prediction and actionable recommendations. Organization-level research relies heavily on ethnographic case studies but limits the opportunities to generalize key insights. Individual-level research grounded in psychology often relies heavily on lab work, which is often criticized for being context specific and not reflecting actual behavior.[58]

No one method can address all the challenges that the natural environment poses to business. Each has its strengths and weaknesses. But the chapters in this Handbook offer multiple suggestions for strengthening the methodological approaches that are used to study B&NE research. Some methodological opportunities include:

- Move beyond a predominant focus on large multinational corporations in dirty industries (such as coal, mining, oil, and timber), and broaden the scope towards small and medium-sized enterprises, as well as new emerging forms of organizations, such as social enterprise, or non-traditional organizations, such as religious or values-based institutions.
- Draw on a wider range of methods, such as ethnographies that bring the researcher closer to the phenomena, and mixed methods that expose multiple perspectives on the phenomena; employ new information sources that permit insights into changes in eco-systems, such as global information systems; or engage in critical analysis, such as narrative and discourse analysis.
- Include multiple levels of analysis, recognizing that an individual's behavior depends on the context of the organization, which further depends on the institutional and natural environments.

Whereas methods shape the way in which we explore an issue, there is also call to shift the focus of the issue that we explore. We are encountering systematic biases in our research focus, which has blinded us to opportunities for new insights that can be encountered by expanding our field of vision. Some of those opportunities are listed below.

---

[58] Devinney, Chapter 21.

- Recognizing that climate change has been the target of much B&NE research, researchers should expand the breadth of environmental issues and corporate goals, including the Millennium Development Goals, which connect natural environmental issues to social and development issues. Critical environmental issues include water scarcity, biodiversity loss and species extinction, fisheries over-exploitation, ecosystem destruction, toxic pollutants, deforestation, nutrient loading and nitrogen fixing, land use changes, and urban sprawl. And with environmental issues rapidly being subsumed into the broader topic of sustainability, the issue domain is expanding into issues of population growth, poverty, widening income disparity between rich and poor; access to food, water and housing, health care and pandemics, and employment and fair wages.
- Focus not only on identifying solutions, but build greater understanding of the problems.
- Focus not only on examples of organizational success, but also organizational failure.
- Expand the focus of research from national activities to both the local as well as the transnational and global spheres. The latter represents an empirical necessity, as companies are embedded in global supply chains, and local environmental movements are increasingly connected internationally.

CONCLUSION

As sustainability alters the global marketplace and the role of the business enterprise within it, questions emerge about how environmental and social sustainability might alter the role of research and education within the contemporary business school. Indeed, the entire field of "management," as we now know it, is faced with new and emerging challenges. Some have begun to question whether business schools are falling out of step and irrelevant to the world of practice (Stewart 2006; Economist 2007; Jacobs 2009; Podolny 2009) and whether the modern business school must fundamentally alter its teaching and research in order to respond to the environmental and sustainability challenges of the twenty-first century.

Khurana (2007), for example, points out that "as things stand, there is little sustained discussion among business school faculty and administrators about whether new technologies, the globalization of trade, demographic trends, the growing inequality between rich and poor, the shifting social norms may be rendering the investor capitalism model unsustainable, if not actually obsolete. Yet these developments in the world since the rise of investor capitalism suggest that a new model . . . may well be called for." Ghoshal (2005) goes further to argue that the financial crises and abuses of the corporate sector are in fact caused by the foundational elements of some of the theories, such as agency theory, that underpin the business-school agenda—elements that the B&NE research agenda often challenges (such as the profit motive being the singular objective of the firm, the value of the environment being measured solely in terms of its commodity value, the firm as socially and environmentally separate from its social context, the unquestioned imperative of economic growth, etc.). In short, the underpinnings of management research and education are being called into question.

A widening circle of business-school academics are raising questions over the "rigor and relevance" of management research (Tushman & O'reilly 2007). Bennis & O'Toole (2005) state: "The root cause of today's crisis in management education is that business schools have adopted an inappropriate—and ultimately self-defeating—model of academic excellence. Instead of measuring themselves in terms of the competence of their graduates, or by how well their faculty members understand important drivers of business performance, they assess themselves solely by the rigor of their scientific research." Schmalensee (2006) concurs. "The academic system's current methods of hiring and rewarding professors don't necessarily attract or encourage the kind of practitioner-oriented faculty we need to make business school research and MBA education much more attuned to meeting today's and tomorrow's management challenges."

But lying within the growing tensions over the role of the modern business school, there exists the opportunity for sustainability research to offer a solution. The focus of B&NE research demands that we cast our eyes on issues, not merely on functions and disciplines. It re-engineers business models to not be self-serving, but to honor the system in which the models are embedded. It restores people and the planet to a central position within business schools, recognizing that businesses can cause great harm and perform enormous good. Addressing environmental issues (and sustainability more broadly) in our research, teaching and outreach (to both scholars and practitioners) holds the promise to restore our field and craft—as well as the profession we serve—towards addressing the pressing needs of our day.

B&NE research forces the kind of problem-based, temporally relevant research that critics and business practitioners demand from business schools. As such, environmental sustainability offers an opportunity for rejuvenation and repurposing of management research and education to reflect changes that are already underway. As problem-based research becomes increasingly common (Biggart & Lutzenhiser 2007; Davis & Marquis 2005), opportunities for environment-centered research (and sustainability-centered research more generally) improve. In fact, few contemporary problems warrant analysis by academics more than environmental and sustainability issues, both for the benefit of the field and for the benefit of society. The opportunities for the field of research represented within the pages of this Handbook are vast and exciting.

References

Barnett, T. (2003). *The Pentagon's New Map*. New York: Berkley Books.

Bennis, W. & O'toole, J. (2005). "How Business Schools Lost Their Way," *Harvard Business Review*, 83(5): 96–124.

Biggart, N. W. & Lutzenhiser, L. (2007). "Economic Sociology and the Social Problem of Energy Efficiency," *American Behavioral Scientist* 50: 1070–1086.

Carson, R. (1962). *Silent Spring*. Boston: Houghton Mifflin Co.

Chu, S. (2010). "China's Clean Energy Successes Represent a New 'Sputnik Moment' for America," Speech before the National Press Club, November 29.

CNA Corporation (2007). *National Security and the Threat of Climate Change*. Alexandria, CAN Corporation.

Davis, G. F. & Marquis, C. (2005). "Prospects for Organization Theory in the Early Twenty-First Century: Institutional Fields and Mechanisms," Organization Science 16: 332–344.

Economist (2007). "Practically Irrelevant? What is the Point of Research Carried Out in Business Schools?" *The Economist*, August 28.

Elkington, J. (2005). Government in the Chrysalis Economy, in R. Olsen and D. Rajeski (eds). *Environmentalism and the Technologies of Tomorrow: Shaping the Next Industrial Revolution*, Washington DC: Island Press, 133–142.

Fischer, K. & Schott, J. (eds.) (1993). *Environmental Strategies for Industry: International Perspectives on Research Needs and Policy Implications*, Washington DC: Island Press.

Florman, S. (1976). *The Existential Pleasures of Engineering*, New York, NY: St. Martins Press.

Friedman, T. (2007). "The Power of Green; What does America Need to Regain its Global Stature?" *New York Times Magazine*, 15 April, 41–67, 71–72.

Gersick, C. (1991). "Punctuated Equilibrium: A Multi-Level Exploration of Revolutionary Change Theories," *Academy of Management Review*, 16, 10–36.

Ghoshal, S. (2005). "Bad Management Theories are Destroying Good Management Practices," *Academy of Management Learning and Education*, 4(1): 75–91.

Gladwin, T., Kenelly, J., & Krause, T. (1995). "Shifting Paradigms for Sustainable Development: Implications for Management Theory and Research," *Academy of Management Review*, 20(4): 874–907.

Hart, S. (1995). "A Natural-Resource-Based View of the Firm," *Academy of Management Review*, 20(4): 986–1014.

Hoffman, A. (2001). *From Heresy to Dogma: An Institutional History of Corporate Environmentalism*, Palo Alto, CA: Stanford University Press.

Jacobs, M. (2009). "How Business Schools Have Failed Business," *Wall Street Journal*, 24 April, A13.

Khurana, R. (2007). *From Higher Aims to Hired Hands: The Social Transformation of American Business Schools and the Unfulfilled Promise of Management as a Profession*. Princeton, NJ: Princeton University Press.

Kuhn, T. (1970). *The Structure of Scientific Revolutions*, Chicago Il: The University of Chicago Press.

Meyerson, D. E. (2003). *Tempered Radicals: How Everyday Leaders Inspire Change at Work*. Boston, MA: Harvard Business School Press.

Millennium Ecosystem Assessment (2005). *Ecosystems and Human Well-Being: Synthesis Report*. Washington DC: Island Press.

National Center For Health Statistics (2004). *Health, United States, 2004*. Washington DC: Department of Health and Human Services.

Podolny, J. (2009). "The Buck Stops (and Starts) at Business School," *Harvard Business Review*, June, 62–67.

Porter, M. & Van Der Linde C. (1995). "Green and Competitive: Ending the Stalemate," *Harvard Business Review*, September–October, 120–134.

Roome, N. (ed.) (1998). *Sustainability Strategies for Industry: The Future of Corporate Strategy.* Washington DC: Island Press.

Schmalensee, R. (2006). "Where's the 'B' in Business Schools?" *Business Week*, November 27, 118.

Schmidheiny, S. (1992). *Changing Course.* Cambridge: MIT Press.

Sexton, K., Marcus, A., Easter, W., Abrahamson, D. & Goodman, J. (eds.) (1998). *Better Environmental Decisions: Strategies for Governments, Businesses and Communities.* Washington DC: Island Press.

Shrivastava, P. (1995). "The Role of Corporations in Achieving Environmental Sustainability," *Academy of Management Review*, 20(4): 936–960.

Smart, B. (1992). *Beyond Compliance.* Washington DC: World Resources Institute.

Starik, M. & Marcus, A. (2000). "New Research Directions in the Field of Management of Organizations in the Natural Environment," *Academy of Management Journal*, 43(4): 539–546.

——— & Rands, G. (1995). "Weaving an Integrated Web: Multi-level and Multi-System Perspectives of Ecologically Sustainable Organizations," *Academy of Management Review*, 20(4): 908–935.

Stead, E. & Stead, J. (1996). *Management for a Small Planet*, 2nd edition, Thousand Oaks, CA: Sage Publications.

Stewart, M. (2006). "The Management Myth," *Atlantic Monthly*, June, 80–87.

Thomas, W. (2002). "Business and the Journey Towards Sustainable Development: Reflections on Progress since Rio," *Environmental Law Reporter*, June 10873–10955.

Tushman, M. & O'Reilly, C. (2007). "Research and Relevance: Implications of Pasteur's Quadrant for Doctoral Programs and Faculty Development," *Academy of Management Journal* 50: 769–774.

UNPRI (2010). *Universal Ownership: Why Environmental Externalities Matter to Institutional Investors* <http://www.unpri.org/files/6728_ES_report_environmental_externalities.pdf> (Accessed 5 October, 2010).

World Resources Institute (1994). *World Resources*, Oxford: Oxford University Press.

PART II

BUSINESS STRATEGY

CHAPTER 2

COMPETITIVE STRATEGY AND THE ENVIRONMENT: A FIELD OF INQUIRY EMERGES

MICHAEL V. RUSSO
AND AMY MINTO

A burst of scholarly activity at the nexus of competitive strategy and the natural environment has generated scholarly excitement, created new knowledge, and helped to establish the broader field of Business and the Natural Environment (B&NE). A precise date for the origin of the research domain formed by competitive strategy and the environment cannot be pinpointed. Tying the date to salient events like Bhopal (1984), the Exxon Valdez (1989), the United Nations Earth Summit in Rio de Janeiro (1992), or the establishment of the Organizations and the Natural Environment Interest Group (1994) appears arbitrary. Using the publication date of a special issue of the *Academy of Management Review* (1995) or *Academy of Management Journal* (2000) that spanned B&NE topics but featured several contributions on competitive strategy and the environment is another possibility, but would be based on a lagging indicator.

Rather than choose a date that may be viewed as arbitrary, we think it best to describe the scholarly heritage of competitive strategy and the environment and illustrate how the field has taken shape. We begin by surveying the literature that bridges business strategy and the environmental imperative, subsequently reviewing the growing literature that peers inside companies to explore dimensions of implementation that can make or break the execution of a chosen strategy. Because competitive strategy research frequently spotlights economic performance implications of firm behavior, we then briefly survey the literature on how environmentally oriented strategies influence profitability. We continue by offering a few notes on the methodologies used in the study of competitive strategy and the environment. We conclude with a critique of knowledge creation in the field of competitive strategy and the environment (hereinafter CSE), presenting final observations and identifying areas that are worthy of further development by scholars.

THE DNA OF CSE

The resource-based view of the firm

The primary theoretical driving force for CSE research has been the resource-based view of the firm. Working from roots in economics (e.g. Penrose 1959; Nelson & Winter 1982; Wernerfelt 1984), Barney (1991) introduced the idea that for resources to contribute to a sustainable competitive advantage they needed to be a) valuable, b) rare, c) difficult to imitate, and d) non-substitutable. The resource-based view of the firm thus breaks free of many of the strictures of neoclassical economic theory by viewing resources and capabilities as heterogeneous across firms and not typically traded in the marketplace (Barney 1991). Further, differences across these bundles of resources and capabilities can be long lived and create the potential for sustained competitive advantages. The internal focus of the resource-based view is attractive to many scholars in the CSE field, because it facilitates studies of sources of competitive advantage that have an environmental foundation, running from ethics (López-Gamero, Claver-Cortés, & Molina-Azorín 2008) to environmental management systems (Delmas 2001) to operations management capabilities (Marcus & Nichols 1999).

Hart (1995) extended the resource-based theory of the firm to embrace ecological limits, which had been systematically excluded from a literature that limited its recognition of factors external to the firm to economic, sociopolitical, and technological forces (Shrivastava 1991). Hart's contribution was to organize and articulate the interconnected methods by which some of the building blocks of resource-based theory—tacitness, social complexity, and rarity—could promote pollution prevention, product stewardship, and ultimately, sustainable development. He also identified external bases for the very valuable resources of legitimacy and reputation, dimensions that would receive further study soon thereafter (Russo & Fouts 1997; Sharma & Vredenburg 1998).

Russo & Fouts (1997) added further granularity to the story linking organizational resources to a firm's environmental performance. By comparing and contrasting the prototypical modes of compliance and prevention, they theorized that there would be systematic differences in the resource bases of firms that employed each approach to environmental management. For example, as opposed to a compliance approach that might employ off-the-shelf technology, pollution prevention leverages capabilities that are causally ambiguous, difficult to observe, and therefore serve as the basis for a competitive advantage. Russo & Fouts (1997) also argued that a strong environmental reputation can be a magnet for superior talent.

Russo & Fouts (1997) provided a regression analysis of how environmental performance drove financial performance, but urged researchers "to identify the full chain of variables" connecting those "two end links." Scholars have begun doing so by applying the resource-based theory.

Extensions of familiar concepts

Several concepts that have roots in the broader business strategy literature have been deployed in CSE research. Shrivastava (1995) worked through the implications of environmental limits on the Porter categories of low-cost, differentiation, and niche strategies. Orsato (2006) argued for a typology that contrasted low-cost and differentiation strategies, each of which could be developed into unique sub-strategies based on whether the company's emphasis was on internal processes or on products and services.

To date, differentiation strategies have received the most significant attention from B&NE researchers. Initial work by Reinhardt (1998) identified three elements needed for environmental differentiation to permit firms to secure a price premium in the marketplace. First, the customer must be willing to pay a premium for the environmental benefit of the product. Second, the information provided to the customer by the firm must be credible. Third, there must be some barrier to imitation of the product (see Gershoff & Irwin [Chapter 20]; and Devinney [Chapter 21] this volume for more information on consumer buying behavior). Delmas, Russo, & Montes-Sancho (2007) explored willingness to pay in a study of renewable power generation by electric utilities. After controlling for many policy and operations variables, they were able to show that renewable power generation was tied to an environmentally enlightened population, especially when deregulation provided the possibility for de-bundling kilowatt hours to create green options. Hull & Rothenberg (2008), looking at corporate social performance, found that CSR-based differentiation was more powerful in low-innovation industries and where products were relatively undifferentiated in other ways. Their results for corporate social performance should apply analogously to corporate environmental performance.

Another concept from business strategy that has contributed to CSE is relatedness within divisions of a firm (Rumelt 1974; 1982). Under this theory, a firm should diversify by extending the reach of its most valuable assets and capabilities. In recent work, Diestre & Rajagopolan (2011) found that beyond product-market relatedness, common emissions profiles predict diversification patterns. They attributed this to the capabilities that a firm develops as it deals with the environmental challenges of a particular portfolio of chemicals. In a theory piece, Sharfman, Shaft, & Tihanyi (2004) argued that higher environmental performance could be linked to greater levels of globalization and diversification (across industries and countries), since pressures for greater performance are increasing and because there are efficiencies in using a common set of policies (Dowell, Hart, & Yeung 2000).

Contributions from adjoining fields

The resource-based view of the firm gives pride of place to the internal dimensions of an organization. It is also at its heart a rational framework. Two more behavioral approaches can be complementary with the resource-based theory: stakeholder management and institution theory. Both of these theories reach well beyond the domain of competitive strategy, but have particular sub-domains that address competitive advantage (for complete reviews of stakeholder management and institution theory, see Kassinis [Chapter 5]; Lounsbury, Fairclough, & Lee [Chapter 12]; and Delmas & Toffel [Chapter 13] this volume).

Stakeholder theory is the main theoretical perspective that influences our understanding of how firms can effectively manage a range of external constituencies to build competitive advantages (Freeman 1984), and numerous scholars have applied the stakeholder concept to the natural environment (e.g. Buysee & Verbeke 2003; Henriques & Sadorsky 1999; Sharma & Vredenburg 1998). The branch of stakeholder theory that has been most frequently applied to CSE is instrumental stakeholder theory, which explores the notion that "corporations practicing stakeholder management will, other things being equal, be relatively successful in conventional performance terms" (Donaldson & Preston 1995: 67).

CSE research has shown that stakeholder management may affect firm performance by allowing firms to access and capitalize on resources (both tangible and intangible) controlled by environmentally sensitive stakeholders. Bansal & Clelland (2004) show that environmentally legitimate firms possess a competitive advantage in the market, but must satisfy key stakeholder groups that control this image. These findings are consistent with those of other scholars (Berrone, Surroca, & Tribo 2007; Surroca, Tribo, & Waddock 2010). Focusing on a more general notion of competitive advantage than is reflected in financial performance metrics, Delmas (2001) demonstrated how external stakeholders were critical to generating firm competitive advantage in the case of the development of ISO 14001. Competitive advantage is likely dependent on the ability to integrate stakeholder capabilities with traditional capabilities such as innovation (Sharma, Aragón-Correa, & Rueda-Manzanares 2007).

Research in institutional theory that bears upon CSE is worth noting for its unusual relationship to competitive strategies. Institutional theory holds that institutions (rules, customs, beliefs, etc.) guide and constrain the behavior of organizations (Scott 2008). Attainment of legitimacy within institutionalized contexts can unlock additional resources and advance organizational goals (DiMaggio & Powell 1983). This advancement, however, generally takes place not through surviving interorganizational competition, but rather through "defensive" forms of CSE that focus more on forestalling aggressive stakeholders who could divert the organization's energies from more important competitive contingencies. The use of certifications and standards plays an important role in institution theory (Terlaak 2007). Studies of the chemical industry's Responsible Care program (King & Lenox 2000) and the ski industry's Sustainable Slopes Program (Rivera, De Leon, & Koerber 2006) demonstrate that there can be collective strategic value in reducing differentiation by adopting common standards toward the environment.

Further evidence that some standards are adopted to erect strategic barriers to change came from Delmas & Toffel (2008), who found that stronger corporate marketing departments were associated with ISO 14001 adoptions. Given that technical units within organizations, such as production and operations departments, are not central to the story, it's not surprising that ISO 14001 may not lead to environmental performance improvements (King, Lenox, & Terlaak 2005; Potoski & Prakash 2005). (Readers interested in non-market strategies such as voluntary regulation and voluntary standards see King, Prado, & Rivera [Chapter 6] this volume.)

Research from both stakeholder management and institutional theory domains indicates that when it comes to competitive strategy and the environment, the notion of capabilities should be widened considerably. We must appreciate that it is not just the direct effect of traditional resources capabilities (superior human resources, first-class production facilities, top-of-mind brand equity, and the like) that can generate a competitive edge. Sound capabilities for managing external constituencies and institutional pressures also can underpin CSE (Aragón-Correa & Sharma 2003). Firms ignore the imperative to build these capabilities at their own risk.

CSE research has produced a rich diversity of literature on the topic of competitive strategy and the environment. Researchers employing a variety of disciplinary lenses have synthesized a body of knowledge that explores the nuances afforded by introducing the natural environment to the strategic equation, respects the value of both rational and behavioral explanations of behavior, and appreciates that we still have much to learn. All of these aspects also are true when we consider the dimension of strategic implementation of strategies.

THE IMPLEMENTATION DIMENSION:
CONNECTING EXTERNAL AND INTERNAL

To understand more fully how competitive strategy unfolds within organizations, we need to flesh out issues of strategy implementation. Here, a number of scholarly contributions are "peeling the onion," by uncovering layers of aggregation and allowing us to perceive the links in the chain that connects the eternal and internal contexts. This task is important to understanding CSE. As Delmas & Toffel (2008) showed, organizations subject to the same set of external pressures will adopt different practices and policies. Studies that bridge external and internal phenomena can help answer this seeming paradox.

Proactivity as the driver of change

An important issue in understanding CSE is how organizations filter the external pressure for environmentally oriented strategic actions at their boundaries (Hoffman 1999;

Murillo-Luna, Garcés-Ayurbe, & Rivera-Torres 2008). Managerial perceptions of stake-holders and their demands are an important determinant of subsequent action (Buysse & Verbeke 2003; Sharma 2000; Henriques & Sadorsky 1999). Being proactive about environmental issues (Aragón-Correa 1998; Hunt & Auster 1990; Roome 1992) is one place to begin looking at how the external environment is translated into organizational action. The source of environmental proactivity (sometimes termed responsiveness) can be associated with different strata within organizations (Bansal & Roth 2000; Wheeler, Fabig, & Boele 2002), and result in several trigger points of constructive change.

Leadership, power, and reward systems

Leadership is perhaps the key variable in the change equation. For Berry & Rondinelli (1998: 45), "because proactive environmental management requires a champion, success depends on securing the backing of top management." Supervisory encouragement can elicit creative responses to the mandate for internal change (Ramus & Steger 2000). Maxwell et al. (1997) agreed, determining that not only was the commitment of senior management essential to successful implementation of environmental initiatives, but also their willingness to actively encourage ideas that emerged from lower levels of the organization. Klassen (2001) also found top managers' attitudes to be critical to driving positive outcomes. Andersson & Bateman (2000) spotlighted the championing of envi-ronmental initiatives, showing that such behavior has many dimensions, including identifying, packaging, and selling the need for action. Branzei et al. (2004) argued that championing behavior by individuals within top management influenced others in the upper echelons to take more pro-environment actions. Not surprisingly, such leaders have a value system that features stronger ecological values (Egri & Herman 2000). Translating the vision for change and educating employees is critical, because wide-spread awareness of environmental issues can elicit improved practices (Jiang & Bansal 2003; Sarkis, Gonzalez-Torre & Adenso-Diaz 2010).

The relative positions of organizational subunits (Howard-Grenville 2006) can also facilitate or impede strategic change. Delmas & Toffel (2008) showed that internal con-stituencies influenced how companies in heavily polluting industries reacted to institu-tional pressure for change. They found that firms with more powerful legal and marketing departments were more responsive to nonmarket and market pressures, respectively. Aragón-Correa, Matías-Reche, & Senise-Barrio (2004) determined that firms having one or more individuals with specific responsibility for the environment had higher levels of commitment to improvement. Analyzing a sample of MNCs in the chemical industry, Christmann (2004) found that the greater the dependence of subsid-iaries on the rest of the company for resources, the greater the level of global standard-ization of policies and communications practices.

Reward systems matter as well. Several studies have spotlighted compensation as a means for eliciting behavior in the service of environmental stewardship. Chinander

(2001) discovered that even though managers in a steel company she studied espoused environmentally sensitive management, the reality on the plant floor was another matter. Accountability was a key to improving employees' environmental performance, as was communicating how their actions had environmental consequences. Analyzing a sample of electronics firms, Russo & Harrison (2005) established that when plant managers had compensation tied to environmental performance, toxic emissions decreased. Berrone & Gomez-Mejia (2009), paradoxically, found that explicitly stated environmental pay policies did not result in differential reward of environmental strategies when compared to companies without such policies. Their result suggests either that firm adoption of such policies may be transitioning from rational to symbolic in orientation, or that reward practices have diffused separately from policy adoption. Further research that explored how incentive systems can change behavior—especially if they included variation on the form of incentives—can reveal highly relevant and actionable findings. A fuller description of internal mechanisms can be found in Forbes & Jermier ([Chapter 30] this volume) and Howard-Grenville & Bertels ([Chapter 11)] this volume).

Developing environmentally oriented capabilities

The development of capabilities to support organizational initiatives toward the environment—or means to direct capabilities to that goal—is the end result of many of the actions we've discussed here. One way to understand what the implications are for capability-building is to integrate environmental issues into strategic planning. Judge & Douglas (1998) determined that such integration significantly influenced environmental performance, a result they attributed to several factors. Planning and information are pivotal to this process. Planning gives top managers an opportunity to access the information necessary to boost environmental performance (Stead & Stead 1995), as well as the opportunity for champions to assert themselves (Winn 1995). In fact, the simple provision of information by those central to organizations can improve prospects for adoption of practices like pollution prevention, especially when that information is not otherwise available (Lenox & King 2004).

Christmann (2000), using survey data, showed that the cost advantages of environmental initiatives like pollution prevention, green innovations, and early timing of changes depended on the presence of complementary assets. Without complementary assets, measured to include process and product innovation, consistent investments in technology, and other more general assets, the effect of the initiatives was weakened. Darnall & Edwards (2006) confirmed the importance of complementary assets by showing that adoption of environmental management systems was more costly for organizations without expertise in continuous improvement.

A literature has emerged to help us understand how companies become energized to pursue environmental improvements, as well as which organizational mechanisms are best suited to eliciting positive change. Further work in this area, particularly that which can tie to "bigger picture" issues that we reviewed in the first section, is most welcome. Although many pieces of the puzzle are in place, we are still some distance from a comprehensive understanding of the skillful implementation of CSE.

THE QUESTION OF ENVIRONMENTAL PERFORMANCE AND FINANCIAL PERFORMANCE

Business strategy is fundamentally concerned with linking firm actions with economic performance. In the sub-field of competitive strategy and the environment, this central focus has motivated one of the dominant research questions about organizations and the natural environment in the past three decades: whether it "pays to be green." Research on this question has generated a wealth of theoretical discussion and empirical analysis that we summarize here for the sake of completeness. This work is important. We suspect that most B&NE researchers genuinely believe that green business is worth doing because it is "the right thing to do." Nonetheless, researchers seem to bear a pragmatic understanding that practitioners aren't looking to us to tell them right from wrong, but rather how "the right thing" can be harnessed to boost profitability. Not all managers need to be lured with a carrot to embrace sustainability, but working to develop a better understanding of how and when environmental strategy can enhance financial performance will provide practitioners and theorists alike with useful guidance in moving competitive strategy toward sustainability.

Debate over whether or not improved environmental performance boosts profitability has persisted so long because, despite persuasive theoretical logic, empirical tests of the relationship between environmental strategy and financial performance have generated mixed results (Margolis & Walsh 2003). The flurry of "pays to be green" research has occurred within the larger theoretical endeavor to link overall corporate social performance to firm financial performance. In this stream, social performance is sometimes deconstructed into purely social and environmental components, to form the "triple bottom line" when added to economic performance (Elkington 1998). Within this literature, several excellent review articles have been published that summarize the debate. In general, the findings of these reviews have been that the link between CEP and CFP is positive, but weak (Margolis, Elfenbein, & Walsh 2009; Orlitzky, Schmidt, & Rynes 2003).

A review of the "pays to be green" literature suggests several explanations for the mixed empirical results. One explanation is that there is rampant inconsistency in how key variables are defined and operationalized across studies (Griffin & Mahon 1997; Orlitzky, Schmidt, & Rhyes 2003; Peloza 2009). We will expand on this point in the following section on methodology. Another concern is that many researchers use single measures of CEP (Peloza 2009) that cannot possibly act as full proxy for a firm's environmental activity. And very few studies mention the fact that improved environmental performance can reduce risk (Sharfman & Fernando 2008). If so, even if a program to improve environmental performance did not increase profits, it would still improve the risk-return profile for the firm and therefore represent a prudent course of action.

One of the biggest contributors of the mixed results seems to be that although the relationship between corporate environmental strategy and financial performance is very likely recursive in nature and highly complex in any case, much of the previous research has relied on relatively simple correlations and direct effect models to test the relationship. Addressing recursiveness, Orlitzky, Schmidt, & Rynes (2003) argue that even treating CEP as an independent variable and CFP as a dependent variable misstates the issue, because environmental and financial performance exist in a "virtuous circle" of bi-directional causality. On the topic of complexity, Peloza (2009) advises researchers to recognize and measure not only CEP and CFP but also the many critical intermediate and mediating variables that contribute to the relationship. Peloza's (2009) list of mediating variables, particularly those in categories he describes as relating to innovation and reputation, tie in well with work by resource-based theorists on corporate environmental strategy.

These arguments suggest a move away from asking "does it pay to be green" to the more nuanced question "when and how does it pay to be green?," a recommendation more than a decade old (Reinhardt 1998). Such a shift in focus echoes a similar one that occurred in strategy and organizational research during the 1960s and 1970s with the advent of contingency theory (Burns & Stalker 1961). The theory pushed researchers to uncover what different attributes determined organizational effectiveness, rather than to attempt to paint all organizations with the same prescriptive brush (Donaldson 2001). Fundamentally, this is the same idea that business strategy and the environment researchers are embracing now. Aragón-Correa & Sharma (2003) argued that many of the general business environment variables first identified by contingency theorists might be important in moderating the relationship between environmental strategy and financial performance.

In any case, we take the position that researchers practicing in the CSE domain concentrate efforts on the links in the causal chain that connect environmental performance to financial performance. Many of these links have been reviewed in the previous sections. While such studies may not allow a researcher to snatch the brass ring represented by a definitive study of the returns to greening, the fact is that this brass ring remains well beyond our reach at this time. At present, our field is like a youngster reaching for the ring, needing further growth to make that attempt successful. We will discuss more about data issues when we offer critiques and recommendations below.

A NOTE ON METHODOLOGY

From its point of origin, CSE has been the subject of much inquiry. It is worth taking a moment to review the progress of the field to date with respect to methodology and identify how it can move forward.

Quantitative analysis

One of the defining characteristics of strategic management research is a focus on financial returns, and work in CSE is no different. Many authors have used profitability ratios. Measures that utilize the stock market, either in terms of a valuation, such as Tobin's q (Dowell, Hart, & Yeung 2000) or market value-added (Hillman & Keim 2001), or in terms of reactions to events and announcements (Klassen & McLaughlin 1996), have been employed with success. All of these approaches are ubiquitous in the greater literature and thus enjoy high levels of "face validity."

The experience with financial performance can be contrasted with the experience with environmental performance. In CSE and elsewhere in the B&NE domain, measurement of environmental performance has been evolving and to an extent remains contested. Several studies of environmental performance utilized third-party assessments by investment advisors. The most popular database of assessments is from Kinder, Lydenberg, & Domini (KLD), which has been used in several studies of the financial impacts of environmental performance (Berman et al. 1999; Hillman & Keim 2001). Other assessments came from an assortment of investment advisors, such as Franklin Research and Development (Russo & Fouts 1997), or groups of socially responsible mutual funds (Barnett & Salomon 2006).

These assessments offer a critical advantage: they are an overall evaluation of a company's environmental performance. Sharfman (1996) showed that the KLD assessments had a good, though not overwhelming, degree of construct validity and Russo & Fouts (1996) reported that the Franklin Research figures they used correlated with toxic releases by firms and fines and penalties tracked by the Investor Responsibility Research Center. Chatterji, Levine, & Toffel (2009) determined that KLD environmental ratings "do a reasonable job of aggregating past environmental performance," (2009: 162), though they were only modestly valuable as predictors of future emissions performance.

Perhaps displaying some lingering skepticism over third-party assessments, other authors have tried to utilize a more direct measure of environmental performance by utilizing emissions data. Several authors have drawn data from the US Environmental Protection Agency's Toxics Release Inventory (TRI), a repository for plant emissions information since 1987. It is instructive to review how this variable has been refined with use. Initially, the total amount of aggregate emissions was used as a measure of environmental performance, typically divided by a company's sales (Dooley & Fryxell 1999; Konar & Cohen 2001). King & Lenox (2000) advanced this concept by recognizing that the variety of pollutants tracked by TRI had very different toxicities, and introduced a scheme that weighted each according to the inverse of a threshold volume (set by the United States Environmental Protection Agency, or EPA) above which a spill must be reported. Toffel & Marshall (2004) took this idea further, by considering the weighting scheme itself as a variable. They surveyed thirteen weighting schemes, finding that there was no single best weighting method but that the choice was contingent on other factors, such as whether the researcher was interested in human or ecosystem impacts.

Thus, there has been progress in measurement of key variables, which has strengthened our confidence in the results of studies in which they appear. We also believe that there has been a decrease in the use of self-reported data in CSE research. CSE researchers are also more likely to address important statistical issues now than they were in initial studies. Just to name one example, strategic management analyses often embody biases by not correcting for endogeneity in regressions (Shaver 1998). When not controlled, omitted variables can create "phantom" associations that suggest artifactual significance. For example, an omitted variable like the presence of strong management or first-class technology can be responsible for both profits and greening. This unobserved heterogeneity can result in spurious findings regarding relationships in this relationship (Telle 2006).

Progress in employing more sophisticated statistical corrections has been paralleled by the development and availability of a number of important databases that will contribute to our research on CSE. For those studying electric utilities (Delmas, Russo, & Montes-Sancho 2007; Delmas & Tokat 2005), the EGrid database has become indispensible. This is because unlike the Toxics Release Inventory, which consists of company estimates, EGrid is based on direct monitoring of actual emissions. It also includes a number of additional pollutants not tabulated in TRI. A database that will play an important role in the future comes from the Carbon Disclosure Project. Both by providing a track record of which companies choose to participate in its voluntary reporting and eventually by providing a consistent database, the CDP will be used to explore how efforts to curtail greenhouse gases impact CSE. A broader model is provided for by the Global Reporting Initiative, which includes a range of variables for both social and environmental measures with a degree of standardization that enhances comparability. Although both the CDP and the GRI are voluntary and involve self-reporting, they may well lead to the development of more credible measures in the future. The EPA's plan to collect standardized greenhouse gas data, for example, offers hope in this regard.

In any case, scholars in the field of CSE must employ a degree of patience in expecting "dream data sets." Public financial reporting is more than a century old, but most of the data used in our studies has been collected for twenty-five or fewer years. The future will see datasets assembled that contain a wider variety of variables included, more careful measurement of these variables, and greater levels of credibility and validity. If there is a "True North," it may be non-financial reporting criteria that are so widely accepted that companies can publish a single report that integrates both financial and non-financial information (Eccles & Krzus 2010).

Qualitative analysis

Like the broader strategic management literature, large-n quantitative studies dominate the CSE literature. That is not to say, however, that smaller-n case and qualitative studies do not play a significant role. Scholars of both positivist and interpretivist leanings have conducted important qualitative CSE studies. These studies are critical to advancing our understanding of CSE—particularly when large quantitative studies generate mixed and/or weak support for theory (as in the case of the CSE-CFP link). Although the studies themselves sacrifice broad external validity in favor of detailed understanding of the processes at play in a single case or industry context, collectively CSE case study researchers have focused on a variety of industries. Thus, an integration of these studies may contribute to a more general research frame. CSE scholars have used qualitative case study methods to explore the petroleum industry (Sharma, Pablo, & Vredenberg 1999; Sharma & Vredenberg 1998), the forestry industry (Brody et al. 2006), chemical and food industries (Roome & Wijen 2006), and semiconductor manufacturing (Howard-Grenville 2006), to name a few.

Given the importance of capabilities as a theme in the CSE literature, understanding the processes that companies employ to harness and develop environmentally relevant capabilities is of obvious importance. Such process-based questions are well suited to qualitative enquiry, the results of which stand on their own value as well as providing greater theoretical grounding for further quantitative testing. That is not to say that case-study researchers have exclusive claim to studies of companies' internal processes. An excellent example can be found by juxtaposing two very different studies with very similar titles that seek to open the "black box" of how companies respond to environmental issues. Howard-Grenville (2006) employs an ethnographic case method to explore how firms generate environmentally responsive practices, whereas Delmas & Toffel (2008) use structural equation modeling (SEM) to analyze a large-n survey of firms, operationalizing different patterns of firm responsiveness based on the roles played by two separate departments. Both studies have advanced CSE, and together stand as an example of how different methods yield results that researchers can use to triangulate toward greater understanding.

CRITIQUES AND RECOMMENDATIONS

The body of research in CSE has expanded very quickly. Numerous ideas have been advanced and a rough set of shared, grounded beliefs about competitive strategy and the environment has materialized. This review has been largely devoted to discussing this corpus, but it is important to pause and offer a critique of our field. In the limited space we have here, we identify two broad shortcomings we think demand attention if the field of CSE is to continue to flourish in the coming years.

Lack of attention to competitive and cooperative interactions

No strategist would ignore competitors, but research on strategy sometimes focuses more on why a firm should take an action than how that decision is influenced by what competitors do. It is true that when we evaluate, for example, how environmental performance can elicit stronger job candidates, implicitly we are assuming that to do so the firm must be greener than its competitors. However, work that explicitly studies strategic initiatives more directly in light of competitors' actions is rare. Nehrt (1996) studied timing of environmental investments, which has the effect of implicitly picking up relative actions, and Russo (2009) contrasted early and later adopters of ISO 14001 adoption. But in both cases, the authors simply considered the place in time of a particular action. No explicit study of how prior decisions affected prospective decisions was made, although these decisions do reflect a firm's existing strategy (Bansal & Hunter 2003). Some appreciation for how managers process the actions of close competitors and others that they benchmark would help the field back up its assumptions about behavior in the executive suite with the corroborating evidence of real-world competitive dynamics.

If we had finer-grained data, or more generalizable studies that featured small samples of firms that were closely studied, we could begin to trace how managers base decisions on competitive strategy in view of the environmental imperative. It may turn out, for example, that in branded product markets, larger companies are taking their cues not from other mainstream companies but the upstarts occupying the fringes of their fields. Unilever keeps a close watch on Colgate-Palmolive, Henkel, and Procter & Gamble. But it also has an eye on Seventh Generation and Method, two smaller companies that make environmental stewardship a cornerstone of their business models. Knowing more about how cutting-edge ideas diffuse through communities of practice, and how competition affects this diffusion would help us to appreciate whether environmental influences are similar to other pressing external influences (e.g., changing technologies) in how they are adopted, and whether or not the "extra-economic" rationales for adoption actually play any role in CSE.

Another area about which we know very little involves cooperative strategies for seeking competitive advantage that have an environmental flavor. In established (and generally not environmentally oriented) fields, the tendency has been to study initiatives like the Sustainable Forestry Initiative or Responsible Care that are intended to forestall stricter initiatives. It would be very instructive to have more stories about how green companies, especially in emerging fields like clean technology, organic foods, and natural care, have employed business associations to further their chances for success. We have evidence from the alternative energy field that such collective strategies yield salutary results (Russo 2001; Sine, Haveman, & Tolbert 2005), but know little about fields that are less subject to government oversight and support. In filling this gap, behavioral frameworks, such as institution theory, may offer significant synergies when blended with more rational frameworks, such as the resource-based theory.

Given the growing pressure for transparency and the responses of companies to this imperative, the role of cooperative strategies for reporting environmental information, via third parties such as The Carbon Disclosure Project and the Global Reporting Initiative, is also ripe for study. How do these organizations negotiate their way through a maze of stakeholders to create a common and consistent reporting language? Do they also exercise control over information in an age of greater transparency? Do they serve as a vehicle of social construction for what should be expected of organizations? These and other pertinent questions deserve answers.

Work in this area may lead to a greater appreciation of how networks of organizations and their environments coevolve over time (Kassinis [Chapter 5] this volume; Porter 2006; Zietsma & Lawrence 2010). In broader terms, the application of systems theories to strategy (Boons & Wagner 2009; Marshall & Brown 2003; Starik & Rands 1995) would appear to offer a promising avenue to appreciating the complexity surrounding strategic actions and how their cascading effects on organizations and environments create corresponding influences and counter-influences (see also Levy & Lichtenstein [Chapter 32] this volume). For example, without considering the actions and reactions of its constellation of related organizations, institutions, and stakeholders, it would be impossible to truly appreciate the trajectory of a firm's strategy for addressing the challenges and opportunities presented by imperatives for climate change action, supply chain stewardship, and dozens of other critical contingencies. Given how institutional forces have been relatively strong with respect to the environmental imperative, studies of how institutions seek to influence and even orchestrate networks can be very revealing (Paquin & Howard-Grenville 2010).

Data-led study contexts, sampling, and model specification

Much of the work in CSE is empirical. As such, the search for data has created several biases that have influenced our choice of topics and samples. First, as noted by Etzion (2007), we have tended to draw samples from dirty industries, such as chemicals, automobiles, wood products, and energy. Using samples from dirty industries may boost chances for significance in environmental variables, since there are wide and meaningful variations in emissions and other environmental indicators across comparable plants. Further, in dirtier industries, a large portion of plants have emissions that exceed TRI thresholds and therefore are mandated to report to the EPA and be included in the database. Thus, studying dirty industries reduces issues associated with missing data, which must be treated as censored for regression purposes.

But there is another bias associated with the tendency to sample companies from dirty industries: they generally sell products to other businesses, not consumers. In this way, CSE researchers have not pushed aggressively enough into the domain of product market competitive strategy. This may be one reason that the empirical literature on environmental differentiation remains so fragmented.

Second, we have tended to focus on phenomena for which there are tabulated records. The foremost example of this is the diffusion and impact of ISO 14001. Although a genuinely interesting platform for the study of institutional theory and competitive strategy, the large number of papers on ISO 14001 does seem to represent a commitment beyond its relative importance as a driver of CSE. And in terms of strategic performance outcomes, frequent use of readily available financial ratios has kept our focus from other, potentially more interesting, outcome measures such as new product innovations and successful partnerships with other companies and organizations.

Our focus on phenomena for which we have data has also drawn our attention away from a number of important topic areas related to CSE that would help fill important gaps in the literature. To cite just one example, Lenox & York ([Chapter 4] this volume) decry the lack of "rigorous empirical research into the central drivers of environmental entrepreneurship." Without question, this paucity of empirical research is due less to a lack of interest by scholars than to a lack of data on small and medium-sized companies. In the same way that new technological innovations come from the fringe of entrepreneurs riding technology's cutting edge, new environmental innovations come from the fringe of entrepreneurs pushing the limits of sustainability (Russo 2010). Therefore, the data-related failure to study environmental entrepreneurs more thoroughly has real consequences for knowledge creation and predictive power in CSE.

A lack of data also interacts with other gaps in our knowledge. Addressing the need for studies of networks that we just noted, if we had better data for supply-chain networks, we could act on the recommendation of Klassen & Vachon ([Chapter 15] this volume) to "keep the greater system in mind." Resulting empirical analysis would generate a deeper understanding of how CSE is reflected in vertical relationships, and how green capabilities can be shared among collaborators.

A third reason, and related to the second, is that we have not done enough to study mediating influences (Peloza 2009) that stand between larger concepts. The most prevalent case of this neglect is represented by the many studies of how environmental performance influences economic performance. Mediating influences such as direct cost savings, employee productivity, and brand impacts all appear in discussions of how environmental initiatives can boost profits, yet are seldom measured (Peloza & Yachnin 2008). Here again, arguably the issue revolves around data. There are two interrelated issues. The first is that most mediating variables are internal in nature and not generally available to outside parties. The second is that, even if such data were available, it might not be comparable across organizations.

One strategy is to obtain this data. It is true that the transparency movement is leading firms to place more of this information in the public domain. But a more complete accounting system of a wider set of variables is necessary. In 1961, the Marketing Science Institute was launched as a way for companies to share data with academics and other researchers through an intermediary. Over time, research collaborations with MSI have addressed issues of clear import to practitioners. It is time for CSE researchers to determine how a parallel repository of internal environmentally oriented data could be assembled. A database of readily available, directly comparable measures of internal dimensions of change would greatly impact our ability to conduct meaningful research that addresses pivotal conceptual questions. Given frequent demands by managers for proof of the instrumental effect of environmental initiatives, it is clear that value would accrue to practitioners as well.

A final thought

In 1997, the *Harvard Business Review* published Stuart Hart's article "Beyond Greening: Strategies for a Sustainable World" (Hart 1997). In the opening paragraphs, reflecting on the progress made by companies since the 1960s and 1970s, he noted, "We have come a long way. But the distance we've traveled will seem small, when in 30 years, we look back at the 1990s (Hart 1997:65)." Shifting forward to 2012, we can draw the same conclusion about the study of competitive strategy and the natural environment. An impressive record of early success reflects well on the field, but we have every reason to expect that the trajectory of our research in the next several decades will mirror Hart's prediction about sustainable development. Great excitement lies ahead.

REFERENCES

Andersson, L. & Bateman, T. (2000). "Individual Environmental Initiative: Championing Natural Environmental Issues in US Business Organizations," *Academy of Management Journal*, 548–70.

Aragón-Correa, J. (1998). "Strategic Proactivity and Firm Approach to the Natural Environment," *Academy of Management Journal*, 41(5): 556–67.

—— Matías-Reche, F. & Senise-Barrio, M. (2004). "Managerial Discretion and Corporate Commitment to the Natural Environment," *Journal of Business Research*, 57(9): 964–75.

—— & Sharma, S. (2003). "A Contingent Resource-Based View of Proactive Corporate Environmental Strategy," *Academy of Management Review*, 71–88.

Bansal, P. & Clelland, I. (2004). "Talking Trash: Legitimacy, Impression Management, and Unsystematic Risk in the Context of the Natural Environmen," *Academy of Management Journal*, 47(1): 197–218.

—— & Hunter, T. (2003). "Strategic Explanations for the Early Adoption of ISO 14001," *Journal of Business Ethics*, 46: 289–299.

—— & Roth, K. (2000). "Why Companies Go Green: A Model Of Ecological Responsiveness," *Academy of Management Journal*, 43(4): 717–36.

Barnett, M. L. & Salomon, R. M. (2006). "Beyond Dichotomy: The Curvilinear Relationship between Social Responsibility and Financial Performance," *Strategic Management Journal*, 27(11): 1101–22.

Barney, J. (1991). "Firm Resources and Sustained Competitive Advantage," *Journal of Management*, 17(1): 99–120.

Berman, S. L., Wicks, A. C., Kotha, S. & Jones, T. M. (1999). "Does Stakeholder Orienation Matter? The Relationship Between Stakeholder Management Models and Firm Financial Performance," *Academy of Management Journal*, 42(5): 488–506.

Berrone, P. & Gomez-Mejia, L. (2009). "The Pros and Cons of Rewarding Social Responsibility at the Top," *Human Resource Management*, 48(6): 959–71.

—— Surroca, J. & Tribó, J. (2007). "Corporate Ethical Identity as a Determinant of Firm Performance: A Test of the Mediating Role of Stakeholder Satisfaction," *Journal of Business Ethics*, 76(1): 35–53.

Berry, M. A. & Rondinelli, D. A. (1998). "Proactive Corporate Environmental Management: A New Industrial Revolution," *Academy of Management Executive*, 12(2): 38–50.

Boons, F. & Wagner, M. (2009). "Assessing the Relationship between Economic and Ecological Performance: Distinguishing System Levels and the Role of Innovation," *Ecological Economics*, 68(7): 1908–14.

Branzei, O., Ursacki Bryant, T., Vertinsky, I. & Zhang, W. (2004). "The Formation of Green Strategies in Chinese Firms: Matching Corporate Environmental Responses and Individual Principles," *Strategic Management Journal*, 25(11): 1075–95.

Brody, S., Cash, S., Dyke, J. & Thornton, S. (2006). "Motivations for the Forestry Industry to Participate in Collaborative Ecosystem Management Initiatives," *Forest Policy and Economics*, 8(2): 123–34.

Burns, T. & Stalker, G. M. (1961). "Mechanistic and Organic Systems of Innovation," *The Management of Innovation*, London: Tavistock Publications, 96–125

Buysse, K. & Verbeke, A. (2003). "Proactive Environmental Strategies: A Stakeholder Management Perspective," *Strategic Management Journal*, 24(5): 453–70.

Chatterji, A., Levine, D. & Toffel, M. (2009) "How Well do Social Ratings Actually Measure Corporate Social Responsibility?" *Journal of Economics & Management Strategy*, 18(1): 125 69.

Chinander, K. (2001). "Aligning Accountability and Awareness for Environmental Performance in Operations," *Production and Operations Management*, 10(3): 276–91.

Christmann, P. (2000). "Effects of 'Best Practices' of Environmental Management on Cost Advantage: The Role Of Complementary Assets," *Academy of Management Journal*, 43(4): 663–80.

—— (2004). "Multinational Companies and the Natural Environment: Determinants of Global Environmental Policy Standardization," *Academy of Management Journal*, 47(5): 747–60.

Darnall, N. & Edwards Jr, D. (2006). "Predicting the Cost of Environmental Management System Adoption: The Role of Capabilities, Resources and Ownership Structure," *Strategic Management Journal*, 27(4): 301–20.

Delmas, M. (2001). "Stakeholders and Competitive Advantage: The Case of ISO 14001," *Production and Operations Management*, 10(3): 343–58.

—— Russo, M. & Montes Sancho, M. (2007). "Deregulation and Environmental Differentiation in the Electric Utility Industry," *Strategic Management Journal*, 28(2): 189–209.

Delmas, M. A & Toffel, M. W. (2008). "Organizational Responses to Environmental Demands: Opening the Black Box," *Strategic Management Journal*, 29(10): 1027–55.

Delmas, M. & Tokat, Y. (2005) "Deregulation, Governance Structures, and Efficiency: The US Electric Utility Sector," *Strategic Management Journal*, 26(5): 441–60.

Diestre, L. & Rajagopolan, N. (2011). "An Environmental Perspective on Diversification: The effects of Chemical Relatedness and Regulatory Sanctions," *Academy of Management Journal*, 54(1): 97–115.

DiMaggio, P. J. & Powell, W. W. (1983). "The Iron Cage Revisited: Institutional Isomorphism and Collective Rationality in Organizational Fields," *American Sociological Review*, 48(2): 147–60.

Donaldson, L. (2001). *The Contingency Theory of Organizations: Foundations for Social Science*. Los Angeles: SAGE Publications

Donaldson, T. & Preston, L. E. (1995). "The Stakeholder Theory of the Corporation: Concepts, Evidence and Implications," *Academy of Management Review*, 20(1): 65–91.

Dooley, R. & Fryxell, G. (1999). "Attaining Decision Quality and Commitment from Dissent: The Moderating Effects of Loyalty and Competence in Strategic Decision-Making Teams," *Academy of Management Journal*, 42(4): 389–402.

Dowell, G., Hart, S. & Yeung, B. (2000). "Do Corporate Global Environmental Standards Create or Destroy Market Value?" *Management Science,* 46(8): 1059–74.

Eccles, R. G. & Krzus, M. P. (2010). *One Report: Integrated Reporting for a Sustainable Strategy.* Hoboken, NJ: Wiley.

Egri, C. & Herman, S. (2000). "Leadership in the North American environmental Sector: Values, Leadership Styles, and Contexts of Environmental Leaders and their Organizations," *Academy of Management Journal,* 43(4): 571–604.

Elkington, J. (1998). *Cannibals with Forks: The Triple Bottom Line of Twenty First Century Business.* Oxford: Capstone.

Etzion, D. (2007). "Research on Organizations and the Natural Environment, 1992–present: A Review," *Journal of Management,* 33(4): 637.

Freeman, R. E. (1984). *Strategic Management: A Stakeholder Approach.* Boston: Pitman.

Griffin, J. & Mahon, J. (1997). "The Corporate Social Performance and Corporate Financial Performance Debate: Twenty-five Years of Incomporable Research," *Business & Society,* 36(1): 5–31.

Hart, S. (1995). "A Natural-Resource-Based View of the Firm," *Academy of Management Review,* 986–1014.

—— (1997). "Beyond Greening: Strategies for a Sustainable World," *Harvard Business Review,* January/February, 66–76.

Henriques, I. & Sadorsky, P. (1999). "The Relationship between Environmental Commitment and Managerial Perceptions of Stakeholder Importance," *Academy of Management Journal,* 42: 87–99.

Hillman, A. & Keim, G. (2001). "Shareholder Value, Stakeholder Management, and Social Issues: What's the Bottom Line?" *Strategic Management Journal,* 22(2): 125–39.

Hoffman, A. J. (1999). "Institutional Evolution and Change: Environmentalism and the U.S. Chemical Industry," *Academy of Management Journal,* 42(4): 351–71.

Howard-Grenville, J. (2006). "Inside the 'Black Box,'" *Organization & Environment,* 19(1): 46.

Hull, C. & Rothenberg, S. (2008). "Firm Performance: The Interactions of Corporate Social Performance with Innovation and Industry Differentiation," *Strategic Management Journal,* 29(7): 781–89.

Hunt, C. B. & Auster, E. R. (1990). "Proactive Environmental Management: Avoiding the Toxic Trap," *Sloan Management Review,* 31(2): 7–18.

Jiang, R. & Bansal, P. (2003). "Seeing the Need for ISO 14001," *Journal of Management Studies,* 40(4): 1047–67.

Judge, W. & Douglas, T. (1998). "Performance Implications of Incorporating Natural Environmental Issues into the Strategic Planning Process: An Empirical Assessment," *Journal of Management Studies,* 35(2): 241–62.

King, A. & Lenox, M. (2000). "Industry Self-Regulation Without Sanctions: The Chemical Industry's Responsible Care Program," *Academy of Management Journal,* 43(4): 698–716.

—— —— & Terlaak, A. (2005). "The Strategic Use of Decentralized Institutions: Exploring Certification with the ISO 14001 Management Standard," *Academy of Management Journal,* 48(6): 1091.

Klassen, R. (2001). "Plant-Level Environmental Management Orientation: The Influence of Management Views and Plant Characteristics," *Production and Operations Management,* 10(3): 257–75.

—— & McLaughlin, C. (1996). "The Impact of Environmental Management on Firm Performance," *Management Science,* 42(8): 1199–214.

Konar, S. & Cohen, M. (2001). "Does the Market Value Environmental Performance?" *Review of Economics and Statistics*, 83(2): 281–89.

Lenox, M. & King, A. (2004). "Prospects for Developing Absorptive Capacity through Internal Information Provision," *Strategic Management Journal*, 25(4): 331–45.

López-Gamero, M., Claver-Cortés, E. & Molina-Azorín, J. (2008). "Complementary Resources and Capabilities for an Ethical and Environmental Management: A Qual/Quan Study," *Journal of Business Ethics*, 82(3): 701–32.

Marcus, A., Nichols, M. & Tyagi, R. (1999). "On the Effects of Downstream Entry," *Management Science*, 45(1): 59–73.

Margolis, J. D., Elfenbein, H. A. & Walsh, J. P. (2009). "Does it Pay to be Good…and Does it Matter? A Meta-Analysis of the Relationship between Corporate Social And Financial Performance." Working paper, Harvard Business School.

—— & Walsh, J. P. (2003). "Misery Loves Companies: Rethinking Social Initiatives by Business," *Administrative Science Quarterly*, 48(2). 268–305.

Marshall, R. S. & Brown, D. (2003). "The Strategy of Sustainability: A Systems Perspective on Environmental Initiatives," *California Management Review*, 46(1): 101–26.

Maxwell, J., Rothenberg, S., Briscoe, F. & Marcus, A. (1997). "Green Schemes: Corporate Environmental Strategies and their Implementation," *California Management Review*, 39: 118–34.

Murillo-Luna, J., Garcés-Ayerbe, C. & Rivera-Torres, P. (2008). "Why do Patterns of Environmental Response Differ? A Stakeholders' Pressure Approach," *Strategic Management Journal*, 29(11): 1225–40.

Nehrt, C. (1996). "Timing and Intensity Effects of Environmental Investments," *Strategic Management Journal*, 17(7): 535–47.

Nelson, R. R. & Winter, S. G. (1982). *An Evolutionary Theory of Economic Change.* Cambridge, MA: Harvard University Press.

Orlitzky, M., Schmidt, F. & Rynes, S. (2003). "Corporate Social and Financial Performance: A Meta-Analysis," *Organization Studies*, 24(3): 403.

Orsato, R. (2006). "Competitive Environmental Strategies: When Does it Pay to be Green?" *California Management Review*, 48(2): 127–43.

Paquin, R. & Howard-Greenville, J. (2010). "Building a Network: Processes and Consequences of Network Orchestration." Working paper.

Peloza, J. (2009). "The Challenge of Measuring Financial Impacts From Investments in Corporate Social Performance," *Journal of Management*, 35(6): 1518–41.

—— & Yachnin, R. (eds.) (2008). *Valuing Business Sustainability: A Systematic Review*, Research Network for Business Sustainability: Ontario.

Penrose, E. (1959). *The Theory of the Growth of the Firm.* John Wiley & Sons: New York.

Porter, T. (2006). "Coevolution as a Research Framework for Organizations and the Natural Environment," *Organization and Environment*, 19(4): 479.

Potoski, M. & Prakash, A. (2005). "Green Clubs and Voluntary Governance: ISO 14001 and Firms' Regulatory Compliance," *American Journal of Political Science*, 49(2): 235–48.

Ramus, C. & Steger, U. (2000). "The Roles of Supervisory Support Behaviors and Environmental Policy in Employee; 'Ecoinitiatives' at Leading-Edge European Companies," *Academy of Management Journal*, 43(4): 605–26.

Reinhardt, F. L. (1998). "Environmental product differentiation: Implications for corporate strategy," *California Management Review*, 40(4): 43–73.

Rivera, J., De Leon, P. & Koerber, C. (2006). "Is Greener Whiter Yet? The Sustainable Slopes Program after Five Years," *Policy Studies Journal*, 34(2): 195–221.

Roome, N. (1992). "Developing Management Environmental Strategies," *Business Strategy and the Environment*, 1(1): 11–24.

—— & Wijen, F. (2006). "Stakeholder Power and Organizational Learning in Corporate Environmental Management," *Organization Studies*, 27(2): 235.

Rumelt, R. (1974). *Strategy, Structure, and Economic Performance*, Boston, MA: Harvard Business School Press.

—— (1982). "Diversification Strategy and Profitability," *Strategic Management Journal*, 3(4): 359–69.

Russo, M. (2001). "Institutions, Exchange Relations, and the Emergence of New Fields: Regulatory Policies and Independent Power Production in America, 1978–1992," *Administrative Science Quarterly*, 46(1): 57–86.

—— (2009). "Explaining the Impact of ISO 14001 on Emission Performance: A Dynamic Capabilities Perspective on Process and Learning," *Business Strategy and the Environment*, 18: 307–319.

—— (2010). *Companies on a Mission: Entrepreneurial Strategies for Growing Sustainability, Responsibility, and Profitability*. Stanford, CA: Stanford University Press.

—— & Fouts, P. (1997). "A Resource-Based Perspective on Corporate Environmental Performance and Profitability," *The Academy of Management Journal*, 40(3): 534–59.

—— & Harrison, N. (2005). "Organizational Design and Environmental Performance: Clues from the Electronics Industry," *Academy of Management Journal*, 48(4): 582.

Sarkis, J., Gonzalez-Torre, P. & Adenso-Diaz, B. (2010). "Stakeholder Pressure and the Adoption of Environmental Practices: The Mediating Effect of Training," *Journal of Operations Management*, 28(2): 163–76.

Scott, W. R. (2008). *Institutions and Organizations: Ideas and Interests*. Los Angeles: SAGE Publications.

Sharfman, M. (1996). 'The Construct Validity of the Kinder, Lydenberg & Domini Social Performance Ratings Data.' *Journal of Business Ethics*, 15(3): 287–96.

—— & Fernando, C. (2008). "Environmental Risk Management and the Cost of Capital," *Strategic Management Journal*, 29(6): 569–92.

Sharfman, M. P., Shaft, T. M., & Tihanyi, L. (2004). "A Model of the Global and Institutional Antecedents of High-Level Corporate Environmental Performance," *Business & Society*, 43(1): 6–36.

Sharma, S. (2000). "Managerial Interpretations and Organizational Context as Predictors of Corporate Choice of Environmental Strategy," *Academy of Management Journal*, 43(4): 681–97.

—— Aragón-Correa, J. A. & Rueda-Manzanares, A. (2007). "The Contingent Influence of Organizational Capabilities on Proactive Environmental Strategy in the Service Sector: An Analysis of North American and European Ski Resorts," *Canadian Journal of Administrative Sciences-Revue Canadienne Des Sciences De L Administration*, 24(4): 268–83.

—— Pablo, A. L. & Vredenburg, H. (1999). "Corporate Environmental Responsiveness Strategies," *The Journal of Applied Behavioral Science*, 35(1): 87.

—— & Vredenburg, H. (1998). "Proactive Corporate Environmental Strategy and the Development of Competitively Valuable Organizational Capabilities," *Strategic Management Journal*, 19(8): 729–53.

Shaver, J. (1998). "Accounting for Endogeneity when Assessing Strategy Performance: Does Entry Mode Choice Affect FDI Survival?" *Management Science*, 44(4): 571–85.

Shrivastava, P. (1991). "Societal Contradictions and Industrial Crises," in S. Jasanoff (ed.) *Learning From Disaster: Risk Management After Bhopal*, Philadephia: University of Pennsylvania Press, 248–68.

—— (1995). "Environmental Technologies and Competitive Advantage," *Strategic Management Journal*, 16(S1): 183–200.

Sine, W., Haveman, H. & Tolbert, P. (2005). "Risky business? Entrepreneurship in the new independent-power sector," *Administrative Science Quarterly*, 50(2): 200–32.

Starik, M. & Rands, G. (1995). "Weaving an Integrated Web: Multilevel And Multisystem perspectives of Ecologically Sustainable Organizations," *Academy of Management Review*, 908–35.

Stead, W. E. & Stead, J. G. (1995). "An Empirical Investigation of Sustainability Strategy Implementation in Industrial Organizations," *Research in Corporate Social Performance and Policy, Supplement*, 43–66.

Surroca, J., Tribó, J. & Waddock, S. (2010). "Corporate Responsibility and Financial Performance: The Role of Intangible Resources," *Strategic Management Journal*, 31(5): 463–90.

Terlaak, A. (2007). "Order without Law? The Role of Certified Management Standards in Shaping Socially Desired Firm Behaviors," *Academy of Management Review*, 32(3): 968–985.

Telle, K. (2006). "'It Pays to be Green' A Premature Conclusion?" *Environmental and Resource Economics*, 35(3): 195–220.

Toffel, M. W. & Marshall, J. D. (2004). "Improving Environmental Performance Assessment: A Comparative Analysis of Weighting Methods Used to Evaluate Chemical Release Inventories," *Journal of Industrial Ecology*, 8:1, 2, 143–72.

Wernerfelt, B. (1984). "A Resource-Based View of the Firm," *Strategic Management Journal*, 5(2): 171–80.

Wheeler, D., Fabig, H. & Boele, R. (2002). "Paradoxes and Dilemmas for Stakeholder Responsive Firms in the Extractive Sector: Lessons from the Case of Shell and the Ogoni," *Journal of Business Ethics*, 39(3): 297–318.

Winn, M. (1995). £Corporate Leadership and Policies for the Natural Environment," in D. Collins & M. Starik (eds.) *Research in Corporate Social Performance and Policy, Supplement:*. Greenwich, CT: JAI Press, 127–61.

Zietsma, C. & Lawrence, T. B. (2010). 'Institutional Work in the Transformation of an Organizational Field: The Interplay of Boundary Work and Practice Work," *Administrative Science Quarterly*, 55:2010, 189–221.

CHAPTER 3

··

INTERNATIONAL BUSINESS AND THE ENVIRONMENT

··

PETRA CHRISTMANN
AND GLEN TAYLOR

IN the past two decades the cross-border activities of firms have increased considerably. Falling barriers to trade and foreign direct investment (FDI) have contributed to large increases in cross-border flows of goods and capital by multinational enterprises (MNEs), defined as firms that own and control value-adding activities in more than one country (Dunning & Lundan 2008). Furthermore, international trade between independent buyers and sellers has created vast global supply chains. These increases in cross-border activities, combined with the fact that government regulations differ across countries, sparked a debate about the environmental implications of the spread of MNEs and global supply chains. This chapter reviews the literature on the environmental conduct of MNEs and global supply chains and on regulating their environmental conduct, and provides directions for future research in this area.

The impact of MNEs and global supply chains on the natural environment is controversial. Some argue that they contribute to improving environmental quality in countries with lax environmental regulations because they face customer and other stakeholder pressures for responsible environmental conduct from abroad (Christmann & Taylor 2001) and because FDI and international trade contribute to transferring advanced environmental practices and technologies to these countries. Others suggest that MNEs and global supply chains take advantage of cross-country differences in environmental regulations by locating polluting activities in countries with lax regulations turning them into pollution havens—production and export platforms for dirty industries (Leonard 1988).

The field of international business (IB) is concerned with the behavior, strategies, and organization of MNEs, their relationships with external institutions and stakeholders, and the effects of their operations on host nations. Given the concerns about environmental impacts of MNE operations it is surprising that only a small number of studies in the IB literature have examined MNEs' environmental conduct. As Madsen (2009: 1299) states: "Oddly, despite the centrality of firm investment behavior to the pollution haven argument, management, international business, and strategy scholars have yet to involve themselves in the…debate." A possible explanation is that the IB literature has tradition-ally focused on positive aspects of MNE activity, while paying less attention to the "dark side" of the MNE (Eden & Lenway 2001). International political economy scholars on the other hand, view MNEs with suspicion, and focus on their negative social and envi-ronmental effects (Eden 1991). Thus, it is not surprising that much of the literature on MNEs' environmental conduct is not well integrated with the mainstream IB theories and literature (Meyer, 2004).

Given the international business field's lack of attention to environmental issues and the failure to integrate work on international environmental issues with IB theories, the pur-pose of this chapter is twofold. First, we review the literature on MNEs' and global supply chains' environmental conduct, on their environmental impact on host nations, and on governance of their environmental conduct in the global economy. Our review focuses on IB research. We also include relevant studies from the economics and international politi-cal economy literature, but do not aim to provide a complete overview of these literatures. Second, to better integrate the study of MNE environmental conduct and impacts with the IB literature, we organize our review around central themes in the IB literature:

1. MNE strategy and organization
2. Impact of MNEs on host countries
3. Global supply chains
4. Regulating the conduct of MNEs and global supply chains

MNEs' ENVIRONMENTAL STRATEGIES AND ORGANIZATION

The international business literature is concerned with international aspects of MNEs' behavior, strategies, and organization. With respect to managing their impacts on the natural environment, MNEs face two strategic decisions: how to design and organize their environmental strategies across their worldwide operations, and how to include environmental considerations in foreign locations decisions. Our review of the litera-ture on MNEs' environmental strategies focuses on these decisions.

Environmental strategies in MNEs: Global standardization versus national fragmentation

How MNEs organize their strategies across the different countries in which they operate is a central issue in the IB field. Bartlett & Ghoshal's (1989) integration-responsiveness framework suggests that MNEs face pressures for global integration of their operations such as common customers' needs across countries, as well as pressures for national responsiveness, such as cross-country differences in government regulations, customer tastes, and resource availability (Yip 2002). MNEs that face pressures for global integration adopt global strategies in which they centralize decision-making and standardize products and practices worldwide, while MNEs that face pressures for national responsiveness adopt multi-domestic strategies, in which they delegate key decision-making responsibilities to country subsidiaries, and tailor products and practices to local conditions.

Managing environmental issues across operations located in different countries is challenging because MNEs face opposing external pressures for global standardization and national fragmentation of their environmental strategies. Given these challenges and the importance of MNEs' cross-country organization of environmental strategies for their overall environmental impact, it is surprising that only a few studies explicitly address how MNEs manage environmental issues across their country subsidiaries.

Evolution of MNEs' global standardization of environmental strategies over time

MNEs' management of environmental issues has changed over time from multi-domestic approaches where country subsidiaries were responsible for managing environmental issues to more global approaches where MNEs standardize environmental practices or performance targets for their operations worldwide. In the 1960s, when environmental issues were not a central concern, MNEs typically assigned the responsibility for managing environmental issues to local production managers (Pearson 1985). Studies conducted in the 1970s and 1980s (Gladwin & Walter 1976; Gladwin & Welles 1976; United Nations 1988) concluded that MNEs' management of environmental issues was decentralized and fragmented. As Gladwin & Welles (1976: 179) state: "For any MNC there are typically as many environmental strategies as there are foreign subsidiaries." However, more recent evidence suggests that most MNEs have shifted to global environmental performance standards and/or more globally uniform environmental policies for their worldwide operations (Brown et al. 1993; Dowell, Hart & Yeung 2000; Epstein & Roy 2007; Rappaport & Flaherty 1992; Sharfman, Shaft & Tihanyi 2004) and that MNEs are transferring environmental practices and technologies across country subsidiaries (Pinske et al. 2010; Rugman & Verbeke 1998). However, specific aspects of MNEs' environmental strategies seem to remain localized. For example, Hunter & Bansal (2006) find that the credibility of environmental communication, that is, the extent to which communication is both transparent and comprehensive, was surprisingly diverse across subsidiaries of the same MNE and tailored to local conditions.

External determinants of MNEs' global standardization of environmental strategies

The IB literature suggests that MNEs face diverse, fragmented and possibly conflicting sets of external pressures (Kostova, Roth, & Dacin 2008) that include home and host country pressures as well as pressures that transcend national borders (Kostova & Zaheer 1999). Managing MNEs' global operations is further complicated by differences in the availability of material, technical, human, and other resources across the countries where they operate. In this section we discuss how external pressures and differences in the country-level availability of resources affect MNEs' decisions to globally organize and manage their environmental strategies.

External pressures for MNE environmental strategy standardization have increased in the past three decades. Early work concluded that the heterogeneity of environmental regulations across countries created fragmenting forces that pushed MNEs towards tailoring or adapting their environmental conduct to local environmental policy environments (Gladwin & Welles 1976). Concerns about the inability of national environmental regulations to effectively protect the environment have increased because, with low barriers to trade and FDI, national governments have incentives to keep environmental regulations low as they compete with other countries to become attractive low-cost locations for production and investment. These concerns, combined with highly visible environmental accidents involving MNEs such as the Bhopal tragedy (Shrivastava 1987), led external stakeholders to pressure MNEs to apply high environmental standards throughout their worldwide operations. Non-governmental organizations (NGOs) and international governmental organizations such as the OECD and the United Nations use a variety of voluntary approaches such as codes of conduct and certifiable standards to affect MNEs' environmental conduct. Customers and investors have become more interested in MNEs' environmental conduct and consider their adoption of global environmental codes and standards in purchasing or investment decisions. These more recent external pressures for environmental responsibility transcend national borders and often originate from areas that are not directly affected by the negative externalities of MNEs' activities.

A small but growing number of studies have examined MNEs' responses to the increased external pressures for global standardization of their environmental strategies. Christmann (2004) concludes that different external drivers for environmental strategy standardization affect MNEs' standardization of different content dimensions of environmental strategies, which suggests that researchers need to explicitly consider the multidimensional nature of the global integration of environmental strategies construct. Government drivers such as international harmonization of environmental regulations affect MNEs' level of global environmental performance standards, while industry pressures cause international standardization of operational environmental practices. Interestingly, customer pressures contribute only to standardizing the content of MNEs' environmental communication across countries, and not to actions that reduce MNEs' environmental impact, possibly because the actual level of MNEs' environmental strategy standardization is not transparent to customers. Thus, mechanisms that increase the transparency of firms' environmental conduct such as certifiable standards are critical for raising the effectiveness of customer pressures for environmental responsibility.

Differences in the availability of resources across countries are fragmenting forces that lower global standardization of MNEs' environmental strategies. The importance of different environmental issues varies across countries because of differences in countries' environmental assimilative capacity, that is, their relative ability to absorb pollutants, which is determined by their relative availability of air, water, and land (Dean 1992). For example, issues of water pollution are more important in countries in which the availability and absorptive capacity of water is low and MNEs may be more likely to transfer advanced water treatment technologies to those countries. In addition, differences in the availability of the skilled human resources required to effectively implement environmental management systems and advanced environmental technologies may impede the transfer of these practices and technologies across MNE subsidiaries (Christmann & Taylor 2003). Differences in local conditions such as the availability of an infrastructure to deal with pollution make it difficult to transfer environmental practices across locations, so that standardizing practices across locations may actually lower environmental performance in some locations (Cebon 1993; Child & Tsai 2005; Levy 1995; Nehrt 1996).

Effects of internal MNE characteristics on global standardization of environmental strategies

MNEs tap into the skill pools of multiple countries to develop and acquire capabilities, practices, and technologies, and leverage these assets by transferring them to their operations in other countries. Global standardization of MNEs' environmental strategies requires transferring environmental practices, procedures, or technologies to all their country subsidiaries across the globe. MNEs develop advanced practices and technologies in response to the stringent environmental regulations they face in some countries (Porter & van der Linde 1995).

Transferring environmental capabilities across country subsidiaries can lead to cost savings in a number of ways (Dowell, Hart, & Yeoung 2000). First, implementing advanced environmental technologies in MNE operations worldwide can result in increased efficiency and reduced materials use. Given that MNEs already possess advanced environmental technologies in their subsidiaries in high regulation countries, transferring these technologies to foreign subsidiaries may be less costly than implementing less advanced technologies. Indeed, using outdated, polluting technologies in low-regulation countries may actually increase MNCs' production costs (Knödgen 1979),

Second, standardizing environmental technologies and practices across country subsidiaries may lower coordination costs, especially for MNEs that operate in many countries. Keeping up with constantly changing national environmental regulations and public expectations in all countries and assuring that all subsidiaries meet these evolving regulations and expectations is complex and costly (Sharfman et al. 2004). Global standardization of environmental strategies by adopting a uniform approach that exceeds regulatory compliance everywhere reduces these complexities.

However, not all MNEs realize the same costs savings from globally integrating their environmental strategies. Many capabilities required to implement environmental strategies are developed by other business functions such as manufacturing or research and development (Christmann 2000; Florida 1996). MNEs that manage other business functions in a globally integrated manner, for example, by standardizing technologies and organizational practices, likely incur lower costs of standardizing their environmental policies globally than firms pursuing multi-domestic strategies. Therefore, MNEs align the cross-country organization of their environmental strategies with their organization of other business functions across countries (Christmann 2004). Furthermore, MNEs pursuing multi-domestic strategies place greater importance on local environmental issues than MNEs following global strategies, possibly because MNEs pursuing multi domestic strategies incur lower costs of identifying and addressing local issues (Husted & Allen 2006).

Inter-subsidiary differences in capabilities also complicate transfers of practices and technologies across MNE subsidiaries. Capability differences can lead to differences in subsidiaries' absorptive capacity, that is, their capacity to assimilate and implement new knowledge from external sources (Cohen & Levinthal, 1990) and in their complementary assets, that is, the assets required to capture the benefits from implementing certain practices, and technologies (Teece 1986). Implementing environmental practices and technologies requires both absorptive capacity and complementary assets (Christmann 2000; Christmann & Taylor 2003; Pinske, Kuss, & Hoffmann 2010), so that a subsidiary's level of these resources likely affects the extent to which environmental practices get transferred to the subsidiary. In emerging economies, subsidiaries' absorptive capacity is related to their workforce's basic education and literacy. Technological capabilities and prior experience with similar management processes can be seen as complementary assets that affect subsidiaries' likelihood of implementing the ISO 14001 environmental management system (EMS) (Christmann & Taylor 2003).

Finally, subsidiary dependence affects the likelihood that headquarters successfully transfer policies, practices, and technologies. Drawing on resource dependence theory (Pfeffer & Salancik 1978) international business scholars suggest that the dependence of subsidiaries on the rest of the MNE for critical resources affects the level of control that headquarters have over subsidiary decisions (Martinez & Ricks 1989; Prahalad & Doz 1987). Because subsidiary managers in low-regulation countries often resist implementing environmental policies, practices, and technologies that they perceive add costs to their operations without any commensurate short-term benefits (Rappaport & Flaherty

1992), headquarter control over subsidiaries affects the extent to which environmental policies are transferred (Christmann 2004).

Effects of environmental issues on MNEs' location decisions

Cross-country differences in environmental regulations provide opportunities for MNEs to lower their production costs by locating polluting activities in countries with less stringent environmental regulations (Leonard 1988). However, empirical studies in the economics literature that examine the effect of differences in environmental regulations on MNE's location choice have not reached conclusive results. Most studies find little evidence that FDI in pollution intensive industries is influenced by the relative stringency of environmental regulations in home and host nations (Eskeland & Harrison 2003; Javorcik & Wei 2004). However, studies that have examined FDI location decisions *within* a given country such as the United States or China find that when making intra-country location decisions firms prefer regions with weaker environmental regulations (Dean, Lovely, & Wang 2009; Keller & Levinson 2002; List and Co 2000). These latter studies suggest that due to large regional variations in environmental regulations within host countries, future research should not focus not on the country level, but on regions within countries.

Given the importance of foreign investment behavior and location choice to international business researchers it is surprising that very few IB studies have addressed the effects of environmental regulations on location choice. One exception is Madsen's (2009) recent firm-level study of MNE location decisions in the automotive industry, which finds that MNEs' environmental protection capabilities moderate the relationship between regulatory stringency and location choice. While a host county's stringency of environmental regulations does on average not affect MNEs' country location choice, MNCs that lack environmental protection capabilities are more likely to locate in countries with weak environmental regulations. This finding is consistent with economics research that found that MNEs from emerging economies, which presumably have lower environmental protection capabilities than other MNEs, are more likely to locate in areas with weak environmental regulations (Dean, Lovely, & Wang 2009). These results point to the importance of considering MNE heterogeneity in future research on the effects of environmental regulations on MNEs' location decisions.

Impact of MNEs on the natural environment in host countries

The international business and the international political economy literature have long been concerned with the conduct and the economic and social impacts of MNE subsidiaries in their host countries. Two central questions in this discussion that have been addressed with respect to environmental issues are how foreign ownership sets MNE subsidiaries apart from locally owned firms and how MNE operations affect the natural environment in developing countries.

Comparing the conduct of MNE subsidiaries and locally owned firms

International business researchers have long argued that MNEs' operations are subject to a liability of foreignness that results in costs not faced by locally owned firms (Hymer 1976; Kindleberger 1969; Zaheer 1995). These costs arise from unfamiliarity with the local environment, from higher public expectations about MNE subsidiaries' conduct in their host countries relative to local firms, and from discrimination against foreign firms by customers, suppliers, and governments. On the other hand, researchers have suggested that MNEs may be able to secure advantages from national governments in their pre-entry negotiations that local businesses cannot obtain. To attract FDI, national governments often give MNEs concessions such as tax breaks and other investment incentives. In addition, MNEs likely have advantages over local firms because the very reason for their existence is that they possess superior resources that they transfer to their foreign subsidiaries (Dunning 1977).

Research has also explored how MNE subsidiaries and local firms differ in their environmental conduct and performance. Many environmental protection activities such as waste or pollution prevention require skills that are tacit and specific to local conditions (see Klassen & Vachon [Chapter 15] this volume; Lifset & Boons [Chapter 17] this volume). The liability of foreignness perspective suggests that this local embeddedness reduces MNE subsidiaries' environmental performance relative to their domestic counterparts because they lack expertise to respond to local conditions (Hymer 1976; Buckley & Casson 1976; Dunning 1977). In addition, information disadvantages make it more difficult for MNE subsidiaries to identify buyers for their waste byproducts in foreign countries, and possible buyers may be reluctant to purchase waste created by foreign firms that use process technologies that they are unfamiliar with (King & Shaver 2001).

MNEs tend to have strong bargaining power in pre-entry negotiations with host governments because they can threaten to locate elsewhere if governments enforce environmental regulations, and because host governments frequently lack adequate information about potential environmental problems associated with proposed industrial plants (Leonard 1988). This bargaining may allow MNEs to secure concessions such as exemptions from complying with specific environmental regulations, which also reduces their environmental performance. While there is only limited evidence that MNE subsidiaries obtain exemptions from complying with environmental regulations, MNEs often make overly optimistic promises about their subsidiaries' environmental quality standards in pre-entry negotiations, only to renegotiate when the facility is operating (Leonard 1988).

Others argue that MNE subsidiaries' environmental conduct and performance is superior to that of domestic firms because MNEs possess superior financial, managerial, and technological capabilities for pollution abatement, and are subject to greater public expectations and external pressures for environmental protection (Pearson 1985). While formal environmental laws apply equally to foreign and domestic firms, governments may single out foreign firms for enforcement actions (Pearson 1985; Mezias 2002).

Most empirical studies of the environmental conduct of MNE subsidiaries versus domestic firms focus on high-income developed countries, possibly due to data availability. Consistent with the liability of foreignness perspective, these studies found that foreign subsidiaries in the United States lag behind domestic firms in waste reduction and environmental performance (Levy 1995; King & Shaver 2001). However, these results are likely specific to developed host countries, where environmental regulations tend to be stringent and where domestic competitors possess strong environmental protection capabilities. In the context of emerging economies, empirical studies show that MNE subsidiaries in Mexico have no worse environmental performance than local firms (Muller & Kolk 2010) and that their environmental conduct in China is superior to that of local firms (Christmann & Taylor 2001). In the next section, we explore MNEs' environmental conduct in emerging economies as well as other effects of MNE operations on the natural environment in these countries.

Effects of MNEs on the natural environment in emerging economies

MNEs play a critical role in linking economies by transferring financial capital, knowledge, capabilities, ideas, and value systems across borders (Meyer 2004). Yet, their impact on economic development and social welfare in emerging economies is controversial. On the one hand, MNEs may transfer advanced technologies and practices to emerging economies and positive knowledge spillovers from MNE operations to local firms may contribute to economic development and social welfare in their host nations. Spillover effects are experienced by local firms other than the MNE subsidiary and do not arise from a deliberate transfer of resources from the MNE to the local partner (Dunning & Lundan 2008). On the other hand, MNEs may crowd out local firms and reduce competition and use their strong bargaining position relative to host country governments to obtain concessions that reduce their economic and social benefits to host nations (Stiglitz 2008; Vacchani 1995; Vernon 1971).

Despite the IB field's interest in the impact of MNEs on host nations, most research on the environmental impact of MNE operations in emerging economies has been performed in other disciplines such as economics and political science. It is argued that MNEs can contribute to improving environmental quality in emerging economy host nations by transferring advanced production technologies and environmental management practices to their subsidiaries in these countries. Such transfers normally result from greenfield FDI, that is, the construction of new facilities in the host country, because MNEs tend to employ their most efficient and cleanest technologies in new foreign operations (Gladwin & Welles 1976; Rugman & Verbeke 1998).

Negative environmental effects of MNE operations on emerging economy host nations can arise from locating dirty operations in these countries to exploit less stringent environmental regulations or regulatory exemptions obtained from host country governments. However, as discussed above, empirical evidence that FDI flows into low-regulation countries and that MNEs are subject to weaker environmental regulations than local firms is limited. Indeed, regulators in emerging economies often tend to focus enforcement efforts on MNEs, possibly because of their greater ability and willingness to pay any possible penalties and fines.

MNE subsidiaries in emerging economies can have broader effects on local firms' environmental conduct through market and non-market relationships. MNEs subsidiaries affect their local suppliers' environmental conduct directly by requiring them to adopt specific environmental management practices (Jeppesen & Hansen 2004). Empirical studies show that in China suppliers to MNE subsidiaries are more likely to adopt the ISO 14001 EMS and have higher environmental performance than firms supplying domestic customers (Christmann & Taylor 2001). Furthermore, host countries' stocks of FDI affect their country-level adoption of ISO 14001 positively (Neumeyer & Perkins 2004; Prakash & Potoski 2007).

Environmental technologies or management practices may also spread to local firms through non-market spillovers. Adoption of advanced technologies and practices by MNE subsidiaries can make local firms aware of these practices and demonstrate that these practices can be implemented in the local environment, which may lead to imitation by local firms. Furthermore, movements of employees who are trained in environmental technologies or practices from MNE subsidiaries to local firms diffuse knowledge about these practices to local firms (Meyer 2007). We are not aware of any empirical research that directly examines these non-market based spillovers in the context of environmental practices.

ENVIRONMENTAL CONDUCT OF GLOBAL SUPPLY CHAINS

Outsourcing and offshoring (see Klassen & Vachon [Chapter 15] this volume) result in complex global supply chains that have contributed to a significant increase in world trade. Surprisingly, the IB literature has paid only limited attention to global supply chains. Studies tend to focus on dyadic cross-country buyer-supplier relationships and their governance.

The most comprehensive body of literature that provides insights in the environmental implications of global supply chains is the international economics literature, where a long-standing debate over the environmental impact of liberalized trade exists (for a review, see Copeland & Taylor 2004). Economic theory suggests that international trade creates benefits by allowing countries to specialize in producing goods that take advantage of country-specific resources. Concerns about the environmental impact of trade arise because some countries may seek to establish comparative advantage in loosely regulated pollution-intensive industries and become pollution havens—export platforms for dirty goods. However, empirical evidence on the existence of pollution havens is largely inconclusive (Copeland & Taylor 2004).

A possible explanation for the inconclusive findings is that external stakeholders increasingly hold companies accountable for the environmental conduct of their foreign suppliers (see King, Prado, & Rivera [Chapter 6] this volume). Such extended responsibility reduces the cost advantage of sourcing from low-regulations countries because suppliers in these countries are pressured to adopt environmental practices or standards that exceed local environmental regulations. Studies confirm the influence of foreign customer pressures on suppliers' environmental conduct. Country-level studies show that exports to regions with high ISO 14001 certification rates such as Europe and Japan increase domestic certification rates (Corbett & Kirsch 2001; Neumayer & Perkins 2004; Prakash & Potoski 2006) and firm-level studies also point to the importance of export levels as antecedents of ISO 14001 certification (Christmann & Taylor 2001). However, this focus on customers' impact on their immediate foreign supplier ignores the environmental conduct of foreign firms that are located at lower tiers in supply chains, which do not have direct contact with foreign customers and are not directly involved in exporting activities (Levy 2008).

REGULATING THE ENVIRONMENTAL CONDUCT OF MNEs AND GLOBAL SUPPLY CHAINS

The international business literature has long been concerned with governing the conduct of MNEs' global operations. Historically, the literature mainly focused on issues such as transfer pricing and taxation, but recently the control of MNEs' environmental and social conduct has gained attention. Furthermore, recent studies have examined how new governance mechanisms affect the environmental conduct of foreign suppliers. A more detailed treatment of these governance mechanisms can be found in King, Prado, & Rivera [Chapter 6] in this volume. Here we focus only on international aspects.

A small but growing number of empirical studies have examined the antecedents of environmental conduct of MNEs and their suppliers. Many of these studies have focused on firms' adoption of international voluntary environmental standards such as ISO 14001, probably due to the difficulty of obtaining other data on the environmental conduct of firms in foreign countries. As discussed above, these studies show the importance of foreign customer pressures and foreign ownership as determinants of ISO 14001 certification. Certification to such standards has in many cases become a de facto requirement for firms engaged in international business (Christmann & Taylor 2001; Cashore 2002).

Commonly agreed upon global environmental standards can lower costs in global supply chains because they reduce the proliferation of requirements for environmentally responsible behavior of exporting firms. Absent global standards, suppliers exporting to different countries may have to satisfy potentially conflicting requirements which increases their costs.

For the remainder of this section we focus on certifiable environmental standards. Firms obtain certification to these standards by passing independent third-party audits. Certifiable standards facilitate trade by reducing information asymmetries in global supply chains. Certification informs foreign customers about firms' or products' environmental attributes that they cannot observe directly (Schuler & Christmann 2011). This allows distant customers to consider suppliers' environmental conduct in purchasing decisions, which increases market pressures for environmental responsibility. Viewed as such, certifiable standards are market-based governance mechanisms for firms' environmental conduct (see Scammon & Mish [Chapter 19] this volume).

Despite their growth in recent years, concerns remain whether certifications to environmental standards are accurate signals of firms' environmental conduct. Weaknesses in third-party monitoring allow some firms to obtain ISO 14001 certification without using the ISO 14001 EMS in their daily operations (Boiral 2007; Christmann & Taylor 2006). Such low quality of ISO 14001 implementation reduces firms' environmental performance (Aravind & Christmann 2011). Problems of third-party monitoring are likely larger in emerging economies where some local third-party auditors may be unable or unwilling to enforce compliance with standards requirements. Auditors in these countries are more likely to lack the industry-specific expertise required for proper verification of compliance (O'Rourke 2003; Boiral 2003; Yeung & Mok 2005) and a culture of corruption which prevails in many emerging economies may allow firms to obtain certification by bribing auditors (Montiel, Husted, & Christmann 2009). As a result, some customers require foreign suppliers to obtain certification from specific auditors (Yeung and Mok 2005), indicating customers are concerned about global variations in auditor quality.

These findings cast doubt on the effectiveness of certifiable standards as market-based governance mechanisms, especially in emerging economies. Market-based governance mechanisms can only work if they provide reliable information about firms' environmental conduct to external stakeholders. Environmental management and IB researchers need to pay closer attention to firms' implementation of international standards in a global context.

CONCLUSIONS

IB research offers many potential ways to expand our understanding of how MNEs and global supply chains impact the natural environment and how these impacts can be regulated in the global economy, as well as about MNEs' role in shaping external pressures for environmental protection. We suggest three areas for future IB research on environmental issues.

Examine other aspects of MNEs' environmental strategies

While the current literature has acknowledged that the global organization of MNEs' environmental strategies is multidimensional across functions such as operations and communication, it has not explored how MNEs vary their strategic responses to different environmental issues. Characteristics of environmental issues such as their geographic scope, their urgency, and their salience to the MNE will likely influence MNEs' strategic responses.

From an IB perspective, it is particularly interesting to explore the geographic scope of environmental issues and the associated external pressures. The geographic scope of external pressures to address an environmental issue can differ from the geographic scope of the issue itself. Clearly, for global issues such as global warming, firms face global pressures. However, even if pollution does not cross national borders, external pressures to address the environmental issue can emerge in other countries. An environmental issue in one country can serve as an exemplar for other similar issues that can potentially arise in other countries, resulting in concerns and pressures regarding the issue in multiple countries across the globe. For example, while the environmental harm caused by BP's Deepwater Horizon accident in 2010 is localized to the Gulf of Mexico environmental activists can use it as an exemplar to question the legitimacy of offshore oil drilling operations worldwide, and the European Commission considered suspending complex drilling projects in Europe until the Deepwater Horizon accident's lessons are understood. This suggests that the geographic scope of environmental pressures changes over time as the issue and its framing evolves. Understanding the geographic scope of environmental pressures is critical for MNEs because it affects whether MNEs adopt a multi-domestic approach (if pressures are purely local) or a global approach (if similar pressures across countries exist) to address the issue. However, we do not know much about the processes through which environmental concerns spread across counties and what the role of key actors (such as international MNCs and NGOs) is in this process. A better understanding of how the concerns and external pressures associated with environmental issues become globalized can help managers to formulate better responses to emerging environmental issues. Longitudinal studies of the emergence and evolution of environmental issues can identify the processes through which environmental issues become international or global.

Research on MNEs' environmental strategies has mainly focused on their operational strategies that are intended to reduce their environmental impact. Only a few studies have examined the strategies that MNEs use to influence the perceptions and pressures of external stakeholders such as communication strategies (Christmann 2004; Hunter & Bansal 2006). Given the political power of MNEs and their ability to shape public opinion we need to know more about political or influence strategies of individual MNEs or groups of MNEs. Furthermore, the interactions of MNEs with global and local NGOs are fruitful areas for future IB research. Research questions that can be addressed include: How do MNEs interact with local and global NGOs? When do MNEs join together to employ political strategies to forestall public expectations for immediate action? What roles do MNEs play in multi-stakeholder processes aimed at global consensus on a wide range of environmental issues?

Revisit the pollution haven hypothesis by testing it at the firm level

Economics research using county-level data to examine the effects of environmental regulations on FDI and trade flows is inconclusive. A possible explanation for these inconclusive findings is that some firms take advantage of cross-country differences in environmental regulations, while others do not. Thus, firm characteristics such as firms' environmental protection capabilities moderate the relationship between national environmental regulations and FDI and trade (Madson 2009; Dean, Lovely, & Wang 2009). Applying the resource based view of the firm (Barney 1991) to MNE location decisions and using firm-level data could identify additional firm characteristics and capabilities that moderate the relationship, such as MNEs' global organization and their capability to transfer environmental technologies. IB researchers and strategy scholars, who have traditionally focused on firm level analysis, are uniquely qualified to examine these issues further.

Inconclusive findings may also be due to sole focus on country-level environmental regulations as determinants of MNE country location decisions. Findings that sub-country (state) level environmental regulations affect MNEs' within-country location decisions suggest that MNEs may consider other factors such as access to resources or human capital when first deciding in which country to locate, and then consider environmental regulations when deciding where to locate within this country. A better understanding of how and when MNEs incorporate environmental considerations in their FDI decisions, and with which levels of government they negotiate environmental performance issues can shed light on the appropriate geographic level of analysis. However, analyzing the effects of regulations at the sub-country level poses challenges of data availability, especially in emerging economies with intra-country differences in the enforcement of formal regulations (Montiel, Husted, & Christmann 2009).

Similar conclusions apply to global supply chains as well. A possible reason for the lack of evidence that low-regulations countries become export platforms for dirty goods is that firms in global supply chains differ in their propensity to take advantage of low environmental regulations. Considering customer, product, and relationship characteristics can identify reasons for these differences. Customer characteristics may moderate the relationship between environmental regulations and trade. For example, customers with strong brand-names risk losing their reputation if they outsource dirty activities to low-regulation countries without taking adequate steps to control their suppliers' conduct. This suggests that the pollution haven hypotheses will more likely hold for global supply chains of firms or industries that do not rely on brand names, a proposition that IB researchers could examine.

Furthermore, product characteristics may moderate the relationship between environmental regulation and trade. Outsourcing the production of components to low-regulation countries may attract little attention compared to outsourcing production of whole products or final assemblies because customers and other external stakeholders are less likely to know from which countries components were sourced. Thus, firms may be likely to outsource component production to low-regulation countries, while being reluctant to outsource production of the whole product or final assembly to these countries.

Finally, relationship characteristics such as the ease of switching to other suppliers may affect the likelihood that customers outsource dirty operations to low-regulation countries. If it is costly to switch suppliers, firms may be reluctant to select suppliers in low-regulation countries. If new or increased pressures to control the environmental conduct of their supply chain emerge, they cannot simply respond by switching to suppliers in higher-regulation countries. Thus, the pollution haven hypothesis will more likely hold for buyer-supplier relationships with low switching costs for buyers.

Controlling firms' environmental conduct in the global economy

The recent expansion of market-based international governance mechanisms gives rise to several interesting research questions. What are the different processes through which governance mechanisms emerge on the global stage? When do they follow on from efforts at a national level and expand? When are they born global? How do MNCs or global suppliers respond when multiple competing international standards or certifications exist? Do they adopt multiple standards or do they choose between standards?

We also need a better understanding of other actions customers can take to control the environmental conduct of their global supply chains in addition to requiring certification to voluntary standards. It is difficult and costly for customers to control the conduct of downstream suppliers that are far removed from them. What actions are customers taking to reach deeper into supply chains? How effective are these actions? What else can be done to extend customers' influence on environmental conduct beyond first- or second-tier suppliers?

In conclusion, we believe that international business researchers can make unique contributions to the debates on the environmental implications of MNEs and global supply chains and on controlling their negative impacts. Taking the analysis to the firm level or within the MNC to the subsidiary level will likely provide new insights that can help to better understand the motivations and incentives of different firms, and to design more effective mechanisms for controlling their environmental conduct. Such research will likely also help MNEs to design strategies to navigate the complexities of competing and often conflicting environmental demands imposed on them by domestic and foreign stakeholders.

REFERENCES

Andrews, R. N. L., Amaral, D., Darnall, N., Gallagher, D. R., Edwards, D., Hutson, A., D'Amore, C., Sun, L. & Zhang, Y. (2003). *Environmental Management Systems: Do They Improve Performance?* Chapel Hill: The University of North Carolina.

Aravind, D. & Christmann, P. (2008). "Institutional and Resource-Based Determinants of Substantive Implementation of ISO 14001," *Best Paper Proceedings of the Academy of Management Conference.*

—— (2011). "Decoupling of Standard Implementation from Certification: Do Variations in ISO 14001 Implementation Affect Facilities' Environmental Performance?" *Business Ethics Quarterly,* 21(1), 73–102.

Barney, J. B. (1991). "Firm Resources and Sustained Competitive Advantage," *Journal of Management,* 17(1): 99–120.

Bartlett, C. A. & Ghoshal, S. (1989). *Managing Across Borders: The Transnational Solution.* Boston: Harvard Business School Press.

Boiral, O. (2003). "ISO 9000: Outside the Iron Cage", *Organization Science,* 14(6): 720–737.

—— (2007). 'Corporate Greening through ISO 14001: A Rational Myth?' *Organization Science,* 18(1): 127–146.

Brown, H. S. Derr, P., Renn, O., & White, A. L. (1993). *Corporate Environmentalism in a Global Economy; Societal Values in International Technology Transfer,* Westport, CT: Quorum Books.

Buckley, P. J. & Casson, M. C. (1976). *The Future of the Multinational Enterprise.* London: Homes & Meier.

Cashore, B. (2002). "Legitimacy and the Privatization of Environmental Governance: How Non-State Market Driven (NSMD) Governance Systems Gain Rule-Making Authority," Governance, 15(4): 504–529.

Cebon, P. (1993). 'Corporate Obstacles to Pollution Prevention'. *EPA Journal.* 19: 20.

Child, J. & Tsai, T. (2005). "The Dynamic Between Firms' Environmental Strategies and Institutional Constraints in Emerging Economies: Evidence from China and Taiwan," *Journal of Management Studies,* 42(1): 95–125.

Christmann, P. (2000). "Effects of 'best practices' of environmental management on cost advantage: The role of complementary assets," *Academy of Management Journal*, 43(4): 663–880.

—— (2004). "Multinational Companies and the Natural Environment: Determinants of Global Environmental Policy Standardization,"*Academy of Management Journal*, 47(5): 747–760.

—— & Taylor, G. (2001). "Globalization and the Environment: Determinants of Firm Self-Regulation in China," *Journal of International Business Studies*, 32(3): 439–458.

—— —— (2002). "Globalization and the Environment: Strategies for International Voluntary Environmental Initiatives," *Academy of Management Executive*, 16(3): 121–135.

—— —— (2006). "Firm Self-Regulation through International Certifiable Standards: Determinants of Symbolic Versus Substantive Implementation," *Journal of International Business Studies*, 37(6): 863–878.

—— —— (2003). "Environmental Self-Regulation in the Global Economy: The Role of Firm Capabilities," in S. Lundan (ed.) *Multinationals, Environment and Global Competition*, JAI/Elsevier, Research in Global Strategic Management, 8: 119–145.

Cohen, W. M. & Levinthal, D. A. (1990). "Absorptive Capacity: A New Perspective on Learning and Innovation," *Administrative Science Quarterly*, 35: 128–152.

Copeland, B. R. & Taylor, M. S. (2004). 'Trade Growth and Environment.' *Journal of Economic Literature*, 17: 7–71.

Corbett C. J. & Kirsch, D. A. (2001). 'International Diffusion of ISO 14000 Certification'. *Production and Operations Management*, 10(3): 327–342.

Dacin, T., Goodstein, J., & Scott, W. R. (2002). 'Institutional Theory and Institutional Change: Introduction to the Special Research Forum'. *Academy of Management Journal*, 45: 45–57.

Dean, J. M. (1992). *Trade and Environment: A Survey of the Literature*, Background Paper for the World Development Report, Washington, DC: World Bank.

——, Lovely, M. E. & Wang, H. (2009). "Are Foreign Investors Attracted to Weak Environmental Regulations? Evaluating the Evidence from China," *Journal of Development Economics*, 90(1): 1–13.

Dowell, G., Hart, S., & Yeung, B. (2000). "Do Corporate Global Environmental Standards Create or Destroy Market Value?" *Management Science*, 46(8): 1059–1076.

Dunning, J. H. (1977). "Trade, Location of Economic Activity and the MNE: A Search for an Eclectic Approach," in B. Ohlin et al. (eds.), *The International Allocation of Economic Activity*, London: Macmillan Press, 395–418,

—— & Lundan, S. (2008). *Multinational Enterprises and the Global Economy*, Second Edition, Edward Elgar, Cheltenham, UK.

Eden, L. (1991). "Bringing the Firm Back In: Multinationals in International Political Economy," *Millennium*, 20(2): 197–224.

—— & Lenway, S. (2001). "The Janus Face of Globalization," *Journal of International Business Studies*, 32(3): 383–400.

Epstein and Roy (2007). "Implementing a Corporate Environmental Strategy: Establishing Coordination and Control within Multinational Companies'. *Business Strategy and the Environment*, 16(6): 389–403.

Eskeland, G. and A. Harrison. (2003). "Moving to Greener Pastures? Multinationals and the Pollution Haven Hypothesis,'. *Journal of Development Economics*, 70: 1–23.

Florida, R. (1996). 'Lean and Green: The Move to Environmentally Conscious Manufacturing'. *Callifornia Management Review*, 39: 80–105.

Gladwin, T. N. & Welles, J. G. (1976). 'Multinational Corporations and Environmental Protection: Patterns of Organizational Adaptation.' *International Studies of Management & Organization*, 6(1–2): 160–184.

—— & Walter, I. (1976). 'Multinational Enterprise, Social Responsiveness, and Pollution Control'. *Journal of International Business Studies*, 7: 57–74.

Hunter, T. and Bansal, P. (2006). 'How Standard is Standardized MNC Global Environmental Communication?' *Journal of Business Ethics*, 71(2): 135–47.

Husted, B. W. & Logsdon, J. M. (1997). "The Impact of NAFTA on Mexico's Environmental Policy," *Growth & Change*, 28(1): 24–48.

—— & Allen, D. B. (2006). "Corporate Social Responsibility in the Multinational Enterprise: Strategic and Institutional Approaches," *Journal of International Business Studies*, 37(6): 838–849.

Hymer, S. H. (1976). *The International Operations of National Firms: A Study of Direct Foreign Investment*. Cambridge, MA: The MIT Press, 1976.

Javorcik, B. S & Wei, S. J. (2004). "Pollution Havens and Foreign Direct Investment: Dirty Secret or Popular Myth?" *Contributions to Economic Analysis & Policy*, 3(2): Article 8.

Jeppesen S. & Hansen, M. W. (2004). "Environmental Upgrading of Third World Enterprises through Linkages to Transnational Corporations. Theoretical Perspectives and Preliminary Evidence," *Business Strategy and the Environment*, 13(4): 261–274.

Keller, W. & Levinson, A. (2002). "Pollution Abatement Costs and Foreign Direct Investment Inflows to U.S. States," *The Review of Economics and Statistics*, 84(4): 691–703.

Kindleberger, (1969). *American Business Abroad*. New Haven: Yale University Press.

King, A. & Lenox, M. (2001). "Lean and Green? An Empirical Examination of the Relationship between Lean Production and Environmental Performance," *Production and Operations Management*, 10(3): 244–256.

King, A. A. & Shaver, J. M. (2001). "Are Aliens Green? Assessing Foreign Establishments' Environmental Conduct in the United States," *Strategic Management Journal*, 22(11): 1069–85.

Knödgen, G. (1979). "Environment and Industrial Siting: Results of an Empirical Survey of Investment by West German Industry in Developing Counties," *Zeitschrift für Umweltpolitik*, 2: 407.

Kostova T. & Zaheer, S. (1999). "Organizational Legitimacy under Conditions of Complexity: The Case of the Multinational Enterprise," *Academy of Management Review*, 24(1): 64–81

—— Roth, K., & Dacin, T. (2008). "Institutional Theory in the Study of MNCs: A Critique and New Directions," *Academy of Management Review*, 33(4): 994–1007.

Leonard, H. J. (1988). *Pollution and the Struggle for a World Product: Multinational Corporations, Environment, and the Struggle for International Comparative Advantage*. Cambridge: Cambridge University Press.

Levy, D. L. (1995). "The Environmental Practices and Performance of TNCs," *Transnational Corporations*, 4(1): 44–68.

—— (2008). "Political Contestation in Global Production Networks," *Academy of Management Review*, 33(4): 943–963.

List, J. A. & Co, C.Y. (2000). "The Effects of Environmental Regulations on Foreign Direct Investment," *Journal of Environmental Economics and Management*, 40: 1–20.

Madsen, P. M. (2009). "Does FDI Drive a 'Race to the Bottom' in Environmental Regulation? A Reexamination Building on the Resource-Based View," *Academy of Management Journal*, 52: 1297–1318.

Martinez Z. L. & Ricks, D. L. (1989). "Multinational Parent Companies' Influence over Human Resource Decisions of Affiliates: U.S. Firms in Mexico," *Journal of International Business Studies*, 20: 465–487.

Meyer, K. E. (2004). "Perspectives on Multinational Enterprises in Emerging Economies," *Journal of International Business Studies*, 34(4): 259–277.

—— (2007). "Social Responsibilities and Impact of Multinational Enterprises in Emerging Economies." Working paper.

Mezias, J. M. (2002). "Identifying Liabilities of Foreignness and Strategies to Minimize their Effects: The Case of Labor Lawsuits Judgments in the United States," *Strategic Management Journal*, 23: 229–244.

Montiel, I. Husted, B. & Christmann, P. (2009). "Corruption and Environmental Certification: The Case of ISO 14001 in Mexico," presentation at the 2009 *Academy of Management Meetings*, Chicago, IL, August.

Muller A. & Kolk, A. (2010). "Extrinsic and Intrinsic Drivers of Corporate Social Performance: Evidence from Foreign and Domestic Firms in Mexico," *Journal of Management Studies*, 47(1): 126.

Nehrt, C.C. (1996). "Timing and Intensity of Environmental Investments," *Strategic Management Journal*, 17(7): 535–547.

Neumayer E. & Perkins, R. (2004). "What Explains the Uneven Take-Up of ISO 14001 at the Global Level? A Panel-Data Analysis," *Environment and Planning*, 36: 823–839.

OECD (2008). *OECD Guidelines for Multinational Enterprises*, Paris, France: OECD Publishing.

O'Rourke, D. (2003). "Outsourcing Regulation: Analyzing Nongovernmental Systems of Labor Standards and Monitoring," *Policy Studies Journal*, 31(1): 1–29.

Pearson, C. S. (1985). *Down to Business: Multinational Corporations: The Environment and Development*. Washington, DC: World Resources Institute.

Pfeffer, J. & Salancik G. R. (1978). *The External Control of Organizations: A Resource Dependence Perspective*. New York, NY: Harper and Row.

Pinkse, J., Kuss, M. J., & Hoffmann, V. H. (2010). "On the Implementation of a 'Global' Environmental Strategy: The Role of Absorptive Capacity," *International Business Review*, 19(2): 160–177.

Porter, M. E., & van der Linde, C. (1995). 'Toward a New Conception of the Environment-Competitiveness Relationship,' *Journal of Economic Perspectives*, 9(4): 97–118.

Potoski, M. & Prakash, A. (2004). "Regulatory Convergence in Nongovernmental Regimes? Cross-National Adoption of ISO 14001 Certifications," *The Journal of Politics*, 66(3): 885–905.

—— —— (2005). "Covenants with Weak Swords: ISO 14001 and Facilities' Environmental Performance," *Journal of Policy Analysis and Management*, 24(4): 745–769.

Prahalad, C. K., and Doz, Y. (1987). *The Multinational Mission: Balancing Local Demands and Global Vision*, New York, Free Press.

Prakash, A. & Potoski, M. (2006). "Racing to the Bottom? Trade, Environmental Governance, and ISO 14001," *American Journal of Political Science*, 50(2): 350–364.

—— —— (2007). "Investing Up: FDI and the Cross-Country Diffusion of ISO 14001 Management System," *International Studies Quarterly*, 51(3): 723–744.

Qinghua, Z. & Sarkis, J. (2004). Relationships between Operational Practices and Performance among Early Adopters of Green Supply Chain Management Practices in Chinese Manufacturing Enterprises, *Journal of Operations Management*, 22(3): 265–289.

Rappaport, A. & Flaherty, M. F. (1992). *Corporate Responses to Environmental Challenges: Initiatives by Multinational Management*. New York: Quorum Books.

Rugman, A. & Verbeke, A. (1998). "Corporate Strategies and Environmental Regulations: An Organizing Framework," *Strategic Management Journal*, 19(4): 363–375.

Schuler, D. A. & Christmann, P. (2011). "The Effectiveness of Market-Based Social Governance Schemes: The Case of Fair Trade Coffee," *Business Ethics Quarterly*.

Shah, K.U. & Rivera, J. E. (2007). "Export Processing Zones and Corporate Environmental Performance in Emerging Economies: The Case of the Oil, Gas, and Chemical Sectors of Trinidad and Tobago," *Policy Sciences*, 40(4): 265–287.

Sharfman, M., Shaft, T. M. & Tihanyi, L. (2004). "A Model of the Global and Institutional Antecedents of High-Level Corporate Environmental Performance," *Business Society*, 43: 6–26.

Shrivastava, P. (1987) *Bhopal: Anatomy of Crisis*. Ballinger Publications.

Spar, D. L. & Yoffie, D. B (2000). 'A Race to the Bottom or Governance from the Top?', in A. Prakash & J. Hart (eds.) *Coping with Globalization*, London: Routledge, 31–51.

Stewart, R. B. (1993). "Environmental Regulation and International Competitiveness," *Yale Law Journal*, 102: 2039–2106.

Stiglitz, J. E. (2008). "Making Globalization Work," *The Economic and Social Review*, 39: 3, (Winter), 171–190.

Teece, D. (1986). "Profiting from Innovation: Implications For Integrity, Collaboration, Licensing, and Public Policy," *Research Policy*, 15: 295–305.

Teegen, H., Doh, J. P. & Vachani, S. (2004). "The Importance of Nongovernmental Organizations in Global Governance and Value Creation: An International Business Research Agenda," *Journal of International Business Studies*, 35: 463–483.

United Nations. (1988). *Transnational Corporations and Environmental Management in Selected Asian and Pacific Developing Countries* (ESCAP/UNCTC Publications Series B, no. 13). New York: United Nations.

Vacchani, S. (1995). "Enhancing the Obsolescing Bargain Theory: A Longitudinal Study of Foreign Ownership of U.S. and European Multinationals," *Journal of International Business Studies*, 26: 159–180.

Vernon, R. (1971). *Sovereignty at Bay: The Multinational Spread of U.S. Enterprises*. New York. NY: Basic Books.

—— (1997). *Storm Over the Multinationals: The Real Issues*. Cambridge, MA: Harvard University Press.

—— (1998). *In the Hurricane's Eye: The Troubled Prospects of Multinational Enterprises*. Cambridge, MA: Harvard University Press.

Yeung, G. and Mok, V. (2005). "What are the Impacts of Implementing ISOs on the Competitiveness of Manufacturing Industry in China?" *Journal of World Business*, 40(2): 139–157.

Yip, G. S. (2002). *Total Global Strategy II.*, 2nd. ed., Prentice Hall.

Zaheer, S. (1995). "Overcoming the Liability of Foreignness," *Academy of Management Journal*, 8(2): 341–363.

CHAPTER 4

....

ENVIRONMENTAL ENTREPRENEURSHIP

....

MICHAEL LENOX
AND JEFFREY G. YORK

We cannot separate organic life and mind from physical nature without also
separating nature from life and mind. The separation has reached the point where
intelligent persons are asking whether the end is to be a catastrophe, the subjection
of man to the industrial and military machines he has created.

John Dewey, *Experience and Nature*, 1925

Environmental entrepreneurs—individuals who create new, often for-profit, ventures
that help address environmental challenges—have become the darlings of environmentalists and business people alike. Yet, until recently, you would be hard pressed to find
entrepreneurs cast as the heroes of the environmental movement. In Hardin's canonical
Tragedy of the Commons, those individuals who recognize and seize opportunity (in
other words, entrepreneurs) are at the root of our environmental dilemma. In Hardin's
words, "Ruin is the destination toward which all men rush, each pursuing his own best
interest in a society that believes in the freedom of the commons" (1968).

Much of the B&NE literature has taken Hardin's view as a starting point: the unbridled self-interest of economic actors cannot be sustained in a world in which resources
are limited. As the chapters in this volume illustrate, the majority of scholarship around
business and the natural environment has focused on large corporations and what can
be done to encourage them to respect and preserve the environmental commons. The
central questions of this literature, such as "When does it pay to be green?", "Can self-
regulation persist?", and "Does environmental responsibility hinder or hamper competitive advantage?", are largely concerned with how to incentivize firms to reduce their own
negative environmental externalities (see Russo & Minto [Chapter 2] this volume; King,
Prado, & Rivera [Chapter 6] this volume).

Entrepreneurship researchers have begun to ask a different set of questions. The nascent field of environmental entrepreneurship asks whether and how entrepreneurs—self-interested individuals who recognize, exploit, and create future markets for goods and services (Venkataraman 1997)—can simultaneously foster economic and ecological benefits for society regardless of whether they themselves contributed to environmental degradation(Hall, Daneke, & Lenox 2010). The possibility that entrepreneurs could solve many of our environmental challenges through the introduction of new environmentally benign products and services has attracted attention from many different quarters in the popular press, so much so that Hall, Daneke, & Lenox (2010) caution against what they refer to as the "panacea hypothesis"—the supposition that entrepreneurship is a solution to all of our environmental problems. As they observe, much more work needs to be done to understand the potential and limits of environmental entrepreneurship.

Despite growing interest in environmental entrepreneurship, the academic literature on the topic is still in a nascent stage. Many early papers, particularly those in journals on sustainable development, focused mainly on defining environmental entrepreneurship. For example Isaak (1997) characterized environmental entrepreneurial ventures as "system-transforming, socially-committed environmental businesses characterized by breakthrough innovation." To a large extent, this early work assumes environmental entrepreneurship is an ethical imperative and does little to explain the underlining drivers of environmental entrepreneurship. However, these early studies do provide some context around what environmental entrepreneurship might be.

Consistent with these early works, the role of the entrepreneur in fostering environmental goods has been of far greater interest to sustainability researchers than entrepreneurship or management researchers. For example, *Greener Management International* published two special issues focused on the topic, the first in 2002 (Isaak 2002; Linnanen 2002; Pastakia 2002; Schaltegger 2002; Schaper 2002; Schick et al. 2002; Volery 2002; Walley & Taylor 2002) and the most recent in 2009 (Gibbs 2009; O'Neill Jr et al. 2009; Parrish & Foxon 2009; Schlange 2009; Tilley & Parrish 2009; Tilley & Young 2009).[1] As of April 2010, no articles focused explicitly on entrepreneurial solutions to environmental degradation had appeared in top US-based management journals such as the *Academy of Management Journal*, the *Academy of Management Review*, the *Strategic Management Journal*, *Administrative Science Quarterly*, and *Organizational Science*, with the exception of a handful of articles focused on entrepreneurial entry into renewable energy (Russo 2003; Sine & Lee 2009). Hall et al. (2010) report that, of the leading entrepreneurship journals,[2] only

[1] For a complete review of published articles pertaining to environmental entrepreneurship, please refer to Hall, Daneke, & Lenox's (2010) lead article to the *Journal of Business Venturing's* special issue on "Entrepreneurship and Sustainable Development."

[2] We considered journals that are listed on Thomson Reuters's Journal Citation Reports and appeared in the Financial Times list of top academic journals in business. Of the journals not listed in The Financial Times "Top 40", *Family Business Review* published one article (Craig and Dibrell 2006), and *Small Business Economics* published another (Bianchi & Noci 1998). As of this writing, there were no substantial publications in *Entrepreneurship Theory and Practice, Strategic Entrepreneurship Journal, International Small Business Journal, Entrepreneurship and Regional Development,* and the *Journal of Small Business Management*.

two papers on the topic of environmental entrepreneurship had been published as of August 2010, both at the *Journal of Business Venturing* (Cohen & Winn 2007; Dean & McMullen 2007). Signs point to an increasing interest in the topic, however, as evidenced by the recently published *Journal of Business Venturing* special issue on "Entrepreneurship and Sustainable Development" (Elsevier 2010).

Overall, work in environmental entrepreneurship has evolved from a variety of fields, including ethics, entrepreneurship, economics, and sustainable development. The nascent environmental entrepreneurship literature has focused primarily on the question of "What drives environmental entrepreneurship?" We identify three main classes of drivers from the literature: economic incentives, personal motivations, and institutional context. In the following sections we examine the existing literature on each of these drivers. Much of the work in this area has been theoretical and prescriptive. We seek to outline existing theories and provide linkages to empirical evidence when possible. After our review, we turn to the future of the field and identify several gaps in the literature and offer potential directions for future research.

ECONOMIC INCENTIVES FOR ENVIRONMENTAL ENTREPRENEURSHIP

The entrepreneurship literature has long focused on entrepreneurs' incentives to discover (Shane 2000; Shane & Venkataraman 2000; Shane 2004) and create (Sarasvathy & Dew 2005; S. Sarasvathy & Venkataraman 2009; Venkataraman 1997) opportunities for new products, services, and markets. Going back to Schumpeter (1934, 1942), scholars have highlighted the role of entrepreneurs as a force of creative destruction in markets. Unlike established economic actors, entrepreneurs have powerful incentives to disrupt the current market status quo and pursue innovations that restructure the competitive ordering.

Larson (2000)extends this view to environmental entrepreneurs, describing how they may be able to restructure the relationship between business and environment in ways that simultaneously create private economic value and public environmental value. In particular, Larson (2000) illustrates the importance of network and supply chain development for discovering and creating environmentally relevant opportunities. She argues "at the core of the entrepreneurship literature are the concepts of opportunity, innovation and future products as well as the processes—including network formation", and that these same concepts are applicable to environmental entrepreneurship.

York & Venkataraman (2010) argue that entrepreneurs are uniquely suited to address sustainability concerns because they can address the root of environmental issues in a manner other actors cannot. They cite three challenges that entrepreneurs are adept at addressing that are endemic to environmental concerns: uncertainty, innovation, and resource allocation. First, entrepreneurs are able to simultaneously create value and profit from the creation process by embracing uncertainty and "privatizing" risk even under conditions in which risk cannot be accurately calculated (Knight 1921). Environmental issues are inherently uncertain and there is no specific timeline for "sustainability", making them particularly well suited to environmental entrepreneurs. Second, entrepreneurship is an important engine of innovation within our society. As demands for sustainability increase, entrepreneurs are well positioned to provide the "creative destruction" that moves us forward. Third, entrepreneurs resolve resource allocation through the application of "alertness" to the inefficient use of resources (Hayek 1978). Because natural resources are limited, a sustainable solution to environmental problems must bring the most efficient method of resource allocation to bear. Entrepreneurs, seeking to reduce uncertainty and foster innovation, can find the best use of available resources.

Dean & McMullen (2007) originate this line of reasoning, focusing on the concept of market failure. They observe that environmental problems are the result of various forms of market failure, including public goods, externalities, monopoly power, government intervention and imperfect information (Dean et al. 2007). These market failures create opportunities that alert and knowledgeable entrepreneurs can capitalize on (Kirzner 1979). Similarly, Cohen & Winn (2007) focus on externalities, imperfect information, inefficient firms, and flawed pricing mechanisms as causes of market imperfection. Flawed pricing refers to the improper or non-existent pricing of natural capital; for example, oil, natural gas, and eco-services. They argue that a free-market economy fails to adequately value exhaustible resources. Renewable resources (bio-diesel, wind power, solar, etc.) are undervalued because the non-renewable resources are priced incorrectly. Entrepreneurs have the opportunity to engage in market correction by bringing newer, low-cost renewable technologies to market in an act of creative destruction.

Anderson & Leal (2001) identify a number of ways in which entrepreneurs are positioned to create environmental benefits while reaping economic gains. Entrepreneurs might devise ways to better market environmental attributes to those who value them (solving information asymmetries with customers), find ways to increase the value of recycled materials and other environmental goods (helping internalize externalities), or create technology which allows property rights to environmental goods to be assigned (helping incentivize the provision of public goods). Anderson & Leal (2001) envision the entrepreneur's primary role is to create the institutions, and particularly property rights, that preserve environmental quality. For example, an entrepreneur may devise a labeling scheme to identify environmentally friendly products or services.

In this way, environmental entrepreneurs could be conceived of as a specific type of institutional entrepreneur (Pacheco et al. 2010a). Institutional entrepreneurs are agents who attempt to mobilize collective action in order to change institutional fields or create new ones (Leca et al. 2008; Pacheco et al. 2010b). Institutional entrepreneurs, as typically referenced, are a broad class of actors including entrepreneurs in for-profit ventures, individual change agents in large organizations, and non-profit and social actors. They pursue change consistent with their personal objectives by changing the various institutional structures that guide economic actions. Does this suggest that all environmental entrepreneurs are institutional entrepreneurs? Not necessarily. Environmental entrepreneurs may have no other objective than to make money and they may be able to do so without changing underlying institutions. To more fully answer this question requires some understanding of the personal motivations of environmental entrepreneurs.

Personal motivations of environmental entrepreneurs

If we are to understand environmental entrepreneurship to be somehow different from general entrepreneurship, it seems logical that we should explore how individual motives for environmental entrepreneurship may differ from motives for entrepreneurship that does not reduce environmental degradation. Are environmental entrepreneurs motivated primarily by their own self-interest (Anderson & Leal 2001) or are they engaged in "a moral act that sustains the earth and the people that live upon it" (Isaak 1999)? If environmental entrepreneurs are differentially motivated, do they also engage in a different process of entrepreneurship?

Entrepreneurial motivation has long interested scholars in the broader field of entrepreneurship. Given the low success rates of new ventures, and the inherent difficulty in starting your own company, why would individuals chose self-employment, especially given that they may have other attractive options? While findings have been far from conclusive, scholars of entrepreneurship have found three recurring motivations for entrepreneurship: 1) a high desire for independence, 2) high need for achievement, and 3) passionate love of work (Shane 2004). One could easily port these motivations to environmental entrepreneurs, and in particular, passion for the specific opportunity and how it relates to resolving an environmental problem would seem a logical extension of findings in the core entrepreneurship literature.

To date, researchers in environmental entrepreneurship have not necessarily relied on research in entrepreneurship to build studies on motivation. For example, Keogh & Polonsky (1998) define entrepreneurship as creating a vision, identifying resources, and marshalling them towards that vision. They argue that individual commitment to environmental issues will generate action and can have three dimensions: affective (emotional), continuant (economic and social), and normative (regulatory). While their theory is quite intuitive, it is far afield from the established view of entrepreneurship as the nexus between an individual and an opportunity (Venkataraman 1997). In a qualitative analysis of six grassroots environmental entrepreneurs based in India, Pastakia (1998) divided entrepreneurs into commercial (maximizing personal gain through identification and exploitation of green business opportunities) and social (seeking to promote an eco-friendly idea/product/technology through market or non-market routes) types. The division between "economic" and "environmental" motivations is a recurring theme in the literature, with scholars finding differences between the motives of traditional vs. environmental entrepreneurs (Choi and Gray 2008; Linnanen 2002; Parrish 2010).

Although many studies have found differences in motivations, few have examined how environmental orientation of individuals, that is, their belief that environmental problems are a serious challenge to society, could impact their ability to recognize opportunity, recruit stakeholders, or engage in other entrepreneurial activities. In an exception, Kuckertz and Wagner (2010) utilized a large-scale survey of engineering and business students and alumni to statistically examine the relationship between a sustainability orientation and intentions to become an entrepreneur. The study shows a positive relationship between sustainability orientation and entrepreneurial which disappears as participants gain greater business education and experience.

If motives are divergent for environmental versus traditional entrepreneurs, it would seem logical to reason the process of initiating and sustaining a new venture may be different as well. Parrish (2010) utilizes in-depth studies of multiple cases to develop the concept of "perpetual reasoning", in which environmental entrepreneurs utilize processes and logics which diverge from the traditional "exploitative reasoning" of entrepreneurship. In a rare study which looks at a struggling venture, Volery (2002) provides an in depth case study in which the founder attempts to wed "stock market capitalism with native wildlife conservation", and struggles to reconcile his goals with the desires of external investors. Schlange (2009) argues that environmental entrepreneurs use a distinctly different method to identify salient stakeholders due to their orientation towards the triple bottom line.

This stream of the environmental entrepreneurship literature shares much in common with the growing literature on social entrepreneurship (Austin et al. 2006; Dees 1998). Social entrepreneurship refers to entrepreneurial ventures with an explicit social mission. While often used as a label for the creation and scaling of new non-profit organizations, reviews of the social entrepreneurship literature (Short et al. 2009; Zahra et al. 2009) highlight that social entrepreneurs are a wide-ranging group, including NGOs, for profit ventures and existing organizations. To the extent that, at least some, environmental entrepreneurs have an explicit social objective beyond profit maximization, we expect greater cross-fertilization between the social and environmental entrepreneurship literatures. Venkataraman (1997) observes that "the connection between the pursuit of a product-market in the future and the creation of social wealth offers both a distinctive voice and a worldview."

INSTITUTIONAL CONTEXT AND ENVIRONMENTAL ENTREPRENEURSHIP

Entrepreneurs, like any other actor, are influenced by the institutional conditions that surround them. Jennings & Zandbergen (1995) argue that an institutional approach could help us to understand how consensus is built around the meaning of sustainability and diffused through organizations broadly. New institutional theory focuses on examining the hidden forces that shape the actions of boundedly rational actors (see Lounsbury, Fairclough, & Lee [Chapter 12] this volume). The core claim of the theory is that actors pursue their interests within the constraints provided by institutions, including rules, norms, culture, and laws (Ingram & Silverman 2002). Actors simultaneously pursue their own interests and create constraints for other actors.

While institutional scholars have not explicitly examined the role of business entrepreneurs in driving the evolution of institutions towards more environmentally friendly practices, several papers have examined how institutional forces have influenced the rate of entrepreneurial entry in sustainability oriented businesses, particularly, renewable energy. Several authors have argued that environmental entrepreneurship can be inhibited by university and government bureaucracy (Isaak 1997)and encouraged by government programs, tax structure (Isaak 2002), and a supportive culture (O'Neill et al. 2009). O'Rourke (2003, 2005; Randjelovic et al. 2003) and her co-authors have explored the actual and potential role of venture capital investors in encouraging environmental entrepreneurship and discuss the impact that regulatory stimulus could have on venture capital and entrepreneurial foundings (O'Rourke, 2005: 135).

A recent stream of research by Russo (2001, 2003) and Sine & Lee (2009) has empirically examined the emergence of environmental entrepreneurs in the energy industry, providing evidence that the emergence of environmental entrepreneurship is indeed closely linked to regulatory, cognitive and normative institutions (Scott 1995).While this stream or research does not explicitly label entry as "environmental entrepreneurship", these studies provide robust empirical evidence and rigorous studies that address a key question for those scholars interested in the relationship between entrepreneurial entry and environmental degradation.

Russo (2001, 2003) provides a clear illustration of how these forces can impact the emergence of environmental entrepreneurship in his studies of entry rates of renewable energy projects. The first study examines the entry of small power producers, particularly those utilizing alternative energy sources (biomass, hydroelectric, municipal waste, solar, and wind) following the passage of laws that forced large utilities to purchase their power. The study analyzes entry rates by small utilities using traditional (coal, natural gas, or oil) versus renewable energy sources and finds that collective action efforts had a greater positive effect on entry for renewable producers, and that macroeconomic conditions had little influence on renewable energy projects.

In a later study focusing on wind energy project foundings in California, Russo (2003) again finds a positive and significant effect for collective action by trade associations on founding rates. Further, this study illustrates the confluence of multiple institutions, finding that positive project economics, prior foundings in the region, and natural resource availability, all provide predictive power for the entry of wind power projects. Sine & Lee (2009) extended these findings by examining the role of social movements, particularly activism by the Sierra Club, in determining entrepreneurial entry in the wind-power industry. The study shows that pro-renewable energy policies contributed to a 14 percent increase in foundings and that a 1000-person increase in Sierra Club membership increased foundings by 17 percent. Further, Sierra Club membership positively moderates the impact of resource availability on founding rates.

Meek and his colleagues (Meek et al. 2010) offer further evidence of the importance of the normative institutional environment for environmental entrepreneurs. Utilizing a panel of solar firm foundings and data on social norms collected by the General Social Survey (GSS), the study finds that higher levels of environmental and family interdependence norms impact the founding rates for solar firms. Further, social norms can impact the efficacy of policy; specifically norms of conformity reduce the efficacy of policy while norms of family interdependence positively moderate policies impact on firm foundings.

This small but growing research stream strongly implies that we must take regulatory and societal surroundings into account in studying environmental entrepreneurship.

FUTURE RESEARCH DIRECTIONS

One clear theme that emerged from our review is the need for rigorous empirical research into the central drivers of environmental entrepreneurship. Qualitative studies have produced a plethora of theories, and empirically testable propositions have been offered by many. We submit that further advancement of this field of study is dependent upon large-scale empirical studies. These studies need not be quantitative in nature, but they should be held to the same standards of rigor imposed on studies that are not exploring environmental issues. In many ways, environmental entrepreneurship research is in a similar situation to what the larger field of entrepreneurship was a decade ago. The path entrepreneurship took offers an instructive historical example of how to move the field forward.

First, the underlying economic incentives and personal motivations for environmental entrepreneurship must be developed further. Given the nascent stage of this area of study, theoretical development is likely to continue for the foreseeable future. However, empirical studies that attempt to differentiate between various drivers of environmental entrepreneurship and help advance our understanding of the conditions under which environmental entrepreneurship is likely to emerge are absolutely critical. Researchers should explore the ways in which economic incentives, personal motivations, and institutional contexts may interact to drive environmental entrepreneurship.

Second, there must be a concerted effort to understand the impact of environmental entrepreneurship on financial and environmental outcomes. In many studies, it is simply presumed that environmental entrepreneurship increases social and environmental welfare. Can we rigorously link the activities of environmental entrepreneurs to positive environmental and/or economic outcomes? As several scholars have pointed out (Hall et al. 2010; Parrish 2010), to frame environmental entrepreneurship as a panacea "neglects the importance of making difficult tradeoffs" (Parrish 2010). While many have theorized on the potential impacts of environmental entrepreneurship (Gibbs

2009; Tilley & Young 2009), in order for research in environmental entrepreneurship to be meaningful, we should examine these trade-offs empirically and understand how they are resolved.

Unfortunately, the empirical research to date on the actual impacts of environmental entrepreneurship is quite limited. Craig & Dibrell (2006) find that family firms which embraced environmentally beneficial policies created more innovations and had better financial performance. However, most quantitative studies have used environmental entrepreneurship as the dependent variable. We could find no empirical studies that examined the direct impacts of environmental entrepreneurship on the preservation of environmental resources, or the adoption of environmentally beneficial practices. For example, early qualitative case studies on the activities of environmental entrepreneurs (Larson 2000; Schaltegger 2002; Solaiman & Belal 1999) have tended to focus on process and motivations, but spend little time differentiating the impact of environmental entrepreneurs. Recent qualitative studies have attempted to draw linkages to the economic and ecological impacts of environmental entrepreneurship. Parrish & Foxon (2009) developed an integrative framework focused on the co-evolution of technology, institutions and business strategy to analyze the case of a US renewable energy firm. In a single case study of a green building start-up, O'Neil and his co-authors (2009) argued for the ability of small firms to impact the adoption of green building practices. While qualitative methods are clearly useful for the crafting of theory and are appropriate for an emerging research stream (Creswell 2009; Yin 2002), they are limited in their ability to differentiate the effect of environmental entrepreneurship in a broad, generalizable context.

Another clearly unaddressed question is differentiating the efforts of entrepreneurs from incumbent firms, social movements, and government in achieving ecological sustainability. For example, how does entrepreneurial entry interact with other institutions to predict the adoption of more environmentally friendly practices? One suggestion is to flip the interdependent and dependent variables of institutional studies of environmental entrepreneurship; in other words, rather than asking how institutions impact entrepreneurs, let us ask, how do entrepreneurs impact institutions? Pacheco and her colleagues (Pacheco et al. 2010a) propose that environmental entrepreneurs may alter or create institutions to encourage incentives for reducing environmental degradation. The role of an environmental entrepreneur can thus be expanded beyond the creation of new markets, products and services (Venkataraman 1997) and into the realm of institutional entrepreneurs (Battilana et al. 2009; Dean & McMullen 2007; Pacheco et al. 2010b). A fruitful question for future researchers would be to look at how the acts of environmental entrepreneurs lead, intentionally or not, to institutional change at a regulatory or socio-cultural level. To take it one step further, how then would those institutional changes impact the rate of entry of environmental entrepreneurs?

Finally, we suggest that studies of environmental entrepreneurship seek to expand the boundaries of their contribution. As outlined above, environmental entrepreneurship scholars have long sought to understand motives for environmental entrepreneurship; in a parallel track, entrepreneurship scholars have made limited progress in understanding motivations of entrepreneurs. For example, an area that has received recent attention in the broader entrepreneurship literature is the role of passion (Cardon et al. 2009). We submit that environmental entrepreneurship scholars are well positioned to examine the role of passion, specifically because the area of passion (addressing environmental issues) is on the surface for many of the ventures studied. Insights garnered from rigorous studies of the role of passion in environmental entrepreneurship could be generalized and provide insight into the broader field of entrepreneurship.

In a related question, what explains the engagement of multiple stakeholders in the environmental entrepreneur's new venture (Schlange 2009)? A central question of entrepreneurship research concerns the puzzle that "some individuals are able to secure resources from different resource controllers, often at very favorable terms, whereby considerable risk is shifted from the entrepreneur to the stakeholders" (Venkataraman 1997). It is commonly assumed that entrepreneurship is the process of alert individuals interacting with pre-existent opportunities in order to create personal gain (Shane 2004). If we instead conceive of entrepreneurship as a creative, as well as a discovery process, how might we address the puzzle of creating stakeholder commitments? By looking at the process of building new stakeholder groups (Freeman 1984) in the entrepreneurial process, we could better understand how environmental entrepreneurs create selective incentives. Similarly, insights from the competitive dynamics of incumbents versus new entrants in emergent, environmentally relevant fields (Hockerts & Wüstenhagen 2010) could contribute to the broader literature in strategic management.

The realm of environmental entrepreneurship offers a rich and fascinating view into how individual beliefs, economic incentives, and broader societal forces can interact to bring about ecologically sustainable practices. Just as Dewey prescribes viewing mind as embodied in nature, we must begin to view environmental entrepreneurship as embodied within larger fields. By seeking to impart empirical rigor and broader theoretical contributions, this field stands to address some of the most pressing and interesting issues faced by management academics and by broader society.

REFERENCES

Anderson, T. L. & Leal, D. R. (2001). *Free Market Environmentalism*, revised edn. New York: Palgrave Macmillan.

Austin, James, Stevenson, Howard, & Wei-Skillern, Jane (2006). "Social and Commercial Entrepreneurship: Same, Different, or Both?" *Entrepreneurship: Theory & Practice*, 30(1): 1–22.

Battilana, J., Leca, B., & Boxenbaum, E. (2009). "How Actors Change Institutions: Towards a Theory of Institutional Entrepreneurship," *The Academy of Management Annals*, 3(1): 65–107.

Bianchi, R. & Noci, G. (1998). "'Greening' SMEs' Competitiveness," *Small Business Economics*, 11(3): 269.

Cardon, M. S. et al. (2009). "The Nature and Experience of Entrepreneurial Passion," *Academy of Management Review*, 34(3): 511–32.

Choi, D. Y. & Gray, Ed. R. (2008). "The Venture Development Processes of 'sustainable' Entrepreneurs," *Management Research News,* 31(8): 558–69.

Cohen, B. & Winn, M. I. (2007). "Market Imperfections, Opportunity and Sustainable Entrepreneurship," *Journal of Business Venturing,* 22(1): 29–49.

Craig, J. & Dibrell, C. (2006). "The Natural Environment, Innovation, and Firm Performance: A Comparative Study," *Family Business Review,* 19(4): 275–88.

Creswell, J. W. (2009). *Research Design : Qualitative, Quantitative, And Mixed Methods Approaches.* Thousand Oaks, Calif.: Sage Publications.

Dean, T. J. & McMullen, J. S. (2007). "Toward a Theory of Sustainable Entrepreneurship: Reducing environmental Degradation through Entrepreneurial Action," *Journal of Business Venturing,* 22(1): 50–76.

Dees, J. G. (1998). "The Meaning of Social Entrepreneurship." Paper given at Stanford University.

Freeman, E. R. (1984). *Strategic Management: A Stakeholder Approach,* ed. Edwin M. Epstein. Pitman Series in Business and Public Policy, Berkley, California: Pitman.

Gibbs, D. (2009). "Sustainability Entrepreneurs, Ecopreneurs and the Development of a Sustainable Economy," *Greener Management International,* (55): 63–78.

Hall, J. K., Daneke, G. A., & Lenox, M. J. (2010). "Sustainable Development and Entrepreneurship: Past Contributions and Future Directions," *Journal of Business Venturing,* 25(5): 439–448.

Hardin, G. (1968). "The Tragedy of the Commons," *Science,* 162 (3859): 1243–48.

Hayek, F. A. (1978). "Competition as a Discovery Process," *New Studies in Philosophy, Politics, Economics, and the History of Ideas,* Chicago: University of Chicago, Chapter 12.

Hockerts, K. & Wüstenhagen, R. (2010). "Greening Goliaths versus Emerging Davids: Theorizing about the Role of Incumbents and New Entrants in Sustainable Entrepreneurship," *Journal of Business Venturing,* 25(5): 481–92.

Ingram, P. L. & Silverman, B. S. (2002). *The New Institutionalism in Strategic Management,* Advances in Strategic Management, vol. 19; Amsterdam; Boston: JAI.

Isaak, R. (1997).'Globalisation and Green Entrepreneurship', *Greener Management International,* (18): 80–90.

—— (2002). "The Making of the Ecopreneur", *Greener Management International,* (38): 81–91.

—— (1999). *Green Logic: Ecopreneurship, Theory, and Ethics.* West Hartford, Conn.: Kumarian Press).

Jennings, P. D. & Zandbergen, P. A. (1995). "Ecologically Sustainable Organizations: An Institutional Approach," *Academy of Management Review,* 20(4): 1015–52.

Keogh, P. D. & Polonsky, M. J. (1998).'Environmental Commitment: A Basis for Environmental Entrepreneurship?', *Journal of Organizational Change Management,* 11(1): 38–49.

Kirzner, I. M. (1979). *Perception, Opportunity, and Profit.* Chicago, IL: University of Chicago Press.

Knight, F. H. (1921). *Risk, Uncertainty and Profit,* reprint edn. Chevy Chase: Beard Books Imprint, Beard Books Incorporated.

Kuckertz, A. & Wagner, M. (2010). "The Influence of Sustainability Orientation on Entrepreneurial Intentions: Investigating the Role of Business Experience," *Journal of Business Venturing,* 25(5): 524–539.

Larson, A. L. (2000). "Sustainable Innovation through an Entrepreneurship Lens," *Business Strategy and the Environment,* 9(5): 304–317.

Leca, B., Battilana, J., & Boxenbaum, E. (2008). "Agency and Institutions: A Review of Institutional Entrepreneurship," Harvard Business School. Working Paper.

Linnanen, L. (2002). "An Insider's Experiences with Environmental Entrepreneurship," *Greener Management International*, (38): 71–80.

Meek, W. R., Pacheco, D. F., & York, J. G. (2010). "The Impact of Social Norms on Entrepreneurial Action: Evidence from the Environmental Entrepreneurship Context," *Journal of Business Venturing*, 25(5): 493–509.

O'Neill, G. D. Jr, Hershauer, J. C., & Golden, J. S. (2009). "The Cultural Context of Sustainability Entrepreneurship," *Greener Management International*, (55): 33–46.

O'Rourke, A. (2003). "The Message and Methods of Ethical Investment," *Journal of Cleaner Production*, 11(6): 683–93.

—— (2005). "Venture Capital as a Tool for Sustainable Development," in Michael Schaper (ed.), *Making Ecopreneurs: Developing Sustainable Entrepreneurship*, Burlington, VT: Ashgate, 122 37.

Pacheco, D. F., Dean, T. J., & Payne, D. S. (2010a). "Escaping the Green Prison: Entrepreneurship and the Creation of Opportunities for Sustainable Development", *Journal of Business Venturing*, 25(5): 464–80.

—— et al. (2010b). "The Co-Evolution of Institutional Entrepreneurship: A Tale of Two Theories," *Journal of Management*, 36(4): 974–1010.

Parrish, B. D. (2010). "Sustainability-Driven Entrepreneurship: Principles of Organization Design," *Journal of Business Venturing*, 25(5): 510–523.

—— & Foxon, T. J. (2009). "Sustainability Entrepreneurship and Equitable Transitions to a Low-Carbon Economy," *Greener Management International*, (55): 47–62.

Pastakia, A. (1998). "Grassroots Ecopreneurs: Change Agents for a Sustainable Society", *Journal of Organizational Change Management*, 11(2): 157–73.

—— (2002). 'Assessing Ecopreneurship in the Context of a Developing Country', *Greener Management International*, (38): 93–109.

Randjelovic, J., O'Rourke, A. R., & Orsato, R. J. (2003). "The Emergence of Green Venture Capital," *Business Strategy & the Environment (John Wiley & Sons, Inc)*, 12(4): 240–53.

Russo, M. V. (2001). "Institutions, Exchange Relations, and the Emergence of New Fields: Regulatory Policies and Independent Power Production in America, 1978–1992", *Administrative Science Quarterly*, 46(1): 57–86.

—— (2003). 'The Emergence of Sustainable Industries: Building on Natural Capital', *Strategic Management Journal*, 24(4): 317–31.

Sarasvathy, S. D. & Dew, N. (2005). "New Market Creation through Transformation," *Journal of Evolutionary Economics*, 15(5): 533–65.

Sarasvathy, S. & Venkataraman, S. (2009). *Made, as Well as Found: Researching Entrepreneurship as a Science of the Artificial*. Yale University Press.

Schaltegger, S. (2002). "A Framework for Ecopreneurship," *Greener Management International*, (38): 45–58.

Schaper, M. (2002). "The Essence of Ecopreneurship," *Greener Management International*, (38): 26–30.

Schick, H., Marxen, S., & F., Jurgen. (2002). "Sustainability Issues for Start-up Entrepreneurs," *Greener Management International*, (38): 59–70.

Schlange, L. E. (2009). "Stakeholder Identification in Sustainability Entrepreneurship," *Greener Management International*, (55): 13–32.

Schumpeter, J. A. (1934). *The Theory of the Economic Development*. Oxford: Oxford University Press.
—— (1942). *Capitalism, Socialism and Democracy*, 6th edn. Abingdon, South Yarra: Routledge, Palgrave Macmillan Distributor.
Scott, W. R. (1995). *Institutions and Organizations*, Foundations for Organizational Science, Thousand Oaks, CA: SAGE.
Shane, S. (2000). "Prior Knowledge and the Discovery of Entrepreneurial Opportunities," *Organization Science*, 11(4): 448–69.
—— (2004). *A General Theory of Entrepreneurship: The Individual-Opportunity Nexus*, New Horizons in Entrepreneurship Series, Northampton: Edward Elgar Publishing Incorporated.
Scott, S. & Venkataraman, S. (2000). "The Promise of Entrepreneurship as a Field of Research," *Academy of Management. The Academy of Management Review*, 25(1): 217–26.
Short, J. C., Moss, T. W., & Lumpkin, G. T. (2009). "Research in Social Entrepreneurship: Past Contributions and Future Opportunities", *Strategic Entrepreneurship Journal*, 3(2): 161–94.
Sine, W. D. & Lee, B. (2009). "Tilting at Windmills? The Environmental Movement and the Emergence of the U.S. Wind Energy Sector," *Administrative Science Quarterly*, 54: 123–155.
Solaiman, M. & Belal, A. R. (1999). "An Account of the Sustainable Development Process in Bangladesh," *Sustainable Development*, 7(3): 121–31.
Tilley, F. & Parrish, B. D. (2009). "Introduction," *Greener Management International*, (55): 5–11.
—— & Young, W. (2009). "Sustainability Entrepreneurs," *Greener Management International*, (55): 79–92.
Venkataraman, S. (1997). "The Distinctive Domain of Entrepreneurship Research," in J. Katz and R. Brockhaus (eds.), *Advances in Entrepreneurship, Firm Emergence, and Growth*, Greenwich, CT: JAI Press.
Volery, T. (2002). "An Entrepreneur Commercialises Conservation," *Greener Management International*, (38): 109–116.
Walley, E. E. & Taylor, D. W. (2002). "Opportunists, Champions,Mavericks…?", *Greener Management International*, (38): 31–43.
Yin, R. K. (2002). *Case Study Research: Design and Methods*, 3rd edn. ASRM Ser.; Thousand Oaks: SAGE Publications Incorporated.
York, J. G. & Venkataraman, S. (2010). "The entrepreneur–environment nexus: Uncertainty, innovation, and allocation," *Journal of Business Venturing*, 25: 449–463.
Zahra, S. A. et al. (2009). "A Typology of Social Entrepreneurs: Motives, Search Processes and Ethical Challenges," *Journal of Business Venturing*, 24(5): 519–532.

CHAPTER 5

....

THE VALUE OF MANAGING
STAKEHOLDERS

....

GEORGE KASSINIS

STAKEHOLDERS matter to firms, as do stakeholder claims and expectations. Evidence suggests that responding (or not) to stakeholder demands entails both costs to, and opportunities for, firms. Therefore, stakeholders can directly or indirectly affect a firm's performance and its ability to create value. In fact, stakeholder theory argues that "firm welfare is optimized by meeting the needs of the firm's important stakeholders in a win-win fashion" (Harrison, Bosse, & Phillips 2010: 60, citing Harrison & St. John 1996 and Walsh 2005).

Pfeffer (2009: 90–91) boldly states that "CEOs are rediscovering stakeholder capitalism"—where CEOs feel responsible to all constituencies and not just investors and where "shareholder returns are just one outcome of management practices that respect all constituencies." He contends that this is ever-more the case as a result of the continuing fallout of the "worst economic meltdown and destruction of wealth since the Great Depression" and the associated political realignments in many countries. Others do not seem to share such a view. Instead, they assert that "the open-ended commitment to economic growth persists, and it is now creating more problems than it is solving." Speth (2009: 18) accuses this fixation on economic growth of undermining "jobs, communities, the environment, a sense of place and continuity...It fuels a ruthless international search for energy and other resources , and it rests on a consumerism that is manufactured by marketers and failing to meet deepest human needs."

The argument that addressing stakeholder needs and demands has value for firms is not new. In fact, it is at the core of Freeman's (1984) seminal work. The stakeholder perspective positions the firm at the center of a complex network of stakeholders (Rowley 1997) through which goods, services, resources, and influence are exchanged. Of course, how and why firms acknowledge the importance of stakeholders and go about realizing such value varies. Early researchers (Berman et al. 1999), for example, make a distinction between "strategic stakeholder management" and "intrinsic stakeholder commitment", thus defining the two ends of a spectrum, as far as managerial motivations regarding firm-stakeholder relationships. In the former, stakeholder relationships and their management are a part of a company's strategy, but do not drive it. Such relationships "enter into [a firm's] strategic calculus and the types of relationships that produce the best prospective outcomes *for the firm* are pursued" (p. 492). In the latter, "certain fundamental moral principles" guide a firm's practices regarding stakeholders rather than "a desire to use those stakeholders solely to maximize profits" (p. 492).

Regardless of where on the spectrum we may be, strategy research accepts that firm decision-making addresses stakeholder interests and demands because this is an integral part of effective firm management. Arguably, also, firms that succeed in managing the complexities surrounding their relationships with their stakeholders over time enhance their value creation opportunities—especially if one considers the potential for value co-creation inherent in such relationships.

In the context of the natural environment, organizations often face a multitude of conflicting stakeholder pressures and demands that arise from diverse, heterogeneous stakeholder groups. These stakeholders can be broadly classified as internal (e.g. employees, customers, stockholders, corporate boards) or external (e.g. regulators, community activists, non-governmental organizations). Other classifications take into consideration whether a contractual or other legal relationship exists between a firm and its stakeholders (Clarkson 1995).

Environmental stakeholders (such as activists) targeting firms because of their poor environmental record can directly cost firms money (financial obligations imposed on firms due to successful lawsuits, for example), or damage firms' reputation in the eyes of investors, suppliers, customers, and potential employees, thus indirectly imposing costs on firms as well (Lenox & Eesley 2009; Sharma & Henriques 2005). However, stakeholders may also contribute to the creation of new market opportunities and encourage entrepreneurship that can lead to firm value creation and improved firm performance. For example, they can help bring about changes in regulatory policies and customer attitudes that foster the creation and sustain the success of new industries, as in the case of the US wind energy sector (Sine & Lee 2009). They may also contribute as co-producers to the improvement of firm environmental performance, as in the case of customers in service settings, for example (Kassinis & Soteriou 2003).

Broadly defined, then, stakeholder management is how a firm responds to the needs and demands of stakeholders while pursuing its objectives. This chapter, through a multidisciplinary perspective, seeks to explore how firms can create value by managing their complex relationships with multiple stakeholders over time. I will organize the discussion around the fundamental question of who matters to firms and why. Research has primarily focused on five main stakeholder groups. Although other categorizations may be adopted, I will review related research under each stakeholder category to offer the reader, where possible, a clearer perspective on the issues involved when considering a firm's polymorphous network of stakeholders and their influences. In the last section, I will discuss directions for future research stressing the importance of considering temporality, change, and the notion of co-creation of value in environmental stakeholder research.

WHO MATTERS TO FIRMS AND WHY?

Stakeholders can influence the practices of organizations by exerting pressures on them, influencing resource flows towards them, imposing costs (directly or indirectly), or creating conditions within which organizations can find it harder or easier to compete. For example, communities and regulators: (i) provide the physical infrastructure and markets that firms utilize and operate in, (ii) promulgate laws and regulations that influence the way firms do business, and (iii) impose taxes and other financial costs on firms (Clarkson 1995; Hillman & Keim 2001; Kassinis & Vafeas 2006). As competition increases, firms can benefit from improved relations with stakeholders (e.g. Berman et al. 1999; Hillman & Keim 2001; Ogden & Watson 1999).

Given the importance of stakeholders, "managing for stakeholders" may "unlock knowledge about stakeholder utility functions", and this knowledge may give rise to "value creation opportunities" over time. Understanding what drives stakeholder utility may allow firms to modify their tactics and re-prioritize the allocation of resources to more effectively and efficiently satisfy stakeholder demands (Harrison et al. 2010: 59–60).

Of course, firms often face a multitude of conflicting stakeholder pressures and demands that make managing these pressures quite challenging. This challenge is intensified if one considers the complexity, diversity, and heterogeneity characterizing the stakeholder groups (especially larger ones) that firms have to interact and build relationships with (Harrison & Freeman 1999; Kassinis & Vafeas 2006; Winn 2001). Researchers have dealt with this complexity by developing typologies to explain why and how managers classify stakeholders in order of importance. For example, Mitchell, Agle, & Wood (1997) and later Agle, Mitchell, & Sonnenfeld (1999) argued that managers prioritize competing stakeholder claims according to three key stakeholder attributes—power, legitimacy, and urgency. The greater the combination of these attributes, the greater the group's importance to managers and, consequently, the more influential it is over firm decisions and outcomes.

Resource dependence theory also provides a useful conceptual foundation for addressing the question of what gives stakeholders the ability to influence firm decisions. As theorists argue, "organizations are not self-contained or self-sufficient" and are dependent on their external environment for resources (Pfeffer & Salancik 1978: 43). A firm's dependence on environmental actors for critical resources gives these actors (e.g. external stakeholders) leverage over a firm (Frooman 1999), and allows them to influence organizational outcomes (Pfeffer & Salancik 1978). Moreover, resource dependence theory assumes that the target organization can actively respond to those stakeholders (Lenox & Eesly 2009; Nohria & Gulati 1994). Stakeholders, then, can influence a firm either directly or indirectly, that is, via another stakeholder (Frooman 1999; Gargiulo 1993). In sum, the more dependent an organization is on a group, the greater the power of that group and the greater its ability to influence organizational outcomes (Kassinis & Vafeas 2006). Key stakeholder categories in the organizational environment that consistently appear in the literature include diverse and internally heterogeneous groups such as regulators, activists, and geographic communities, customers, employees, and corporate boards. Interestingly, the literature, implicitly if not explicitly, treats each group as a self-contained entity, despite the multiple overlaps that exist among the groups. In the following paragraphs, I will synthesize research that broadly falls under each of these stakeholder groups.

Regulators

The regulatory environment (such as governments and legislatures) affects a firm's competitive position and performance as a vast number of issues are formulated in a public policy process—issues that may create uncertainty and increase the transaction costs for firms (Hillman & Hitt 1999; Shaffer 1995; Williamson 1979). In fact, it is argued that there is a high degree of interdependence between a firm's competitive environment and public policy (Baron 1995), as regulators have the power to alter the size or affect the structure of markets and influence product demand (through taxes, for example). Moreover, legislators can alter the cost structure a firm faces—through environmental protection legislation (Hillman & Hitt 1999). In sum, they have the power to channel valuable resources towards or away from a firm.

In effect, regulators can use the multiple carrots and sticks at their disposal to pressure firms to embrace environmental protection as part of the way they do business (Buysse & Verbeke 2003; Rugman & Verbeke 1998; Hart 1995; Shrivastava 1995). The effect of environmental regulation on firms and its role as a driver of environmentally sustainable innovation remains an issue of ongoing discussion in the literature (Greenstone 2002; Majumdar & Marcus 2001; Porter & van der Linde 1995). In the U.S. context, for example, in a study of firms convicted and penalized for violating environmental law, regulatory stringency appeared to have no effect on the likelihood of environmental wrongdoing (Kassinis & Vafeas 2002). In other studies, no relationship was found between proxies for the regulatory capacities of US environmental agencies and the environmental performance of US firms (Kassinis & Vafeas 2006). In the Canadian context, however, where directors and company executives can face personal liability for environmental violations, regulation appears as an influential driver of improved environmental practices (Sharma & Henriques 2005).

In the context of regulatory stakeholders, researchers have also looked at legislative stakeholders and explored how voting records on major environmental issues in the US Congress are related to the environmental records of firms located in the Congressional districts of the members of Congress with a pro- or anti-environment voting record. Legislators' environmental voting record may be a signal of their willingness to use their capacity to exert pressures on firms to improve their environmental performance. This is especially so given the resource flows towards a firm legislators can influence or outright control (for example, in the form of physical or other infrastructure, favorable or unfavorable changes in taxes or subsidies etc.). Although no statistically significant relationship between voting records and environmental performance was reported in the literature (e.g. Kassinis & Vafeas 2002; 2006), this relationship may warrant further examination especially when combined with research on environmental activism (e.g. Lenox & Eesley 2009).

Voting records reflect the diversity of environmental opinions within a state and, hence, the degree of heterogeneity of the environmental preferences of that state's electorate. Researchers stress the importance of legislators' electoral constituencies in determining their legislative actions and public-choice models emphasize the electoral self-interest of legislators and the significance of their relevant constituencies in shaping their behavior while in office. As a result, legislators have a strong interest in responding to their politically active constituencies because gaining or maintaining their support is crucial to winning re-election (Keim & Zeithaml 1986; Lord 2000). These politically active constituents, such as members of environmental organizations, and their public policy or issue preferences may or may not be representative of the larger population a legislator represents in Congress. However, they represent those who are likely to stay actively involved in the public policy and electoral processes (unlike the majority who are generally uninvolved) (Baron 1994; Baysinger, Keim, & Zeithaml 1985; Keim 1985; Keim & Zeithaml 1986). This is an indication of the indirect power and influence of such stakeholders on firms—via the resource flows they can affect (Frooman 1999; Pfeffer & Salancik 1978; Pfeffer 1992).

Clearly, regulatory stakeholders are complex, diverse, and heterogeneous (see, also, Coglianese & Anderson [Chapter 8] this volume). How such heterogeneity is related to the stakeholders' capacity to pressure and influence a firm and, in turn, how a firm responds to such varying pressures deserves further investigation. With respect to regulatory stakeholders, within-group heterogeneity is first associated with this group's multi-layered composition—something that is especially pronounced in a federal political system such as that of the United States. For example, the policies that affect firms are made at various levels (national, state etc.). Moreover, the regulatory infrastructures and institutions associated with such policy-making functions may have different capacities (e.g. in terms of resources) to influence firms located and operating in their jurisdictions. Complexity, diversity, and heterogeneity surely characterize regulatory stakeholders in the European Union context, an empirical setting that can surely provide the background for fruitful research in the future.

Activists and geographic communities

Eesley & Lenox (2006) build on and extend the work of Mitchell et al. (1997) by examining firm responses to secondary stakeholder actions (which can have both direct and indirect, reputational costs for the firm). Conceptually, their work broadens and deepens our understanding of stakeholder importance. They argue that the salience of stakeholder claims depends "not only on stakeholder attributes but also on the nature of the request and the attributes of the targeted firm" (p. 767). The empirical part of this study is noteworthy for its unique dataset, which, unlike most studies in this area, consists of longitudinal data (1971–2003) on secondary stakeholder actions drawn from a variety of publicly available sources such as LexisNexis and the Investor Responsibility Research Center. In a more recent study, Lenox & Eesly (2009) delve deeper into environmental activist actions aimed at changing individual firm behavior by examining activists' political strategies including boycotts, protests, and civil suits (Baron 2001; 2003). Using a longitudinal data set of environmental activist campaigns targeting US firms in the period 1988–2003, they find evidence that larger, more profitable, advertising-intensive, and more polluting firms are more likely activist targets. Also, they find that the greater the cash reserves and the worse the environmental record of a firm, the lower the likelihood that it will acquiesce to activists' demands. In both papers, resources and the resource balance between firms and stakeholders, directly or indirectly, play a role in firms' willingness or capacity to respond to stakeholder demands.

In addition to imposing costs, activist groups (by interacting with other stakeholders such as regulators) may help create market opportunities for environmentally friendly investments, products, or services. Sine & Lee (2009), for example, examine how social movements (in their study, the Sierra Club, the Audubon Society, the Union of Concerned Scientists, and Friends of the Earth) influenced the development of the wind energy sector in the US by articulating problems associated with the use of fossil fuels for the production of energy and advocating wind energy as an environmentally benign solution (p. 147). By mobilizing thousands of activists at state and local levels, through educational programs, public relations efforts, and lobbying campaigns directed at state governments and regulators, these stakeholders helped create awareness, contributed to regulatory changes that increased, supported, and sustained entrepreneurial activity in the wind-power sector. More fundamentally, Sine and Lee show how environmental stakeholders "developed and advocated *an alternative set of values and norms* [emphasis added] that justified the use of a unique set of resources and technologies to produce electricity through environmentally benign methods" (p. 148). According to the authors, such activities may have precipitated or even catalyzed the influence of other supportive stakeholder actions such as those of industry associations and regulators, as shown in earlier work on the subject of independent power production in the US (Russo 2001; 2003; Sine, Haveman & Tolbert 2005; Sine, David, & Mitsuhashi 2007).

A different, critical perspective to the above is offered by Hart & Sharma (2004), who argue that firms must move beyond engaging "known, salient, or powerful" groups and towards a systematic identification and integration of the views (and knowledge) of "fringe" stakeholders ("the poor, weak, non-legitimate") (p. 7). By preemptively developing the capability to do so (what Hart & Sharma term "radical transactiveness"), firms can "design and execute disruptive new business strategies" and pave the path of "competitive imagination for the future" (p. 17).

Overall, activist groups may represent, in whole or in part, broader community interests (see, also, King, Prado, & Rivera [Chapter 6], Weber & Soderstrom [Chapter 14], and Delmas & Toffel [Chapter 13] this volume). As mentioned in the context of regulatory stakeholders, politically active members of a geographic community may be involved in public policy and electoral processes and thus be able to exert stronger pressures on polluting firms. However, the majority are generally silent and opt out of the political processes at large. The uninvolved majority in geographic communities is not homogeneous and may differ in terms of per capita income, residential density, and, of course, its environmental preferences (Kassinis & Vafeas 2006). Questions are raised as to how such heterogeneity is related to the stakeholders' capacity to pressure and influence a firm and, in turn, how a firm responds to such potentially varying pressures. For example, to what extent can stakeholders of various levels of income pressure firms to reduce environmental impacts in the area in which they live? Research shows that plants located in richer areas are less polluting (Kassinis & Vafeas 2006). As Grossman & Krueger (1995: 371–372) show "the strongest link between income and pollution is via an induced policy response. As nations or regions experience greater prosperity, their citizens demand that more attention be paid to the non-economic aspects of their living conditions." Thus, they pressure firms indirectly through the policy process, which controls resource flows towards firms (e.g. directly via taxes or subsidies or indirectly via the costs or benefits associated with favorable or unfavorable legislation).

Environmental justice research also argues that most hazardous waste facilities tend to be located in poor, minority neighborhoods. This is because their residents lack the political and financial resources, and hence the power, to challenge corporate polluters (Bryant & Mohai 1992; Grant et al. 2002). Unable to voice their demands through the political process (Hamilton 1995) residents of such areas lack the power to affect corporate policies. By implication, we also expect facilities in highly polluting industries to do a less effective job of managing their emissions when located in such communities—or even expand their production capacity in such communities as a profit-maximizing decision based on compensation and liability cost considerations (Boyce et al. 1992; Hamilton 1995). In sum, there exists an imbalance in resource dependence favoring firms, as poorer communities may be more dependent on firms for resources (e.g. jobs, taxes) than the other way around (Frooman 1999; Pfeffer & Salancik 1978).

Customers

Firms are very sensitive to the way customers perceive them since customers are directly responsible for the firms' well-being and performance. Individually, customers express their preferences (and their indirect approval of firm decisions) through their purchasing decisions; thus they have the power to "reward" or "punish" firms for their environment-related actions. Also, either alone or in collaboration with other firm stakeholders (activists, regulators, media), a firm's customers can target the firm if unhappy with its environmental performance record (through boycotts or customer-induced policy action, for example).

From existing research we know that firms' environmental practices are affected by customer pressures (see Gershoff & Irwin [Chapter 20] and Scammon & Mish [Chapter 19] this volume). For example, as Sharma & Henriques (2005) show in the context of the Canadian forestry industry, managerial perceptions regarding customer demands for information on product sustainability or certification affect the types of sustainability practices their firms adopt. Satisfying the demands of environmentally conscious customers becomes a critical consideration for firms, given the established relationship between customer satisfaction and performance. In fact, research has shown that customer satisfaction and loyalty mediate the relationship between the implementation of environmental practices and firm performance (Kassinis & Soteriou 2003).

Responding to the demands of customers for information regarding what environmental practices firms adopt and how effective such practices are is crucial, especially in order to overcome consumer suspicions of firm motives. The provision of credible information or signals regarding such practices may reduce information asymmetries, increase customer satisfaction (if customers are convinced that firms are environmentally responsible) and yield performance benefits for the firms involved. Although not examining customer issues directly, studies by Bansal & Clelland (2004)—who show that environmental information has both an immediate and a long-term influence on how investors assess a firm's environmental legitimacy—or King, Lenox, & Terlaak (2005) on ISO 14001 certification can provide useful insights for research on this topic.

The potential influence of customers on firm performance and value creation becomes more complex when one considers their role as co-producers, especially in the service portion of a firm's value chain, or the linkages between sustainable consumption and production. Although largely unexplored in existing strategy research, work in other fields such as operations management or industrial ecology can provide strategy researchers with a basis to begin work in this area (see Klassen & Vachon [Chapter 15], Abbey & Guide [Chapter 16], Lifset & Boons [Chapter 17] this volume). For example, in the former, work on customer efficiency in service coproduction and its effect on the performance of service delivery systems and firm performance (Xue, Hitt, & Harker 2007) can provide insights into mutually beneficial, value-adding firm-stakeholder interactions. Also, research on service operations failures and their effect on customer satisfaction and firm performance can shed light on how environment-related firm "failures" (accidents, worsening pollution records, lawsuits etc.) can influence stakeholder satisfaction. Drawing from research in consumer psychology, such work shows that customers seek reasons for service failures, and that attributions of blame moderate the effects of failure on the level of customer satisfaction (Anderson, Baggett, & Widener 2009).

Recent industrial ecology literature focuses on customer-firm (or user-producer) interactions in the promotion of household energy innovations (Heiskanen & Lovio 2010). It also examines firm strategies to promote energy conservation by customers (Gram-Hanssen 2010), and even the extent to which information on the life cycle cost of products can influence purchase decisions (Deutsch 2010; Kaenzig & Wustenhagen 2010). These are interesting empirical contexts for further exploring customer-firm interactions.

Finally, work that draws from the identity-related literature, which argues that people identify with an organization based on their perception of its core characteristics (Bhattacharya & Sen 2003; Dutton, Dukerich, & Harquail 1994; Gershoff & Irwin [Chapter 20] this volume; Homburg, Wieseke, & Hoyer 2009), can provide food for thought with respect to the conditions under which stakeholders (such as customers) identify with a firm and are prone to act favorably towards it. In the same context, since customer-company identification serves as a motivator to act on behalf of a group, it can also increase the consumer's willingness to pay for the firm's products or services (Arnett, German, & Hunt 2003)—an important determinant of firm financial performance. Customer-company identification is also linked with customer loyalty, a construct related with firm financial performance (Reicheld & Sasser 1990; Froehle, Roth, Chase, & Voss 2000).

Employees

Almazan, Suarez, & Titman (2009) argue that stakeholders appreciate "the benefits of being associated with a successful firm, that is, a winner" and, therefore, a firm's success may be "tied to how it is perceived, both internally, by its employees, and externally, by its customers and suppliers." Moreover, as Enz & Siguaw (1999) show all environmental best-practice champions in the US lodging industry indicated that such practices had a positive impact on employee morale (and thus satisfaction) and enhanced the staff's pride in the hotel. Similar results are reported by Goodman (2000). More generally, how employees perceive environmental issues appears to be critical for a firm's success, since enhanced employee awareness leads to improved individual behavior and practices (Andersson & Bateman 2000; Jiang & Bansal 2003)—provided that employee predisposition towards environmental protection and willingness to participate in it fits with firm efforts to reduce operating costs (Bansal 2003) and when firms perceive environmental issues as opportunities for growth (Sharma 2000). Naturally, employees are at the heart of organizational efforts to facilitate the transfer of knowledge regarding best practices and the eventual adoption of such practices that improve environmental performance (Lenox & King 2004; May & Flannery 1995; Sharma & Henriques 2005). Finally, an interesting finding worthy of further exploration in the environmental context is reported by de Luque et al. (2008) who show that "stakeholder values...provide better decision making criteria for executives", "assigning a greater level of importance to stakeholders in decision making results in the leader being perceived by subordinates as more visionary and less autocratic." Such "visionary leadership encourages extra effort, which translates into improved firm performance (p. 646).

Corporate boards

Corporate boards can influence firm attitudes towards the natural environment, but it is unclear whether they are an effective mechanism for translating, or even transferring, stakeholder concerns into managerial action (Hillman, Keim, & Luce 2001). Boards, for example, do not seem to reward CEOs for effective stakeholder management (Coombs & Gilley 2005). Interestingly, also, in a longitudinal study of environmental performance and executive pay in US firms, Berrone & Gomez-Mejia (2009) find that firms with an explicit environmental pay policy and an environmental committee do not reward environmental strategies more than those without such structures, suggesting that these mechanisms play a symbolic role. This may be explained, at least in part, by the fact that few individuals who clearly represent environmental interests serve on corporate boards (Prasad & Elmes 2005).

Kassinis & Vafeas (2002) examined board characteristics in some depth and found that such characteristics are related to firm environmental performance. They found that larger boards are less effective in preventing behavior that leads to environmental lawsuits than smaller ones, that the likelihood of lawsuit increases with the fraction of directors in peer firms, and that the likelihood of a lawsuit decreases with the number of directorships held by outside directors. There is, in fact, a broader debate regarding the effect of board size on the quality of board decisions. Although a resource-dependence view may suggest, for example, that larger boards enhance company performance by strengthening a firm's ability to secure critical resources from its external environment, or providing management with otherwise unobtainable expert advice, others disagree. They indicate that larger boards are less cohesive and participative than smaller ones and thus not as apt to initiate strategic action. Further, agency theory suggests that larger boards experience process losses, while they also hinder the free exchange of ideas among board members (see Goodstein, Gautam, & Boeker 1994; Zahra & Pearce 1989). This may also cause opportunistic CEOs to sidestep unwelcome board monitoring on environmental matters. Regarding board composition, governance research has focused on the importance of board independence as a measure of board effectiveness in monitoring managerial actions. Fruitful directions for research may further explore how board composition may play a role in the firm's ability to address stakeholder concerns and promote stakeholder-firm win-win outcomes.

Clearly the board's attitude towards environmental issues has the potential of influencing not only firm environmental practices directly but also the way firms respond to environmental stakeholder demands. As such, its broader role in firm decision-making involving environmental stakeholder concerns is worthy of further research considering that boards are at the apex of the decision-making process in public corporations and that every major operational or strategic decision must go through the board. Therefore, even though boards sometimes exert little real power over decision-making, they are ultimately responsible for corporate environmental strategy, whether that strategy is proactively pursued or just rubber-stamped. To address environmental issues, boards may create separate committees to deal with them. Further, they have the discretionary power to seek legal or other expert advice as an additional resource for ensuring sound environmental policy. Finally, the extent, depth, and sincerity of discussion on environmental matters in the boardroom itself are likely to determine, to a great extent, the quality of corporate environmental policies.

Future research and concluding remarks

There are many promising directions for further research focused on the stakeholder-business-environment relationship. Of those, two follow directly from the preceding discussion: the first revolves around the idea of studying stakeholders as co-producers or co-creators of value, and the second relates to the explicit adoption of a network perspective in studying firm—stakeholder interactions and outcomes. Within the latter, I stress the importance of considering temporality and change when studying firm-stakeholder relationships.

Stakeholders as co-producers of value

Researchers, mostly in the disciplines of operations management and marketing (see, for example, Xue & Field 2008), but also in strategy (e.g. Prahalad & Ramaswamy 2000; 2004), have discussed, and some have even empirically examined, the impact of customer actions or involvement on different dimensions of firm performance, such as efficiency, productivity, quality, and customer satisfaction. Interdisciplinary research that extends work from operations and marketing and considers the involvement of all important stakeholders as value co-producers and environment-related aspects of performance would certainly be enlightening.

In fact, the strategic management literature routinely stresses the importance of considering the value chains of a firm's stakeholders (such as suppliers and forward-channel allies, for example) when examining that firm's ability to create value and achieve competitiveness. More explicitly, a firm and its stakeholders are all involved in the value creation process, the resulting value being the outcome of a co-production process. In this process, stakeholders have essential "production" roles that, if not fulfilled, will affect the nature of the intended outcome. In studying the co-production of environmental value through stakeholder involvement, researchers can consider the most relevant characteristics of the stakeholder as a co-producer. In other words, research could explore a stakeholder's capacity to participate in the co-production of environmental value. In fact, gaps in stakeholder capabilities may result in inefficiencies in the value-creation process and thus compromise the ability of the organizations involved to achieve their objectives. A firm's actions to deal with such stakeholder-capability gaps, through, for example, changes in its design efforts (for products and services) (see Cachon & Harker 2002, for example) and their effect on firm performance may be interesting to consider in future research. In the same context, it would be worthwhile to consider how the acquisition, transfer. and use of environment-related information (Bettencourt et al. 2002; Skjolsvik et al. 2007)—the information and knowledge exchange process between a firm and its stakeholders—would affect the value-creation efforts of a firm.

Firm-stakeholder networks and opportunities for value creation

Firms and their stakeholders interact within a dynamic network of relationships to produce value. Thus, social network research may offer conceptual and empirical guidance to stakeholder researchers. For example, as discussed earlier, stakeholder influences on, and interactions with, a firm are not merely dyadic but web-like, with interactions among stakeholders also influencing a focal organization. Rowley (1997), for example, uses social network analysis to construct theory about stakeholder influences that predict how organizations respond to multiple stakeholder demands.

It is important to note that it is difficult to understand how firms and their stakeholders interact if time is abstracted away. Arguably, then, a temporal approach is essential to fully studying phenomena such as those involving firms and their stakeholders (Ancona, Okhuysen, & Perlow 2001). Intimately connected to such an approach is the notion of change: firm-stakeholder relations are dynamic and evolve/change over time. Change occurs when organizations interact with their stakeholders "to solve problems that are atypical" (Tsoukas & Chia 2002)—as is the case with the multifaceted environmental challenges organizations face, and will continue to face, in the future.

One way organizations can strive to stay current (with constantly changing environments) is to change their networks and relationships (Kim, Oh, & Swaminathan 2006; Ring & Van De Ven 1994). Future research can examine how firms, in response to changes in both their external and internal environments, redefine *who* their stakeholders are and how improved awareness of *what* these stakeholders want can influence firm performance (Harrison et al. 2010). Responding to this challenge may require firms to learn about the factors that drive stakeholders' utility functions and to translate such information into the creation of additional value by fine-tuning strategies and tactics over time to offer what is really important to stakeholders. For example, nuanced understanding of stakeholders' needs, claims, and constraints may put a firm in a better position to successfully address them by completing 'transactions' with them more efficiently than rivals do. This, in turn, may also increase the stakeholders' willingness to cooperate with the firm in the future, thus enhancing its growth prospects and even its competitiveness (Bosse, Phillips, & Harrison 2009). This process of devising new ways of satisfying the needs of stakeholders may be viewed as a "creative envisioning process that requires entrepreneurial intuition and imagination" (Harrison et al. 2010: 66), and clearly is worthy of further examination.

Related to the above are questions of how familiarity, mutual knowledge and trust between firms and their stakeholders *over time* fuel the process of change, growth, and value creation (Hansen 1999; Harrison et al. 2010; Tsai 2000; 2001; 2002). As Podonly (1994) also points out, status and reputation enhance the likelihood of cooperation because they signal the skill and trustworthiness of potential partners.

Lastly, stakeholder actions contribute to organizational transformations and influence organizations' ability to fulfill their mission over time. The process of forming, reforming, modifying, and even dissolving, stakeholder relationships is challenging for any organization, however. In fact, research on networks that adopts a process-based perspective (e.g. Ebers 1999; Podolny & Page 1998; Kim et al. 2006) emphasizes the constraints and costs associated with such transitions. Future research inspired by these ideas can also enrich our understanding of the firm-stakeholder-environment interaction.

In conclusion, this chapter contends that, through managing complex stakeholder demands over time, firms can create value. Numerous worthwhile venues for interdisciplinary research exist, as outlined above. The interested reader will confirm, by perusing this Handbook, that the study of the firm-stakeholder-environment relationship can be approached from many different perspectives, touching all aspects of organizational research. It is now crucial for researchers to move beyond establishing empirical relationships between constructs and variables of interest. Instead, it is time to explore what drives these relationships and how they affect organizational outcomes over time.

REFERENCES

Agle, B. R., Mitchell, R. K., & Sonnenfeld, J. A. (1999). "Who Matters to CEOs? An Investigation of Stakeholder Attributes and Salience, Corporate Performance, and CEO Values," *Academy of Management Journal*, 42: 507–525.

Almazan, A., Suarez, J., & Titman, S. (2009). "Firm's Stakeholders and the Costs of Transparency," *Journal of Economics & Management Strategy*, 18: 871–890.

Ancona, D., Okhuysen, G., & Perlow, L. (2001). "Taking Time to Integrate Temporal Research," *Academy of Management Review*, 26: 512–529.

Anderson, S. W., Baggett, L. S., & Widener, S. K. (2009). "The Impact of Service Operations Failures on Customer Satisfaction: Evidence on how Failures and their Source Affect what Matters to Customers," *Manufacturing & Service Operations Management*, 11: 52–69.

Andersson, L. & Bateman, T. (2000). "Individual Environmental Initiative: Championing Natural Environmental Issues in U.S. Business Organizations," *Academy of Management Journal*, 43: 548–570.

Arnett, D., German, S., & Hunt, S. (2003). "The Identity Salience Model of Relationship Marketing Success: The Case of Nonprofit Marketing," *Journal of Marketing*, 67(4): 89–105.

Bansal, P. (2003). "From Issues to Actions: The Importance of Individual Concerns and Organizational Values in Responding to Natural Environmental Issues," *Organization Science*, 14: 510–527.

Bansal, T. & Clelland, I. (2004). "Talking Trash: Legitimacy, Impression Management, and Unsystematic Risk in the Context of the Natural Environment," *Academy of Management Journal*, 47: 93–103.

Baron, D. P. (1994). "Electoral Competition with Informed And Uninformed Voters," *American Political Science Review*, 88: 33–47.

—— (1995). "Integrated Strategy: Market and Non-Market Components. *California Management Review*, 37(3): 47–65.

—— (2001). "Private Politics, Corporate Social Responsibility, and Integrated Strategy," *Journal of Economics & Management Strategy*, 10: 7–45.

—— (2003). "Private Politics," *Journal of Economics & Management Strategy*, 12: 31–66.

Baysinger, B. D., Keim, G. D., & Zeithaml, C. P. (1985). "An Empirical Evaluation of the Potential for Including Shareholders in Corporate Constituency Programs," *Academy of Management Journal*, 28: 180–200.

Berman, S., Wicks, A. C., Kotha, S., & Jones, T. M. (1999). "Does Stakeholder Orientation Matter? The Relationship between Stakeholder Management Models and Firm Financial Performance," *Academy of Management Journal*, 42: 488–506.

Berrone, P. & Gomez-Mejia, L. (2009). "Environmental Performance and Executive Compensation: An Integrated Agency-Institutional Perspective," *Academy of Management Journal,* 52: 103–126.

Bettencourt, L. A., Ostrom, A. L., Brown, S. W., & Roundtree, R. I. (2002). "Client Co-Production in Knowledge-Intensive Business Services," *California Management Review,* 44(4): 100–128.

Bhattacharya, C. B. & Sen, S. (2003). "Consumer-Company Identification: A Framework for Understanding Consumers' Relationships with Companies," *Journal of Marketing,* 67(4): 76–88.

Bosse, D. A., Phillips, R. A., & Harrison, J. S. (2009). "Stakeholders, Reciprocity, and Firm Performance," *Strategic Management Journal,* 30(4): 447–456.

Boyce, R. R., Brown, T. C., McClelland, G. H., Peterson, G. L., & Schulze, W. D. (1992). "An Experimental Examination of Intrinsic Values as a Source of WTA-WTP Disparity," *American Economic Review,* 82: 1366–1373.

Bryant, B. & Mohai, P. (1992). *Race and The Incidence of Environmental Hazards.* Boulder, CO: Westview.

Buysse, K. & Verbeke, A. (2003). "Proactive Environmental Management Strategies: A Stakeholder Management Perspective," *Strategic Management Journal,* 24: 453–470.

Cachon, G. & Harker, P. (2002). "Competition and Outsourcing with Scale Economies," *Management Science.* 48: 1314–1333.

Clarkson, M. B. (1995). "A Stakeholder Framework for Analyzing and Evaluating Corporate Social Performance," *Academy of Management Review,* 20: 92–117.

Coombs, J. E. & Gilley, K. M. (2005). "Stakeholder Management as a Predictor of CEP Compensation: Main Effects and Interactions with Financial Performance," *Strategic Management Journal,* 26: 827–840.

de Luque, Washburn, N. T., Waldman, D. A., & House, R. J. (2008). "Unrequited Profit: How Stakeholders and Economic Values Relate to Subordinates' Perceptions of Leadership and Firm Performance," *Administrative Science Quarterly,* 53: 626–654.

Deutsch, M. (2010). "Life-Cycle Cost Disclosure, Consumer Behavior, and Business Implications: Evidence from an Online Field Experiment," *Journal of Industrial Ecology,* 14(1): 103–120.

Dutton, J. E., Dukerich, J. M, & Harquail, C. V. (1994). "Organizational Images and Member Identification," *Administrative Science Quarterly,* 39: 239–263.

Ebers, M. (1999). "The Dynamics of Inter-Organizational Relationships," *Research in the Sociology of Organizations,* 16: 31–56.

Eesley, C. & Lenox, M. J. (2006). "Firm Responses to Secondary Stakeholder Action," *Strategic Management Journal,* 27: 765–781.

Enz, C. A. & Siguaw, J. A. (1999). "Best Hotel Environmental Practices," *Cornell Hotel and Restaurant Administration Quarterly,* 40(5): 72–77.

Freeman, R. E. (1984). *Strategic Management: A Stakeholder Approach.* Pitman: Boston, MA.

Froehle, C. M., Roth, A. V., Chase, R. B., & Voss, C. A. (2000). "Antecedents of New Service Development Effectiveness: An Exploratory Examination of Strategic Operations Choices," *Journal of Service Research,* 3(1): 3–17.

Frooman, J. (1999). "Stakeholder Influence Strategies," *Academy of Management Review,* 24: 191–205.

Gargiulo, M. (1993). "Two-Step Leverage: Managing Constraint in Organizational Politics," *Administrative Science Quarterly,* 38: 1–19.

Goodman, A. (2000). Implementing Sustainability in Service Operations in Scandic Hotels. *Interfaces,* 30(3): 202–214.

Goodstein, J., Gautam, K., & Boeker, W. (1994). "The Effects of Board Size and Diversity on Strategic Change," *Strategic Management Journal,* 15: 241–250.

Gram-Hanssen, K. (2010). "Standby Consumption in Households Analyzed with a Practice Theory Approach," *Journal of Industrial Ecology*, 14(1): 150–165.

Grant, D. S., Jones, A. W., & Bergesen, A. J. (2002). "Organizational Size and Pollution: The Case of the U.S. Chemical Industry," *American Sociological Review*, 67: 389–407.

Greenstone, M. (2002). "The Impacts of Environmental Regulations on Industrial Activity: Evidence from the 1970 and 1977 Clean Air Act Amendments and the Census of Manufactures," *Journal of Political Economy*, 110: 1175–1219.

Grossman, G. M. & Krueger, A. B. (1995). "Economic Growth and the Environment. *Quarterly Journal of Economics*, 110: 353–377.

Hamilton, J. T. (1995). "Testing for Environmental Racism: Prejudice, Profits, Political Power?" *Journal of Policy Analysis and Management*, 141: 107–132.

Hansen, M. (1999). "The Search-Transfer Problem: The Role of Weak Ties in Sharing Knowledge across Organization Subunits," *Administrative Science Quarterly*, 44(1): 82–111.

Harrison, J. S., Bosse, D. A., & Phillips, R. A. (2010). "Managing for Stakeholders, Stakeholder Utility Functions, and Competitive Advantage," *Strategic Management Journal*, 31: 58–74.

—— & Freeman, R. E. (1999). "Stakeholders, Social Responsibility, and Performance: Empirical Evidence and Theoretical Perspectives," *Academy of Management Journal*, 42: 479–485.

—— & St. John, C. H. (1996). "Managing and Partnering with External Stakeholders," *Academy of Management Executive*, 10(2): 46–60.

Hart, S. L. (1995). "A Natural Resource-Based View of the Firm," *Academy of Management Review*, 20: 986–1014.

—— & Sharma, S. (2004). "Engaging Fringe Stakeholders for Competitive Imagination," *Academy of Management Executive*, 18(1): 7–18.

Heiskanen, E. & Lovio, R. (2010). "User-Producer Interaction in Housing Energy Innovations: Energy Innovation as a Communication Challenge," *Journal of Industrial Ecology*, 14(1): 91–102.

Hillman, A. & Hitt, M. (1999). "Corporate Political Strategy Formulation: A Model of Approach, Participation, and Strategy Decisions," *Academy of Management Review*, 24: 825–842.

—— & Keim, G. (2001). "Stakeholder Value, Stakeholder Management, and Social Issues: What's the Bottom Line?" *Strategic Management Journal*, 22: 125–139.

—— & Luce, R. (2001) "Board Composition and Stakeholder Performance: Do Stakeholder Directors Make a Difference?" *Business & Society*, 40(3): 295–314.

Homburg, C., Wieseke, J., & Hoyer, W. D. (2009). "Social Identity and the Service-Profit Chain," *Journal of Marketing*, 73(3): 38–54.

Jiang, R. J. & Bansal, P. (2003). "Seeing the Need for ISO 14001," *Journal of Management Studies*, 40: 1047–1067.

Kaenzig, J. & Wustenhagen, R. (2010). "The Effect of Life Cycle Cost Information on Consumer Investment Decisions Regarding Eco-Innovation," *Journal of Industrial Ecology*, 14(1): 121–136.

Kassinis, G. & Soteriou, A. (2003). "Greening the Service Profit Chain: The Impact of Environmental Management Practices," *Production and Operations Management*, 12: 386–403.

Kassinis, G. & Vafeas, N. (2002). "Corporate Boards and Outside Stakeholders as Determinants of Environmental Litigation," *Strategic Management Journal*, 23: 399–415.

—— (2006). "Stakeholder Pressures and Environmental Performance," *Academy of Management Journal*, 49: 145–159.

Keim, G. (1985). "Corporate Grassroots Programs in the 1980s," *California Management Review*, 28: 110–123.

——— & Zeithaml, C. P. (1986). "Corporate Political Strategy and Legislative Decision Making: A Review and Contingency Approach," *Academy of Management Review*, 11: 828–843.

Kim, T., Oh, H., & Swaminathan, A. (2006). Framing Interorganizational Network Change: A Network Inertia Perspective. *Academy of Management Review*, 31(3): 704–720.

King, A. A., Lenox, M. J., & Terlaak, A. (2005). "The Strategic Use of Decentralized Institutions: Exploring Certification with the ISO 14001 Management Standard," *Academy of Management Journal*, 48: 1091–1106.

Lenox, M. J. & Eesley, C. (2009). "Private Environmental Activism and the Selection and Response of Firm Targets," *Journal of Economics & Management Strategy*, 18: 45–73.

——— & King, A. A. (2004). "Prospects for Developing Absorptive Capacity through Internal Information Provision," *Strategic Management Journal*, 25: 331–345.

Lord, M. D. (2000). "Corporate Political Strategy and Legislative Decision Making: The Impact of Corporate Legislative Influence Activities," *Business & Society*, 39(1): 76–93.

Majumdar, S. K. & Marcus, A. A. (2001). "Rules Versus Discretion: The Productivity Consequences of Flexible Regulation," *Academy of Management Journal*, 44: 170–179.

May, D. R. & Flannery, B. L. (1995). "Cutting Waste with Employee Involvement Teams," *Business Horizons*, 38(5): 28–38.

Mitchell, R. K., Agle, B. R., & Wood, D. J. (1997). "Toward a Theory of Stakeholder Identification and Salience: Defining the Principle of Who and What Really Counts," *Academy of Management Review*, 22: 853–886.

Nohria, N. & Gulati, R. (1994). "Firms and their Environments," in N. J. Smelser & R. Swedberg (eds.), *Handbook of Economic Sociology*, Princeton, NJ: Princeton University Press, 529–555.

Ogden, S. & Watson, R. (1999). "Corporate Performance and Stakeholder Management: Balancing Shareholder and Customer Interests in the UK Privatized Water Industry," *Academy of Management Journal*, 42: 526–538.

Pfeffer, J. (1992). *Managing with Power: Politics and Influence in Organizations*. Boston, MA: Harvard Business School Press.

——— (2009). "Shareholders First? Not so Fast...," *Harvard Business Review*, July–August, 90–91.

——— & Salancik, G. R. (1978). *The External Control of Organizations: A Resource Dependence Perspective*, New York: Harper and Row.

Podolny, J. (1994). "Market Uncertainty and the Social Character of Economic Exchange," *Administrative Science Quarterly*, 39(3): 458–483.

——— & Page, K. (1998). "Network Forms of Organizations," *Annual Review of Sociology*, 24(1): 57–76.

Porter, M. E. & van der Linde, C. (1995). "Toward a New Conception of the Environment-Competitiveness Relationship," *Journal of Economic Perspectives*, 94: 97–118.

Prahalad, C. K. & Ramaswamy, V. (2000). "Co-opting Customer Competence," *Harvard Business Review*, January–February, 79–87.

——— ——— (2004). *The Future of Competition: Co-creating Unique Value with Customers*. Boston, MA: Harvard Business School Press.

Prasad, P. & Elmes, M. (2005). "In the Name of the Practical: Unearthing the Hegemony of Pragmatics in the Discourse of Environmental Management," *Journal of Management Studies*, 42: 845–867.

Ramaswamy, V. & Gouillart, F. (2010). "Building the Co-Creative Enterprise," *Harvard Business Review.* October, 100–109.

Reichheld, F. F. & Sasser, W. E. (1990). "Zero Defections: Quality Comes to Services," *Harvard Business Review*, 68(5): 105–111.

Ring, P., & Van De Ven, A. (1994). "Developmental Processes of Cooperative Interorganizational Relationships," *Academy of Management Review*, 19(1): 90–118.

Rowley, T. J. (1997). "Moving beyond Dyadic Ties: A Network Theory of Stakeholder Influences," *Academy of Management Review*, 22: 887–910.

Russo, M. (2001). "Institutions, Exchange Relations, and the Emergence of New Fields: Regulatory Policies and Independent Power Production in America, 1978–1992," *Administrative Science Quarterly*, 46: 57–86.

—— (2003). "The Emergence of Sustainable Industries: Building on Natural Capital," *Strategic Management Journal*, 24: 317–331.

Shaffer, B. (1995). "Firm-Level Responses to Government Regulation: Theoretical and Research Approaches," *Journal of Management*, 21: 495–514.

Sharma, S. (2000). "Managerial Interpretations and Organizational Context as Predictors of Corporate Choice Of Environmental Strategy," *Academy of Management Journal*, 43: 681–697.

—— & Henriques, I. (2005). "Stakeholder Influences on Sustainability Practices in the Canadian Forest Products Industry," *Strategic Management Journal*, 26: 159–180.

Shrivastava, P. (1995). "The Role of Corporations in Achieving Ecological Sustainability," *Academy of Management Review*, 20: 936–960.

Sine, W. D., David, R., & Mitsuhashi, H. (2007). "From Plan to Plant: Effects of Certification on Operational Start-Up in the Emergent Independent Power Sector," *Organization Science*, 18: 578–594.

—— Haveman, H. A., & Tolbert, P. S. (2005). "Risky Business? Entrepreneurship in the New Independent Power Sector," *Administrative Science Quarterly*, 50: 200–232.

—— & Lee, B. H. (2009). "Tilting at Windmills?. The Environmental Movement and the Emergence of the U.S. Wind Energy Sector," *Administrative Science Quarterly*, 54: 123–155.

Skjolsvik, T., Lowendahl, R., Kvalshaugen, S., & Fosstenlokken, S. M. (2007). "Choosing to Learn and Learning to Choose: Strategies for Client Co-Production and Knowledge Development," *California Management Review*, 49(3): 110–128.

Speth, J. G. (2009). "Doing Business in a Postgrowth Society," *Harvard Business Review*, September, 18–19.

Tsai, W. (2000). "Social Capital, Strategic Relatedness and the Formation of Intraorganizational Linkages," *Strategic Management Journal*, 21(9): 925.

—— (2001). "Knowledge Transfer in Intraorganizational Networks: Effects of Network Position and Absorptive Capacity on Business Unit Innovation and Performance," *Academy of Management Journal*, 44(5): 996–1004.

—— (2002). "Social Structure of "Coopetition" within a Multiunit Organization: Coordination, Competition, and Intraorganizational Knowledge Sharing," *Organization Science*, 13(2): 179–190.

Tsoukas, H. & Chia, R. (2002). "On Organizational Becoming: Rethinking Organizational Change," *Organization Science*, 13(5): 567–582.

Walsh, J. P. (2005). "Taking Stock of Stakeholder Management," *Academy of Management Review*, 30: 426–438.

Williamson, O. (1979). "Transaction Cost Economics: The Governance of Contractual Relations," *Journal of Law and Economics*, 26: 233–261.

Winn, M. (2001). "Building Stakeholder Theory with a Decision Modeling Methodology," *Business and Society*, 40: 133–166.

Xue, M., & Field, J. M. (2008). "Service Coproduction and with Information Stickiness and Incomplete Contracts: Implications for Consulting Services Design," *Production and Operations Management*, 17: 357–372.

—— Hitt, L. M., & Harker, P. T. (2007). "Customer Efficiency, Channel Usage, and Firm Performance in Retail Banking," *Manufacturing & Service Operations Management*, 9: 535–558.

Yermack, D. (1996). "Higher Market Valuation of Companies with a Small Board of Directors," *Journal of Financial Economics*, 40: 185–213.

Zahra, S. & Pearce, J. (1989). "Boards of Directors and Corporate Financial Performance: A Review and Integrative Model," *Journal of Management*, 15: 291–334.

PART III

POLICY AND NON-MARKET STRATEGIES

CHAPTER 6

INDUSTRY SELF-REGULATION AND ENVIRONMENTAL PROTECTION

ANDREW KING,
ANDREA M. PRADO,
AND JORGE RIVERA

ENVIRONMENTAL problems are no longer local or regional, or even continental. They are global. And their solution requires coordination and regulation at the global level. Solving these problems will require governing institutions with global reach, massive resources, and an incentive to protect the environment. Who can take on this job?

One potential list of candidates starts with the world's top 100 economies. The list begins with some familiar names—the European Union, the United States, China, and Brazil. Certainly all will have a role to play, but one can easily envision barriers each might face. Then, somewhere around the twelfth rank, an odd thing occurs: the names shift from those of nations to those of corporations. For the remainder of the list, corporations become common. In fact, about half of the top "economies" in the world are private corporations. Some of the comparisons are staggering. Exxon's revenues are larger than Australia's GDP, Volkswagen's bigger than Pakistan's, Costa Rica's economy smaller than that of Lowe's.

The list of the world's top economies is jarring in part because it inverts our thinking about how the economic "game" is played—in particular who are the "players" and who are the "umpires". People tend to think of companies as players in a game umpired by governments and civil society. Institutions (e.g., regulating states) set the rules of the game, and firms compete within those rules. But firms actually have a much more complicated role. They also act as umpires that shape the rules of the competition.

In this chapter, we look at some of the ways that corporations coordinate to set the rules of business competition. Such coordination is often called "industry self-regulation" because it involves regulation of business activities without the direct aid of central government. However, none of the words that make up this title is perfectly appropriate. "Industry self-regulation" is sometimes created by actors that are not "industrial". Its enforcement may not be "self" regulated, but rely instead on the sanctions of outsiders. And, how much it regulates behavior remains an open question.

"Industry self-regulation" (ISR) is distinguished mostly by what it is not. It is not regulation by government. And this lack of governmental authority is what makes it so problematic, provocative, and so potentially important. No effective world government exists, and thus solutions for many important problems will require cooperative agreements that are self-regulating and self-enforcing. Self-regulation among firms may be one vehicle for solving wide-spread environmental problems. Thus, whether or not firms, with their massive resources and global reach, can self-regulate represents one of the most important questions we must answer in determining how best to make this planet more sustainable.

This chapter starts by discussing the difficulties and promises of self-regulation as a mechanism to address environmental problems.

The peril and promise of industry self-regulation

Adam Smith famously remarked, "People of the same trade seldom meet together, even for merriment and diversion, but the conversation ends in a conspiracy against the public, or in some contrivance to raise prices." Such a conspiracy represents a kind of agreement, and since it is done without the aid or support of government, it is a form of "industry self-regulation." Such collusion is not the type of self-regulation we consider in this chapter, but Adam Smith's comment should provide us with both hope and concern. The prevalence he describes should make us hopeful that firms can indeed cooperate and self-regulate. The result that such cooperation often ends in a "conspiracy against the public" should remind us of the potential risks of any self-regulated industry agreement.

The form of self-regulation that we explore in this chapter creates value to society—or at least that is what is claimed and hoped. By colluding on a set of rules, firms do not conspire against the public. Rather, they improve public welfare as well. How can they be both raising their own profits and bettering society? They can do this, economic models suggest, because sometimes the rules of the business competition are so out of whack that they are ruining the "game" for everyone—firms, customers, and stakeholders. Changing the rules can make a better competition and make everyone better off. Economists call these cases where market exchange is out of whack and needs correction "market failure."

Market failures occur when free exchange does not produce an efficient allocation of goods and services. The rules of the competition and trade somehow produce an inferior outcome. Everyone is made poorer—the players, the audience, and the rule makers. The only good news is that this very inefficiency creates an opportunity to form better rules that make everyone better off. It is this potential for general gain that makes the idea of industry self-regulation so intriguing. If new and better rules will benefit large and powerful corporations, perhaps these companies will be motivated to lead such rule changes.

Such is the hope, but there is also a great risk when firms are allowed to shape the rules of competition. New rules might benefit everyone, or they might, as Adam Smith warned, benefit the firms at the expense of the public. If firms are indeed going to be important agents of change, they must be disciplined by knowledgeable stakeholders. They should be rewarded when they act in the common interest. The research reviewed in this chapter attempts to better understand the promise and danger of industrial attempts to create self-regulatory solutions to environmental problems.

Animal, vegetable, or mineral? Categorizing the common forms of ISR

Self-regulatory agreements are "institutions" and they shape, in the words of Douglass North, "the rules of the game" (North 1990). But, if there is any advantage to new rules, then the old ones must have been incomplete or inefficient. What are the problems of the rules that these new self-regulations may be attempting to solve? Scholars have proposed two main options.

The first problem that may drive self-regulation is that existing rules leave information "asymmetrically distributed." This problem is not limited to environmental goods and services, but it is unusually common for them because the environmental attributes of most products and services are invisible. Take, for example, a pound of coffee. It is impossible for a consumer to determine if that coffee was grown in a sustainable manner (for example, under a forest canopy of native trees). As a result, producers know the environmental attributes of their products, but consumers do not. In the presence of such asymmetric information, consumers reasonably doubt unverified claims by producers. When this doubt is greatest, a "market for lemons" can arise in which only low-quality goods are traded. For environmental goods and services, such conditions lead to a market where only environmentally damaging products are provided.

The second problem that may drive self-regulation is that the cost of environmental harm is borne by others than those that caused the harm. Environmental effects are usually "externalities" that do not appear on the polluter's balance sheet. The rights to many environmental resources are not clearly defined, held, or protected. The Earth's atmosphere, for example, is commonly held by all, and thus the services it provides are "free" goods. People can use it to carry their pollution away and, given that is free and commonly held, they will tend to abuse it in ways that harm everyone.

Considered together, these problems form a two-by-two matrix in which some sort of institutional control is needed in three of the Quadrants (see Figure 6.1). Over the last fifteen years, scholars interested in business and environmental regulation have tried to distinguish which self-regulations were addressing which of these problems. They have done so by first hypothesizing some basic stylized predictions for which firms might participate in the institution, how they might be affected by participation, and who might benefit from the institution.

Quadrant 1 (Q1): Certifications

When asymmetric information causes inefficient exchange, self-regulation might provide a way to convey to the customer or stakeholder unobservable information about the product. For example, certification of compliance with certain practices can communicate to the customer that the product is "organic"—that is, pesticides and herbicides have not been used in the production of the good. This attribute, "organic" production, illustrates a common problem for environmental products: the environmental attributes of the product often relate to the way it was produced—and these

	Substantial Externalities	No Externalities
Asymmetric Information	**Quadrant 4: Mixed-Method** *Goal*: To communicate unobservable attributes to stakeholders and to respond to a shared threat *Mechanism*: Differentiate "good" and "bad" firms, but also improve performance of all members. *Participants*: Indeterminate *Effects*: Indeterminate	**Quadrant 1: Certifications** *Goal*: To communicate unobservable attributes to stakeholders *Mechanism*: Credibly distinguish "good" and "bad" performers *Participants*: "Good" performers *Effects*: Participating firms and stakeholders benefit
Shared Information	**Quadrant 3: Collective Responsibility** *Goal*: To respond to a shared threat and protect members from stakeholders *Mechanism*: Performance improvement of members is enough to reduce the shared threat (e.g., forestall regulatory or stakeholder action) *Participants*: Industry members with greater interest in common welfare (usually those with greater market share) *Effects*: Industry members and stakeholders benefit	**Quadrant 2:** Self-Regulation Not Needed

FIGURE 6.1 Categorization of Industry Self-Regulation

attributes are not apparent to the consumer. As a result, many of these programs set standards for these unobservable management practices. In some cases, the sponsors of these programs explicitly state that their goal is to help stakeholders distinguish products from "good" and "bad" firms.

Industry self-regulations of this type have been organized by a variety of sponsors, including firms, non-governmental organizations, and multi-stakeholder initiatives. One of the most influential sponsors is the International Organization for Standardization (ISO). ISO constitutes an example of certification-type self-regulation. ISO certifications include ISO 9000, ISO 14000, and ISO 26000. These standards encompass a set of guidelines to implement quality, environmental management systems and social responsibility practices. For instance, ISO 14000 specifies a set of environmental management systems, including the development of environmental objectives and policies, the provision of training and documentation, delegation of responsibilities, and internal performance audits (Delmas 2002). In order to obtain certification, firms go through an audit that certifies compliance with the standard requirements. ISO relies on a system of third-party auditors that conduct inspections around the world.

Q1: Empirical Evidence

Most scholarly research on certification programs has attempted to demonstrate that the program matches simple stylized facts from a signaling model (see Figure 6. 1). The models suggest that certified organizations should have higher (but otherwise unobservable) performance, and should gain some financial reward (such as a price premium) relative to non-certified organizations (King, Lenox, & Terlaak 2005; Terlaak & King 2006; Corbett, Montes-Sancho, & Kirsch 2005). Clearly, demonstrating either of these hypotheses is a difficult empirical challenge. It requires the scholar to measure quality that is not observable to stakeholders as well as changes in financial performance of heterogeneous participants (including private and publicly owned organizations). Most scholars have tried to use archival data to identify the attributes of the participant organizations that may predict their propensity to gain certification under a particular program (Albernini & Segerson 2002; Christmann & Taylor 2001; Delmas & Montiel 2009; King, Lenox, & Terlaak 2005; Rivera & deLeon 2004). To understand the effect on performance, scholars tried to distinguish the performance of firms before and after they join (Terlaak & King 2006). In some cases, both approaches are used. In the most advanced research, the performance of participating firms is compared to non-members that are as similar as possible (e.g., the control group) (Corbett, Montes-Sancho, & Kirsch 2005).

Q 1: Do Certification Systems Reveal Superior Environmental Performers?

Contrary to predictions, few studies of US firms find that certified organizations have superior performance to non-certified organizations. Only Toffel (2006) finds that participants have superior performance, measured as the change in the facility's chemical emissions (not the degree to which these emissions are greater or lesser than comparable others). Potoski & Prakash (2005) also find that ISO 14001 certified facilities reduce their pollution emissions faster compared with non-participants. Outside of the US context, Dasgupta, Hettige, & Wheeler (2000) report that adoption of environmental management practices along the lines prescribed by ISO 14001 improved Mexican manufacturers' self-reported compliance with public law.

Evaluating ISO 14000 certifiers in the US, King, Lenox, & Terlaak (2005) are unable to demonstrate that certifying facilities have superior performance to non-certifiers, but argue that performance improvement is precisely what certifying firms are trying to communicate to their exchange partners. The authors try to validate their claim by showing that facilities are more likely to adopt ISO 14000 when their exchange partners are less able to monitor internal efforts to improve. They demonstrate, for example, that facilities are more likely to certify when they have distant or foreign-exchange partners. Similarly, Welch, Mori, & Aoyagi-Usui (2001) argue that ISO 14000 is being used to communicate performance efforts at facilities to remote corporate officers. Consistent with this claim, the authors show that decentralized organizations are more likely to adopt ISO 14001. They also find that adopters are subject to more local regulation, which might imply that some organizations use adoption to signal to regulators their commitment to compliance.

In contrast with research on ISO 14000, research on other certification programs generally fails to find any evidence that participation in the program reveals superior performance. Research suggests that corporate codes of conduct to promote labor practices (Locke, Qin, & Brause 2007; Locke, Amengual, & Mangla 2009) and sustainability certifications for agricultural commodities (Blackman & Rivera 2010) do not reveal superior working conditions or environmental practices respectively.

Q1: Do Participants Benefit?

The second stylized fact that has been explored in the literature is the degree to which participants benefit from certifications. If certifications are indeed signaling superior performance in order to obtain a sales premium, participating organizations should benefit from their participation.

Once again, research has mostly explored the effect of ISO standards in the United States. This research suggests that participants do indeed gain a measureable benefit: either a financial return or a sales winning advantage (Corbett et al. 2005; Terlaak & King 2006). Corbett shows that ISO 9000 certified firms achieved significant financial gains. Terlaak & King (2006) show that facilities grow faster following certification, and that this effect is greater in industries with higher asymmetric information between buyers and suppliers. These results are consistent with predictions from a simple signaling model.

Few studies have been able to measure financial gains from certifications other than those sponsored by ISO. In one notable exception, Rivera (2002) shows that participation in the Costa Rican sustainable tourism certification program is significantly related to higher prices (Rivera 2002). He shows, however, that is it only certification at the highest levels of the program which allows price premiums (Rivera 2010).

Q1: *Questions Raised by Research on Certifications*

The stylized results presented above raise some fundamental questions. If most programs do not provide credible evidence of superior performance, what role are they playing? And, if they fail to separate "good" and "bad" actors, why do firms choose to certify? Finally, if stakeholders are mostly unable to use certifications to assess the unobserved quality of goods, why do they seem to reward firms for certifying?

Stakeholder Confusion

Research is beginning to suggest that stakeholders give undue credence to certifications. A recent experiment by Hiscox & Smyth (2008) testing whether or not customers will pay more for "sustainable" goods revealed the credulousness of consumers. In the experiment, he placed a fake certification tag on some towels and candles in a New York department store. The tag claimed that the towels had been produced in a manner that protected workers and the environment. The fact that customers paid more for these products revealed that customers are willing to pay a price premium for "sustainable" products. The fact that they did so because of a fake certification also revealed that customers are willing to believe unsupported certification claims (see Devinney [Chapter 21] and Gershoff & Irwin [Chapter 20] of this volume for similar studies).

Certification programs may add to customer confusion. Certifications come in a dizzying array of forms and use a wide variety of rules and mechanisms (Darnall & Carmin 2005). Moreover, the criteria necessary for participation in the different initiatives tend be complex, technical, and involve multiple performance dimensions (Smith & Fischlein 2010). Finally, some of these institutions have multiple objectives, such as providing a means to differentiate good and bad performing firms while also providing a useful best practice guideline (Terlaak 2007). As a result, stakeholders often have difficulty interpreting what participation reveals about unobserved environmental performance.

The names, acronyms, and labels of some certification programs can add to stakeholder confusion. In forestry, the Sustainable Forestry Initiative (SFI) and the Forestry Stewardship Council (FSC) are often confused, but one is sponsored by industry and the other is independent. By the end of 2009, the website ecolabelling.org identified more than 300 different industry self-regulation programs (Harbaugh, Maxwell, & Roussillon 2010). In the presence of multiple programs, consumers are often unsure of the exact quality standard—is it a relatively easy or difficult standard (Harbaugh, et al. 2010)? As a result, consumers, buyers, and producers have a hard time understanding the difference among these programs. See Baron & Lyon (Chapter 7) of this volume for further discussion.

Social Explanations

If stakeholders cannot make accurate inferences from certifications or if certification programs do not separate "good" and "bad" actors, the economic logic of the programs no longer holds. Accordingly, economists predict that such programs should cease to exist. Yet, we see many examples where participation continues and programs are given credence by stakeholders. What other theories might explain this behavior?

Scholars such as Magali Delmas and Andrew Hoffman have attempted to provide an answer by drawing on sociological theories (Delmas 2002; Delmas & Toffel 2004; Hoffman 1999; Hoffman 2001). They note that pre-conscious constraints prevent rational consideration because powerful schemas provide rigid frames for decision-making (Berger & Luckmann 1966). Similarly, post-conscious constraints cause decision-makers to fail to recognize their interests or to be able to do so effectively (DiMaggio 1988). Hoffman (1999) argues, for example, that over time metaphors for "pollution" shifted from being an obligation to a strategic choice. Decisions, he argues, were made within the frames of these metaphors. Delmas (2002: 91) concludes that normative and cognitive "aspects of a country's institutional environment explain the differences in adoption [of ISO 14000] across countries."

Boiral (2007) uses case studies to argue that ISO 14001 might be operating as a 'rational myth' that spurs 'ceremonial behavior.' Despite the often idealized statements about the standard's advantages, the author finds only relative improvements in environmental practices and performance. Rational myths were maintained to justify the implementation of ISO 14001, give it a more legitimate appearance, help dissimulate internal contradictions, and avoid jeopardizing the continuity of the system.

Quadrant 3 (Q3): Collective Responsibility

In Quadrant 3, externalities or missing markets cause inefficient use of communal resources. Since this usually means that firms do not bear the full cost of the social problems they create, why would managers want to change the situation through industry self-regulation?

One reason is that stakeholders take actions to impose these "external" costs on offending firms (see Baron and Lyon [Chapter 7] of this volume for further discussion on private politics). They lobby for increased government regulation or they engage in direct action to penalize firms. If such regulation were effectively targeted to impose appropriate costs on each offending firm, there would be no need for self-regulation. Often, however, regulation penalizes all firms, be they good or bad. Stakeholders also impose a common cost on all firms in an industry by sanctioning firms collectively or randomly.

In response to these industry-wide pressures, firms may choose to create industry self-regulation as a collective defense mechanism. A number of potential explanations have been offered for how this might work. A common argument is that firms seek to forestall regulatory or stakeholder action by improving just enough that regulators or stakeholders no longer have sufficient motivation to incur in a fixed cost of regulating (Rivera 2010; Segerson & Dawson 2001). As a result, firms incur some cost of regulation, but avoid a much higher cost. In this model, everyone gains: stakeholders gain improved environmental performance, and firms, regulators, and customers avoid costly regulatory administration.

Q3: Empirical Evidence

Research suggests a few stylized predictions for the effect of these programs. As with self-regulation in Quadrant 1, both firms and stakeholders should benefit from these institutions. In this case, however, the benefit could spill over to all firms, not just the participants and the entire industry should be rewarded. For their additional support of the industry, stakeholders should gain some consideration—for example, improved environmental protection.

These predicted patterns of general improvement make empirical analysis of these programs very difficult. Nevertheless, some scholars have uncovered intriguing evidence.

Q3: Do Participants Improve Environmental Performance?

Studies provide mixed evidence on the degree to which these self regulations improve the environmental performance of firms. For example, Rees (1994) notes that the Institute of Nuclear Power Operation (INPO) was successful because it was able to support its internal sanctions through a threat to reveal non-compliance to the Nuclear Regulatory Commission (Rees 1994). In contrast, studies of several other programs show that participating firms do not improve their performance compared with non-participants (Darnall & Sides 2008; King & Lenox 2000; Howard, Nash, & Ehrenfeld 2000; Rivera & deLeon 2004).

King & Lenox (2000) demonstrate that participants in the Responsible Care program do not improve their environmental performance faster than non-participants. Howard-Grenville, Nash, & Coglianese (2008) find that in many participating firms; managers did not have the knowledge or resources needed to implement the required standards. Rivera & deLeon (2004) find similar results for the Sustainable Slopes Program. Participating ski areas were also more likely to have lower third-party environmental performance ratings (Rivera & deLeon 2004).

Why are these programs not meeting their aspirations? A common problem seems to be that these programs lack mechanisms for verifying compliance with the agreed standard and/or a viable means for sanctioning non-compliance. In 1999, *Chemical Week* reported that members of the chemical industry were becoming concerned with the lack of internal compliance to the Responsible Care program and had as a result taken the "velvet glove" off (Barnett & King 2008).

Various researchers have suggested that tighter requirements, such as explicit sanctions for non-compliers, public disclosure, and independent monitoring and verification mechanisms can improve the performance of these institutions (King & Lenox 2000; Rivera & deLeon 2005). Lenox & Nash (2003) argue that self-regulatory institutions that have demonstrated a serious commitment to expel non-compliant members are less likely to suffer from adverse selection. In support of this claim, they found empirical evidence that a forestry trade association's self-regulation program, which featured a credible threat of expulsion, attracted a disproportionate number of participants that exhibited superior environmental performance.

Q3: Does the Industry Benefit?

In contrast to evidence that programs in Quadrant 3 have provided little environmental benefit, several studies have found evidence that the programs provide financial benefits to the industry. Some scholars have looked at the financial benefits that a self-regulation initiative generates for all industry members. Lenox (2006) finds that the creation of the Responsible Care program generated dramatic financial benefits to most firms in the industry. Barnett & King (2008) find that the Responsible Care program reduces the tendency that a negative event of a firm such as a chemical accident, could have in decreasing the stock price of another firm. Thus, empirical evidence suggests that, as predicted by theory, the financial benefits of programs in Quadrant 3 go not to participating firms, but to the industry as a whole.

Q3: Questions Raised by Research on Collective Responsibility

Many questions remain about self-regulation in Quadrant 3. Most critically, scholars are puzzled by the apparent contradiction in the empirical evidence concerning the functioning of these institutions. On the one hand, they seem to provide no apparent benefit to stakeholders. On the other, they are used as a vehicle for stakeholder outreach, and they apparently provide firms with a financial benefit. What could be going on?

Barnett & King (2008) propose that the purpose of one prominent program, Responsible Care, may have been misunderstood. Rather than an agreement to improve environmental performance, it was, they argue, an agreement to disclose information. This disclosure of information helped reduce concerns about chemical risks and reduced the degree to which accidents at one firm would harm the reputation of another. Their argument modifies existing models, but retains their basic structure. The program, they argue, provides a benefit to stakeholders (information) which reduces the tendency for stakeholders to punish the industry.

Other scholars have used theories from sociology to argue that self-regulation may take on meaning that it does not deserve. These institutions, by their prominence and their affiliation, may gain a sense of "legitimacy." This legitimacy could cause stakeholders to reward participating firms whether or not the program provides real benefits to stakeholders (D'Aveni 1990).

Scholars have also pondered how these programs get initiated. For example, what allows firms to come together to create a common strategy and common set of rules? Anecdotal evidence seems to suggest that major negative events tend to spark the formation of these programs. For example, the nuclear accident at Three Mile Island sparked the nuclear industry to form the Institute of Nuclear Power Operations (INPO). Similarly, the Responsible Care Program of the chemical industry was formed after an accident in Bhopal, India, killed approximately 10,000 people and may have injured up to 100,000. Other evidence seems to point to the importance of a leading actor to help coordinate agreement on a standard. Rees (1997) reports that in the case of Responsible Care, Robert Kennedy, CEO of Union Carbide, played this important role.

Quadrant 4: Mixed-Method Approaches

Programs in Quadrant 4 have been least studied. Although the founders of several programs expressed the hope that they would accomplish both objectives, scholars have noted that attempting to accomplish both goals may be difficult or even counter-productive (Terlaak 2007). This is because accomplishing the two goals seems to involve conflicting strategies (see Table 6.1). As shown in Table 6.1, when the goal of the self-regulatory institution is improvement of all firms in an industry, membership should include all relevant firms, but when the goal is to separate "good" from "bad" firms, only the better should participate. Similarly, because it is less costly for the worst performers to improve, self regulatory institutions who seek to improve collective performance should allocate resources to improve the worst performers. However, if the self-regulatory institution is designed to separate "good" and "bad" performers, no special assistance should be provided to the worst performers. Finally, the financial returns are distributed differently in the two examples. In the case of collective responsibility, the entire industry benefits by the improved reputation that the program provides. For certifications, only the participants benefit from the higher price premiums they can charge by having distinguished themselves from the low-performing firms.

Example

The best example of a program in Quadrant 4 is the Equator Principles. This agreement was formed among banks engaged in project finance, and it was designed to address growing concern among stakeholders about the environmental and social costs caused by project finance and among investors concerned with the potential for loan default. A few high-profile projects (e.g., the Holcim Vietnam Plant) threatened to damage the reputation of the entire industry. According to the founders of the Equator Principles, the program was intended to reassure stakeholders that leading banks were acting to reduce the propensity for social harm and reassure investors that investments had undergone proper due diligence.

Table 6.1 Strategies of Mixed–Method Self-Regulation

	Collective Responsibility	Certifications
Membership	Include all	Include the better performing
Environmental Performance	Worst improve most	Average improve to meet standard
Financial Performance	Entire industry benefits	Participants benefit

GENERAL PRINCIPLES FOR EFFECTIVE
SELF-REGULATION

All of the studies on industry self-regulation note that the institutions begin with some claim to creating gains for society. For example, when the Responsible Care program was initiated, its proponents claimed it would reduce accidents, assuage stakeholders, eliminate the need for costly regulation, and maintain the profitability of the industry. Although such claims might simply represent public relations, notes from internal documents and reports suggest that such feelings are held by some founders and important members. Research on self-regulation seems to confirm a functional explanation of institutions (i.e. institutions arise to improve inefficient market exchange). However, there are still various challenges to overcome for these institutions to teach their potential and maximize the gains for society.

What principles have emerged from the empirical studies reviewed in this chapter? Research has shown that the effectiveness of these initiatives is subject to the credible enforcement of their rules and their interactions with other institutions. Scholars must build on the knowledge generated so far regarding these two principles and seek a better understanding on how these mechanisms and relationships operate. For instance, it is important to explore potential trade-offs or unintended consequences that the strengthening of the sanctioning mechanism or the development of relationships with different stakeholders can have in the adoption and impact of the these institutions.

Credible Enforcement of Rules

Research on industry self-regulation has considered the importance of visible verification of rule compliance and credible enforcement of rules. In the majority of cases, scholars have concluded that both visibility and credible enforcement are critical to the effective functioning of self-regulation.

The mechanism for achieving visibility varies across the institutions being analyzed. Self-regulation in Quadrant 3 seem to have the greatest difficulty in developing systems for allowing visibility. Few of these institutions include effective verification systems. Instead, they seem to rely on "incestuous" relations to passively provide visibility. Rees (1997), for example, argues that the tendency of chemical firms to be connected in complex supplier/buyer relationships allows firms in the industry to monitor compliance with the Responsible Care program. The participants in the Equator Principles also rely on these nested relations to provide oversight. Banks tend to syndicate in numerous loans, and therefore have insight on the extent to which other firms are following agreements.

Certification programs tend to have more direct and credible mechanisms for maintaining visibility. In most cases, these programs rely on official inspection and certification of compliance with rules. To make the result of these inspections credible to stakeholders, the inspector usually needs to be independent from the institutional governance, or the sponsor of the institution must have interests that are clearly aligned with the stakeholders and not with the firm. Environmental goods are usually credence goods, thus the "quality" of the good cannot be verified even after the purchase. As a result, stakeholders must infer the credibility of the certification by gauging the interests of the certifier.

Independent certification represents a major problem for many self-regulatory programs. In many cases, certifiers pay auditors to assess their compliance. As a result, firms are inclined to select lenient auditors (Swift, Humphrey, & Gor 2000). In all cases, auditing only validates compliance at periodic times, when audits are scheduled. However, real compliance with management system standards is an ongoing activity (O'Rourke 2002). Thus, the implementation of the standards can be more of a symbolic than a substantive act (Christmann & Taylor 2006).

The ability of the auditor can influence the accuracy of the information provided by certification. Some auditors may lack sufficient business knowledge (Swift et al. 2000) or technical knowledge of specific industries (Boiral 2003; O'Rourke 2002; Yeung & Mok 2005). As audited firms need to provide documentation to external auditors, less qualified auditors may uncritically accept the internal report prepared by the firm (Yeung & Mok 2005). As a result, one auditor might certify a firm while another one would fail the same firm (Boiral 2003; Yeung & Mok 2005). These concerns are being addressed by certifying organizations through initiatives such as ISEAL Alliance.

Several studies argue that sanctions are necessary for maintaining the efficiency of a self-regulatory program. In a comparison of four self-regulation programs, the one with explicit sanctions for malfeasance was the one that was able to avoid adverse selection problems (Lenox & Nash 2003). For sanctions to work, however, they must be available and credible. The cost to the sanctioner of applying them must be less than the benefit the sanctioner obtains. Many of the programs discussed in this chapter fail this test because collective sanctions require removing a participant from the group, and this raises problems for the group. Removing non-compliers from the group suggests that participants have not maintained compliance with the program.

Sanctioning is a particularly difficult problem for self regulatory programs in Quadrant 3. Anti-trust regulation prevents certain types of sanctioning behavior, and bi-lateral sanctions do not leverage the advantage of the collective agreement. Such bi-lateral sanctions are also vulnerable to free-riding behavior as each actor waits for another to take on the costly role of sanctioner. One effective means of sanctioning is noted by Rees (1994) in his study of the Institute of Nuclear Power Operations. In that program, violators of the industry program are turned over to the government for further inspection and potential enforcement. Such transfers need not be public, and their existence reassures the Nuclear Regulatory Commission that the INPO is functioning.

Sanctioning is much easier for certifications than for collective responsibility programs. Both types of programs have two main components: the set of guidelines or requirements and the monitoring and sanction mechanisms (Gereffi, Garcia-Johnson, & Sasser 2001). The mechanism for sanctioning for non-compliance in the case of certifications is straightforward. Certifications are not provided, not renewed, or removed for violations of rules. In practice, however, misaligned incentives may prevent effective sanctioning. Sponsors of certifications often have a financial or reputational interest in their program, and they seek to encourage adoption by avoiding sanctioning. The current business model for certifiers also reduces the incentive for sanctioning. Certifiers are often paid by the firm, and thus face conflict incentives when performing audits.

Supportive Institutional Environment

Most of the research on industry self-regulation has been done in nations with highly developed regulatory environments. This makes comparison of the effect of the institutional environment difficult. Nevertheless, several studies note connections to national institutions as particularly important in allowing self-regulation (see Christmann & Taylor [Chapter 3] this volume).

Although some scholars have proposed that industry self-regulation could substitute for missing state institutions, existing evidence suggests that regulation actually complements the functioning of these institutions. Greater reporting requirements, such as the US Toxic Release Inventory, allow stakeholders a means for analyzing the efficacy of programs. Correspondingly, the threat of state regulation helps provide the incentive for self-regulation, and state regulators can provide a credible enforcement mechanism for voluntary programs. Finally, government oversight can directly reduce the tendency for firms to violate self-regulatory agreements (Khanna & Damon 1999).

Evidence also suggests that informed customers and intermediaries support the functioning of self-regulatory institutions. For example, Prado (2010) notes that flower producers often choose the weakest certifications—except when they are importing to Switzerland. She notes Swiss consumers buy more flowers per capita than any other nation, and are known to be very discerning customers. She hypothesizes that these Swiss customers are more likely to require the most stringent environmental certification.

The adoption of programs often requires new management practices or creates opportunities in unexpected places. For instance, firms interested in promoting responsible labor practices could address the root causes of poor working conditions by enabling suppliers to better schedule their work and to improve quality and efficiency (Locke et al. 2007). Locke et al. (2009) find that responsible sourcing practices more focused on joint problem solving, information exchange, and diffusion of best practices, than on compliance with a code of conduct have led to improvements in working conditions in factories around the world. Finally, an active community of local non-governmental organizations can be helpful in monitoring and supporting participation in self-regulatory programs.

FUTURE DIRECTIONS

After more than a decade of research on industry self-regulation, it is important to highlight a basic agenda for future research. The literature has focused on a limited number of programs—including ISO 14001, ISO 9000, Responsible Care, Sustainable Slopes, and the Forestry Stewardship Council—pointing to a couple of obvious gaps in the literature.

First, we still do not know if the emerging findings about key program characteristics can be generalized to the hundreds of other initiatives currently being implemented around the world. Second, most existing research has focused on examining self-regulation in manufacturing and natural resource extraction industries. We know very little about the effects of institutions in other sectors of the economy, such as banking or insurance. Third, we do not understand what happens to the environmental and financial performance of participating firms that drop-out or are expelled from a program.

Additionally, most empirical studies have examined industry self-regulation in developed countries. We know little about the effectiveness of initiatives diffusing in developing countries, where these institutions often become the only de facto policy tool available for attempting to promote environmental practices within the business community. More research is necessary to understand why firms in these countries are adopting self-regulatory initiatives, and what types of programs are more likely to improve businesses' environmental and financial performance.

As discussed previously, these initiatives need performance-based standards, third-party oversight, and a sanctions/reward system in order to function effectively. Yet, we know very little about what are the optimal levels of stringency that would make these conditions sufficient to avoid opportunism. After all, a draconian program that doesn't attract enough business participation may also be as ineffective as a lax one that promotes minimal environmental protection.

Another stream of research that is worth exploring is the relationship of self-regulation and government intervention. This relationship is a source of debate among scholars. There are those who argue that these programs "crowd-out" more thorough government interventions (Esbenshade 2004). While others argue that they help strengthen government enforcement of national laws (O'Rourke 2003; Rodriguez-Garabito 2005). More research is necessary to understand when either of these positions accurately predicts the effects of industry self-regulation.

In terms of research methods it is essential that future studies to evaluate the effects of participation in industry self-regulation, consider what would have been the firms' situation without participation in the program. Blackman & Rivera (2010) found that from thirty-seven studies that have sought to measure the environmental and socio-economic impacts of certifications, only fourteen make a serious attempt to construct a credible counterfactual, and therefore can be considered tests of causal impacts. Heckman correction and propensity score-matching are statistical techniques to address self selection problems (Greene 2000; Maddala 1986; Rosenbaum & Rubin 1983).

CONCLUSIONS AND IMPLICATIONS

We began this chapter by noting that business enterprises represent one of the few actors with the power, global reach, and incentive to respond to growing environmental problems. As we discussed in our introduction, the resources available to business enterprises rival all but the largest nations, and their independence allows them free-dom of action not available to most nations. In addition, business enterprises may have the incentive to act to create institutions which better regulate market exchange to pre-vent the inefficiencies caused by missing property rights and asymmetric information. Other stakeholders, such as non-governmental or multi-stakeholder organizations, can also participate in the creation of these institutions.

The research reviewed in this chapter shows that self-regulatory programs created by business enterprises take forms that appear to be designed to solve exchange problems. Some seem to resolve problems caused by asymmetric information. Others seem to help regulate externalities. A very few appear to try to do both. The rapid growth of these pro-grams appears to some eyes to suggest a proactive response from businesses and other organizations to growing environmental problems.

Existing research both confirms earlier findings on self-regulation of common pool resources and reveals new questions for scholars of industry self-regulation. The body of this research suggests, however, that self-regulatory programs often fail to live up to their promise. Evidence on many of the programs suggests that they fail to provide benefits to the stakeholders that they claim to protect. Why then do these programs garner support from stakeholders? One possibility is that the very hope that these programs embody creates the conditions that cause them to fail. Customers buy goods with suspect labels because they think that doing so supports good intentions. Regulators provide members of industry self-regulations with regulatory relief because they assume that they must be somewhat better than non-members.

Academics too fall victim to this kind of destructive wishful thinking. At a confer-ence in 2010 at which several papers were presented demonstrating the failure of self-regulatory programs, a well-known scholar chastised the panel for emphasizing the failure and not the promise of these programs. Failed attempts at self-regulation, he argued, raised awareness of issues and thereby aided environmental causes. In fact, we believe that nothing could be further from the truth. A lack of attentive stakeholder oversight allows these programs to operate "out of equilibrium." Without oversight, firms can garner private benefits from self-regulation without providing social benefits. Firms can create misleading programs that substitute good feeling for good action. If one message comes out of research on self-regulatory institutions it is that the risk of a "conspiracy against the public" is always present. Scholars have a duty to accurately report the effect of self-regulatory programs.

Where does the existing body of reporting leave us? It leaves the authors of this chapter both skeptical and hopeful. Stakeholders—including the government—must stop creating or endorsing strictly voluntary programs that do not include the institu-tional conditions for maintaining compliance with institutional rules. This includes the necessity of credible and public evaluation and the visible sanctioning of rule breakers. Without such disciplined oversight, the promise of industry self-regulation will go unmet. If, however, stakeholders can effectively police the use of industry self-regulation, businesses and other organizations may indeed help create the new rules needed to achieve a more sustainable planet.

REFERENCES

Alberini, A. & Segerson, K. (2002). "Assessing Voluntary Programs to Improve Environmental Quality," *Environmental and Resource Economics*, 22(1–2): 157–184.

Barnett, M. L. & King, A. A. (2008). "Good Fences Make Good Neighbors: A Longitudinal Analysis of an Industry Self-Regulatory Institution," *Academy of Management Journal*, 51(6): 1150–1170.

Berger, P. & Luckmann, T. (1966). *The Social Construction of Reality*. New York: Doubleday.

Blackman, A. & Rivera, J. (2010). "Environmental Certification and the Global Environment Facility," *Advisory Report*, Washington, DC: United Nations' Global Environmental Facility.

Boiral, O. (2003). 'ISO 9000: "Outside the Iron Cage," *Organization Science*, 14(6): 720–737.

——(2007). "Corporate Greening through ISO 14001: A Rational Myth?" *Organization Science*, 18(1): 127–146,

Christmann, P. & Taylor, G. (2001). "Globalization and the Environment: Determinants of Firm Self-Regulation in China," *Journal of International Business Studies*, 32(3): 439–458.

——— (2006). "Firm Self-Regulation through International Certifiable Standards: Determinants of Symbolic versus Substantive Implementation," *Journal of International Business Studies*, 37(6): 863–878.

Corbett, C. J., Montes-Sancho, M. J. & Kirsch, D. A. (2005). "The Financial Impact of ISO 9000 Certification in the United States: An Empirical Analysis," *Management Science*, 51(7): 1046–1059.

D'Aveni, R. (1990). "Top Managerial Prestige and Organizational Bankruptcy," *Organization Science*, 1(2): 187–220.

Darnall, N. & Carmin, J. (2005). "Greener and Cleaner? The Signaling Accuracy of US Voluntary Environmental Programs," *Policy Sciences*, 38(2–3): 71–90.

—— & Sides, S. (2008). "Assessing the Performance of Voluntary Environmental Programs: Does Certification Matter?" *Policy Studies Journal*, 36(1): 95–117.

Dasgupta, S., Hettige, H. & Wheeler, D. (2000). "What Improves Environmental Compliance? Evidence from Mexican Industry," *Journal of Environmental Economics and Management*, 39(1): 39–66.

Delmas, M. A. (2002). "The Diffusion of Environmental Management Standards in Europe and in the United States: An Institutional Perspective," *Policy Sciences*, 35(1). 91–119.

—— & Montiel, I. (2009). "Greening the Supply Chain: When Is Customer Pressure Effective?" *Journal of Economics and Management Strategy*, 18(1): 171–201.

—— & Toffel, M. W. (2004). "Stakeholders and Environmental Management Practices: An Institutional Framework," *Business Strategy and the Environment*, 13: 209–222.

DiMaggio, P. J. (1988). "Interest and Agency in Institutional Theory," in L. G. Zucker (ed.), *Institutional Patterns and Organizations: Culture and Environment*, Cambridge, MA: Ballinger.

Esbenshade, J. (2004). *Monitoring Sweatshops: Workers, Consumers and the Global Apparel Industry,* Philadelphia: Temple University Press.

Gereffi, G., Garcia-Johnson, R. & Sasser, E. (2001). "The NGO-Industrial Complex," *Foreign Policy*, 125: 56–65.

Greene, W. (2008). *Econometric Analysis,* Upper Saddle River, N.J.: Prentice Hall, Inc.

Harbaugh, R., Maxwell, J. W. & Roussillon, B. (2010). "Uncertain Standards." Working Paper, Kelley School of Business, Indiana University.

Hiscox, M. J. & Smyth, F. B. (2006). "Is There Consumer Demand for Improved Labor Standards? Evidence from Field Experiments in Social Product Labeling." Working Paper, Department of Government, Harvard University.

Hoffman, A. J. (1999). "Institutional Evolution and Change: Environmentalism and the US Chemical Industry," *Academy of Management Journal*, 42(4): 351–371.

—— (2001). "Linking Organizational and Field-Level Analyses: The Diffusion of Corporate Environmental Practice," *Organization and Environment*, 14(2): 133–156.

Howard, J., Nash, J. & Ehrenfeld, J. (2000). "Standard or Smokescreen? Implementation of a Voluntary Environmental Code," *California Management Review*, 42(2): 63–82.

—— —— & Coglianese, C. (2008). "Constructing the License to Operate: Internal Factors and their Influence on Corporate Environmental Decisions," *Law and Policy*, 30(1): 73–107.

Khanna, M. & Damon, L. A. (1999). "EPA's Voluntary 33/50 Program: Impact on Toxic Releases and Economic Performance of Firms," *Journal of Environmental Economics and Management*, 37(1): 1–25.

King, A. A. & Lenox, M. J. (2000). "Industry Self-Regulation without Sanctions: The Chemical Industry's Responsible Care Program," *Academy of Management Journal*, 43(4): 698–716.

—— —— & Terlaak, A. (2005). "The Strategic use of Decentralized Institutions: Exploring Certification with the ISO 14001 Management Standard," *Academy of Management Journal*, 48(6): 1091–1106.

Lenox, M. J. (2006). "The Role of Private Decentralized Institutions in Sustaining Industry Self-Regulation," *Organization Science*, 17(6): 677–690.

—— and Nash, J. (2003). "Industry Self-Regulation and Adverse Selection: A Comparison across Four Trade Association Programs," *Business Strategy and the Environment*, 12: 343–356.

Locke, R. M., Amengual, M. & Mangla, A. (2009). "Virtue out of Necessity? Compliance, Commitment, and the Improvement of Labor Conditions in Global Supply Chains," *Politics and Society*, 37(3): 319–351.

—— Qin, F. & Brause, A. (2007). "Does Monitoring Improve Labor Standards? Lessons from Nike," *Industrial and Labor Relations Review*, 61(1): 3–31.

Maddala, M. (1986). *Limited-Dependent and Qualitative Variables in Econometrics*, Cambridge. UK: Cambridge University Press.

North, D. C. (1990). *Institutions, Institutional Change, and Economic Performance*, Cambridge, UK: Cambridge University Press.

O'Rourke, D. (2002). "Monitoring the Monitors: A Critique of Corporate Third-Party Labor Monitoring," in R. Jenkins, R. Pearson, and G. Seyfang (eds.), *Corporate Responsibility and Ethical Trade: Codes of Conduct in the Global Economy*. London: Earthscan.

—— (2003). "Outsourcing Regulation: Analyzing Non-Governmental Systems of Labor Standards and Monitoring," *Policy Studies Journal*, 31(1): 1–29.

Potoski, M. and Prakash, A. (2005). "Covenants with Weak Swords: ISO 14001 and Facilities' Environmental Performance," *Journal of Policy Analysis and Management*, 24(4): 745–769.

Prado, A. M. (2010). "Choosing among Environmental and Labor Certifications: An Exploratory Analysis of Producer Adoption," Working Paper, New York University.

Rees, J. (1994). *Hostages of Each Other: The Transformation of Nuclear Safety since Three Mile Island*. Chicago: University of Chicago Press.

—— (1997). "Development of Communitarian Regulation in the Chemical Industry," *Law and Policy*, 19: 477–528.

Rivera, J. (2002). "Assessing a Voluntary Environmental Initiative in the Developing World: The Costa Rican Certification for Sustainable Tourism," *Policy Sciences,* 35(4): 333–360.

——— (2010). "Business and Public Policy: Responses to Environmental & Social Protection Processes," Cambridge, UK: *Cambridge University Press.*

——— & deLeon, P. (2004). "Is Greener Whiter? Voluntary Environmental Performance of Western Ski Areas," *Policy Studies Journal,* 32(2–3): 417–437.

——— ——— (2005). "Chief Executive Officers and Voluntary Environmental Performance: Costa Rica's Certification for Sustainable Tourism," *Policy Sciences,* 38(2): 107–127.

Rodriguez-Garavito, C. A. (2005). "Global Governance and Labor Rights: Codes of Conduct and Anti-Sweatshop Struggles in Global Apparel Factories in Mexico and Guatemala," *Politics and Society,* 33(2): 203–233.

Rosenbaum, P. & Rubin, D. B. (1983). "The Central Role of the Propensity Score in Observational Studies for Causal Effects," *Biometrika,* 70: 41–55.

Segerson, K. & Dawson, N. L. (2001). "Environmental Voluntary Agreements: Participation and Free-Riding," in E. W. Orts and K. Deketelacre (eds.) *Environmental Contracts: Comparative Approaches to Regulatory Innovation in Europe and the United States.* Dordrecht: Kluwer Law International.

Smith, T. M. & Fischlein, M. (2010). "Rival Private Governance Networks: Competing to Define the Rules of Sustainability Performance," *Global Environmental Change,* 20(3): 511–522.

Swift, T. A., Humphrey, C. & Gor, V. (2000). "Great Expectations?: The Dubious Financial Legacy of Quality Audits," *British Journal of Management,* 11(1): 31–45.

Terlaak, A. (2007). "Order without Law? The Role of Certified Management Standards in Shaping Socially Desired Firm Behaviors," *Academy of Management Review,* 32(3): 968–985.

——— & King, A. A. (2006). "The Effect of Certification with the ISO 9000 Quality Management Standard: A Signaling Approach," *Journal of Economic Behavior and Organization,* 60(4): 579–602.

Toffel, M. W. (2006). "Resolving Information Asymmetries in Markets: The Role of Certified Management Programs." Working Paper, Harvard Business School.

Welch. E. W., Mori, Y. & Aoyagi-Usui, M. (2001). "Voluntary Adoption of ISO 14001 in Japan: Mechanisms, Stages and Effects," 11(1): 43–62.

Yeung, G. & Mok, V. (2005). "What are the Impacts of Implementing ISOs on the Competitiveness of Manufacturing Industry in China?" *Journal of World Business,* 40(2): 139–157.

CHAPTER 7

ENVIRONMENTAL GOVERNANCE

DAVID P. BARON
AND THOMAS P. LYON

THIS chapter presents an analytical framework for studying the institutions society uses to mitigate environmental externalities. Our analysis is rooted in the economic approach to human behavior.[1] We treat individual actors as intelligent agents that pursue their own objectives, which may include altruism as well as financial gain, receiving recognition from others, and feeling good about themselves. Because the natural environment is a shared resource, individuals must come together via collective action to protect it.[2] We sketch the outlines of a unified theory of environmental governance, which identifies the key players affecting environmental outcomes and their objectives, the institutions within which they interact, and the expected results of their interactions. In doing so, we incorporate a number of key ideas from political science, and take initial steps toward integrating non-governmental organizations (NGOs) into the overall theory.

The field of environmental governance has its roots in the question "What is the best policy for mitigating environmental externalities?" Environmental economics has provided detailed answers to this question. But governments often fail to implement the best solution. This has led researchers to ask "When political constraints block the implementation of the best policy, what is the second-best policy?" Unfortunately, this question is much more difficult to answer than the first one, but an extensive literature on the political economy of regulation provides at least partial answers. When government failure becomes severe, NGOs increasingly turn to private politics, and engage directly with businesses to change their behavior. This area of inquiry is much more recent, and asks "How do NGOs influence corporate environmental behavior?" and "How does the NGO industry function?" Research into these

---

[1] Becker (1978) provides an overview of this perspective.
[2] Ostrom (1990) offers many insights into the challenges of collective action.

issues is still in its early stages and is likely to occupy many of the next generation of scholars in environmental governance.

WHAT IS ENVIRONMENTAL GOVERNANCE?

Until recently, governance was generally equated with government. In this view, environmental externalities cause markets to fail, and government must enact policies that overcome these market failures. This is not to say that the task of government is easy—policymakers face many tough questions. What is the right policy instrument for a particular problem? Should the problem be addressed at the local, state, federal, or international level? Is regulation needed at all, or is tort liability sufficient? Nevertheless, it has been widely believed that there is a bright line dividing the responsibilities of the marketplace from the responsibilities of the political systems. Indeed, this is the heart of Friedman's (1970) argument that "the social responsibility of business is to increase its profits."

During the 1970s and early 1980s, legislative victories such as the Clean Air Act, the Clean Water Act, and the Resource Conservation and Recovery Act appeared to validate the "governance as government" view. Yet achieving full compliance with the new laws proved slower than many had expected, and new environmental challenges such as toxic chemical pollution and climate change proved difficult to address using traditional regulatory tools. By the 1990s, regulators increasingly turned to new tools such as information disclosure and voluntary partnership programs. Furthermore, as environmental activists grew increasingly frustrated with government as a tool for achieving environmental improvements, they began to directly engage companies through the marketplace. It became increasingly clear that government policy was only one tool available to those pressing for environmental protection.

The economics literature traditionally assumed consumers and investors ignore the environmental externalities associated with their market activities, but their behavior appears to have changed in recent years. Indeed, an important research issue is the extent to which firms are rewarded in the marketplace for their environmental improvements. If they are sufficiently rewarded, they will voluntarily adopt environmental governance programs. Firms could be rewarded by investors for their environmental or other social performance as identified by Graff-Zivin & Small (2005) and Baron (2008, 2009), but identifying this effect using financial market analysis is a formidable research challenge. Firms could also be rewarded by employees through higher retention rates, improved hiring, or lower wages. Consumers can directly reward firms with a record of environmental accomplishment by paying a premium for their products. Moreover, to the extent that environmental performance provides product differentiation, competition may be lessened, resulting in higher prices and profits.

The actual willingness of consumers to pay for green goods remains difficult to assess econometrically, although Elfenbein & McManus (2010), Kiesel & Villas-Boas (2007), and Casadesus-Masanell et al. (2009) present empirical evidence that some consumers

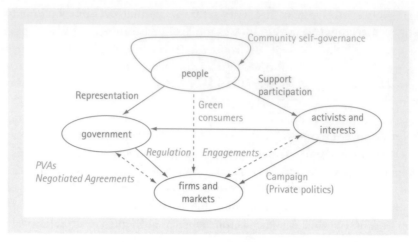

FIGURE 7.1 Environmental Governance

David Baron, Stanford University

are willing to pay a premium for them. In addition, experiments have begun to provide evidence on the phenomenon (Hiscox & Smyth 2006).

Today, environmental governance is understood to include the full set of pressures and incentives that motivate business to improve its environmental performance. This includes markets for green products and investments, regulatory relationships, and NGO/corporate engagements, as illustrated in Figure 7.1. This chapter provides a broad framework for understanding this complex set of forces.

REGULATION OF ENVIRONMENTAL EXTERNALITIES

Since A. C. Pigou (1932), economists have argued that environmental policy should "internalize externalities" through a tax equal to the marginal social damage created by the sale of each product. If policy "gets the prices right", consumers need not research the environmental and social impacts of the products they buy—prices convey all the information consumers need. This "first-best" solution of a Pigouvian tax (enforced via perfect coercion) provides the appropriate starting point for the study of environmental governance. In a sense, it presents an upper bound on society's ability to solve its environmental problems.

Political constraints and the second best

If the first-best solution is politically infeasible, environmental economists take constraints into account and seek a constrained optimum, which is called the "second-best" solution. This may involve a tax that is not set at the optimal level, or switching to a different policy instrument altogether. One example of such a constraint is an explicit prohibition on taking the costs of environmental protection into account in setting regulatory requirements, as was done in the US Clean Water Act. It should be no surprise that such constraints make traditional environmental regulation economically inefficient.[3]

Interest-group politics is one of the most important constraints on environmental policy. Olson (1965) puts the problem in stark terms: small groups with a lot at stake have strong incentives to organize and influence the policy process, but large groups whose members individually have little at stake face collective action problems that are often insurmountable. As a result, special interests tend to dominate the policy process, at the expense of the public. In the environmental arena, a polluting industry often has strong incentives to fight environmental legislation, whereas individual citizens have an incentive to free ride, resulting in little if any political action. This powerful logic imposes a constraint on the political process that often makes first-best policy solutions unattainable.

Some analysts argue that there are so many political constraints that there is little point in seeking optimal solutions. Instead, they advocate making head-to-head comparisons of alternative policies that appear feasible in light of political realities. Such "comparative institutional analysis" has been forcefully advocated by Williamson (1985) in other contexts, but the idea applies just as well in the environmental arena.

Comparative institutional analysis becomes increasingly important as one considers challenges in developing countries as opposed to developed nations, since the former generally have much weaker systems of environmental law and particularly of enforcement. A further list of constraints emerges when one considers global rather than local externalities, among them the inability to make binding international agreements when there is no encompassing system of international law.

Virtually all environmental and energy policy reflects the limitations of government. Climate policy is a perfect example. Historically, the largest emitter of greenhouse gases (GHGs) has been the United States, which has not passed a carbon tax, the policy most economists consider to be first-best. Hence, many analysts advocate a cap-and-trade scheme that would limit total GHG emissions and allow the trading of emissions permits. Although neither policy has been adopted at the federal level in the United States, states have implemented their own policies. The most common of these is the "renewable portfolio standard" (RPS), which requires electric utilities to obtain a certain percentage of their supplies from renewable sources. Unfortunately, many states attempt to use an RPS as a protectionist tool to build a renewable energy industry within the state (Lyon & Yin 2010). As a result, what carbon policy there is in the United States is far from a second-best policy.

Government failure can arise from many sources. Perhaps the most important of these is distributive politics, which is motivated by the economic impact of policies on

---

[3] Peltzman (1991) provides a more extensive critique of the inefficiency of environmental regulation.

employment and the profits of firms, and can block policies such as the regulation of GHGs. Information problems are also rife within government, ranging from difficulties measuring the severity and causes of problems to private information that provides individual agents with influence in the political process. Even without blatant manipulation of the process, the familiar Principal/Agent problem can distort the will of the people (the ultimate political principals) as it is expressed in actions of their representatives (or agents) working through the complex structures of government. In addition, democratic voting processes can fail to have a correspondence between the preferences of the citizenry and voting outcomes (Condorcet's Paradox), or can impose unethical outcomes on minority populations. If these sources of failure are severe enough, it can be better to tolerate market failures than to try and fix them through government action.

Regulation and instrument choice

Much research has been devoted to assessing which policy instruments(e.g. effluent fees, subsidies, standards, etc.) are best suited to solve particular environmental problems. Familiar textbook treatments show that in simple, static, deterministic settings of full information, where monitoring and enforcement are not a problem, any of a range of instruments can be used equally effectively to internalize an externality. However, when one relaxes these restrictive assumptions, the choice between alternative policy instruments matters. Coglianese & Anderson ([Chapter 8] this volume) explore environmental law and regulation in more detail. Here we provide a relatively brief overview, focusing on key economic insights.

As mentioned earlier, an emissions tax is often considered the best solution to an externality problem. A common alternative is an environmental standard, which may specify the allowed rate of emissions per unit of output or the technology to be used to reduce emissions. The term "command and control regulation" is often used as a broadside to denigrate government regulation as clumsy and inflexible. In our view, the term should be limited to regulations that mandate specific technologies, such as rules that require the use of "Best Available Control Technology" (BACT). All other forms of environmental regulation allow for at least some flexibility. For example, emissions standards limit a firm's discharge of pollutants, but allow the firm to choose how to accomplish the reduction. Nevertheless, environmental taxes provide stronger incentives for innovation than do standards, since standards offer no reward for going beyond compliance. Taxes also allow society's environmental goals to be met more cheaply than do standards, since a tax induces more abatement from firms with the lowest costs of emissions reduction.

Tradable emissions permits have become the instrument of choice for many regulators. Initially proposed by Dales (1968), such permits are attractive because they allow the use of a quantity instrument but also allow firms to trade abatement burdens until marginal abatement costs are equalized across emitters, thereby minimizing social costs. Tradable permits are also attractive from a political perspective, since politicians can designate the initial permit allocations for favored constituents, thereby increasing the political acceptability of the policy. The best-known example of permit trading comes from the 1990 Clean Air Act Amendments, which created tradable permits for sulfur dioxide emissions. The allocation of sulfur dioxide permits favored producers, but public utility regulation transferred the benefits to consumers. The success of the SO_2 trading program has led to the use of tradable permits in other contexts, such as nitrogen oxide trading in southern California and carbon trading in the European Union.

Solving some environmental problems, such as global warming, requires substantial research and development (R&D). Designing policy instruments to induce desired levels of R&D is challenging, because R&D is largely a public good: knowledge can be shared without being used up, and it is hard to exclude rivals from learning one's breakthroughs. Thus, markets underinvest in R&D, even when environmental taxes internalize externalities. In the area of climate change, Popp (2006) finds that combining R&D subsidies with a carbon tax is better than either policy alone, and that if one can only implement a single policy then a carbon tax is more beneficial than R&D subsidies alone.

Instrument choice becomes increasingly challenging when one accounts for the characteristics of the political process. For example, firms worry that present regulations might be ratcheted up in the future. In turn, regulators worry that firms may have enough political clout to block implementation of the best policy. In such situations, regulators have turned increasingly to new instruments such as voluntary programs and information disclosure.

Voluntary approaches

One of the most striking trends in environmental governance over the past twenty years has been the shift toward the use of voluntary, as opposed to mandatory, approaches. In a negotiated agreement, the regulator and a firm or industry group jointly set environmental goals and the means of achieving them; such agreements consequently tend to be heterogeneous in nature. In public voluntary programs, the regulatory agency sets program goals and then invites firms to make good faith efforts to meet them; in return, firms receive technical assistance and/or favorable publicity from the government (Lyon & Maxwell 2004). These alternative approaches to governance cannot be understood in isolation from traditional regulation; indeed, many voluntary actions actually occur under threat of regulation, while others are taken precisely because the threat of regulation is weak. A complete theory of environmental governance must incorporate the economics of instrument choice, and monitoring and enforcement, as well as the political economy of environmental policy.

Negotiated agreements can be of two types: target-oriented or implementation-oriented (OECD 2003). The former are designed to preempt legislative threats, whereas the latter are designed to provide greater flexibility in complying with regulation. Segerson & Miceli (1998) show that if there is a strong background threat of legislation, both the regulator and the industry can benefit from a target-oriented negotiated agreement because it lowers transaction costs relative to traditional regulation.

Negotiated agreements are more common in Europe and Japan than in the United States, perhaps because the corporatist structure of many of these countries allows industry to negotiate as a unit with government. In addition, the parliamentary systems of Europe and Japan ensure that the legislative and executive branches of government are controlled by the same political coalition, potentially making legislative threats more credible. However, the OECD (2003) argues that target-oriented negotiated agreements generally accomplish little in terms of environmental goals. Implementation-oriented negotiated agreements, however, do appear to be effective in reducing the costs of implementation without weakening environmental performance.

In public voluntary programs (PVPs), regulatory "sticks" are abandoned altogether in favor of carrots. The US EPA offers dozens of these programs; among its better known partnership programs have been the 33/50 Program, Climate Leaders, and WasteWise. This new generation of regulatory programs has been celebrated by some as a superior, low-cost instrument that can be used in preference to traditional, inefficient, regulation. Alternatively, however, they can be seen as small "carrots" used when political opposition makes the "stick" of environmental regulation infeasible (Lyon & Maxwell 2003).

The empirical evidence on the effectiveness of PVPs is mixed, and the academic literature has reached a consensus that PVPs have at best limited potential (Morgenstern & Pizer 2007; Lyon & Maxwell 2007). However, the appropriate question may not be "Do PVPs work?" but rather, "*When* do PVPs work?" The challenge at this point is to identify more precisely exactly where the potential of PVPs lies. Lyon & Maxwell (2007) argue that studies focusing on whether PVP participants improved more than non-participants completely miss the possibility that PVPs actually accomplished what they set out to do: create a market transformation that raises a whole industry's performance. Lange (2008) finds that this is exactly what was accomplished by the Coal Combustion By-Products Program. Furthermore, most empirical studies have not controlled for program design. A revisionist view of PVPs is gradually emerging that may identify when they are likely to be useful.

Information disclosure

When constraints such as high transaction costs, weak political institutions, or a lack of information on pollution damages make it hard to implement traditional regulations, regulators increasingly turn to mandatory information disclosure programs (Dasgupta, Wang, & Wheeler 2007). The most thoroughly studied of these is the Toxic Release Inventory (TRI), mandated by the US Emergency Planning and Community Right-to-Know Act of 1986, which requires reporting on releases of hundreds of toxic chemicals. Similar programs exist in other countries, including Canada and Mexico. Such programs hold out the potential that citizens will use the reported data to pressure toxic emitters to reduce their emissions, avoiding the need for inefficient government regulations. Unfortunately, measuring the impact of information disclosure programs is difficult, since there is often no data on corporate performance prior to the onset of reporting requirements. Nevertheless, Blackman et al. (2004) find that the worst polluters in Indonesia reduced their emissions after the country implemented a program to rate firms' environmental performance. Delmas et al. (2010) find that electric utilities reduced emissions after being forced to report information on their polluting behavior to consumers via monthly bill inserts. Powers et al. (2011) find that the worst polluters in India's pulp and paper industry improved their performance after an environmental NGO began rating them publicly.

Corporations increasingly make voluntary disclosures through annual sustainability reports, but the reports may not provide a complete picture of a firm's environmental impacts. Thus, there is an important role for third parties in shaping the nature of voluntary disclosures. Some NGOs attack perceived corporate greenwash, as exemplified by the website <www.stopgreenwash.org> (Lyon & Maxwell 2011). Others create certification programs encouraging firms to disclose their environmental performance, as in the Forest Stewardship Council (FSC) program for timber harvesting. Sometimes, industry creates its own standards and certification programs, such as the Sustainable Forestry Initiative (SFI). These non-governmental programs are especially attractive in trade-intensive industries that cannot be controlled by any single nation, but their effectiveness remains unclear. Heyes & Maxwell (2004) show that certification is valuable as a complement to regulation but can be welfare-reducing if it substitutes for regulation. Fischer & Lyon (2010) show that competition between eco-labels can worsen environmental damages. Harbaugh, Maxwell, & Roussillon (forthcoming) show that if consumers are uncertain about the stringency of alternative labels, markets can produce poor results.

Instrument choice with weak regulatory capacity

Instrument choice in developing countries is just beginning to attract serious academic attention. Many developing countries have weak political institutions, which render traditional policy instruments and their enforcement ineffective. For example, Bell & Russell (2002) question whether markets for tradable emissions permits make much sense in developing countries, which may lack the political infrastructure to make permit systems work. Blackman, Lyon, & Sisto (2006) argue that voluntary programs may play a useful role in developing countries when regulatory capacity is weak.

Monitoring and Enforcement

Much of the academic literature simply assumes that regulators have the ability to perfectly enforce the regulations they promulgate. In reality, however, regulatory authorities generally lack the resources to ensure that laws are enforced with full compliance, and they are often constrained by statutes that limit penalties for non-compliance. Gray & Shimshack (2011) report that in 2008, the median fine imposed by the EPA for an environmental violation was $2,300—hardly enough to put the fear of God into a corporate polluter. Yet compliance rates among regulated entities remain high (Cohen 1999). One simple explanation for high compliance rates is that the managers of firms believe in complying with the law in their corporate lives as they do in their private lives.

Much research effort has gone into explaining the apparent contradiction between weak regulatory threats and high compliance rates. Harrington (1988) and others have developed dynamic models exploring firms' incentives to comply today so as to avoid more aggressive regulatory enforcement tomorrow. Furthermore, Shimshack & Ward (2010) find that the EPA targets enforcement resources towards firms with a history of non-compliance. And indeed the empirical record suggests that inspections, or at least the threat of inspections, positively influence firm compliance. (Gray & Deily 1996; Shimshack & Ward 2005). Other studies have looked for non-regulatory costs to explain high compliance rates. Konar & Cohen (2001) found that large firms' asset values are reduced by an average of $380 million as a result of poor environmental performance. Further research is needed in this area, however, since financial markets may simply be reflecting the punishments expected to be imposed upon poor environmental performers by other governance devices. Furthermore, in recent years there has been a regulatory shift toward higher fines and holding corporate officers and directors personally liable for environmental damages. Both of these trends may be driving better compliance and merit detailed empirical investigation (see Cho, Patten, & Roberts [Chapter 24] and Bauer & Derwall [Chapter 25] this volume, for a discussion of market responses to firm disclosures).

A good compliance record may pay dividends in a variety of ways. Decker (2003) has shown that it can significantly shorten the time it takes for a firm to receive a permit to build or to discharge pollutants. Since production delays can cost up to one million dollars a day in lost revenues, the value of preventing permitting delays can easily dwarf expected regulatory penalties from noncompliance. Considerably more research is needed to deepen our understanding of what motivates environmental compliance.

Inducing compliance becomes increasingly difficult as the number of firms covered grows. For "non-point sources" of pollution such as agricultural run-off or small sources of greenhouse gases or toxic chemicals, monitoring and enforcement may be prohibitively expensive. In these cases, good environmental governance may need to rely on community norms or voluntary approaches to environmental protection.

A full theory of environmental governance must incorporate interest-group politics and industrial organization, taking into account the institutional setting of particular issues. The biggest gap in developing a comprehensive theory of environmental governance lies in understanding the role of NGOs, both within public politics and—even more urgently—in the domain of private politics. It is to these topics that we turn next.

Private politics, NGOs,
and social pressure

Some environmental governance mechanisms are private and involve the voluntary participation of firms, often in the presence of social pressure and in the shadow of government. The motivation for these mechanisms is varied, ranging from an attempt to forestall social pressure (Baron & Diermeier 2007) or government regulation (Maxwell, Lyon, & Hackett 2000) to an attempt to respond to consumer preferences to a commitment to the social goal of environmental improvement. The Sustainable Forestry Initiative (SFI) is a response to social pressure led by the NGOs backing the Forest Stewardship Council (FSC). Certification programs for Internet privacy protection have helped forestall government regulation of the Internet, and self-regulation by the movie industry has helped the industry avoid government regulation. NGOs have participated in some of these private initiatives, with Conservation International and Environmental Defense Fund helping in the development of the standards adopted by the SFI, whereas other NGOs such as Greenpeace that support the FSC view the SFI standards as not going far enough.

The principal research challenges pertaining to private environmental governance include: explaining the rise of these private governance mechanisms, understanding the relationship between private governance and public governance, identifying the circumstances under which each arises, and evaluating the efficacy of private governance. Private politics plays a central role in the answer to these questions.

What is private politics?

Private politics refers to actions taken by a private (non-government) party intended to change the behavior of an economic actor. Private politics is conducted outside of government institutions, but the participants may have recourse to government institutions such as the courts or they may participate in public politics in conjunction with private politics. Just as public politics is strategic, private politics is strategic, and involves a competition of strategies implemented by the participants. For example, an environmental NGO could organize a boycott of a firm or industry viewed as responsible for environmental degradation, and the target could adopt strategies to contest the boycott. Often the supply-side instrument of private politics is social pressure.

Social pressure has been studied within the social movement sub-field of sociology with a focus on social pressure directed toward government on issues such as suffrage, civil rights, and worker rights (see Weber & Soderstrom [Chapter 14] this volume). More recently, social movement theory has studied the environmental movement with an emphasis extending beyond public politics and into private politics (Ingram, Yue, & Rao 2010). Private politics in economics and management was introduced by Baron (2001, 2003).

Private politics differs from public politics on a number of dimensions. The incentives for private parties to engage in public politics are structured by the institutions of government, including legislatures, regulatory agencies, administrative agencies, and courts, whereas formal institutions are largely absent in the realm of private politics.

In the past several decades, private politics has grown, in part because of a recognition that private parties could more readily attain their objectives outside of government institutions. The environmental movement achieved early success with a flurry of legislation in the 1970s, but subsequent achievements have been slowed or thwarted by government gridlock, bureaucratic inaction, and court challenges. As a result of the fili-buster in the US Senate and the presidental veto, supermajorities in Congress are required to enact new legislation.[4] Regulatory actions can also be slowed by due proc-ess requirements, congressional pressure, and requirements that costs and benefits be considered. In contrast, private politics is largely outside these constraints and can be activated at any time.

Market failures associated with environmental externalities are widespread, and gov-ernments have responded with a myriad of regulations and market-based mechanisms. Some externalities remain unaddressed, as in the case of global climate change. Whether these are examples of government failure is not entirely clear, since the government may not have acted because the public does not support additional regulation. Private poli-tics, however, can mitigate market failures or government failures to the extent that it can cause private parties to mitigate unregulated externalities.

Whereas public politics requires a majority or supermajority in public institutions, private politics can be advanced by minorities, and the success of their efforts depends on the social pressure that can be imposed on their targets. A majority of the public can oppose a proposed public policy resulting in government inaction, but activists can carve out their own policy and force responses by private parties. The scope of those responses is generally narrower than what government can do, but private politics can force targets to adopt practices where government has not acted. Minorities thus can go where majorities do not.

Public politics is also limited by the enacted law. Suppose that a first-best environ-mental regulation is in place. Enforcement activity cannot go beyond the enacted stand-ard, but private politics can go beyond it. For example, activists use the annual release of the Toxics Release Inventory (TRI) to direct social pressure towards firms emitting toxic substances, and that pressure has led many firms to reduce their emissions below those allowed by law and regulations. If the legal limits on emissions have been set efficiently, private politics and social pressure can reduce emissions below efficient levels resulting in excessive costs of abatement. This can occur when social pressure is motivated by dis-tributive concerns rather than social efficiency, as in NIMBY ("Not In My Back Yard") activities. That is, the emissions remaining after socially efficient regulation could still pose a threat to the environment or human health, and activists could seek to reduce that threat even though it would be socially inefficient to do so.

Some private politics results from self-interested NIMBY preferences, as in the case of homeowners opposing a license application for a hazardous waste disposal facility pro-posed for their neighborhood (Hamilton 1993). A more recent form of environmental NIMBYism warrants fresh research, since it pits one set of environmental interests against a different set of environmental interests. California, for example, had adopted regulations requiring 20 percent renewable energy by 2010, yet many renewable power generation proposals have met with environmental opposition. This includes coastal

---

[4] See Krehbiel (1998, 1999) for an analysis of pivotal politics.

wind farms, solar farms in the Mojave desert, geothermal facilities, and the transmission lines needed to take the power generated to where the demand is located. Does the opposition to these projects reflect traditional NIMBY self-interest, an unwillingness to make trade-offs, or a preference for one environmental performance dimension over another?

NGOs can have social efficiency objectives, and they can also have distributive objectives that from their perspective can take precedence over efficiency considerations. As in Rawls' (1971, 2001) theory of justice, the distributive objectives could focus on those who are less advantaged, which is the subject of environmental justice, or they could focus on the risk averse, as in the case of the precautionary principle. NGOs could also have retributive justice objectives focusing on punishing those who have committed environmental wrongs. Private politics can thus go beyond the economist's concept of social efficiency and embrace other objectives, such as distribution and justice.[5]

THE INDUSTRIAL ORGANIZATION
OF ENVIRONMENTAL ACTIVISM

Economists study the organization of industries, typically focusing on the supply side of the market. Somewhat surprisingly, there is little economic work that examines the spectrum of NGOs that form the backbone of the environmental movement, such as the Sierra Club, the National Audubon Society, the World Wildlife Federation, Environmental Defense Fund, and Greenpeace. Bosso (2005) provides a descriptive treatment of many of the research issues, though he does not develop formal models of their behavior or test hypotheses using statistical techniques. Lyon (2010) provides a survey of how sociologists, political scientists and economists approach the study of NGOs and their attempts to influence business behavior.

In our view, the tools of industrial organization can be applied to provide new insights into how these groups compete and cooperate. A key objective in this line of research is to identify the locus of private politics, including the environmental issues on which NGOs focus, which targets they select, and what strategies they employ. This is a considerable research challenge, and an even greater challenge is to identify and measure the outcomes of private politics.

Private politics by environmental NGOs can be directed at influencing public sentiment on an issue, but in most cases it focuses on specific targets, typically firms. Given the large number of diverse environmental NGOs and the broad set of potential targets, environmental NGOs both focus and select. They frequently focus on a few issue areas and then select targets where a difference can be made. This can be thought of as an involuntary matching game where potential targets can affect their demand; that is, the likelihood that they are the recipients of social pressure. Eesley & Lenox (2006) and

---

[5] Lyon (2010) contains chapters by a number of environmental NGOs.

Lenox & Eesley (2009) categorize activist campaigns and identify outcomes based on reports in the media.

Little systematic is known about the selection of targets. Some NGOs target the worst offenders, and others select "soft" targets that are likely to agree to their demands. Some NGOs have concluded that it is better to target the markets in which firms operate rather than the environmentally offending firms themselves. To stop the harvesting of old growth timber, NGOs targeted not the timber firms but instead the retailers that sell lumber made from old growth timber. The rationale was that the retailers had a public face and brand equity that could be harmed and thus would be more responsive to social pressure than were the timber companies. The retailers then would pressure their suppliers.[6]

The launching of market campaigns was facilitated by the Internet, which allowed mass communication about campaigns and their targets as well as direct communication to participants in the campaign. The Internet has reduced the costs of organization, coordination, and execution of campaigns, and it may have increased the success rate of campaigns through broader threats to the reputation and public face of their targets. Funding for the environmental movement has also been strengthened by the Internet, since NGOs can more easily raise funds directly from the public, as the experience of Move-On has dramatically demonstrated.

CONFRONTATION AND COOPERATION

NGOs are differentiated, not only by their focus on selected issues such as wildlife, forests, oceans, and climate change, but also by their approach to issues and targets. The focus of this section is on cooperation and confrontation, or, in the language of Lyon (2010), on whether an NGO chooses to act as a "good cop" or a "bad cop."

Confrontation can be viewed as an NGO demanding that a target change its practices, with the target then choosing whether or not to accept the demand. If the target does not accept, the activist can launch a campaign and threaten the target with harm. The activist campaign succeeds if there is sufficient support from consumers and the public that the target changes its practices and fails otherwise. One frequent strategy of NGOs is to call for a boycott of a target's products. Boycotts have received research attention (Innes 2006, Baron & Diermeier 2007), but the theory leaves much yet to be studied, and the empirical studies of boycotts yield mixed conclusions about their effectiveness (Friedman 1999). When faced with a campaign mounted by a confrontational NGO, targets have a variety of strategies to contest the campaign (Baron and Diermeier 2007). These strategies include fighting, negotiation and compromise, reputation management, communication with interest groups and the public, and stonewalling.

[6] See Asmus et al. (2006) for more details.

NGOs with a competence or a degree of expertise on an environmental issue may adopt a cooperative strategy. An NGO could invite a target to join in identifying the benefits and costs from an environmental action, as in the case of Environmental Defense Fund working with McDonald's to reduce behind-the-counter waste and packaging. The NGO thus helps the target discover the consequences of a change in environmental practices, where ex ante neither the NGO nor the target knows the exact benefits and costs that might be discovered. The target may accept the invitation with the understanding that it will change its practices when it makes business sense to do so. That may be when the change will increase its profits, or when it is justified by its corporate social responsibility policy.

The weakness of the cooperative approach is that the social benefits from the change in practices could be positive, but the change is rejected because it would reduce profits. A cooperative approach could be strengthened by greater bargaining power of the NGO. A strength of the cooperative approach is that resources are not expended in a campaign, but resources must be expended to develop expertise. Developing the expertise to be able to identify the gain in a cooperative relationship requires an investment that could be funded by donors that share the environmental objectives of the NGO. A cooperative NGO must also be able to certify credibly that the firm has changed its practices.

The matching of NGOs with targets depends on the characteristics of targets as well as on the approaches chosen by NGOs. Some firms are easier to threaten with harm, as in the case of consumer goods companies, companies with a public face, and companies with high brand equity.[7] Other firms that do not have a public face and do not sell directly to consumers or through retailers can be more difficult to harm. Firms can also differ in terms of their own capabilities to deal with environmental issues. DuPont can readily identify the costs and benefits associated with an environmental issue, whereas smaller chemical companies may not be able to do so.

Confrontational NGOs rely on the credible threat of harm, and thus should prefer targets that are vulnerable to harm to their reputation, brand equity, or public face. Cooperative NGOs should be indifferent to the potential for harm and should prefer targets for which their expertise is valuable. Both cooperative and confrontational NGOs should prefer targets with substantial opportunities for improvement and large potential environmental benefits.

The matching of NGOs and targets is strategic. A (potential) target with its own capabilities may obtain little benefit from working with a cooperative NGO, but may choose to do so if that shields it from a confrontational NGO.[8] A confrontational activist may prefer a target with its own expertise if the target can readily be harmed, since that expertise would aid in making the change in environmental practices efficiently.

Confrontational NGOs can create a demand for engagements with cooperative NGOs, as in the bad cop–good cop analogy. The threat of a campaign against a firm can

---

[7] For a detailed discussion of these targeting issues, see Conroy (2007).
[8] The effectiveness of shields remains an open research question.

cause it to seek a cooperative NGO with which to work. Moreover, potential targets that recognize that they could be targeted by a confrontational NGO could seek engagements with cooperative NGOs to pre-empt targeting. This also means that an NGO that chooses a cooperative approach need not also develop the capability to confront firms. NGOs thus can specialize in their approach to achieving environmental improvements.

Matching can also involve networks and collective action. NGOs frequently partner with other NGOs in their campaigns as a means of sharing the cost and increasing social pressure. Targets also may act together when threatened, as in the case of the formation of the Sustainable Forestry Initiative in response to demands by the NGOs supporting the Forest Stewardship Council.

The strategic matching of NGOs and targets is largely an open research issue, as is the path to the development of expertise and credibility on the part of NGOs. In their choice between confrontation and cooperation, NGOs may have an eye on donors, since success brings financial support. The funding of NGOs and how it depends on their strategies is a largely unexplored research topic.

CONCLUSIONS

The literature on environmental governance has emerged from a growing awareness of the limitations of traditional regulation as a tool for solving environmental problems. Lack of political will, lack of conclusive scientific information, and lack of resources for monitoring and enforcement, all constrain the effectiveness of regulation. At the same time, businesses face a variety of new pressures for environmental improvement. Markets increasingly provide incentives for companies to green themselves, through the demands of consumers, employees, and investors. Environmental NGOs have moved into private politics, deploying a portfolio of strategies for direct engagement with business, many of which they view as more effective than engaging in traditional public politics. The penetration of information technology into every crevice of modern life continues to change the set of strategies available to both activists and firms. The combination of these forces makes the study of environmental governance a dynamic and exciting research field.

There are a number of areas in which research is especially promising. As markets for green products continue to grow, it is clear that consumers have very limited cognitive capacity for processing detailed information about the environmental footprints of the products they buy. Behavioral economics can shed new light on how consumers process information, which will inform both green marketing strategies as well as the evolution of the market for ecolabels. The role of the media in shaping the emergence of new environmental demands badly needs further study. Social norms have the potential to play a powerful role in building greater consumer demand for green products, but our understanding of how norms emerge and how they are related to the passage of new laws and regulations is extremely limited. Supply chains are attracting much attention from activists as a way to influence environmental behavior in developing countries with weak regulatory capacities, and this is another area in need of more research. Perhaps most important, our understanding of the industrial organization of the NGO industry is rudimentary, and much more work remains to be done in this area: both theoretical and empirical work in this area is in short supply.

References

Asmus, P., Hank C., & Maroney. K. (2006). "Case Study: Turning Conflict into Cooperation," *Stanford Social Innovation Review*, Fall, 52–61.

Baron, D. P. (2001). "Private Politics, Corporate Social Responsibility, and Integrated Strategy," *Journal of Economics & Management Strategy*, 10: 7 45.

—— (2003). "Private Politics," *Journal of Economics & Management Strategy*, 12: 31 66.

—— (2008). "Managerial Contracting and Corporate Social Responsibility," *Journal of Public Economics* 92: 268–288.

—— (2009). "A Positive Theory of Moral Management, Social Pressure, and Corporate Social Performance," *Journal of Economics and Management Strategy*. 18: 7–43.

—— & Diermeier, D. (2007). "Strategic Activism and Nonmarket Strategy," *Journal of Economics and Management Strategy*, 16: 599–634.

Becker, G. S. (1978). *The Economic Approach to Human Behavior*, Chicago: University of Chicago Press.

Bell, R. G. & Russell, C. (2002). "Environmental Policy for Developing Countries," *Issues in Science and Technology*. 18: 63 70.

Blackman A, Af., S., & Ratunanda, D. (2004). "How does public disclosure work? Evidence from Indonesia's PROPER program," *Human Ecology Review*, 11(3): 235–46.

Blackman, A., Lyon, T., P., & Sisto, N. (2006). "Voluntary Environmental Agreements when Regulatory Capacity is Weak," *Comparative Economic Studies*, 48: 682–702.

Bosso, C. J. (2005). *Environment, Inc.: From Grassroots to Beltway*. Lawrence, KS: The University of Kansas Press.

Casadesus-Masanell, R., Crooke, M., Reinhardt, F., and Vasishth, V. (2009). "Households' Willingness to Pay for 'Green' Goods: Evidence from Patagonia's Introduction of Organic Cotton Sportswear," *Journal of Economics and Management Strategy*. 18: 203–233.

Chavis, L. & Leslie, P. (2009). "Consumer Boycotts: The Impact of the Iraq War on French Wine Sales in the U.S.," *Quantitative Marketing and Economics*. 7: 37–67.

Cohen, M. (1999). "Monitoring and Enforcement of Environmental Policy," *International Yearbook of Environmental and Resource Economics*, v. III, edited by Thomas Tietenberg and Henk Follmer, Edward Elgar Publishers.

Conroy, M. E. (2007). *Branded! How the Certification Revolution is Transforming Global Corporations*. Gabriola Island, British Columbia, Canada: New Society Publishers.

Dales, J. H. (1968). "Land, Water and Ownership," *Canadian Journal of Economics*, 1: 791–804.

Dasgupta, S., Wheeler. D., & Wang, H. (2007). "Disclosure Strategies for Pollution Control", in Teitenberg T, Folmer H (eds). *International Yearbook of Environmental and Resource Economics 2006/2007: A Survey of Current Issues*, Edward Elgar, Northampton, Massachusetts.

Decker, C. (2003). "Corporate Environmentalism and Environmental Statutory Permitting," *Journal of Law and Economics*, 46: 103–129.

Delmas M., Montes-Sancho M., Shimshack J. (2010). "Information Disclosure Policies: Evidence from the Electricity Industry," *Economic Inquiry*, 48: 483–498.

Eesley, C. & Lenox, M. (2006). "Firm Responses to Secondary Stakeholder Action," *Strategic Management Journal*. 27: 765–781.

Elfenbein, D. W. & McManus, B. (2010). "A Greater Price for a Greater Good? Evidence that Consumers Pay More for Charity-Linked Products," *American Economic Journal: Economic Policy*, 2: 28–60.

Fischer, C. & Lyon, T. P. (2010). "Competing Environmental Labels." Working Paper, Ross School of Business, University of Michigan.

Friedman, M. (1970). "The Social Responsibility of Business is to Increase Profits," *The New York Times Magazine*, 13 September, New York: The New York Times.

—— (1999). *Consumer Boycotts*. Routledge: New York.

Graff-Zivin, J. & Small, A. (2005). "A Modigliani-Miller Theory of Altruistic Corporate Social Responsibility," *Topics in Economic Analysis*, 5: Article 10.

Gray, W. B. & Deily, M. E. (1996). "Compliance and Enforcement: Air Pollution Regulation in the U.S. Steel Industry," *Journal of Environmental Economics and Management* 31(1): 96–111.

—— & Shimshack, J. P. (2011). "The Effectiveness of Environmental Monitoring and Enforcement: A Review of the Empirical Evidence," *Review of Environmental Economics and Policy*, 5, 3–24.

Hamilton, J. T. (1993). "Politics and Social Costs: Estimating the Impact of Collective Action on Hazardous Waste Facilities," *Journal of Economics*, 24 (Spring): 101–125.

Harbaugh, R., Maxwell, J. W., & Rousillon, B. (2010). "Uncertain Standards." RAND *Management Science*.

Harrington, W. (1988). "Enforcement Leverage when Penalties are Restricted," *Journal of Public Economics*, 37: 29–53.

Heyes, A. G. & Maxwell, J. W. (2004). "Private vs. Public Regulation: Political Economy of the International Environment," RAND/Management Science *Journal of Environmental Economics and Management*, 48: 978–996.

Hiscox, M. J. & Smyth, N. F. B. (2006). "Is There Consumer Demand for Improved Labor Standards? Evidence from Field Experiments in Social Product Labeling." Working paper, Harvard University.

Ingram, P., Yue, L. Q., & Rao, H. (2010). "Trouble in Store: The Emergence and Success of Protests against Wal-Mart Store Openings in America," *American Journal of Sociology*, 116: 53–92.

Innes, R. (2006). "A Theory of Consumer Boycotts under Symmetric Information and Imperfect Competition," *Economic Journal*. 116: 355–381.

Kiesel, K. & Villas-Boas, S. B. (2007). "Got Organic Milk? Consumer Valuations of Milk Labels after the Implementation of the USDA Organic Seal," *Journal of Agricultural & Food Industrial Organization*: 5(1): 4.

King, A. A. & Lenox, M. J. (2000). "Industry Self-Regulation without Sanctions: The Chemical Industry's Responsible Care Program," *Academy of Management Journal*. 43: 698–716.

—— —— (2002). "Exploring the Locus of Profitable Pollution Reduction," *Management Science*. 48: 289–299.

Konar, S. & Cohen, M. (2001). "Does the Market Value Environmental Performance?," *Review of Economics and Statistics*, 83: 281–289.

Krehbiel, K. (1998). *Pivotal Politics: A Theory of U.S. Lawmaking*, Chicago, IL: University of Chicago Press.

—— (1999). "Pivotal Politics: A Refinement of Nonmarket Analysis for Voting Institutions," *Business and Politics*, 1 (April).

Lange, I. (2008). "Evaluating Voluntary Measures with Spillovers: The Case of Coal Combustion Products Partnership." Working Paper, University of Stirling.

Lenox, M. J. & Eesley, C. E. (2009). "Private Environmental Activism and the Selection and Response of Firm Targets," *Journal of Economics and Management Strategy*. 18: 45–73.

Lyon, T. P. (2010). *Good Cop/Bad Cop: Environmental NGOs and Their Strategies towards Business*, editor, Washington, DC: Resources for the Future Press.

——and Maxwell J. W. (2003). "Self-Regulation, Taxation, and Public Voluntary Environmental Agreements," *Journal of Public Economics*, 87: 1453–1486.

—— —— (2004). *Corporate Environmentalism and Public Policy*, Cambridge, UK: Cambridge University Press.

—— —— (2007). "Environmental Public Voluntary Programs Reconsidered," *Policy Studies Journal*, 35: 723–750.

—— (2011). "Greenwash: Corporate Environmental Disclosure under Threat of Audit," *Journal of Economics and Management Strategy*, 20(1).

—— & Yin, Haitao (2010). "Why Do States Adopt Renewable Portfolio Standards? An Empirical Investigation," *The Energy Journal*, 31: 131–155.

Maxwell, J. W., P. Lyon, & S. C. Hackett (2000). "Self-Regulation and Social Welfare: The Political Economy of Corporate Environmentalism," *Journal of Law and Economics*, 43: 583–618.

Morgenstern, R. & W. Pizer (2007). *Reality Check: The Nature and Performance of Voluntary Environmental Programs in the United States, Europe, and Japan*, Washington, DC: Resources for the Future Press.

Organization for Economic Cooperation and Development (2003). *Voluntary Approaches for Environmental Policy: Effectiveness, Efficiency and Usage in Policy Mixes*. Paris, France.

Olson, M. (1965). *The Logic of Collective Action: Public Goods and the Theory of Groups*. Cambridge, MA: Harvard University Press.

Ostrom, E. (1990). *Governing the Commons: The Evolution of Institutions for Collective Action*, Cambridge: Cambridge University Press.

Peltzman, S. (1991). "The Handbook of Industrial Organization: A Review Article," *Journal of Political Economy*, 99: 201–217.

Pigou, A. C. (1932). *The Economics of Welfare*. 4th ed., London: Macmillan.

Popp, D. (2006). "R&D Subsidies and Climate Policy: Is there a Free Lunch?," *Climatic Change*, 77: 311–341.

Powers, Nicholas, Blackman, A. Lyon, T. P. & Narain, U. (2011). "Does Public Disclosure Reduce Pollution? Evidence from India's Pulp and Paper Industry," *Enviromontal and Resource Economics*, Published on line 12 April 2011.

Rawls, J. (1971). *A Theory of Justice* Cambridge, MA: Belknap Press.

—— (2001). *Justice as Fairness: A Restatement*, (ed.) Erin Kelly, Harvard University Press: Cambridge, MA.

Segerson, K. & T. Miceli (1998). "Voluntary Environmental Agreements: Good or Bad News for Environmental Protection?," *Journal of Environmental Economics and Management*, 36: 109–130.

Shimshack, J. & M.Ward (2005). "Regulator Reputation, Enforcement, and Environmental Compliance," *Journal of Environmental Economics and Management* 50(3): 519–40.

—— (2010). "Repeat Offenders, Enforcement, and Environmental Compliance." Working Paper, Tulane University.

Williamson, O. (1985). *The Economic Institutions of Capitalism*. New York: Free Press.

CHAPTER 8

BUSINESS AND ENVIRONMENTAL LAW

CARY COGLIANESE
AND RYAN ANDERSON

GOVERNMENTS around the world have used law to influence business behavior so as to reduce pollution and conserve energy and other natural resources. The dramatic expansion in the scope, volume, and detail of environmental law over the past several decades has made law a ubiquitous factor that cannot be ignored in any attempt to understand the relationship between business and the environment. Researchers investigating environmental law have made considerable progress in categorizing and analyzing the advantages and disadvantages of discrete types of environmental laws, in studying the ways that government inspection authorities enforce environmental law, in identifying the factors that explain business compliance with law, and finally in empirically evaluating the ultimate impact of law on both environmental and business conditions.

SOURCES OF ENVIRONMENTAL LAW

Environmental law emanates from a variety of sources, as shown in Table 8.1. At a global level, treaties and other international agreements addressing a variety of environmental problems have emerged in recent decades. These treaties range from the Convention on International Trade in Endangered Species (CITES) to the Montreal Protocol on Substances that Deplete the Ozone Layer, from the UN Convention on the Law of the Sea to the Framework Convention on Climate Change. Although international law does not directly impose legal obligations on businesses, the obligations that treaties impose on nation-states typically require passage of domestic laws that impose enforceable legal duties on businesses. In establishing laws enforceable on businesses, nation-states face

Table 8.1 Sources of Environmental Law

Source	Examples
International Law	• Convention on International Trade in Endangered Species • United Nations Framework Convention on Climate Change • Montreal Protocol on Substances that Deplete the Ozone Layer • UN Convention on the Law of the Sea • European Union Council Directive 2008/50/EC on Ambient Air Quality
Domestic Law: National	• US Clean Air Act • US Clean Water Act • US EPA Rule on Control of Hazardous Air Pollutants from Mobile Sources • German Environmental Code (Umweltgesetzbuch, UGB) • Japanese Water Pollution Prevention Law
Domestic Law: State or Local	• Hawaii Global Warming Solutions Act • California Safe Drinking Water and Toxic Enforcement Act (Proposition 65) • Massachusetts Toxic Use Reduction Act • Rome, Italy Ordinance on Waste Disposal and Recycling
Informal "Law"	• United Nations' Forest Principles • ISO 14000 Environmental Management System Standards • US Green Building Council's Leadership in Energy and Environmental Design (LEED) Green Building Rating System

not only obligations under international *environmental* law but also constraints on their authority under international *trade* law. The General Agreement on Tariffs and Trade, as well as rules created under the framework of the World Trade Organization (WTO), may preclude nations from adopting certain environmental standards if doing so would discriminate against foreign importers (Bernasconi-Osterwald et al. 2006).

The European Union (EU) is a creature of international law, originating in 1957 primarily as a trading alliance but gaining new authority over the years through additional treaties, so that today EU institutions possess legal authority over certain environmental matters. As with international law more generally, EU *directives* impose obligations on member states rather than directly on private parties. But some EU *regulations,* such as the EU's 2007 regulation of chemicals known as REACH, do impose obligations directly on private businesses (Applegate 2008). As a result, collectively, EU law may more appropriately be considered a source of "quasi-international law."

In Germany, the Netherlands, Spain, and some other European countries, national constitutions contain provisions obligating the government to establish environmentally protective laws, although these provisions tend to be aspirational rather than judicially binding (Seerden, Heldeweg, & Deketelaere 2002). The United States has no comparable constitutional provision guaranteeing a right to a clean environment, but constitutional language granting authority to the US national government to regulate interstate commerce must nevertheless provide the basis for Congress to adopt federal environmental legislation.

With the exception of certain EU regulations, then, domestic legal authorities constitute the primary source of law that directly imposes obligations on businesses—as well as the source of any corresponding punishment for failure to comply with these obligations. Within each country, business obligations arising from domestic law may emanate from constitutional provisions (which are treated as the highest legal authority in a country), legislation (or statutes), and, finally, rules and policies adopted by ministries or administrative agencies. These laws, especially statutes and administrative rules, can be adopted by national governments or by state or local authorities, at least when governmental authority is subdivided along federal-state lines within a country.

In the United States, as in other developed countries, federal legislation now establishes the overarching framework of environmental law obligations to which businesses are subjected. For example, the US Clean Water Act makes it illegal for any company to discharge pollution into a waterway without a government permit, while the Endangered Species Act makes it illegal for private landowners to kill or destroy the habitat of endangered or threatened species (Lazarus 2004). Such national legislation often authorizes national environmental ministries or agencies to create more specific regulatory standards or regulations. The US Clean Air Act, for example, authorizes the Environmental Protection Agency (EPA) to develop motor vehicle emissions standards and impose these standards on manufacturers of cars and trucks.

In addition to national legislation and regulations, domestic environmental law can emanate from states or provinces as well as from local governments. For example, Rome has its own municipal recycling laws and California has its own rules on toxic pollution. Even when national legislation sets a broad framework for environmental standards, actual implementation may depend on state legal authorities. For example, although the US Clean Air Act authorizes the EPA to set national air quality standards, the actual emissions limits that factories must meet are creatures of state law, crafted under plans approved by the national EPA. The US environmental law system can be described as one of "cooperative federalism" because of the coordination of laws adopted at both the national and state levels of government (Percival 1995).

Finally, although not technically "laws," various non-binding, sometimes even non-state, rules or norms affect and constrain businesses in their environmental management. These so-called soft laws include aspirational statements by international organizations (see Delmas & Toffel [Chapter 13] this volume), such as the United Nations' non–legally binding principles on the management and sustainable development of forests, the "Forest Principles," adopted at the United Nations' 1992 environmental conference in Rio de Janeiro. Soft law also includes principles and standards adopted by nongovernmental organizations that create norms of business practice or that customers may sometimes require their suppliers to implement, such as the International Organization of Standardization (ISO) standards on environmental management systems (Prakash & Potoski 2006). Although failure to comply with these standards may elicit no formal, government-imposed penalty, customer and community pressures at times may make them function as effectively as if they were binding law.

MAKING ENVIRONMENTAL LAW

As should be evident, sources of environmental law can be distinguished by their legal pedigree, that is, by the types of institutions from which they emanate. An entirely different way to think of the "sources" of environmental law is to focus on its political origins. Political scientists and legal scholars have written widely on the sources of environmental law in this latter sense, emphasizing the social and political factors giving rise to the growth in environmental regulation in the developed world over the last thirty years (Elliott et al. 1985; Coglianese 2001; Keohane, Revesz, & Stavins 1998; Vig & Kraft 2009). Expanding economic development has tended to lead to greater public support for environmental quality (Inglehart 1997). Dramatic environmental disasters such as oil spills and leakage from hazardous waste dumps have also played a role in making salient certain environmental issues and inducing legislative responses (Coglianese 2001).

In the making of environmental law, businesses play significant roles (Kamieniecki 2006). Businesses seek to influence the stringency and design of environmental law by lobbying legislators and officials at environmental agencies. Such governmental officials often welcome and encourage input from the businesses they regulate, because business possesses information government officials need to write effective regulations (Coglianese 2007). Although businesses can and do shape environmental laws, this does not mean that business groups always succeed (Kraft & Kamieniecki 2007). On the contrary, environmental regulations continue to be adopted, even though many of them impose substantial burdens on business firms.

Sometimes business groups play a formal, collaborative role in the development of environmental regulations. In Europe, for example, some countries have institutionalized the role of business in policymaking through more permanent—so-called corporatist—policy structures that give industry associations an official function in the development of new environmental policies. Scruggs (2001) has suggested that European countries with such corporatist policy structures achieved, somewhat surprisingly, greater environmental gains in the 1980s and 1990s than other countries without such structures. However, subsequent work by Neumayer (2003) shows that the strength of progressive and green political parties, rather than corporatist structures, best explains variation in pollution levels across Europe.

In the United States, the EPA has on a few occasions experimented with *negotiated rulemaking*, a process by which the agency explicitly invites business firms (and other interested organizations) to meet with agency officials to seek a consensus on the parameters of a new regulation (Coglianese 1997). Most of the time, however, the agency develops regulations through a process called *notice-and-comment rulemaking*, during which businesses offer input and feedback about rules proposed and developed by agency staff. Whether through informal or formal means, businesses provide information and seek to influence environmental law, although the existence of strong environmental groups, political parties, and publics that are broadly supportive of environmental concerns have ensured that such laws remain intact even during difficult economic times.

DESIGNING ENVIRONMENTAL LAW

Environmental law takes many forms. It can require businesses to install specific types of equipment (*means standards*) or it can call on them to achieve specified outcomes (*performance standards*). These two types of regulatory designs have been used extensively throughout the history of environmental law. More recently, nations have experimented with innovative approaches to environmental law, including *market-based instruments*, *information disclosure*, and *management-based regulation*. Social scientists and policy analysts have studied each of these five basic types of regulatory designs and have reached a series of generalizations about the advantages and disadvantages of each type.

Under the first type of regulatory design—what we call means standards, or others have called *specification* or *technology standards*—businesses are required to install pollution-control technologies or adopt specific practices used in their production processes. For example, government can mandate that large, coal-powered utility plants install scrubbers that remove pollutants that go up through the plants' smokestacks. Such technology standards usually are, relatively speaking, easy to administer. When the government mandates that a specific technology be used in a plant, its costs of inspecting for compliance are relatively low because agency inspectors simply need to see if the plant has the required technology installed. Means standards' ease of administration, however, comes at the cost of efficiency. By forcing all firms to adopt the same technologies, firms are unable to use other means that would achieve the same level of pollution control but at a lower cost.

The second type of regulatory design—performance standards—reduces some of the inflexibility of means standards. Performance standards limit firms' emissions levels but leave it up to them to decide the means they will use to achieve those levels. In this way, performance standards give firms the opportunity to innovate and find less costly ways of achieving environmental goals (Coglianese, Nash, & Olmstead 2003; Viscusi 1983). Of course, from the standpoint of the government, performance standards can be more difficult to administer because determining compliance requires measuring actual emissions levels rather than just observing whether a firm has installed a specific type of technology. In the case of coal-powered utility plants, for example, measuring performance may require installing monitoring equipment in smokestacks or running tests in the area around a plant.

Although performance standards provide more flexibility to regulated firms than means standards, they too have been criticized for inflexibility in requiring all firms to achieve the same outcomes. For certain kinds of environmental problems, namely those that arise from pollutants that build up in a common watershed or air quality region, a third type of regulatory design—market-based instruments—can prove more cost-effective than either means or performance standards. Market-based instruments can take the form of environmental taxes or emissions trading (Tietenberg 1990).

Environmental taxes place a price on the incremental release of pollution. If the government can set the marginal tax rate at a level equal to the social costs the pollution imposes, firms should reduce their pollution to the socially optimal level. However, if rates are set too high, a lower-than-optimal level of pollution will result. Firms will end up paying to control more emissions than is needed, given lower corresponding social gains from those extra levels of control. On the other hand, if tax rates are set too low, then more pollution will be generated than desirable. To achieve the full advantages of environmental taxes, then, government must be able to set the correct rates.

Emissions trading can be used when government does not know the optimal tax rate but does have in mind a preferred or acceptable overall level of emissions. Under emissions trading, the government establishes an overall cap on emissions at the desired level and distributes permits that allow firms to release increments of pollution that add up to the level of the cap (Hahn & Hester 1989). Firms can then trade these permits among themselves. Firms that can abate pollution cheaply have an incentive to reduce to below their permitted level and sell their excess credits to other firms that face higher abatement costs. For society, the same overall level of emissions reductions can be obtained at costs lower than if all firms had to meet uniform emissions limits (Stavins 1998).

The fourth regulatory design is mandated information disclosure. One of the most prominent examples of this type is the US Toxics Release Inventory (TRI), which requires certain businesses to report publicly how much toxic pollution they emit. Consumers and community members can use the information to place pressure on firms to reduce their pollution (Hamilton 2005). Another example of information disclosure can be found in regulations promulgated under the US Securities Act and the Exchange Act. Although securities laws have long required disclosure of financial information, the US Securities and Exchange Commission now requires disclosure of information about certain aspects of environmental management when legal compliance and liability have significant material effects on publicly traded companies' financial positions (Monsma & Olson 2007).

Finally, the fifth basic type of regulatory design is management-based regulation (Coglianese & Lazer 2003; Braithwaite 1982). Under this design, firms must undertake specific management activities, such as environmental planning. For example, the US EPA requires large chemical facilities to develop Risk Management Plans to identify hazards and implement actions designed to reduce accidents. Another example is the Massachusetts Toxics Use Reduction Act, which requires large chemical facilities to develop written plans to reduce their use of toxic substances—although firms are not actually required to implement their plans, just to develop them (Bennear 2007). Even though management-based regulations do not always require firms to disclose their plans to the public or even implement the plans they develop, by mandating planning government officials seek to focus the attention of firms' managers on environmental problems and spur them to identify steps they can take to improve environmental performance.

ENFORCING ENVIRONMENTAL LAW

However they are designed, environmental laws and regulations matter to businesses because they are backed up by the threat of penalties for noncompliance. For example, many US environmental statutes provide for the imposition of up to $25,000 in civil penalties *per day* of violation, which means that fines imposed on an individual firm can easily reach in the millions of dollars just for a single ongoing offense. Given how extensive and complex environmental regulations have become, even a modestly straightforward business operation can have a difficult time conducting its operations in full compliance, and therefore runs the risk of violating numerous different environmental requirements, each with its own associated daily penalties. In addition, especially egregious and dangerous environmental violations can be punished with criminal fines imposed on either the firm or its management. As a result, business owners and corporate officers can and do spend time in jail for violating environmental regulations (Cohen 1992).

Researchers have sought to explain variation in the frequency of regulatory inspections, the frequency and size of penalties, and the overall "style" of regulatory enforcement. Such enforcement styles have generally been characterized as either adversarial or cooperative (Hawkins 1984). Inspectors exhibit an adversarial style when they "go by the book," viewing their primary role as law enforcers and rigidly imposing fines according to the letter of the law in order to punish offenders. By contrast, cooperative inspectors tend to see their role more as problem solvers, seeking to identify areas in need of improvement and working collaboratively with firms to ensure that they come into compliance with environmental rules. In reality, most enforcement officials' behavior probably lies somewhere between the extremes of this cops-to-consultants continuum, and it may vary over time or across interactions, even with the same firms (May & Winter 1999). Informed by the insights of game theory, regulatory scholars have suggested that regulators may be more effective if they adapt their style to the behavior of the business firm (Scholz 1984; Ayres & Braithwaite 1992). In other words, inspectors can initiate interaction in a cooperative manner, but then shift to an adversarial mode if their cooperation is not reciprocated by a regulated firm.

Empirical research reveals a number of factors that affect regulators' enforcement behavior. First, political culture appears to matter. An adversarial, by-the-book style appears more likely when regulators and their discretion meet with mistrust by the public or by other government officials (Bardach & Kagan 1982). Researchers have pointed to the division of governmental authority in the United States as contributing to greater adversarialism because inspectors better avoid criticism and charges of so-called regulatory capture when they go by the book.

Second, regulatory enforcement can be affected by the political ideology of the officials in charge of enforcement agencies. For example, federal and state environmental enforcement patterns in the United States appear to vary depending on the political party in control of the White House or the governor's office (Atlas 2007; Ringquist 1995). Enforcement agencies appear to have a tendency toward less stringent environmental enforcement under Republican administrations than under Democratic ones. Legislators can also influence regulatory agencies' enforcement strategies through investigations and budgetary control (Wood & Waterman 1991).

Third, regulatory enforcement may be affected by jurisdictional competition. Pressures to attract business investment may lead states or other political subdivisions to compete with each other in a "race to the bottom," as each jurisdiction reduces enforcement scrutiny to lower levels to become business friendly (Atlas 2007). Although such race-to-the-bottom pressures can be real, the game of regulatory competition in practice is more complicated, as regulatory agencies not only face pressures to encourage economic development but also confront countervailing pressures emanating from the public to maintain a quality environment (Konisky 2007; Vogel 1995).

Finally, regulatory officials' enforcement behavior can be affected by characteristics of businesses themselves. Large, public companies appear to find themselves on the receiving end of more cooperative enforcement strategies than do smaller companies (Shover et al. 1984). This may be because they have their own teams of internal compliance professionals who share a common orientation with regulatory inspectors; they may also have a greater incentive to respond cooperatively to initial overtures of cooperation by inspectors because they believe they have more to lose by becoming the target of adversarial confrontations. Firms that do a better job of complying with environmental law— and even go above and beyond legal requirements in their pollution control efforts—appear also to receive more relaxed scrutiny by enforcement officials (Decker 2005; Sam & Innes 2008).

COMPLYING WITH ENVIRONMENTAL LAW

Why do some firms do a better job managing their environmental performance? Government enforcement is clearly part of the answer—but it is only part. Researchers have identified three sets of factors that explain variations in firms' environmental performance: regulatory, social, and economic. Together, these factors effectively constitute each firm's "license to operate," as the firm must respond to each type of pressure in order to survive (Gunningham, Kagan, & Thornton 2003).

As already suggested, business managers can be expected to respond to regulatory pressures because of the threat of penalties for noncompliance. Their decisions (assuming they are fully and not boundedly rational) will balance the benefit to be received—or costs to be saved—from failing to comply with the law against the probability of getting caught for noncompliance and the penalty they would face if they were caught. If the expected penalty (that is, probability times penalty) is higher than the benefits of non-compliance, they will comply with the law (Becker 1968). Gunningham, Kagan, & Thornton (2003) point to tightening water pollution regulations as a primary factor explaining why pulp-and-paper mills around the world have installed expensive pollution-control equipment.

Social pressures tend to reinforce regulatory pressures (see Lounsbury, Fairclough, & Lee [Chapter 12] this volume). Aoki & Cioffi (1999) show that, despite fewer inspections, Japanese firms actually comply with waste disposal regulations more consistently than US firms do—perhaps as a result of stronger social pressures to comply in Japan. Social pressures can also offer reasons for businesses to take environmentally protective measures even if they are not required to do so by law. Individuals and community groups may exert this pressure either directly by seeking to influence facility managers or indirectly by activating increased scrutiny by governmental officials. As Gunningham, Kagan, & Thornton (2003: 37) observe, "a company's failure to meet social expectations concerning environmental performance can impair the firm's reputation, adversely affecting recruiting, and trigger demands for more stringent and intrusive legal controls."

Often working against social and regulatory pressures are the economic pressures that bear down on firms. Firms respond to shareholder demands for returns on their investments. In competitive markets, firms that assume additional costs for environmental controls beyond those required by law may be less able to compete for market share, risking not only reduced shareholder returns but, at some point, even their own survival (Thornton, Kagan, & Gunningham 2008). Of course, in some cases firms have been able to use their image as responsible environmental actors to their economic advantage (Reinhardt 2000), although it is far from clear how strong or widespread such advantages might be. Given the need for environmental regulation, presumably the economic advantages from investments in environmental management are neither strong nor widespread enough to generate socially optimal levels of environmental control.

The concept of a license to operate highlights how external regulatory, social, and economic pressures come together to affect business behavior. Because these external pressures can vary for different firms, they may help explain the different levels of pollution control and legal compliance achieved by different firms. Of course, even firms that confront similar external pressures may nevertheless vary in their environmental behavior and performance. As much as external pressures matter, so too do the characteristics of businesses themselves as well as their internal organizational features. Easily observable internal features such as the size and age of businesses may make a difference to their levels of environmental compliance, but so too can less tangible qualities such as management style or commitment (Gunningham, Kagan, & Thornton 2003; Coglianese & Nash 2001). Businesses appear to be affected by an "internal license" consisting of factors such as organizational culture or identity and management incentives (Howard-Grenville, Nash, & Coglianese 2008). Internal factors such as organizational norms or managers' personal commitments to the environment may create independent pressures for environmental excellence (Vandenbergh 2003). These internal factors also influence how managers perceive and respond to the external pressures bearing down on their firms.

IMPACTS OF ENVIRONMENTAL LAW

Judging from progress made over the past several decades, it would appear that environmental law has had a substantial impact on pollution levels. According to a number of measures, developed countries have exhibited a substantial decline in pollution in the years following the widespread adoption of environmental regulation (Davies & Mazurek 1998; Bok 1996). Environmental conditions ranging from air and water quality to cleaned-up hazardous waste sites have shown improvement across much of the developed world, as some of the most visible environmental problems—such as belching smokestacks or burning rivers—have been ameliorated (Coglianese 2001). Yet, whether these improvements stem from regulation and its enforcement or from other factors, such as a shift away from manufacturing and other pollution-intensive industries toward a service-based economy, is ultimately an empirical question that requires careful analysis.

Too often, policy analysts and scholars have observed the passage of a law and a subsequent decline in pollution, and then jumped to the conclusion that the law must explain the observed decline. For example, the passage of the US Toxic Release Inventory (TRI) in the late 1980s—an information disclosure regulation—has been said to have led to a decline of more than 40 percent in toxic emissions (Fung & O'Rourke 2000). Thaler & Sunstein (2008: 192) call TRI "the most unambiguous success" of any US environmental regulation, "spurring large reductions in toxic releases throughout the United States." But to determine whether TRI actually caused a decline calls for making an inference about what would have happened to toxic emissions in the absence of TRI. If such emissions were already on the decline before the passage of TRI, then not all of the decline after its passage should be attributed to TRI. Similarly, if the US government's passage of new (non-TRI) hazardous air pollutant regulations in 1990 led to reductions in releases of toxic chemicals, then again not all of the observed decline after 1990 should be attributed to TRI (Hamilton 2005).

The empirical record overall shows that some environmental laws appear to have resulted in improvements while others have not had their intended effects (Bennear 2007; McKitrick 2007; Hamilton & Viscusi 1999; Davies & Mazurek 1998; Revesz & Stewart 1995; Ackerman & Hassler 1981). Even when environmental law does lead to improved environmental conditions, the improvements properly attributable to law (as opposed to other factors) can sometimes fall short of the full degree of environmental improvements observed. For example, Greenstone's (2004) study of the effects of the US Clean Air Act on sulfur dioxide concentrations shows that the areas designated under the Act as "non-attainment," and therefore subject to more stringent regulation, do see more significant reductions in sulfur dioxide (SO_2) in the ambient air. But when other factors are controlled for, the additional reductions either disappear or become substantively quite small.

In addition to affecting underlying environmental conditions, environmental law can impact other policy criteria, such as technological innovation, the distribution of environmental risks, compliance costs to regulated firms, and corporations' international competitiveness. The annual costs associated with environmental law in the United States, for example, have been estimated to reach into the hundreds of billions of dollars (Jaffe et al. 1995). Critics of environmental law have sometimes claimed that imposing environmental compliance costs on businesses lowers their competitiveness, contributing to a flight of manufacturing jobs overseas. Although clear differences do exist across countries in environmental laws and the resulting costs of compliance (Hammitt et al. 2005; Stewart 1993), and some research does indeed suggest that environmental standards can be associated with job flight (Greenstone 2002), manufacturing flight from countries such as the United States appears instead to stem primarily from other, more significant differences in economic conditions, such as labor costs (Cole & Elliott 2007; Jaffe et al. 1995).

Business scholar Michael Porter has suggested that stricter environmental regulations can actually enhance businesses' competitiveness. He argues that businesses respond to regulatory demands by finding more innovative and efficient ways to operate, ways that not only reduce pollution but also deliver cost-savings or other bottom-line advantages (Porter & Van der Linde 1995). Numerous anecdotes seem to support this win-win or "green-to-gold" hypothesis (Reinhardt 2000; Esty & Winston 2006). Yet, although businesses can sometimes profit from going the extra mile in the way they manage their environmental impacts, this does not mean that they generally reap rewards from pollution control measures or that environmental regulation yields only positive net effects for companies. If firms could generally benefit from investing in pollution abatement technology, one would expect that, given their underlying profit motive, they would do much more such abatement on their own. The fact that countries find environmental regulation to be needed in the first place to address the negative side effects of business operations would suggest that firms do not, on their own, have enough of a private gain from pollution control (Palmer, Oates, & Portney 1995). Business lobbying groups' rather consistent mobilization opposing additional environmental regulation would seem to belie the view that regulation constitutes a clear economic advantage to business (Kraft & Kaminecki 2007).

Environmental law in the global society

The global reach of business in today's economy, combined with the global scope of some of the most salient environmental problems, increasingly creates new challenges for business and environmental law. One set of challenges centers on the complexity—even, at times, the inconsistency—of the legal environment within which multinational corporations and other businesses engaged in global transactions must operate (see Christmann & Taylor [Chapter 3] this volume). Multi-national corporations may desire to coordinate their business and production activities to reap economies of scale, but they also need to take into account the fact that the different jurisdictions within which they operate may impose vastly differing environmental standards (Kagan & Axelrad 2000). These regulatory differences may at times impede more efficient business practices or the development of new technologies, particularly in cutting-edge fields such as biotechnology or nanotechnology. If nothing else, transnational regulatory conflicts can increase the transaction costs of global business and, at the extreme, can also wreak havoc on global trade if environmental standards become a ruse for protectionism.

In an effort to respond to concerns about the ill effects of regulatory competition and transnational legal conflicts, national environmental officials do engage in crossnational dialogue and efforts at regulatory harmonization through international forums. In addition, the World Trade Organization (WTO) has on occasion ruled against national environmental standards that do not apply equally to both domestic and foreign businesses. In 1996, for example, the WTO ruled against the United States over an EPA regulation on reformulated gasoline because the standards for importers of foreign fuel were more strict than those for domestic oil refiners (McCrory & Richards 1998).

The global nature of some of the most pressing environmental problems has also created a related set of challenges associated with achieving international cooperation and coordination. Environmental problems such as climate change cannot be readily solved by each individual country deciding whether to set its own standards. Global climate change demands collective action because, even if one country succeeds in reducing emissions of greenhouse gases within its own borders, if other countries do nothing the problem will not lessen (Wiener 2007). Pollutants emitted in one country enter the atmosphere and can affect climate everywhere, which means that countries must act in concert to reduce the risks posed by emissions in any significant way.

International collective action is not easy, as the checkered history of cooperation to address climate change attests. Not only does scientific uncertainty mean that different actors assess the benefits of emissions control regulation differently, but the costs of control also vary considerably. Emerging economic powerhouses such as China and India argue that they should not be subject to the same level of emissions abatement as developed economies such as the United States and Western Europe, which long ago exploited carbon-based energy as the backbone of their economic development. In return, developed countries argue that, although they did emit more carbon dioxide in the past, they were unaware of the dangers it caused to the environment and therefore should not be held responsible for those past emissions. Further complicating international cooperation have been the general incentive effects—such as free riding and holdouts—that work against collective action in any setting (Olson 1968). For all these reasons, when environmental problems go global, the legal responses to those problems grow ever more challenging to implement.

AVENUES FOR FUTURE RESEARCH

Whether addressing global or domestic problems, environmental law raises numerous important questions for researchers interested in law and business. Many of these research questions have been reflected in the issues we have considered in this chapter. Each of these issues—the making, designing, enforcing, and complying with environmental law, as well as its overall impact on the environment and the economy—remains open for, and in need of, additional research. In part, this need exists because of the relative newness of environmental law and its study. On some questions, only a handful of studies exist, and their results are sometimes mixed, if not even conflicting. More fundamentally, what makes environmental law challenging as a field of empirical research is the sheer complexity of the phenomena under study. Not only does the environment raise difficult questions of natural and public health science, but we have also seen that the law itself is complex—not only in its technical density but also in its varied sources (international, national, state, local, and nongovernmental), its varied designs (means standards, performance standards, market-based regulation, information disclosure, and management-based regulation), and its varied methods of implementation and enforcement (adversarial, cooperative, and hybrid). Environmental law and its enforcement also function in a complex—and often high-stakes—political and economic environment. Law in this area seeks to shape the behavior of heterogeneous entities that are the target of law's power—namely, businesses ranging from sole proprietorships to multinational corporations, not to mention individuals, nonprofit organizations, and even other governmental entities. Consequently, to study environmental law requires understanding more than just environmental science and principles of public law. Ultimately it calls for an ability to analyze the dynamic and complex phenomena of human and organizational behavior, and then to discern the impact of that behavior on another highly complex system, the environment.

To date, the study of environmental law has proceeded, quite sensibly, by trying to isolate and understand separate pieces of this larger, complex puzzle. Scholars have given considerable attention to the analysis of individual regulatory designs, generating important knowledge about the advantages and disadvantages of each particular approach. But the research community has done much less by way of making systematic empirical comparisons across different regulatory designs. We do not know, for example, whether the TRI's information disclosure approach has contributed more (or less) to the decline in toxic air pollution in the United States than the Clean Air Act's hazardous air pollutant performance standards. We also know less than we should about the interaction among different ways of making, designing, and enforcing environmental law. What political economy factors favor conventional means or performance standards over market-based regulation (Keohane, Revesz, & Stavins 1998)? Do different regulatory designs tend to lead to (or benefit distinctively from) different approaches to enforcement? In the end, how do regulatory designs and enforcement styles interact to affect business behavior? How do different businesses and industrial operations respond to different types of design-and-enforcement combinations? Do environmental quality and economic growth benefit more from having both TRI and hazardous air pollutant performance standards than from each one separately? Do local, state, and national laws responding to global climate change productively link up together, or do they impede more effective global legal responses?

These questions will not be easy to answer. But there are at least three reasons to be optimistic that environmental law researchers will be able to answer some of these questions better over the next twenty years than they have over the past twenty years (Coglianese & Bennear 2005). First, environmental law is no longer new, which means that researchers can now exploit longitudinal analysis in ways that were simply unavailable in earlier times. Second, political interest in empirical research on environmental law appears to be growing. The environmental problems many developed countries have already tackled (e.g., water pollution discharged from industrial pipes) have tended to be simpler or less costly to address than the more subtle and complex environmental problems remaining to be tackled (e.g., water pollution from run-off from farms and parking lots). Pressures for increased regulatory analysis—sometimes through political initiatives traveling under the banner of "smart" regulation (Gunningham, Grabosky, & Sinclair 1998)—have apparently intensified in a number of developed countries in recent years.

Finally, recent and likely future advances in measurement, data availability, and analytic techniques will make it more feasible for researchers to bring new analysis to bear on old research questions as well as to examine new questions altogether. For example, although the US EPA previously kept disparate data on firms' environmental performance in its different offices, it now posts many data online and has established a Facility Registry System that makes it easier to combine data about the same facility from different sources. More generally, advances in remote sensing and data-mining capabilities can be expected to facilitate important new analysis in the coming decades.

CONCLUSION

As much as scholars have already learned about business and environmental law, still more research opportunities abound. The study of the intersection of business and environmental law will remain vital in the years to come because answers to the kinds of research questions addressed by scholars in this field—as well as answers to questions still to be studied—will help inform decision-making by legislators and regulatory officials as well as business leaders. Knowing more about how and why different businesses act the way they do when faced with different regulatory designs and different enforcement tactics will clearly be a necessary condition to navigating more effectively in the future toward the goals of environmental protection and economic growth.

REFERENCES

Ackerman, B. & Hassler, W. T. (1981). *Clean Coal/Dirty Air: Or How the Clean Air Act Became a Multibillion-Dollar Bail-Out for High-Sulfur Coal Producers and What Should be Done About It*. New Haven, CT: Yale University Press.

Aoki, K. & Cioffi, J. (1999). "Poles Apart: Industrial Waste Management Regulation and Enforcement in the United States and Japan," *Law and Policy*, 21: 213–45.

Applegate, J. S. (2008). "Synthesizing TSCA and REACH: Practical Principles for Chemical Regulation Reform," *Ecology Law Quarterly*, 35: 721–769.

Atlas, M. (2007). "Enforcement Principles and Environmental Agencies: Principal-Agent Relationships in a Delegated Environmental Program," *Law and Society Review*, 41: 939–80.

Ayres, I. & Braithwaite, J. (1992). *Responsive Regulation*. New York: Oxford University Press.

Bardach, E. & Kagan, R. A. (1982). *Going by the Book: The Problem of Regulatory Unreasonableness*. Philadelphia, PA: Temple University Press.

Becker, G. S. (1968). "Crime and Punishment: An Economic Approach," *Journal of Political Economy*, 76: 169.

Bernasconi-Osterwald, N. Magraw, D. Olivia, M. J., Orellana, M., & Tuerk, E. (2006). *Environment and Trade: A Guide to WTO Jurisprudence*. London: Earthscan.

Bennear, L. (2007). "Are Management-Based Regulations Effective? Evidence from State Pollution Prevention Programs," *Journal of Policy Analysis and Management*, 26: 327–48.

Bok, D. C. (1996). *The State of the Nation: Government and the Quest for a Better Society*. Cambridge, MA: Harvard University Press.

Braithwaite, J. (1982). "Enforced Self Regulation: A New Strategy for Corporate Crime Control," *Michigan Law Review*, 80: 1466–1507.

Coglianese, C. (1997). "Assessing Consensus: The Promise and Performance of Negotiated Rulemaking," *Duke Law Journal*, 46: 1255–349.

—— (2001). "Social Movements, Law, and Society: The Institutionalization of the Environmental Movement," *University of Pennsylvania Law Review*, 150: 85–118.

—— (2007). "Business Interests and Information in Environmental Rulemaking," in M. E. Kraft & S. Kamieniecki (eds.), *Business and Environmental Policy: Corporate Interests in the American Political System*, Cambridge, MA: Massachusetts Institute of Technology.

—— & Bennear, L. S. (2005). "Program Evaluation of Environmental Policies: Toward Evidence-Based Decision Making," in National Research Council, *Social and Behavioral Science Research Priorities for Environmental Decision Making*. Washington, DC: National Academies Press.

—— & Lazer, D. (2003). "Management-Based Regulation: Prescribing Private Management to Achieve Public Goals," *Law & Society Review*, 37: 691–730.

—— Nash, J., & Olmstead, T. (2003). "Performance-Based Regulation: Prospects and Limitations in Health, Safety, and Environmental Regulation," *Administrative Law Review*, 55: 705–729.

——— (2001). *Regulating from the Inside: Can Environmental Management Systems Achieve Policy Goals?* Washington, DC: Resources for the Future Press.

Cohen, M. A. (1992). "Environmental Crime and Punishment: Legal/Economic Theory and Empirical Evidence on Enforcement of Federal Environmental Statutes," *Journal of Criminal Law and Criminology*, 82: 1054–1108.

Cole, M. & Elliott, R. (2007). "Do Environmental Regulations Cost Jobs? An Industry-Level Analysis of the UK," *The B.E. Journal of Economic Analysis and Policy*, 7: 1–25.

Davies J. and Mazurek J. (1998). *Pollution Control in the United States: Evaluating the System.* Washington, DC: Resources for the Future.

Decker, C. (2005). "Do Regulators Respond to Voluntary Pollution Control Efforts? A Count Data Analysis," *Contemporary Economic Policy,* 23: 180–94.

Elliott, E. D., Ackerman, B. A. & Millian, J. C. (1985). "Toward a Theory of Statutory Evolution: The Federalization of Environmental Law," *Journal of Law, Economics and Organization,* 1: 313–40.

Esty, D. C. & Winston, A. S. (2006). *Green to Gold: How Smart Companies Use Environmental Strategy to Innovate, Create Value, and Build Competitive Advantage.* New Haven, CT: Yale University Press.

Fung, A. & O'Rourke, D. (2000). "Reinventing Environmental Regulation from the Grassroots Up: Explaining and Expanding the Success of the Toxics Release Inventory," *Environmental Management,* 25: 115–27.

Greenstone, M. (2002). "The Impacts of Environmental Regulation on Industrial Activity: Evidence from the 1970 and 1977 Clean Air Act Amendments and the Census of Manufacturers," *Journal of Political Economy,* 110: 1175–219.

—— (2004). "Did the Clean Air Act Amendments Cause the Remarkable Decline in Sulfur Dioxide Concentrations?," *Journal of Environmental Economics and Management,* 47: 585–611.

Gunningham, N., Kagan, R., & Thornton, D. (2003). *Shades of Green: Business, Regulation, and Environment.* Palo Alto, CA: Stanford University Press.

—— Grabosky, P. N., & Sinclair, D. (1998). *Smart Regulation: Designing Environmental Policy,* Oxford: Oxford University Press.

Hahn, R. W. & Hester, G. L. (1989). "Marketable Permits: Lessons for Theory and Practice," *Ecology Law Quarterly,* 16: 361–406.

Hamilton, J., (2005). *Regulation Through Revelation: The Origin and Impacts of the Toxics Release Inventory Program.* New York. Cambridge University Press.

—— & Viscusi, W. K. (1999). *Calculating Risks? The Spatial and Political Dimensions of Hazardous Waste Policy.* Cambridge, MA: MIT Press.

Hammitt, J. K., Wiener, J. B., Swedlow, B., Kall, D., and Zhou, Z. (2005). "Precautionary Regulation in Europe and the United States: A Quantitative Comparison," *Risk Analysis,* 25: 1215–28.

Hawkins, K. (1984). *Environment and Enforcement: Regulation and the Social Definition of Pollution.* Oxford: Clarendon Press.

Howard-Grenville, J. A., Nash, J., & Coglianese, C. (2008) "Constructing the License to Operate: Internal Factors and their Influence on Corporate Environmental Decisions," *Law & Policy,* 30: 73–107.

Inglehart, R. (1997). *Modernization and Postmodernization: Cultural, Economic and Political Change in 43 Societies.* Princeton, NJ: Princeton University Press.

Jaffe, A. B., Peterson, S. R., Portney, P. R., and Stavins, R. N. (1995). "Environmental Regulation and the Competitiveness of U.S. Manufacturing: What Does the Evidence Tell Us?" *Journal of Economic Literature,* 33: 132–63.

Kagan, R. A. & Axelrad, L. (2000). *Regulatory Encounters: Multinational Corporations and American Adversarial Legalism.* Berkeley, CA: University of California Press.

Kamieniecki, S. (2006). *Corporate America and Environmental Policy: How Often Does Business Get Its Way?* Palo Alto, CA: Stanford University Press.

Keohane, N. O., Revesz, R. L., & Stavins, R. N. (1998). "The Choice of Regulatory Instruments in Environmental Policy," *Harvard Environmental Law Review,* 22: 313.

Konisky, D. (2007). "Regulatory Competition and Environmental Enforcement: Is There a Race to the Bottom?" *American Journal of Political Science,* 51: 853–72.

Kraft, M. E. & Kamieniecki, S. (eds.) (2007). *Business and Environmental Policy: Corporate Interests in the American Political System*. Cambridge, MA: Massachusetts Institute of Technology.

Lazarus, R. J. (2004). *The Making of Environmental Law*. Chicago: University of Chicago Press.

McCrory, M. A. & Richards, E. L. (1998). "Clearing the Air: The Clean Air Act, GATT and the WTO's Reformulated Gasoline Decision," *UCLA Journal of Environmental Law & Policy*, 17: 1.

McKitrick, R. (2007). "Why Did US Air Pollution Decline After 1970?," *Empirical Economics*, 33, 491–513.

May, P. & Winter, S. (1999). "Regulatory Enforcement and Compliance: Examining Danish Agro-Environmental Policy," *Journal of Policy Analysis and Management*, 18: 625–51.

Monsma, D. & Olson, T. (2007). "Muddling Through Counterfactual Materiality and Divergent Disclosure: The Necessary Search for a Duty to Disclose Material Non-Financial Information," *Stanford Environmental Law Journal*, 26: 137.

Neumayer, E. (2003). "Are Left-Wing Party Strength and Corporatism Good for the Environment? Evidence from Panel Analysis of Air Pollution in OECD Countries," *Ecological Economics*, 45: 203–20.

Olson, Mancur, Jr. (1968). *The Logic of Collective Action*. New York: Schocken Books.

Palmer, K., Oates, W., & Portney, P. (1995). "Tightening of Environmental Standards: The Benefit-Cost or the No-Cost Paradigm?" *Journal of Economic Perspectives*, 9: 119–32.

Percival, R. V. (1995). "Environmental Federalism: Historical Roots and Contemporary Models," *Maryland Law Review*, 54: 1141–1182.

Porter, M. E. & Van der Linde, C. (1995). "Green and Competitive: Ending the Stalemate," *Harvard Business Review*, September–October, 120–34.

Prakash, A. & Potoski, M. (2006). *The Voluntary Environmentalists: Green Clubs, ISO 14001, and Voluntary Environmental Regulation*. Cambridge: Cambridge University Press.

Reinhardt, F. L. (2000). *Down to Earth: Applying Business Principles to Environmental Management*. Boston, MA: Harvard Business School Press.

Revesz, R. L. & Stewart, R. B. (eds.) (1995). *Analyzing Superfund: Economics, Science and Law*. Washington, DC: Resources for the Future Press.

Ringquist, E. (1995). "Political Control and Policy Impact in EPA's Office of Water Quality," *American Journal of Political Science*, 39: 336–63.

Sam, A. & Innes, R. (2008). "Voluntary Pollution Reductions and the Enforcement of Environmental Law: An Empirical Study of the 33/50 Program," *Journal of Law and Economics*, 51: 271–96.

Scholz, J. T. (1984). "Cooperation, Deterrence, and the Ecology of Regulatory Enforcement," *Law & Society Review*, 18: 179–224.

Scruggs, L. (2001). "Is There Really a Link Between Neo-Corporatism and Environmental Performance? Updated Evidence and New Data for the 1980s and 1990s," *British Journal of Political Science*, 31: 686–92.

Seerden, R. J. G. H., Heldeweg, M. A., & Deketelaere, K. R. (2002). *Public Environmental Law in European Union and US: A Comparative Analysis*. The Hague, Netherlands: Kluwer Law International.

Shover, N., Lynxwiler, J., Groce, S., and Clelland, D. (1984). "Regional Variation in Regulatory Law Enforcement: The Surface Mining Control and Reclamation Act," in K. Hawkins and J. T. Thomas (eds.), *Enforcing Regulation*. Boston, MA: Kluwer-Nijhoff.

Stavins, R. N. (1998). "What Can We Learn from the Grand Policy Experiment? Positive and Normative Lessons from SO2 Allowance Trading," *Journal of Economic Perspectives,* 12: 69–88.

Stewart, R. B. (1993). "Environmental Regulation and International Competitiveness," *Yale Law Journal,* 102: 2039–2106.

Thaler, R. H. & Sunstein C. R. (2008). *Nudge: Improving Decisions about Health, Wealth, and Happiness.* New Haven, CT: Yale University Press.

Thornton, D., Kagan, R. A., & Gunningham, N. (2008). "Compliance Costs, Regulation, and Environmental Performance: Controlling Truck Emissions in the U.S," *Regulation & Governance,* 2: 275–292.

Tietenberg, T. H. (1990). "Economic Instruments for Environmental Regulation," *Oxford Review of Economic Policy,* 6: 17–33.

Vandenbergh, M. (2003). "Beyond Elegance: A Testable Typology of Social Norms in Corporate Environmental Compliance," *Stanford Environmental Law Journal,* 22: 55–144.

Vig, N. J. & Kraft, M. E. (2009). *Environmental Policy: New Directions for the Twenty-First Century* (7th ed.). Washington, DC: CQ Press.

Viscusi, W. K. (1983). *Risk by Choice: Regulating Health and Safety in the Workplace.* Cambridge, MA: Harvard University Press.

Vogel, D. (1995). *Trading Up: Consumer and Environmental Regulation in a Global Economy.* Cambridge, MA: Harvard University Press.

Wiener, J. B. (2007). "Think Globally, Act Globally: The Limits of Local Climate Policies," *University of Pennsylvania Law Review,* 155: 1961–1979.

Wood, D., & Waterman, R. (1991). "The Dynamics of Political Control of the Bureaucracy," *American Political Science Review,* 85: 801–828.

PART IV

··

ORGANIZATIONAL BEHAVIOR AND THEORY

··

CHAPTER 9

COGNITIVE BARRIERS TO ENVIRONMENTAL ACTION: PROBLEMS AND SOLUTIONS

LISA L. SHU
AND MAX H. BAZERMAN

THE preceding chapters have offered many excellent business and non-market strategies to promote environmental sustainability initiatives. Together, these chapters offer novel interventions at the corporate, policy, and organizational levels to help society move toward better environmental solutions. In this chapter, we turn inward to explore interventions at the micro level—the level of the individual—from both the citizen and policymaker perspectives. We focus on recognized cognitive barriers from the behavioral decision-making literature. In particular, we highlight three cognitive barriers that impede sound individual decision-making that have particular relevance to behaviors impacting the environment. We then discuss possible ways to overcome these cognitive barriers, first from the perspective of the individual citizen and then from the perspective of the policymaker.

In 2002, the Nobel Committee broke with tradition by awarding its Prize in Economics to Daniel Kahneman. Kahneman, together with the late Amos Tversky, carved out a field devoted to systematic and predictable mistakes people make in everyday decision-making (Tversky & Kahneman 2002). At its core, the field of behavioral decision-making presumes that all people rely on simplifying strategies, or cognitive heuristics, when facing judgments and choices. These heuristics evolved to equip us with faster decision-making abilities that can withstand the numerous complexities of everyday life. But speed comes at a cost: As Tversky & Kahneman identified, heuristics also lead people to systematic and predictable errors. Decision-making errors, or biases, are defined as pervasive departures from rational thought in predictable directions. The long list of specific biases that have been identified has hugely impacted the existing models of decision-making in the fields of economics, financial markets, consumer behavior, negotiation, medicine, and organizational behavior (see Bazerman & Moore 2008).

The behavioral decision-making perspective is oftentimes considered the diametric opposite of the neoclassical economics perspective. In actuality, the two approaches have much more in common than the academic debate suggests. Research on decision-making biases does not discredit all models of economic rationality; rather, the behavioral perspective aims to uncover predictable departures from economic rationality (in specific domains and decision contexts) to better improve existing models of behavior.

The field of behavioral decision-making has documented a long list of biases (Bazerman & Moore 2008), many of which are relevant to faulty environmental decisions (Hoffman & Bazerman 2007). In order to provide a deeper understanding of how behavioral decision-making research can be used, we focus on three biases that we believe are particularly relevant to behaviors that impact the environment. First, despite claiming that they want to leave the world in good condition for future generations, people intuitively discount the future to a greater degree than can be rationally defended. Second, positive illusions lead us to conclude that energy problems do not exist or are not severe enough to merit action. Third, we interpret events in a self-serving manner, a tendency that causes us to expect others to do more than we do to solve energy problems. We then propose ways in which these biases could actually be used to our advantage in steering ourselves toward better judgment. At the end of this chapter, we outline the key questions on the research frontier from the behavioral decision-making perspective, and debunk the myth that behavioral and neoclassical economic perspectives need be in conflict.

COGNITIVE BIASES OVERVIEW

Discounting the future

Would you prefer to receive $10,000 today or $12,000 a year from now? People faced with this question often say they would prefer to receive $10,000 today, ignoring the opportunity to earn a 20 percent return on their investment. Similarly, homeowners often fail to insulate their homes appropriately or to purchase energy-efficient appliances and fluorescent lighting, even when the long-term rate of return would be huge. Research demonstrates that people too often use an extremely high discounting rate regarding the future—that is, they tend to focus on or overweight short-term considerations (Loewenstein & Thaler 1989).

Organizations are also guilty of discounting the future (see Howard-Grenville & Bertels [Chapter 11] and Banerjee [Chapter 31] this volume). One top university undertook a significant renovation of its infrastructure without using the most cost-efficient products from a long-term perspective (Bazerman, Baron, & Shonk 2001). Facing capital constraints on construction, the university implicitly placed a very high discount rate on construction-related decisions, emphasizing the minimization of current costs over the long-term costs of running the building. As a result, the university passed on returns that its financial office would have enjoyed receiving on its investments. By contrast, as part of its Green Campus Initiative, Harvard University set up a fund to finance worthwhile projects for different colleges within the university that, due to short-term budget pressures, might otherwise have been overlooked. The Green Campus Initiative helps university departments avoid making poor long-term decisions that could result from the tendency to overly discount the future.

Over-discounting the future can contribute to a broad array of environmental problems, ranging from the overharvesting of the oceans and forests, to the failure to invest in new technologies to address climate change. Hoffman & Bazerman (2007) document the disastrous impact of extremely high discount rates on the global fishing crisis. Eleven of the seventeen world's largest fishing basins have been depleted. High-tech equipment and government subsidies have allowed fishers to deplete the oceans. The subsidization of the global fishing fleet has helped produce enough boats, hooks, and nets to catch far more fish than the entire resource. Too many boats are chasing too few fish, and international skirmishes over poaching have resulted.

Ecological economist Herman Daly has observed that many of our environmental decisions are made as if the Earth "were a business in liquidation" (Gore 1992). We are most likely to discount the future when the future is uncertain, distant, and when intergenerational distribution of resources is involved (Wade-Benzoni 1999) (see also Tost & Wade—Benzoni [Chapter 10] this volume). Specifically, when people espouse the view that the Earth's resources should be preserved, they tend to think about their descendants. But when consumption opportunities arise today that would inflict environmental costs on future generations, they begin to view "descendants" as vague groups of people living in a distant time. In their book, *Priceless: On Knowing the Price of Everything and the Value of Nothing*, Frank Ackerman & Lisa Heinzerling connect discounting of the future to phenomena such as species extinction, the melting of polar ice caps, uranium leaks, and failure to deal with hazardous waste. From a societal perspective, overweighting present concerns can be viewed as both foolish and immoral, as it robs future generations of opportunities and resources (Ackerman & Heinzerling 2004; Stern 2007).

Positive illusions

Many countries' borders are likely to be substantially altered by the effects of climate change in the form of more destructive hurricanes and the submersion of oceanfront land. Yet most governments continue to ignore opportunities to play a constructive role in addressing climate change and fail to take steps to control or reduce their countries' reliance on fossil fuels. Contributing to this problem has been political action by the groups most threatened by aggressive responses to climate change, such as heavy manufacturing businesses, oil and gas companies, and elected officials closely tied to these industries (see Weber & Soderstom [Chapter 14] this volume). But average citizens also contribute to the problem by failing to modify their energy usage, at least until the price of gas skyrockets. Why do we make such egregious long-term mistakes?

Our positive illusions about the future are a likely culprit. In general, we tend to see ourselves, our environment, and the future in a more positive light than is objectively the case (Taylor and Brown 1988). Such positive illusions have benefits, as they can enhance self-esteem, increase commitment to action, and encourage persistence at difficult tasks and strength in the face of adversity (Taylor 1989). But, research also shows that positive illusions also reduce the quality of decision-making and prevent us from acting in time to address significant problems (Bazerman & Watkins 2004; Bazerman & Moore 2008).

We all hold a wide variety of positive illusions, yet two are particularly relevant to inattention to energy and climate change: unrealistic optimism and the illusion of control (Bazerman, Baron, & Shonk 2001). Unrealistic optimism can be described as the tendency to believe that one's own future will be better and brighter than that of others, and also better and brighter than an objective analysis would imply (Taylor 1989). Undergraduates and graduate students alike tend to expect that they are far more likely than reality suggests to graduate with honors, get a good, high-paying, and enjoyable job, and be featured in the newspaper. People also assume that they are less likely than their peers are to develop a drinking problem, get fired or divorced, or suffer from physical or mental ailments. In alignment with these tendencies, we believe and act as if the repercussions of climate change will be far less significant than the scientific community predicts.

We also tend to think that we can control uncontrollable events (Crocker 1982). Experienced dice players, for example, believe that "soft" throws help them roll lower numbers; gamblers also believe that the silence of observers affects their success (Langer 1975). Such illusory beliefs result from a false sense of control over the most uncontrollable of events. In the realm of climate change, this type of positive illusion translates to the common expectation that scientists will invent new technologies to solve the problem. Unfortunately, despite claims such as those made by Steven D. Levitt & Stephen J. Dubner in their best-selling book *Freakonomics* (Harper 2009), little concrete evidence exists that a new technology will solve the problem in time. In fact, such claims make the task of climatologist all the harder. As a result, the unrealistic illusion that a new technology will emerge serves as an ongoing excuse for the failure to act today.

Egocentrism

Who is to blame for climate change? As we saw in Copenhagen in 2009, parties are likely to have different assessments of their proportionate blame and responsibility for the problem. Emerging nations such as China and India tend to blame Western countries for their past and present industrialization and excessive consumption. Meanwhile, the US government failed to contribute to an agreement in part because China and India accepted little responsibility for their increasing contributions to climate change. Developed economies tend to blame emerging nations for burning rainforests and for unchecked economic and population expansion.

These opposing views are consistent with the common tendency to be egocentric—that is, to be biased in a self-serving manner (Babcock & Loewenstein 1997; Messick & Sentis 1983). A bias related to the positive illusions described above, egocentrism refers more specifically to the tendency to make self-serving judgments regarding allocations of blame and credit, a phenomenon that in turn leads people to differing assessments of what a fair solution to a problem might be.

Psychologists David Messick and Keith Sentis have found that we tend to first determine our preference for a certain outcome on the basis of self-interest. Next, we justify this preference on the basis of fairness by changing the importance of the attributes affecting what is fair (Messick & Sentis 1985). Thus, each government might indeed seek a climate change agreement that is fair to all parties, but its view of what is fair is biased by self-interest. Unfortunately, egocentrism leads all parties involved to believe that it is honestly fair for them to bear less responsibility for reversing climate change than an independent party would judge as fair. The problem is worsened not by a desire to be unfair but by an inability to view information objectively.

It is important to note that energy issues tend to be highly complex, lacking conclusive scientific and technological data. This uncertainty can allow egocentrism to dominate (Wade-Benzoni, Tenbrunsel, & Bazerman 1996; Wade-Benzoni et al. 2002). When data are clear and obvious, the mind's ability to manipulate fairness is limited; by contrast, extreme uncertainty exacerbates egocentrism. Philosopher John Rawls proposed that we should assess fairness under a "veil of ignorance"—that is, we ideally should judge a situation with no knowledge of the role we play in it (Rawls 1971). From Rawls's perspective, egocentrism describes the difference between our perceptions with and without the effects of a veil of ignorance.

The three biases just discussed—positive illusions, egocentrism, and the tendency to discount the future—can have an interactive effect. After insisting for decades that the scientists are flat-out wrong, many of those who have strongly opposed efforts to reduce climate change for self-interested reasons have changed their tune. No longer arguing that climate change does not exist, that humans do not contribute to climate change, or that others are to blame for the problem, they now argue that it would be too costly to respond to the problem. This transition in argument—from "There is no problem" to "We aren't responsible" to "It's too expensive to fix"—allows the current generation to receive small benefits in exchange for high costs to future generations. The opponents of climate change action may be correct about certain details and proposals, but little evidence suggests that they are interested in having their assertions tested through an objective, cost-benefit analysis.

OVERCOMING COGNITIVE BARRIERS

The three cognitive barriers we have just discussed are innate and pervasive roadblocks that prevent individuals from adopting energy-efficient behaviors and technologies. Decades of research confirming these biases paint a bleak picture of the difficulty of overcoming hard-wired patterns. However, recent scholars have begun to see a silver lining in our reliance on heuristics. Armed with the knowledge that people act in predictably irrational ways, we can structure choices in a way that optimally exploits our stubborn reliance on heuristics to gently nudge us toward better decisions. In particular, Richard Thaler & Cass Sunstein, the champions of such "choice architecture," have identified several ingenious ways of seamlessly designing choice environments to avoid systematic pitfalls in decision-making (2008).

The behavioral decision-making literature has shown the difficulty of fully debiasing human judgment (Milkman, Chugh, & Bazerman 2009). We see greater potential to design decision-making contexts in ways that lead to wiser choices (Thaler & Sunstein 2008). In the spirit of choice architecture, we propose harnessing the following tools to help citizens and policymakers overcome the pitfalls of our decision biases.

The power of defaults

Given innate cognitive barriers to environmental solutions to climate change, how can we guide people to adopt better behaviors? A simple intervention would be to make use of existing human tendencies. Notably, people have an exaggerated tendency to stick with a default option. Bill Samuelson & Richard Zeckhauser (1988) observed this effect when Harvard University switched from enrolling its faculty members in a default healthcare plan to allowing faculty members to choose their own plans. Faculty members overwhelmingly chose to remain with their existing plans; having become accustomed to the original default as a reference point, they were reluctant to switch from an established status quo.

An even more powerful demonstration of the power of defaults was conducted by Eric Johnson and Daniel Goldstein in their investigation of organ donation behavior (2003). Using the variation in timing of the shift in European Union countries from opt-in organ donation policies to opt-out policies that enrolled all citizens by default, the authors revealed a staggering difference caused simply by the established default. Countries with opt-in policies had donor consent rates of 4.25 to 27.5 percent; countries with opt-out policies had effective consent rates of 85.9 percent to 99.98 percent (Johnson & Goldstein 2003).

Given the established strength of defaults and the widespread reluctance to move away from them, we recommend that governments and organizations make greener options the norm with the goal of steering people toward better behavior. Maintaining the status quo turns out to be a powerful driver of choice precisely because it takes advantage of people's tendency to avoid choosing. In the consumer arena, car manufacturers that offer both hybrid and non-hybrid models could move toward making the hybrid model the default. Default settings for all home electronics, such as air conditioners, refrigerators, and computer monitors could be tuned to lower factory presets while still giving the user the same range of power.

Small changes across numerous domains could drive a move toward ever-more energy-conserving choices. In the process, individuals could become incrementally more tempered consumers of energy without making any explicit effort or even being consciously aware of foregone choices. Setting wise defaults is a powerful tool, as it demands little conscious effort within the individual to steer everyone toward better decision-making. However, such reliance on effortless influence is not sufficient to counteract a problem as staggeringly large as energy conservation.

Making energy costs salient

Despite their strong desire to maintain the status quo, people are not impervious to new information. Seligman & Darley (1977) conducted one of the first studies demonstrating the effect of feedback on energy consumption. The researchers gave homeowners feedback on their daily rates of electricity usage as a fraction of actual consumption over predicted consumption determined by usage history. Feedback was displayed four times a week over the course of a month. Compared to a control group that started with the same baseline levels of energy consumption, homeowners who received feedback used 10.5 percent less electricity.

More recent work highlights the specific form such feedback messages should take. P. Wesley Schultz (1999) studied the effect of feedback on community curbside recycling in 120 households, each of which received one of the following five treatments: a plea to recycle, a plea plus individual-level written feedback, a plea plus neighborhood-level written feedback, a plea plus information about recycling, or no treatment (control group). The results indicated significant increases from baseline recycling for groups that received feedback interventions (either individual or neighborhood-level information), but no observed increases in other conditions. This work suggests that feedback itself is not sufficient to change behavior and that behavior change produced through feedback needs to coexist with norm activation.

Furthermore, the units in which energy consumption is reported matters. Richard Larrick & Jack Soll (2008) exposed the fact that measuring fuel efficiency as miles per gallon (MPG) leads consumers to systematically misinterpret their automobile fuel usage. The "MPG illusion" refers to people's false belief that the amount of gas a car consumes decreases linearly as a function of a car's MPG, when the actual relationship is curvilinear. More specifically, the illusion leads one to assume that the same fuel savings occur under the following scenarios: trading a 10 MPG car for a 15 MPG car, and trading a 20 MPG car for a 25 MPG car. In actuality, the first scenario will save much more fuel than the second, holding miles driven constant. The 5 MPG improvement from 10 to 15 MPG has much more impact on fuel savings than the same 5 MPG improvement from 20 to 25 MPG.

Larrick & Soll (2008) offer gallons per mile (GPM) as an alternative unit measure of fuel efficiency that would more accurately reflect consumption and savings. Fuel consumption actually does decrease linearly with GPM, thereby correcting the misperception caused by the MPG illusion. Participants in Larrick & Soll's study more accurately chose fuel-efficient cars when consumption was expressed as GPM as opposed to MPG. While Europe, Canada, and Australia have already moved to volume over distance measures such as GPM, the United States, Japan, and India have yet to correct the MPG illusion.

Policy bundling to reduce loss aversion

One of the most robust findings in behavioral decision research is that losses loom larger than gains (Kahneman & Tversky 1979; Tversky & Kahneman 1991). People expect and experience the pain of a loss to be larger than the pleasure of an equal-sized gain. This suggests that legislators face an uphill battle when proposing legislation that has both costs and benefits, due to the expected overweighting of losses relative to gains. Wise environmental legislation has benefits that outweigh the costs, but people's tendency to overweight the costs can be a barrier to the passage of such legislation. Thus, we believe that strategies are necessary to help policymakers overcome their loss aversion.

Research cited earlier in this chapter highlights policy applications of loss aversion. A knowledge of people's tendency to view any deviation from the status quo as an aversive loss can help policymakers understand the enormous implications of defaults on important issues such as organ donation (Johnson & Goldstein 2003) and 401k participation (Madrian & Shea 2001). As noted, Johnson & Goldstein found that countries with an opt-out organ donation system have far greater donation rates than countries that require citizens to opt-in to participate. In the 401k context, employers can encourage retirement savings by assuming that new employees want to enroll in the retirement system, rather than requiring them to proactively sign up. Similarly, Samuelson & Zeckhauser's demonstration of faculty reluctance to switch from the default healthcare option (1988) shows that Harvard University faculty exhibits loss aversion. Older faculty members were unwilling to switch unless the possible benefits dramatically outweighed the possible costs, while new faculty experienced no such loss aversion.

We believe that knowledge of a strategy for overcoming loss aversion through bundling could also help policymakers pass better legislation. It is common for legislators to combine *unrelated* policies into a single bill to increase support for their legislation. Milkman et al. (2011) propose a different type of policy bundling technique, where the goal is to combine *related* bills in a way that reduces the harmful effects of the tendency to irrationally overweight losses relative to gains. They show that it is possible to combine one bill that has costs in Domain A (e.g. job losses in Town X) and benefits in Domain B (e.g. acres of forest preserved in Town X) with a matched bill that has the inverse structure: benefits in Domain A (e.g. job gains in Town Y) and costs in Domain B (e.g. acres of forest lost in Town Y).

Each piece of legislation in the Milkman et al. (2011) study was either a single bill or a combined bill in which the costs and benefits of two separate bills summed to generate net benefits in two domains. For example, participants were randomly assigned to view one of the following three bills:

- *Bill 1*: A law to establish new park areas in Community X where logging would be prohibited, costing the community 100 jobs but preserving 60,000 acres of forest;
- *Bill 2*: A law to eliminate a protected park area in Community Y, which would allow logging on 50,000 acres of previously protected forest, destroying that forest region but creating 125 new jobs;
- *Combined Bill*: A bundled bill presenting the proposals in both *Bill 1* and *Bill 2* as two components of a single piece of legislation.

Eighty-three percent of participants indicated they would vote for the *Combined Bill*, a significantly greater percentage than for either *Bill 1* (54%) or *Bill 2* (45%). Each individual bill suffered from loss aversion on the dimension where a sacrifice was required. This study demonstrated that policy bundling may be an effective tool for policymakers hoping to pass legislation that is advantageous overall, but that contains necessary costs

Milkman et al. (2011) confirm across a set of four legislative domains that this bundling technique increases support for bills that have both costs and benefits. Single pieces of legislation often fail to gain the necessary support because they are too narrowly specified, preventing legislators from overcoming loss aversion. Bundling may help legislators move beyond the irrational reluctance to support wise legislation that loss aversion can induce.

The benefit of slightly delaying wise policies

In many cases, passing wise environmental legislation consists of doing what we know we *should* do, but not what we *want* to do (Bazerman, Tenbrunsel, & Wade-Benzoni 1998). We know we should reduce our consumption of goods, conserve energy by reducing our use of fossil fuels, and generally avoid destroying our eco-system. The best-intentioned among us confidently expect that we will take such actions in the future (Epley & Dunning 2000). Yet, when the moment of decision arrives, we often fail to do what we established we should do. Why? Because at the moment of decision, we tend to experience intra-subjective conflict between what we should do and what we want to do (Tenbrunsel et al. 2011).

The tension that underlies these inconsistencies between expected preferences and actual behaviors has been metaphorically called the "multiple selves" phenomenon (see Schelling 1984). Bazerman, Tenbrunsel, & Wade-Benzoni (1998) describe the two selves as the "want" self and the "should" self. The former refers to what people affectively feel they want to do at the moment. The "should" self refers to what people more deliberatively think they should do. The want–should tension often, though not always, coincides with a tension between an individual's short-term and long-term interests.

Citizens are often asked to consider policies that trade short-term interests for long-term ones. An example of a contemporary issue that could benefit from steering a future choice towards the "should" option is the question of how to reduce domestic consumption of fossil fuels that contribute to global climate change. While the vast majority of citizens agree that the US needs to reduce its contribution to this global problem, most legislative efforts face stiff opposition. Rogers & Bazerman (2008) argue that one strategy that would help policymakers is to leverage the benefits of what they call "future lock-in." They show that people are more likely to choose based on the interests of their *should* selves when choosing in the present for the future than when choosing in the present for immediate implementation.

Many wise environmental policies require people to make a small-to-medium current sacrifice in return for larger benefits in the future (or to avoid larger future harms). Such proposals often fail because people overweigh the immediate costs of implementation. People are more likely to support environmentally friendly policies that have initial costs and long-term benefits when the policies will be implemented in the future—even in the near future—rather than today. While a slight delay may create inefficiency, large increases in support may be possible with even this delay in implementation. Effectively, the slight delay persuades people to look beyond the steep slope of their emotional dislike of incurring the immediate costs of implementation.

Rogers & Bazerman (2008) first identified a set of policies that people report feeling they *should* support but do not *want* to support. In a pre-study, participants were asked to evaluate the extent to which they felt they *should* support the policy and the extent to which they *wanted* to support the policy. A policy was classified as a *should* policy when participants reported feeling significantly more strongly that they *should* support than they *wanted* to support it. The policies that Rogers & Bazerman (2008) identified as *should* policies included a policy that would increase the price of gasoline to reduce pollution, and a policy limiting the number of fish that could be caught to reduce ocean overharvesting, along with three other non-environmentally relevant policies.

For the fish-harvesting issue, participants were asked to consider a policy to limit the amount of fish that could be caught by the fishing industry. The policy would increase the price of fish for all consumers, reduce the number of jobs in the fishing industry, protect the fish stocks in the oceans, and extend and sustain the survival of the fishing industry. Participants were randomly assigned to evaluate this proposal—either assuming that the policy would go into effect as soon as possible or four years from now. The latter condition dramatically increased the receptivity of the policy.

Rogers & Bazerman (2008) suggest that delaying the time to implementation may be a useful strategy for policymakers who are trying to bolster support for policies that people feel they *should* support but do not *want* to support. While the vast majority of citizens agree that the United States needs to do more to reduce its contribution to the global environmental problem, most proposed initiatives face strong opposition from legislators and citizens. Advocating for reforms that would go into effect in the future, policymakers might be able to leverage the benefits of the future lock-in effect to increase the proportion of people who support *should* reforms.

In some cases, applying future lock-in to public policy would be practically costless. Many laws are already designed to go into effect well into the future, yet are communicated in language that evokes immediate, self-interested concerns. Rogers & Bazerman

(2008) show that future lock-in can occur even under minimal conditions. They asked a national sample of subjects about how favorably they would view a policy that would increase the price of gas by 53 cents in two years, but which they would vote on in a few months. All participants in their study read the following:

If passed, this policy would reduce gas consumption by increasing the price of a gallon of gas by 53 cents. In doing this, the policy would reduce US contribution of carbon emissions into the atmosphere, which is one of the leading causes of global climate change. This policy would also reduce US dependence on oil from foreign countries, especially the Middle East. This 53 cent price increase in a gallon of gas would also make gas more expensive for Americans, and increase the costs of all forms of travel, especially driving. It would also probably cost jobs in the short term as the gas price increase would slow economic growth.

Half the participants read the policy would go into effect two years in the future; the other half of the participants read that it would be voted on by Congress as soon as possible. Participants were then asked "How strongly would you oppose or support this policy?" Participants who read the version wherein there was a two-year delay in enactment indicated that they supported the policy significantly more and were significantly more likely to vote for the policy than participants who read the version without mention of delay. Essentially, delaying implementation reduced the emotive reaction that comes from immediately facing losses.

Independent of how much support people give to *should* legislation that will take effect in the distant future, an additional benefit of delaying a policy's implementation is that it gives people time to prepare for the legislation's impact. For example, passing stronger fuel-efficiency legislation that would take effect a few years in the future allows vehicle owners to enjoy more years of value out of the vehicles they currently own and allows producers to gradually increase their capacity to manufacture more efficient vehicles.

One obvious risk of passing policies designed to take advantage of the future lock-in effect is that future legislatures could overturn the legislation. Rogers & Bazerman (2008) counter that this danger is not as risky as one might fear, since initially passing a policy is very different from overturning an existing one. Once implemented, citizens anticipate its instatement, and the policy gradually comes to be viewed as the default or status quo. As we reviewed above, defaults are powerful (Johnson & Goldstein 2003), and people are averse to changes from the status quo (Samuelson & Zeckhauser 1988).

REMAINING QUESTIONS: RESEARCH FRONTIER

While most research in the environmental management arena has focused on technology innovation and organizational change (Bazerman & Hoffman 1999), we have highlighted research relevant to environmental change that focuses on the minds of decision makers. We are not the first to do so. Related efforts have been published (Bazerman & Hoffman 1999; Bazerman, Baron, & Shonk 2001; Hoffman & Bazerman 2007; Hoffman & Henn 2008). And these related works cover other decision biases (e.g. mythical fixed-pie, overconfidence, etc.), and in some cases, focus on specific environmental issues (see Bazerman [2006] for an application to climate change). We continue to believe that powerful insights can be obtained by thinking about the faulty decisions that negatively affect the environment. The goal of the current paper has been to highlight exemplars of the decision effects that we see as most important, and to focus on how to change environmentally destructive decisions.

We admit to a long history of disappointment in the ability of decision researchers to debias judgment (Fischhoff 1982; Bazerman & Moore 2008). Nevertheless, we believe in leveraging the insights of behavioral decision researchers to change systems in a manner that takes positive advantage of the mind's natural tendencies. Specifically this involves changing the choice environment by framing choices in ways that would advantage pro-environmental interventions. The choice architecture perspective that we have overviewed is in its infancy, and its application to environment issues remains minimal. We view it as a significant opportunity.

One popular myth that future research could help debunk is the myth that there is a battle between the different techniques of behavioral economists and neoclassical economists in designing interventions to help people and policymakers make wiser decisions. Though the two groups recommend very different solutions for the same problems (e.g. neoclassical economists rely on increasing prices—both sticker price and opportunity costs—to discourage behaviors with high environmental costs), there is great benefit to combining the recommendations of both groups. The different recommendations for the same problem from behavioral and neoclassical thinkers are oftentimes complementary instead of competing. One specific example could be decreasing gasoline consumption by increasing the price of gasoline (neoclassical approach) as well as measuring fuel efficiency by gallons per mile to more accurately reflect gasoline consumption (behavioral approach). The two approaches do not have to be in opposition; rather, the behavioral approach can actually be used to supercharge the incentive-compatible recommendations of the neoclassical approach.

Methodologically, we also see an important change coming from behavioral decision research and behavioral economics. Over the past quarter century, most of this research has been conducted in the lab, and pure experimental methods have been used. While we believe lab research has proven to generalize amazingly well (Bazerman & Moore 2008), it is also clear that strong evidence from the field can create a powerful desire to change. One interesting observation from behavioral economists is that if you give a good idea to an organization, it should have an interest in working with researchers to test the idea in order to use and diffuse it more broadly. Ideally, field experiments should be conducted so that causality can be inferred. We believe that this will be very useful in helping organizations and nations think about wise interventions in the future.

One question in particular that could benefit from field evidence is which behaviors leading to energy conservation are easiest to change. We have decent measures of how behavioral change can impact our energy footprints, but relatively poor measures of how likely people are to engage in such behaviors. Researchers and practitioners are natural partners in helping each other answer this type of question. By identifying the behaviors that are ripest for change—the lowest-hanging fruit with regard to intervention—we will be able to gain the most impact from their respective efforts.

REFERENCES

Ackerman, F. & Heinzerling, L. (2004). *Priceless: On Knowing the Price of Everything and the Value of Nothing*. New York: New Press.

Babcock, L., Lowenstein, G., & Issacharoff, S. (1997). "Creating Convergence: Debiasing Biased Litigants," *Law and Social Inquiry Journal of the American Bar Foundation*, 22(4): 913–925.

Baron, J., Bazerman, M., & Shonk, K. (2006). "Enlarging the Societal Pie through Wise Legislation: A Psychological Perspective," *Perspectives on Psychological Science*, 1(2): 123–132.

Bazerman, M. H. (2006). "Climate Change as a Predictable Surprise," *Climatic Change*, 1–15.

——, Baron, J., & Shonk, K. (2001). *You Can't Enlarge the Pie: Six Barriers to Effective Government*. New York: Basic Books.

Bazerman, M. H. & Hoffman, A. J. (1999). "Sources of Environmentally Destructive Behavior: Individual, Organizational, and Institutional Perspectives," in R. I. Sutton and B. M. Staw (eds.), *Research in Organizational Behavior*, Volume XXI. Stamford, CT: JAI Press.

—— & Moore, D. (2008). *Judgment in Managerial Decision Making*, 7th ed. New York: Wiley.

—— Tenbrunsel, A. E., & Wade-Benzoni, K. A. (1998). "Negotiating with Yourself and Losing: Understanding and Managing Conflicting Internal Preferences," *Academy of Management Review*, 23(2): 225–241.

—— & Watkins, M. D. (2004). *Predictable Surprises: The Disasters You Should Have Seen Coming and How to Prevent Them*, Boston: Harvard Business School Press.

Benabou, R. & Tirole, J. (2006). "Incentives & Prosocial Behavior," *American Economic Review*, 96(5): 1652–1678.

Crocker, J. (1982). "Biased Questions in Judgment of Covariation Studies," *Personality & Social Psychology Bulletin*, 8(2): 214–220.

Epley, N. & Dunning, D. (2000). "Feeling 'Holier than Thou': Are Self-Serving Assessments Produced by Errors in Self- or Social Prediction," *Journal of Personality and Social Psychology*, 79(6): 861–875.

Fischhoff, B. (1982). "Debiasing," in D. Kahneman, P. Slovic & A. Tversky (eds.), *Judgment under Uncertainty: Heuristics and Biases*, Cambridge: Cambridge University Press.

Gimbel, R., Strosberg, M. A., Lehrman, S. E., Gefenas, E., & Taft, F. (2003). *Progress in Transplantation*, 13(1): 17–23.

Gore, A. (1992). *Earth in the Balance*, New York: Penguin.

Hoffman, A., & Bazerman, M. H. (2007). "Changing Practices on Sustainability: Understanding and Overcoming the Organizational and Psychological Barriers to Action," in S. Sharma,

M. Starik & B. Husted (eds.), *Organizations and the Sustainability Mosaic*, Edward Elgar Publishing,

Hoffman, A. & Henn, R. (2008). "Overcoming the Social and Psychological Barriers to Green Building" *Organization & Environment*, 21(4): 390–419.

Johnson, E. J. & Goldstein, D. G. (2003). "Do Defaults save Lives?" *Science*, 302(5649): 1338–1339.

Kahneman, D. & Tversky, A. (1979). "Prospect Theory: An Analysis of Decision under Risk" *Econometrica*, 47: 263–291.

Langer, E. J. (1975). "The Illusion of Control," *Journal of Personality & Social Psychology*, 32(2): 311–328.

Larrick, R. P. & Soll, J. B. (2008). "The MPG Illusion," *Science*, 320 (5883): 1593–1594.

Levitt, S. D. & Dubner, S. J. (2009). *Freakonomics: A Rogue Economist Explores the Hidden Side of Everything*. New York: Harper Perennial.

Loewenstein, G. & Thaler, R. H. (1989). "Anomalies: Intertemporal choice," *Journal of Economic Perspectives*, 3(4): 181–193.

Madrian, B. C. & Shea, D. F. (2001). "The Power of Suggestion: Inertia in 401(k) Participation and Savings Behavior," *Quarterly Journal of Economics*, 116(4): 1149–1187.

Messick, D. M. & Sentis, K. P. (1983). "Fairness, "Preference, and Fairness Biases," in D. M. Messick & K. S. Cook (eds) *Equity Theory, Psychological and Sociological Preferences*, New York: Praeger, 66–94,

—— (1985). "Estimating Social and Nonsocial Utility Functions from Ordinal Data." *European Journal of Social Psychology*, 15(4): 389–399.

Milkman, K. L., Mazza, M. C., Shu, L. L., Tsay, C., & Bazerman, M. H. (2011). "Policy Bundling to Overcome Loss Aversion: A Method for Improving Legislative Outcomes." Organizational Behavior and Human Decision Processes. In press

—— Chugh, D., & Bazerman, M. H. (2009). "How Can Decision Making Be Improved?" *Perspectives on Psychological Science*, 4(4): 379–383.

Rawls, J. (1971). *A Theory of Justice*. Cambridge, MA: Harvard University Press.

Rogers, T., & Bazerman, M. H. (2008). "Future Lock-in: Future Implementation Increases Selection of 'Should' Choices," *Organizational Behavioral and Human Decision Processes*, 106(1): 1–20.

Samuelson, W. F. & Zeckhauser, R. (1988). "Status Quo Bias in Decision Making," *Journal of Risk and Uncertainty*, 1(1): 7–59.

Schelling, T. C. (1984). *Choice and Consequence: Perspectives of an Errant Economist*. Cambridge, MA: Harvard University Press.

Schultz, P. W. (1999). "Changing Behavior with Normative Feedback Interventions: A Field Experiment on Curbside Recycling," *Basic and Applied Social Psychology*, 21(1): 25–36.

Seligman, C. & Darley, J. M. (1977). "Feedback as a Means of Decreasing Residential Energy Consumption," *Journal of Applied Psychology*, 62(4): 363–368.

Taylor, S. E. (1989). *Positive Illusions: Creative Self-Deception and the Healthy Mind*. New York: Basic Books.

—— & Brown, J. D. (1988). "Illusion and Well-Being: A Social Psychological Perspective on Mental Health," *Psychological Bulletin*, 103(2): 193–210.

Tenbrunsel, A. E., Diekmann, K. A., Wade-Benzoni, K. A., & Bazerman, M. H. (2011). "Why We Aren't as Ethical as We Think We Are: A Temporal Explanation," in B. M. Staw and A. Brief (eds.), *Research in Organizational Behavior*.

Thaler, R. H. & Sunstein, C. R. (2008). *Nudge: improving Decisions about Health, Wealth, and Happiness.* New Haven, CT: Yale University Press.

Tversky, A., & Kahneman, D. (1991). "Loss Aversion in Riskless Choice: A Reference-Dependent Model," *Quarterly Journal of Economics*, 106(4): 1039–1061.

—— —— (2002). "Judgment under uncertainty: Heuristics and biases," in D. J. Levitin (ed.), *Foundations of Cognitive Psychology: Core Readings*, Cambridge, MA: MIT Press, 585–600.

Wade-Benzoni, K. A. (1999). "Thinking about the Future: An Intergenerational Perspective on the Conflict and Compatibility between Economic and Environmental Interests, *American Behavioral Scientist*, 42(8): 1393–1405.

—— Tenbrunsel, A. E., & Bazerman, M. H. (1996). "Egocentric Interpretations of Fairness in Asymmetric, Environmental Social Dilemmas: Explaining Harvesting Behavior and the Role of Communication," *Organizational Behavior & Human Decision Processes*, 67(2): 111–126.

Wade-Benzoni, K. A. Okumura, T., Brett, J. M., Moore, D. A. Tenbrunsel, A. E., & Bazerman, M. H. (2002). "Cognitions and Behavior in Asymmetric Social Dilemmas: A Comparison of Two Cultures," *Journal of Applied Psychology*, 87: 87–95.

CHAPTER 10

INTERGENERATIONAL BENEFICENCE AND THE SUCCESS OF ENVIRONMENTAL SUSTAINABILITY INITIATIVES IN ORGANIZATIONAL CONTEXTS

LEIGH PLUNKETT TOST
AND KIMBERLY A. WADE-BENZONI

ENVIRONMENTAL sustainability refers to a status that an organization achieves when it functions such that the environmental benefits (e.g. natural resources) that will be passed on to future generations are not decreased, the environmental burdens (e.g. toxic waste) to future others are not increased, and the capacity of individual stakeholders to reach their potential is progressively enhanced. In order to achieve this status, it is crucial that organizational decision makers take a long-range temporal perspective on the activities of the organization and come to place a positive value on protecting and promoting the interests and needs of future others. In this chapter, we discuss research on psychological factors that impact the likelihood that individuals will value outcomes to future others and consequently sacrifice their present self-interest to ensure environmental sustainability.

To examine this issue, we begin by describing how individuals psychologically experience dilemmas in which they face a tradeoff between their own self-interests in the present and the interests of future others. In doing so, we describe the psychological

Table 10.1 Negative and positive factors impacting intergenerational beneficence

Negative influences	Mechanisms	How to Counter-Act	Areas for Future Research
Intergenerational distance (interpersonal + intertemporal distance)	Distance-based discounting	Promote intergenerational affinity and intergenerational identification	What might be the effects of loosening some of the boundary conditions that have characterized previous research in this area? What if decision-makers are not immediately removed from the social context but instead have some chance of experiencing both the present and future consequences of their decisions?
Positive influences	**Mechanisms**	**How to Cultivate**	**Areas for Future Research**
Reciprocity	Social norms	Emphasize positive behavior from previous generations	What moderates the likelihood that norms of intergenerational reciprocity are adhered to? When might the behavior of previous generations be viewed as an example of "what not to do"? Does greater intertemporal distance diminish the modeling effect of previous generations? Or does the modeling effect of previous generations' behavior gain in import and stature as intertemporal distance increases, because it is endowed with a greater symbolic and tradition-based import?
Power	Feelings of social responsibility	Promote norms of social responsibility; emphasize the power of present decision-makers	How would the dynamics of power change if present decision-makers do not have unilateral control over present decisions? How might these dynamics change if multiple present decision-makers must negotiate to reach a collective decision about allocations to the present vs. future?
Legacy Motive	Death awareness prompts symbolic immortality striving	Promote legacy-building activities across organizational levels	What factors activate the legacy motive? What determines the content of the legacies that individuals seek to create?

dynamics that impact individuals' inclinations to sacrifice their present self-interest to protect or promote the interests of future others (See Table 10.1 for summary). In addition, we describe the implications of this research for how organizations can promote environmental sustainability.

THE PSYCHOLOGICAL APPROACH TO STUDYING INTERGENERATIONAL BENEFICENCE

Intergenerational dilemmas are decisions in which the interests of present decision-makers are in conflict with the interests of future others. A central goal of psychological research on intergenerational dilemmas has been to identify the factors that impact the likelihood that decision-makers will engage in intergenerational beneficence, which occurs when a present decision-maker sacrifices his or her present interests for the interests of future others. This area of research has adopted a broader definition of "generation" than the conventional use of the term as applying to a twenty- to thirty-year timeframe within society and family contexts. Instead, psychological research on intergenerational behavior has conceived of a generation as consisting of any individual or group that occupies a role for a limited time period and then transitions out of that role when another individual or group transitions in (see Wade-Benzoni 2002a for a thorough discussion of how generations are defined in this research). In this sense, past, present, and future cohorts of organizational members can be thought of as different "generations" in organizations. In addition, the time delay can be of any length—organizational members may hold their roles for weeks, years, or decades.

Thus, in research on intergenerational dilemmas, the critical defining features of the decision-making situation include a conflict of interests between present actors and future others, as well as some degree of time delay between the decisions made in the present and the outcomes experienced by future others. In this sense, intergenerational dilemmas are marked by two critical types of psychological distance: the social distance that separates the decision-maker from the future others who will also experience the impact of the decision, and the temporal distance between the timing of the decision and the timing of the impacts to future others. This intersection of social and temporal distance creates the features of intergenerational dilemmas that make the psychological experience of those decisions particularly unique. Some of these features include a lack of direct reciprocity across generations, uncertainty about the outcomes to future others, and power asymmetry between present actors and future others.

For these reasons, previous research on the psychological dynamics of intergenerational decisions has been characterized by two primary boundary conditions. First, previous research on intergenerational dilemmas has focused on decision contexts in which the present generation has complete and unilateral decision-making power over decisions with consequences for future generations. In other words, future generations have no voice in these decisions. Second, previous work in this area has examined situations in which social actors are removed from the social exchange context over time, and thus do not benefit or suffer from the later consequences of their prior decisions. A key implication of this second boundary condition is that future generations do not have an opportunity to directly reciprocate the good or bad given to them by prior generations. Thus, these boundary conditions have differentiated the study of intergenerational dilemmas from more typical inter-group situations in which other parties have their own voice, and from traditional social dilemmas in which the decision-maker remains part of the collective when the consequences of his or her decisions materialize. One direction for future research on intergenerational beneficence is, therefore, to consider how the psychological dynamics of intergenerational decisions might change when these boundary conditions are loosened. We discuss some of these potential directions below, but first we focus on reviewing previous research in this area.

TWO DIMENSIONS OF DISTANCE

Intergenerational dilemmas are characterized by a combination of interpersonal and intertemporal dimensions. In other words, in intergenerational dilemmas, the decisions and behaviors of one person or group affect outcomes to another person or group (the interpersonal dimension), and actions in the present affect outcomes in the future (the intertemporal dimension). These two dimensions represent domains of psychological distance, which is the psychological feeling of being removed from any direct experience of reality or of lacking a sense of psychological immediacy (Bjorkman 1984; Henderson, Trope, & Carnevale 2006; Liberman, Trope, & Stephan 2007; Loewenstein 1996, Trope & Liberman 2003; Wong & Bagozzi 2005).

In the research we review below, we describe how the independent effects of these two types of distance in intergenerational contexts can combine to diminish intergenerational beneficence, and thus lead to intergenerational discounting.

Interpersonal distance

Interpersonal psychological distance is a function of the extent to which an individual experiences an affinity with another individual or group (Hernandez, Chen, & Wade-Benzoni 2006). Affinity refers to a combination of perceived oneness, empathy, and perspective-taking and is a function of the extent to which the decision maker feels empathetic toward, and connected with, the others who will be impacted by the decision (Wade-Benzoni 2008). When interpersonal psychological distance is great, and thus affinity is low, decision-makers tend to place less weight on the consequences of their decisions for others relative to the weight they put on the consequences to themselves (Loewenstein 1996). This phenomenon is referred to as social discounting (see Shu & Bazerman [Chapter 9] this volume), which occurs when the value of a good is discounted when it accrues to others rather than to the self (Loewenstein, Thompson, & Bazerman 1989; Rachlin & Raineri 1992). For example, an individual may be willing to work for thirty minutes to acquire $5 for him- or herself, but that same individual may only be willing to work for a few minutes to acquire the same amount of money for another person. Critically, research into social discounting has demonstrated that greater levels of interpersonal distance lead to greater degrees of social discounting (Jones & Rachlin 2006). Given that interpersonal psychological distance is often high in intergenerational contexts (e.g. the present decision-maker may have never met the future others who will be impacted by the decision), social discounting is likely to have a substantial negative effect on intergenerational beneficence.

Indeed, recent research has provided some support for the presence of this effect in intergenerational contexts. In a study based on the real-life crisis in the ocean's fisheries, Wade-Benzoni (2008) documented a positive relationship between affinity for future fishers and intergenerational beneficence in decisions regarding present fish consumption. Affinity with future generations appeared to cause the outcomes to future generations to feel more immediate and personal. Thus, when affinity with future others is high, decision-makers may come to conceive of future others as part of themselves, which consequently aligns self-interest with the interests of the future others, reduces psychological distance, and promotes intergenerational beneficence (Wade-Benzoni 2008). When this type of affinity is low, however, the effects of social distance and social discounting have a negative impact on intergenerational beneficence.

This phenomenon of social distance also contributes negatively to the likelihood of intergenerational beneficence by exacerbating egocentric perceptions of fairness. A substantial amount of previous research has documented that when the interests of two individuals or groups are opposed, individuals who are personally involved in the situation exhibit biased perceptions of the fairness of potential and actual outcomes, such that they view their preferred outcome as the fairest outcome (Babcock et al. 1995; Bazerman & Neale 1982; Neale & Bazerman 1983; Wade-Benzoni, Tenbrunsel, & Bazerman 1996; Walster, Walster, & Berscheid 1978). This bias emerges due to the dual motivations that tend to characterize individuals in social contexts. Specifically, on the one hand, individuals are motivated to perceive and present themselves as fair-minded, ethical, and generous. On the other hand, individuals are also motivated to promote and protect their own self-interest by obtaining benefits for themselves and avoiding burdens. The power of biased perceptions of fairness lies in the fact that this type of bias allows individuals to fulfill both motives simultaneously because the bias produces the perception that the self-interested action, outcome, or interpretation of events is also the most ethically legitimate one. As a consequence, the decision-maker is freed from the dilemmatic aspect of the decision and can move forward to pursue his or her self-interests unimpeded by concerns about justice, ethics, or fairness. Research has indicated that, in making these types of judgments, individuals typically do not realize that their judgments are characterized by a self-serving bias

(Wade-Benzoni et al. 2002). Furthermore, greater levels of social distance are expected to exacerbate this tendency.

Previous research on intergenerational beneficence has demonstrated the persistence of egocentric biases in intergenerational contexts. Specifically, findings from a recent study indicate that individuals judge lower allocations to future generations to be fairer when those individuals are part of the current generation of decision-makers than when they are part of the future generation who experiences the consequences of those decisions (Wade-Benzoni et al. 2008). Thus, this research shows that members of present generations exhibit egocentric biases in their interpretations of intergenerational allocations (in comparison to neutral third-party judges), and these biases in turn produce a tendency to act in favor of the self and against the interests of future others (Wade-Benzoni et al. 2008).

Intertemporal distance

Not only are present decision-makers socially removed from the future others who will be impacted by their decisions, they are also temporally removed. That is, in intergenerational contexts, there is not only an effect of the social distance between the decision-maker and others, there is also a time delay that occurs between the decision and the consequences to others. In this sense, future others are doubly removed from the decision-maker's immediate experience. The intertemporal dimension of intergenerational dilemmas produces two key features that can exacerbate egocentric biases on the part of present decision-makers: time discounting and uncertainty.

First, extensive research has shown that time delay between decisions and consequences can have systematic effects on resource allocations. Specifically, research on intertemporal choice demonstrates that people discount the value of resources that will be consumed in the future, exhibiting an inherent preference for immediate over postponed benefits or consumption (see Loewenstein 1992 for a review). This intertemporal form of discounting occurs because long time horizons limit cognition, such that potential decision outcomes feel less realistic and become less salient and harder to discriminate as time delay increases (Pigou 1920; von Bohm-Bawerk 1889). Consequently, time delay leads people to have greater difficulty fully envisioning and understanding the consequences of their decisions. In addition to these types of cognitive limitations, motivational effects, such as the immediate pain of deferral, can also contribute to intertemporal discounting. Consistent with research on intertemporal personal choice, research on intergenerational dilemmas suggests that a greater time delay between decisions made in the present and the consequences of those decisions to future others tends to diminish the likelihood of intergenerational beneficence (Wade-Benzoni 1999; 2008).

Second, as intertemporal distance between decisions and outcomes increase, there is inevitably greater uncertainty about the nature and extent of the future impacts of present decisions. Specifically, as time delay increases, the expected or intended outcomes of present actions can be disrupted by unexpected events. For example, environmental scholars have suggested that the consequences of continued emissions of greenhouse gases could range from severe global warming to barely any environmental changes, to even a cooling of certain areas of the globe. Because of this type of outcome uncertainty, decision-makers often exhibit an optimistic bias in decisions that involve time delay, in which they assume that the future outcomes of their decisions will be unrealistically positive. This optimism bias can exacerbate the dynamics of egocentric interpretations of fairness. Specifically, when present decision-makers are faced with a decision of foregoing present benefits to preserve benefits for future others, they tend to evaluate the prospective availability of the benefits in question for future others as much higher than objective evidence indicates. In this way, individuals capitalize on temporal uncertainty by assuming that outcomes that favor themselves will also produce positive outcomes in the future (Budescu, Rapoportd, & Suleiman 1990; Gustafsson, Biel, & Garling 1999; 2000; Weinstein 1980).

Intergenerational discounting

We refer to the combined effects of intertemporal and social discounting described above as intergenerational discounting, which is the tendency to prefer smaller benefits for the self in the present as opposed to larger benefits for others in the future (Wade-Benzoni 1999; 2002a; 2008). Thus, the degree of intergenerational discounting reflects how much the interests of future generations are represented in current decisions. As intergenerational discounting increases, the interest of future others are valued less relative to the interests of the self in the present, and therefore greater levels of intergenerational discounting produce lower levels of intergenerational beneficence.

Critically, the effects of intergenerational discounting are often magnified because the consequences to future generations often escalate over time. Specifically, future generations can experience more serious negative consequences as a result of the present generation leaving burdens for them than would be experienced by the present generation if they had handled the burdens themselves. For example, the negative impact of dumping toxic waste can escalate over time as it seeps into ground water and contaminates broader water sources. Similarly, when a present generation foregoes present benefits in order to maintain those benefits for future generations, the positive impacts can accumulate over time, as in the case of long-term financial investments. This escalation of consequences can add intensity to the psychological dynamics of intergenerational dilemmas.

Thus, intergenerational discounting represents a combined effect of intertemporal and social discounting and its consequences can escalate over time. Consequently, the distinct negative effects of the two different dimensions of discounting on beneficence may be compounded in intergenerational contexts, leading to quite high levels of intergenerational discounting. In other words, when decision-makers experience both the effects of time delay and social distance, they may be particularly inclined to prioritize their present self-interests over the interests of future others. Research on the psychological dynamics of intergenerational decision making, however, has demonstrated that the interaction of these two dimensions of distance may not necessarily be additive in a negative fashion under all circumstances (see Wade-Benzoni & Tost 2009 for a review). Specifically, the combination of these two dimensions of distance can produce unexpected effects that are unique to intergenerational dilemmas and have the potential to increase the likelihood that individuals will be inclined to promote and protect the interests of future others, as we explain below.

POSITIVE INFLUENCES
ON INTERGENERATIONAL BENEFICENCE

While the combined effects of intertemporal and social discounting seem to imply that prospects for promoting environmental sustainability in organizational contexts are fairly bleak, research on intergenerational beneficence has also shown that norms established by previous generations can sometimes overpower these discounting tendencies, and that there are even circumstances in which the effects of time delay can be reversed. In the following sections, we review some of this research, pointing to directions for future research on these effects.

Reciprocity

As one of the most fundamental norms in social relationships (Gouldner 1960; Haidt 2004; McLean Parks 1997), considerations of reciprocity naturally emerge from the interpersonal dimension of intergenerational dilemmas. The special form it takes in intergenerational contexts, however, is a function of the combined intertemporal and interpersonal dimensions. Reciprocity typically refers to the direct and mutual exchange of benefits or burdens characterized by a quid pro quo mentality (e.g. Trivers 1971). Theorists have typically identified the absence of any potential for direct reciprocity in intergenerational contexts (due to the time delay between decisions and outcomes) as a major inhibitor of intergenerational beneficence (e.g. Care 1982). Specifically, because future generations often cannot reciprocate the behavior of the present generation, the present generation is able to make a self-interested decision without considering the potential for retribution from future others. Psychological research on intergenerational dilemmas, however, has shown that reciprocity can take on a more generalized form in intergenerational contexts such that people can "reciprocate" the good or bad left to them by previous generations by behaving similarly to the next generation (Wade-Benzoni 2002a). In this way, individuals can behave toward future others similarly to how past others behaved toward them, thus passing on the benefits (or burdens) to future generations as a matter of retrospective obligation (or retaliation) for the good (or bad) received from past generations. This type of reciprocity is referred to as "intergenerational reciprocity" (Wade-Benzoni 2002a). Intergenerational reciprocity can thus function as either a barrier to, or a facilitator of, intergenerational beneficence, depending on the behavior of prior generations. In addition, the phenomenon of intergenerational reciprocity means that the norms set by a previous generation of decision makers can set a powerful example with effects carrying over many generations.

Previous research on intergenerational behavior documents the phenomenon of intergenerational reciprocity and further suggests that a combination of mechanisms underlie this effect—including reciprocal obligation and the establishment of an intergenerational norm (Wade-Benzoni 2002a). Specifically, consistent with notions of generalized exchange reciprocity, this research indicates that a key motivation of intergenerational beneficence is a sense of moral obligation and a need to "repay the debt" in the cases in which the prior generation was particularly generous. In addition, these studies have indicated that the behavior of previous generations can function as a source of information about what might constitute appropriate intergenerational behavior.

While this previous research has done a great deal to establish the basic phenomenon of intergenerational reciprocity and to suggest some mechanisms that underlie it, a number of critical questions remain open for further inquiry. For example, while previous research has established that the behavior of previous generations functions as a model that is emulated by present decision-makers, researchers do not yet understand when this modeling effect is likely to emerge and when it is likely to be ignored. For example, when will the behavior of previous generations be viewed as an example of "what not to do"? Similarly, does greater intertemporal distance diminish the modeling role of previous generations? Or does the modeling effect of previous generations' behavior gain in import and stature as intertemporal distance increases, because it is endowed with a greater symbolic and tradition-based import?

Power

As described above, outcome uncertainty associated with time delay between decisions and consequences can have a negative effect on intergenerational beneficence. It is important to point out, however, that there are some circumstances in which uncertainty can have a positive effect. Specifically, research has indicated that if the uncertainty involves not just a question of how much future generations will benefit from a decision, but instead involves a question of whether or not they will benefit at all, the effect of uncertainty can become positive (Wade-Benzoni et al. 2008). This research suggest that this effect of such dramatic levels of outcome uncertainty may emerge because this degree of uncertainty heightens decision-makers' awareness of the nature of the power asymmetry that characterizes the decision context, and causes decision-makers to feel a sense of social responsibility for the outcomes that accrue to others (Tost, Hernandez, & Wade-Benzoni 2008; Wade-Benzoni et al. 2008).

These unexpected findings with respect to outcome uncertainty led researchers to examine the role of power in intergenerational decisions in more detail. Indeed, power asymmetry is a critical feature of intergenerational contexts that contributes substantially to the psychological dynamics of intergenerational decisions (Wade-Benzoni 2002a; 2003; Wade-Benzoni et al. 2008). As described above, in intergenerational dilemmas, present decision-makers may have complete control over how resources will be allocated to subsequent generations, and future generations do not have an opportunity to reciprocate that behavior. This power asymmetry is even more dramatic given that, in intergenerational situations, the consequences of decisions tend to increase over time. As a result, the individuals who have control over the decision (present decision-makers) are not the individuals with the most at stake (future generations). In this sense, the powerlessness of future generations, and the power of present decision-makers, is intensified.

For these reasons, an understanding of how the psychological effects of power might impact intergenerational beneficence is critical. Do people who feel a high level of power feel an obligation to protect the interests of future others? Or does power instead contribute to feelings of entitlement that would lead powerholders to promote their own interests at the expense of the interests and needs of future others? Previous research in non-intergenerational contexts has produced mixed findings regarding the relationship between power and moral and ethical behavior. For example, research has demonstrated that the experience of social power leads to enhanced views of the self and derogation of others (Georgesen & Harris 1998; 2000; Kipnis 1972; Sachdev & Bourhis 1985), as well as a diminished capacity for empathizing with and considering the perspectives of others (Galinsky et al. 2006; Van Kleef et al. 2008). Other work, however, has documented a positive effect of power on feelings of social responsibility (Frieze & Boneva 2001; Wade-Benzoni et al. 2008). For example, research on dictator games, a paradigm used by experimental economists in which decision-makers have unilateral choice about the outcomes to themselves and others (e.g., Bolton, Katok, & Zwick 1998; Forsythe et al. 1994; Hoffman, McCabe, & Smith 1996), has suggested that extreme forms of power imbalance can heighten feelings of social responsibility and produce a prosocial motivation to protect the interests of powerless others (Handgraaf et al. 2008).

The surprising finding that extreme outcome uncertainty (i.e. levels of outcome uncertainty that include the possibility of complete resource depletion) in intergenerational contexts can lead to feelings of social responsibility and beneficence behavior toward future others suggests that time delay between decisions and outcomes may be another moderating factor that impacts the relationship between power and moral behavior. Indeed, Wade-Benzoni et al. (2008) found that priming present decision-makers with power, similar to the effect of high levels of outcome uncertainty, led to greater feelings of social responsibility and beneficence toward future generations.

Importantly, the level of power of present decision-makers is not inherently tied to the powerlessness of future others, and recognition of this disconnect points to important avenues of future research in this area. For example, future others may remain powerless, but present decision-makers may be beholden to the interests of other present actors. In such situations, present decision-makers may have to negotiate with other present parties in order to settle on a course of action with implications for future others. How might present decision-makers' obligations to other contemporary stakeholders impact feelings of responsibility or beneficent behavior toward future others? Does this type of dynamic diminish awareness of power asymmetry, thereby diminishing the potential for feelings of responsibility and intergenerational beneficence, or instead do such situations increase decision-makers' perspective taking and empathy for future others, increasing intergenerational beneficence?

Legacies

A legacy is an enduring meaning attached to one's identity and manifested in the impact that one has on others beyond the temporal confounds of the lifespan. Thus, legacies are intergenerational phenomena, because they are characterized by both intertemporal and interpersonal dimensions: when an individual leaves a legacy, that individual has established an impact that will persist into the future and have an effect on other individuals in some way. Recent theory and research on the nature of the motive to establish an enduring legacy has suggested that the legacy motive can encourage intergenerational beneficence if properly harnessed in organizational contexts (Fox, Tost, & Wade-Benzoni 2010).

The legacy motive is closely tied to the concept of generativity, which refers to the desire to invest one's substance in forms of life and work that will outlive the self (Kotre 1984) by exhibiting a concern and commitment to the well-being of future generations (McAdams & de St. Aubin 1992). Building on this view of generativity, we conceptualize the legacy motive as the personal motive to engage in generative action for the purpose of achieving a feeling of symbolic immortality. Symbolic immortality refers to the sense of self-extension that individuals achieve when they create a lasting legacy by affiliating themselves with other individuals, institutions, and value systems that will outlive them. In this sense, the motive to leave a positive legacy involves a basic human desire to be part of the larger progression of life, to have a positive impact on the world, and to feel as though one has mattered. Thus, the legacy motive involves a desire to establish meaning to one's life, and the legacy itself functions as the carrier of that meaning, extending the self into the future through one's impacts on future others.

A great deal of social psychological research has demonstrated that people desire personal meaning in their lives (Heine, Proulx, & Vohs 2006; Keyes, Shmotkin, & Ryff 2002; McGregor & Little 1998; Ryff & Keyes 1995; Steger et al. 2008; Zika & Chamberlain 1992). Heine and colleagues (2006) argue that meaning is "what links people, places, objects, and ideas to one another in expected and predictable ways" (89). Building on this conceptualization of meaning, one's personal life meaning can be thought of as a set of linkages between one's existence and something external to the self, such as other individuals, institutions, or value systems. In this sense, the pursuit of meaning is the pursuit of linkages between the self and things external to the self.

Consistent with research on generativity and meaning, theory on intergenerational behavior has held that intergenerational beneficence can function as a form of symbolic self-extension and generative behavior, and that intergenerational beneficence is consequently enhanced when individuals are motivated to leave a positive legacy (Wade-Benzoni 2002b; 2006). This insight prompts an important question: what activates the legacy motive?

A primary avenue of research into this issue has focused on the role of death awareness as a source of activation of the legacy motive. Specifically, research has suggested that awareness of one's own mortality activates in individuals a desire to connect the self to future others. In other words, death awareness activates the legacy motive, which in turn inspires intergenerational beneficence as a mechanism for establishing a lasting legacy. Indeed, in a recent series of experiments, Wade-Benzoni and her colleagues (Wade-Benzoni et al. 2010) found that death awareness reversed the effect of time delay on resource allocations in intergenerational contexts. In other words, in the absence of death awareness, time delay between decisions and outcomes to future others led to diminished intergenerational beneficence. When individuals were reminded of their mortality, however, time delay actually increased the level of beneficence. Thus, in those studies, it appeared that participants were using intergenerational allocations as a vehicle for carrying a positive legacy. An important implication of these studies is, therefore, that acting on behalf of future others can help to buffer death anxiety and to fulfill needs for symbolic immortality, while acting on the behalf of contemporary others does not perform these functions.

What is crucial about this insight is that it identifies the legacy motive as a mechanism by which decision-makers' self-interest can be channeled to promote the long-term interests of the collective. In this sense, legacies produce an alignment between the interests of the self and the interests of future others. An important avenue for further research on this topic, therefore, involves the determination of other types of factors that might activate the legacy motive. Recent theorizing has suggested that the allocation of burdens (Wade-Benzoni, Sondak, & Galinsky 2010) and the activation of the decision-maker's moral identity may represent two additional mechanisms that activate the legacy motive (Fox, Tost, & Wade-Benzoni 2010). In addition, another important avenue for future research in this area concerns the determinants of the content of the legacy that individuals seek to create. For example, theorists have suggested that death awareness can come in different forms (e.g. death anxiety and death reflection; see Grant & Wade-Benzoni 2009), and recent discussions have suggested that different forms of death awareness can lead individuals to pursue different forms of legacies. Specifically, Fox, Tost, & Wade-Benzoni (2010) have suggested that legacy building behaviors that stem from death anxiety will tend to focus on one's in-group as the beneficiary of the legacy, such as accumulating wealth to leave to one's family. In contrast, those that arise from death reflection will focus instead on providing the maximum benefit to a more inclusive understanding of future generations, such as protecting the environment for all to enjoy in the future. Theorists have also suggested that cultural factors and work-value orientation may moderate the content of the legacies that people pursue (Fox, Tost,

& Wade-Benzoni 2010). This avenue of empirical inquiry could be quite fruitful for future research.

IMPLICATIONS FOR INSTITUTING ENVIRONMENTAL SUSTAINABILITY INITIATIVES IN ORGANIZATIONS

In this final section, we review some of the implications of the findings of psychological research on intergenerational behavior for promoting environmental sustainability in organizations. In doing so, we describe ways to counteract the factors that negatively impact intergenerational beneficence and ways to promote the factors that positively impact intergenerational beneficence.

While the temporal distance that separates present decision-makers from future others may appear to be a challenging impediment to creating intergenerational affinity, research has shown that decision-makers need not interact with future others to feel affinity for them; rather, they need only identify themselves as part of a common group with future others (Wade-Benzoni 2008). Intergenerational identification refers to the feeling or perception that one shares a common group identity with other (past and/or future) generations of actors within one's group or organization (Wade-Benzoni 2003). Thus, the concept of identification is highly related to the concept of affinity because, as an individual feels a greater sense of common ingroup identity with other generations of organizational actors, that individual is also more likely to feel connected to those actors, to have empathy for them, and to consider their perspectives.

Theorists have therefore suggested that one mechanism for promoting environmental sustainability in organizations may be to enhance organizational actors' levels of intergenerational identification (Wade-Benzoni & Tost 2009). A variety of factors that affect the extent of intergenerational identification have been identified, such as the decision maker's motivation for self-enhancement, the decision-maker's holistic needs, the specificity with which future others are identified, decision framing, and aspects of group social identity (see Wade-Benzoni 2003, for a detailed review).

Most recently, theorists have focused on two potential avenues for enhancing intergenerational identification and thus promoting environmental sustainability: focusing on long-term group goals and emphasizing the role of past generations in producing present group identity (Wade-Benzoni & Tost 2009). First, research on group entitativity, or the extent to which group members perceive the group as a single coherent entity or unit, has indicated that groups that share common goals are more entitative (Lickel et al. 2000). On the basis of this finding, researchers have argued that establishing long-term group goals that can only be ultimately realized by future generations of group members is likely to promote environmental sustainability by encouraging present decision-makers to feel a sense of identification and entitativity, not only among current group members, but also across generations because multiple generations would be required to work toward and achieve common goals (Wade-Benzoni & Tost 2009). Future research should explore this possibility.

Second, research has indicated that individuals' understandings of the past can have a powerful impact on feelings about the future (Sherif 1966). In addition, theorists have suggested that, in intergenerational contexts, enhancing identification with past generations may be more feasible than enhancing identification with future generations, because past group members are more readily identified and specified than future ones (Wade-Benzoni & Tost 2009). Furthermore, the role that past group members have played in creating the present group situation can render the connection between past and present more identifiable and definable than the impact of the present on the future, which as we have already discussed is marked by a high level of uncertainty. Fortunately, when an individual identifies with past generations of group or organizational actors, that individual has come to view different generations of the group as members of one common ingroup, which can facilitate identification with future generations. In this way, increasing awareness of how past actors have affected the present can in turn encourage present decision-makers to view group decisions as having impacts that last over time and across sequences of generations. These perceptions can enhance intergenerational identification as well as awareness of the responsibilities of present generations to future generations, thereby encouraging individuals to value environmental sustainability. Empirical research into the impact of identification with past generations on affinity for, and beneficence toward, future others is therefore a critical avenue of future inquiry.

CONCLUDING REMARKS

The importance of taking a long-term environmental sustainability-based view of organizational decisions, strategies, and processes is becoming increasingly critical, as present-day decision-makers have an unprecedented power to affect the outcomes of future generations of organizational members and external stakeholders. In this chapter, we have reviewed some of the key findings from psychological research on intergenerational behavior in order to identify some of the critical factors that impact the likelihood that decision-makers will value environmental sustainability. We have also pointed to future research on these issues and have identified potential mechanisms by which organizational leaders might be able to encourage organizational members to value environmental sustainability.

Intergenerational decisions have considerable impact within organizations and society. Current decisions can affect the long-term strategic options available to future leaders, affect the organization's public image decades into the future, shape the leadership pipeline to determine which future leaders are able to attain leadership positions, and influence the long-term survivability of the organization in numerous other ways. The study of intergenerational decision-making therefore provides critical insight into the ways that organizations achieve long-term environmental sustainability and viability. Our hope, therefore, is that the types of research reviewed in this chapter can be used to guide the development and change of organizational policies and procedures in ways that are productive and beneficial for long-term success both of organizations and society.

References

Arndt, J., Greenberg, J., Pyszczynski, T., Solomon, S., & Simon, L. (1997a). "Subliminal Presentation of Death Reminders Leads to Increased Defense of the Cultural Worldview," *Psychological Science, 8:* 379–385.

—— —— —— —— ——(1997b). "Suppression, Accessibility of Death-Related Thoughts, And Cultural Worldview Defense: Exploring the Psychodynamics of Terror Management," *Journal of Personality and Social Psychology, 73:* 5–18.

Babcock, L., Loewenstein, G., Issacharoff, S., & Camerer, C. (1995). "Biased Judgments of Fairness in Bargaining," *American Economic Review, 85:* 1337–43.

Bazerman, M., & Neale, M. A. (1982). "Improving Negotiation Effectiveness under Final Offer Arbitration: The Role of Selection and Training," *Journal of Applied Psychology, 67:* 543–548.

Becker, E. (1973). *The Denial of Death.* New York: Free Press.

Bjorkman, M. (1984). "Decision Making, Risk Taking, and Psychological Time: Review of Empirical Findings and Psychological Theory," *Scandinavian Journal of Psychology, 25:* 31–49.

Bolton, G., Katok, E., & Zwick, R. (1998). "Dictator Game Giving: Fairness Versus Random Acts of Kindness," *The International Journal of Game Theory, 27:* 269–299.

Budescu, D. V., Rapoport, A., & Suleiman, R. (1990). "Resource Dilemmas with Environmental Uncertainty and Asymmetric Players," *European Journal of Social Psychology, 20:* 475–487.

Care, N. S. (1982). "Future Generations, Public Policy, and the Motivation Problem," *Environmental Ethics, 4:* 195–213.

Forsythe, R., Horowitz, J. L., Savin, N. E., & Sefton, M. (1994). "Fairness in Simple Bargaining Experiments," *Games and Economic Behavior, 6:* 347–369.

Fox, M., Tost, L. P., & Wade-Benzoni, K. A. (2010). "The Legacy Motive: A Catalyst for Sustainable Decision Making in Organizations," *Business Ethics Quarterly* 20(2): 153–185.

Frieze, I. H. and B. S. Boneva (2001). "Power Motivation and Motivation to Help Others," in *The Use and Abuse of Power: Multiple Perspectives on the Causes of Corruption.* A. Y. Lee-Chai and J. T. Bargh (eds.), Philadelphia: Psychology Press: 75–89.

Galinsky, A., Magee, J. C., Inesi, M. E., & Gruenfeld, D. H. (2006). "Power and Perspectives Not Taken," *Psychological Science, 17:* 1068–1074.

Georgesen, J. C. & Harris, M. J. (1998). "Why's my Boss Always Holding Me Down? A meta-analysis of Power Effects on Performance Evaluations," *Personality and Social Psychology Review, 2:* 184–195.

——(2000). "The Balance of Power: Interpersonal Consequences of Differential Power and Expectancies," *Personality and Social Psychology Bulletin, 26:* 1239–1257.

Gouldner, A. W. (1960). "The Norm of Reciprocity," *American Sociological Review, 25:* 161–167.

Grant, A. M., & Wade-Benzoni, K. A. (2009). "The Hot and Cool of Death Awareness at Work: Mortality Cues, Aging, and Self-Protective and Prosocial Motivations," *Academy of Management Review, 34:* 600–622.

Gustafsson, M., Biel, A., & Garling, T. (1999). "Outcome-Desirability Bias in Resource Management Problems," *Thinking and Reasoning*, 5: 327–337.

——— ——— ——— (2000). "Eogism Bias in Social Dilemmas with Resource Uncertainty," *Group Processes and Intergroup Relations*, 3: 351–365.

Haidt, J. (2004). "The Emotional Dog gets Mistaken for a Possum," *Review of General Psychology*, 8: 283–290.

Handgraaf, M., Van Dijk, E., Vermunt, R. C., Wilke, H. A. M. & De Dreu, C. K. W. (2008). "Less Power or Powerless? Egocentric Empathy Gaps and the Irony of Having Little Versus No Power in Social Decision Making," *Journal of Personality and Social Psychology*, 95: 1136–1149.

Heine, S. J., Proulx, T., & Vohs, K. D. (2006). "The Meaning Maintenance Model: On the Coherence of Social Motivations," *Personality and Social Psychology Review*, 10: 88–110.

Henderson, M. D., Trope, Y., & Carnevale, P. J. (2006). "Negotiation from a Near and Distant Time Perspective," *Journal of Personality and Social Psychology*, 91: 712–729.

Hernandez, M., Chen, Y. R., & Wade-Benzoni, K. A. (2006). Toward an Understanding of Psychological Distance Reduction between Generations: A Cross-Cultural Perspective," in Y.-R. Chen (ed.), *National Culture and Groups*, Vol. 9, Elsevier, JAI Press.

Hoffman, E., McCabe, K., & Smith, V. L. (1996). "Social Distance and Other-Regarding Behavior in Dictator Games," *American Economic Review*, 86: 653–660.

Jones, B., & Rachlin, H. (2006). "Social Discounting," *Psychological Science*, 17: 283–286.

Keyes, C. L. M., Shmotkin, D., & Ryff, C. D. (2002). "Optimizing Well-Being: The Empirical Encounter of Two Traditions," *Journal of Personality and Social Psychology*, 82: 1007–1022.

Kipnis, D. (1972). "Does Power Corrupt?" *Journal of Personality and Social Psychology*, 24: 33–41.

Kotre, J. (1984). *Outliving the Self: Generativity and the Interpretation of Lives*. Baltimore: Johns Hopkins University Press.

Liberman, N., Trope, Y., & Stephan, E. (2007). "Psychological Distance," in E. T. Higgens & A. W. Kruglanski (Eds.), *Social Psychology: Handbook of Basic Principles*, Vol. 2. New York: Guilford.

Lickel, B., Hamilton, D. L., Wieczorkowska, G., Lewis, A., Sherman, S. J., & Uhles, A. N. (2000). "Varieties of Groups and the Perception of Group Entitativity," *Journal of Personality and Social Psychology*, 78: 223–246.

Loewenstein, G. (1992). "The Fall and Rise of Psychological Explanations in the Economics of Intertemporal Choice," in G. Loewenstein & J. Elster (eds.), *Choice over time* (3–34). New York: Russell Sage Foundation.

—— (1996). "Behavioral Decision Theory and Business Ethics: Skewed Trade-Offs Between Self and Other," in D. M. Messick & A. E. Tenbrunsel (eds.), *Codes of Conduct: Behavioral Research into Business Ethics*, New York: Russell Sage Foundation, 214–227.

——, Thompson, L., & Bazerman, M. H. (1989). "Social Utility and Decision Making in Interpersonal Contexts," *Journal of Personality and Social Psychology*, 57: 426–441.

McAdams, D. P. & de St. Aubin, E. (1992). A Theory of Generativity and its Assessment through Self-Report, Behavioral Acts, and Narrative Themes in Autobiography, *Journal of Personality and Social Psychology*, 62: 1003–1015.

McGregor, I., & Little, B. R. (1998). Personal Projects, Happiness, and Meaning: On Doing Well and Being Yourself," *Journal of Personality and Social Psychology*, 74: 494–512.

McLean Parks, J. (1997). "The Fourth Arm of Justice: The Art and Science of Revenge," in R. J. Lewicki, R. J. Bies, & B. H. Sheppard (eds.), *Research on Negotiation in Organizations*, Volume 6. Greenwich, CT: JAI Press.

Neale, M. A., & Bazerman, M. H. (1983). "The Role of Perspective-Taking Ability in Negotiating under Different Forms of Arbitration," *Industrial and Labor Relations Review*, 36: 378–388.

Overbeck, J. R., & Park, B. (2001). "When Power Does Not Corrupt: Superior Individuation Processes among Powerful Perceivers," *Journal of Personality and Social Psychology*, 81: 549–565.

—— (2006). "Powerful Perceivers, Powerless Objects: Flexibility of Powerholders' Social Attention," *Organizational Behavior and Human Decision Processes*, 99: 227–243.

Pigou, A. C. (1920). *The Economics of Welfare*, London: Macmillan.

Pyszczynski, T., Greenberg, J., & Solomon, S. (1999). "A Dual-Process Model of Defense against Conscious and Unconscious Death-Related Thoughts: An Extension of Terror Management Theory," *Psychological Review*, 106: 835–845.

Rachlin, H. & Raineri, A. (1992). "Irrationality, Impulsiveness, and Selfishness as Discount Reversal Effects," in G. Loewenstein & J. Elster (eds.), *Choice over Time*, New York: Russell Sage Foundation.

Ryff, C. D., & Keyes, C. L. M. (1995). "The Structure of Psychological Well-Being Revisited," *Journal of Personality and Social Psychology*, 69: 719-727.

Sachdev, I. & Bourhis, R. Y. (1985). "Social Categorization and Power Differentials in Group Relations," *European Journal of Social Psychology*, 15: 415–434.

Sherif, M. (1966). *In Common Predicament: Social Psychology of Intergroup Conflict and Cooperation*. Boston, MA: Houghton Mifflin.

Simon, L., Greenberg, J., Harmon-Jones, E., Solomon, S., Pyszczynski, T., & Arndt, J. (1997). "Terror Management and Cognitive-Experiential Self-Theory: Evidence that Terror Management Occurs in the Experiential System," *Journal of Personality and Social Psychology*, 72: 1132–1146.

Steger, M. F., Kashdan, T. B., Sullivan, B. A., & Lorentz, D. (2008). "Understanding the Search for Meaning in Life: Personality, Cognitive Style, and the Dynamic Between Seeking and Experiencing Meaning," *Journal of Personality*, 76: 199–228.

Törnblom, K. Y. (1988). "Positive and Negative Allocation: A Typology and Model for Conflicting Justice Principles," in E. Lawler & B. Markovsky (eds.), *Advances in Group Processes*, (5): 141–165, Greenwich, CT: JAI Press.

Tost, L. P., Hernandez, M., & Wade-Benzoni, K. A. (2008). "Pushing the Boundaries: A Review and Extension of the Psychological Dynamics of Intergenerational Conflict in Organizational Contexts," in Martocchio, J. J. (ed.), *Research in Personnel and Human Resources Management*, (27): 93–147, Greenwich, CT: JAI Press.

—— & Wade-Benzoni, K. A. "Power Corrupts in the Present but Ennobles over Time: The Roles of Power and Responsibility in Intergenerational Dilemmas." Working Paper: Duke University

Trivers, R. L. (1971). "The Evolution of Reciprocal Altruism," *The Quarterly Review of Biology*, 46: 35–57.

Trope, Y., & Liberman, N. (2003). "Temporal Construal," *Psychological Review*, 110: 403–421.

Van Kleef, G. A., Oveis, C., Van der Lowe, I., LuoKogan, A., Goetz, J., & Keltner, D. (2008). "Power, Distress, and Compassion: Turning a Blind Eye to the Suffering of Others," *Psychological Science*, 19: 1315–1322.

von Bohm-Bawerk, E. (1889). *Capital and Interest*. South Holland, IL: Libertarian Press.

Wade-Benzoni, K. A. (1999). "Thinking about the Future: An Intergenerational Perspective on the Conflict and Compatibility between Economic and Environmental Interests," *American Behavioral Scientist*, 42: 1393–1405.

—— (2002a). "A Golden Rule over Time: Reciprocity in Intergenerational Allocation Decisions," *Academy of Management Journal*, 45: 1011–1028.

—— (2002b). "'Too Tough to Die: September 11, Mortality Salience, and Intergenerational Behavior," *Journal of Management Inquiry*, 11: 235–239.

—— (2003). "Intergenerational Identification and Cooperation in Organizations and Society," in M. Neale, E. Mannix, & A. Tenbrunsel (eds.), *Research on Managing Groups and Teams*, Vol. 5: 257–277, Greenwich, CT: JAI Press.

—— (2006). "Legacies, Immortality, and the Future: The Psychology of Intergenerational Altruism," in M. Neale, E. Mannix, & A. Tenbrunsel (eds.), *Research on Managing Groups and Teams*, Vol. 11: 247–270, Greenwich, CT: Elsevier Science Press.

—— (2008). "Maple Trees and Weeping Willows: The Role of Time, Uncertainty, and Affinity in Intergenerational Decisions," *Negotiation and Conflict Management Research*, 1: 220–245.

——, Hernandez, M., Medvec, V. H., & Messick, D. (2008). "In Fairness to Future Generations: The Role of Egocentrism, Uncertainty, Power, & Stewardship in Judgments of Intergenerational Allocations," *Journal of Experimental Social Psychology*, 44: 233–245.

—— Okumura, T., Brett, J. M., Moore, D., Tenbrunsel, A. E., & Bazerman, M. H. (2002). "Cognitions and Behavior in Asymmetric Social Dilemmas: A Comparison of Two Cultures," *Journal of Applied Psychology*, 87: 87–95.

—— Sondak, H., & Galinsky, A. D. (2010). "Leaving a Legacy: Intergenerational Allocations of Benefits and Burdens," *Business Ethics Quarterly*, 20: 7–34.

—— Tenbrunsel, A. E., & Bazerman, M. H. (1996). "Egocentric Interpretations of Fairness in Asymmetric, Environmental Social Dilemmas: Explaining Harvesting Behavior & the Role of Communication," *Organizational Behavior and Human Decision Processes*, 67: 111–126.

—— & Tost, L. P. (2009). "The Egoism and Altruism of Intergenerational Behavior," *Personality and Social Psychology Review*, 13: 165–193.

—————— Hernandez, M., & Larrick, R. (2010). "Intergenerational Beneficence as a Death Anxiety Buffer." Working paper, Duke University.

Walster, E., Walster, G. W., & Berscheid, E. (1978). *Equity: Theory and Research*. Boston: Allyn & Bacon.

Weinstein, N. D. (1980). "Unrealistic Optimism about Future Life Events," *Journal of Personality and Social Psychology*, 5: 806–820.

Wong, N. Y., & Bagozzi, R. P. (2005). "Emotional Intensity as a Function of Psychological Distance and Cultural Orientation," *Journal of Business Research*, 58: 533–542.

Zika, S., & Chamberlain, K. (1992). "On the Relation Between Meaning in Life and Psychological Well-Being," *British Journal of Psychology*, 83: 133–145.

CHAPTER 11

ORGANIZATIONAL CULTURE AND ENVIRONMENTAL ACTION

JENNIFER HOWARD-GRENVILLE
AND STEPHANIE BERTELS

PREVIOUS chapters in this volume have addressed the strategic importance of implementing improved environmental practices for companies. Yet, integrating environmental concerns into "the DNA of a business" remains a major challenge for most companies (Bertels et al. 2010; Ceres 2010). Many still struggle to move beyond compliance with existing environmental regulations, and only a very few make environmental sustainability an everyday, guiding principle within the organization. This chapter addresses how organizational culture shapes the uptake (or not) of environmental practices, and considers how culture might be leveraged to embed environmental considerations across organizations.

Organizational culture is often colloquially referred to as "the way things are done around here," and it captures the distinct patterns of meanings that circulate in an organization and inform its members' day-to-day actions (Martin 2002). Nike recognized the power of organizational culture when it was creating a set of design principles to guide environmentally favorable material choices for its shoes and apparel. It was only when sustainability experts tapped the existing, broader culture of innovation—and competition—at the firm that they gained traction on this issue with design teams. By pitting design teams against one other in their quests to earn "gold," "silver," or "bronze" ratings on the 'Considered Design' index, Nike unleashed the competitive culture within the company, and soon saw some of its most mainstream products, like the Michael Jordan basketball shoe, earn 'gold' (Mackrael 2009). One Nike manager explained "Nike's culture is one of innovation, so we have very consciously ... stresse[d] sustainability as an opportunity for innovation and business growth" (Severn 2010). Culture can be a powerful vehicle for change, as this example suggests, when new issues are made resonant with it. However, as often as not, culture can act as a powerful inhibitor of change. Understanding how culture influences employees' actions on environmental issues is therefore critical to understanding how needed transformations in business practice may actually be brought about.

Work in the area of business and the natural environment (B&NE) has only begun to directly explore organizational culture. However, it does connect to a rich body of more general scholarship on the topic (Martin 2002) and recent interest in theorizing culture in more dynamic ways (Swidler 2001; Hatch 2004; Weber & Dacin 2011). This chapter draws on this more general literature to explore several ways in which organizational culture influences members' actions, integrating findings from a number of business and environment studies to explain how culture can shape action on environmental issues. While the B&NE studies that are included here do not all explicitly probe culture, they do shed light on cultural aspects of organizing.

An internal, cultural perspective on B&NE complements those that offer a more micro-level analysis of individual's cognitive biases and psychological states (see Shu & Bazerman [Chapter 9]; and Tost & Wade-Benzoni [Chapter 10] this volume). While individuals put culture to use, cultural meaning is generally regarded as residing at a higher, collective level of analysis (Swidler 2008; see also Forbes & Jermier [Chapter 30] this volume). An organizational culture lens is also complementary to, but distinct from, those that emphasize broader institutional and social movement dynamics (see Lounsbury, Fairclough, & Lee [Chapter 12]; and Weber & Soderstrom [Chapter 14] this volume). Organizational culture never operates in a vacuum, and meanings in wider circulation are translated and brought into use within organizations (Creed et al. 2002; Zilber 2008). However, organizational culture is not simply an assemblage of these broader logics, for it comprises a distinct pattern of meaning and action that has accumulated over time and in response to an organization's unique trajectory of internal reflection and external change (Ravasi & Schultz 2006; Rindova et al. 2010).

The chapter begins with a brief overview of the concept of organizational culture (for comprehensive reviews see Martin 2002, Martin et al. 2006, Hatch 2010). Next, it outlines three main mechanisms through which organizational culture shapes business and environment interactions, with each one reflecting a somewhat different perspective on culture. Finally, we outline some directions for future research and suggest productive ways in which a cultural lens can be leveraged to lead to new insights on B&NE.

WHAT IS ORGANIZATIONAL CULTURE?

Culture has been a prominent concept in organizational research for more than three decades, yet there has long been considerable variation in how researchers view and study the concept (Smircich 1983; Martin 2002). Despite definitional debates (Martin 2002; Weeks 2004), most scholars and most members of organizations recognize an organization's culture as a distinct pattern of meanings that circulate in an organization and shape members' thoughts and actions about what is appropriate and valued in that setting. Anthropologist Clifford Geertz offered an influential metaphor, noting that a culture comprises the "webs of significance [meaning]" that people themselves spin (1973: 5). Organizational scholars have used this metaphor to call attention to two aspects of culture. First, members of an organization operate within a web of meaning that guides their day-to-day actions. And second, through these very actions, members continuously recreate what is meaningful within the organization. Because of this reinforcing cycle, culture is often regarded as having a stabilizing effect on organizational action.

Some early proponents saw culture as so stabilizing that it could supplant structural and other forms of organizational control (Ouchi 1981). These authors urged managers to manipulate culture as if it was a 'variable' (Smircich 1983), causally related to important organizational outcomes such as employee commitment and performance (Ouchi 1980; Ouchi 1981; Deal & Kennedy 1982; Peters & Waterman 1982; Wilkins 1989). Other organizational scholars drew from anthropology and saw culture as "a root metaphor for conceptualizing organization" (Smircich 1983: 342), constituting something an organization "is," rather than something it "has" (Smircich 1983).

This latter perspective withstood a test of time that the former did not (Martin et al. 2006; Hatch 2010), yielding insight into the durability of even 'negative' cultures (Weeks 2004) and the complexity of culture when meanings are unevenly shared across an organization (Meyerson & Martin 1987; Kunda 1992). Of particular importance to the study of B&NE is the existence and interactions of subcultures that can form around occupational groupings, organizational roles, and hierarchical levels (Van Maanen & Barley 1985; Jermier et al. 1991; Golden 1992; Schein 1996; Stevenson & Bartunek 1996), for it is often through a particular occupational group or other subculture that environmental issues enter an organization and are brought to the attention of others (Bansal 2003; Howard-Grenville 2006).

How does organizational culture shape interpretations of and actions on environmental issues?

This section outlines three different perspectives on the means by which culture shapes how members of an organization interpret and act on issues, including environmental issues. These perspectives—culture as shared norms or values; culture as a frame or filter; and culture as a 'toolkit'—each derive from somewhat different scholarly traditions, although they are united in regarding culture as something that an organization 'is.' Each also holds promise for understanding the relationship between organizational culture and B&NE. When culture is regarded as expressed through *shared norms or values*, this perspective can help explain how members connect their work in an organization to larger concerns such as environmental protection, and whether they interpret actions related to the environment as being a priority for the organization and for themselves. When culture is regarded as *a filter or frame for meaning*, this perspective illustrates how information and ideas related to environmental issues either gain traction and penetration or get filtered out of the everyday discourse in organizations. Finally, when culture is regarded as a *'tool-kit'* and enacted in everyday practices, we can gain an understanding of how actions might be altered to create new meaning and understanding of environmental issues.

Below we discuss these three mechanisms and review empirical contributions in each area. We incorporate empirical work on B&NE that we regard as having relevance to one of these cultural perspectives through its consideration of values, leader behavior, framing, and other practices, even when authors did not explicitly use the term 'organizational culture.' By doing this, we hope to take the first step in building the groundwork of studies that are consistent with a cultural perspective and that can inform future research in this area.

CULTURE AS SHARED NORMS OR VALUES

One prevalent model of organizational culture asserts that culture is expressed at three levels, through artifacts, espoused values, and assumptions (Schein 1992). While artifacts such as behavior, dress, and physical arrangements are relatively obvious features of an organization, they are only suggestive of the 'real' culture that resides in the underlying assumptions of members. Assumptions capture the 'taken for granted' norms that have accumulated as members of an organization work together over a period of time to solve their problems of internal integration and external alignment (Schein 1992). According to Schein, founders or leaders disproportionately influence cultural norms or values as these are often explicitly developed early in an organization's life, and capture founders' visions of what will make the organization unique (1992). Over time, new members are socialized to these assumptions, values, and norms, learning that they capture "the correct way to perceive, think, and feel in relation to [specific] problems" (Schein 1992: 12).

Other scholars depict culture as shared understandings, but they elaborate the role of symbols as carriers of culture, and suggest that several types of evidence—artifacts, behaviors, and interactions—must be pieced together to yield a "multifaceted and complex picture of the various kinds of symbol systems and their associated meanings" (Smircich 1983: 351). Schein's model excludes symbols from explicit consideration, and has been critiqued for undertheorizing dynamic relationships between artifacts, symbols, assumptions, and values (Hatch 1993). Nonetheless, norms and values, and their underlying sustaining assumptions, are often taken as a starting point for understanding an organization's culture, whereas the degree to which these are uniformly shared can be considered an empirical question (Meyerson & Martin 1987).

Several specific mechanisms connect shared norms with organizational action on environmental issues. First, shared norms promote commitment to, acceptance of, and internal communication around actions that are congruent with these norms (Dutton & Dukerich 1991; Bansal 2003; Ravasi & Schultz 2006). Second, norms can act as both a guide and inspiration to individuals who are making organizational decisions in areas where few precedents exist, which is often the case in the rapidly evolving field of environmental practice. They can be leveraged by individuals who seek to champion issues within an organization since championing is most effective when it aligns at least partially with broader concerns and understandings in the organization (Meyerson & Scully 1995; Creed et al. 2002; Bansal 2003). Third, strong shared norms can elicit and shape responses to unusual circumstances or crises that reveal and build organizational strengths and capabilities (Dutton et al. 2006; Christianson et al. 2009). In this way, norms empower individuals to act and accelerate collective responses.

Outlined below is B&NE research that addresses the work undertaken by individuals in their organizations. This includes leader and champion actions and the creation of specific roles related to the environment. The work undertaken by individuals is followed by an examination of other mechanisms of signaling that environmental practices are consistent with an organization's shared values, including the allocation of resources, the use of incentives, and the existence of corporate policies.

Leadership actions

Considerable B&NE research has explored the role of the senior leadership in signaling the importance of the natural environment for business operations and in turn, shaping the norms and values of employees related to the environment. Several researchers found links between top management support for environmental initiatives and the enactment of environmental behaviors (Cordano & Frieze 2000; DuBose 2000; Goodman 2000; Ramus & Steger 2000; Sharma 2000; Bansal 2003; Molnar & Mulvihill 2003; Werre 2003; Berry 2004; Dixon & Clifford 2007; Ángel del Brío et al. 2008; Esquer-Peralta et al. 2008; Adriana 2009; Holton et al. 2010). In particular, Andersson et al. (2005) found that when values of ecological sustainability are strongly espoused among top management, supervisors translate and enact these values in their everyday interaction with subordinates at the operational levels of the organization. Backing-up subordinates when they make a decision to prioritize sustainability is another way to send a strong signal (Howard-Grenville et al. 2008). Yet, Harris & Crane (2002) caution that while positive signaling on the part of senior leadership can have positive effects, a negative instance of signaling can severely dampen greening efforts. For a detailed discussion of the role of the senior leadership on the path to environmental sustainability see Elkington & Love ([Chapter 36] in this volume).

Environmental champions

Champions recognize the importance of the environment for the organization and are able to bring the issue onto the organizational agenda (Andersson & Bateman 2000). Environmental champions can act both as models of behaviors and ambassadors for values. The B&NE work on championing has mainly focused on comparing the tactics and characteristics of champions. In a study of 146 environmental champions, Andersson & Bateman (2000) found that coalition building and inspirational appeal were two successful influence tactics, along with enlisting help or endorsement from others. Internal champions appear to be more likely to be successful than outsiders (Bansal 2003), and senior managers and board members can be particularly effective champions due to their positions and influence (Harris & Crane 2002). While individual champions are important, it often takes a 'team' of champions to advance the sustainability agenda (Molnar & Mulvihill 2003). In contrast to previous work that emphasizes the characteristics of champions, Markusson (2010) takes the perspective that organizations contain a range of potential environmental champions based on a combination of skills and interest, who—given the right opportunity—may engage in environmental championing as a behavior.

The creation of roles

Several authors point to the creation of specific roles related to the environment as having a legitimizing effect within the organization (DuBose 2000; Smith & Brown 2003; Ángel del Brío et al. 2008; Cheung et al. 2009; Lee 2009; Holton et al. 2010) and reinforcing management's commitment (Smith & Brown 2003). In other cases, a failure to create roles and assign responsibility stood in the way of effective implementation of environmental programs (Balzarova et al. 2006).

Moving beyond the role of individuals in connecting shared norms with organizational action on environmental issues, prior work reveals three other mechanisms that signal that environmental practices are consistent with an organization's shared values. These include the allocation of resources, the use of incentives, and corporate policies.

Allocation of resources

Beyond espousing the value of addressing environmental concerns, senior leadership can allocate resources to sustainability or signal their intent to allocate such resources. Allocating time and money to an issue helps place it on an organization's strategic agenda (Andersson & Bateman 2000; DuBose 2000; Buysse & Verbeke 2003; Dunphy 2003; Chamorro & Bañegil 2006; Darnall & Edwards 2006) and supports the implementation of sustainability and/or acts as a signal to stress its importance for the organization (DuBose 2000; Sharma 2000; Molnar & Mulvihill 2003; Wei-Skillern 2004; Roome 2005; Holton et al. 2010).

Incentives

Prior research also suggests that rewarding individual efforts can help build commitment to environmental objectives (Smith & Brown 2003; Ángel del Brío et al. 2008), and that linking performance incentives to environmental measures can shape behaviors (DuBose 2000; Douglas 2007). Jones (2000) proposes that financially rewarding individuals for their personal contribution towards sustainability encourages them to participate in firm activities and recognizes those who participate over those who don't.

Corporate policies

Corporate policies make expected behaviours explicit and promote a set of shared values related to sustainability. The existence of corporate environmental policies may serve to signal the organization's commitment to sustainability for employees (Harris & Crane 2002; Andersson et al. 2005) and may also encourage employees to generate more creative environmental ideas (Ramus & Steger 2000).

Because many of the B&NE studies mentioned did not explicitly examine organizational culture, we caution against concluding that these mechanisms can or will create norms supportive of environmental actions that are shared across an organization. Such questions are ripe for further empirical study. The organizational literature on culture reveals that norms and values are frequently not uniformly shared or adhered to (Meyerson & Martin 1987; Van Maanen 1991; Kunda 1992; Weeks 2004). Companies that push espoused values on to their employees may find that cynical detachment, rather than enhanced commitment, results (Kunda 1992). In other cases, strong norms in one group or subculture, and an imbalance of power that is inherent in organizational relations, can lead to some members having much more of a 'say' than others in which issues get attended to and acted upon (Hallett 2003; Howard-Grenville 2006). Further research is needed on whether and how the practices above contribute to widely shared norms or values, and whether in some cases norms may actually impede, or only imperfectly support, environmental actions. This is particularly important because environmental issues often challenge traditional corporate cultural norms (Emerson and Welford 1997; Meima 1997).

Culture as filter and frame for meaning

A related, but somewhat different, perspective on culture to that above emphasizes culture as a continually recreated "web of meaning" (Geertz 1973). This perspective is less concerned with shared values or norms that may be associated with these meanings, and more concerned with the recursive connections between members' day-to-day actions and the meanings associated with them. In the course of the day-to-day, members rarely question cultural meaning and it tends to guide their actions and decisions, contributing, as in the perspective above, to culture acting as a form of "deep structure" (Swidler 2001: 163) that is relatively stable and durable. However, consistent with symbolic interactionism (Fine 1984), the stability of culture is only dynamically so. According to this perspective, meanings are recreated and perhaps renegotiated through people's interactions (Fine 1984) and those who can manipulate meaning for others gain power (Hallett 2003).

Two main mechanisms connect culture as recreated meaning with organizational actions. First, as systems of meaning, cultures are also schemes of classification that shape what their members pay attention to and what they ignore (Douglas 1978), and what they count as 'normal' and what they do not (Douglas 1966). In this way, culture can 'filter' the information that organizations obtain from beyond their boundaries, and hence have an important impact on the issue agenda within the organization (Howard-Grenville & Hoffman 2003). Schön refers to this filtering process at the individual level as problem 'setting,' noting that "we select what we will treat as the 'things' of the situation, we set the boundaries of our attention to it, and we impose upon it a coherence which allows us to say what is wrong and in what directions the situation needs to be changed" (1983: 40). Operating like problem setting but at the organizational level of analysis, firms shape their interpretations of external threats in a manner that preserves internal authenticity and consistency (Ravasi & Schultz 2006). In the B&NE literature, Howard-Grenville (2006, 2007a) found that the dominant engineering subculture in a high-tech manufacturing company filtered information such that it paid most attention to issues that were presented as 'data,' those that needed to be solved on a very short time horizon, and that could be solved through the application of hard work and technical savvy. This created challenges for those seeking to infuse consideration of environmental impacts into the work of this engineering group, for the environmental issues often involved uncertain data, and long time horizons, and could only be solved by working with many stakeholders inside and outside the company.

A second mechanism focuses not on how culture as meaning filters incoming information, but how it is used by members to frame their messages and shape an internal conversation. Framing derives from social movement theory and refers to members' use of "collective processes of interpretation" (McAdam et al. 1996: 2) to inspire and shape action consistent with meanings more widely shared by a group or organization (Snow & Benford 1988). Skilled members of an organization can frame new issues as worthy of attention by carefully crafting messages that translate specific concerns into a language that is legitimated within the organization (Creed et al. 2002; Howard-Grenville 2007b; Zilber 2008).

B&NE research has both explored different approaches to framing environmental issues as well as the impact that language has on the tractability of the environmental message. Andersson & Bateman (2000) found that framing environmental issues as urgent, framing them as a financial opportunity, and making use of everyday business language increased the likelihood of success. They advise first emphasizing potential financial pay-off and then tying environmental issues to other strategic priorities or conversations being undertaken in the organization. They caution that unlike appeals to the general public, dramatic and emotional language is not as effective as a business case when discussing environmental issues within companies (exceptions may occur when the organization already has strong environmental values). Similarly, Bansal (2003) found that environmental values are more likely to lead to change if they are framed as concerns, and that frames that tap organizational values or priorities and use organizational language will be better received.

Part of the process of infusing environmental considerations across an organization appears to involve translating abstract environmental concepts into language that enables employees to understand their application in day-to-day business (Cramer et al. 2004; Wei-Skillern 2004; Esquer-Peralta et al. 2008). Cross-functional work groups can be helpful in this translation process (Reverdy 2006). Terms like sustainability can be viewed as 'jargon' (Jenkins 2006). Companies may elect to avoid these terms entirely, instead ensuring that their actions clearly and consistently demonstrate a commitment to the environment (Molnar & Mulvihill 2003). Andersson & Bateman (2000) found that the use of metaphor and symbolism can be another powerful means of conveying environmental messages, while Howard-Grenville (2007b) found that experiences that led employees to understand the meanings that *others* brought to bear on environmental issues helped them re-craft their messages to better resonate with others.

Culture as a toolkit

A third and quite distinct perspective on culture derives from a practice perspective which foregrounds individuals' situated behavior—what people actually do—and is less concerned with underlying motives or values. Consistent with the symbolic interactionist perspective, this perspective extends it and encourages explicit attention to action, backgrounding power, and the manipulation of meaning. Swidler's influential work focuses on the individual, and argues that individuals act knowledgeably by drawing cultural resources from a 'toolkit' and enacting 'strategies of action' that are meaningful within the culture (Swidler 1986; Swidler 2001). Swidler argues that "we are still too wedded to the view that what we are seeing when we observe culture is an internalized complex of meaning and practices, rather than people's knowledge of how a set of publicly available codes and situations operate" (2001: 180). Where the 'culture as a toolkit' perspective differs most from those reviewed above is through its identification of the potential for cultural adjustment and change. Rather than seeing people as "cultural dopes" (Swidler 1986: 277), blinded by the potentially constraining effects of culture, Swidler sees them as knowledgeable and skillful actors. Accordingly, culture may change and evolve because: "there are not simply different cultures: there are different ways of mobilizing and using culture, different ways of linking culture to action" (Swidler 2001: 23).

The idea of culture as a toolkit has recently gained attention in organizational studies. Some authors use this perspective to empirically demonstrate how culture is made malleable by individual actors who use cultural resources in new ways, drawing on cases where individuals sought to infuse environmental practices within their organizations (Howard-Grenville et al. 2011). Others consider how organizations as a whole develop cultures that are informed by much broader industry or societal cultural toolkits (Weber 2005; Weber et al. 2008). Changes in an organization's cultural toolkit can in turn lead to the development of new strategies and practices (Rindova et al. 2011).

Few B&NE studies to date portray culture as a toolkit, but in their systematic review of the academic and practitioner literature on embedding sustainability into organizational culture, Bertels et al. (2010) adopted a similar perspective by identifying *how* organizations were going about the task of trying to build or strengthen cultures that encourage environmental and social decision-making. These authors grouped these activities according to how companies were going about infusing sustainability, generating a set of practices that might fit well in a variety of organizational settings. Consistent with a toolkit approach, these authors emphasize the need for companies to reflect on their current cultural resources and to make use of a diversified portfolio of practices that include both informal and formal approaches aimed at fulfilling current commitments *and* developing innovative new ways of doing things.

FUTURE DIRECTIONS

As we reflect on the research work related to B&NE undertaken within the three perspectives outlined above, we see several particularly promising paths for further research.

Make culture more explicit

There is considerable scope for further empirical work in the area of B&NE that specifically addresses organizational culture. Relatively little work has been undertaken in this area that explicitly takes a cultural perspective, yet a fair amount of existing literature speaks to issues that are cultural, namely values, communication, and behavioral patterns within organizations. In adding to this literature, researchers should aim to gather data that can capture multiple expressions of culture—for example, language, artifacts, and behavior—at multiple levels within an organization. Only then can a complex picture be painted from which to analyze more fundamentally cultural questions. For example, researchers could study how the provision of resources or incentives to encourage environmental practices is interpreted by recipients. To what extent are these resources or incentives in line with what a group already values and acts on, or not? What are the consequences? In undertaking this work, scholars must carefully consider the perspective they take on culture. As noted above, no single definition or understanding of organizational culture is dominant in the literature, which itself is not problematic if scholars are clear about which perspective they are adopting, understand the assumptions inherent in it, and design their data collection and analysis methods accordingly.

Move beyond success stories

We have many more 'success' stories of cultures supporting the uptake of environmental practices than we have stories of 'failure' or studies that explore how current cultures impede change (Bertels et al. 2010). Yet, environmental initiatives in most companies meet at least some resistance, and in many cases considerable resistance because they simply do not fit with 'how we do things here.' Probing how culture impedes the adoption of environmental practices (see, for example, Howard-Grenville 2006) can build understanding of the possibilities for culture change, given that removing barriers to infusing environmental practices in the day-to-day can be more important than communicating the need for such practices. Conducting comparative studies that consider culture within multiple companies adopting similar environmental practices would greatly enhance our understanding of how culture might shape successful versus unsuccessful uptake of such practices. However, the need to generate rich empirical data, often through direct observation or ethnographic methods (Van Maanen 1988), somewhat limits the number of companies a researcher can practically compare and the generalizability of the cultural insights. One productive approach might be to study, for example, the implementation of a common environmental management system by two or more divisions or plant sites within a single company that are known to have different subcultures.

Distinguish what makes environmental issues unique

Scholars must remain acutely aware that issues of B&NE create different demands for an organization's culture than many other issues or initiatives. Environmental issues often are presented as having greater scientific uncertainty, broader (and more diffuse) responsibility, and much longer time horizons than most business decisions. An effort to change culture is inherently confined to the boundaries of an organization and limited in its ability to either shape or respond to a broader societal agenda that extends beyond the organization. Key levers required for change may be beyond the control of the organization and may reside in the organization's supply chain or with external stakeholders. How does organizational culture influence a company's interactions in these spheres? How does a cultural change effort interact with interorganizational collaboration? Can one trigger another? Finally, to what degree do environmental issues demand fundamental cultural change? Can incremental change to 'business as usual' actually attain the paradigm-breaking approaches that are demanded? Scholars studying such questions by longitudinally tracing the movement of issues across organizational boundaries and capturing unfolding patterns of action and interaction would considerably advance work on B&NE, and also contribute to much-needed theorizing on the interactions between institutional logics, social movements, and culture (Aten et al. 2012). While such multi-level longitudinal studies may be daunting, recent exemplars exist (Chiles et al. 2004; Ravasi and Schultz 2006; Rindova et al. 2011).

Consider links to close conceptual cousins (identity and institutions)

Given that environmental concerns and actions extend well beyond single organizations, studies in the domain of B&NE are well-suited to answering calls to cultivate ties between cultural and other theories that are near neighbors in organizational studies. For example, cultural and institutional approaches share an interest in understanding how meaning shapes action within and between organizations, and each can inform the other by considering more closely how meaning within organizations both reflects and shapes broader institutional norms (Aten et al. 2012). Similarly, recent work theorizes and demonstrates links between organizational culture and identity (Ravasi & Schultz 2006; Kreiner 2011), suggesting another route by which culture shapes and is informed by an organization's interactions with external stakeholders. We see great promise in looking explicitly at interactions between culture and identity, image, and reputation in the domain of business and environment. Prior work on voluntary environmental standards, reporting, certification, and sustainability awards and rankings, affirms the importance of external stakeholder perceptions and external norms in shaping organizational action (Howard et al. 1999; Bertels & Peloza 2008; Beske et al. 2008; Howard-Grenville et al. 2008; Herremans et al. 2009). Others argue that the uptake of such practices is influenced significantly by a firm's internal management and culture (Gunningham et al. 2003; Howard-Grenville et al. 2008). Further understanding these interactions between the internal and the external will significantly advance our understanding of B&NE while also contributing to the development of organizational theory at the interstices of culture, institutions, and identity.

Conduct more longitudinal work that addresses change

Ultimately, work on B&NE needs to inform and offer novel pathways for change. Common to much early work on organizational culture was an often implicit tendency to treat culture as a context pressuring individuals to act in a prescribed way (Trice & Beyer 1993), obscuring attention to cultural change. However, recent work on culture regards it much more dynamically (Hatch 1993; Hatch 2004), and hence available as a tool of insider-driven change (Weber et al. 2008; Howard-Grenville et al. 2011), not simply a source of stability. We see the 'culture as toolkit' perspective as particularly important for re thinking cultural change, for it engages with what a culture 'is' while also imagining what culture 'could be.' It also offers a way of thinking about cultural change as emergent and insider-driven, which is consistent with much of the literature to date on how environmental practices have been introduced to companies. We see further work on the processes of cultural change as particularly important to include in the growing literature on B&NE. As the Nike example at the opening of this chapter suggests, integrating environmental considerations into an organization's everyday life demands, if not a wholesale shift in culture, at least its intentional crafting in service of such change efforts. Further work should look specifically at the processes of cultural change, and the barriers to these, while also taking a longitudinal approach to consider change or implementation at different stages. More work is also needed to understand which practices are most effective at various stages as organizations try to embed environmental sustainability into their cultures and operations, and whether certain 'bundles' of practices are more effective than others (Bertels et al. 2010).

CONCLUSION

This chapter presents an overview of the ways in which organizational culture influences actions on environmental issues and the work that has been undertaken in the B&NE field to address this relationship. Beginning with a brief overview of the concept of organizational culture, we outlined three different perspectives on the cultural mechanisms of embedding environmental sustainability. We propose that these three different perspectives—culture as shared norms or values; culture as a frame or filter; and culture as a 'toolkit'—yield insights into our understanding of how culture may both support and restrict these efforts. Our review of the prior B&NE work related to culture reveals that our understanding of the interactions between organizational culture and environmental sustainability is still in its infancy. Clearly, there is much work that remains to be done.

As the B&NE field continues to gain more prominence and structure (as reflected in the creation this Handbook), addressing the relationship between culture and environmental sustainability needs to be high on the research agenda. In this chapter, we point to several particularly promising paths, including making culture more explicit in B&NE research: moving beyond success stories; addressing how the multidimensionality of environmental issues may impact culture change; considering the link between culture and identity or institutions; and taking a more longitudinal perspective in order to study the process of embedding environmental sustainability into an organization's culture. By laying the groundwork and pointing to the ways in which the B&NE literature can be informed by different perspectives on organizational culture, this chapter opens a number of pathways for future research.

References

Adriana, B. (2009). "Environmental Supply Chain Management in Tourism: The Case of Large Tour Operators," *Journal of Cleaner Production,* 17: 1385–1392.

Andersson, L., Shivarajan, S., & Blau, G. (2005). "Enacting Ecological Sustainability in the MNC: A Test of an Adapted Value-Belief-Norm Framework," *Journal of Business Ethics,* 59: 295–305.

Andersson, L. M. & Bateman, T. S. (2000). "Individual Environmental Initiative: Championing Natural Environmental Issues in US Business Organizations," *The Academy of Management Journal,* 43: 548–570.

Ángel del Brío, J., Junquera, B., & Ordiz, M. (2008). "Human Resources in Advanced Environmental Approaches-a Case Analysis," *International Journal of Production Research,* 46: 6029–6053.

Aten, K., Howard-Grenville, J. & Ventresca, M. (2012). "A Conversation at the Border of Culture and Institutions (in press)," *Journal of Management Inquiry.*

Balzarova, M. A., Castka, P., Bamber, C. J. & Sharp, J. M. (2006). "How Organisational Culture Impacts on the Implementation of ISO 14001:1996: a UK Multiple-Case View," *Journal of Manufacturing Technology Management,* 17: 89–103.

Bansal, P. (2003). "From Issues to Actions: The Importance of Individual Concerns and Organizational Values in Responding to Natural Environmental Issues," *Organization Science,* 510–527.

Berry, G. R. (2004). "Environmental Management The Selling of Corporate Culture," *Journal of Corporate Citizenship,* 16: 71–84.

Bertels, S., Papania, L. & Papania, D. (2010). "Embedding Sustainability in Organizational Culture: A Systematic Review of the Body of Knowledge." Available at: <http://www.nbs.net/knowledge/culture>

—— & Peloza, J. (2008). "Running Just to Stand Still? Managing CSR Reputation in an Era of Ratcheting Expectations," *Corporate Reputation Review,* 11: 56–72.

Beske, P., Koplin, J. & Seuring, S. (2008). "The Use of Environmental and Social Standards by German First-Tier Suppliers of the Volkswagen AG," *Corporate Social Responsibility & Environmental Management,* 153: 68–75.

Buysse, K. & Verbeke, A. (2003). "Proactive Environmental Strategies: A Stakeholder Management Perspective," *Strategic Management Journal,* 24: 453–470.

Ceres (2010). "The 21st Century Corporation: The Ceres Roadmap for Sustainability," Available at <http://www.ceres.org/ceresroadmap>

Chamorro, A. & Bañegil, T. M. (2006). "Green Marketing Philosophy: A Study of Spanish Firms with Ecolabels," *Corporate Social Responsibility & Environmental Management*, 13: 11–24.

Cheung, D. K. K., Welford, R. J., & Hills, P. R. (2009). "CSR and the Environment: Business Supply Chain Partnerships in Hong Kong and China," *Corporate Social Responsibility & Environmental Management*, 16: 250–263.

Chiles, T. H., Meyer, A. D. & Hench, T. J. (2004). "Organizational Emergence: The Origin and Transformation of Branson, Missouri's Musical Theaters", *Organization Science*, 15: 499–519.

Christianson, M. K., Farkas, M. T., Sutcliffe, K. M. & Weick, K. E. (2009). "Learning Through Rare Events: Significant Interruptions at the Baltimore & Ohio Railroad Museum," *Organization Science*, 20: 846–860.

Cordano, M. & Frieze, I. H. (2000). "Pollution Reduction Preferences of U.S. Environmental Managers: Applying Ajzen's Theory of Planned Behavior," *The Academy of Management Journal*, 43: 627–641.

Cramer, J., Jonker, J., & van der Heijden, A. (2004). "Making Sense of Corporate Social Responsibility," *Journal of Business Ethics*, 55: 215–222.

Creed, W. E. D., Scully, M. A., & Austin, J. R. (2002). "Clothes Make the Person? The Tailoring of Legitimating Accounts and the Social Construction of Identity," *Organization Science*, 13: 475–496.

Darnall, N. & Edwards, D. (2006). "Predicting the Cost of Environmental Management System Adoption: The Role of Capabilities, Resources and Ownership Structure," *Strategic Management Journal*, 27: 301–320.

Deal, T. & Kennedy, A. (1982). *Corporate Cultures*. Reading, MA, Addison-Wesley.

Dixon, S. E. A. & Clifford, A. (2007). "Ecopreneurship: A New Approach to Managing the Triple Bottom Line," *Journal of Organizational Change Management*, 20: 326–345.

Douglas, M. (1966). *Purity and Danger: an Analysis of Concepts of Pollution and Taboo*. New York, NY, Routledge & K. Paul.

—— (1978). "Cultural Bias." Occasional Paper No. 35 of the Royal Anthropological Institute of Great Britain and Ireland. Royal Anthropological Institute.

Douglas, T. (2007). "Reporting on the Triple Bottom Line at Cascade Engineering," *Global Business & Organizational Excellence*, 26: 35–43.

DuBose, J. R. (2000). "Sustainability and Performance at Interface, Inc," *Interfaces*, 30: 190–201.

Dunphy, D. (2003). *Organizational Change for Corporate Sustainability*. New York, NY, Routledge.

Dutton, J. E. & Dukerich, J. M. (1991). "Keeping an Eye on the Mirror: Image and Identity in Organizational Adaptation," *The Academy of Management Journal*, 34: 517–554.

——Worline, M. C., Frost, P. J. & Lilius, J. (2006). "Explaining Compassion Organizing," *Administrative Science Quarterly*, 51: 59–96.

Emerson, T. & Welford, R. (1997). "Power, Organizational Culture and Ecological Abuse," in R. Welford (ed.), *Corporate Environmental Management:Culture and Organizations*. London: Earthscan, 57–75.

Esquer-Peralta, J., Velazquez, L. & Munguia, N. (2008). "Perceptions of Core Elements for Sustainability Management Systems (SMS)," *Management Decision*, 46: 1027–1038.

Fine, G. A. (1984). "Negotiated Orders and Organizational Cultures," *Annual Review of Sociology*, 10: 239–262.

Geertz, C. (1973). *The Interpretation of Cultures: Selected Essays*. New York, NY, Basic Books.

Golden, K. A. (1992). "The Individual and Organizational Culture: Strategies for Action in Highly-Ordered Contexts," *Journal of Management Studies*, 29: 1–21.

Goodman, A. (2000). "Implementing Sustainability in Service Operations at Scandic Hotels," *Interfaces*, 30: 202–214.

Gunningham, N., Kagan, R. & Thornton, D. (2003). *Shades of Green: Business, Regulation, and Environment*. Stanford, CA, Stanford University Press.

Hallett, T. (2003). "Symbolic Power and Organizational Culture," *Sociological Theory*, 21: 128–149.

Harris, L. C. & Crane, A. (2002). "The Greening of Organizational Culture: Management Views on the Depth, Degree and Diffusion of Change," *Journal of Organizational Change Management*, 15: 214–234.

Hatch, M. J. (1993). "The Dynamics of Organizational Culture," *Academy of Management Review*, 18: 657–693.

—— (2004). "Dynamics in Organizational Culture," in M. S. Poole and A. Van de Ven (eds.), *Handbook of Organizational Change and Innovation*. Oxford, UK: Oxford University Press, 190–211.

—— (2010). "Culture Stanford's way," in M. D. Lounsbury (ed.), *Research in the Sociology of Organizations*. Emerald Group Publishing Limited, 71–95.

Herremans, I., Herschovis, M. & Bertels, S. (2009). "Leaders and Laggards: The Influence of Competing Logics on Corporate Environmental Action," *Journal of Business Ethics*, 89: 449–472.

Holton, I., Glass, J. & Price, A. D. F. (2010). "Managing for Sustainability: Findings from Four Company Case Studies in the UK Precast Concrete Industry," *Journal of Cleaner Production*, 18: 152–160.

Howard-Grenville, J. A. (2006). "Inside the 'Black Box': How Organizational Culture and Subcultures Inform Interpretations and Actions on Environmental Issues," *Organization & Environment*, 19: 46–73.

—— (2007a). *Corporate Culture and Environmental Practice: Making Change at a High-Technology Manufacturer*. Cheltemham, UK, Edward Elgar.

—— (2007b). "Developing Issue-Selling Effectiveness over Time: Issue Selling as Resourcing," *Organization Science*, 18: 560–577.

—— Golden-Biddle, K., Irwin, J. & Mao, J. (2011). "Liminality as Cultural Process for Cultural Change," *Organization Science*: 22: 522–39.

Howard-Grenville, J. A. & Hoffman, A. J. (2003). "The Importance of Cultural Framing to the Success of Social Initiatives in Business," *The Academy of Management Executive* 17: 70–86.

—— Nash, J., & Coglianese, C. (2008). "Constructing the License to Operate: Internal Factors and Their Influence on Corporate Environmental Decisions," *Law & Policy*, 30: 73–107.

Howard, J., Nash, J., & Ehrenfeld, J. (1999). "Industry Codes as Agents of Change: Responsible Care Adoption by US Chemical Companies," *Business Strategy and the Environment*, 8: 281–295.

Jenkins, H. (2006). "Small Business Champions for Corporate Social Responsibility," *Journal of Business Ethics*, 67: 241–256.

Jermier, J. M., Slocum Jr, J. W., Fry, L. W. & Gaines, J. (1991). "Organizational Subcultures in a Soft Bureaucracy: Resistance Behind The Myth and Facade of an Official Culture," *Organization Science*, 2: 170–194.

Jones, D. R. (2000). "A Cultural Development Strategy for Sustainability," *Greener Management International*, 71–85.

Kreiner, G. E. (2011). "Identity in Organizations: A Look at Culture's Conceptual Cousin," in N. M. Ashkanasy, C. P. M. Wilderom and M. P. Peterson (eds.), *Handbook of Organizational Culture and Climate, 2nd Edition*. Thousand Oaks, CA: Sage Publications, 463–480.

Kunda, G. (1992). *Engineering Culture: Control and Commitment in a High-Tech Corporation.* Philadelphia, PA, Temple University Press.

Lee, K.-H. (2009). "Why and How to Adopt Green Management into Business Organizations? The Case Study of Korean SMEs in Manufacturing Industry," *Management Decision,* 47: 1101–1121.

McAdam, D., McCarthy, J. D. & Zald, M. N. (1996). "Introduction: Opportunities, Mobilizing Structures, and Framing Processes—Toward a Synthetic, Comparative Perspective on Social Movements," in D. McAdam, J. D. McCarthy, and M. N. Zald (eds.), *Comparative Perspectives on Social Movements.* New York: Cambridge University Press, 1–20.

Mackrael, K. (2009). "A Natural Step Case Study: NIKE", *available at* <http://www.naturalste-pusa.org/storage/case-studies/Nike%20Case%20Study_Jan2009.pdf>

Markusson, N. (2010). "The Championing of Environmental Improvements in Technology Investment Projects," *Journal of Cleaner Production,* 18: 777–783.

Martin, J. (2002). *Organizational Culture: Mapping the Terrain.* Thousand Oaks, CA, Sage Publications Inc.

—— Frost, P. J., & O'Neill, O. A. (2006). "Organizational Culture: Beyond Struggles for Intellectual Dominance," in S. Clegg, W. Hardy and T. Lawrence (eds.), *Handbook of Organization Studies.* London: Sage, 599–621.

Meima, R. (1997). "The Challenge of Ecological Logic: Explaining Distinctive Organizational Phenomena in Corporate Environmental Management," in R. Welford (ed.), *Corporate Environmental Management:Culture and Organizations,* London: Earthscan, 26–56.

Meyerson, D. & Martin, J. (1987). "Cultural Change: An Integration of Three Different Views," *Journal of Management Studies,* 24: 623–647.

—— & Scully, M. A. (1995). "Tempered Radicalism and the Politics of Ambivalence and Change," *Organization Science,* 6: 585–600.

Molnar, E. & Mulvihill, P. R. (2003). "Sustainability-Focused Organizational Learning: Recent Experiences and New Challenges," *Journal of Environmental Planning & Management,* 46: 167–167.

Ouchi, W. (1981). *Theory Z: How American Business can Meet the Japanese Challenge.* New York, NY, Avon Books.

—— (1980). "Markets, Bureaucracies, and Clans," *Administrative Science Quarterly,* 25: 129–141.

Peters, T. J. & Waterman, R. H. (1982). *In Search of Excellence : Lessons from America's Best-Run Companies.* New York, NY, Harper & Row.

Ramus, C. A. & Steger, U. (2000). "The Roles of Supervisory Support Behaviors and Environmental Policy in Employee 'Ecoinitiatives' at Leading-Edge European Companies," *The Academy of Management Journal,* 43: 605–626.

Ravasi, D. & Schultz, M. (2006). "Responding to Organizational Identity Threats: Exploring the Role of Organizational Culture," *The Academy of Management Journal,* 49: 433–458.

Reverdy, T. (2006). "Translation Process and Organizational Change: ISO 14001 Implementation," *International Studies of Management and Organization,* 36: 9–30.

Rindova, V., Dalpiaz, E. & Ravasi, D. (2011). "A Cultural Quest: A Study of Organizational Use of New Cultural Resources in Strategy Formation," *Organization Science,* 22(2): 413–431.

Roome, N. (2005). "Stakeholder Power and Organizational Learning in Corporate Environmental Management," *Organization Studies,* 27: 235–263.

Schein, E. (1992). *Organizational Culture and Leadership: A Dynamic View.* San Francisco, CA, Jossey-Bass.

—— (1996). "Culture: The Missing Concept in Organization Studies," *Administrative Science Quarterly,* 41: 229–240.

Schön, D. (1983). *The Reflective Practitioner: How Professionals Think in Action*. New York, Basic Books.

Severn, S. (2010). New Ceres Report Delivers Powerful Message and Roadmap for Companies. See: <http://www.nikebiz.com/responsibility/considered_design/features/2010_SarahSevern CeresRoadmapBlog.html>

Sharma, S. (2000). "Managerial Interpretations and Organizational Context as Predictors of Corporate Choice of Environmental Strategy," *The Academy of Management Journal*, 43: 681–697.

Smircich, L. (1983). "Concepts of Culture and Organizational Analysis," *Administrative Science Quarterly*, 28: 339–358.

Smith, D. & Brown, M. S. (2003). "Sustainability and Corporate Evolution: Integrating Vision and Tools at Norm Thompson Outfitters," *Journal of Organizational Excellence*, 22: 3–14.

Snow, D. A. & Benford, R. D. (1988). "Ideology, Frame Resonance, and Participant Mobilization," *Int.Soc. Mov. Res*, 1: 197–218.

Stevenson, W. B. & Bartunek, J. M. (1996). "Power, Interaction, Position, and the Generation of Cultural Agreement in Organizations," *Human Relations*, 49: 75–104.

Swidler, A. (1986). 'Culture in Action: Symbols and Strategies.' *American Sociological Review*, 51: 273–286.

—— (2001). *Talk of Love: How Culture Matters*. Chicago, University Of Chicago Press.

—— (2008). "Comment on Stephen Vaisey's 'Socrates, Skinner, and Aristotle: Three Ways of Thinking About Culture in Action,'" *Sociological Forum*, 23: 614–618.

Trice, H. M. & Beyer, J. M. (1993). *The Cultures of Work Organizations*. Englewood Cliffs, NJ, Prentice-Hall.

Van Maanen, J. (1988). *Tales of the Field: On Writing Ethnography*. Chicago, IL, Chicago University Press.

—— (1991). "The Smile Factory: Work at Disneyland," in P. Frost, L. Moore, M. Louis, C. Lundberg and J. Martin (eds.), *Reframing Organizational Culture*. Newbury Park, CA.: Sage, 58–76.

—— & Barley, S. R. (1985). "Cultural Organization: Fragments of a Theory," in P. J. Frost, L. F. Moore, M. R. Louis, C. C. Lundberg and J. Martin (eds.), *Organizational Culture*. Beverly Hills: Sage Publications.

Weber, K. (2005). "A Toolkit for Analyzing Corporate Cultural Toolkits," *Poetics*, 33: 227–252.

—— & Dacin, T. (2011). "The Cultural Construction of Organizational Life: Introduction to the Special Issue," *Organization Science*, 22: 287–98.

—— Heinze, K. L. & DeSoucey, M. (2008). "Forage for Thought: Mobilizing Codes in the Movement for Grass-fed Meat and Dairy Products," *Administrative Science Quarterly*, 53: 529–567.

Weeks, J. R. (2004). *Unpopular Culture: Lay Ethnography as Cultural Critique*. Chicago, University of Chicago Press.

Wei-Skillern, J. (2004). "The Evolution of Shell's Stakeholder Approach: A Case Study," *Business Ethics Quarterly*, 14: 713–728.

Werre, M. (2003). "Implementing Corporate Responsibility: The Chiquita Case," *Journal of Business Ethics*, 44: 247–260.

Wilkins, A. (1989). *Developing Corporate Character: How to Successfully Change an Organization Without Destroying it*. San Francisco, CA, Jossey-Bass.

Zilber, T. B. (2008). "The work of meanings in institutional processes and thinking," in R. Greenwood, C. Oliver, K. Sahlin and R. Suddaby (eds.), *Sage Handbook of Organizational Institutionalism*. Los Angeles, CA: Sage, 151–169.

....

CHAPTER 12

INSTITUTIONAL APPROACHES TO ORGANIZATIONS AND THE NATURAL ENVIRONMENT

....

MICHAEL LOUNSBURY, SAMANTHA FAIRCLOUGH, AND MIN-DONG PAUL LEE

> A peaceful place or so it looks from space
> A closer look reveals the human race
> Full of hope, full of grace, is the human face
> But afraid, we may lay our home to waste
>
> Lyrics to *Throwing Stones* by the Grateful Dead

In his 23 September 2009 address to the United Nations General Assembly, US President Barack Obama emphasized that alongside disarmament, peace and security, and ensuring equal opportunity in an expanding global economy, "preservation of the planet" was one of the four key pillars that was fundamental to America's goals on the world stage. This attention to the natural environment is remarkable given that concern for the environment was miniscule just a few decades ago (Kneese & Schultze 1975). Obama's focus on the natural environment not only highlights its contemporary importance as a policy issue but, given the target audience of his speech, also highlights that the construction and implementation of such policies are transnational in scope and comprise varied geo-political considerations. This elevation of the natural environment as a policy issue of such magnitude, as well as the difficulty of addressing such complicated planetary concerns in a coordinated fashion, suggests the need to understand issues and problems related to the natural environment as embedded in institutional dynamics.

By institutional dynamics, we refer to the wider socio-historical processes within which organizational behavior and individual action occur (see Greenwood et al. 2008). While there are a wide variety of institutional theoretic approaches in organizational theory, neoinstitutional theory has provided a dominant lens—emphasizing how broader cognitive, normative, and regulative forces constitute and shape the behavior of actors (Scott 2008). Neoinstitutionalism has proven to be valuable in informing a great deal of contemporary scholarship on ecological dynamics and corporate environmentalism (e.g. Bansal & Roth 2000; Hoffman 1999; Jennings & Zandbergen 1995; Lounsbury 2001; Lounsbury, Ventresca, & Hirsch 2003), and provides a robust framework to guide future research on these topics.

For instance, a focus on institutional dynamics can deepen our understanding of current discourse and practice on pressing issues related to sustainable development or climate change—such as on how greenhouse gas pollution from a variety of industry sectors as well as other human activities related to resource extraction and farming is threatening the extinction of different kinds of species (Rockström et al. 2009). While such issues are informed by contemporary scientific advances, interest in these issues and the very existence of resources to support such scientific investigation is made possible by a great deal of prior environmental activism and institutional entrepreneurship—that is, institutional dynamics. Thus, institutional analysis directs the gaze of researchers to the historical processes and events that inform and situate current issues, in order to understand how prior activity constrains as well as enables what policy and social responses might be subsequently possible and appropriate.

To wit, appreciating the history of modern environmental activism is crucial to any neoinstitutional analysis of contemporary environmental issues. As is well documented, the modern environmental movement took shape in the post-World War II boom era, when the rapid growth of mass consumerism and associated environmental degradation (Packard 1960), including growing industrial pollution (Beamish 2002) and problems of toxicity in the food supply (e.g. see Maguire 2004; Maguire & Hardy 2009; Szasz 1994) generated heightened public and political scrutiny of environmental issues (e.g. Crenson 1971).[1] The mounting momentum of the environmental movement culminated on 22 April 22 1970 in a massive public demonstration called "Earth Day" that brought 20 million Americans out onto the streets in the name of environmentalism. In partial response to this disquiet, the US Environmental Protection Agency (EPA) was created in 1970, providing an authoritative governmental agency to oversee policy-making and regulation in respect of environmental problems, such as polluted air and water, rapidly filling waste dumps, and toxicity.

And while Reagan-era politics led to rollbacks in the creation, funding and policing of certain environmental policies, environmental issues continued to gain visibility on the national policy agenda (e.g. Dunlap 1992). In addition, the creation of formal, institutional mechanisms such as the EPA and varied professionalized social movement organ-

---

[1] One measure of growth of the environmental movement is the Sierra Club membership numbers, which grew from only 7,000 members in 1950 to 200,000 in 1980. The acceleration began mostly in the 1960s when the membership grew more than seven-fold from 16,000 in 1960 to 114,000 in 1970.

izations (e.g. Natural Resources Defense Council, Environmental Defense Fund, National Wildlife Federation, Sierra Club) redirected attention away from the claims of more radical social movement organizations (e.g. Earth First!) and towards mainstream policy negotiation (Hoffman & Ventresca 2002). Moreover, environmental problems emerged as key transnational policy issues that were informed and shaped by the growth of international environmental discourse and treaties (Frank 1997), the rise of new communities of environmental scientific experts (Haas 2003) and international environmental non-governmental organizations (Frank, Hironaka, & Schofer 2000).

Our understanding of these issues, especially more recent trends towards international regulation and surveillance, remains limited and should provide an important focus for future research. Our core assertion is that the growing salience of efforts to address sustainable development and climate change via industry-focused policies such as "cap-and-trade" emissions, reduction systems, and technologically-oriented entrepreneurial movements such as cleantech, are best understood as an outcome of broader institutional dynamics linked to social movement mobilization and the development of a growing infrastructure of expertise that helps to define the environmental issue agenda and concomitant policy-responses (see also Weber & Soderstrom [Chapter 14] this volume). In addition, our understanding of the more general relationship of organizations to the natural environment, as well as policy issues related to corporate environmentalism, is usefully enhanced by conceptualizing organizations as receptor sites of broader institutional dynamics, creating heterogeneous responses that are moderated by intermediary factors that exist in organizations' immediate environment or within organizations themselves.

Our chapter will proceed as follows. First, we will provide a brief overview of research on institutional dynamics, emphasizing neoinstitutional theory in organizational analysis (Greenwood et al. 2008; Powell & DiMaggio 1991; Scott 2008). In order to assess gaps and opportunities for the study of institutional dynamics at the interface of business and the environment, we then provide a brief review of the extant literature. We conclude with a discussion of opportunities for future institutionally oriented research.

RESEARCH ON INSTITUTIONAL DYNAMICS

The study of institutional dynamics is informed by work in sociology, economics, and political science that variously addresses cognitive, normative, and regulative dimensions of institutions and how they relate to the behavior of actors in a social system (see Scott 2008 for an overview). To analyze the disparate dimensions of institutional analysis, many institutionalists employ the notion of *field* (see Wooten & Hoffman 2008 for a review). This approach incorporates attention to various stakeholders (e.g. see Kassinis [Chapter 5]; and Delmas & Toffel [Chapter 13] this volume), but goes beyond conventional stakeholder theory to emphasize the embeddedness of organizations in a more extensive system of interaction that is informed and shaped by diverse institutional forces which delineate how actors in a particular field behave and, to a significant degree, share a common mindset and collective identity. DiMaggio & Powell (1991: 65) define an organizational field as "those organizations that, in the aggregate, constitute a recognized area of institutional life: key suppliers, resource and product consumers, regulatory agencies, and other organizations that produce similar services and products." In a somewhat related fashion, Scott (1995: 56) conceptualizes fields as comprising a "community of organizations that partakes of a common meaning system and whose participants interact more frequently and fatefully with one another than with actors outside the field."

As a broad corpus of scholarship, the institutional literature addresses policy prescription and analysis, as well as the historical construction of dominant social issues and fields of activity. Thus, institutional theoretic approaches address the sources and consequences of institutions, and can be harnessed for both normative and positive approaches. Scott (1995: 34) argues that institutional environment consists of "three pillars"—that is, regulative, normative and cognitive systems—and institutional scholarship mostly developed by stressing one or another of the three pillars. Below, we briefly highlight works that focus on regulatory, normative, and cognitive institutional forces within this school of thought.

Regulatory forces

The regulative dimension of institutional analysis tends to feature the study of regulatory agencies, as well as formal laws and policies and their enforcement, emphasizing how rule systems aim to *coerce* actors into certain behaviors. Roland (2004) characterizes formal rule systems as "fast-moving institutions," that are more likely to be shallow or superficial in their effects—as compared with normative and cognitive institutional forces (see Scott 2008). To the extent that formal rules are superficial, and difficult to enforce, actors can more easily "game the system" and deviate from the expectations of authorities. Researchon formal rule systems, regulatory constraints, and incentives by economists and rational choice political scientists (e.g. North 1990) exemplifies research in this vein, and typically employs more instrumental approaches to actors and agency.

However, in contradistinction to the analysis of regulatory arenas as mainly comprising shallow rules that are easily manipulated, sociologists and institutionally oriented political scientists have highlighted the need to understand rules, and their varied sources and consequences, as embedded in more complex fields of activity (Streeck & Thelen 2005; Zald & Lounsbury 2010). This richer approach to rule systems was pioneered by the development of iron triangle theory that examined the interrelationships between industry and special interest groups, Congressional committees, and regulatory agencies (e.g. Adams 1981; Allison & Zelikow 1999; Baumgartner and Jones 2005). In sociology, these issues have been addressed by research on the social control of industries (e.g. Zald 1978), industry governance (Campbell, Hollingsworth, & Lindberg 1990), business systems (e.g. Morgan, Whitley, & Moen 2004; Whitley 2007), and the evolutionary dynamics of rules (e.g. Baron, Dobbin, & Jennings 1986; Dobbin & Dowd 1997). Some of the more recent work, connected to the law and society literature, has sought to highlight the endogenous and complex nature of law creation and implementation (Sutton et al. 1994; Edelman, Abraham, & Erlanger 1992; Edelman & Suchman 2007).

With regard to research on business and the environment, the work of Russo and colleagues (e.g. Delmas, Russo, & Montes-Sancho forthcoming; Russo 1992; Russo & Harrison 2005) is exemplary in demonstrating the effects of regulatory institutional forces on energy producers (see also Russo & Minto [Chapter 2] this volume). Highlighting the importance of understanding the structure of governance systems, Hoffman (1999) showed how the creation of the Environmental Protection Agency shaped the way in which the field of environmental practice emerged and developed. Focusing on the dynamics of rule systems, Jennings and colleagues (2005) traced how the enactment of regional water laws varied over time as a result of multiple factors such as the interpretation of the law by the courts, changes in political parties, and exogenous shock events such as war. While this work has enhanced our understanding of regulatory forces in the domain of corporate environmentalism, much more research is needed on the wider structuring of environmental governance systems and on the varied effectiveness of different governance regimes.

Normative forces

Normative forces introduce "a prescriptive, evaluative, and obligatory dimension into social life" (Scott 2008: 32). The role of norms has always been central in sociological variants of institutional analysis—especially the institutional analysis of Selznick (e.g. 1949) and his contemporaries (see Hirsch & Lounsbury 1997). This literature tends to emphasize how behavior is driven by commitments linked to values and norms that were internalized as a result of varied socialization processes. The notion of norm relates to broadly accepted societal expectations of appropriate behavior such as the "norm of reciprocity" (e.g. Gouldner 1960); violations of such widely shared expectations can lead to sanction. The role of professionals (DiMaggio & Powell 1983) and other third-party arbiters (e.g. Zuckerman 1999) are theorized as key promulgators and enforcers of institutionalized norms.

A focus on normative institutional forces has been a dominant theme in the literature on business and the environment. The work of King and colleagues, for example, has highlighted the importance of industry self-regulatory norms of environmental performance and management (e.g. Barnett & King 2008; King & Lenox 2000) (see also King, Prado, & Rivera [Chapter 6] this volume) as well as the role of certification and certification agencies such as ISO in catalyzing better environmental performance (e.g. Bansal & Bogner 2002; King, Lenox, & Terlaak 2005). Similarly, based on their qualitative analysis of firms from the United Kingdom and Japan, Bansal & Roth (2000) argued that institutional legitimacy is one of the central factors shaping corporate ecological responsiveness. It would be useful to build on this work to examine the construction and effectiveness of norms within and across organizations and fields, and how normative forces can supplement more formal regulatory approaches to environmental problems.

Cognitive forces

Institutional research also stresses the importance of broader *taken-for-granted* cognitive forces such as logics and other cultural beliefs that pre-consciously structure cognition, direct attention, and shape behavior (Meyer, Boli, & Thomas 1987; Powell & DiMaggio 1991). For instance, researchers have shown that institutional logics fundamentally shape cognition and decision-making (Thornton & Ocasio 1999), and that the creation of new practices often requires a shift in dominant logics (e.g. Haveman & Rao 1997). Compared to regulative and normative forces, cognitive institutional forces tend to have more profound and pervasive effects because they tend to remain unquestioned. In contrast to the instrumental action that is focalized in economic analyses of regulation, research on cognitive forces emphasizes the constitutive nature of institutions—how cultural elements such as categories, scripts and conventions enable action and "create the very possibility of certain activities" (Searle 1995: 64).

A handful of studies even explore the relationship of cognitive institutional forces to the environmental practices of corporations. For instance, Lounsbury, Ventresca, & Hirsch (2003) showed that it was not until the broader field frame of resource recovery which valorized waste-to-energy incineration over recycling practices in the US solid waste field was dismantled to enable the creation of recycling as a separate discourse category, that recycling practices gained mainstream acceptance and diffused into the broader cultural milieu. As a result, traditional solid waste haulers became advocates and key beneficiaries of curbside recycling and international recycling markets. In a similar vein, Maguire (2004) showed how finding an appropriate substitute for insecticidal DDT, the toxic chemical targeted by Rachel Carson (1962), was bound up in discursive dynamics. While this work has demonstrated the power of field-level cognitive forces, it would be especially useful to complement these efforts with attention to how such broader categories and discourses actually shape individual- and organization-level cognition.

Even though different scholars place varied emphases on regulative, normative, and cognitive institutional forces and dynamics, it is important to note that it is very difficult to parse these three dimensions empirically, and much of the research in this tradition often blends all three. For instance, Hoffman's (1997) institutional history of corporate environmentalism showed how the unfolding of the 1960s' environmental social movement led to corresponding changes in the perceptions and practices of large-scale corporations in the chemical and petroleum industries. He demonstrates how norms, rules and beliefs change in tandem across four periods: from Industrial Environmentalism (1960–1970) to Regulatory Environmentalism (1970–1982) to Environmentalism as Social Responsibility (1982–1988) to Strategic Environmentalism (1988–1993). Thus, despite the theoretical usefulness of segregating regulative, normative and cognitive forces, we suggest that research should focus less on disentangling these different forces, and more on highlighting how varied constellations of institutional forces relate to different kinds of organizational behaviors and outcomes.

As this brief overview of institutional dynamics research highlights, a broad array of topics and theoretical foci pervade the literature. However, this corpus of scholarship is united by a shared interest in understanding how organizational action is embedded in wider fields of activity, as well as how constellations of regulative, normative, and cognitive forces fundamentally shape the behavior of actors in fields. The subject matter of organizations and the natural environment inherently lends itself to institutional analysis. For example, as Hoffman (1997) cleverly expresses it, environmentalism has undergone a dramatic institutional transformation from "heresy to dogma" in the business community. The transformation is clearly not driven by market forces, but rather there are many institutional factors which have contributed to the emergence of pro-environmental corporate practices. Environmental movement organizations and government agencies such as the Environmental Protection Agency and Occupational Safety and Health Administration have, for instance, become a strong coercive force monitoring and regulating corporate environmental practices. As for normative institutional forces, the growing number of environmental self-regulations (e.g. Responsible Care and ISO 14000), as well as the corpus of academic studies which advocate the financial and social benefits of improved environmental management, have continued to sustain social pressure upon firms. Lastly, during the previous two decades, environmentalism and green management have emerged as alternative institutional cognitive frames, challenging the traditional market logics of profit and unfettered growth.

THE STUDY OF INSTITUTIONAL DYNAMICS IN THE BUSINESS AND ENVIRONMENT LITERATURE

Before we chart out fruitful directions for future research, we would like to briefly situate research on institutional dynamics within the field of organizationally based environmental scholarship. To do this, we reviewed all research articles in one of the leading specialty journals in the field, *Organization & Environment*, for the period 1997–2009, to gain an understanding of which research problems related to business and the environment have garnered significant attention by researchers. This enabled us to develop a cursory understanding of possible research gaps and opportunities for the study of institutional dynamics at the business–environment nexus. From our review of published articles in *Organization & Environment*, we identified four main research foci that attracted concentrated attention from organizational scholars: (1) how corporations respond to environmental problems, (2) the organizational dimensions of the environmental movement, (3) environmental justice, and (4) sustainability.

How corporations respond to environmental problems

One of the most popular topics of study among research published in *Organization & Environment* relates to the adoption (voluntarily or otherwise) of corporate environmental practices or programs. For instance, in a particularly intriguing study, Howard-Grenville (2006) examined the role of organizational culture and subcultures in shaping companies' interpretations of, and actions towards, environmental issues (see also Howard-Grenville & Bertels [Chapter 11] this volume). Drawing more directly on institutional theory, Hoffman (2001) studied why companies incorporate environmental concerns into their strategies and actions, and suggests a conceptual model linking various constituencies of the institutional field—such as investors and consumers—with the structural and cultural routines that become enacted within firms. A similar topic is addressed by Moon & DeLeon (2007), who identify the institutional pressures that encourage firms to commit resources to voluntary environmental strategies in order to obtain legitimacy. Analogous themes are explored by Marshall and Standifird (2005), who look at how isomorphic pressures impact organizations in the organic certification industry, and Luke (2001), who analyzed Ford's attempt to reinvent itself as a green business leader.

We believe that this stream of research is particularly fruitful and expect to see a great deal of future research on the topic. While extant research that has focused on institutional dynamics has tended to stress a single dominant institutional logic and top-down isomorphic processes, we believe future research will draw more on contemporary developments in institutional theory that emphasize the fragmented nature of organizational environments, the pluralistic nature of organizations, and the heterogeneous responses of corporations to varied institutional pressures (e.g. Kraatz & Block 2008; Lounsbury 2007). We elaborate on these directions in our discussion.

The Organizational Dimensions of the Environmental Movement

Another locus for empirical and theoretical consideration is the organizations which constitute a critical part of the environmental movement. Research has examined the culture, structure and operation of NGOs, "grassroots" organizations, and other types of environmental interest group (e.g. Carmin & Balser 2002; Dreiling & Wolf 2001; Dreiling et al. 2008). In addition, many scholars have focused on the factors determining the success of such organizations in preserving natural resources, opposing industrial development, and effecting behavioral change for the environmental good (e.g. Kaczmarski &

Cooperrider 1997; Weinberg 1997; Widener 2007). Other researchers have focused on the increasing public mistrust of science-based environmental information, and how environmental movement organizations can mobilize by contesting or engaging policy issues via scientific expertise (McCormick 2009; Schrader-Freschette 1997).

Of course, the study of environmental movement organizational processes has also been the focal point for institutional theory research on the sources and consequences of such organizations and movement dynamics (e.g. Lounsbury 2001; Lounsbury, Ventresca, & Hirsch 2003), and we expect that research on the institutional dynamics of movements provides a key direction for scholarship (see also Weber & Soderstrom [Chapter 14] this volume). A focus on the institutional dynamics of such interface between movements and institutions can shed important light on the mobilization efforts of environmental activist groups, the success of their action repertoires, and how ecological restoration and environmental justice movements may bring about reparation or regime change.

Environmental justice

A related research strand among articles in *Organization & Environment* focuses on the inequitable distribution of environmental burdens among socially and economically disadvantaged populations such as women, indigenous groups, racial minorities, the poor, and peoples from less developed countries. These so-called "environmental justice" studies intersect with the environmental movement literature where they examine the organizations which represent these communities, and/or their attempts at ecological restoration (e.g. Gedicks 2004; Tomblin 2009). Other researchers are interested in the effect of pollution, industrial development, and other forms of environmental degradation upon ethnic, minority, and other disadvantaged groups. Jorgensen (2007), for example, studied the extent to which foreign investment harms the environment in less developed countries; similarly, Whiteman (2004) examined the impact of a hydroelectricity project on the aboriginal people of James Bay, Quebec.

While issues of environmental justice highlight inequities in the distribution of power across geographic space, a focus on institutional dynamics could contribute to a deeper understanding of the processes by which different kinds of groups in different kinds of locations become targets for corporate polluting behavior, as well as how varied groups are able to successfully contest corporate power. The pressing need for such research is echoed by the writings of Jermier et al. (2006) who, in discussing the 'new corporate environmentalism', suggest "perverse forms of politics" have been institutionalized, and that "nationally based environmental organizations and local forms of environmental activism" are completely inadequate to deal with the power corporations have to dictate the environmental agenda (see p. 624). Emerging scholarship that brings institutional and social movement theory together begins to shed some light on how various institutional entrepreneurs such as shareholder activists are overcoming the power imbalance to significantly affect corporate environmental behavior (Lee & Lounsbury forthcoming).

Sustainability

Sustainable development—the notion of balancing economic growth with environmental protection so that the needs of the present day are met without affecting the well-being of future generations (Roumasset 1990)—provides a key topic of growing interest among researchers. For instance, Gould's (1999) fascinating case study examined the development of sustainable nature-based tourism in the rainforests of Ecuador and Belize. Other researchers have analyzed corporate discourse in sustainability values reports (Livesey & Kearins 2002), and the development of a 'sustainability business model' (Stubbs & Cocklin 2008).

Institutional dynamics also figure prominently in this stream of research. Hoffman & Henn (2008) examined the constraining effect of institutional forces in their study, which considers the taken-for-granted beliefs obstructing the adoption of green building practices and environmentally sustainable building design and delivery in the construction industry. Srikantia & Bilmoria (1997) construct an analogous argument in their review of the sustainability literature. They find it dominated by a corporate model perpetuated by scholars and managers whereby isomorphic pressures have transformed the meaning of sustainability into one which accords with the practices of mainstream business organizations. While it has been over fifteen years since Jennings & Zandbergen (1995) laid out an agenda for the use of institutional theory to study ecologically sustainable organizations, we believe that much remains to be done, and that their agenda continues to provide some useful guideposts.

FUTURE OPPORTUNITIES AND
RESEARCH DIRECTIONS

Research on business and the environment is a robust and growing area of research, and we believe that there are a number of opportunities that zoom in on institutional processes to both enhance our understanding of key issues, as well as to contribute to policy. As our overview of the literature indicates, institutional theory questions the fundamental sources of environmental destruction and action, offering insights about how regulative, normative and cognitive forces shape social perception and environmental behavior (Scott 2008). However, it is important to note that contemporary institutional research has begun to shift away from a focus on top-down isomorphic pressure and towards a focus on institutional pluralism and organizational heterogeneity (Kraatz & Block 2008; Lounsbury 2007; Reay & Hinings 2009; Thornton & Ocasio 2008). We encourage researchers interested in institutional dynamics to engage with this wider theoretical conversation to shed new light on the corporation–environment linkage. While we believe that there are many research opportunities related to the topics reviewed in the previous section, here we would like to briefly highlight opportunities to expand the scope of research on institutional dynamics by focusing on the topics of (1) Greenwashing, (2) Climate Change, (3) Movements and Counter Movements, and (4) Policy.

Greenwashing

Given recent trends in institutional analysis towards an understanding of varied organizational responses to institutional pressures, of particular interest could be the topic of greenwashing—empty policies, or a façade of practices, which appear to be environmentally proactive (Beder 1997) (see Jermier & Forbes [Chapter 30] this volume). In contrast to a focus on isomorphism, such research would probe the extent to which organizations are able to decouple their behavior from institutional prescription, thereby developing symbolic responses that satisfy stakeholders and other interested actors (e.g. see Westphal & Zajac 1994). We propose that institutional dynamics offer much latent explanatory promise in understanding how corporate environmental impacts are perpetuated and/or tolerated, and in accounting for the behavior of corporations in their adoption of green business practices. Since institutional theory encourages critical inquiry into the fundamental sources of environmental destruction or action, it may offer fresh insights about how social perception and the enactment of environmental issues are influenced by regulative, normative and cognitive forces (Scott 2008). These dimensions combine in an amalgam of institutional pressure that drives corporate action, whether it be for profit or environmental protection.

A focus on the institutional dynamics of greenwashing may assist in identifying the extent to which corporate environmental practices are real or ceremonial, and how regulation, professional and social codes of conduct, and shared cognitions and logics legitimate or condemn various types of corporate behavior. A focus on the concrete mechanisms that enable different kinds of organizations to greenwash to different extents, or not at all, would be particularly valuable, and would contribute not only to theory, but also to the design of policy and the strategic approaches of stakeholders and activists.

Climate change

Despite the advocacy of former Vice-President Al Gore and others (e.g. Gore 2006), there remains considerable skepticism about the real ecological threat from greenhouse gas emissions (Hoggan 2009). Norgaard (2006) found that Norwegian apathy, despite repeated warnings of the consequences of global warming, was at least partially explained by a form of socially approved organized denial linked to Norwegian economic interests. But much more research is needed on how and why different nation states and communities of actors differentially contribute to and respond to climate change discourse. It is absolutely crucial to develop a richer appreciation of the media and how the production and evolution of discourse fundamentally shapes the saliency of environmental problems and how people understand and react to them (e.g. Lawrence & Phillips 2004; Phillips, Lawrence, & Hardy 2004).

Such institutionally oriented research would shed light on the ways in which global environmental problems related to climate change have been addressed, or may be successfully tackled in the future. One need only recall the refusal of the United States to ratify the Kyoto Protocol on global climate change to demonstrate how a conflict of opinion or policy—undoubtedly rooted in the differing institutional logics of nation states—can derail global environmental initiatives. It would be especially useful to develop comparative research designs that examine the role of scientific knowledge in addressing and framing environmental concerns in the media and the public sphere across different countries (Djelic & Sahlin-Anderson 2005; Djelic & Quack 2003).

Movements and counter-movements

Expanding upon research on the institutional dynamics of environmental movements, we believe that more sustained attention needs to be paid to the dynamic and interactive relationship between corporations and environmental movement organizations (see Weber & Soderstrom [Chapter 14] this volume), and the spread of environmentalism in the form of environmental justice networks. We note how the environmental movement of the 1960s dramatically altered the corporate landscape by impacting the philosophies of businesses and government to shape the institutional environment (Hoffman 1999). In an oral history interview series conducted by the EPA, its first administrator, William Ruckelshaus (1993: 1), maintained that public opinion was "absolutely essential for anything to be done on behalf of the environment. Absent that, nothing will happen because the forces of the economy and the impact on people's livelihood are so much more automatic and endemic. Absent some countervailing public pressure for the environment, nothing much will happen." Mounting public pressure on politicians and law-makers resulted in the rapid institutionalization of environmental regulations in the 1970s, and the resulting emergence of the 'green consumer'.

However, corporations quickly responded to these institutional changes by bolstering their political lobbying activities. By the early 1980s, political support for environmental groups was weakening and the pendulum of environmental institutions had shifted in the opposite direction. In particular, President Reagan's Executive Order 12291, which required all major federal regulations to be subject to a cost-benefit analysis before being carried out, dramatically changed the institutional environment by severely limiting the EPA's ability to carry out its mandate. These changes in the institutional environment, in turn, forced environmental movement organizations to reinvent themselves and professionalize their movement tactics and activities (e.g. shareholder activism, mainstream policy engagement, corporate consultation and production of relevant research).

In addition to those broader movement/counter-movement dynamics, it would be useful to examine how corporations differentially respond to movement pressure. As Davis et al. (2008: 390) suggest "some corporations respond to pressures by social movements by changing their strategies, structures, and routines. Others are obdurate in their resistance. Still others create Potemkin Village counter-movements to articulate their perspective—known as 'astroturf organizing,' in contrast to grassroots organizing." Why do firm responses differ so dramatically? What is the possibility for corporations to resist such pressure, or collective mobilize to create an effective counter-mobilization? A focus on the institutional dynamics which impact the relationship between organizations and the natural environment can effectively expand our research horizons and provide insights into the social mechanisms by which environmental impairments or safeguards are produced, perpetuated, or prevented.

Policy

Finally, we believe that research on institutional dynamics is especially crucial because it can fruitfully contribute to policy formulation, design, and implementation (see Zald & Lounsbury 2010). This was clearly signaled by the publication of *Organizations, Policy, and the Natural Environment: Institutional and Strategic Perspectives* (Hoffman & Ventresca 2002), a collection of empirical papers and thought pieces that demonstrated the utility of institutional analysis for informing environmental management and policy debates. The scope of this compilation is wide-ranging in its application of an institutional perspective to green management theory, including explanations of the contestation and field structure of environmentalism; the influence of isomorphism and decoupling in response to regulation, uncertainty and custom; the enabling and constraining power of institutions in discourse and policy; and how differences in field-level cognitive models, discourses, and communities can influence organizational strategies and behaviors. However, the promise of this Handbook is yet to be realized, and we encourage a more concerted effort by business and environment researchers to focus on policy-relevant issues and engage policymakers. While theory and criticism are important, our scholarship will ultimately have little impact unless we can mobilize and translate our research findings to help shape policy debate, or otherwise develop policy recommendations that aim to make a better world.

In sum, contemporary environmental threats, such as global warming and its concomitant hazards, such as rising sea levels, glacier retreat, and species extinction, and the role of governments and the media in shaping public perceptions of these threats, provide a germane and challenging focus for institutionally oriented environmental management research. It would be useful for researchers to focus more intently on how such environmental "crises" are constructed and variously generate intense media scrutiny, public anger, and corporate vilification. One need only think of the enormous and critical attention paid by the U.S. government and the media to BP's massive oil spill in the

Gulf of Mexico in 2010, while worse oil spills which continue to wreak damage upon human health and livelihoods in Nigeria and Ecuador are ignored (Khor 2010). These situations demonstrate how government and media attention is shaped by institutionalized political and cultural interests. Clearly, there is still much to uncover about how institutional rules and beliefs underpin the environmental actions of corporations as well as the development and implementation of policy by regimes around the world. Institutional theory provides the tools to assess the context within which environmental policy is shaped, and to investigate how issues and problems are defined, attended to, and addressed. In turn, an increased understanding of how corporations and the environment are embedded in wider institutional dynamics will enable a richer discussion about policy options and a more informed approach to the creation of policy responses.

REFERENCES

Adams, G. (1981). *The Iron Triangle: The Politics of Defense Contracting.* NY: Council on Economic Priorities.

Allison, G. T. & Zelikow, P. (1999). *Essence of Decision: Explaining the Cuban Missile Crisis,* 2nd edition. NY: Pearson Longman.

Bansal, P. & Bogner, W. C. (2002). "Deciding on ISO 14001: Economics, Institutions and Context," *Long Range Planning,* 35: 269–290.

Bansal, P. & Roth, K. (2000). "Why Companies Go Green: A Model of Ecological Responsiveness," *Academy of Management Journal,* 43: 717–736.

Barnett, M. & King, A. (2008). "Good Fences Make Good Neighbors: A Longitudinal Analysis of an Industry Self-Regulatory Institution," *Academy of Management Journal,* 51: 1150–1170.

Baron, J. P., Dobbin, F., & Jennings, P. D. (1986). "War and Peace: The Evolution of Modern Personnel Administration in U.S. Industry," *American Journal of Sociology,* 92: 250–283.

Baumgartner, F. R. & Jones, B. D. (2005). *The Politics of Attention: How Government Prioritizes Problems.* Chicago: University of Chicago Press.

Beamish, T. D. (2002). *Silent Spill: The Organization of Industrial Crisis.* Cambridge, MA: MIT Press.

Beder, S. (1997). *Global Spin: The Corporate Assault on Environmentalism.* White River Junction, VT: Chelsea Green.

Campbell, J. L., Hollingsworth, J. R., & Lindberg, L. N. (1990). *Governance of the American Economy.* Cambridge: Cambridge University Press.

Carmin, J., & Balser, D. (2002). "Selecting Repertoires of Action in Environmental Movement Organizations: An Interpretive Approach," *Organization & Environment,* 15(4): 365–388.

Carson, R. (1962). *Silent Spring.* Boston, MA: Houghton Mifflin.

Crenson, M. A. (1971). *The Un-Politics of Air Pollution.* Baltimore, MD: Johns Hopkins Press.

Davis, G. F., Morrill, C., Rao, H., and Soule, S. A. (2008). "Introduction: Social Movements in Organizations and Markets," *Administrative Science Quarterly,* 53(3): 389–394.

Delmas, M., Russo, M. V., & Montes-Sancho, M. (forthcoming). "Deregulation and Environmental Differentiation in the Electric Utility Industry," *Strategic Management Journal.*

DiMaggio, P. J. & Powell, W. W. (1991). "Introduction," in W. W. Powell & P. J. DiMaggio (eds.) *The New Institutionalism in Organizational Analysis*: 1–40. Chicago: University of Chicago Press.

———— (1983). "The Iron Cage Revisited: Institutional Isomorphism and Collective Rationality in Organizational Fields," *American Sociological Review*, 48: 147–160.

—— & Quack, S. (eds.) (2003). *Globalization and Institutions: Redefining the Rules of the Economic Game*. Cheltenham (Grande-Bretagne): Edward Elgar Publishing.

——Djelic, M. & Sahlin, K. (eds.) (2006). *Transnational Governance: Institutional Dynamics of Regulation*. Cambridge, U.K.: Cambridge University Press.

Dobbin, F. & Dowd, T. (1997). "How Policy Shapes Competition: Early Railroad Foundings in Massachusetts," *Administrative Science Quarterly*, 42: 501–529.

Dreiling, M., Jonna, R., Lougee, N., and Nakamura, T. (2008). "Environmental Organizations and Communication Praxis: A Study of Communication Strategies among a National Sample of Environmental Organizations," *Organization & Environment*, 21(4): 420–445.

—— & Wolf, B. (2001). "Environmental Movement Organizations and Political Strategy: Tactical Conflicts over NAFTA," *Organization & Environment*, 14(1): 34–54.

Dunlap, R. (1992). *American Environmentalism: The U.S. Environmental Movement, 1970–1990*. New York: Taylor and Francis.

Edelman, L. B., Abraham, S. E., & Erlanger H. S. (1992). "Professional Construction of Law: The Inflated Threat of Wrongful Discharge," Law & Society Review, 26(1): 47–84.

—— & Suchman, M. C. (eds.) (2007). *The Legal Lives of Private Organizations*. Surrey, U.K: Ashgate.

—— Uggen, C., & Erlanger, H. (1999). "The Endogeneity of Legal Regulation: Grievance Procedures as Rational Myth," *American Journal of Sociology*, 105: 406–54.

Frank, D. J. (1997). Science, Nature, and the Globalization of the Environment. *Social Forces*, 76, 409–435.

—— Hironaka, A., & Schofer, E. (2000). "The Nation-State and the Natural Environment over the Twentieth Century," *American Sociological Review*, 65: 96–116.

Gedicks, A. (2004). "Liberation Sociology and Advocacy for the Sokaogon Ojibwe," *Organization & Environment*, 17(4): 449–470.

Gore, A. (2006). *An Inconvenient Truth: The Planetary Emergency of Global Warming and What We Can Do About It*. New York: Rodale.

Gould, K. A. (1999). "Tactical Tourism: A Comparative Analysis of Rainforest Development in Ecuador and Belize," *Organization & Environment*, 12(3): 245–262.

Gouldner, A. W. (1960). "The Norm of Reciprocity: A Preliminary Statement," *American Sociological Review*, 25: 165–170.

Greenwood, R., Oliver, C., Sahlin, K., and Suddaby, R. (eds) (2008). *Handbook of Institutional Theory*. London: SAGE.

Haas, P. M. (ed.) (2003). *Environment in the New Global Economy*. New York: Edward Elgar.

Haveman, H. A. & Rao, H. (1997) "Structuring a Theory of Moral Sentiments: Institutional and Organizational Co-Evolution in the Early Thrift Industry," *American Journal of Sociology*, 102: 1606–1651.

Hirsch, P. M. & Lounsbury, M. (1997). "Ending the Family Quarrel: Towards a Reconciliation of "Old" and "New" Institutionalism," *American Behavioral Scientist*, 40: 406–418.

Hoffman, A. J. (1997). *From Heresy to Dogma: An Institutional History of Corporate Environmentalism*. San Francisco, CA: New Lexington Press.

—— (1999). "Institutional Evolution and Change: Environmentalism and the U.S. Chemical Industry," *Academy of Management Journal,* 42: 351–371.

—— (2001). "Linking Organizational and Field Level Analyses: The Diffusion of Corporate Environmental Practice," *Organization & Environment*, 14(2): 133–156.

—— & Henn, R. (2008). "Overcoming the Social and Psychological Barriers to Green Building," *Organization & Environment*, 21(4): 390–419.

Hoffman, A. J. & Ventresca, M. J. (eds.) (2002). *Organizations, Policy, and the Natural Environment: Institutional and Strategic Perspectives*. Stanford, CA: Stanford Business Books.

Hoggan, J. (2009). *Climate cover-up: The Crusade to Deny Global Warming*. Vancouver, B.C.: Greystone Books.

Howard-Grenville, J. A. (2006). "Inside the 'Black Box': How Organizational Culture and Subcultures Inform Interpretations and Actions on Environmental Issues," *Organization & Environment*, 19(1): 46–73.

Jennings, P. D., Schulz, M., Patient, D., Gravel, C., and Yuan, K. (2005). "Weber and Legal Rule Evolution: The Closing of the Iron Cage?" *Organization Studies*, 26: 621–653.

—— & Zandbergen, P. A. (1995). "Ecologically Sustainable Organizations: An Institutional Approach," *Academy of Management Review*, 20(4): 1015–1052.

Jermier, J. M., Forbes, L. C., Benn, S., and Orsato, R. J. (2006). "The New Corporate Environmentalism and Green Politics," in S. Clegg, C. Hardy, T. Lawrence, & W. Nord (eds.), *Handbook of Organizational Studies*, 2nd ed., London: SAGE, 619–650.

Jorgensen, A. K. (2007). "Does Foreign Investment Harm the Air we Breathe and the Water we Drink? A Cross-National Study of Carbon Dioxide Emissions and Organic Water Pollution in Less-Developed Countries," 1975–2000. *Organization & Environment*, 20(2): 137–156.

Kaczmarski, K. M. & Cooperrider, D. L. (1997). "Constructionist Leadership in the Global Relational Age: The Case of the Mountain Forum," *Organization & Environment*, 10(3): 235–258.

Khor, M. (2010). "The Double Standards of Multinationals," *The Guardian*, 25 June 2010. Retrieved on 29 July 29 2010 from <http://www.guardian.co.uk/commentisfree/cif-green/2010/jun/25/double-standards-multinationals-ecological-disasters>

King, A. & Lenox, M. (2000). "Industry Self-Regulation Without Sanctions: The Chemical Industry's Responsible Care Program," *Academy of Management Journal*, 43(4): 698–716.

—— —— & Terlaak, A. (2005). "The Strategic Use of Decentralized Institutions: Exploring Certification with the ISO 14001 Management Standard," *Academy of Management Journal*, 48(6): 1091–1106.

Kneese, A.V. & Schultze, C. L. (1975). *Pollution, Prices, and Public Policy: A study sponsored jointly by Resources for the Future, Inc. and the Brookings Institution*. Washington: Brookings Institution.

Kraatz, M. S., & Block, E. S. (2008). "Organizational Implications of Institutional Pluralism," in R. Greenwood, C. Oliver, K. Sahlin & R. Suddaby (eds.) *Handbook of Organizational Institutionalism*, London: SAGE, 243–275.

Lawrence T. B, & Phillips N. (2004). "From Moby Dick to Free Willy: Macro-Cultural Discourse and Institutional Entrepreneurship in Emerging Institutional Fields," *Organization*, 11: 689–711.

Lee, M-D., & Lounsbury, M. (forthcoming). "Domesticating Radical Rant and Rage: An Exploration of the Consequences of Environmental Shareholder Resolutions on Corporate Environmental Performance," *Business & Society*.

Livesey, S. M. & Kearins, K. (2002). "Transparent and Caring Corporations? A Study of Sustainability Reports by The Body Shop and Royal Dutch/Shell," *Organization & Environment*, 15(3): 233–258.

Lounsbury, M. (2007). "A Tale of Two Cities: Competing Logics and Practice Variation in the Professionalizing of Mutual Funds," *Academy of Management Journal*, 50: 289–307.

——(2001). "Institutional Sources of Practice Variation: Staffing College and University Recycling Programs," *Administrative Science Quarterly*, 46: 29 56.

——Ventresca, M., & Hirsch, P. (2003). "Social Movements, Field Frames and Industry Emergence: A Cultural-Political Perspective on U.S. Recycling," *Socio-Economic Review*, 1: 71–104.

Luke, T. W. (2001). "SUVs and the Greening of Ford: Reimagining Industrial Ecology as an Environmental Corporate Strategy in Action," *Organization & Environment*, 14(3): 311–335.

McCormick, S. (2009). "From 'Politico-Scientists' to Democratizing Science Movements: The Changing Climate of Citizens and Science," *Organization & Environment*, 22(1): 34–51.

Maguire, S. (2004). "The Co-Evolution of Technology and Discourse: A Study of Substitution Processes for the Insecticide DDT," *Organization Studies*, 25(1): 113–134.

——& Hardy, C. (2009). Discourse and Deinstitutionalization: The Decline of DDT. *Academy of Management Journal*, 52(1): 148–178.

Marshall, R. S. & Standifird, S. S. (2005). "Organizational Resource Bundles and Institutional Change in the U.S. Organic Food and Agricultural Certification Sector," *Organization & Environment*, 18(3): 265–286.

Meyer, J. W., Boli, J., & Thomas, G. M (1987). "Ontology and Rationalization in the Western Cultural Account," in G. M. Thomas et al. (eds.) *Institutional Structure: Constituting State, Society, and the Individual*, Thousand Oaks, CA: SAGE, 12–37.

Moon, S-G., & DeLeon, P. (2007). "Contexts and Corporate Voluntary Environmental Behavior: Examining the EPA's Green Lights Voluntary Program," *Organization & Environment*, 20(4): 480–496.

Morgan, G., Whitley, R., & Moen, E. (eds.) (2004). *Changing Capitalisms? Internationalisation, Institutional Change and Systems of Economic Organisation*. Oxford: Oxford University Press.

Norgaard, K. (2006). We Don't Really Want to Know: The Information-Deficit Model, Environmental Justice and Socially Organized Denial of Global Warming in Norway. *Organization & Environment*, 19(3): 347–370.

North, D. C. (1990). *Institutions, Institutional Change and Economic Performance*. Cambridge, UK: Cambridge University Press.

Packard, V. (1960). *The Waste Makers*. New York, NY: D. McKay Co.

Phillips N., Lawrence T. B., & Hardy C. (2004). "Discourse and Institutions," *Academy of Management Review*, 29: 635–652.

Powell, W. W., & DiMaggio, P. J. (eds.) (1991). *The New Institutionalism in Organizational Analysis*. Chicago: University of Chicago Press.

Reay, T. & Hinings, C. R. (2009). "Managing the Rivalry of Competing Institutional Logics," *Organization Studies*, 30: 629–652.

Rockström, J., Steffen, W., Noone, K., Persson, Å., Chapin, F. S. III, Lambin, E. F., Lenton, T. M., Scheffer, M., Folke, C., Schellnhuber, H. J., Nykvist, B., de Wit, C. A., Hughes, T., van der Leeuw, S., Rodhe, H., Sörlin, S., Snyder, P. K., Costanza, R., Svedin, U., Falkenmark, M., Karlberg, L., Corell, R. W., Fabry, V. J., Hansen, J., Walker, B., Liverman, D., Richardson, K., Crutzen, P., and Foley. J. A. (2009). "A Safe Operating Space for Humanity," *Nature*, 461(24): 472–475.

Roland, G. (2004). "Understanding Institutional Change: Fast-Moving and Slow-Moving Institutions," *Studies in Comparative International Development*, 4: 109–31.

Roumasset, J. (1990). Economic Policy for Sustainable Development," *Development*, 3(4): 38–41.

Ruckelshaus, W. D. (1993). "William D. Ruckelshaus: Oral History Interview," edited by Environmental Protection Agency: Environmental Protection Agency. Retrieved on November 16, 2009 from <http://www.epa.gov/history/publications/print/ruck.htm.>

Russo, M. V. (1992). "Power Plays: Regulation, Diversification, and Backward Integration in the Electric Utility Industry," *Strategic Management Journal*, 13: 13–27.

—— & Harrison, N. S. (2005). "Internal Organization and Environmental Performance: Clues from the Electronics Industry," *Academy of Management Journal*, 48: 582–593.

Schrader-Freschette, K. (1997). Elite Folk Science and Environmentalism. *Organization & Environment*, 10(1): 23–25.

Scott, W. R. (2008). *Institutions and Organizations: Ideas and Interests* 3rd edition. Thousand Oaks, CA: SAGE.

—— (1995). *Institutions and Organizations*. Thousand Oaks, CA: SAGE.

—— (1995). *The Construction of Social Reality*. New York: Free Press.

Selznick, P. (1949). *TVA and the Grass Roots*. New York: Harper and Row.

Streeck, W., & Thelen, K. (eds.) (2005). *Beyond Continuity: Institutional Change in Advanced Political Economies*. Oxford, UK: Oxford University Press.

Srikantia, P. & Bilmoria, D. (1997). "Isomorphism in Organization and Management Theory: The Case of Research on Sustainability," *Organization & Environment*, 10(4): 384–406.

Stubbs, W. & Cocklin, C. (2008). Conceptualizing a Sustainability Business Model. *Organization & Environment*, 21(2): 103–127.

Sutton, J., Dobbin, F., Meyer, J. & Scott, W. R. (1994). "The Legalization of the Workplace," *American Journal of Sociology*, 99: 944–971.

Szasz, A. (1994). *Ecopopulism*. Minneapolis, MN: University of Minnesota Press.

Thornton, P. H. & Ocasio, W. (1999). "Institutional Logics and the Historical Contingency of Power in Organizations: Executive Succession in the Higher Education Publishing Industry, 1958–1990," *American Journal of Sociology*, 105: 801–843.

—— (2008). "Institutional Logics," in R. Greenwood, C. Oliver, S. K. Andersen, and R. Suddaby (eds.) *Handbook of Organizational Institutionalism*, 99–129. Thousand Oaks, CA: Sage.

Tomblin, D. C. (2009). "The Ecological Restoration Movement: Diverse Cultures of Practice and Place," *Organization & Environment*, 22(2): 185–207.

Weinberg, A. S. (1997). "Local Organizing for Environmental Conflict: Explaining Differences between Cases of Participation and Non-Participation," *Organization & Environment*, 10(2): 194–216.

Westphal, J. & Zajac, E. J. (1994). "Substance and Symbolism in CEOs' Long-Term Incentive Plans," *Administrative Science Quarterly*, 39: 367–390.

Whiteman, G. (2004). "The Impact of Economic Development in James Bay, Canada: The Cree Tallymen Speak Out. *Organization & Environment*, 17(4): 425–448.

Whitley, R. (2007). *Business Systems and Organizational Capabilities: The Institutional Structuring of Competitive Competences*. Oxford, U.K.: Oxford University Press.

Widener, P. (2007). Oil Conflict in Ecuador: A Photographic Essay. *Organization & Environment*, 20(1): 84–105.

Wooten, M. & Hoffman, A. J. (2008). "Organizational Fields: Past, Present and Future," in R. Greenwood, C. Oliver, K. Sahlin & R. Suddaby (eds.), *Handbook of Institutional Theory*, London: SAGE, 130–148.

Zald, M. N. (1978). "On the Social Control of Industries," *Social Forces*, 57: 79–102.

—— & Lounsbury, M. (2010). "The Wizards of OZ: Towards an Institutional Approach to Elites, Expertise and Command Posts," *Organization Studies*, 31: 963–996.

Zuckerman, E. W. (1999). "The Categorical Imperative: Securities Analysts and the Illegitimacy Discount," *American Journal of Sociology*, 104: 1398–438.

CHAPTER 13

....

INSTITUTIONAL PRESSURES AND ORGANIZATIONAL CHARACTERISTICS: IMPLICATIONS FOR ENVIRONMENTAL STRATEGY

....

MAGALI A. DELMAS
AND MICHAEL W. TOFFEL[1]

WHY do some firms adopt environmental management strategies that go beyond regulatory compliance while others do not? A broad literature has emerged over the past decades demonstrating that firms' environmental strategies and practices are influenced by external stakeholders and institutional pressures, including from regulators and competitors (Aragón-Correa 1998; Christmann 2000; Dean & Brown 1995; Delmas 2003; Hart 1995; Nehrt 1996; Nehrt 1998; Russo & Fouts 1997; Sharma & Vredenburg 1998) and non-governmental organizations (NGOs) (Lawrence & Morell 1995).

Such findings are consistent with institutional sociology, which emphasizes the importance of regulatory, normative, and cognitive factors in shaping firms' decisions to adopt specific organizational practices, above and beyond their technical efficiency (DiMaggio & Powell 1983; Lounsbury, Fairclough, & Lee [Chapter 12] this volume). Several authors have built on institutional theory to explain firms' environmental strategies. Jennings & Zandbergen (1995) argue that because coercive forces

[1] The authors gratefully acknowledge the excellent research assistance provided by Jenna Bernhardson, and financial support from the Division of Research and Faculty Development at the Harvard Business School.

—primarily in the form of regulations and regulatory enforcement—have been the main impetus of environmental management practices, firms within each industry have implemented similar practices. Delmas (2002) proposed an institutional perspective to analyze the factors that led companies in Europe and in the United States to adopt the ISO 14001 Environmental Management System (EMS) international standard. She described how the regulatory, normative, and cognitive aspects of the institutional environment within a specific country affect the costs and potential benefits of ISO 14001 adoption, and how this would lead to different adoption rates across countries. Other researchers have explored how companies operating in different organizational fields are subject to different institutional pressures.

However, the institutional perspective does not address a fundamental issue of business strategy: why do organizations subject to the same institutional pressures pursue different strategies? In other words, how might institutional forces lead to heterogeneity, rather than homogeneity, within an industry? Hoffman (2001) argues that while organizations do not simply react to the pressures dictated by the organizational field, they also do not act completely autonomously without the influence of external bounds. Institutional and organizational dynamics are tightly linked.

Other research has analyzed how organizational characteristics affect firms' adoption of "beyond compliance" strategies. These studies have examined the influence of organizational context and design (Ramus & Steger 2000; Sharma 2000; Sharma, Pablo, & Vredenburg 1999) and organizational learning (Marcus and Nichols 1999). Others have focused on individuals and managers, examining the role of leadership values (Egri and

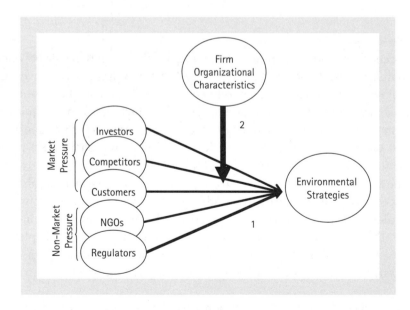

FIGURE 13.1 Institutional pressures, organizational characteristics, and environmental strategies

Herman 2000), and managerial attitudes (Cordano & Frieze 2000; Sharma 2000; Sharma et al. 1999).

While each study has provided a piece of the puzzle, there is still a lack of understanding of the conditions under which institutional pressures and organizational characteristics explain the adoption of beyond compliance strategies (see Figure 13.1). In this chapter, we first describe the empirical research that examines how pressures from constituents of firms' institutional environments affect their adoption of environmental strategies (relationship #1 in Figure 13.1). We then review the research that examines the moderating role of organizational characteristics on this relationship (relationship #2 in Figure 13.1). Finally, we offer some directions for future research.

Environmental strategies

Firms can adopt various types of voluntary environmental strategies that seek to reduce the environmental impacts of operations beyond regulatory requirements. For example, firms can implement EMS elements by creating an environmental policy, developing a formal training program, or instigating routine environmental auditing (Delmas 2000). In addition, management can choose to have the comprehensiveness of their EMS validated by a third party by seeking certification to the ISO 14001 Environmental Management System Standard (Toffel 2000). Management can also convey the importance of environmental management by including it as a criterion in employee performance evaluations (Nelson 2002).

Companies can also seek to improve relations with regulators and signal a proactive environmental stance by participating in government or industry sponsored voluntary programs (Delmas & Terlaak 2002; Delmas & Montes-Sancho 2011; Short & Toffel 2010; Toffel & Short forthcoming). Indeed, the US Environmental Protection Agency (EPA), some industry associations, and several NGOs have created voluntary standards to provide incentives for firms to go beyond minimal regulatory requirements. For example, the US EPA has developed several voluntary agreements between governmental agencies and firms to encourage technological innovation and pollution reduction by providing relief from particular procedural requirements (Delmas & Terlaak 2001). Industry programs include Responsible Care and Sustainable Slopes (King & Lenox 2000; Rivera & de Leon 2003), and NGO programs include The Natural Step and the Global Reporting Initiative Guidelines (Bradbury & Clair 1999; Hedberg von Malmborg 2003).

Companies can also work directly with customers and suppliers to improve their environmental performance. Furthermore, they may engage in "systematic communication, consultation and collaboration with their key stakeholders…(and) host stakeholder forums and establish permanent stakeholder advisory panels at either the corporate level, the plant level, or to address a specific issue" (Nelson 2002: 18).

INSTITUTIONAL PRESSURES: INFLUENCE
ON ENVIRONMENTAL STRATEGIES

The new institutional perspective suggests that firms obtain legitimacy by conforming to the dominant practices within their institutional field (DiMaggio & Powell 1983; Scott 1992). An organizational field includes "those organizations that...constitute a recognized area of institutional life: key suppliers, resource and product consumers, regulatory agencies, and other organizations that produce similar services or products" (DiMaggio & Powell 1983: 148).

Several scholars have argued that examining only institutional forces is not sufficient to explain divergent organizational change (D'Aunno, Succi, & Alexander 2000; Kraatz & Zajac 1996). Kraatz & Zajac (1996) investigated the effect of both the institutional and technical or market environment on organizational change and found pressures from the technical environment to be an important driver of organizational change. D'Aunno, Succi, & Alexander (2000: 700–1) argue that "both institutional and market forces are likely to affect divergent change to varying degrees in different organizational fields and, probably, in different historical periods. Moreover, institutional and market forces may interact in important ways to affect organizational change, and future research should aim to specify their roles more precisely." This speaks to the need to define precisely the external forces that pressure firms to engage in organizational change.

In this chapter, instead of characterizing market forces as being in opposition to institutional forces, we consider that institutional forces can bound and define rational argument and approaches (Fligstein 1990). With this approach, we differentiate two main sets of agents within the organizational field: market and non-market constituents (Baron 1995) and argue that both may impose institutional pressure. In doing so, we build on Hoffman's (2001) insight that buyers and other market actors are constituents within an organizational field.

Firms engage with market constituents (e.g., customers, suppliers, competitors, shareholders) via economic transactions, whereas non-market constituents (e.g., regulators, environmental organizations) are interested in social, political, and legal issues (Baron 1995; Baron 2000). Non-market and market constituents frame environmental management issues differently (Hoffman & Ventresca 1999). For example, market constituents tend to view environmental issues primarily within the rubric of business performance, focusing on their cost and efficiency implications. On the other hand, non-market constituents such as regulators and activist groups typically view environmental issues as negative externalities and often operate via the legal system and the mass media (e.g., as a court of public opinion).

In this section, we review the empirical evidence that various institutional actors have influenced organizations' environmental practices, focusing on politicians, regulators, local communities, customers, competitors, and shareholders (owners).

Pressures from non-market constituents

Political and regulatory pressures

Government is perhaps the most obvious institutional constituent that influences firms' adoption of environmental practices. Legislation authorizes government agencies to promulgate and enforce regulations, a form of coercive power. Whereas political pressure refers to the level of political support for broader or more stringent laws and regulations, regulatory pressure represents the extent to which regulators threaten to or actually impede a company's operations based on their environmental performance (Delmas & Toffel 2004).

Many researchers have focused on the influence of enforced legislation and regulations on firms' environmental practices (Carraro, Katsoulacos, & Xepapadeas 1996; Delmas & Montes-Sancho 2010; Delmas 2002; Majumdar & Marcus 2001; Rugman & Verbeke 1998). One study found government regulations to be the most frequently cited source of pressure in the adoption of environmental management practices (Henriques & Sadorsky 1996a).

Several studies have compared institutional environments across different countries, many of which demonstrated that more stringent regulatory environments were associated with higher levels of adoption of beyond-compliance environmental practices. Christmann (2004) found that a positive relationship between managers' perception of the stringency of governmental environmental regulation in the country in which they operated and the stringency of their company's internal environmental policy. Governments have also played an important role in firms' decision to adopt ISO 14001 (Delmas & Montes-Sancho 2011; Delmas 2002). Governments can signal their endorsement of ISO 14001 by, for example, enhancing the reputation of adopters. Governments can also facilitate adoption by reducing information and search costs by providing technical assistance to potential adopters. Regulatory pressure was also found to be an important driver of firms' participation in government led voluntary programs (Delmas & Terlaak 2002). Delmas & Terlaak (2002) argued that institutional environments that strengthen the regulator's ability to credibly commit to the objectives of governmental programs were key to the implementation of the voluntary programs.

Within individual countries, research has shown that government pressure, measured by environmental inspections or the threat of legal liabilities, has increased the adoption of voluntary environmental practices. For example, one study showed that companies facing a greater threat of legal liability adopted more environmental management practices (Khanna & Anton 2002a). Furthermore, the threat of liabilities in a firm's industry, as well as regulations aimed at other industries, was shown to increase the likelihood a firm will publicly disclose environmental practices and strategies (Reid & Toffel 2009). Firms were more likely to self-disclose environmental regulatory compliance violations if they recently experienced an enforcement measure (like an inspection or being issued a violation) and if they received immunity from prosecution for self-disclosed violations (Laplante & Rilstone 1996; Short & Toffel 2008). There is also fairly consistent evidence across many national government voluntary programs that regulatory pressures were important in motivating participation (Delmas & Montes-Sancho 2010; Delmas & Terlaak 2001; Maxwell, Lyon, & Hackett 2000; Rivera & de Leon 2004; Segerson & Miceli 1998). In at least one instance, this relationship changed over time, as Delmas & Montes-Sancho (2010) found that regulatory pressure significantly influenced the participation of early adopters of the US Climate Challenge voluntary program but found no evidence that it influenced late adopters.

Community and environmental interest group pressures

Local communities can also impose coercive pressure on companies through their vote in local and national elections, via environmental activism within environmental NGOs, and by filing citizen lawsuits. Several studies have found that company decisions to adopt environmental management practices have been influenced by the desire to improve or maintain relations with their communities (Florida & Davison 2001). Studies have found that pressure from community groups have influenced firms to adopt environmental plans (Henriques & Sadorsky 1996a) and government-sponsored voluntary environmental programs (Darnall, Potoski, & Prakash 2010). Another study based on a survey of ISO 14001 certified companies across fifteen countries found that one of the strongest motivating factors to pursue certification was the desire to be a good neighbor (Raines 2002).

Some communities may be better able than others to encourage plants to adopt environmental practices. Communities with larger minority populations, lower incomes and less education had greater exposure to toxic emissions (Arora & Asundi 1999; Brooks & Sethi 1997; Khanna & Vidovic 2001). Communities with higher incomes, higher population density, and greater participation in environmental and conservation organizations had less exposure to toxic emissions (Kassinis & Vafeas 2006). One study found that adoption of a US EPA voluntary program was more likely in communities with higher median household income, suggesting that socioeconomic community characteristics could affect plants' decisions to adopt environmental management practices (Khanna & Vidovic 2001). Greater declines in toxic emissions have been observed among plants located in communities with higher voting rates (Hamilton 1999), and in states with higher membership in environmental interest groups (Maxwell et al. 2000), both proxies for a community's propensity for collective action.

There are many examples where companies have amended their environmental practices in response to environmental group pressures (Baron 2003; Lawrence and Morell 1995; Sharma & Henriques 2005). For instance, after Mitsubishi Corporation was subject to a protracted consumer boycott led by the Rainforest Action Network (RAN), Mitsubishi announced it would no longer use old-growth forest products (World Rainforest Movement 1998).

Pressures from Market Constituents

In addition to the non-market pressures described above, market pressures can also lead firms to adopt environmental management practices. Below, we review the literature that explores the influences of customers, industries, and shareholders.

Customer pressures

Pressure from buyers is perhaps the primary mechanism through which quality management standards have diffused (Anderson, Daly, & Johnson 1999), and it has also played a significant role in motivating firms to adopt environmental practices (Delmas & Montiel 2008). Several studies have found evidence that customer pressure has motivated firms to adopt environmental management practices, with one study noting customers' influence was second only to that of government pressure (Henriques & Sadorsky 1996b). A recent empirical analysis found customer pressure to be an important determinant of the likelihood of adopting the ISO 14001 standard (Delmas & Toffel 2008). Others have found that companies customize their response to customer demands depending on the types of information being requested. For example, firms facing customer demand for information on the sustainability of products improved input processes, whereas firms that faced customer demand for product certification embarked on more fundamental changes to their operations including improving environmental efficiency in product design and packaging (Sharma & Henriques 2005). In addition, companies adopted more comprehensive environmental practices if they sold goods and services directly to consumers (Anton, Deltas, & Khanna 2004; Khanna & Anton 2002b). This suggests that managers perceive retail consumers (as opposed to commercial and industrial customers) as exerting more pressure on companies to adopt environmental management practices.

Industry pressure

Industry pressure is another important market pressure. For example, multinationals are widely recognized as key agents in the diffusion of practices across national borders by transmitting organizational techniques to subsidiaries and other organizations in the host country (Arias & Guillen 1998). Firms may also mimic practices that successful leading firms have adopted. In addition, firms respond to customer requirements. Industry trade associations are also a strong driver of firm environmental behavior (Christmann 2004; Delmas & Montes-Sancho 2010; King & Lenox 2000; Lenox & Nash 2003).

Competitor pressure can also encourage the adoption of EMS (Bremmers et al. 2007). In the US hazardous waste management industry, local competition increased compliance with environmental regulation, though the effect diminished in larger markets (Stafford 2007). One study found that firms facing little competition were less likely than firms in more competitive markets to decrease their environmental impact (Darnall 2009).

Several studies have found that industry associations have motivated firms to adopt environmental management practices or participate in voluntary programs (Christmann 2004; Delmas & Montes-Sancho 2010; Delmas & Terlaak 2002; Gunningham 1995; Lenox & Nash 2003; Rivera & de Leon 2004). The decisions of whether to pursue certification and which EMS standard to pursue (ISO 14001 or the European Union's Eco-Audit and Management Scheme) were found to be strongly influenced by pressure from industry associations as well as from regional chambers of commerce, suppliers, and regulators (Kollman & Prakash 2002). Trade conferences and seminars, representing industry pressure, can also influence environmental aspects of procurement decisions (Sharma & Henriques 2005). Industry concentration may also affect environmental management practices: firms with fewer competitors were found to be less likely to reduce their environmental impacts (Darnall 2009). Trade associations also employ a variety of informal mechanisms to encourage compliance with their own program requirements (Lenox & Nash 2003). Lenox & Nash (2003) describe how a number of trade associations convene meetings to share implementation experiences among members, and how such meetings impose pressure on managers of firms that are falling behind.

The creation of industry self-regulatory institutions often occurs as a result of an accident or controversy, as a way to proactively manage more stringent regulation that would be imposed as a result of the event. The Three Mile Island incident prompted industry executives to create the Institute of Nuclear Power Operation (Rees 1994). The chemical industry's Responsible Care program was borne out of a deadly accident in Bhopal, India (Gunningham 1995). As a caveat, some industry-created self-regulatory programs attracted more heavily polluting firms, which can be viewed as a form of adverse selection (Lenox & Nash 2003).

Industry groups have created other institutions such as the Global Climate Coalition in response to threats of environmental regulations. This group was financed by firms and trade groups in the oil, coal, and auto industries, among others, and campaigned against the idea that the release of greenhouse gases led to global climate change. Its public relations campaigns were sufficiently effective to stir public debate and likely delayed government action (Revkin 2009).

Firm characteristics vis-a-vis adoption of industry standards have also been investigated. Previous adoption of voluntary environmental standards, such as Responsible Care and ISO 9000, spur diffusion of subsequent standards, like ISO 14001 (Delmas & Montiel 2008). Larger companies and those with better-known brands and corporate names, more intensive polluters, and companies in sectors with higher emissions were more likely to participate in the Chemical Manufacturers Association's Responsible Care Program (King & Lenox 2000).

Shareholder pressures

Several studies have examined efforts of shareholders to influence the environmental management practices of firms. Institutional investor ownership, measured through public pension-fund ownership, was found to positively affect corporate social performance (Chatterji & Listokin 2009). While shareholder resolutions on environmental topics seldom attract enough votes to pass, Reid & Toffel (2009) found that the very presence of an environmental shareholder resolution (many of which called for greater transparency) being targeted at a firm subsequently led its management to become more transparent by publicly reporting its climate change strategy and greenhouse gas emissions. Such shareholder proposals not only had a direct effect on the targeted company, but also a spillover effect on firms in the same industry as a targeted firm, who also became more transparent (Reid & Toffel 2009).

Many scholars have observed that shareholder resolutions prompt companies to change their environmental practices through private meetings between management and activists during which the companies agree to adopt some of the proposals' specifications in exchange for the activists withdrawing their proposals (O'Rourke 2003; Proffitt & Spicer 2006; Rehbein, Waddock, & Graves 2004). For example, Amoco resisted calls by nine religious groups that proposed a shareholder resolution that called for the company to adopt the Valdez Principles, but reached a negotiated settlement. In exchange for the withdrawal of the proposal, the company agreed to abide by one of the principles and to publish an environmental progress report (Hoffman 1996). The company subsequently enacted several other management practices aligned with the Valdez Principles. One study found that this compromise between activists and management was strongly related to more robust (or thorough) disclosure of environmental practices (Marshall, Brown, & Plumlee 2007).

Examining how companies respond to environmental ratings is another approach to discern the influence of investors on managerial behavior. Chatterji & Toffel (2010) analyzed how firms responded to KLD's corporate environmental ratings and found that firms that initially received poor ratings subsequently improved their environmental performance more than firms that had more positive initial ratings and more than firms that were never rated. Such improvements were most substantial among poorly rated firms that were able to make low-cost environmental improvements and that were in highly regulated industries (Chatterji & Toffel 2010).

Combined pressures

It is important to note that while we have been referring to the institutional pressures individually, several studies examine a combination of institutional pressures and compare the differential effects of these pressures or combine them through factor analyses (Delmas 2001; Delmas & Toffel 2008). Furthermore the interaction between these institutional pressures is likely to moderate their individual influence on company practices (Bansal & Clelland 2004). For example, Bansal & Clelland (2004) provided insights about how competitors, regulators, and customers can influence investors' assessments of firms' environmental legitimacy. As another example, the pressure from environmental groups may encourage the formulation of more stringent regulations. This, in turn, can induce industry leaders to encourage laggard firms to adopt environmental practices. Similarly, following its chemical disaster in Bhopal in 1984, Union Carbide along with other large chemical companies faced mounting public pressure for more stringent safety and environmental regulations. In response, the chemical industry developed and promoted a set of environment, health and safety (EHS) management practices—the Responsible Care program—to chemical industry associations in Canada and the United States (King & Lenox 2000; Prakash 2000).

ORGANIZATIONAL CHARACTERISTICS MODERATING THE IMPACT OF INSTITUTIONAL PRESSURES ON ENVIRONMENTAL STRATEGIES

Institutional theory has traditionally described how isomorphic institutional pressures lead to common organizational practices. In the traditions of this framework, persistent heterogeneity among various firms within the same industry might be attributed to differences in the *composition* of their organizational fields. For example, firms located in different states would face different institutional pressures, which could result in dissimilar organizational practices. Differing *levels* of institutional pressure could also lead to heterogeneous activities during any specific period, but ultimately these are purported to result in common organizational structures and practices to ensure legitimacy. As a consequence, few have employed institutional theory to understand questions of strategy which focus on *persistent differences among organizations that share common organizational fields*. We therefore need more informed theories about how and why organizations respond differently to institutional pressures. While scholars have made significant advances in analyzing how institutional pressures affect firms' decisions to pursue 'beyond compliance' strategies, there remains very limited research about how organizational factors moderate these relationships. Levy & Rothenberg (2002) describe several mechanisms by which institutionalism can encourage heterogeneity. First, they argue that institutional forces are transformed as they permeate an organization's boundaries because they are filtered and interpreted by managers according to the firm's unique history and culture. Second, they describe how an institutional field may contain conflicting institutional pressures that require prioritization by managers. Third, they describe how multinational and diversified organizations operate within several institutional fields— both at the societal and organizational levels—which expose them to different sets of institutionalized practices and norms. In this section, we review the empirical research on the interaction between institutional pressures and organizational characteristics.

Organizational functions

One line of research examines how differences in organizational functions moderate how institutional pressures affect firms' responses. Hoffman (2001) theorized that organizations channel institutional pressures to different subunits, which frame these pressures according to their typical functional routines. For example, legal departments interpret pressures in terms of risk and liability, public affairs does so in terms of company reputation, environmental affairs in terms of ecosystem damage and regulatory compliance, and sales departments in terms of potential lost revenues. Consequently, the pressure is managed according to the cultural frame of the unit that receives it: either as an issue of regulatory compliance, human resource management, operational efficiency, risk management, market demand, or social responsibility (Hoffman 2001). Delmas & Toffel (2008) extend this to hypothesize and demonstrate that corporate assignments of responsibilities to specific departments lead firms to differ in their receptivity to pressures from various stakeholders. In their framework, pressures from external stakeholders are channeled to different organizational functions, which influence how they are received by facility managers. These differences in receptivity are critical because they, in turn, influence organizations' responses in terms of adopting management practices. In other words, some organizations will allow pressures from stakeholders to permeate the organization. For example, firms with powerful legal departments will be more responsive to pressures from regulators, while firms with powerful marketing departments will be more responsive to pressures from customers. These functional departments influence managers' sensitivity and responses to institutional pressures in the form of adopting different environmental management practices. Analyzing survey and archival data, Delmas & Toffel (2008) find that organizations that were more receptive to institutional pressure from market constituents (controlling for the amount of pressure exerted) were more likely to adopt the ISO 14001 Environmental Management System Standard, and that organizations that were more receptive to institutional pressure from non-market constituents (controlling for the amount of pressure exerted) were more likely to adopt government-initiated voluntary programs and less likely to adopt ISO 14001.

Environmental Management Efficiency

Chatterji & Toffel (2010) argue that firms facing lower-cost opportunities to improve their environmental performance are more likely to respond to stakeholder pressures that besmirch their reputation. They find that less eco-efficient firms (those with above-average pollution levels given their size and industry) were particularly likely to respond to poor environmental ratings from KLD, a major socially responsible investment rating agency, by improving their environmental performance.

Buyer–Supplier Relations

The relationship between firms and their customers also affects firms' responses to customer pressure. Delmas & Montiel (2009) revealed the importance of buyer–supplier relationships to moderate firms' responses to customer pressures to adopt ISO 14001.

Examining ISO 14001 adoption by automotive suppliers, Delmas & Montiel (2009) found that adoption was more likely among suppliers that were younger, which used ISO 14001 certification to gain legitimacy and signal their environmental practices; suppliers that had highly specialized assets and were thus more dependent on their current customers; suppliers that were headquartered in Japan and thus had a greater need to reduce the information asymmetries arising from the physical and cultural distance to the US; suppliers that reported to the US EPA's Toxic Release Inventory and therefore received higher levels of public scrutiny of their environmental management practices (Delmas & Montiel 2009). Firms were more likely to adopt ISO 14001 if they were located far from their potential buyers (King, Lenox, & Terlaak 2005) and adopted more comprehensive environmental practices if they sold goods and services directly to consumers (Christmann & Taylor 2001).

Industry characteristics

Others have focused on industry characteristics as moderators of institutional pressures on firm behavior. Lyon & Maxwell (2011) predict greater transparency among firms in industries that have socially or environmentally damaging impacts. Cho & Patten (2007) found that firms in environmentally sensitive industries were especially likely to respond to pressures for transparency by disclosing some forms of environmental information (e.g., expenditures on pollution control and abatement) in their annual reports (10-Ks) because such firms "face greater exposure to the public policy process than companies from non-environmentally sensitive industries." In their analysis of corporate disclosure of climate change strategy and greenhouse gas emissions, Reid & Toffel (2009) found that firms targeted by environmental shareholder resolutions were more likely to disclose this information, and that this relationship was especially pronounced for firms in environmentally sensitive industries. They also found that firms in industries with more environmental shareholder resolutions (i.e., targeting their competitors) were also more likely to disclose this information, even when the focal firm had not itself been targeted. Similarly, Chatterji & Toffel (2010) find that firms in more intensively regulated industries are particularly likely to respond to poor environmental ratings by improving their environmental performance.

CONCLUSION AND FUTURE RESEARCH

This chapter reviews the literature that describes how stakeholders including politicians, regulators, local communities, customers, competitors, and shareholders impose institutional pressures on firms and how these pressures influence firms to adopt beyond-compliance environmental strategies (see Kassinis [Chapter 5] this volume for a complementary approach to stakeholder perspectives). In addition, this chapter reviews research that reveals how organizational factors moderate how managers perceive and act upon these pressures. These moderating factors, which can magnify or diminish the influence of institutional pressures, include organizational structure and functions, environmental management efficiency, buyer–supplier relations, and industry characteristics. This novel research stream contributes to institutional theory by exploring how institutional pressures interact with organizational characteristics in influencing managerial decisions in general, and environmental strategies in particular.

We also believe that this novel approach can reveal conditions under which firms are more likely to resist institutional pressure. Most prior studies predict and show positive relationships between institutional pressures and the adoption of environmental strategies. In most cases, more pressure is associated with the adoption of more environmental management practices. However, incorporating moderating effects of firm characteristics in the model can yield substantial insights such as inverted relationships. For example, Delmas & Toffel (2008) found that, controlling for the level of regulatory pressure, ISO 14001 was less likely to be adopted by organizations that had strong legal departments. This approach allows researchers to identify factors that enable firms to resist institutional pressures. Likewise, Delmas & Montiel (2009) analyzed the motivations for automotive suppliers to resist the mandate of the Big Three US automotive manufacturers to adopt ISO 14001 by 2003. They found that suppliers resisting adoption by the deadline tended to be older, smaller, and to produce less specialized products. In addition, many resistant firms were less visible to regulators and environmental NGOs because they were not required to report their emissions to the US EPA Toxic Release Inventory (TRI).

In seeking to understand the factors that contribute to corporate environmental strategy, further studies have highlighted the importance of additional organizational characteristics, including firms' capabilities, resources, and ownership structure (Darnall & Edwards 2006; Sharma 2000; Sharma & Vredenburg 1998), board size (Kassinis & Vafeas 2002), corporate identity and managerial discretion (Sharma 2000), the characteristics of individual managers (Bansal & Roth 2000, Cordano & Frieze 2000), and corporate culture (Howard-Grenville & Bertels [Chapter 11] this volume). Future research could investigate how characteristics moderate how firms perceive and respond to institutional pressures. For example, future work might examine the extent to which managers' personal characteristics and professional experiences influence their perception of particular institutional pressures. It seems feasible that a facility manager's nationality could imbue similar cultural-based sensitivities to those we ascribed to the influence of the headquarters country. In addition, corporate marketing and legal affairs department managers' prior experience with stakeholders (e.g., when these managers were employed at other firms) could influence their current sensitivity to institutional pressures. A richer understanding of such personal attributes would provide an important supplement to the organizational characteristics identified in this chapter.

Further promising areas of research stem from considering the dynamics of the interactions between institutional pressures and organizational characteristics. Just as Delmas & Montes-Sancho (2010, 2011) found that institutional pressures exerted a more powerful influence on firms when particular environmental management practices were just emerging, future research could explore whether, how, and why the moderating role of organization characteristics change over time. An example of such a study might examine the factors that lead organizations' perceptions of institutional pressures to change over time, such as accumulating positive experiences engaging with particular stakeholders or the shock of being targeted by regulators, community protests, or activist campaigns.

Exploring how organizational factors moderate firms' responsiveness to institutional pressures represents an important opportunity to develop institutional theory while enhancing its ability to foster a better understanding of why companies pursue different environmental strategies and environmental management practices.

References

Anderson, S. W., Daly, J. D., & Johnson, M. F. (1999). "Why Firms Seek ISO 9000 Certification: Regulatory Compliance or Competitive Advantage?" *Production & Operations Management*, 8(10): 28–43.

Anton, W. R. Q., Deltas, G., & Khanna, M. (2004). "Incentives for Environmental Self-Regulation and Implications for Environmental Performance," *Journal of Environmental Economics and Management*, 48(1): 632–654.

Aragón-Correa, J. A. (1998). "Strategic Proactivity and Firm Approach to the Natural Environment," *Academy of Management Journal*, 41: 556–567.

Arias, M. E. & Guillen, M. F. (1998). "The Transfer of Organizational Management Techniques," in J. L. Alvarez (ed.), *The Diffusion and Consumption of Business Knowledge*, 110–137. London: Macmillan.

Arora, A. & Asundi, J. (1999). *Quality Certification and the Economics of Contract Software Development: A Study of the Indian Software Industry*. NBER Working Paper 7260. Cambridge, MA: National Bureau of Economic Research.

Bansal, P. & Clelland, I. (2004). "Talking Trash: Legitimacy, Impression Management, and Unsystematic Risk in the Context of the Natural Environment," *Academy of Management Journal* 47(1): 93–103.

—— & Roth, K. (2000). "Why Companies go Green: A Model of Ecological Responsiveness," *Academy of Management Journal*, 43(4): 717–736.

Baron, D. P. (1995). "Integrated Strategy: Market and Nonmarket Components," *California Management Review*, 37(2): 47–65.

—— *Business and Its Environment*, 3rd edition. Upper Saddle River, NJ: Prentice Hall.

—— (2003). "Private Politics," *Journal of Economics & Management Strategy*, 12(1): 31–66.

Bradbury, H., & Clair, J. A. (1999). "Promoting Sustainable Organizations with Sweden's Natural Step," *Academy of Management Executive*, 13(4): 63–74.

Bremmers, H. Omta, O., Kemp, R., and Haverkamp, D.-J. (2007). "Do Stakeholder Groups Influence Environmental Management System Development in the Dutch Agri-Food Sector?" *Business Strategy and the Environment*, 16: 214–231.

Brooks, N. & Sethi, R. (1997). "The Distribution of Pollution: Community Characteristics and Exposure to Air Toxics". *Journal of Environmental Economics and Management*, 32(2): 233–250.

Carraro, C., Katsoulacos, Y., & Xepapadeas, A. (eds.). (1996). *Environmental Policy and Market Structure*. Boston: Kluwer Academic Publishers.

Chatterji, A. & Listokin, S. (2009). "The Economic and institutional Motivations for Corporate Social Responsibility." *Working Paper, Duke Fuqua School of Business*.

—— & Toffel, M. W. (2010). How Firms Respond to Being Rated. *Strategic Management Journal*, 31(9): 917–945.

Cho, C. H. & Patten, D. M. (2007). "The Role of Environmental Disclosures as Tools of Legitimacy: A Research Note," *Accounting, Organizations and Society*, 32(7–8): 639–647.

Christmann, P. (2000). "Effects of Best Practices of Environmental Management on Cost Advantage: The Role of Complementary Assets," *Academy of Management Journal*, 43: 663–680.

—— (2004). "Multinational Companies and the Environment: Determinants of Global Environmental Policy Standardization," *Academy of Management Journal*, 47(5): 747–760.

—— & Taylor, G. (2001). "Globalization and the Environment: Determinants of Firm Self-Regulation in China," *Journal of International Business Studies*, 32(3): 439–458.

Cordano, M. & Frieze, I. H. (2000). "Pollution Reduction Preferences of US Environmental Managers: Applying Ajzen's theory of Planned Behavior," *Academy of Management Journal*, 43(1): 627–641.

D'Aunno, T., Succi, M., & Alexander, J. A. (2000). "The Role of Institutional and Market Forces in Divergent Organizational Change," *Administrative Science Quarterly*, 45(4): 679–703.

Darnall, N. (2009). "Regulatory Stringency, Green Production Offsets, and Organizations' Financial Performance." *Public Administration Review*, May/June, 418–434.

—— & Edwards, D. J. (2006). "Predicting the Cost of Environmental Management System Adoption: The Role of capabilities, Resources, and Ownership Structure," *Strategic Management Journal*, 27(4): 301–320.

——, Potoski, M., & Prakash, A. (2010). "Sponsorship Matters: Assessing Business Participation in Government- and Industry-Sponsored Voluntary Environmental Programs," *Journal of Public Administration Research and Theory*, 20(2): 283–307.

Dean, T. J. & Brown, R. L. (1995). "Pollution Regulation as a Barrier to New Firm Entry: Initial Evidence and Implications for Future Research," *Academy of Management Journal*, 38: 288–303.

Delmas, M. A. (2000). "Barriers and Incentives to the Adoption of ISO 14001 by Firms in the United States," *Duke Environmental Law & Policy Forum*, 11(1): 1–38.

—— (2001). "Stakeholders and Competitive Advantage: The Case of ISO 14001," *Production and Operations Management*, 10(3): 343–358.

—— (2002). "The Diffusion of Environmental Management Standards in Europe and the United States: An Institutional Perspective," *Policy Sciences*, 35: 91–119.

—— (2003). *In Search of ISO: An institutional perspective on the adoption of international management standards*. Stanford, CA: Stanford Graduate School of Business Working Paper 1784.

—— & Montes-Sancho, M. (2010). "Voluntary Agreements to Improve Environmental Quality: Symbolic and Substantive Cooperation," *Strategic Management Journal*, 31(6): 576–601.

—— —— (2011). "An Institutional Perspective on the Diffusion of International Management System Standards: The Case of the Environmental Management Standard ISO 14001," *Business Ethics Quarterly*, 21(1): 1052–1081.

Delmas, M. & Montiel, I. (2008). "The Diffusion of Voluntary International Management Standards: Responsible Care, ISO 9000, and ISO 14001 in the Chemical Industry," *The Policy Studies Journal*, 36(1): 65–93.

—— —— (2009). "Greening the Supply Chain: When are Customer Pressures Effective?" *Journal of Economics & Management Strategy*, 18(1): 171–201.

—— & Terlaak, A. (2001). "A Framework for Analyzing Environmental Voluntary Agreements," *California Management Review*, 43(3): 44–63.

—— —— (2002). "Regulatory Commitment to Negotiated Agreements: Evidence from the United States, Germany, The Netherlands, and France," *Journal of Comparative Policy Analysis: Research and Practice*, 4: 5–29.

—— & Toffel, M. W. (2004). "Stakeholders and Environmental Management Practices: An Institutional Framework," *Business Strategy and the Environment*, 13(4): 209–222.

—— —— 2008. "Organizational Responses to Environmental Demands: Opening the Black Box," *Strategic Management Journal* 29(10), 1027–1055.

DiMaggio, P. J. & Powell, W. W. (1983). "The Iron Cage Revisited: Institutional Isomorphism and Collective Rationality in Organizational Fields," *American Sociological Review*, 48(2): 147–160.

Egri, C. & Herman, S. (2000). "Leadership in the North American Environmental Sector: Values, Leadership Styles and Contexts of Environmental Leaders and their Organizations," *Academy of Management Journal*, 43: 571–604.

Fligstein, N. (1990). *The Transformation of Corporate Control*. Cambridge, MA: Harvard University Press.

Florida, R. & Davison, D. (2001). "Gaining from Green Management: Environmental Management Systems inside and outside the Factory," *California Management Review*, 43(3): 64–84.

Gunningham, N. (1995). "Environment, Self-Regulation, and the Chemical Industry: Assessing Responsible Care." *Law & Policy*, 17(1): 57–109.

Hamilton, J. T. (1999). "Exercising Property Rights to Pollute: Do Cancer Risks and Politics Affect Plant Emission Reductions?" *Journal of Risk and Uncertainty*, 18(2): 105–124.

Hart, S. L. (1995). "A Natural-Resource-Based View of the Firm," *The Academy of Management Review.*, 20(4): 986–1014.

Hedberg, C.-J. & von Malmborg, F. (2003). "The Global Reporting Initiative and Corporate Sustainability Reporting in Swedish Companies." *Corporate Social Responsibility and Environmental Management*, 10(3): 153–164.

Henriques, I. & Sadorsky, P. (1996a). "The Determinants of an Environmentally Responsive Firm: An Empirical Approach," *Journal of Environmental Economics & Management*, 30(3): 381–395.

—— (1996b). "The Determinants of an Environmentally Responsive Firm: An Empirical Approach," *Journal of Environmental Economics and Management*, 30(3): 381–395.

Hoffman, A. J. (1996). "Trends in Corporate Environmentalism: The Chemical and Petroleum Industries, 1960–1993," *Society and Natural Resources*, 9(1): 47–64.

—— (2001). "Linking Organizational and Field-Level Analyses: The Diffusion of Corporate Environmental Practice," *Organization & Environment*, 14(2): 133–156.

—— & Ventresca, M. (1999). "The Institutional Framing of Policy Debates," *American Behavioral Scientist*, 42(8): 1368–1392.

Jennings, P. D. & Zandbergen, P. A. (1995). "Ecologically Sustainable Organizations: An Institutional Approach," *Academy of Management Review*, 20(4): 1015–1052.

Jermier, J. & Forbes, L. (2011). "Greening Organizational Culture," in A. J. Hoffman & T. Bansal (eds). *Oxford Handbook of Business and the Environment,* Oxford, UK: Oxford University Press.

Kassinis, G. & Vafeas, N. (2002). "Corporate Boards and Outside Stakeholders as Determinants of Environmental Litigation," *Strategic Management Journal*, 23(5): 399–415.

—— (2006). "Stakeholder Pressures and Environmental Performance," *Academy of Management Journal*, 49(1): 145–159.

Khanna, M. & Anton, W. Q. (2002a). "Corporate environmental Management: Regulatory and Market-Based Pressures," *Land Economics*, 78(4).

—— —— (2002b). "Corporate Environmental Management: Regulatory and Market-Based Incentives," *Land Economics*, 78(4): 539–558.

Khanna, N. & Vidovic, M. (2001). *Facility Participation in Voluntary Pollution Prevention Programs and the Role of Community Characteristics: Evidence From the 33/50 Program*. Binghamton University Economics Department Working Paper.

King, A. A. & Lenox, M. J. (2000). "Industry Self-Regulation Without Sanctions: The Chemical Industry's Responsible Care program," *Academy of Management Journal*, 43(4): 698–716.

—— & Terlaak, A. (2005). "Strategic Use of Decentralized Institutions: Exploring Certification with the ISO 14001 Management Standard," *Academy of Management Journal*, 48(6): 1091–1106.

Kollman, K. & Prakash, A. (2002). "EMS-Based Environmental Regimes as Club Goods: Examining Variations in Firm-Level Adoption of ISO 14001 and EMAS in U.K., U.S. and Germany," *Policy Sciences*, 35: 43–67.

Kraatz, M. S. & Zajac, E. J. (1996). "Exploring the Limits of the New Institutionalism: The Causes and Consequences of Illegitimate Organizational Change," *American Sociological Review*, 61(5): 812–836.

Laplante, B. & Rilstone, P. (1996). "Environmental Inspections and Emissions of the Pulp and Paper Industry in Quebec," *Journal of Environmental Economics and Management*, 31(1): 19–36.

Lawrence, A. T. & Morell, D. (1995). "Leading-Edge Environmental Management: Motivation, Opportunity, Resources and Processes," in D. Collins & M. Starik (eds.), *Special Research Volume of Research in Corporate Social Performance and Policy, Sustaining the Natural Environment: Empirical Studies on the Interface Between Nature and Organizations*, Greenwich, CT. JAI Press, 99–126.

Lenox, M. J. & Nash, J. (2003). "Industry Self-Regulation and Adverse Selection: A Comparison across Four Trade Association Programs," *Business Strategy and the Environment*, 12: 343–356.

Levy, D. L. & Rothenberg, S. (2002). Heterogeneity and Change in Environmental Strategy: Technological and Political Responses to Climate Change in the Global Automobile Industry," in A. J. Hoffman & M. J. Ventresca (eds.), *Organizations, Policy and the Natural Environment: Institutional and Strategic Perspectives*. Stanford: Stanford University Press.

Lounsbury, M., Fairclough, S & Lee, M-D P. (2011). "Institutional Dynamics," in A. J. Hoffman & T. Bansal (eds), *Oxford Handbook of Business and the Environment*. Oxford, UK:Oxford University Press.

Lyon, T. P. & Maxwell, J. W. (2011). "Greenwash: Corporate Environmental Disclosure Under Threat of Audit," *Journal of Economics & Management Strategy*, 20: 3–41.

Majumdar, S. K. & Marcus, A. A. (2001). "Rules Versus Discretion: The Productivity Consequences of Flexible Regulation," *Academy of Management Journal*, 44(1): 170–179.

Marcus, A. A. & Nichols, M. L. (1999). "On the Edge: Heeding the Warnings of Unusual Events," *Organization Science*, 10: 482–499.

Marshall, R. S., Brown, D., & Plumlee, M. (2007). "'Negotiated' Transparency? Corporate Citizenship Engagement and Environmental Disclosure," *Journal of Corporate Citizenship*, 28: 43–60.

Maxwell, J. W., Lyon, T. P., & Hackett, S. C. (2000). "Self-Regulation and Social Welfare: The Political Economy of Corporate Environmentalism," *Journal of Law and Economics*, 43(2): 583–619.

Nehrt, C. (1996). "Timing and Intensity Effects of Environmental Investments," *Strategic Management Journal*, 17: 535–547.

—— (1998). "Maintainability of First Mover Advantages when Environmental Regulations Differ between Countries," *Academy of Management Review*, 23: 77–97.

Nelson, J. (2002). "From the Margins to the Mainstream: Corporate Social Responsibility in the Global Economy," in N. Højensgård & A. Wahlberg (eds.), *Campaign Report on European CSR Excellence 2002–2003: It Simply Works Better!* Copenhagen: The Copenhagen Centre, CSR Europe and the International Business Leaders' Forum, 14–19.

O'Rourke, A. (2003). "A new Politics of Engagement: Shareholder Activism for Corporate Social Responsibility," *Business Strategy and the Environment*, 12(4): 227–239.

Prakash, A. (2000). *Greening the Firm: The Politics of Corporate Environmentalism*. New York: Cambridge University Press.

Proffitt, W. T. & Spicer, A. (2006). "Shaping the Shareholder Activism Agenda: Institutional Investors and Global Social Issues," *Strategic Organization*, 4(2): 165–190.

Raines, S. S. (2002). "Implementing ISO 14001—An International Survey Assessing the Benefits of Certification," *Corporate Environmental Strategy*, 9(4): 418–426.

Ramus, C. A. & Steger, U. (2000). "The Roles of Supervisory Support Behaviors and Environmental Policy in Employee 'Ecoinitiatives' at Leading-Edge European Companies," *Academy of Management Journal*, 43(4): 605–626.

Rees, J. V. (1994). *Hostages of Each Other: The Transformation of Nuclear Safety Since Three Mile Island*. Chicago: University of Chicago Press.

Rehbein, K., Waddock, S., & Graves, S. (2004). "Understanding Shareholder Activism: Which Corporations are Targeted?" *Business and Society*, 43(3): 239–267.

Reid, E. M. & Toffel, M. W. (2009). "Responding to Public and Private Politics: Corporate Disclosure of Climate Change Strategies," *Strategic Management Journal*, 30(11), 1157–1178.

Revkin, A. C. (2009). "On Climate Issue, Industry Ignored its Scientists," *The New York Times*. New York.

Rivera, J. & de Leon, P. (2003). "Voluntary Environmental Performance of Western Ski Areas: Are Participants of the Sustainable Slopes Program Greener?" Paper presented at the Annual Research Conference of the Association for Public Policy Analysis and Management, Washington DC.

—— —— (2004). Is Greener Whiter? The Sustainable Slopes Program and the Voluntary environmental performance of western ski areas. *Policy Studies Journal*, 32(3): 417–437.

Rugman, A. M. & Verbeke, A. (1998). "Corporate Strategies and Environmental Regulations: An Organizing Framework," *Strategic Management Journal*, 19(4): 363–375.

Russo, M. V. & Fouts, P. A. (1997). "A Resource-Based Perspective on Corporate Environmental Performance and Profitability. "*Academy of Management Journal*, 40: 534–559.

Scott, W. R. (1992). *Organizations: Rational, Natural, and Open Systems,* 3rd ed., Englewood Cliffs NJ: Prentice Hall.

Segerson, K. & Miceli, T. J. (1998). "Voluntary Environmental Agreements: Good or Bad News for Environmental Protection?" *Journal of Environmental Economics and Management*, 36: 109–130.

Sharma, S. (2000). "Managerial Interpretations and Organizational Context as Predictors of Corporate Choice of Environmental Strategy," *Academy of Management Journal*, 43: 681–697.

—— & Henriques, I. (2005). "Stakeholder Influences on Sustainability Practices in the Canadian Forest Products Industry," *Strategic Management Journal*, 26: 159–180.

—— Pablo, A. L., & Vredenburg, H. (1999). "Corporate Environmental Responsiveness Strategies: The Importance of Issue Interpretation and Organizational Context," *Journal of Applied Behavioral Science*, 35(1): 87–108.

—— & Vredenburg, H. (1998). "Proactive Corporate Environmental Strategy and the Development of Competitively Valuable Organizational Capabilities," *Strategic Management Journal*, 19: 729–753.

Short, J. L. & Toffel, M. W. (2008). "Coerced Confessions: Self-policing in the Shadow of the Regulator," *Journal of Law, Economics, & Organization*, 24(1): 45–71.

—— —— (2010). "Making Self Regulation More than Merely Symbolic: The Critical Role of the Legal Environment," *Administrative Science Quarterly*, 55(3): 361–396.

Stafford, S. L. (2007). "Should you Turn Yourself In? The Consequences of Environmental Self-Policing," *Journal of Policy Analysis and Management*, 26(2): 305–326.

Toffel, M. (2000). "Anticipating Greener Supply Chain Demands: One Singapore Company's Journey to ISO 14001," in R. Hillary (ed.), *ISO 14001: Case Studies and Practical Experiences*, Sheffield, UK: Greenleaf Publishing.

Toffel, M. W. & Short, J. L. (forthcoming). "Coming Clean and Cleaning Up: Does Voluntary Self-Reporting Indicate Effective Self-Policing?" *Journal of Law & Economics*.

World Rainforest Movement (1998). "End of Boycott: 'Eco-Agreement' between RAN and Mitsubishi," *World Rainforest Movement Bulletin*.

CHAPTER 14

SOCIAL MOVEMENTS, BUSINESS, AND THE ENVIRONMENT

KLAUS WEBER
AND SARA B. SODERSTROM

WHEN sifting through the business sections of major newspapers in recent years, we can read about corporate actions such as FedEx introducing hybrid delivery trucks, WalMart imposing environmental standards on its suppliers, and consortia of multinational corporations adopting voluntary environmental standards (e.g. the 4C association of coffee growers) and lobbying in favor of climate change legislation (e.g. the USCAP group in the United States). Corporate environmentalism is *en vogue*, or at least it has become acceptable enough to not create much surprise or raise eyebrows. It is, however, easy to forget that this role of business in addressing environmental issues is a relatively recent phenomenon. While a number of other explanations for this behavior are addressed in other chapters in this Handbook, we review the historical and contemporary role of social movements in defining the relationship between business and the natural environment. Arguably, without the modern environmental movement, there would not be much to write about on the topic of corporate environmentalism.

Social movements are informal coalitions that take sustained action with a goal of contesting and changing prominent social and cultural practices (McAdam et al. 2001; Diani 1992). Key characteristics of movements are their diffuse membership and limited formal organization, the articulation of a conflict with societal practices in the name of a greater good, and the sustained nature of these efforts. Movements can also be understood as a historically evolved form of politics that contests authority through a distinctive set of political repertoires, such as street protests, boycotts, and law suits (Tilly 2004). From a more functionalist perspective, movements articulate collective interests and moral grievances—such as environmental degradation or justice—and translate them into societal concerns (Alexander 2006). The study of movements therefore excludes such collective behaviors as isolated episodic conflict (e.g. spontaneous protests), mobilization for or against trivial practices (e.g. fashion fads), and interest politics pursued by formal organizations (e.g. corporate lobbying). Businesses may be part of movement alliances, for example when climate change activism helps create demand for renewable energy providers, but to qualify as social movement dynamics, such effort must be embedded in coalitions and causes that transcend corporate self interest.

The unique contribution of a social movement perspective on business–environment relations is a conceptual and empirical toolkit for analyzing *patterns of sustained collective action* outside the formal political system. While movements often include activists and formal organizations engaged in private politics (see Baron & Lyon [Chapter 7] this volume), stakeholders of focal companies (see Kassinis [Chapter 5] this volume), and institutional entrepreneurs (see Lounsbury, Fairclough, & Lee [Chapter 12] this volume), social movement researchers hold that the actions and effectiveness of any specific actor must be understood as embedded in a broader network of activity and societal force—the movement (see, e.g. Rootes 2003; Rootes 2007). Social movement theory and research thus privilege collective and societal level models of behavior that focus on processes of social influence, collective identity, and cultural and institutional change that unfold over longer timeframes.

Social movements can be seen as a form of informal social control of business, a civil-society based complement to state and contractual regulations. But some movements also more fundamentally contest economic systems. They may thus play a creative or destructive, in addition to a regulative, role. While many social movements have been successful in influencing governments, a unique challenge for movements in affecting business is that commercial corporations are constituted as private concerns, which by design are relatively closed to direct control by external claimants other than owners (Weber et al. 2009). Critical questions of a social movement perspective on business and the environment therefore center on the process of movement influence: When and how do collective environmental movements emerge? What issues do they choose to address and what targets do they confront? How do businesses respond? How do movement activities translate into business practices? When are movements successful?

The chapter is organized around these process questions. We begin with an outline of the historical significance of the environmental movement for corporate environmental practices. Next we review the basic processes and mechanisms that lead from the identification of grievances and collective mobilization to the response and internalization of such challenges in businesses. Then we assess the success of social movements in affecting environmentally relevant practices of businesses, and finally we outline implications and emergent directions of research in studies of the environmental movement and businesses. At each stage we outline key concepts and ideas, and review example studies to assess the state of research in each area.

THE HISTORICAL ROLE OF THE ENVIRONMENTAL MOVEMENT FOR BUSINESS

The environmental movement developed in a specific historical and geographic context, and these initial conditions still shape current environmentalism. Like many social movements, movements concerned with the natural environment can be traced back to the social changes of the Industrial Revolution and early modernity. From the beginning, the environmental movement was therefore concerned with economic activities carried out by private enterprises(for more history of this period, see Post [Chapter 29] this volume).

It is useful to distinguish two movement waves: The first or early environmental movement, which arose in direct response to industrialization in Europe and North America in the late 1800s and early 1900s, and a second or new environmental movement that formed in response to new technologies, globalization and environmental degradation in North America and Europe in the 1960s and 1970s.

The environmentalism of the nineteenth century had its intellectual roots in European romanticism and in transcendentalism, a yearning for a pre-modern, spiritual and pastoral past. Key thinkers of this period are, for example, Emerson and Thoreau in North America, and Rudolph Steiner in Europe; as well as activists like John Muir, who founded the Sierra Club in 1892. Their thoughts and actions were fueled by a broader movement that shared core ideas about nature and paths for improving human societies. Early environmentalism was primarily a cultural movement, with limited mass mobilization and protest capacity to disrupt authority or stop the course of industrialization. It did, however, have a profound effect on thinking about the natural environment and its relationship to human activity. Ideas of the conservation, preservation, and restoration of nature were articulated at this time. "Nature" became a value-infused, often spiritual, category as opposed to simply a resource for human livelihood. The idyllic and stable state of untouched nature was seen as separate from the sphere of human activity, and in need of protection. These ideas gave rise to conservationist organizations such as the Sierra Club, and also the subsequent, and quite enduring, focus of environmentalists on the pollution and contamination of natural systems through human activity. The same understandings also laid the foundations for the development of some business practices, for example organic agriculture.

The second wave of environmentalism was only partly connected to the earlier tradition (Dunlap & Mertig 1992). The discontinuity can be attributed to two changes in the intervening decades. One is the dramatic expansion of science and rational models of knowledge about nature (Meyer et al. 1997; Frank 1997); the other is the emergence of an anti-establishment and politically left-leaning critique of capitalism after World War II (Belasco 2007; Rootes 2003). In North America, the birth of the new environmentalism as a social movement is often associated with the publication of Rachel Carson's book *Silent Spring* in 1962—not accidentally a science-based critique of the environmental effects of pesticides and an attack on the chemical industry and supporting government agencies. The movement gathered pace in the late 1960s, showing its increasing capacity for mass mobilization with the first Earth Day event in 1970. During this period, concerns with environmental degradation were infused with broader counter-cultural ideas in the United States, and more leftist ideologies in Western Europe, both of which shared a deep suspicion of large corporations and the capitalist system. The new environmentalists formed an uneasy coalition with the older more conservative group of conservationists, who were inspired by the first wave of environmentalism. The newer environmentalists imported frames, networks, and protest repertoires from the civil rights and peace movements, giving rise to ideas of environmental justice, consumer rights, and sustainability. A key difference to older environmental groups was the concern with reforming industrial production itself instead of protecting pockets of untouched nature at the fringes of industrial societies. Business activity therefore became a much more central focus.

In the new environmentalism of the second half of the twentieth century, earlier ideas of protecting nature from human interference persist in a focus on water and air pollution, and on the risks of new nuclear and genetic technologies. The common denominator of these concerns is the concept of contamination, the spoiling of a 'clean,' healthy state of nature through 'unnatural' products of industrial technologies. In addition to this continuity, new understandings emerged, many of which can be linked to the expansion of environmental sciences (Frank 1997). For example, the *Club of Rome* publications noted threats to global ecosystems and human survival, and critiqued global capitalism. Scientific concepts such as ecosystem and biodiversity translated into a new type of issues, such as closed-loop recycling, saving endangered species, and sustainable global development. These new concerns are significant because they partly reverse the separation between the spheres of nature and human activity in early environmentalism. If natural systems are dynamic, and human activity is part of them, concerns with nature cannot be addressed without reference to social and economic practices. Intervention and management, rather than conservation and separation is needed (Brulle 1996; Gottlieb 2005). The environmental movement achieved important successes in its efforts to change business practices over the past fifty years. Most developed countries have created government agencies and legislation that regulates industrial production, and have also seen some changes that are driven by more cultural change, for example higher voluntary recycling rates, the rise of alternative agriculture and eco-friendly products, and technology development in the area of renewable energy.

The new environmental movement thrived in Western Europe and more recently in North America (Rucht 1999). However, despite many transatlantic connections, movements in different countries often developed in parallel due to different political systems and local concerns. For example, progressive and conservationist groups began to form alliances and fuse in some European countries in the 1980s, in the context of forming Green parties that sought and gained parliamentary representation (Rootes 1999; Rucht 1999). This process did not occur until later in countries without proportional representation electoral systems, such as the United States. And new concerns, such as biotechnology and GM food, garnered more attention in countries such as France, Italy, and

Germany than in the United States, in part because of the movement's greater political foothold via parliamentary Green parties. In both North America and Europe, the environmental movement has to some extent become less counter-cultural and increasingly "mainstream" and institutionalized (Hoffman 2001). This trend is evidenced by the professionalization and institutionalization of its organization in the form of political parties and NGOs, and the legitimacy of the voluntary corporate environmentalism depicted at the outset of this chapter.

The movement's global impact on business is more mixed (Özen & Özen, 2009; Crotty 2006). On the one hand, Western ideas of environmentalism were exported to some developing and developed countries in Eastern Europe, Asia, South America, and Africa, where they often connect with local activism against multinational enterprises and post-colonial sentiments (Frank et al. 2000; Ignatow 2007). On the other hand, the ideas and priorities of the Western environmental movement are not always shared by local populations and sometimes resisted as an imperialist view that does not address pressing material and social issues. The local mobilization ability of environmental movements varies strongly across countries and regions, which in turn has created opportunities for businesses to evade pressures by relocating their operations (Welker 2009; Gould 1991). The globalization of the environmental movement itself has often taken the form of participating in international policy-making and targeting multinational companies headquartered in developed countries, and less successfully of planting local movements across the globe.

DYNAMICS OF MOVEMENTS: GRIEVANCES, MOBILIZATION, TARGETS

Compared to more company-centered approaches to business and the environment, social movement scholars treat the construction of environmental issues and the processes of stakeholder mobilization as endogenous and central to understanding corporate environmentalism. A large body of middle-range theory and empirical studies examines the dynamics of how various environmental concerns originate, become articulated and framed, and how activists gain enough power to trigger corporate responses. We review three central conditions of movement emergence: the origin and construction of grievances, the collective mobilization processes that turn latent causes into a movement, and the selection of strategies and targets of contestation.

Origins and construction of grievances

The question of when and how movements emerge is not a trivial one. Most movement scholars believe that failures of markets or states to satisfy the needs of a population or provide public goods are insufficient explanations. In terms of theory, a majority of current movement research treats self-interests, identities, and deprivation—common sources of grievances—as socially constructed in the course of mobilization, rather than as entirely pre-existing (Goodwin et al. 2001; Polletta & Jasper 2001). Empirically, movements often fail to emerge in the presence of manifest local and persistent environmental deprivation (e.g. deforestation, displacement, and pollution in extractive industries in developing countries). At the same time, successful mobilization has occurred around issues that seemingly have little immediate impact on those that mobilize (e.g. biodiversity activists in North America).

While historically some social movements could be directly linked to the self-interest of disadvantaged groups, such as the working class and discriminated social minorities, the environmental movement is largely a movement that acts "on behalf of others," including future generations, wildlife, or abstract notions of the planet or nature. It is therefore more than other movements reliant on the cultural and scientific construction of the reality of these interests (Meyer et al. 1997; Yearly 1992)—see, for example, the contention about the reality of global warming. Three main accounts have been put forward for the construction of a common interest around the natural environment in the modern environmental movement.

One explanation focuses on environmental deprivation that affects the material or ideational livelihood of some part of the population. As the term "deprivation" implies, grievances arise from environmental conditions falling short of some standard. Awareness of deprivation is created by man-made disasters, such as oil and toxin spills, and the pollution or decline of natural resources at the heart of human health and survival such as air, water, and soil. While clearly applicable to many causes of environmental mobilization that address current conditions, such as water pollution or acid rain that damages forests, environmental degradation arguments are open to counter-evidence of many failures of movements to emerge under similar conditions. They are also open to questions as to how risk-based movement causes, such as global warming and GMOs can be accommodated in the absence of current manifest effects.

A second source of environmental grievances has come from evoking the notion of environmental justice and environmental rights. Borrowing from notions of human rights and social justice, this perspective suggests that grievances about the natural environment are closely intertwined with social, political, and economic inequalities and inequities. Mobilization about environmental issues is at the same time about social emancipation from broader institutions (Banerjee 2000; Banerjee 2003). One prominent example of this perspective is the "treadmill of production" model. This model links greater environmental deprivation of socially disadvantaged communities to the design of global models of industrial production: the "treadmill" of corporations and aligned political interests moves most of the benefits of economic growth to the rich and leaves the poor with the environmental fallout (see also Banerjee [Chapter 31] this volume). Some empirical evidence supports, for example, that low-income communities experience higher environmentally induced health risks, and access to clean water and air have been cast as a basic right for everyone by several movements.

Yet, the environmental movement in the United States and Western Europe has been particularly successful in mobilizing the better educated and affluent parts of the population, who are most shielded from environmental degradation and are on the advantaged end of environmental justice. A third, and perhaps most prominent account for the source of environmental grievances, therefore, looks at the crafting and expression of identity as pivotal. Research under the umbrella of "new social movements" (Polletta & Jasper 2001; Melucci 1996), sees environmentalism as less motivated by the material impacts of environmental change, than by cultural and ideological processes that allow activists to claim a positive and distinctive identity in relation to other societal groups. Movement participation is as much about group membership as it is about being personally affected in terms of health or livelihood.

Mobilization

Much like general attitudes, experienced grievances of whatever type do not, however, automatically lead to collective action. The process that turns latent dissatisfaction into a movement that can, for example, challenge companies' practices or fuel new technologies, is mobilization—getting people to act together in a coordinated and directed way. Social movement research has identified three main ingredients to mobilization (McAdam et al. 1996): favorable political opportunities, existing mobilizing structures such as networks and organizations, and framing processes that communicate movement goals effectively.

Political opportunities can take the form of disunity of existing elites or an ideological legitimacy crisis of a regime. Both reduce the ability of those in power to undermine or suppress mobilization. In the case of the environmental movement, ideological divisions among leftist parties in Europe allowed green causes and Green Parties to rally supporters around environmental causes. The legitimacy crisis of the chemical industry in the wake of earlier environmental disasters allowed anti-biotech activists to attack the same companies for genetically engineered organisms (Schurman 2004; Schurman 2009).

Existing networks among activists and movement organizations facilitate collective action by diffusing protest tactics, building trust, and aligning ideologies. The network aspect is particularly salient at the local level for creating turnout for protest events, and at the macro level for coordinating actions internationally and across different movements (Diani 1995). One path of recruitment to activism and of continued commitment is via close personal relationships with other participants (Jasper & Poulsen 1995). Formal movement organizations also provide the infrastructure and at times the funding for more sustained campaigns, for example in pushing for renewable energy use at the local level (Vasi 2010; Sine & Lee 2009).

Recent research on movement mobilization has placed increasing emphasis on another pathway: issue framing—the rhetorical structure and emotional power of public appeals. Frames serve diagnostic, prognostic, and motivational purposes: they explain what the problem is, direct the search of likely solutions, and motivate action (Benford & Snow 2000; Gamson & Meyer 1996; Gamson & Modigliani 1989). Many movements, including environmental ones, use a limited set of "master frames," such as rights, sustainability or freedom, that act as broad umbrella concepts for alliances (Snow & Benford 1992). Frames work when they resonate with audience understandings, due to, for example sharing broader cultural codes or experiential bases (Johnston & Klandermans 1995; Weber et al. 2008). Stories and personal narratives are particularly effective ways to frame often more abstract environmental issues.

Strategies and tactics

Mobilization addresses the question of how movements grow in influence by increasing membership and the willingness of members to engage in activism. The other question for understanding movements' impact is what specific issues they pursue, what tactics they use, and to whom they apply the tactics. Traditionally, the environmental movement employed mainly confrontational tactics, such as protests, calls for boycotts or shareholder resolutions designed to apply pressure to companies (King & Soule 2007). While still prevalent, this emphasis has changed and given rise to more reformist strategies, such as collaboration with companies on specific issues (Yaziji & Doh 2009).

The issue agenda of the environmental movement has been shown to vary significantly over time and between countries (Dalton 1994; Rootes 2003). Concerns with acid rain, recycling, and nuclear power in the 1980s have to some extent given way to concerns such as climate change and renewable energy in the 2010s. As mobilization often occurs around specific issues, activist organizations chose issues not only based on ideology, but also pragmatically, for their mobilization potential, and reactively, in response to specific events that garner public attention (Hoffman & Ocasio 2001). For example, vivid issues and events, such as catastrophes, the occurrence of major political events, and damage in the immediate environment are more likely to be pursued.

A related question is what targets movements chose. To the extent that business is a target of contestation, movements are more likely to contest and scrutinize producers of branded goods, large facilities, and those in prominent positions or with troubled histories. Movements do, therefore, not always select target firms and practices for campaigns based on their environmental impact or actions. From a company perspective this has been labeled as the "social risk" of businesses (Yaziji & Doh 2009).

How movements affect business organizations

Social movements can influence businesses' environmental practices through several distinct pathways. One form of influence is indirect: by changing the general operating environment of all firms in an industry or economy. Organized activism is often aimed at governments, leading to the formulation of new public policies and regulations, such as carbon pricing or wastewater treatment requirements, that in turn affect industry. Another path is via more diffuse cultural change in public sentiment that alters the social environment of businesses, for example in the form of consumer preferences and employee skills and identities. Another form of influence is more direct, where movements interact with organizations. A prominent direct pathway is pressure campaigns launched against specific target firms for their environmental practices. Such campaigns use familiar protest repertoires such as boycotts, lawsuits, and media and street protests, to threaten a company's reputation and disrupt its operations. In addition to this more traditional form of influence, recent research draws attention to two other direct pathways. One is the role of the environmental movement in creating alternatives to incumbent organizations by fueling the creation of new technologies, enterprises and markets. The other path is via social movement organizations that use cooperative rather than conflictual engagement with companies to create voluntary company policies and offer certification or audit services. The question of how movements change environmental practices of companies has generated a considerable body of empirical and theoretical knowledge, but the extent of available research addressing each alternative pathway varies.

We discussed the cultural influence of the environmental movement on broader understandings in the section on the history of environmentalism above. Environmental movements can "shift standards of good conduct…and empower local communities" (Wapner 1995: 311) to change the general cultural and discursive standards according to which businesses have to legitimate their conduct (Maguire & Hardy 2009). Such broad understandings and standards of legitimacy influence how corporate stakeholder groups, such as consumers, employees, investors and communities, come to understand their interests. The impact on corporations of the diffuse cultural change created by the environmental movement is therefore often mediated by political processes within and between different stakeholder groups (Soule 2009). Movements play an additional role in translating broad cultural understandings into public interpretations and sentiments regarding specific issues, such as new technologies and business practices (Douglas & Wildavsky 1982). For example, companies located in areas where a large part of the population cares about the environment have been shown to be more exposed to environmentalist ideas and more influenced by concerns about their environmental reputation than companies elsewhere (Weber et al. 2009; Sine & Lee 2009).

Much traditional research has measured the success of the environmental movement on its ability to affect environmental regulations and policies at national and international levels, and a large body of research illuminates conditions for success in different domains. As the implementation of environmental regulations is often assumed to be automatic, studies in this realm largely focus on identifying mobilizing strategies and tactics that prompt governments to take action. For example, during NAFTA's negotiations, environmental activists were able to gain significant concessions, even from a relatively low power position and with few resources (Evans & Kay 2008). This was because of their ability to successfully broker alliances and resources, adapt their frames, and intersect multiple fields.

Activists have also directly confronted incumbent organizations in attempts to change organizational behaviors. Environmental movements act to disrupt and change operations by mobilizing organizational stakeholders, such as shareholders, workers, and consumers (Luders 2006). One common mode of contestation is shareholder resolutions. Reid & Toffel (2009) found that shareholder resolutions about climate change filed against a firm or others in its industry increased a firm's likelihood to engage in activities aligned with the activists' interests. Another frequent action is a call for a consumer boycott. Boycotts calls are most effective when the target organization had a recent decline in sales or reputation and when paired with significant media attention (King 2008). While the economic interruption caused by consumer boycotts are often negligible, their effect on corporate reputation is important and often more effective. Environmental activists also attempt to undermine reputation through street protests, law suits and media campaigns. For example, in the early 2000s, Greenpeace and the NRDC waged a five-year media campaign (and boycotts) against Kimberly-Clark for its policies on using fiber from "virgin" forests. In 2009 Kimberly-Clark agreed to stop these practices.

In recent decades, movement organizations have increasingly used cooperative in addition to confrontational tactics with corporations. Yaziji & Doh (2009), for example, show that movement-based NGOs engage in a range of activities, ranging from radical challenges to advocacy to service provision. Cooperative influence channels take the form of stakeholder dialogue, partnering on corporate environmental projects, or facilitating voluntary industry standards. These relationships have been well documented in the area of forestry and sustainable development (Bartley 2007), and are becoming increasingly common as the environmental movement becomes more institutionalized. Some observers are critical of cooperation and fear the cooptation of environmentalist groups and their objectives, others see it as an effective complementary strategy (Hoffman 2009).

In addition to targeting incumbent organizations, environmental movements have a direct influence on entrepreneurship and markets (Vasi 2010; Lounsbury et al. 2003). The mobilizing capacity of the environmental movement can help overcome barriers to developing alternative technologies, enterprises, and markets. In a study of the emergence of a new category for grass-fed meat and dairy products, Weber, Heinze, & DeSoucey (2008) found that movement processes helped recruit and inspire entrepreneurs, facilitated the creation of collective market identities, and allowed producers and consumers to understand and price new product categories. And a large sample study by Sine & Lee (2009) found that a greater density of environmental activists in a local community had a larger impact on entrepreneurial activity around wind energy than the presence and quality of wind itself. Environmental movements thus can direct technological and social innovation aligned with movement goals, create consumer demand for these products, and develop legitimacy and positive reputations for organizations that address their concerns.

INTERNALIZATION OF MOVEMENT INFLUENCE

However they gain attention, environmental issues ultimately have to filter into the firm's internal decision processes to change its environmental policies and practices. This process may seem clear-cut in cases of regulative compliance, but in many instances, crossing the organization's boundary is not trivial. A growing body of research investigates translation mechanisms between organizations and their environment and internal organizational dynamics to understand the impact of the environmental movement and specific campaigns on corporate environmental practice. This literature has identified a number of common pathways (Zald et al. 2005; Weber et al. 2009): via access to formal governance structures, such as shareholder meetings and boards, through boundary-spanning units dedicated to environmental issues (e.g. sustainability or environmental compliance officers), by altering the economic cost-benefit calculations used to evaluate alternative options (Luders 2006), via peer pressure and competitive benchmarking with other companies, reputation and status motivations, and through activists inside the company who hold environmentalist identities (Scully & Segal 2002).

Social movements can take advantage of structural aspects of organizations to push for specific demands. Boundary-spanning units can amplify and/or adopt movement goals. For example, the public relations and legal divisions all interface with social movement organizations as part of their business operations. The connections between movement activists and these divisions can improve the perception of the movement goals and aid communication between the different groups. Managers and employees can also hold personal movement-related identities, and participate in related networks. These connections can aid activists in understanding the organization and getting access to key decision-makers.

The internal organization of the target firm also influences its susceptibility to influence from environmental activists. Organizations vary in their capacity and commitment to address the movement demands (Zald, Morrill, & Rao 2005). Organizations with low capacity may be unable to implement movement objectives, even if the organization is committed to them. On the other hand, organizations with sufficient capacity may resist implementing movement objectives due to low commitment by organizational actors. An organization's internal power system also influences its reactions to movement demands. In the case of early biotechnology in Germany, for example, movements affected pharmaceutical companies' decision processes via status threats to scientists and executives as well as via perceptions of investment uncertainty, but importantly, both effects were contingent on the unity of the companies' elites (Weber et al. 2009).

Even when an organization is committed to meeting movement demands or comply with regulations, it must implement any changes. Its internal organization, and especially the presence of champions, are important in this regard (Scully & Segal 2002). The number and distribution of internal activists affects the prominence of an issue, as does the ability of champions to forge coalitions and mobilize collective resources and energy.

Research on issue selling, for example, has examined how middle managers bring environmental concerns to the attention of organizational leaders (Bansal 2003; Bansal & Roth 2000).

BUSINESS RESPONSES TO ENVIRONMENTAL MOVEMENTS

Corporations can respond to environmental movements in a variety of ways. They can comply, either sincerely or symbolically. More often, they resist movement demands through counter-mobilization and political strategies. They can also seek to co-opt pressure groups, turning confrontation in to advantageous collaboration. Or they can address potential movement demands proactively by integrating environmental stewardship into their operations and identity and gaining strategic advantage from these actions.

When corporations do not want to take action on environmental demands, they often counter-mobilize to actively work against the demands. One example of this is the automotive manufacturer's response to corporate average fuel economy (CAFE) standards. The standards were initially passed by US Congress in 1975 after the 1973 oil embargo. Automotive manufacturers lobbied against any CAFE standards using numerous approaches, such as arguing that they are ineffective and sponsoring research by economists to show that the standards are not economical. However, there are also times when organizations simply comply with movement demands. This is more likely to occur when the target organization faces costs of non-compliance, such as penalties or fines, decreases in reputation, and negative media attention (King & Soule 2007).

A concern of environmental movements is that the compliance is only symbolic. In other words, there is a concern that organizations say they will meet the movement demands, but decouple their actions from their statements and do not end up complying (Westphal & Zajac 2001). In the environmental area, a common concern is "greenwashing"—or stating a specific environmental policy or attribute but not implementing it (see also Jermier and Forbes [Chapter 30] this volume). Ramus & Montiel (2005) found, for example, that the chemical manufacturing industry was as likely as other industries to commit to a toxic use reduction policy; however, they were less likely to implement such a policy.

Organizations may proactively address the concerns generated by the cultural and public agenda impact of environmental movements. This may be to preemptively deal with regulatory uncertainty or to gain strategic advantage. For example, the Global Roundtable on Climate Change is a group of leaders from business, civil society, NGOs, and research institutions who are working together to develop consensus around climate change and how to address it. The consortium has developed recommendations and guidelines for regulations—in part trying to influence the regulatory environment towards goals that they would like to, or are able to, achieve. At times, individual organizations also proactively address environmental concerns. For example, many companies voluntarily joined the Chicago Climate Exchange, working towards carbon neutral operations. Their actions help them develop a reputation as leaders in environmental issues and have influenced other, more reactive companies.

Proactive attempts to address environmental issues are, however, in practice hard to distinguish from symbolic compliance and attempts at co-opting environmental advocacy groups. Co-optation is when organizations integrate new elements, in this case environmental activists, into its leadership or policy-determining structure as a means of avoiding threats (Selznick 1949). For example, Murphree, Wright, & Ebaugh (1996) followed an attempted cooptation by a toxic waste company. The company gained agreement with established activist leaders to negotiate, but the negotiation was structured beneficially for the waste company. By engaging the activists in the negotiation, the waste company was able to avoid having those activists participate in other adversarial activities. This attempt at co-optation eventually failed to achieve its goal—gaining a permit for a new toxic waste site—because other activists who were not engaged in the negotiation mobilized local opposition.

Empirical research has so far mainly studied the internal dynamics and tactics of the environmental movement, at the expense of counter-strategies by industry and the relative effectiveness of mobilization and counter-mobilization efforts (for exceptions, see Rucht 1990; Gould 1991; Maguire & Hardy 2009).

FUTURE RESEARCH DIRECTIONS

Research on the environmental movement has produced a substantial body of work, as has research on corporate environmentalism. Yet, for most of the past decades, these streams have developed in parallel. Only recently have we seen a surge of studies at the intersection of these two perspectives. This dialog and partial convergence have opened up important new perspectives and areas of research, for example in understanding collaboration between businesses and advocacy groups, the role of movement activism in market and technology evolution, and in a better understanding of the origin of stakeholder groups' varying influence. As this research expands, we observe a number of trends that affect the relationship between business and the environmental movement. Some are prompted by the continued evolution of the environmental movement; others by theoretical puzzles or inconsistencies.

One empirical trend is a shift from political confrontation between environmental activists and corporations towards more diverse types of relations, where SMOs take on the role of adversary, collaborator, monitor of soft regulation, ally in influencing governments, or service provider. This trend is prompted, not only by the ideological and organizational diversification of the movement, but also by changing corporate views of environmental issues. In this fast-changing arena, questions arise about how these new relationships are structured, and how portfolios of different relationships are managed, and about their effectiveness for achieving environmental and economic goals. A related question is the role of business influence on environmental movements. Almost all existing research sees movements as an independent force and looks at influence directed at businesses. Yet, as businesses increasingly use movement-like tactics and become more sophisticated in managing activist pressure, they begin to play a role in directing, sponsoring or undermining environmental mobilization against other companies or the state (for a rare example of such research, see Walker 2009).

Another area of increasing interest is in moving beyond conceptions of firms, movements, and movement organizations as relatively unitary actors, towards taking seriously the internal organization of companies and movements in understanding their interactions (Weber et al. 2009). For example, the effectiveness of movement campaigns may have as much to do with the internal political dynamics of the targeted company as with the strength of the movement's mobilizing ability. The implication is that movement scholars have to become better organization theorists and students of market processes, while organizational and economic scholars have to become better students of politics and collective action processes.

A third trend is a shift in the focus of research from local and national activities to issues and mobilization in the transnational and global spheres. This is in part an empirical necessity, as companies are embedded in global supply chains and local environmental movements are increasingly connected internationally (Smith 2001; Rucht 1997; Bartley 2007). Yet, the ability of environmental movements to mobilize campaigns internationally remains uncertain, as does their capacity to affect business practices, support international regulatory regimes and pursue global objectives in the face of often local impacts. The fact that many environmental issues are interconnected or global in nature calls for more extensive research in this area.

Fourth, the role of new communication technologies in facilitating social movements has captured much public attention but is rather understudied. For example, it is not at all clear what role networks mediated solely by social media platforms can play in mobilization, and how they impact movement and corporate tactics. High stakes and sustained activism that is often needed to start broader or more radical campaigns, such as blockades, acts of civil disobedience or violence, has historically been found to require strongly embedded relationships among activists (Mcadam 1986). Can weak ties among strangers fulfill a similar function, or are they more suitable for short-lived and feeble movement actions? Do they allow for better coordination between local environmental groups, or create new inequalities? Do they make companies more vulnerable or afford them more influence?

Lastly, while most recent research has focused on middle-range theory building and empirical analyses at the intersection between movements and business actors, these interactions cannot be completely understood without a greater appreciation for their embeddedness in civil society and political institutions. Much of the current research, for example, implicitly assumes a backdrop of a Western liberal democracy with a strong state and a sizeable civil society sector. This assumption clearly does not hold in other parts of the world or at in the international sphere (Rootes 1999). To find answers to some of the more sticky questions, such as why environmental movements do not emerge in some places and for some issues, it is necessary for empirical studies to more explicitly take into account contextual dimensions, and for theoretical development to more directly address the multi-level and networked nature of social movements and the modern economy.

REFERENCES

Alexander, J. C. (2006). *The Civil Sphere*. New York, Oxford University Press.

Banerjee, S. B. (2000). "Whose Land is it Anyway? National Interest, Indigenous Stakeholders and Colonial Discourses: The Case of the Jabiluka Uranium Mine," *Organization & Environment*, 13: 3–38.

—— (2003). "Who Sustains Whose Development? Sustainable Development and the Reinvention of Nature," *Organization Studies*, 24: 143–180.

Bansal, P. (2003). "From Issues to Actions: The Importance of Individual Concerns and Organizational Values in Responding to Natural Environmental Issues," *Organization Science*, 14: 510–527.

—— & Roth, K. (2000). "Why Companies go Green: A Model of Ecological Responsiveness," *Academy of Management Journal*, 43: 717–736.

Bartley, T. (2007). "Institutional Emergence in an Era of Globalization: The Rise of Transnational Private Regulation of Labor and Environmental Conditions," *American Journal of Sociology*, 113: 297–351.

Belasco, W. J. (2007). *Appetite for change: How the Counterculture Took On the Food Industry*. Ithaca, NY, Cornell University Press.

Benford, R. D. & Snow, D. A. (2000). "Framing Processes and Social Movements: An Overview and Assessment," *Annual Review of Sociology*, 26: 611–639.

Brulle, R. J. (1996). "Environmental Discourse and Social Movement Organizations: A Historical and Rhetorical Perspective on the Development of US Environmental Organizations," *Sociological Inquiry*, 66: 58–83.

Crotty, J. (2006). "Reshaping the Hourglass? The Environmental Movement and Civil Society Development in the Russian Federation," *Organization Studies*, 27: 1319–1338.

Dalton, R. J. (1994). *The Green Rainbow: Environmental Groups in Western Europe*. New Haven, CT, Yale University Press.

Diani, M. (1992). "The concept of social movement," *The Sociological Review*, 40: 1–25.

—— (1995). *Green Networks: A Structural Analysis of the Italian Environmental Movement*. Edinburgh, Edinburgh University Press.

Douglas, M. & Wildavsky, A. (1982). *Risk and Culture: An Essay on the Selection of Technical and Environmental Dangers*. Berkeley, CA, University of California Press.

Dunlap, R. & Mertig, A. G. (eds.) (1992). *American Environmentalism: The U.S. Environmental Movement, 1970–1990*. Washington, DC, Taylor & Francis.

Evans, R. & Kay, T. (2008). "How Environmentalists 'greened' Trade Policy: Strategic Action and the Architecture of Field Overlap," *American Sociological Review*, 73: 970–991.

Frank, D. J. (1997). "Science, Nature, and the Globalization of the Environment, 1870–1990," *Social Forces*, 76: 409–435.

—— Hironaka, A. & Schofer, E. (2000). "The Nation-State and the Natural Environment over the Twentieth Century," *American Sociological Review*, 65: 96–116.

Gamson, W. A. & Meyer, D. S. (1996). "Framing Political Opportunities," in Mcadam, D., Mccarthy, J. D., & Zald, M. N. (eds.) *Comparative Perspectives on Social Movements: Political Opportunities, Mobilizing Structures, and Cultural Framings,* Cambridge, UK, Cambridge University Press.

—— & Modigliani, A. (1989). "Media Discourse and Public Opinion on Nuclear Power: a Constructionist Approach," *American Journal of Sociology*, 95: 1–37.

Goodwin, J., Jasper, J. M. & Polletta, F. (eds.) (2001). *Passionate Politics: Emotions and Social Movements.* Chicago, IL, University of Chicago Press.

Gottlieb, R. (2005). *Forcing the Spring: The Transformation of the American Environmental Movement.* Washington, DC, Island Press.

Gould, K. A. (1991). "The Sweet Smell of Money: Economic Dependency and Local Environmental Political Mobilization," *Society & Natural Resources*, 4: 133–150.

Hoffman, A. J. (2001). *From Heresy to Dogma: An Institutional History of Corporate Environmentalism.* Stanford, CA, Stanford University Press.

—— (2009). "Shades of Green," *Stanford Social Innovation Review*, Spring: 40–49.

—— & Ocasio, W. (2001). "Not All Events Are Attended Equally: Toward a Middle-Range Theory of Industry Attention to External Events," *Organization Science*, 12: 414–434.

Ignatow, G. (2007). *Transnational Identity Politics and the Environment.* Lanham, MD, Lexington.

Jasper, J. M. & Poulsen, J. D. (1995). "Recruiting Strangers and Friends: Moral Shocks and Social Networks in Animal Rights and Anti-Nuclear Protests," *Social Problems*, 42: 493–512.

Johnston, H. & Klandermans, B. (eds.) (1995). *Social Movements and Culture.* New York, Routledge.

King, B. G. (2008). "A Political Mediation Model of Corporate Response to Social Movement Activism," *Administrative Science Quarterly*, 53: 395–421.

—— & Soule, S. A. (2007). "Social Movements as Extra-Institutional Entrepreneurs: The Effect of Protest on Stock Price Returns," *Administrative Science Quarterly*, 52: 413–442.

Lounsbury, M., Ventresca, M. J., & Hirsch, P. (2003). "Social Movements, Field Frames and Industry Emergence: A Cultural–Political Perspective on US Recycling," *Socio-Economic Review*, 1: 71–104.

Luders, J. (2006). "The Economics of Movement Success: Business Responses to Civil Rights Mobilization," *American Journal of Sociology*, 111: 963–998.

Mcadam, D. (1986). "Recruitment to High-Risk Activism: The Case of Freedom Summer," *American Journal of Sociology*, 92: 64–90.

—— Mccarthy, J. D., & Zald, M. N. (1996). *Comparative Perspectives on Social Movements: Political Opportunities, Mobilizing Structures, and Cultural Framings.* Cambridge, UK, Cambridge University Press.

—— Tarrow, S., & Tilly, C. (2001). *Dynamics of Contention,* Cambridge, UK, Cambridge University Press.

Maguire, S. & Hardy, C. (2009). "Discourse and Deinstitutionalization: The Decline of DDT," *Academy of Management Journal*, 52: 148–178.

Melucci, A. (1996). *Challenging Codes: Collective Action in the Information Age.* Cambridge, UK, Cambridge University Press.

Meyer, J. W., Frank, D. J., Hironaka, A., Schofer, E. & Tuma, N. B. (1997). "The Structuring of a World Environmental Regime, 1870–1990," *International Organization*, 51: 623–651.

Murphee, D. W., Wright, S. A., & Ebaugh, H. R. (1996). "Toxic Waste Siting and Community Resistance: How Cooptation of Local Citizen Opposition Failed," *Sociological Perspectives*, 39: 447–463.

Özen, Ş. & Özen, H. (2009). "Peasants against MNCs and the State: The Role of the Bergama Struggle in the Institutional Construction of the Gold-Mining Field in Turkey," *Organization*, 16: 547–573.

Polletta, F. & Jasper, J. M. (2001). "Collective Identity and Social Movements," *Annual Review of Sociology*, 27: 283–305.

Ramus, C. A. & Montiel, I. (2005). "When are Corporate Environmental Policies a Form of Greenwashing?" *Business and Society*, 44: 377–414.

Reid, E. & Toffel, M. W. (2009). "Responding to Public and Private Politics: Corporate Disclosure of Climate Change Strategies," *Strategic Management Journal*, 30: 1157–1178.

Rootes, C. (1999). "Environmental Movements: From the Local to the Global," *Environmental Politics*, 8: 1–12.

—— (2003). "Environmental movements," in Snow, D. A., Soule, S. A., & Kriesi, H. (eds.) *The Blackwell Companion to Social Movements*. Malden, MA, Blackwell.

—— (2007). "Environmental Movements," in Ritzer, G. (ed.) *Blackwell Encyclopedia of Sociology*. Malden, MA, Blackwell.

Rucht, D. (1990). "Campaigns, Skirmishes and Battles: Anti-Nuclear Movements in the USA, France and West Germany," *Organization & Environment*, 4: 193–222.

—— (1997). "Limits to Mobilization: Environmental Policy for the European Union. in Smith, J., Chatfield, C., & Pagnucco, R. (Eds.) *Transnational Social Movements and Global Politics: Solidarity beyond the State*. Syracuse, NY, Syracuse University Press.

—— (1999). "The Impact of Environmental Movements in Western Societies," in Guigni, M., Mcadam, D., & Tilly, C. (eds.) *How Social Movements Matter*. Minneapolis, MN, University of Minnesota Press.

Schnaiberg, A. & Gould, K. A. (1994). *Environment and society: The enduring conflict*, Caldwell, NJ, Blackburn Press.

Schurman, R. (2004). "Fighting 'Frankenfoods': Industry Opportunity Structures and the Efficacy of the Anti-Biotech Movement in Western Europe," *Social Problems*, 51: 243–268.

—— (2009). "Targeting Capital: A Cultural Economy Approach to Understanding the Efficacy of Two Anti–Genetic Engineering Movements," *American Journal of Sociology*, 115: 155–202.

Scully, M. A. & Segal, A. (2002). "Passion with an Umbrella: Grassroots Activists in the Workplace," *Research in the Sociology of Organizations*, 19: 125–168.

Selznick, P. (1949). *TVA and the Grass roots*. New York, Harper & Row.

Sine, W. D. & Lee, B. H. (2009). "Tilting at Windmills? The Environmental Movement and the Emergence of the U.S. Wind Energy Sector," *Administrative Science Quarterly*, 54: 123–155.

Smith, J. (2001). "Globalizing Resistance: The Battle of Seattle and the Future of Social Movements," *Mobilization*, 6: 1–19.

Snow, D. A. & Benford, R. D. (1992). "Master Frames and 'Cycles of Protest'. in Morris, A. D. & Mcclurg Mueller, C. (eds.) *Frontiers of Social Movement Theory*. New Haven, Yale University Press.

Soule, S. A. (2009). *Contention and Corporate Social Responsibility*. New York, Cambridge University Press.

Tilly, C. (2004). *Social Movements, 1768–2004,* Boulder, CO, Paradigm Publishers.

Vasi, B. (2010). *Winds of Change: The Environmental Movement and the Global Development of the Wind Energy Industry*. Cambridge, MA, Oxford University Press.

Walker, E. T. (2009). "Privatizing Participation: Civic Change and the Organizational Dynamics of Grassroots Lobbying Firms," *American Sociological Review*, 74: 83–105.

Wapner, P. (1995). "Politics beyond the State: Environmental Activism and World Civic Politics," *World Politics*, 47: 311–340.

Weber, K., Heinze, K. & DeSoucey, M. (2008). "Forage for Thought: Mobilizing Codes in the Movement for Grass-Fed Meat and Dairy Products," *Administrative Science Quarterly*, 53: 529–567.

—— Rao, H. & Thomas, L. G. (2009). "From Streets to Suites: How the Anti-Biotech Movement Affected German Pharmaceutical Firms," *American Sociological Review*, 74: 106–127.

Welker, M. (2009). "Corporate Security Begins in the Community: Mining, the Corporate Social Responsibility Industry, and Environmental Advocacy in Indonesia," *Cultural Anthropology*, 24: 142–179.

Westphal, J. D. & Zajac, E. J. (2001). "Explaining Institutional Decoupling: the Case of Stock Repurchase Programs," *Administrative Science Quarterly*, 46: 202–228.

Yaziji, M. & Doh, J. (2009). *NGOs and Corporations: Conflict and Collaboration*. New York, Cambridge University Press.

Yearly, S. (1992). "Green Ambivalence about Science: Legal-Rational Authority and the Scientific Legitimation of a Social Movement," *British Journal of Sociology*, 43: 511–532.

Zald, M. N., Morrill, C., & Rao, H. (2005). "The Impact of Social Movements on Organizations: Environment and Responses," in Davis, G. F., Mcadam, D., Scott, W. R., & Zald, M. N. (eds.) *Social Movements and Organization Theory*. New York, Cambridge University Press.

PART V

OPERATIONS AND TECHNOLOGY

CHAPTER 15

....

GREENER SUPPLY
CHAIN MANAGEMENT

....

ROBERT D. KLASSEN
AND STEPHAN VACHON[1]

ESTABLISHING THE CONTEXT

....

During the last two decades, customers, investors, regulators, and the public have increasingly focused their attention on aspects of firms' operations and supply chains that extend far beyond traditional measures like cost, quality, and profitability. Concerns about hazardous materials in products, large volumes of used products and waste in both developing and developed countries, and sizable carbon footprints are but a few of the issues that have garnered media and, more recently, managerial attention. Moreover, new regulations seek to simultaneously protect both the environment and human health. For example, the Registration, Evaluation and Authorisation of Chemicals (REACH) regulation in the European Union, forces companies to evaluate the human health and environmental impact of a broad range of chemicals, and then track them throughout their supply chain.

Environmental and social concerns are not unique to one region, one industry, or one type of firm. Instead, these issues cut across the entire supply chain, which is a complex network of firms—from raw materials, to components, to logistics and other services—that collectively provides a particular good or service to consumers or end-users (Beamon 1999). A critical aspect is the inter-organizational flows and hand-offs of materials, information, and energy. Early efforts to translate the environmental dimension of sustainable development into corporate practices highlighted the importance of closing material cycles (now termed closed-loop supply chains), saving energy through improved efficiency, and improving quality to extend the life of products, thereby potentially reducing the demand for resources (Cramer & Schot 1993).

However, firms in a supply chain do not work in isolation: one supply chain partner's activities may affect many customers indirectly, as materials and information pass

[1] The authors would like to thank the Social Sciences and Humanities Research Council of Canada (SSHRC) for financial support of this research.

through several tiers of suppliers. With supply chains now extending their reach in multiple ways—that is geographically, to become truly global; vertically, to recover used products after their use; and horizontally, to transform the wastes of one firm into the inputs for another—environmental management in supply chain presents both difficult challenges and significant opportunities to redefine customer value. As a result, performance appraisal within supply chains must shift toward a more comprehensive set of environmental and operational indicators that reflect a broader conceptualization of customer value.

EMERGING APPROACHES TO ENVIRONMENTAL MANAGEMENT

To clarify how environmental issues influence the management of supply chains, it is helpful to step back and examine a fundamental assumption implicitly or explicitly held by many managers. For most, their attention has tended to focus on the financial bottom line based on the presumption that if the firm is making money (legally), the firm is managing its resources well. This perception was mirrored in the minds of stakeholders: economic performance was the primary focus of investors, lenders, and analysts when ranking peer firms. In contrast, environmental issues were perceived to be peripheral by managers, and environmental performance was the domain of regulators, community groups, and other non-governmental organizations (NGOs).

In the early 1990s, several leading firms started to consider the environmental implications of internal practices and expenditures, colloquially termed *green manufacturing*. For example, several studies explored environmental management systems within operations (Melnyk et al. 2003), environmental technologies (Klassen & Whybark 1999), and internal pollution reduction (King & Lenox 2002). In some cases, linkages between green manufacturing and traditional areas of competitiveness, such as quality (Pil & Rothenberg 2003), lean systems (Florida 1996) and product design (Chen 2001), continue to provide an important foundation for our more recent understanding of green supply chains.

In an effort to better capture environmental aspects, researchers and managers have advanced the notion that firms and their supply chains should assess both environmental and financial performance (Carter & Rogers 2008). Moreover, international standards and certification schemes are shaping environmental attributes of product design, process design, technology choices, and management practices. For example, certifications such as those of Fairtrade (e.g. agricultural products) and Forest Stewardship Council (FSC) (i.e. harvesting of timber) consider specific environmental and social criteria related to raw material supply. Integrative frameworks, such as the Global Reporting Initiative (2006) go further, and provide a structured approach to report key environmental indicators in consultation with stakeholders (Seuring & Müller 2008).

Managers can also use these standards to diagnose points of weakness and target improvements in supply chains. If the major impact is identified within suppliers, whether first-tier or further upstream, firms can change their purchase criteria or collaborate with suppliers to change deficient environmental components or practices (Van Hoek 1999). Alternatively, if the primary impact occurs with the firm itself, product designs can be altered, new process technologies explored or management practices adjusted (Gungor & Gupta 1999). Finally, if customer-use generates the largest impact (including energy use, misuse of the product, etc.), then changes in product design, end-of-life product recovery or customer education may yield the greatest environmental returns (Klassen & Greis 1993).

Expanding stakeholder groups

Stakeholder theory emphasizes the need to consult and manage multiple levels of individuals and groups with an interest in a business process, product, or service. Thus, assessing the environmental performance of a firm's operations in isolation, that is, green manufacturing, only captures the narrowest range of possible impacts (internal). Beyond the firm's operations, a second level of interaction exists between a buying firm and its multiple tiers of suppliers and customers (supply chain). Finally, with increasing accountability being demanded by regulators, communities, and NGOs, many firms with international supply chains must extend their consideration of stakeholders to actively encompass those outside the supply chain (external) (see Kassinis [Chapter 5] this volume).

For a firm midway along a supply chain, these three levels are illustrated in Figure 15.1. Supply chain stakeholders (e.g. customers) and external stakeholders (e.g. regulators, competitors, and NGOs) have been explicitly identified as important drivers of green supply chain management practices (Mollenkopf et al. 2010; Walker et al. 2008). The importance of considering multiple levels is not limited only to developed economies, for example internal, supplier, and customer dimensions were empirically identified in large-scale study in China (Zhu & Sarkis 2004). With complex globally supplied goods and services, it is not surprising that increased transparency between supply chain partners and external stakeholders is a growing demand (New 2010). Collectively, all three levels must be engaged and leveraged to better manage and improve environmental performance (see Figure 15.1).

Thus, any definition of greener supply chain management must capture design; material selection, extraction, and sourcing; manufacturing; logistics and delivery; and end-of-life management, including such options as recycling, remanufacturing or disposal (Carter & Rogers 2008; Gungor & Gupta 1999; Srivastava 2007). Synthesizing multiple perspectives together with stakeholder considerations, greener supply chain management is defined as the strategic and transparent integration of material, information, and capital flows to achieve environmental and economic objectives through the systemic coordination of key inter-organizational business

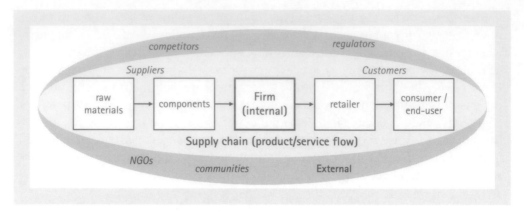

FIGURE 15.1 Three levels of stakeholders span the supply chain

processes. These objectives are derived from customer and stakeholder requirements, must reflect evolving scientific understanding, and must maintain or enhance firm competitiveness over the long term.

Three related supply chain trends

Off-shoring of operations

One implication of increasing globalization is off-shoring—a supply chain strategy that involves moving internal processes and operations from one, usually developed, country to another, usually less developed or emerging country. Direct control of processes is maintained, although other supply chain partners may be leveraged for local expertise through a joint venture. Not surprisingly, a key motivator tends to be cost, but other advantages such as local market responsiveness also can be gained. For example, a global electronics firm might move some assembly operations to India, both to reduce cost and to improve local market access for its products. Naturally, environmental regulations and firm performance might (or might not) differ between North American and Indian operations.

From an environmental management perspective, off-shoring has significant implications if the monitoring and enforcement of environmental standards by local regulators differ significantly between countries. In response, firms may have to develop and substitute their own management systems for the nascent or absent regulatory policies in developing economies. Significant investments might be needed to develop new information systems, controls, and communication and review mechanisms, along with new organizational structures. Without deeper thoughtful analysis, managers can overlook sizable incremental costs and risks.

Outsourcing of non-strategic processes

In contrast to off-shoring, outsourcing addresses the degree to which a firm is vertically integrated, that is, the range of activities, processes, or operations that are directly performed in-house. Over the last two decades there has been a strong trend toward focusing on a few strategic activities in-house, and relying on a set of supply chain partners to perform a myriad of additional activities, such as designing products and services, supplying materials and components, transferring and processing information, and transporting goods across the supply chain. Multiple factors have driven this specialization: lower cost resulting from deeper expertise or greater economies of scale; greater flexibility; access to higher quality materials or components; improved design; and more responsive logistics.

If viewed very simplistically, one might argue that the firm is no longer "responsible" for environmental emissions and treatment of wastes, given the arms-length transactions now taking place – it is now solely within the purview of suppliers. But that conclusion is rather one-dimensional and ill-informed, as many community, NGO, and customer stakeholders do not perceive that to be the case (New 2004). And the complications of outsourcing increase beyond those of off-shoring. The supply chain tends to grow longer, that is, more tiers, and more complex, with different external stakeholder expectations. Supply chain partners in developing economies also are viewed as being under the influence of downstream firms (and customers) in developed countries. In effect, the firm retains much of the accountability, possibly with less control, which in turn translates into increased risk.

Increasing clockspeed of supply chains

In essence, clockspeed is the rate at which products, processes, and organizational systems evolve in an industry and in its supply chain (Fine 1998).[2] Not all supply chains progress at the same rate, with significant implications for industries that derive competitive advantage from innovation or fast changing supply chain relationships. For example, supply chains in the personal computer, automobile, and electricity generation industries have high, medium, and low clockspeeds, respectively.

As a result, the design of the supply chain has become a core competency for maintaining competitive advantage. In faster clockspeed supply chains, the ability to introduce greener innovations that improve environmental performance is potentially easier than in those that view product, process, and organizational change from the timescale of decades, not years or months. In part, change permits the upgrade of processes and technologies, and facilitates changes in supplier relationships that might be used to advance environmental performance. In contrast, slow clockspeed industries tend to be commodity-based, which favours an efficient supply chain with incremental, cost-focused improvements, and transactional relationships (Vachon et al. 2009), which is not conducive for environmental innovation (Prokesch 2010).

---

[2] N.B. Clockspeed is based on the rate at which industries introduce products, processes, and organizational innovations, and should not be confused with the typical time that is required for a product to move along a supply chain from raw materials to final customer.

Rethinking supply chain design

Greener approaches

The supply chain has been traditionally defined as a one-way process that captures activities whereby raw materials are converted into final products, then delivered to customers (Figure 15.1). A simple first step beyond green manufacturing is the inclusion of environmental concerns as additional criteria in purchasing decisions of materials or components, for example minimum recycled content in paper (Min & Galle 1997). A growing understanding of the complexity and inter-connectedness of environmental issues, driven by multiple stakeholders, has forced managers to expand this narrow view of green purchasing to capture a broader system (Beamon 1999). For example, local optimization of a small portion of the supply chain might, in fact, simply shift the environmental burden elsewhere in the supply chain through outsourcing. Greener supply chain management has been divided characteristically into three separate, but strongly related dimensions: (i) strategic considerations; (ii) extending and broadening green operations, including activities such as remanufacturing and waste management; and (iii) green design, including life-cycle assessment (LCA) and other tools to enable environmentally conscious design (Ilgin & Gupta 2010; Srivastava 2007).

Drawing from and paralleling similar views in corporate strategy, researchers have tended to characterize greener strategies for supply chains along a continuum from reactive to integrative (or sustainable) (Vachon & Klassen 2006; Van Hoek 1999). Thus, cross-functional and inter-firm processes must be addressed related to product design, suppliers' processes, evaluation systems, and inbound logistics. Commonly accepted practices, such as just-in-time deliveries of parts and supplies, need to be re-examined depending on the geographic dispersion of the supply chain, modes of transport, and the use of returnable packaging (Angell & Klassen 1999). The competitive opportunity that emerges is one of developing new strategic resources related to product-, process-, or organizational aspects of supply chains (Carter & Rogers 2008) that vary based on clockspeed (Fine 1998).

Barriers to greener supply chain practices include cost, legitimacy, poor supplier commitment, and regulation, to name several (Min & Galle 1997; Walker et al. 2008). For example, legitimacy can be hard to achieve if past efforts by the firm, its suppliers, or its customers have been perceived as "green-washing." Powerful suppliers also might withhold information about some critical aspects, such as chemical composition necessary for product redesign (Dillon & Baram 1993), industry-specific norms might slow the adoption of greener practices, and customers might resist new concepts (Mollenkopf et al. 2010).

Extending the supply chain

Recent regulations in Asia, Europe, and North America have spurred OEMs in many supply chains to manage their products when they become waste. In addition, some firms have chosen voluntarily to manage their used products for competitive reasons (Toffel 2003). As supply chains are extended to capture product disposal, take-back and re-use, the concept of a closed loop or reverse supply chain emerges (Figure 15.2) (Ilgin & Gupta 2010). Not only are the classic 3Rs included (i.e. reduce, reuse, and recycle), but also a fourth and fifth "R", namely recondition and remanufacturing, must be actively developed (Figure 15.2).

While related research is further detailed in Abbey & Guide ([Chapter 16] this volume), it is important to recognize several important elements related to the overall development of a greener supply chain. First, the scope of supply chain decision-making must expand from an initial sale to service delivery and product use (and post use), thus better managing the environmental impact throughout the entire life of a service or product. For manufactured goods, closed loop systems have the potential both to be profitable, and to reduce environmental impact by reusing materials, reducing energy use, and reducing the need for disposal (Guide et al. 2000).

Second, the key activities related to extended supply chains differ greatly from those in traditional supply chains. For example, firms must design and maintain collection networks, possibly using new partners, to gather and transport used products from end-users to upstream supply chain partners. Unfortunately, the volume, quality, and timing of used product, material and waste flows (which may not match the demand for "new" products) are uncertain, which in turn makes inventory management and logistics for the collection of end-of-life products difficult. Moreover, new process technologies and partnerships for recycling and remanufacturing may be required. Thus, managers must develop new capabilities to accommodate or reduce uncertainty in the timing and quantity of returns, to balance return

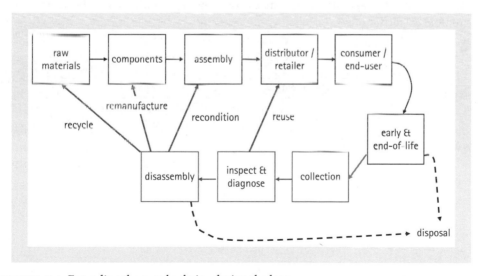

FIGURE 15.2 Extending the supply chain: closing the loop

Note: Wastes can be generated at each tier in the supply chain.

Adapted from Beamon (1999)

rates with demand rates, and to make the quality of recovered materials and parts more predictable.

Broadening the supply chain

Thus far we have explored two major extensions of the operations system: first, from operations at a single firm to operations across the supply chain; and second, from the one-way supply chain to the closed loop. A third extension starting to tentatively emerge can be characterized as lateral, whereby non-competing supply chains are linked to reduce waste, recycle materials, and use by-products, sometimes termed industrial symbiosis (Ehrenfeld & Gertler 1997) (Figure 15.3). Thus, new linkages are created between firms to improve efficiency of material and energy flows from a *cluster* of processes, usually located in close geographic proximity.

Research in industrial symbiosis is further detailed by Lifset & Boons ([Chapter 17] this volume). Several subtle, but important operational implications are critical. Some firms, when viewed independently in isolation, may appear to be less efficient or carry a heavier environmental burden than competitors. Yet, the overall environmental performance can be superior because of symbiotic linkages. Also, the tight coupling of by-products as raw materials or energy for other firms' processes requires two or more firms to jointly manage overall production levels, to identify alternative uses or disposal options for by-products, and to substitute virgin materials as needed. As the number of connections between supply chains grows, the evolving set of symbiotic links in a specific location gives rise to a network termed an industrial ecosystem (Graedel & Allenby 1995). The classic example is the industrial district at Kalundborg, Denmark, where eleven physical linkages transfer wastes, by-products, and energy between firms (Ehrenfeld & Gertler 1997).

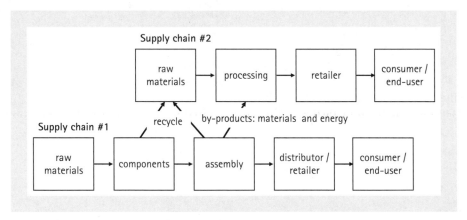

FIGURE 15.3 Broadening the supply chain: horizontal linkages created by industrial symbiosis

Note: Horizontal-linked supply chains usually involve non-competitors offering different products and serving different markets.

For greener supply chains, two observations from industrial ecosystems are of partic-ular importance. First, the co-location of distinct, but now connected, supply chains did not occur by insightful planning and forethought. Instead, a sequential series of inde-pendently negotiated, bi-lateral arrangements that made both economic and environ-mental sense organically build the inter-connected system (Ehrenfeld & Gertler 1997). Yet, the system that emerges can become much greater than the sum of its parts as a dense network of relationships develops (Bansal & McKnight 2009). Moreover, the ben-efits of industrial symbiosis, confined to a small geographic space, stand in sharp con-trast to the long supply chains that result from off-shoring and outsourcing.

Second, most of the firms linked into industrial ecosystems are partners in supply chains with slower clockspeeds. In fact, of the multiple supply chains linked together at Kalundborg (energy, agriculture, building materials, and pharmaceuticals), none is a fast clockspeed, and only two are medium. A similar observation can be made for other examples (Bansal & McKnight 2009). The prevalence of slow clockspeed supply chains might change as public policies actively promote the scale-up of industrial symbiosis, thereby reducing the managerial search costs of finding suitable partners and facilitat-ing the exchange of information and contracting (e.g. Paquin & Howard-Grenville 2009).

Influence on supply chain partners and stakeholder accountability

Within the supply chain, a firm's responsibility for particular environmental issues is derived from having information available, and having the ability to intervene and bring about improvement (New 2004; Parmigiani et al. 2011). In essence, both the degree of *influence* exercised by a firm over its supply chain partners, and the degree of *accounta-bility* required by stakeholders from a firm, shape how environmental issues can be man-aged across a supply chain.

Influence is defined as the capability to persuade, pressure or control action and change; it reflects the degree to which managers in a firm have direct or implied control and power to deal with specific issues, make business decisions independently, or affect outcomes either through action or inaction. Influence can be achieved through multiple means (Hall 2000), either directly through incentives and threats, or indirectly through complex appeals to norms, best practice, and aspirations of industry leadership. Outsourcing has provided one means by which firms can attempt to shift their environmental obligations to supply chain partners. However, external stakeholders continue to focus on the degree of influence derived through economic power that a firm has on its suppliers.

In contrast to influence, accountability captures the extent to which firms (and man-agers) are required or expected to justify their decisions and actions, regardless of the degree of influence present. Basically, managers must report, answer for, and explain outcomes. If a firm's influence is low, possibly because of its small relative size, yet

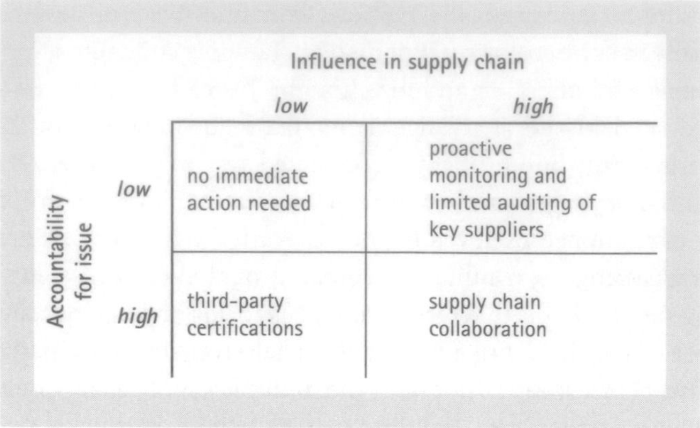

Influence in supply chain

		low	high
Accountability for issue	low	no immediate action needed	proactive monitoring and limited auditing of key suppliers
	high	third-party certifications	supply chain collaboration

FIGURE 15.4 Identifying critical supply chain issues: accountability and influence

Adapted from Parmigiami et al. (2011)

accountability is high, managers might work with other high-influence supply chain partners using inter-organizational teams to foster consensus-based improvements. The levels of influence and accountability vary by type of issue, nature of the supply chain, and geographic location.

Both influence (Green et al. 1998; Hall 2000) and accountability (Walton et al. 1998) affect how a firm might position itself within the supply chain on particular environmental issues, and the means available to manage performance (Figure 15.4). Separating influence from accountability also helps to explain why changes might be required when managing some environmental issues, but not others. To illustrate the distinction, consider sourcing commodities in food supply chains and linkages to rainforest preservation. Managers of a global food retailer might choose to purchase raw materials, such as soya, from a variety of international suppliers. And only a very small fraction of those raw materials might be harvested from land where rainforest deforestation occurred. Yet, despite the minor influence (if any) that the firm has over deforestation, stakeholders still can hold management strongly accountable. In anticipation of being a target of NGOs, management might proactively change its sourcing, or work with the suppliers to alter rainforest practices.

ENVIRONMENTAL IMPACT

Life cycle assessment

Environmental performance within the supply chain is often assessed by resource and energy use (i.e. eco-efficiency), and waste generation (including toxicity and quantity) (Beamon 1999). Yet a critical question is difficult to answer: how should any assessment capture environmental outcomes that extend beyond the boundary of the firm? One methodological approach, life cycle assessment (LCA), attempts to quantify the complete environmental impact of a product or service. This methodology has evolved significantly since the initial focus on energy consumption during the 1970s: it now captures the environmental impact of a product from cradle-to-grave (Fava et al. 1991) across the supply chain (Dillon & Baram 1993), or better yet, from cradle-to-cradle (McDonough & Braungart 2002). In essence, a product's use of materials and energy and all associated environmental burdens throughout its extended supply chain are identified and weighted. Thus, in some respects, an LCA forms a natural bridge from traditional topics such as quality and lean systems to product stewardship.

An LCA is much more than a simple accounting exercise: increased scientific understanding of the interaction between supply chains, product use, service consumption and the natural environment often have failed to resolve difficult uncertainties. The number of chemical substances that must be considered continues to grow, and efforts to weight and integrate energy and materials by media (i.e. releases to air, water, or land), by composition, and by toxicity to various organisms are complex and open to controversy. Moreover, consumption patterns evolve, regulations proliferate, and new technological innovations are frequently introduced. In response to these difficulties, managers, NGOs, regulators, and consumers have generally embraced measurement approaches that focus on a small set of environmental performance criteria across a small number of tiers in the supply chain (Faruk et al. 2001). For example, the "carbon footprint" traces the greenhouse gas emissions of goods or services

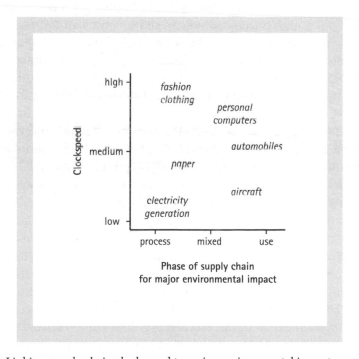

FIGURE 15.5 Linking supply chain clockspeed to major environmental impacts

created by one or more tiers in the supply chain (converting all greenhouse gases to equivalent carbon dioxide).

At the simplest level, environmental burdens occur in two phases: consumption of a good or service (use-based impact), and processes associated with creating and delivering that good or service (processes-based impact). Thus, the major environmental burden for a supply chain can be thought of as falling somewhere along a continuum from process to use (Figure 15.5). Use-based impact includes the energy spent to "consume" the product (e.g. gasoline for car, propane for grill cooking, electricity for appliances), and waste or by-products resulting from consumption (e.g. flashlight's batteries, printed paper from computers, fast-food containers). Process-based impact captures environmental aspects of sourcing decisions, manufacturing, product packaging, and transportation. While the lines might blur somewhat with services such as restaurants that directly involve a real-time combination of customers and products, it is still reasonable to point to the use phase, including energy, versus the process phase, including food and even building materials.

To illustrate, Apple has reported the environmental burden for at least one dimension of its popular products. The 13-inch MacBook Pro has a carbon footprint of 440 kg of carbon dioxide-equivalent, of which 68 percent comes from the supply chain *process*, including production (59%), transport (8%) and recycling (1%)(Apple 2010). In contrast, the 27-inch iMac has a much larger carbon footprint, at 1,970 kg, of which the majority of this arises from customer *use* (56%). Thus, major efforts to reduce the environmental burden of each conceivably should focus on different phases, that is, product design related to energy efficiency for the iMac (use), and product or process design related to material selection, manufacturing technology, and supply chain for the MacBook Pro (process). However, trade-offs may exist between process- and use-based improvements. For example, fluorescent lamps consume much less energy during use than incandescent bulbs, but also require small amounts of mercury as a key material. As a result, additional supply chain activities might reduce hazards from fluorescent lamp manufacturing and disposal.

Given the expanding emphasis on LCA, product design has emerged as a major stream of research to green supply chains (Srivastava 2007). At a minimum, environmental concerns can become a criterion in the product design similar to other attributes such as quality, cycle time, and cost (Chen 2001), and included early on in product development and redesign (Green et al. 1998). Much of the product design research has focused on multi-criteria techniques that allow for the simultaneous consideration of environmental, economic, consumer and material requirements (Ilgin & Gupta 2010). But if viewed more strategically (Sarkis 2003), design-for-the-environment should be driven by life-cycle principles: product design should consider the entire set of environmental impacts from raw material to consumption, and beyond. Tools based on LCA and design protocols such as cradle-to-cradle (McDonough & Braungart 2002) are starting to guide managers in the complex challenges of less toxic materials, increased recycling, and closed-loop product/service systems.

Challenges of global supply chains

As supply chains reach around the globe, partly related to off-shoring, outsourcing, and new market opportunities, multinational firms are pushed by some customers in developed economies and external stakeholders (e.g. NGOs) to monitor gaps in environmental performance. Public third-party certifications, such as ISO 14001, Fairtrade, FSC or SA8000, can set expectations for suppliers, as well as routinely monitoring compliance. Using such standards can help to establish legitimacy and reorient a firm's approach toward supply chain management. Alternatively, larger firms or industry associations can develop policies that set expectations for suppliers, monitor their environmental performance, and closely track hazardous materials or products.

Influencing supply chain partners becomes more difficult as distance increases, as this makes it more challenging to establish trust and maintain rich exchanges of information. Distance is a multidimensional construct, encompassing geographic location, cultural differences between firms, and the number of tiers in a supply chain (Awaysheh & Klassen 2010). For example, customer and supplier plants may attach similar importance to conscientiously handling hazardous wastes despite being thousands of kilometres apart in Europe and Asia because they are both owned by parent firms located in Europe (i.e. small cultural distance). On the other hand, two neighbouring Asian plants in a supply chain may have very different views of environmental performance because one has a European parent and the other an Asian parent (i.e. large cultural distance). Moreover, potential conflicts can arise within global supply chains where some partners focus on lowest cost, and others focus on environmental issues such as safe disposal of toxic substances (Mollenkopf et al. 2010). As noted earlier, outsourcing and off-shoring can also shift local environmental burdens from developed to developing countries.

Supply chain traceability and transparency also confound monitoring and improvement efforts. Supply chain traceability tracks products from raw material sourcing to supply chain partners, to manufacturing, to distribution, to end-consumer use (and quite possibly, beyond to disposal) (Pullman et al. 2009). For example, growing segments of customers are concerned about such aspects as genetically modified plant ingredients in food and a product's carbon footprint. Transparency reflects the extent to which this information is readily available to supply chain partners and customers in a meaningful format (New 2010). Distance can exacerbate the difficulties of gathering information, auditing, and coordination.

MANAGING ACROSS THE SUPPLY CHAIN

In many countries, environmental policies have evolved from managing the risk of toxic chemicals, to pollution prevention, to life-cycle management. When viewed broadly, three approaches to greening the supply chain have emerged to varying degrees: risk mitigation, supply chain improvement, and the pursuit of new opportunities (Min & Galle 1997; Seuring & Müller 2008).

Risk mitigation

Generally, the management of risk is designed to decrease potential liabilities from environmental damage, reduce the likelihood of unwanted media or NGOs attention, and limit fines from non-compliance (Cousins et al. 2004). Risks can arise from relying on a limited number of technologies that have a large environmental burden, or from the use of a small number of suppliers that have large environmental risks of their own. As such, these risks can be embedded subtly and deeply in the supply chain. Alternatively, increased exposure can result from a firm's interactions with customers and external stakeholders as new environmental issues gain attention, and these groups impose accountability on the firm and its supply chain. The firm can manage its risk exposure by working with existing suppliers, finding new suppliers, altering manufacturing processes, attempting to "educate" customers, or broadly communicating with the public in an effort to change perceptions.

Efforts are underway at a number of firms to classify their supply bases according to the environmental risk and positioning (tier) in the supply chain. Risk is evaluated based on location (e.g. local standards and enforcement), manufacturing process (i.e., chemical-intensive manufacturing and labour-intensive assembly), supply chain relationships (size of contracts, branded products, and length of relationship), and historical information, including certification using external auditors (Hewlett Packard 2008). Other approaches try to differentiate between risk and influence, thereby separating out the relational aspect of the supply chain (Figure 15.6). These factors suggest different options to mitigate risk. It is important to stress that both the issue and the supply chain partner

		Influence in supply chain	
		low	high
Risk	low	**2nd best** • screening: self-assessment by supplier • tracking of performance	**Optimal** • screening: self-assessment by supplier • contracting with spectic requirements • tracking of performance
	high	**Avoid if possible** • encourage third-party ceritication • if possible, contracting with specific requirements • tracking of performance	**"Handle with care"** • active monitoring and tracking • collaboration, including training and capability building • rewards and penalties in contracts

FIGURE 15.6 Supply chain influence, risk, and environmental improvement

Adapted from Klassen (2009)

must be considered jointly: Figure 15.4 assesses the firm's accountability and influence on *specific environment issues*, whereas Figure 15.6 evaluates overall risk for *each supply chain partner*. For example, high influence occurs with long-term relationships, and a high proportion of supplier's revenue flowing from the firm (Klassen 2009).

Carried one step further, one could question how a firm should deal with supply chain partners with high environmental risks? This concern is partially addressed by transaction cost analysis (TCA), where costs related to environmental issues with suppliers are driven by uncertainty, frequency of transactions, and asset specificity (Zsidisin & Siferd 2001). Thus, monitoring and contract enforcement for environmental performance also create additional supply chain costs for outsourcing and off shoring. However, much more research is needed to explore how to quantify the implied costs of monitoring versus correcting problems and accidents after they occur.

Supply chain improvement

Supplier screening can be viewed as a simplistic means of improving environmental performance if clear-cut criteria can be established, alternative suppliers are available, and costs are reasonable (Dillon & Baram 1993). Early efforts for green purchasing also focused on packaging decisions (Min & Galle 1997), driven in part by groundbreaking "Grüne Punkt" (green dot) regulations for consumer packaging in Germany. In general, green purchasing policies can employ *inclusionary* criteria, such as recycled content and low-carbon footprint materials, *exclusionary* criteria such as no cadmium, or *process specifications* such as using returnable containers (Cramer & Schot 1993).

Characterizing efforts to green the supply chain along the lines of monitoring and collaboration holds many parallels to the traditional intra-firm approaches of pollution control and pollution prevention, respectively (Vachon & Klassen 2006). While monitoring is primarily about "controlling" risk, collaboration emphasizes the potential to create new value. Environmental collaboration reflects two-way interactions between supply chain partners, including such aspects as joint environmental goal setting, shared environmental planning, and working together to reduce pollution or other environmental burdens. Collaboration requires a good understanding of each other's responsibilities and capabilities for environmental management, and can be directed either upstream toward suppliers to improve suppliers' processes and materials selection (Walton et al. 1998) or downstream toward customers (Vachon & Klassen 2006). Collaboration is most likely to occur on environmental issues for which the firm has both high accountability and a modest degree of influence in the supply chain (Figure 15.4, lower right quadrant). As influence decreases, the firm might find it more effective to shift away from collaboration toward relying on third-party certifications during supplier selection.

The potential competitive advantage generated by environmental collaboration is two-fold. First, case evidence supports the linkage to improved productivity (Geffen & Rothenberg 2000), while survey evidence points to improved product and process quality

(Vachon & Klassen 2008), better supplier performance, and stronger financial performance (Carter et al. 2000). Second, environmental collaboration is directly associated with a proactive environmental management orientation in the supply chain, implying capabilities related to the natural resource based view of the firm (Bowen et al. 2001). However, detailed empirical evidence continues to be limited, no doubt partly attributable to the difficulty of measuring competitive and environmental performance for supply chain (or at least multiple partners) rather than only a single firm.

New opportunities

Green innovation, whether derived from collaboration or internal development, is critical for developing new products, processes, supply chain capabilities, and business models (Seuring & Müller 2008). For many consumers, environmental characteristics and performance are only beginning to surface in many markets as purchasing criteria, for example, organic foods, all-natural household cleaners, and carbon offsets for tourism. However, in other markets, green consumerism is well aligned with traditional product-based innovation, for example, energy efficiency for refrigeration or air conditioning.

Environmental innovations tend to diffuse upstream from a customer firm to a supplier firm, that is, B2B relationship (Hall 2000). Based on case studies in the UK and Japan, environmental innovations can emerge if a supply chain member has sufficient influence over their suppliers, technical competencies, and are themselves under specific environmental pressure. Thus, firms with high accountability and influence on particular environmental issues (Figure 15.4, lower-right quadrant) are best positioned and most likely to reap competitive benefits from fuelling green innovation.

Tightening environmental legislation generates opportunities to introduce new value-added services and products. For example, European Union's Waste Electrical and Electronics Equipment (WEEE) regulation requires the collection and recycling of air conditioning equipment by either individual firms or an industry consortium. One large manufacturer developed a logistics system for independent field installers to recycle its *own and competitors'* end-of-life products, thereby prompting increased loyalty and stronger incentives for new customers. The business proposition was simple: scrapped products could be safely and efficiently removed as new products were sold, without further storage and handling by the installer. Moreover, as economies of scale grew, financial results improved; the model then was expanded to a second country in the EU (Klassen 2009).

For identifying and developing specific new product-related requirements, as described earlier, life cycle assessment encourages firms to look beyond first-tier suppliers to the entire supply chain. Similar to new product introductions, a large sophisticated firm (e.g. OEM with strong branding) must direct and collaborate with key suppliers. Criteria for improvement do not only relate to the final products, which conceivably can be directly tested by consumers (e.g. free of contaminants), but also to processes along the supply chain (e.g. chemical transport, storage and monitoring) (Seuring & Müller 2008). The influential firm can lead by its own example where possible, provide incentives such as additional sales volume, or impose threats, such as loss of contracts (Klassen 2009). More generally, there is need for cooperation among more tiers of the supply chain, as new greener opportunities demand much 'deeper' information flows (Seuring & Müller 2008) and new capabilities (De Bakker & Nijhof 2002).

Looking forward: developing research trends

Two major areas hold much promise for both research and practice in the short to medium term: system based measurement; and stronger integration of the social bottom line in supply chains. First, to the credit of many researchers who are actively exploring how the greening of supply chains can occur competitively, their efforts attempt to keep the larger system in mind rather than simply dyadic linkages between adjacent tiers (e.g. buyer–supplier transaction). However, a significant challenge remains to transition managers beyond a narrow internal focus on their firm's processes. Process-based standards, such as ISO 14001, are only good starting points, and more detailed certifications such as FSC and Fairtrade help to expand the supply chain scope. However, even these efforts emphasize only a few tiers upstream in the supply chain, at most, and fail to include the entire supply chain. Broader, stakeholder-driven reporting systems, such as GRI (2006), are coming closer to a systems perspective, at least so far as the reporting firm exercises a high degree of influence. An intermediate stopgap measure might be to adapt a balanced scorecard for the design and evaluation of green supply chain management performance (Hervani et al. 2005).

Like other areas of management, it is likely that refined measurement must precede better practice. Measurement of environmental performance for the supply chain, and subsequent labeling is codified for a few metrics, such as a product's energy use, in several industries, for example automobiles, computers, etc. Other metrics based on LCA, such as carbon footprint, are attracting much interest from customers and external stakeholders, but also much controversy. Unlike energy use, these metrics vary by specific supply chain partners, their processes, and even seasonality. For example, fresh fruit might be grown locally in summer, and imported in winter from a wide variety of suppliers, each with their own farm-specific factors. Thus, research and practice must converge to develop rigorous environmental accounting systems that track a small number of key environmental metrics in supply chains, likely subject to impartial third-party audits. Slow clockspeed supply chains might offer the best starting point for developing better methodologies, identifying key parameters, and developing transparent reporting systems for customers and other stakeholders.

Second, research on the sustainability of supply chain continues to be dominated by environmental issues. Social issues, performance, and the integration of the three dimensions of triple bottom line are still rare (Seuring & Müller 2008). However, the management complexity grows dramatically when trying to account for the triple bottom line of global supply chains (Mollenkopf et al. 2010). Social performance also derives from process- and use-based phases of the supply chain, including suppliers' employees safety, product safety for consumers, and suppliers' fair wages. While some international standards focus specifically on social issues only (e.g. SA8000), others such as Fairtrade combine both environmental and social criteria.

So can managers be expected to improve all three bottom lines simultaneously to the same degree? While this might appear to be ideal, it is also very unlikely. Our personal observations suggest that waves of improvement in environmental, social and financial performance might be related to three factors that ebb and flow, and act in different supply chains at different rates: regulatory pressures, evolving customer demands, and perceived risks. Limited time, technology, and financial resources have forced managers to shift attention from one bottom line to another, partly driven by the supply chain clockspeed. Thus, triple bottom line success might be demonstrated best by raising all three bottom lines slowly, unevenly, but relentlessly, over a long period of time.

REFERENCES

Angell, L. C. & Klassen, R. D. (1999). "Integrating Environmental Issues into the Mainstream: An Agenda for Research in Operations Management," *Journal of Operations Management*, 17(5): 575–98.
Apple (2010). "Apple and the Environment", [website], <www.apple.com/environment/reports/>, accessed May 10.
Awaysheh, A. & Klassen, R. D. (2010). "Supply Chain Structure and Its Impact on Supplier Socially Responsible Practices," *International Journal of Production and Operations Management*, 30(12): 1246–68.
Bansal, P. & McKnight, B. (2009). "Looking Forward, Pushing Back and Peering Sideways: Analyzing the Sustainability of Industrial Symbiosis," *Journal of Supply Chain Management*, 45(4): 26–37.
Beamon, B. (1999). "Measuring Supply Chain Performance," *International Journal of Operations & Production Management*, 19(3): 275–92.
Bowen, F., Cousins, P. D., Lamming, R. C., and Faruk, A. C. (2001). "The Role of Supply Management Capabilities in Green Supply," *Production and Operations Management*, 10(2): 174–89.
Carter, C. R. & Rogers, D. S. (2008). "A Framework of Sustainable Supply Chain Management: Moving toward New Theory," *International Journal of Physical Distribution & Logistics Management*, 38(5): 360–87.
—— Kale, R., & Grimm, C. M. (2000). "Environmental Purchasing and Firm Performance: An Empirical Investigation," *Transportation Research. Part E, Logistics & Transportation Review*, 36E(3): 219–28.
Chen, C. (2001). "Design for the Environment: A Quality-Based Model for Green Product Development," *Management Science*, 47(2): 250–63.
Cousins, P. D., Lamming, R. C., & Bowen, F. (2004). "The Role of Risk in Environment-Relaed Supplier Initiatives," *International Journal of Operations & Production Management*, 24(5–6): 554–65.

Cramer, J. & Schot, J. (1993). "Environmental Comakership among Firms as a Cornerstone in the Striving for Sustainable Development," in K. Fischer and J. Schot (eds.), *Environmental Strategies for Industry*, Washington, DC: Island Press, 311–28.

De Bakker, F. & Nijhof, A. (2002). "Responsible Chain Management: A Capability Assessment Framework," *Business Strategy and the Environment*, 11(1): 63–75.

Dillon, P. S. & Baram, M. S. (1993). "Forces Shaping the Development and Use of Product Stewardship in the Private Sector," in K. Fischer and J. Schot (eds.), *Environmental Strategies for Industry*, Washington, DC: Island Press, 329–41.

Ehrenfeld, J. & Gertler, N. (1997). "Industrial Ecology in Practice: The Evolution of Interdependence at Kalundborg," *Journal of Industrial Ecology*, 1(1): 67–79.

Faruk, A. C., Lamming, R. C., Cousins, P. D., & Bowen, F. E. (2001). "Analyzing, Mapping, and Managing Environmental Impacts Along Supply Chains," *Journal of Industrial Ecology*, 5(2): 13–36.

Fava, J. A., Denison, R., Jones, B., Curran, M. A., Vigon, B., Selke, S., & Barnum, J. (eds.) (1991). *A Technical Framework for Life-Cycle Assessments*. Washington, DC. Society of Environmental Toxicology and Chemistry (SETAC).

Fine, C. H. (1998). *Clockspeed: Winning Industry Control in the Age of Temporary Advantage*. Reading, Mass.: Perseus Books, xv, 272.

Florida, R. (1996). "Lean and Green: The Move to Environmentally Conscious Manufacturing," *California Management Review*, 39(1): 80–105.

Geffen, C. A. & Rothenberg, S. (2000). "Suppliers and Environmental Innovation," *International Journal of Operations & Production Management*, 20(2): 166–86.

Global Reporting Initiative (2006). *Sustainability Reporting Guidelines*. Amsterdam, The Netherlands: Stichting Global Reporting Initiative (GRI).

Graedel, T. E. & Allenby, B. R. (1995). *Industrial Ecology*. Englewood Cliffs, NJ: Prentice Hall.

Green, K., Morton, B., & New, S. (1998). "Green Purchasing and Supply Policies: Do They Improve Companies' Environmental Performance," *Supply Chain Management*, 3(2): 89–95.

Guide, V. D. R., Jayaraman, V., Srivastava, R., & Benton, W. C. (2000). "Supply Chain Management for Recoverable Manufacturing Systems," *Interfaces*, 30(3): 125–42.

Gungor, A. and Gupta, S. M. (1999). "Issues in Environmentally Conscious Manufacturing and Product Recovery: A Survey," *Computers and Industrial Engineering*, 36: 811–53.

Hall, J. (2000). "Environmental Supply Chain Dynamics," *Journal of Cleaner Production*, 8(6): 455–71.

Hervani, A. A., Helms, M. M., & Sarkis, J. (2005). "Performance Measurement for Green Supply Chain Management," *Benchmarking: An International Journal*, 12(4): 330–53.

Hewlett Packard (2010). "Hp Fy07 Global Citizenship Report" [website], <www.hp.com/hpinfo/globalcitizenship/07gcreport/pdf/hp_fy07_gcr.pdf>, accessed May 28.

Ilgin, M. & Gupta, S. M. (2010) "Environmentally Conscious Manufacturing and Product Recovery (Ecmpro): A Review of the State of the Art," *Journal of Environmental Management*, 91(3): 563–91.

King, A. & Lenox, M. (2002). "Exploring the Locus of Profitable Pollution Reduction," *Management Science*, 48(2): 289–99.

Klassen, R. D. (2009). "Improving Social Performance in Supply Chains: Exploring Practices and Pathways to Innovation," Leuven, Belgium: Flanders DC and Vlerick Leuven Gent Management School, 79.

—— & Greis, N. P. (1993). "Managing Environmental Improvement through Product and Process Innovation: Implications of Environmental Life Cycle Assessment," *Industrial and Environmental Crisis Quarterly*, 7(4): 293–318.

Klassen, R. D. & Whybark, D. C. (1999). "The Impact of Environmental Technologies on Manufacturing Performance," *Academy of Management Journal*, 40(6): 599–615.

McDonough, W. & Braungart, M. (2002). *Cradle to Cradle: Remaking the Way We Make Things*. New York: North Point Press.

Melnyk, S. A., Sroufe, R. P., & Calantone, R. (2003). "Assessing the Impact of Environmental Management Systems on Corporate and Environmental Performance," *Journal of Operations Management*, 21(3): 329–51.

Min, H. & Galle, W. P. (1997). "Green Purchasing Strategies: Trends and Implications," *International Journal of Purchasing and Materials Management*, 33(3): 10–17.

Mollenkopf, D., Stolze, H., Tate, W. L., & Ueltschy, M. (2010). "Green, Lean, and Global Supply Chains," *International Journal of Physical Distribution & Logistics Management*, 40(1–2): 14–41.

New, S. (2004). "The Ethical Supply Chain," in S. New and R. Westbrook (eds.), *Understanding Supply Chains: Concepts, Critiques and Futures*. Oxford, UK: Oxford University Press, 253–80.

—— (2010). "The Transparent Supply Chain," *Harvard Business Review*, 88(10): 76–82.

Paquin, R. L. & Howard-Grenville, J. (2009). "Facilitating Regional Industrial Symbiosis: Network Growth in the Uk'S National Industrial Symbiosis Programme," in J. Howard-Grenville & F. A. Boons (eds.) *Industrial Ecology and the Social Sciences*. London, UK: Edward Elgar.

Parmigiani, A., Klassen, R. D., & Russo, M. V. (2011). "Efficiency Meets Accountability: Performance Implications of Supply Chain Configuration, Control, and Capabilities," Journal of Operations Management, 29(3): 212–223.

Pil, F. K. & Rothenberg, S. (2003). "Environmental Performance as a Driver of Superior Quality," *Production and Operations Management*, 12(3): 404–15.

Prokesch, S. (2010). "The Sustainable Supply Chain," *Harvard Business Review*, 88(10) 70–72.

Pullman, M. E., Maloni, M. J., & Carter, C. R. (2009). "Food for Thought: Social Versus Environmental Sustainability Practices and Performance Outcomes," *Journal of Supply Chain Management*, 45(4): 38–54.

Sarkis, J. (2003). "A Strategic Decision Framework for Green Supply Chain Management," *Journal of Cleaner Production*, 11(4): 397–409.

Seuring, S. and Müller, M. (2008). "From a Literature Review to a Conceptual Framework for Sustainable Supply Chain Management," *Journal of Cleaner Production*, 16(15): 1699–710.

Srivastava, S. K. (2007). "Green Supply-Chain Management: A State-of-the-Art Literature Review, £ International Journal of Management Reviews, 9(1): 53–80.

Toffel, M. W. (2003). "The Growing Strategic Importance of End-of-Life Product Management," *California Management Review*, 45(3): 102–29.

Vachon, S. and Klassen, R. D. (2006). "Extending Green Practices across the Supply Chain; the Impact of Upstream and Downstream Integration," *International Journal of Operations & Production Management*, 26(7): 795–821.

—— —— (2008). "Environmental Management and Manufacturing Performance: The Role of Collaboration in the Supply Chain," *International Journal of Production Economics*, 111(2): 299–315.

—— Halley, A., and Beaulieu, M. (2009). "Aligning Competitive Priorities in the Supply Chain: The Role of Interactions with Suppliers," *International Journal of Operations and Production Management*, 29(4): 322–40.

Van Hoek, R. I. (1999). "From Reversed Logistics to Green Supply Chains," *Supply Chain Management*, 4(3): 129–34.

Walker, H., Sisto, L. D., & McBain, D. (2008). "Drivers and Barriers to Environmental Supply Chain Management Practices: Lessons from the Public and Private Sectors," *Journal of Purchasing & Supply Management,* 14(1): 69–85.

Walton, S. V., Handfield, R. B., & Melnyk, S. A. (1998). "The Green Supply Chain: Integrating Suppliers into Environmental Management Processes," *International Journal of Purchasing and Materials Management,* 34(2): 2–11.

Zhu, Q. & Sarkis, J. (2004). "Relationships between Operational Practices and Performance among Early Adopters of Green Supply Chain Management Practices in Chinese Manufacturing Enterprises," *Journal of Operations Management,* 22(3): 265–89.

Zsidisin, G. A. & Siferd, S. P. (2001). "Environmental Purchasing: A Framework for Theory Development," *European Journal of Purchasing and Supply Management,* 7(1): 61–73.

CHAPTER 16

....

CLOSED-LOOP SUPPLY CHAINS

....

JAMES D. ABBEY
AND V. DANIEL R. GUIDE, JR.

A closed-loop supply chain (CLSC) incorporates design, control, and operation of a system to maximize value creation over the entire life cycle of a product with dynamic recovery of value from different types and volumes of returns over time (Guide & Van Wassenhove 2009). For many firms, a well-designed and implemented CLSC can provide the foundation for an economically and environmentally sound business system.

UNDERSTANDING THE DEFINITION OF CLSC

....

As the definition implies, a CLSC must evolve over time to take advantage of different product return types and volumes as well as changing market conditions. Consequently, the design, operation, and control of a CLSC are not static, one-time process decisions. Rather, the CLSC is an ever-evolving set of processes and related performance measurements. Generally, implementing a CLSC involves multiple decisions at the operational, tactical, and strategic levels. In addition, to make a business case for closing the loop, managers must focus on the value creation as opposed to mere cost avoidance. In business, doing the right thing needs to add to the bottom line. Hence, aligning both the strategic and tactical incentives of managers and their departments usually will prove vital in the implementation of a CLSC—a topic in need of continued research.

CLOSED-LOOP SUPPLY CHAIN
CHAPTER STRUCTURE

This chapter begins with an exploration of CLSC as a process flow, followed by a discussion of how forward and reverse supply chains differ, with a specific focus on the coordination of forward and reverse supply chain flows in a CLSC. The chapter then moves into the evolution of closed-loop supply chains as a fundamental piece of the broader B&NE related framework of reduce, reuse, and recycle. Multiple research issues arise through the discussion of product design, legislative issues, and closed-loop supply chain design ramifications. The chapter closes with a discussion of various gaps in extant research, including the lack of interdisciplinary research with industrial ecology and marketing, as well as the need for greater consideration of competition in the current economics models. Though the chapter does cover many topics regarding remanufacturing and closed-loop supply chains for both original equipment manufacturers and third-party remanufacturers, most of the forward supply chain discussion is left to multiple external references and the Klassen & Vachon chapter on supply chain management (see Klassen & Vachon [Chapter 15] in this volume). Moreover, in-depth discussion of industrial ecology (see Lifset & Boons [Chapter 17] in this volume) and the marketing topics (see Gershoff & Irwin [Chapter 20] as well as Scammon & Mish [Chapter 19] in this volume) is left to other contributing authors.

EXAMINING CLSC AS A PROCESS FLOW

Closed-loop supply chains consist of multiple activities within a process flow. Both forward and reverse chain activities combine in a CLSC with additional constraints on the reverse supply chain activities. Figure 16.1 provides a graphical examination of general CLSC process flows and related constraints.

The rectangular bars across the flow arrows represent potential constraints on the system. As Figure 16.1 displays, the forward supply chain usually has relatively unconstrained flows as shown in the top row of the figure. The main constraints on a forward supply chain often are based in cost, quality, lead-time, and other measureable metrics. After product demand and use, products may be available for collection for a variety of reasons, including commercial returns, end-of-use (EOU), or end-of life (EOL). Commercial returns are products returned due to issues such as customer dissatisfaction or overstocks by a reseller. Generally, commercial returns are still in a current life cycle phase that allows some value extraction. End-of-use products are still functional but no longer produced—products that are one generation or more behind the current technology. End-of-life products are no longer current technology (e.g. cathode-ray tube televisions) and often offer little in the way of reuse potential aside from recycling.

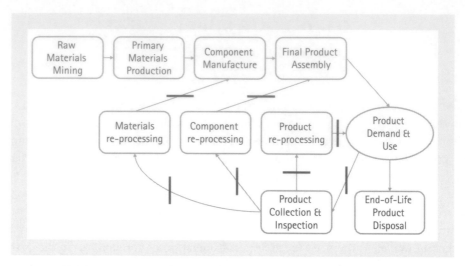

FIGURE 16.1 CLSC as a constrained process flow

Adapted from Guide & Van Wassenhove (2005).

In the reverse portion of the supply chain of Figure 16.1—the closed-loop segment—a firm must work to collect and inspect products for reprocessing at the product, component, and materials levels. In each case, multiple constraints can impact the system. The overarching constraint on any closed-loop supply chain is the production from the forward supply chain. Returns only can be collected from previously produced products (see Geyer et al. 2007 for a complete discussion). Even when a sufficient supply of returns exists for a remanufacturing firm, access to and collection of the used products can be a challenge, depending on the nature of the product as represented by the bar constraints in Figure 16.1. Large products, such as heavy construction equipment, generally can be monitored and serviced by the Original Equipment Manufacturer (OEM) under lease agreements. Such leases allow the OEM to maintain tight control over the flow of goods. Conversely, consumer goods generally prove much harder to monitor and collect as the usage by consumers tends to be more widely spread. Assuming the product can be collected effectively, a firm has to develop technical competency to repair or remanufacture the product for resale into a generally constrained market segment. Such technical competency relies on effective methods to test, sort, and dispose of the products, components, and materials.

As Figure 16.1 and the related discussion make clear, a firm that follows a closed-loop supply chain strategy faces many challenges and constraints. Of course, those challenges allow proactive firms to find profits that may be missed by competitors. Firms that reuse past materials, energy, and labor in a CLSC system can also improve environmental performance, gain insights into the life cycle of their products, find means to improve processes, and more (Lund 1984).

FORWARD AND REVERSE SUPPLY CHAINS

Multitudes of material cover an enormous breadth of concepts in forward supply-chain design, control, and operation. Some general texts that give an excellent overview include Jacobs and Chase's recently updated text regarding both operations and supply chain management (Jacobs & Chase 2010) and Harrison, Lee, & Neale's text on convergence between supply chain theory and practice (Harrison, Lee, & Neale 2005). Martin provides a more specific six-sigma oriented text (Martin 2006). Therefore, this section predominantly will focus on how reverse supply chains differ from forward chains, what activities drive a reverse supply chain, and how a closed-loop supply chain coordinates the forward and reverse supply chains.

UNDERSTANDING THE FUNDAMENTAL
DIFFERENCES FROM A FORWARD SUPPLY CHAIN

After a firm has a clear understanding of their forward supply chain, the differences in a closed-loop reverse supply chain become quite apparent. For instance, the product life cycle as defined by Levitt (Levitt 1965) is no longer solely a marketing concept of market development, growth, maturity, and decline. Rather, the product life cycle becomes an issue of how end-users consume and dispose of the product. The product life cycle in a CLSC context includes the value that will be left in the product at the first end-of-use cycle, the second end-of-use cycle, and eventually the end of life for the product. Ideally, the product design specifically will include multiple life cycle considerations. However, when the product design does not include consideration of multiple life cycles, design for serviceability and reparability can allow value extraction from a product throughout multiple life cycles. In effect, firms already designing a product to be serviceable and repairable have a great advantage when transitioning to a true CLSC.

Another difference from a forward supply chain is the inherent input–output nature of a CLSC. Past production output becomes the input for future returns. Using the previously produced parts allows a firm to utilize past expenditures in energy and labor as well as materials. Of course, the trade-off is increased complexity in dealing with quality and quantity variability in the returns. Additionally, the technology embodied in past production often needs updating to meet current market demands. If the technological update is predominantly software based, the upgrades can be exceptionally simple. Conversely, if the technological update is hardware based, the firm must evaluate carefully how to extract value from the prior production. For example, GE transportation faces the issue of diesel locomotive engine control units requiring frequent updates while the locomotive engines themselves may last decades with appropriate but less frequent maintenance. Even with careful design, hardware can become obsolete. If prior production has little value in meeting the current technological requirements, a firm faces a marketing challenge to determine the right customer segment for older generation products that still have value.

Exploring reverse supply chains

This section provides specific details regarding development and implementation of elements in a reverse supply chain. The predominant focus of this section will be reuse—a major topic later in this chapter for the discussion of the reduce, reuse, and recycle (3R) hierarchy. Before reuse can occur, the products must be reacquired from end users and transported from the point of use to the point of evaluation for testing, sorting, and disposition to determine the most profitable reuse options in redistribution and marketing. Additionally, many well-designed CLSC systems incorporate repair and service functions to meet warranty obligations with reclaimed parts from the reverse supply chain.

Product recovery options

Before commencing collection, firms need to understand potential disassembly, quality, and resulting product outcomes. Table 16.1 is adapted from the Thierry et al. (1995) paper regarding strategic product recovery.

The definitions in Table 16.1 may draw too fine a line for some products and industries. For instance, refurbishment often refers to technology-based products (e.g. inkjet printers). On the other hand, remanufacturing generally refers to more standard mechanical products or heavy equipment. In effect, both refurbishment and remanufacturing involve tearing down a product to the module or part level for inspection and rebuilding to a pre-specified standard. Though the differences in the terms seem thinly defined, the general concepts should be adaptable as guidelines for firms to examine product reuse options.

Product acquisition management

Product acquisition management focuses on obtaining the used products from the user (Blackburn et al. 2004). As described by Guide & Van Wassenhove (2001), product acquisition management (PrAM) systems have three core facets. First, they describe how reuse activities must create value. Second, the research describes how product returns must be managed systematically to compete profitably through remanufacturing. The authors use an economic value added (EVA®) framework to explore the financial potential of product recovery activities (Young 1997). Third, the authors show how the management of product returns drives operational issues. The core of the paper is that firms need to

Table 16.1 Product Recovery Guidelines

	Level of Disassembly	Quality Requirements	Resulting Product
Repair	Product	Restoration to Original Product Specification	Like new
Refurbishment	Module/Part Level	Inspection of Modules/Parts for Restoration to Original Product Specification	Pre-specified standard or like new with potential for upgrades
Remanufacturing	Module/Part Level	Inspection of Modules/Parts for Restoration to Original Product Specification	Pre-specified standard using a combination of used and new modules/ parts
Service Parts	Module/Part Retrieval	Inspection and Extraction of Modules/Parts to Meet Service Requirements	Selective module/part retrieval with recycling or scrap of remainder
Recycling	Materials	Varies by materials recovered	Materials used to produce new parts or alternative uses

Adapted from the Thierry et al. (1995) paper regarding strategic product recovery

proactively monitor and manage the acquisition market for returned goods. The acquisition management could entail the use of inexpensive and quick visual inspection systems, such as those used by the ReCellular (a third-party remanufacturer of cellular devices), to classify high profit and low profit returns (Guide & Van Wassenhove 2001). Other systems might need to monitor prices in active returns markets or even create the markets from scratch. The most successful remanufacturing firms must work proactively to control the quality, quantity, and timing of returned products to maximize profitability.

A quick examination of the economic value added concepts reveals that managers need to document carefully operational process costs such as materials, labor, and acquisition prices. Additionally, the potential revenues for the remanufactured products must be monitored and evaluated continuously. In fact, pricing of remanufactured products represents one of the least understood areas of CLSC. Therefore, the authors of this chapter are involved actively with multiple companies and are completing multiple studies to shed light on the difficult pricing topic. Other considerations in the EVA model include taxation, current capital equipment, capital asset usage rates, cost of capital considerations, and more. In other words, the EVA model takes an in-depth, holistic look at the profitability paths involved in the decision to employ PrAM.

Reverse logistics

Reverse logistics are the processes required to transport the recovered products to a facility for inspection, sorting, and disposition (Blackburn et al. 2004). In general, reverse logistics network design follows similar principles to forward logistics network design. Many of the same principles of facility location apply (Fleischmann et al. 2001). In general, firms must evaluate whether the forward and reverse chains can be set up as independent entities (sequential) or integrated entities (simultaneous). The authors find that the answer lies in the nature of the product flows to match supply and demand. In many cases, the forward and reverse chains can be treated as separate entities even when sharing resources. The ability to manage the two chains separately greatly simplifies management requirements. Further, the authors show that supply uncertainty appears to have little impact on the network design, and that relatively simple models work well. However, distinct differences emerge based on the industry examined. For very high volume return industries that have regulatory requirements due to high environmental impacts (e.g. paper), an integrated network design with multiple forward and reverse facility locations might prove necessary (Bloemhof-Ruwaard et al. 1996; Fleischmann et al. 2001). The general findings indicated that most firms should be able to avoid the high costs of setting up a dedicated set of facilities for reverse logistics and can rely instead ontransportation networks to bring goods back to forward supply chain facilities.

An additional consideration in the reverse logistics design is whether to insource or outsource the reverse logistics tasks. Current research finds that there are many trade-offs involved in the decision to insource, mix, or outsource reverse supply chain activities (Martin et al. 2010). For strong brands with a customer-service orientation and a high marginal value of time in the returning products, insourcing is likely wise as a means to maintain full control over the timing and flow of products. Outsourcing of the reverse logistics often makes sense for firms with lower marginal value of time products, and for firms that do not already have a large investment in a transportation and logistics network.

Testing, sorting, and disposition

The processes of testing, sorting, and disposition assess the condition of the return and determine the most profitable decision for reuse (Blackburn et al. 2004). In general, recovery systems that allow quick and effective inspection and testing of returned products can lead to significant cost savings. Other research showed that savings from inspection and testing rise quickly when the general quality levels of returned products are lower—products that are in good condition are more valuable (Aras et al. 2006). Additionally, Galbreth & Blackburn (2010) describe means to assessacquisition quantities in the face of high uncertainty in the return quality. Related work provides a detailed analysis of how many quality grades a firm should employ, how many units should be processed, and what type of inventory policies are appropriate for the different grades (Ferguson et al. 2009). The overall results demonstrate that firms should match the processing of units to the demand (assuming the returns are sufficient), and that quality grading usually will improve profitability, particularly when return volumes are large.

Interestingly, the research also shows that five or fewer quality grades should be sufficient for most firms, and two quality grades can be sufficient in some cases.

In general, firms need simple, inexpensive means to test and sort products. As a result, firms such as Bosch and Hewlett Packard (HP) designed simple memory chips to record vital usage information about the product (i.e. maximum operating temperature, usage hours, and number of prints) to make quick decisions about remanufacturing or recycling the product (Klausner 1998). The products that meet quality standards then can be sorted and eventually reprocessed in coordination with demand.

Repair, service, and warranty considerations

For many firms, tying the product returns into the repair and service network can reduce greatly the module and part costs. The cost reduction can be invaluable for service and repair of older machines when the procurement of new parts can be prohibitively expensive due to large minimum-order quantities. Harvesting parts from product returns often allows a firm to continue providing service for a product longer than would be possible through standard forward supply chain procurement methods. When harvesting parts, firms need to estimate the volume and timing of returns to regulate the inventory of the modules and parts in the repair network. Research has shown that a modified base stock policy seems to work well when determining how much inventory of replacement parts should be held for the service network (Huang et al. 2008). Additionally, a research study at IBM focused on when to recover, what channels to use for recovery, and how to coordinate spare-part supply sources (Fleischmann et al. 2003). The research showed that IBM could realize significant cost savings by procuring used parts instead of new. The study also demonstrated cost savings that far outweighed any additional reverse logistics costs, particularly when the parts, rather than the entire machine, became the focus of acquisition. In agreement with the Huang et al. paper, modified base-stock policies appeared to work well in controlling the spare-parts inventory. Further, though not a specific consideration in the IBM paper, the life-cycle effect of increasing new procurement costs for older parts likely would have a significant effect of increasing the profitability from use of returned parts for spares.

Putting the pieces together at Hewlett-Packard

A 2002 INSEAD business case examines management of product returns at Hewlett Packard. The case provides an excellent picture of how to integrate the activities described throughout this section (Kumar, Van Wassenhove, & Guide 2001). The case shows the benefits of HP's adopting a value-creation perspective, rather than treating the product returns as a nuisance and focusing on cost-minimization. Though the details of the HP case are too numerous to include in this chapter, the discussion of the business case, marketing opportunities, and reverse logistics network, as well as some specific examples of testing, sorting, and disposition could prove useful for both practitioners and academics who wish to further examine the CLSC process.

Coordinating Forward and Reverse Chains as a CLSC

Product recovery via a CLSC is not philanthropy. In fact, a well-designed and executed product-recovery system can be highly profitable for a stand-alone third-party remanufacturer (3PR). For example, third-party remanufacturing firms such as ReCellular, Inc. do not manufacture new cellular phones. Instead, ReCellular focuses on reclaiming value and profits from mobile communications devices produced by other companies (Guide & Van Wassenhove 2001). ReCellular also generates unanticipated additional value from information about usage patterns, design flaws, and causes for product failure. At the same time, ReCellular prevents the materials and energy embodied in the prior production from entering the waste stream and landfills.

If a third-party remanufacturer such as ReCellular can form an entire business as a reverse supply chain, then firms that design, control, and operate both the forward and reverse supply chains should have even more opportunities to make profits than firms only focused on one direction. By capturing the profits in all phases of a product's life cycle, firms gain proactive means to enhance profits, improve environmental performance, increase the range of customer segments, and gain insight into process improvements, all while gaining information about product design ramifications.

This section has provided a broad overview of many of the components of a reverse supply chain in the CLSC context. For the interested reader, further details can be found in Guide & Van Wassenhove's early text on business aspects of CLSC (Guide & Van Wassenhove 2003). The text contains numerous topics, including an investigation of the retail reverse logistics, product recovery strategies, contracting coordination, reverse logistics network design, production planning, inventory control, forecasting product returns, and more. A more recent book, edited by Ferguson & Souza, covers CLSC with a focus on sustainability related business practices (Ferguson & Souza 2010). Additional works of interest include a book by Flapper, van Nunen, & Van Wassenhove (Flapper, van Nunen, & Van Wassenhove 2005) as well as an earlier text by Klose, Speranza, & Van Wassenhove (Klose, Speranza, & Van Wassenhove 2002).

PRODUCT RECOVERY AS A FOUNDATION FOR CLSC

Though product reuse is often a primary focus of a CLSC, reuse alone can be too myopic a focus for a fully developed closed-loop supply chain. Therefore, the reduce, reuse, and recycle (3R) hierarchy can be used to gain a more holistic view of CLSCs. Many CLSCs will concentrate on the reuse portion, but not to the exclusion of recycling and reduction.

The reduce, reuse, and recycle ordering is representative of the rough environmental impact level of the three actions. The first action is to reduce the materials and energy load. The second action is to reuse—the prime focus of many CLSC systems. The third action is to recycle, which is really a last resort only to be used once a firm exhausts the previous two options. Unfortunately, using the reduce, reuse, and recycle hierarchy is not always simple. For example, materials reduction without consideration of shrinking product life cycles can lead to a net increase in the materials load over time. Additionally, recycling can yield products that are inferior to virgin materials, particularly when dealing with plastics. Accordingly, reduction of plastics often would prove much more beneficial than planning to recycle plastics at the end of life. In general, reduction, reusing, and recycling often need to be considered in conjunction rather than isolation. Additionally, due to legislative pressures, simplicity of implementation, and a host of other issues, the priorities tend to be recycling first, reduction second, and reuse a distant third. Figure 16.2 displays what seems to be the current state of the reduce, reuse, and recycle hierarchy.

3M maintains a focus on reduction as a dominant strategy along with integrated recycling and reuse. 3M's Pollution Prevention Pays (3P) process oriented philosophy seems to integrate nicely with the basic tenets of the reduce, reuse, and recycle concept (Ochsner 1995). Though the details are beyond the scope of this chapter, 3M's pollution prevention pays program seeks to ingrain at every level of the firm the intrinsic benefits

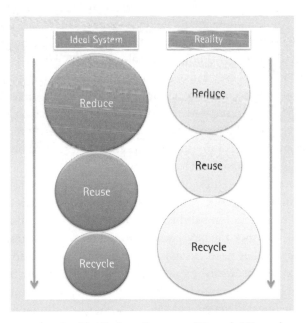

FIGURE 16.2 The Reduce, Reuse, and Recycle Hierarchy

of monitoring waste reduction, starting from the early phases of product design all the way through the product's life cycle to end of life. The end result has been both cost and waste reduction through a focus on the entire life cycle of the various products.

Reduce: the need for materials and energy reduction in a CLSC

In many ways, the reduction of materials, energy, and labor inputs derives from various quality initiatives. In fact, one of the main results of both the ISO 9000 and ISO 14000 process certifications is waste reduction in materials, energy, and toxic releases. Even earlier work in TQM and other quality initiatives focused on the process orientation to remove waste from the system. The authors' own work indicates a need for firms to evolve into learning organizations with operational performance excellence (LOOPE).

Servicizing represents one example of a paradigm shift in mode of consumption to reduce waste through extended producer responsibility. Servicizing allows a firm to sell use of a good, rather than the physical good, so that the user receives the full benefits of ownership without concern for maintenance, repair, and end-of-life disposal issues. In other words, a servicizing firm does provide a good in the form of a service, usually though leasing or contractual arrangements. A report from Tellus Institute (White et al. 1999) provides great detail on the many facets of servicizing. As the Tellus Institute report notes, servicizing does not automatically yield environmental benefits. For instance, when the service entity and the manufacturing entity are not appropriately coordinated, less efficient products may remain in the market too long when newer more efficient products would reduce the total energy usage. The report notes that without explicit policies to terminate the life of the product in the market, the product efficiency gains may be delayed too long. Additionally, multiple challenges seem to have prevented the widespread acceptance of servicizing in many markets. In many ways, the disposable product culture and general market acceptance appear to represent some of the greatest challenges to a servicizing transition. As a consequence, before any firm attempts to use a servicizing strategy, the likely customer response must be analyzed and understood thoroughly. Servicing also has ramifications in reuse as described below in the section titled 'Servicizing: Building reuse into consumption.'

Shared savings contracts represent another form of potential materials reduction that often can be similar to servicizing. A classic example of a shared savings contract comes from the chemical solvents industry (Corbett & DeCroix 2001). Under a traditional sales volume contract, the buyer wishes to reduce consumption of the chemical solvents, while the supplier needs to make sales quotas. Under a shared savings contract, the buyer makes some form of guaranteed payment to ensure the supplier's profits remain acceptable while incentivizing the supplier to allow consumption reduction. For instance, the chemical management fee contract is quite similar to servicizing—the supplier makes the guarantee to provide chemical solvents to the buyer for a fixed fee.

As a result, the supplier can save cost by not providing excess chemicals, while the buyer is less concerned with usage rates. The true shared savings contract also employs a fixed-fee arrangement with the addition of terms that share the savings from any reduction in the use of the chemicals, thereby incentivizing both parties to reduce consumption. Interestingly, the savings come not only from reduction in the chemical solvents but also in the form of reduced disposal and handling fees. In all cases, when a reduction of chemical use occurs, both the supply chain profits and environmental performance can improve.

Reuse: understanding reuse in a CLSC context

In many ways, reuse is the core activity of a CLSC. As the definition states, a CLSC dynamically extracts value from product returns over the entire product life cycle. Additionally, a well-designed reuse system can provide tremendous profit potentials by tapping previously unexplored market segments. The value in reuse comes from extraction of previously procured materials as well as prior expenses in energy and labor—a topic extensively covered by Lund's World Bank report on remanufacturing (Lund 1984). As Lund notes, reuse leads to social and economic benefits, such as lower cost of core acquisition (i.e. the used product) versus buying new materials. Also, the reuse can lead to significant energy to materials leverage ratios of five-to-one or better. Lund further notes that both original equipment manufacturers and third parties have relatively low barriers to entry for reuse when compared to designing and manufacturing a product from raw materials.

One of the most typical objections against a CLSC heard from an OEM is the threat of cannibalizing new product sales. Recent research demonstrates that firms should be less concerned about cannibalization and more concerned about expanding their product portfolio through appropriate pricing strategies for the remanufactured products (Atasu et al, 2010). Another objection to reuse regards logistics. The argument tends to be that the transportation of the old products has to be too costly. Fortunately, for a CLSC that appropriately matches the marginal value of time for returns, the profits often can outweigh significantly the related reverse logistics costs (see Blackburn et al. 2004). For short product life-cycle goods, such as computers, the marginal value of time tends to be very high. In effect, firms seeking to extract value from such high marginal value of time goods must act quickly to refurbish and return the product to the market. Products with more stable, longer life cycles, such as power tools, tend to have a lower marginal value of time, which allows the firm extracting value from reuse more time to collect and resell the products.

As the preceding discussion made clear, reuse is not the only facet in the interlinked nature of a CLSC. In fact, a myopic focus on materials reduction without consideration for reuse or recycling can lead to a significantly worse overall environmental result for an industry. Moreover, ignoring the value embodied in previous production can give rise to third-parties that extract the value that OEMs missed. Additionally, firms need to consider the full product life cycle through careful examination of life cycle assessments (LCA) or other available tools.

The business case: reuse as a profit center

For some firms, simply aligning the forward supply chain to provide the right product to the right place at the right time can be a challenge. Hence, the concept of reuse often seems a distant afterthought, particularly during the introduction of a new product to the market. Additionally, employing a reverse supply chain as an afterthought can add significant complexity and cost to a system that already may have slim margins. Therefore, some firms simply ignore the potential of reuse as too costly and unprofitable. Yet, such an attitude can open the door to a third-party remanufacturer who does see CLSCs and remanufacturing as profit for the taking rather than costs to be avoided. Moreover, changing the perspective of reuse from a cost to a profit center can be a challenge. Many firms, such as Bosch, that successfully make the transition view the products as a portfolio of goods and services. In other words, the firm must decide if adding a reuse operation adds to the overall profitability and competitive position within a portfolio of product and service options.

As the process diagram in Figure 16.3 displays, the nature of the reverse supply chain can be vertical (in-house), mixed, or outsourced, depending on the core competencies and structure of the firm.

Vertical reverse supply chains largely derive from strong brand image and a need for high levels of customer service. Firms that employ a mixed strategy often do so due to a lack of remanufacturing as a core competence or product complexity issues. The prime impetus behind full outsourcing often stems from a lack of manufacturing competence. Such a lack of internal competence generally occurs in firms that predominantly employ outsourced contract production for forward supply chain. Of course, intellectual property risks and loss of control increase when moving from a vertical to an outsourced configuration. In general, firms can move easily from vertical to outsourced configurations. However, moving out of an outsourced configuration can be difficult because of knowledge-loss issues. Thus, the configuration decision should be made carefully due to the long-term strategic implications of the various choices.

Commercial returns and false failures

Commercial returns are products returned by customers for any reason within up to ninety days of sale, and the manufacturer must credit the retailer and then determine the best way to extract the remaining value from the return (Blackburn et al. 2004). For firms dealing in business-to-consumer (B2C) goods, commercial returns are a difficult challenge to manage. The problem becomes even more prominent when many of the returns are false failures—returns that are fully functional but do not meet some

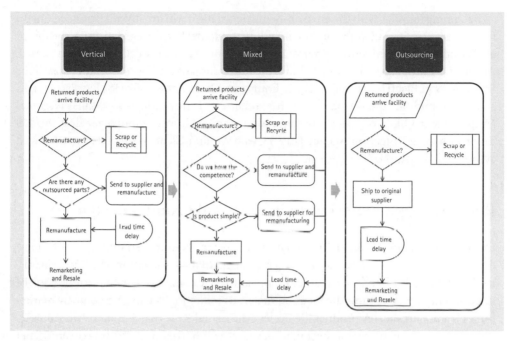

FIGURE 16.3 Reverse Supply Chain Configuration

Martin et al (2010)

customer requirement (Ferguson et al. 2006). Unfortunately, differentiating between the legitimate product returns (i.e. returns due to a defect) and false failures can be difficult. In general, retailers have little incentive to expend resources in examining and testing a return for appropriate disposition. Thus, finding an appropriate contract or other means to align the incentives can prove crucial for acquiring the returned products.

Legislation as a reuse driver

Some firms have made the decision to employ reuse based on a proactive assumption that governmental regulation of markets will force some type of reduction, reuse, or recycling programs. For example, 3M's pollution prevention pays program was at least in part a means to prepare proactively for the potential issues with governmental regulation, such as the Clean Air and Clean Water acts. Additionally, firms such as BMW took an active role in developing internal standards that made transition to legislative standards, such as the Waste Electrical and Electronic Equipment (WEEE), relatively easy. A recent work by Atasu et al. (2009) discusses means to alter take-back legislation for improved environmental performance and fairness of the legislation. Take-back legislation represents an active area for continued research.

Becoming familiar with the environmental legislation will greatly aid firms seeking to implement a CLSC. Full information including the actual WEEE legislation can be found at European Commissions Environment section (European Commission 2010). Additional European legislation includes the Restriction of the Use of Certain Hazardous Substances in Electrical and Electronic Equipment Regulations (RoHS) legislation, and can be found at the Department for Business Innovation and Skills National Measurement Office of the United Kingdom (2003). Information regarding the US Environmental Protection Agency (EPA) Clean Air and Clean Water acts can be found at the EPA's website (US EPA 2010).

Reuse through materials reduction and product design

In the mobile-phone industry, the quantity of materials used certainly seems to have diminished over the past two decades—a significant dematerialization. However, shrinking life cycles in the hands of consumers appear to have come along with the reduction of materials inputs. Over time, the focus on materials reduction can be overcome by market forces leading to shorter product life cycles. The net effect is that a system without adequate planning for reuse and eventual recycling will have a potentially worsening net impact over time. Additionally, if the OEM simply releases their product to market without further thought for the eventual disposition of the product, third parties such as ReCellular will be able to move into the market to reclaim value the OEMs ignore.

In many ways, planning for reuse is a function of product design. Design principles such as component/module minimization, use of screws instead of welds, common frames across product lines, and ease of module accessibility all facilitate reuse. In effect, many of the principles of design for reuse also apply in making the product easier to service and repair in the field. A discussion of some of the design issues appears in recent text edited by Ferguson & Souza (Ferguson & Souza 2010). Specifically, the chapter on product design, by Bras (2010), goes through many of the issues surrounding product design that are applicable in a closed-loop system. For instance, the presence of external entities that will extract value from the product through remanufacturing or recycling may seem parasitic to the OEM. Accordingly, the OEM might make design decisions directly aimed at preventing a third-party remanufacturer from entering the market. The OEM may go so far as to design the product to make recycling difficult to deter any value extraction after the initial sale. Bras (2010) also discusses issues regarding what level of remanufacturing or value extraction should occur. For example, a firm may not wish to remanufacture the entire product but merely harvest some components. Usually, such decisions should be made at the product design phase as noted in the Office of Technology Assessment in their report regarding green product design choice (Congress of the United States 1992). The report goes on to note that no one dimension, such as recyclability, should dominate product design. On the contrary, firms must commit to full life-cycle assessments and adapt to changing technological trade-offs in green design.

Servicizing: Building reuse into consumption

The Tellus Institute (White et al. 1999) describes servicizing as a means to change the way products are made, used, and disposed of through sales of functionality of a product rather than a transactional sale of the product. The paper also discusses the potential learning cycle involved in servicizing operations. Yadav et al. (2003) discuss the development of a servicizing business for trucking fleet tires. Unfortunately, the number of documented servicizing firms remains small. In general, a servicizing firm maintains product ownership through leasing, employs a take/buy-back system, or employs some other form of extended producer responsibility. As a result, the servicizing firm has the opportunity to reclaim value from the product after each end-of-use cycle from a customer. Information regarding differing usage patterns, replacement rates, and repair requests can prove invaluable for future product design, materials procurement, and production decisions. Additionally, the Tellus Institute (White et al. 1999) report goes so far as to argue that knowledge and information will become the core competencies of servicizing firms, as opposed to more traditional core competencies focused on finding more efficient manufacturing for transactional sales.

Recycle: evaluating the role of recycling in a CLSC

In general, recycling has the least benefits in terms of environmental impact. Recycling requires multiple operations including transportation, teardown, shredding, melting, and other steps to yield usable materials. Metals tend to be particularly well suited for recycling by firms such as Alcoa. The EPA provides a large list of products with recommended uses (EPA website 2010). Due to technological limitations, many of the products cannot be made entirely from recycled materials. Thus, the placement of recycling last in the reduce, reuse, and recycle hierarchy is both a cost and environmental placement. Recycling might seem to be an easy fix to prevent waste stream and landfill issues, but reduction and reuse generally offer greater environmental benefits, cost savings, and potential profits. Curiously, recycling has taken a prominent role for many firms, perhaps due to the ability to free-ride on existing recycling networks, meet governmental regulatory requirements (e.g. WEEE in Europe), and maintain visibility of environmental concern in the eyes of customers. However, for manufacturing firms interested in increasing profitability, recycling should not be a prime focus. Rather, reduction and particularly reuse usually will be much more fruitful choices.

Even though recycling should not be the first choice, some industries have found profitable solutions. For example, paper recycling can be both environmentally friendly and profitable. The main issue faced by paper recyclers in Europe was that paper mills tended to be far from the points of use in major cities. Hence, the reverse logistics network design had to be adapted such that reclamation and recycling could be completed close to the point of use. Unfortunately, not all industries are adaptable to profitable recycling networks. Redesigning the entire reverse logistics network also might not be a viable option for many firms when the end result is only losing less money (i.e. simple cost reduction). In some cases, firms might need to make integrated decisions simultaneously for both the forward and reverse logistics network design before deployment.

FINAL DISCUSSION AND RESEARCH OPPORTUNITIES

The beginning of this chapter gives the definition of a CLSC as 'a closed-loop supply chain (CLSC) that incorporates design, control, and operation of a system to maximize value creation over the entire life cycle of a product with dynamic recovery of value from different types and volumes of returns over time.' The previous sections of this chapter cover the basics of why CLSCs can be profitable, environmentally friendly, and good business practice. The following providesa brief summary of open questions for continued research. More comprehensive reviews of open research topics in remanufacturing and CLSC can be found in Guide & Van Wassenhove's work on the evolution of CLSC (Guide & Van Wassenhove 2009) and work on product reuse economics by Atasu et al. (Atasu et al. 2008).

Design of the CLSC

To understand the means to close the loop in a supply chain, a firm must have a thorough understanding of the forward supply chain. Before designing a CLSC, a firm often will need to examine and map carefully the nature of the forward supply chain system— a business process that requires continued research. Other areas for further research include product usage and disposal patterns for improved product and CLSC design. As noted, the reacquisition can be relatively easy for firms that deal in large business-to-business equipment under lease agreements. On the other hand, difficulties mount rapidly for smaller, less expensive consumer goods sold into various markets and widely dispersed geographic regions. An open question for future research concerns the marginal value of time for reacquisition of the used products. Products with a high marginal value of time that lose value rapidly, such as high-tech goods, need a responsive reverse supply chain to maximize value recovery, but optimal value maximization as a function of time remains an area for continued research. The design of CLSCs includes many interlinked processes including elements of product design, disassembly processes, and reverse logistics network design as well as testing, sorting, and disposition of returns. Though reverse logistic network design is relatively well understood, the related topics of product design, disassembly processes, and integration into existing reverse logistic network design remain open topics for continued research.

Control and operation of the CLSC

Once the firm has a reasonable understanding of how to design and implement the closed-loop system, the CLSC will require control mechanisms. Continued improvement of control mechanisms requires research into both consumer and business customer segments to better understand attitudes and valuations of remanufactured and recycled products. Some researchers assert the existence of a "green market" of consumers willing to pay a premium for green product brands—an assertion that requires further research and rigorous empirical validation. As discussed earlier, CLSCs may have high return stream instability, which leads to the need for research into improved inventory controls in a multiple life-cycle context. Furthermore, the CLSC must be designed to allow for continuous improvement and process learning—a topic that lends itself both to classical operations management modeling as well as synergies with more traditional management research. Due to the ever-expanding product portfolios of many firms, product proliferation often represents an ever-growing challenge for firms attempting to extract value from returns. Improved models for handling product proliferation in a multiple life-cycle context could prove to be a fruitful area for future research. Additional research into the impact of shrinking product life cycles, increasing competitive pressures, and smaller margins all add impetus for researchers to analyze effective ways to extract value out of both the forward and reverse supply chain.

The need for interdisciplinary research

Researchers also need to examine whether a portfolio of products including product reuse will add more market segments, improve brand visibility, generate knowledge about product use across multiple life cycles, reduce environmental impact, and increase profits. Each of these topics lends itself to interdisciplinary research through improved economic modeling of competition, greater awareness of marketing models, improved handling of time effects in traditional operations management models, and increased involvement of industrial ecologists in improving the synergy of business with the natural environment. Researchers also need to generate better models to both understand current legislation as well as identify areas for improvement in future legislation. In other words, the future of CLSC will require a more holistic view of closed-loop supply chains across multiple business disciplines. Such a view will prove invaluable for both researchers and managers in the quest to improve profitability while aiding environmental performance—the core of integrating business and the natural environment.

REFERENCES

Aras, N., Boyaci, T., & Verter, V. (2006). "The Effect of Categorizing Returned Products in Remanufacturing," *IIE Transactions*, 36: 319–331.

Atasu, A., Guide, V. D. R. Jr. & Van Wassenhove, L.N. (2010). "So What if Remanufacturing Cannibalizes my New Product Sales?" *California Management Review*, 52(2): 56–76.

—— Van Wassenhove, L. N., & Sarvary, M. (2009). "Efficient Take-Back Legislation," *Production and Operations Management*, 18(3): 243–258.

—— Guide, V. D. R. Jr. & Van Wassenhove, L.N. (2008). "Product Reuse Economics in Closed-Loop Supply Chain Research," *Production and Operations Management*, 17(5): 483–497.

Blackburn, J. D., Guide, V. D. R., Jr., Souza, G. C., & Van Wassenhove, L. N. (2004). "Reverse Supply Chains for Commercial Returns," *California Management Review*, 46(2): 6–22.

Bloemhof-Ruwaard et al. (1996). "An Environmental Lifecycle Optimization Model for the European Pulp and Paper Industry," *Management Science*, 24(6): 615–629.

Bras, B. (2010). "Product Design Issues," in Ferguson, M. E. and Souza, G. C. (eds.) *Closed-Loop Supply Chains New Developments to Improve the Sustainability of Business Practices*, Boca Raton: CRC Press.

Congress of the United States (1992). *Green Products by Design Choices for a Cleaner Environment*. Washington, D.C: Congress of the United States Office of Technology Assessment.

Corbett, C. J. & DeCroix, G. A. (2001). "Shared-Savings Contracts for Indirect Materials in Supply Chains: Channel Profits and Environmental Impacts," *Management Science*, 47(7): 881–93.

Department of Business and Innovation National Measurement Office (2003). "Official Journal of the European Union Directive 2002/95/EC of the European Parliament and of the Council," Available at <http://www.rohs.gov.uk/Docs/Links/RoHS%20directive.pdf,> accessed June 2010.

European Commission "Waste Electrical and Electronic Equipment," European Commission Environment website: <http://ec.europa.eu/environment/waste/weee/legis_en.htm>, accessed June 2010.

Ferguson, M., Guide, V. D. R. Jr., & Souza, G. C. (2006). "Supply Chain Coordination for False Failure Returns," *Manufacturing & Service Operations Management*, 8(4): 376–393.

Ferguson, M. E. & Souza, G. C. (2010). *Closed-Loop Supply Chains New Developments to Improve the Sustainability of Business Practices*. Boca Raton: CRC Press.

Ferguson, M., Guide, V. D. R., Jr., Koca, E., & Souza, G. C. (2009). "The Value of Quality Grading in Remanufacturing," *Production and Operations Management*, 18(3): 300–14.

Flapper, S. D. P, van Nunen, J. A. E. E., & Van Wassenhove, L. N. (2005). *A Business View on Closed-Loop Supply Chains*. Berlin: Springer-Verlag.

Fleischmann, M., van Nunen, J. A. E. E., & Grave, B. (2003). "Integrating Closed-Loop Supply Chains and Spare-Parts Management at IBM," *Interfaces*, 33(6): 44–56.

—— Beullens, P., Bloemhof-Ruwaard, J. M., and Van Wassenhove, L. N. (2001). "The Impact of Product Recovery on Logistics Network Design," *Production and Operations Management*, 10(2): 156–73.

Galbreth, M. R., and Blackburn, J. D. (2010). "Optimal Acquisition Quantities in Remanufacturing with Condition Uncertainty," *Production and Operations Management*, 19(1): 61–70.

Geyer, R., Van Wassenhove, L. N., & Atasu, A. (2007). "The Economics of Remanufacturing Under Limited Component Durability and Finite Product Life Cycles," *Management Science*, 53(1): 88–100.

Guide, V. D. R. & Van Wassenhove, L. N. (2001). "Managing Product Returns for Remanufacturing," *Production Operations Management*, 10: 142–155.

—— (2003). "Business Aspects of Closed-Loop Supply Chains," in Guide, V. D. R. Jr., & Van Wassenhove, L. N. (eds.), *Business Aspects of Closed-Loop Supply Chains Exploring the Issues*, Pittsburgh: Carnegie Mellon University Press.

—— (2005). "Evolution of Closed-Loop Supply Chain Research," Presentation for the Evolution of CLSC.

—— (2009). "The Evolution of Closed-Loop Supply Chain Research," *Operations Research*, 57(1): 10–21.

Harrison, T. P., Lee, H. L., & Neale, J. J. (2005). *The Practice of Supply Chain Management: Where Theory and Application Converge*. New York: Springer.

Huang, W., Kulkarni, V., Swaminathan, J. M. (2008). "Managing the Inventory of an Item with a Replacement Warranty," *Management Science*, 54(8): 1441–52.

Jacobs, R. F., & Chase, R. (2010). *Operations and Supply Chain Management*. New York: McGraw-Hill/Irwin.

Klausner, Markus. (1998). "Design and Analysis of Product Takeback Systems: An Application to Power Tools." Ph.D. diss., Carnegie Mellon University.

Klose, A., Speranza, M. G., & Van Wassenhove, L. N. (2002). *Quantitative Approaches to Distribution Logistics and Supply Chain Management*. Berlin: Springer-Verlag.

Kumar, N., Van Wassenhove, L. N., & Guide, V. D. R., Jr. (2001). "Product Returns at Hewlett-Packard Company," INSEAD Teaching Case Series, 03/2001, 4940.

Levitt, T. (1965). "Exploit the Product Lifecycle," *Harvard Business Review*, 43: 81–94.

Lund, R. (1984). *Remanufacturing: The Experience of the United States and Implications for Developing Countries*. Washington, DC: World Bank.

Martin, P., Guide, V. D. R., Jr., & Craighead, C. W. (2010). "Supply Chain Sourcing in Remanufacturing Operations: An Empirical Investigation of Remake Versus Buy," *Decision Sciences*, 41(2): 301–24.

Martin, J. (2006). *Lean Six Sigma for Supply Chain Management*. New York: McGraw-Hill.

Ochsner, M., Chess, C., & Greenberg, M. (1995). "Pollution Prevention at the 3M Corporation," *Waste Management*, 15(8): 663–72.

Thierry, M., Salomon, M., Van Nunen, J., & Van Wassenhove, L. N. (1995). "Strategic Issues in Product Recovery Management," *California Management Review*, 37(2): 114–35.

US EPA (United States Environmental Protection Agency). *Wastes: Resource Conservation Comprehensive Procurement Guidelines*. <http://www.epa.gov/waste/conserve/tools/cpg/products/index.htm>, accessed October 2010.

US EPA (United States Environmental Protection Agency). *EPA Laws & Regulations*. <http://www.epa.gov/lawsregs/laws/index.html>, accessed June 2010.

White, A. L., Stoughton, M., & Feng, L. (1999). "Servicizing: The Quiet Transition to Extended Producer Responsibility," Washington, DC: US Environmental Protection Agency Office of Solid Waste.

Yadav, P., Miller, D., Schmidt, C., & Drake, R. (2003). "McGriff Treading Company Implements Service Contracts under Shared Savings." *Interfaces*, 33(6): 18–29.

Young, D. (1997). "Economic Value Added: A Primer for European Managers," *European Management Journal*, 14(4): 335–343.

CHAPTER 17

···

INDUSTRIAL ECOLOGY:
BUSINESS MANAGEMENT
IN A MATERIAL WORLD

···

REID LIFSET
AND FRANK BOONS

INDUSTRIAL ecology (IE) is an ensemble concept that specifies ways in which firms can and are currently starting to deal with their environmental impact. It builds on a metaphor of natural ecological phenomena to analyze and develop tools and prescriptions for industrial systems that are, for the most part, larger than a single firm. The normative goal of industrial ecology is to optimize resource efficiencies and close material loops within this more encompassing system boundary as part of the pursuit of sustainable production and consumption. The field is often said to have started with the publication of an article "Strategies for Manufacturing" by two senior executives from General Motors in a 1989 special issue of *Scientific American*, though the field has much more extensive roots and antecedents (Erkman 1997). In that widely-read piece, Frosch & Gallopolous (1989) argued that industrial activities could be made more environmentally-benign, if natural systems were viewed as a potential model for the organization of industry. The notion, variously called the biological or ecological analogy (or metaphor),[1] views natural systems as highly efficient in using and reusing resources. It is this interest in ecological models that prompts the name industrial *ecology*.[2]

A major inspiration in the field has been the evolution of collaboration among firms in the Danish town of Kalundborg (Ehrenfeld & Gertler 1997). Over a period of several decades, industry managers created a network of exchanges of by-products and wastes

---

[1] Whether the relationship is one of analogy or metaphor is the basis of lively scholarly debate, but not directly germane to this chapter.

[2] The "ecology" in industrial ecology is also meant to allude to concern with environmental sustainability, irrespective of the ecological analogy.

among a cluster of facilities including a power plant, an oil refinery, a pharmaceutical plant, and a plasterboard factory, reducing emissions and conserving resources. Similar examples of such regional industrial ecosystems are now studied under the label "industrial symbiosis", defined by Chertow (2007: 12) as "engaging traditionally separate industries in a collective approach to competitive advantage involving physical exchange of materials, energy, water, and by-products. The keys to industrial symbiosis are collaboration and the synergistic possibilities offered by geographic proximity."

A central premise of industrial ecology is that environmental problems and remedies should be viewed from a systems perspective in order to understand the biophysical and social processes at play and to avoid partial understandings and managerial and policy solutions that displace rather than resolve environmental threats. The systems approach is most frequently manifest in a life-cycle perspective,[3] that is, environmental assessment of products, facilities, technologies, or services is achieved by examining the inputs to, and outputs from, the processes involved in their production, use, and disposal. A product such as disposable diapers is thus assessed (or compared to cotton diapers) by looking at environmental impacts in all activities from resource extraction and materials processing, to product manufacture and distribution, through consumption, and then to waste disposal. This cradle-to-grave framework can be informal and qualitative or highly quantitative and complex, as in the case when formal life-cycle assessment is employed. Life-cycle assessments (LCAs) have become familiar elements of public discourse and environmental management.

The systems perspective is also manifest in the attention to the multiplicity of environmental concerns that are often assessed together. Rather than examining just, for example, greenhouse gas emissions or waste generation, the analysis addresses an entire range of environmental endpoints—climate change, energy consumption, ozone depletion, human and ecosystem toxicity, eutrophication, etc.—making the framing and analysis of environmental issues in industrial ecology fundamentally multi-attribute.

The concern with resource efficiency and systems analysis leads to a reliance on the tracking of stocks and flows of resources that is a hallmark of the field. In the words of the then-president of the US National Academy of Engineering (White 1994: V):

> Industrial ecology is the study of the flows of materials and energy in industrial and consumer activities, of the effects of these flows on the environment, and of the influences of economic, political regulatory and social factors on the flow, use and transformation of resources.

Industrial ecology is *industrial* because industry is seen as a locus of technological expertise and a point of leverage, both of which can be used to accomplish environmental remedies. At the time of the field's early development, the view of the role of the busi-

---

[3] Terminology is confusing here as industrial ecology uses the term "product life cycle" to refer to processes through which products and materials pass in a physical sense from resource extraction to final disposal. In marketing, the same term refers to the commercial stages of a product vis-a-vis its position in the market, going from market introduction to growth of market share to maturity of market share to saturation and decline. In this chapter, the term is used in its physical sense.

ness sector was changing from one of villain to one of potential pro-active actor that can participate in the pursuit of environmental goals and strategies (Boons 2009).

In its genesis, industrial ecology was forward-looking by intent—emphasizing the need and opportunity to avoid costly and damaging environmental mistakes through the conscious use of design for environment (DfE). This entailed a deliberate turning away from matters of corporate environmental compliance as well as environmental remediation. Attention in the field to the history of environmental phenomena, management, and policy, however, has grown over time as researchers have discovered that some of the key tools in the field allow reconstruction of the pattern of pollution in ways that are relevant to policy and scholarship.

The emphasis on forward-looking environmental management and policy leads industrial ecologists to focus on technological change and its relationship to the environment in several guises—research quantifying environmental benefits of technological change (e.g. Wernick et al. 1997), characterization of the mechanisms of environmental innovation and societal level transitions (e.g. Green & Randles 2006), and debates over the efficacy of technological change to bring about desired environmental results (e.g. Huesemann 2003).

The attention to technology and the focus on material and energy flows as the foundation for analysis also reflects the origins of the field—many of the pioneers came from an engineering background as manifest in the concern with product design (mechanical engineering), mass balances (chemical engineering), and infrastructure (environmental and civil engineering).

The systemic perspective of industrial ecology requires an explicit definition of the boundary of the system that is analyzed. Here the field displays its diversity by including not only the analysis of product life cycles, but also individual firms as a focal actor within resource networks; regionally bounded groups of firms (a boundary that has received substantial attention under the label of industrial symbiosis); the global stocks and flows of a particular substance such as phosphates, mercury, or copper; and material flows in cities, and nation states. System boundaries can thus be based on social, geographic, and technical criteria. Considering such a wide range of systems has led to insights concerning the consequences of using different boundaries. Such consequences relate to associated management issues (Boons & Baas 1997) as well as to the relative importance of environmental impacts.

RELATIONSHIP OF INDUSTRIAL ECOLOGY
TO BUSINESS FUNCTIONS

Business strategy

Business strategy fundamentally refers to the way in which the firm operates within its wider context. Management-driven research typically defines this context in terms of social actors and their interrelations. Industrial ecology challenges this definition in two ways: (1) it extends beyond the social context to include physical and ecological phenomena, and (2) it proposes a system boundary for addressing environmental impact that goes beyond the individual firm. The second challenge is not unique as other concepts analyze networks of firms as a potential source of competitive advantage (Porter 1985; Porter 1990; Gereffi et al. 2005). The regional and product chain system boundaries from industrial ecology run parallel to concepts such as industrial clusters, supply chain management, global value chains, and reverse logistics (see Chapters 15 and 16).

The extent to which industrial ecology mainly emphasizes improvement of the efficiency of existing activities rather than focusing on more fundamental changes of industrial systems (Commoner 1997; Oldenburg & Geiser 1997) is an ongoing concern. This discussion may be translated into the question about the extent to which industrial ecology is taken up as a strategic, rather than operational, activity by firms. Industrial ecology may provide competitive advantage, especially when it concerns exploiting resource efficiencies that contribute to cost leadership, but closing material loops[4] may also lead to additional costs, such as in the case where products are recycled and an infrastructure for collection needs to be developed. Also, adopting principles of design for environment (DfE) may lead to the development of products that require alternative business models and for which consumer demand is not evident.

There are also positive examples of business strategies where principles of industrial ecology are central. Some of these centre on increased resource productivity through interlinked production activities, as shown by Luke (2001) in a study of developments within Ford Motor Company (FMC) to deal with the ecological impact of its processes and products. Another interesting case is the Guitang Group, a Chinese conglomerate firm producing sugar. According to Zhu et al. (2007), the conglomerate has been implementing an industrial ecology strategy for over four decades, building linkages among its production processes and thus developing an integrated set of activities including alcohol and paper production. Thus, a strategy of vertical integration has been combined with principles of loop closing. The case is also illustrative in showing the fragility of such a conglomerate; due to the large amount of linkages, it is vulnerable to outside events and increased competitiveness on any of its markets.

Conceptually, the wider system boundaries of industrial ecology may combine with the strategic ambition of firms to transform existing systems of production and consumption. Such a strategy requires specific systemic capabilities that enable the firm to develop its resource networks in such a way that a new technological trajectory is put in place (Boons 2009). Through design for environment, firms such as GE Medical Services may be able to align their business strategy with improved environmental performance (Finster et al. 2001). And the concept of product-service systems has been adopted by several firms as a viable business model to lease rather than sell their products to customers (Mont et al. 2006).

---

[4] Loops in this context allude to the cycling of resources in natural systems. Closing a loop thus entails capturing a resource so that it may be used again. With respect to post-consumer waste, it connotes the recycling of materials back into the same product. For other types of waste, the notion is expansive and less specific.

The latter examples make clear that industrial ecology can facilitate the incorporation of environmental concerns into business strategy through new product development. Interestingly, some of the tools of industrial ecology serve the strategic purpose of risk reduction. Within the sustainable supply-chain literature, mitigating risks has been identified as an important motive (Seuring & Müller 2008). In that context, risk is interpreted mainly in terms of the extent to which a firm may lose legitimacy due to the social and environmental impacts of its activities and products. Recently, however, the issue of security of supply is gaining increased interest. As resources become scarcer, and the places where they are extracted more politically volatile, supply security is endangered. Analysis of this issue is aided by material flow analysis (described later in this chapter) (Alonso et al. 2007).

Governance and coordination

By definition, industrial ecology requires that a number of firms coordinate their activities to enable the exchange of materials and energy. Such exchanges are at the heart of economic systems. Markets, networks, and organizations are distinct mechanisms to coordinate them, each with their specific advantages and disadvantages (Williamson 1975; Powell 1990). The ubiquity of such mechanisms in economic systems has led to the approach of 'uncovering symbiosis', where 'kernels' of environmentally sustainable linkages in regional clusters are discovered and then provide a basis for further development (Chertow 2007).

Implicitly or explicitly, the concept of industrial ecology adds two specific conditions to such coordination:

1. it signifies an increase of linkages over time among economic actors (loop closing), or increased importance of an existing link (increased flow);
2. the linkages must result in improved environmental performance of the larger system.

Industrial ecology researchers differ in the extent to which they consider these conditions as necessary or sufficient. The first condition implies that industrial ecology must be studied over time. An important part of the literature seeks to gain insight into the process through which actors in industrial systems can increase the closing of loops. Based on widely used economic models of individual and organizational actors, the consequences of incentive structures and transaction costs can be assessed for their effect on loop closing by economic actors (Andrews 2000).

Each of the different system boundaries—product chain, regional cluster, sector of industry—provides different initial conditions in terms of the existing coordinating structure (Boons & Baas 1997). Several case studies indicate that the process to develop this initial structure in such a way that it supports increased linkages is a long one: it requires the building of trust but also of concrete organizational arrangements for knowledge exchange, standard setting, and monitoring (Ehrenfeld & Gertler 1997; Seuring 2004; Ashton 2009).

The second condition adds that the linkages must in some way contribute to increased environmental sustainability. This makes industrial ecology an issue of governance, that is, the coordination of the activities of actors to solve a collective problem (Sharfman et al. 1997; Koppenjan & Klijn 2004). This condition adds complexity because it introduces the need to balance environmental concerns and economic value. The extent to which the integration of these values can be accomplished primarily by market mechanisms has been a continuing debate in the field. Desrochers (2000) has argued vigorously for this possibility, but his definition of industrial ecology is narrow (see Boons 2008a). More moderately, it is often argued that industrial ecology depends on the initiative of firms to engage in such exchanges.

At the same time, governmental control is not seen by many as a viable alternative to reliance on market exchanges; in fact, it is often revealed as a barrier to realizing industrial ecology. Moreover, based on an extensive survey of eco-industrial parks, Gibbs et al. (2005) found that most of these did not materialize beyond shared visions and plans. In the case of extended producer responsibility (EPR), a strategy that assigns responsibility to firms for the environmental impacts of their products throughout their life cycle especially at end of life, results have been modest and often fail to meet initial goals. Rather than have firms incorporate life-cycle impacts into their core concerns (thus providing an incentive to design for environment), the dominant response has been to develop organizations for dealing collectively with post-consumer waste on behalf of individual firms (Lifset & Lindhqvist 2008).

In another vein, authors have searched for actors serving as information brokers and facilitators in regional networks (Burström & Korhonen 2001). A successful example of such a broker is the National Industrial Symbiosis Program (NISP)[5] in the UK, which provides information and actively connects firms that can exchange waste streams (Paquin & Howard-Grenville 2009).

A complex systems approach has been proposed by several authors to provide a theoretical basis for these insights into various governance mechanisms (Boons 2008b; Chertow 2009; Dijkema & Basson 2009). Such a systems approach makes clear the conditions for self-organization, which in terms of industrial ecology would mean that firms voluntarily develop linkages that increase the environmental sustainability of the system. Such self-organization requires that certain conditions are fulfilled, such as availability of information about the supply of waste and potential uses within the system, but also the existence of legal institutions that allow contracts among private parties dealing with wastes. Actors may also be able to organize a system of self-governance, where they develop monitoring and sanctioning rules to guide their activities, as in the case of certification systems such as Fair Trade coffee, where economic actors have developed standards that are monitored by independent auditors (Raynolds 2002). In terms of complex systems, governmental agencies can be viewed as external agents that may seek to manage the system. They may try to do so by planning future linkages, but

---

[5] See http://www.nisp.org.uk

they can also manage by providing the conditions that then lead to specific patterns of self-organization or governance.

Each of these governance types (self-organization, self-governance, governments setting conditions, external control) can be instrumental in providing the coordination necessary for industrial ecology. Their application may change in the same system over time, as in the case of the industrial complex in the Rotterdam harbor (Boons 2008b); also, industrial systems are embedded in different national economic and political systems, which leads to different governance types being dominant in different countries (Heeres et al. 2004; Zhu et al. 2007).

Operations and Technology

Industrial ecology intersects with operations management and research primarily in three ways:

1. through its focus on resource efficiency,
2. through efforts to accomplish loop-closing,[6] and
3. through insights that emerge from the ecological analogy.

The link with technology arises from industrial ecology's strong interest in design as a vehicle for environmental improvement on the product and process level and in technological innovation as the basis for improvements in resource efficiency. Product design takes on a character distinctive of industrial ecology when the design is done in a life-cycle framework (Keoleian & Menerey 1993). However, the attention to design is not limited to conventional product development. The supra-firm focus of industrial ecology also leads to considerations of design of product chains, symbiotic networks and infrastructure, in pursuit of resource efficiency and the closing of loops. Much of what industrial ecology contributes here is in the form of substantive environmental assessment and in analytical tools for assessment and improvement.

Concern with efficient use of resources is a central preoccupation of industrial ecology. At the conceptual level, the focus is motivated by a broad-based concern with environmental sustainability and, more specifically, by the implications of the ecological analogy. Resources in this context can be defined narrowly as raw materials or, in the view of some, more broadly to include ecosystem services (Ayres 1993). The focus in industrial ecology on resource efficiency typically extends beyond the boundaries of individual firms to encompass supply chains, entire product life cycles, and industrial clusters. Much of the research and practice at the firm level falls under the rubric of cleaner production, a field that emerged in Europe at roughly the same time as industrial ecology, and whose boundaries and membership vis-à-vis industrial ecology are blurry (Jackson 2002). Cleaner production, tracing its routes to pollution prevention, a related

---

⁶ See Klassen & Vachon ([Chapter 15] this volume) for further insights on resource efficiency and Abbey & Guide ([Chapter 16] this volume) for further insights on loop-closing.

field in the US, started with a focus on process and firm-level reduction of toxic materials use and similar environmental improvements (e.g. energy and water efficiency) and subsequently broadened to encompass life-cycle-wide concerns of the sort that are central to industrial ecology. The notion of eco-efficiency emerged in the 1990s as a business response to environmental pressures. By asking how companies might produce a given level of output with less environmental damage or fewer environmental resources, the business community sought to identify win-win opportunities. The concept was subsequently taken up by scholars and eventually became the focus of a ongoing research literature (Huppes & Ishikawa 2005).[7]

The analysis of eco-efficiency is very similar to cost benefit analysis (CBA) where either the costs or the benefits are expressed in terms of environmental damage or resource consumption, that is, the cost can be expressed, for example, in tons of pollutant released or the benefits expressed as reduction of those same releases. Eco-efficiency differs from cost benefit analysis (CBA) in the greater attention given to the specifics of the environmental impacts and in the practice of avoiding monetization of the impacts so as to minimize loss of crucial biophysical information in the metric.

The overlap between operational issues as seen through an eco-efficiency lens and technology issues is substantial. As noted above, technological innovation and change are viewed as important means of increasing the efficiency of resource use or environmental impact reduction. Dematerialization, the reduction in the quantity of materials used to accomplish a task, is typically discussed on the level of industrial sectors, regions and economies (Wernick & Ausubel 1995; Adriaanse et al. 1997). It is viewed as a means of decoupling resource use from economic growth.

The business implications of such a perspective are clearest in sectoral analyses. For example, Wernick et al. (1997) examined the technological improvements in the forest products chain, assessing the reductions in materials intensity of use at each life-cycle stage with an eye to asking "how much land can be spared for nature" as a result of improvements in resource efficiency. Ruth & Harrington (1997) modeled the paper industry's goals ("Agenda 2020") for reduction of energy use and utilization of recycled content, and quantified the extremely ambitious changes that would be entailed by the simultaneous pursuit of those objectives.

In a different vein, attention to life-cycle management (LCM) has grown in industrial ecology. Viewed as the managerial analog to life-cycle assessment (Jensen & Remmen 2006), life-cycle management is a portfolio of policies, systems, concepts, tools and data for a product-based approach to environmental management. It has developed in parallel to other research that takes a product chain perspective—reverse logistics and closed-loop supply chains topics dominated by business scholars based in operations research who investigate the management of product returns (Abbey & Guide [Chapter 16] this volume; Guide & Van Wassenhove 2009).

---

[7] See the special issue of the Journal of Industrial Ecology on eco-efficiency, volume 9, number 4, for an extended treatment of eco-efficiency.

Marketing

The relationship of industrial ecology to marketing began with the environmental assessment of products, providing the analytical tools and foundation to address the knotty question of "Is X green?" or put another way, the paper-vs-plastic debate (writ large). Thus, industrial ecology has critical connections to green marketing, environmental labeling, and environmental certification. More recently, industrial ecology has attended to questions of consumption, paying greater attention to the intersection of consumer behavior and environmental impact (including the rebound effect).

The focus of much research in industrial ecology has been the evaluation of the environmental impact of materials, processes, products, technologies, and facilities. Typically, evaluation has been accomplished using life-cycle assessment, but other methods such as ecological foot-printing and eco-efficiency analysis are also used. Thus, industrial ecology provides the analytical or scientific basis for efforts to substantiate green marketing claims.

Green marketing and the environmental claims on which it relies are frequently contested, either because the claims make or imply a position of superiority relative to competitors or because, in the often politicized world of business and environment, they raise policy issues about the environmental desirability of products, and thus become the focus of disagreements with activist groups or governments. The relative environmental superiority or even non-comparative claims of benefits are inherently subject to dispute for a variety of reasons: (1) assessments are sensitive to how evaluations are framed, especially with respect to system boundaries (i.e. what parts of the economy and what indirect impacts are included in the analysis), (2) key components of the assessment are necessarily value-laden and (3) substantial analytical and data-based uncertainties are unavoidable. Thus, the result is the answer to "is X greener?" is "it depends."

These challenges have led to the development of standards on how to conduct life-cycle assessments (ISO 2009), which harmonize practice in the field but cannot resolve the underlying issues. The challenges also engender sensitivity to the inherently normative nature of such issues, an ongoing debate in the field.

The environmental assessment activities embodied in life-cycle assessments provide a foundation for managerial and public policy approaches based on a life-cycle framework. Life-cycle management is paralleled by integrated product policy (IPP), the life-cycle-based notion in the realm of public policy (Rubik 2006). Among the analytical and programmatic concepts that comprise life-cycle management and integrated product policy, the components of greatest relevance to marketing are environmental labeling and environmental certification. Environmental labeling refers to the provision to consumers of information about the environmental quality or performance of product (see Gershoff & Irwin [Chapter 20] this volume). Some, but not all, environmental labels are based on life-cycle considerations and thus overtly involve tools and concepts from industrial ecology.

Environmental certification is closely related to labeling in that it is a means to influence consumer and producer behavior through the provision of information. While labels are often certified in various fashions, and certification usually leads to some sort of label, certification, as the term is typically used in environmental management and policy, differs from labeling in that it typically is initiated or run by non-governmental organizations (NGOs) and has generally focused on the manner in which natural resource-based commodities are harvested, processed and/or marketed. Because of their origins and focus on mitigating the impacts of resource extraction, they less typically involve a life-cycle framework in their assessment.

Industrial ecology is increasingly broadening its ambit to include the relationship of consumption to environmental outcomes, and thus intersecting with marketing not only on the supply side, but also on the demand side. The distinctive contributions of industrial ecology in the understanding of the environmental role of consumption lie in placing consumption in the life-cycle framework, in quantifying the magnitude of environmental impacts by consumption category (Tukker & Jansen 2006) and in expanding and reframing discussions of the rebound effect (Hertwich 2005). The use phase of products (distinguished from the production and disposal phases) has distinctive environmental impacts; for example, tailpipe emissions from automobiles and waste water from home appliances, as well as subtler environmental emissions such as the portion of tires that are released in the course of normal wear and become non-point source water pollution associated with roadways.

The identification of food, mobility, and housing as the product categories responsible for a disproportionate share of environmental impacts across the economy (Huppes et al. 2006) has potentially strong implications for prioritization of environmental policy-making and thus for corporate strategy and marketing. The rebound effect, a concept famously developed by Jevons in the early 1900s, and subsequently explored by energy analysts (Greening et al. 2000), poses a different sort of challenge for marketing. The rebound effect refers to increase in demand for services that can occur as a result of the increased efficiency of a product. As a result of income, substitution, and a variety of macroeconomic mechanisms, improvements in efficiency can have perverse effects, either leading to resource savings that are less than would be otherwise expected, or even net increases in demand. Because industrial ecology employs a multiple-attribute environmental framework, the implications of the rebound effect are more complicated, with both positive and negative results (Hertwich 2005).

Industrial ecology, through its contributions to identification of green products and related endeavors of communicating those findings to the public and assessing the magnitude and environmental significance of consumption, can thus inform, shape, and even constrain corporate marketing activities.

Accounting and finance

Industrial ecology views the world primarily through a biophysical, especially a material-based, lens. This engenders the need for new and expanded measurement systems.

Industrial ecology has substantial implications for accounting and finance as it requires accounting methods that fit with its more encompassing system boundaries.

Tools in industrial ecology range in application from very narrow scales—unit processes, facilities, and firms—to broader, supra-firm groupings and entities—supply and product chains, industrial clusters, cities and regions, industry sectors, and national economies. These tools thus complement conventional accounting approaches, posing the challenge of integrating the biophysically oriented accounting with conventional approaches.

Material flow analysis (MFA), a key tool in industrial ecology, quantifies the inputs, outputs, and accumulation of materials at various scales. Substance-flow analysis (SFA), one form of material flow analysis, can be applied at the narrowest and most detailed level. Substance-flow analysis tracks the stocks and flows of a specific substance or material through a specified system on a comprehensive basis. Substance-flow analysis emerged in part from efforts to reduce the use of toxic substances in manufacturing, which in turn relied on materials accounting that has sometimes been mandated by government.[8] A related process- and firm-level form of accounting known as materials flow cost analysis (MFCA), which measures material flows in both physical and monetary terms, also emerged in the last decade, but has been less widely adopted. Materials flow cost analysis allocates costs on the basis of material flows as a means of identifying opportunities for resource efficiency (Jasch 2009).

The detailed accounting for specific substance flows can be used to identify emissions of pollutants that are overlooked activities based on end-of-pipe controls, allowing firms to improve process efficiency and to meet emissions controls targets or obligations.[9] It can also enable innovative approaches to materials use such as chemical management services (CMS) where "a customer contracts with a service provider to supply and manage the customer's chemicals and related services and where the provider's compensation is tied primarily to quantity and quality of services delivered, not chemical volume" (CMS Forum 2010). Material flow analysis can take a second form, sometimes known as economy-wide material flow analysis (EW-MFA) or material and energy flow analysis (MEFA). In EW-MFA, all materials are tracked through an entity or geographic region, providing a quantitative description of the biophysical resource flows in aggregate. EW-MFA is most typically applied at the regional or national level as a means of understanding trends (or their absence) such as dematerialization.[10] While there are

[8] The US Toxic Release Inventory (TRI) contains information on toxic chemical releases and waste management activities in industry (http://www.epa.gov/TRI/), but usually does not generate sufficiently comprehensive data to stand as the basis for SFA. Massachussetts and New Jersey, however, have laws mandating corporate materials accounting which provide more of a basis for SFA.

[9] See, for example, the identification of "missing" mercury in the chlor-alkali production process by Ayres (1997).

[10] Accounting methods in industrial ecology intersect with macroeconomic accounting—national accounts—via the System of Environmental and Economic Accounts (SEEA) and National Accounting Matrix including Environmental Accounts (NAMEA), but the import for business is less immediate (Pedersen & de Haan 2006).

occasional efforts to apply EW-MFA at the firm level (e.g. Liedtke et al. 1998), and a method of environmental assessment has been proposed for products and processes based on EW-MFA,[11] this tool has been used more for scholarly and policy research than for business management.

Much of the accounting in industrial ecology focuses at scales larger than the individual firm. This is especially salient in the use of input–output tables and input–output analysis (IOA), which is a method of economic analysis that describes the structure of an economy in terms of interactions among industries, and is typically applied to regional and national economies. Because it allows the tracking of resource use through the stages of production across the economy, input–output analysis is increasingly being adopted in industrial ecology as a means of capturing indirect environmental impacts on a comprehensive basis in life-cycle assessment and as a stand-alone form of analysis in its own right through the augmentation of monetary input–output tables with environmental and resource data (Hendrickson et al. 2006; Suh 2009). Input–output analysis can be applied at the firm level (e.g. Lin & Polenske 1998), but is not common.

The practical implications of input–output analysis, especially when used as part of life-cycle assessment, is that environmental assessment of products (or services, facilities, etc.) can be done on an economy-wide basis, encompassing the impacts of all tiers of a supply chain, not merely those that are salient to observers. Lenzen (2000) has shown that conventional process based life-cycle assessment, by excluding environmental impacts from higher-order upstream stages of the production process, can suffer "truncation" errors on the order of 50 percent. Thus notions of where environmental hotspots lie in product life cycles or industrial sectors may be invalidated. Assessment tools based on input–output analysis with the capability to quantify environmental impacts of supply chains on a rigorous, replicable basis are emerging that have direct relevance for corporate environmental management (Wiedmann et al. 2009).

Other environmentally oriented forms of accounting are consistent with and complementary to industrial ecology, but do not emerge from its core focus. Total cost assessment (TCA) is a form of capital budgeting that seeks to quantify, not only those costs and savings conventionally considered in corporate cost accounting, but also those associated with environmental impacts. Such costs are often hidden in overhead and not allocated to the source of the impact (Rosselot & Allen 2002). Life-cycle costing (LCC)—not to be confused with life-cycle assessment—is used to assess the cost of a project from its inception to its retirement. Because environmental costs and savings often arise in later stages of the life of a project rather than in the purchase or first costs (e.g. durable goods reveal their value through their longevity and energy efficient goods exhibit their net savings in later years of the product's usage), life-cycle costing has important environmental implications, even if the technique was not developed for environmental purposes.

Industrial ecology has a less distinctive connection to finance. The question of whether and how industrial ecology concepts and approaches can be applied to business

---

[11] Material intensity per unit of service (MIPS) was proposed by Schmidt-Bleek et al. (1998) as a way of measuring resource use scaled to the quantity of desired services delivered.

activities on a profitable basis is a key concern in the field (Esty & Porter 1998; Jackson & Clift 1998) and there is an emerging interest in identifying business models that mesh well with the practices that are emblematic of industrial ecology (e.g. loop-closing, industrial symbiosis). The premise in industrial ecology that environmental gains can be accompanied by financial gains has generated contributions to the does-it-pay-to-be-green literature (King & Lenox 2001; Koellner et al. 2007; Russo & Minto [Chapter 2] this volume).

DISCUSSION AND CONCLUSION

Industrial ecology provides a rich set of concepts and tools that enables a systemic analysis of the environmental impact of industrial systems. Through its focus on systems that have industrial processes at their heart, it is of central concern to the study of firms within the natural environment. There are several contributions that the field has to offer. First, it provides a welcome antidote to the danger of conceptualizing environmental management and policy mainly in social terms. It also helps to avoid inadequate operationalizations of the environmental impact of organizations and larger social systems (Whiteman & Cooper 2000; Baumann & Tillman 2004). Through its explicit focus on material and energy streams, the concept of industrial ecology allows the interplay between social and ecological systems to take a more central role.

A second contribution is based on the systems perspective. While business administration has concepts that match this perspective (most notably organization ecology; (Aldrich & Ruef 2006; Dimaggio & Powell 1983), influential theories such as the natural resource based view (Hart 1995) have a tendency to deal with firms in an atomistic way. The systemic perspective is useful in contextualizing business activities within a wider social system (Hoffman 2003).

The anchoring of industrial ecology in a physical conception of environment that challenges the monopoly of conventional approaches to management is also a key source of a central dilemma for the field—how to incorporate social, political, and economic considerations while still maintaining its distinctive identity and contribution. The field's aspirations to systematic analysis, even a kind of technical holism, demand that nonphysical factors be addressed. Industrial ecology has not yet, however, developed consensus about the extent to which its boundaries can be expanded while retaining a coherent character. This tension has played out, for example, in research on social and behavioral factors related to sustainable consumption (Lifset 2008).

Social science research is thus beginning to be part of the interdisciplinary dialog in the field (Boons & Howard-Grenville 2009). Research on business administration may help to further develop the field of industrial ecology. The fields are similar in their inclusion of a variety of concepts, tools, and system boundaries. With respect to the latter, research on firms has led to useful insights on the way in which firm behavior interacts to produce business networks and sectoral and national business systems (Whitley 1998). Given the longer tradition of research on these topics in business administration, industrial ecologists can usefully incorporate lessons learned there.

Also, the issue of power asymmetries remains underexplored in the analysis of industrial ecosystems. Economic factors may force others into patterns of behavior they would not normally choose, and these may affect the amount and distribution of environmental impact of industrial ecosystems (Jackson & Clift 1998). The study of organizations has a rich tradition in exploring questions of power within and among organizations (Clegg 1989), and the field of industrial ecology would do well to include such insights in order to further build towards realistic models of social systems and the way in which these produce material and energy flows.

REFERENCES

Adriaanse, A. Bizingezu, S., Hammond, A., Moriguichi, Y., Rudenburg, E., Rogich, D., & Schütz, H. (1997). *Resource Flows: The Material Basis of Industrial Economies.* Washington, DC: World Resources Institute.

Aldrich, H. & Ruef, M. (2006). *Organizations Evolving.* Thousand Oaks: Sage.

Alonso, E., Gregory, J., Field, F., & Kirchain, R. (2007). "Material Availability and the Supply Chain: Risks, Effects, and Responses," *Environmental Science & Technology,* 41(19): 6649–6656.

Andrews, C. J. (2000). "Building a Micro Foundation for Industrial Ecology," *Journal of Industrial Ecology,* 4(3): 35–52.

Ashton, W. S. (2009). "The Structure, Function, and Evolution of a Regional Industrial Ecosystem," *Journal of Industrial Ecology,* 13(2): 228–246.

Ayres, R. U. (1993). "Cowboys, Cornucopians and Long-Run Sustainability." *Ecological Economics,* 8(3): 189–207.

——— (1997). "The Life-Cycle of Chlorine, Part I: Chlorine Production and the Chlorine-Mercury Connection," *Journal of Industrial Ecology,* 1(1): 81–94.

Baumann, H. & Tillman, A. (2004). *The Hitchhiker's Guide to LCA: An Orientation in Life Cycle Assessment Methodology and Application.* Lund: Studentlitteratur AB.

Boons, F. A. A. (2009). *Creating Ecological Value: An Evolutionary Approach to Business Strategies and the Natural Environment,* Cheltenham: Edward Elgar Publishing

——— (2008a). "History's Lessons: A Critical Assessment of the Desrochers Papers," *Journal of Industrial Ecology,* 12(2): 148–158.

——— (2008b). "Self-Organization and Sustainability: The Emergence of a Regional Industrial Ecology," *Emergence: Complexity and Organization,* 10(2): 41–48.

——— & Baas, L. W. (1997). "Types of Industrial Ecology: The Problem of Coordination," *Journal of Cleaner Production,* 5(1–2): 79–86.

Boons, F. A. A. & Howard-Grenville, J. (2009). *The Social Embeddedness of Industrial Ecology.* Cheltenham: Edward Elgar.

Burström, F. & Korhonen, J. (2001). "Municipalities and Industrial Ecology: Reconsidering Municipal Environmental Management," *Sustainable Development,* 9(1): 36–46.

Chertow, M. R. (2007). "'Uncovering' Industrial Symbiosis," *Journal of Industrial Ecology,* 11(1): 11–30.

——— (2009). "Dynamics of Geographically Based Industrial Ecosystems," in M. Ruth & B. Davidsdottir (eds.), *The Dynamics Of Regions And Networks In Industrial Ecosystems.* Cheltenham: Edward Elgar Publishing, 6–27.

Clegg, S. (1989). *Frameworks of Power*. London: Sage Publications.

CMS Forum (2010). Defining CMS. Available at <http://www.cmsforum.org/cms_definition.html> [Accessed April 28, 2010].

Commoner, B. (1997). "The Relation between Industrial and Ecological Systems," *Journal of Cleaner Production*, 5(1–2): 125–129.

Desrochers, P. (2000). "Market Processes and the Closing of 'Industrial Loops': A Historical Reappraisal," *Journal of Industrial Ecology*, 4(1): 29–43.

Dijkema, G. P. J. & Basson, L. (2009). "Complexity and Industrial Ecology," *Journal of Industrial Ecology*, 13(2): 157–164.

Dimaggio, P. J. & Powell, W. W. (1983). "The Iron Cage Revisited: Institutional Isomorphism and Collective Rationality in Organizational Fields," *American Sociological Review*, 48(2): 147–160.

Ehrenfeld, J. R. & Gertler, N. (1997). "Industrial Ecology in Practice: The Evolution of Interdependence at Kalundborg," *Journal of Industrial Ecology*, 1(1): 67–79.

Erkman, S. (1997). "Industrial Ecology: An Historical View," *Journal of Cleaner Production*, 5(1–2): 1–10.

Esty, D. C. & Porter, M. E. (1998). "Industrial Ecology and Competitiveness: Strategic Implications for the Firm," *Journal of Industrial Ecology*, 2(1): 35–43.

Finster, M., Eagan, P. & Hussey, D. (2001). "Linking Industrial Ecology with Business Strategy: Creating Value for Green Product Design," *Journal of Industrial Ecology*, 5(3): 107–125.

Frosch, R. & Gallopoulos, N. (1989). "Strategies for Manufacturing," *Scientific American*, 261(3): 94–102.

Gereffi, G., Humphrey, J. & Sturgeon, T. (2005). "The Governance of Global Value Chains," *Review of International Political Economy*, 12(1): 78–104.

Gibbs, D., Deutz, P., & Proctor, A. (2005). "Industrial Ecology and Eco-Industrial Development: A Potential Paradigm for Local and Regional Development?" *Regional Studies*, 39(2): 171–183.

Green, K. & Randles, S. (2006). *Industrial Ecology and Spaces of Innovation*. Cheltenham: Edward Elgar Publishing.

Greening, L. A., Greene, D. L., & Difiglio, C. (2000). "Energy Efficiency and Consumption—the Rebound Effect: A Survey," *Energy Policy*, 28(6–7): 389–401.

Guide, V. D. R. & Van Wassenhove, L. N. (2009). "OR FORUM—The Evolution of Closed-Loop Supply Chain Research," *Operations Research*, 57(1): 10–18.

Hart, S. L. (1995). "A Natural-Resource-Based View of the Firm," *The Academy of Management Review*, 20(4): 986–1014.

Heeres, R., Vermeulen, W., & De Walle, F. (2004). "Eco-Industrial Park Initiatives in the USA and the Netherlands: First Lessons. *Journal of Cleaner Production*, 12(8–10): 985–995.

Hendrickson, C., Lave, L., & Matthews, S. (2006). *Environmental Life Cycle Assessment of Goods and Services: An Input-Output Approach*. Washington DC: Resources for the Future.

Hertwich, E. G. (2005). "Consumption and the Rebound Effect: An Industrial Ecology Perspective," *Journal of Industrial Ecology*, 9(1–2): 85–98.

Hoffman, A. J. (2003). "Linking Social Systems Analysis to the Industrial Ecology Framework," *Organization & Environment*, 16(1): 66–86.

Huesemann, M. H. (2003). "Recognizing the Limits of Environmental Science and Technology," *Environmental Science and Technology*, 37(13) 259–261.

Huppes, G. & Ishikawa, M. (2005). "A Framework for Quantified Eco-Efficiency Analysis," *Journal of Industrial Ecology*, 9(4): 25–41.

——, De Koning, A., Suh, S., Heijungs, R., Van Oers, L., Nielsen, P., & Guinée, J. (2006). "Environmental Impacts of Consumption in the European Union: High-Resolution Input-Output Tables with Detailed Environmental Extensions," *Journal of Industrial Ecology*, 10(3): 129–146.

ISO (International Organization of Standardization). (2009). *Environmental Management: The ISO 14000 Family of International Standards.* Geneva: ISO.

Jackson, T. (2002). "Industrial Ecology and Cleaner Production," in R. U. Ayres & L. W. Ayres (eds.), *A Handbook of Industrial Ecology.* Cheltenham: Edward Elgar Publishing, 36–43.

—— & Clift, R. (1998). "Where's the Profit in Industrial Ecology? *Journal of Industrial Ecology,* 2(1): 3–5.

Jasch, C. (2009). *Environmental and Material Flow Cost Accounting: Principles and Procedures.* New York: Springer Verlag.

Jensen, A. A. & Remmen, A. (2006). *Background Report for a UNEP Guide to LIFE CYCLE MANAGEMENT—A Bridge to Sustainable Products.* Paris: United Nations Environment Programme.

Keoleian, G. A. & Menerey, D. (1993). *Life Cycle Design Guidance Manual: Environmental Requirements and the Product System.* Washington DC: U.S. Environmental Protection Agency.

King, A. A. & Lenox, M. J. (2001). "Does it Really Pay to be Green? An Empirical Study of Firm Environmental and Financial Performance," *Journal of Industrial Ecology,* 5(1): 105–116.

Koellner, T., Suh, S., Weber, O., Moser, C., & Scholz, R. (2007). "Environmental Impacts of Conventional and Sustainable Investment Funds Compared Using Input-Output Life-Cycle Assessment," *Journal of Industrial Ecology,* 11(3): 41–60.

Koppenjan, J. F. M. & Klijn, E. (2004). *Managing Uncertainties in Networks: A Network approach to problem solving and decision making.* London. Routledge.

Lenzen, M. (2000). "Errors in Conventional and Input-Output-Based Life-Cycle Inventories," *Journal of Industrial Ecology,* 4(4): 127–148.

Liedtke, C., Rohn, C., Kuhndt, M., & Nickel, R. (1998). "Applying Material Flow Accounting: Ecoauditing and Resource Management at the Kambium Furniture Workshop," *Journal of Industrial Ecology,* 2(3): 131–147.

Lifset, R. (2008). "The Quantitative and the Qualitative in Industrial Ecology," *Journal of Industrial Ecology,* 12(2): 133–135.

—— & Lindhqvist, T. (2008). "Producer Responsibility at a Turning Point?" *Journal of Industrial Ecology,* 12(2): 144–147.

Lin, X. & Polenske, K. R. (1998). "Input-Output Modeling of Production Processes for Business Management," *Structural Change and Economic Dynamics,* 9(2). 205–226

Luke, T. W. (2001). "SUVs and the Greening of Ford," *Organization & Environment,* 14(3): 311–335.

Mont, O., Singhal, P., & Fadeeva, Z. (2006). "Chemical Management Services in Sweden and Europe: Lessons for the Future," *Journal of Industrial Ecology,* 10(1–2): 279–292.

Oldenburg, K. U. & Geiser, K. (1997). "Pollution Prevention and…or Industrial Ecology?" *Journal of Cleaner Production,* 5(1–2): 103–108.

Paquin, R. & Howard-Grenville, J. (2009). "Facilitating Regional Industrial Symbiosis: Network Growth in the UK's National Industrial Symbiosis Programme," in F. A. A. Boons & J. Howard-Grenville (eds.), *The Social Embeddedness of Industrial Ecology.* Cheltenham: Edward Elgar Publishing, 103–127.

Pedersen, O. G. P. & de Haan, M. (2006). "The System of Environmental and Economic Accounts: 2003 and the Economic Relevance of Physical Flow Accounting," *Journal of Industrial Ecology,* 10(1–2): 19–42.

Porter, M. E. (1985). *Competitive Advantage: Creating and Sustaining Superior Performance.* New York: Free Press.

—— (1990). *The Competitive Advantage of Nations*. New York: Free Press.

Powell, W. W. (1990). "Neither Market nor Hierarchy: Network Forms of Organization," *Research in Organizational Behavior*, 1: 295–336.

Raynolds, L.T. (2002). "Consumer/Producer Links in Fair Trade Coffee Networks," *Sociologia Ruralis*, 42(4): 404–424.

Rosselot, K. S. & Allen, D. (2002). "Environmental Cost Accounting," in D. T. Allen & D. Shonnard (eds.), *Green Engineering: Environmentally Conscious Design of Chemical Processes*. Upper Saddle River: Prentice Hall PTR, 397–416.

Rubik, F. (2006). Policy Profile: Integrated Product Policy: Between Conceptual and Instrumental Approaches in Europe," *European Environment*, 16(5): 307–302.

Ruth, M. & Harrington, T. (1997). "Dynamics of Material and Energy Use in U.S. Pulp and Paper Manufacturing," *Journal of Industrial Ecology*, 1(3): 147–168.

Schmidt-Bleek, F., Bringezu, S., Hinterberger, F., Liedtke, C., Spangenberg, J. H., & Welfens, M. J. (1998). *MAIA, Einfürung In Die Material-Intensitätsanalyse Nach Dem MIPS-Konzept (MAIA— Introduction: The Material-Intensity Analysis According to the MIPS Concept)*. Bern: Birkhäuser.

Seuring, S. (2004). "Integrated Chain Management and Supply Chain Management Comparative Analysis and Illustrative Cases," *Journal of Cleaner Production*, 12(8–10): 1059–1071.

—— & Müller, M. (2008). "From a Literature Review to a Conceptual Framework for Sustainable Supply Chain Management," *Journal of Cleaner Production*, 16(15) 1699–1710.

Sharfman, M., Ellington, R. T. & Meo, M. (1997). "The Next Step in Becoming 'Green': Life-Cycle Oriented Environmental Management," *Business Horizons*, 40(3): 13–22.

Suh, S. (2009). *Handbook of Input-Output Economics in Industrial Ecology*. Dordrecht: Springer.

Tukker, A. & Jansen, B. (2006). "Environmental Impacts of Products: A Detailed Review of Studies," *Journal of Industrial Ecology*, 10(3): 159–182.

Wernick, I. K. & Ausubel, J. H. (1995). "National Materials Flows and the Environment," *Annual Review of Energy and the Environment*, 20(1): 463–492.

—— Waggoner, P. E. & Ausubel, J. H. (1997). "Searching for Leverage to Conserve Forests: The Industrial Ecology of Wood Products in the United States," *Journal of Industrial Ecology*, 1(3): 125–145.

White, R. (1994). "Preface", in B. R. Allenby & D. Richards (eds.) *The Greening of Industrial Ecosystems*. Washington, D.C.: National Academy Press.

Whiteman, G. & Cooper, W. H. (2000). "Ecological Embeddedness," *The Academy of Management Journal*, 43(6): 1265–1282.

Whitley, R. (1998). "Internationalization and Varieties of Capitalism: The Limited Effects of Cross-National Coordination of Economic Activities on the Nature of Business Systems," *Review of International Political Economy*, 5(3): 445–481.

Wiedmann, T. O., Lenzen, M. & Barrett, J. R. (2009). "Companies on the Scale: Comparing and Benchmarking the Sustainability Performance of Businesses," *Journal of Industrial Ecology*, 13(3): 361–383.

Williamson, O. E. (1975). *Markets and Hierarchies, Analysis and Antitrust Implications: A Study in the Economics of Internal Organization*. New York: Free Press.

Zhu, Q., Lowe, E., Wei, Y-A., & Barnes, D. (2007). Industrial Symbiosis in China: A Case Study of the Guitang Group. *Journal of Industrial Ecology*, 11(1): 31–42.

CHAPTER 18

INFORMATION SYSTEMS, BUSINESS, AND THE NATURAL ENVIRONMENT: CAN DIGITAL BUSINESS TRANSFORM ENVIRONMENTAL SUSTAINABILITY?

NIGEL P. MELVILLE

WE live in an increasingly digital world. Yet the scholarly discourse on business and the natural environment has proceeded, for the most part, according to business as usual. Perhaps this was reasonable in earlier eras, when information systems (IS) played only a modest role in enabling business processes, such as the use of decision-support systems to support regulatory compliance. However, in the Internet era, IS has shifted from being an enabler to being transformative. Gen. Y grew up on the Internet, lives on texting, and expects all aspects of their lives to be digitally and socially networked. Indeed, from music to financial services, industry after industry is being transformed by digital business innovations. Is digital business poised to transform environmental sustainability, and if so, how? In this chapter, I will examine this question.

In the next section I provide a brief review of the evolution of IS for environmental sustainability, examining IS as both hero (transformative force for the better) and villain (voracious energy user, e-waste, etc.). Then, I examine three ways in which IS might transform environmental sustainability by changing individual beliefs, transforming environmental practices, and ultimately impacting both the financial and environmental performance of organizations. Next, I describe complexities, challenges, and business opportunities in a specific context: carbon emission data management at a large university. I conclude by providing a few examples of how researchers might contribute to knowledge in this dynamic, emergent domain of environmental sustainability.

INFORMATION SYSTEMS AND ENVIRONMENTAL SUSTAINABILITY: FROM AUTOMATION TO TRANSFORMATION

Managers in industries as diverse as elevator manufacturing and haute couture fashion have applied information systems innovatively to automate business processes, process and distribute information, and in many cases, transform the very basis of competition. Consider the music industry, which until recently was controlled by a few large record labels and distributors, but is now controlled in large part by consumer products companies such as Apple and Amazon. Study of how such IS-enabled innovation changes industries suggests that early applications focus on automation and efficiency of existing business processes, which gives way to informating them by centralizing, processing, and distributing information, which ultimately leads to transformation by changing what is possible and altering the basis of competition (Zuboff 1984). Might this pattern—automate, informate, transform—also apply to environmental sustainability?

In the early 1990s, institutional pressure from regulators (see Delmas & Toffel [Chapter 13] this volume), such as the Eco-Management Audit Scheme in the European Union, led to the emergence of decision-support systems and other types of information systems to reduce paperwork and facilitate compliance (Kleindorfer & Snir 2001; Sen, Moore, & Hess 2000). Another automation example is voluntary environmental standards such as ISO 14001, which triggered the use of information systems to automate aspects of environmental planning and enable firms to meet shifting technological, regulatory, and user requirements (Dray & Foster 1996). Slowly, the era of automation gave way to informating. Business process redesign applied to the health, safety, and environmental function drove adoption of information systems to increase efficiencies, support enhanced collaboration between environmental staff and business units, and improve information and knowledge-sharing (Heptinstall 2001). Another example of informating is observed in supply chains, in which networked information systems enabled strategic benefits in the context of life-cycle oriented environmental management (Shaft et al. 1997; Shaft, Sharfman, & Swahn 2002).

After several decades of automation and informating, we are now observing the beginnings of transformation, towards what might be called Environmental Sustainability 2.0 (ES 2.0). Environmental data that were once considered esoteric and limited to the "Environmental, Health, and Safety" groups within corporations are surging in collection, storage, and distribution. Consider carbon emissions data, which is increasingly demanded by institutional investors as well as customers—respondents to the Carbon Disclosure Project rose tenfold from 235 in 2003 to 2,456 in 2010 (Carbon Disclosure Project 2010). In response to these market pressures (and enacted and potential regulation), innovative firms are adopting carbon management software systems and social media to transform the very idea of what constitutes a "Sustainability Report"—from a static, unidirectional, and text-based approach (do people really read these?), to dynamic, user customizable, graphical, socially networked online dashboards (SAP 2010). Beyond carbon emissions, Intel uses social media such as wikis and blogs to advance its environmental sustainability programs, grow communities of interest across its organization, and promote its efforts to external stakeholders (Rowley 2009). Even Greenpeace realizes that ES 2.0 is the future, developing its "Facebook: Unfriend Coal" campaign that uses Facebook's own social network to foster protest groups to pressure Facebook into using 100 percent renewable energy (Greenpeace 2010). Energy is another area, as described by Tom Friedman: "all the energy programming and monitoring that thousands of global companies are going to be undertaking in the early 21st century to either become carbon neutral or far more energy efficient" is "going to be the next big global business transformation" (Friedman 2007).

Further evidence of an emergent ES 2.0 is contained within the slew of government and industry reports appearing in recent years that analyze the impact of IS on environmental sustainability. For example, the Climate Group's Global e-Sustainability Initiative estimates that IS reduces global carbon emissions by 15 percent of business as usual in 2020 (7.8 GtCO2e) by providing solutions that "enable us to 'see' our energy and emissions in real time and could provide the means for optimizing systems and processes to make them more efficient" (Howard 2008: 7). Similarly, the European Commission's Institute for Prospective Technological Studies finds beneficial environmental impacts in the areas of supply chain management, virtual meetings, e-business, waste management, facilities management, and production process management (Erdmann et al. 2004). Recognizing a lucrative business opportunity, global management consulting firms have also analyzed the role of IS in transforming environmental sustainability (Boccaletti, Loffler, & Oppenheim 2008; Dittmar 2010; Shehadi et al. 2010).

Despite the potential of ES 2.0, decades of IS scholarship suggest two significant hurdles: significant implementation complexity coupled with negative (and often unanticipated) consequences (Markus & Robey 2004). IS may not achieve its intended consequences due to the combination of complexity and managerial incompetence (Avison, Gregor, & Wilson 2006; Nelson 2007). Business managers blame IT personnel, and IT personnel blame managers. In the realm of negative consequences, computers and related equipment have short lifetimes, resulting in a proliferation of e-waste containing toxic materials, such as lead, arsenic, and mercury, which pollute the natural environment (Wong et al. 2007). Also, information systems are themselves energy using, and may even enable new forms of greenwash. Unanticipated outcomes include the possibility that innovative IS used to lower energy may involve a rebound effect (Berkhout, Muskens, & Velthuijsen 2000), or may yield only transient energy reductions (van Dam, Bakker, & van Hal 2010). The use of videoconferencing to reduce carbon emissions may lead to reduced employee attachment to employers. Other unanticipated negative outcomes include user reinvention to subvert management intentions, unreliable data, inaccurate transactions, operational breakdowns, security breaches, and fraud (Markus & Robey 2004). In sum, despite the potential of IS to transform environmental sustainability, significant hurdles exist. Decades of IS scholarship demonstrate the managerial difficulties inherent to converting expected into actual outcomes, and there is no reason to believe that the natural environment context will be any different.

Unfortunately, there is a dearth of research at the nexus of IS, business, and the natural environment (Melville 2010; Watson, Boudreau, & Chen 2010), so we know little about "what is" and "what might be." As a first step to addressing this knowledge gap, we now describe three ways in which IS might transform environmental sustainability by changing individual beliefs, transforming environmental practices, and ultimately impacting both the financial and environmental performance of organizations.

TRANSFORMATIONAL OPPORTUNITIES TO APPLY INFORMATION SYSTEMS: BELIEFS, ACTIONS, OUTCOMES

Core constructs in IS scholarship include systems, people, processes, organizations, and markets. Problems addressing environmental sustainability issues expand this scope to include the natural environment, such as how to reduce e-waste or how to manage carbon emissions. Beyond constructs, expansion in the scope of IS scholarship makes certain mechanisms and theories more relevant, such as altruism, values, and social norms. The belief-action-outcome (BAO) framework is intended to address the expanded scope of IS scholarship by incorporating how agents form their beliefs and expectations with respect to the natural environment and the role of information systems therein, how information systems enable new managerial actions, practices, routines, etc. that address environmental sustainability, and how the former might impact both environmental and organizational performance.

Coleman's (1986, 1994) model of micro-macro relations is an approach to synthesizing macro and micro phenomena and has been extended to the organizational sphere (Felin & Foss 2006). I adapt this approach to the IS and environmental sustainability sphere (Melville 2010). There are three main phenomena of interest. First, beliefs about the environment are shaped by both organizational and societal structure (Andersson, Shivarajan, & Blau 2005), which may be mediated or moderated by information provided within purposively designed information systems. Second, action formation represents the link between beliefs and individual action (Fishbein and Azjen 1975; Sharma & Yetton 2009). Third, combined individual actions within organizations impact macro-level variables such as the behavior of the social system and organization (Berkes & Folke 2000). In sum, organizational and societal spheres inform beliefs about the natural environment (e.g. the salience of energy use reduction to environmental and economic performance), which lead to managerial actions (e.g. adoption of systems for measuring, mitigating, and reporting carbon emissions), which impact the behavior of organizations and the natural environment (e.g. reduced costs and lower carbon footprint), as well as the possibility of reverse causality.

How can information systems transform environmental sustainability belief formation?

Where do beliefs and attitudes about sustainability originate and what role might information systems play in informing such beliefs? Beliefs are what individuals take to be true about the world. They may arise from direct observation of the world or from indirect inference. As suggested by the BAO framework, beliefs may also arise from information provided by an outside source, such as the organization in which an individual works or society in which she lives (see Howard-Grenville & Bertels [Chapter 11] and Lounsbury, Fairclough, & Lee [Chapter 12] this volume). A distinction is drawn by Fishbein & Azjen (1975) between believing that something is true and believing that an outside source has provided information that something is true—salient in the natural environmental context in which information about climate change may be provided by external sources within an information system and rarely observed directly.

In an exploratory study of the formation of ethical beliefs in consumers, Shaw & Clark (1999) conclude that beliefs of individuals are formed jointly by normative beliefs (corporations, religion, social, and social sphere) and information (literature, labeling, advertising, etc.). This finding suggests that information systems, if designed effectively, may play a role in environmental sustainability belief formation, a view consistent with that of Dumont & Franjeska-Nicole (2008): "at the heart of the environmental crisis are the critical issues of information acquisition and attitude formation, for it becomes clear that in the absence of information, one cannot formulate attitudes toward an issue, whether positive or negative in content" (Dumont & Franjeska-Nicole 2008: 5). There is some evidence from the cognitive science literature suggesting that designed IS artifacts might be effective in informing individuals about the environment (Abrahamse et al. 2005; Seligman & Darley 1977). However, despite numerous examples from practice, we could identify few scholarly studies examining the role of information systems in sustainability belief formation. Below, we outline a few nascent research contexts and suggest research directions.

In eco-visualization, information about the environment is presented visually, whether online or in public spaces, to inform, excite, shock, etc. Many examples of eco-visualization are emerging. For example, an information kiosk uses trees with leaves to represent real-time energy use and greenhouse gas emissions of an office building (Holmes 2006). Another example is mapping applications, such as the Urban EcoMap displaying greenhouse gas intensity by zip code within cities such as Amsterdam (Urban Ecomap 2010) as well as those displaying the sources of materials used in everyday goods such as computers (Sourcemap 2010). Design research, which involves building such systems and testing their efficacy (Hevner, March, & Park 2004; Peffers et al. 2007), might be employed to examine whether such systems inform the beliefs of individuals. Human-computer interaction studies might also be conducted to examine the specific details of such systems to determine what is effective and what is not (Blevis 2007). For example, to what extent does personalization and interactivity matter in the formation of beliefs and attitudes, and do demographic characteristics (e.g. age, gender, etc.) make a difference? Findings from cognitive science (see Shu & Bazerman [Chapter 9] this volume) may inform such studies.

Integrated assessment is another approach that may be examined from the perspective of information systems. To what extent might a purposively designed information system that forms the core of integrated assessment information affect environmental sustainability beliefs (Morgan and Dowlatabadi 1996; Pereira and O'Connor 1999)? In one study, researchers designed and developed an information system to provide residents with information about local dimensions of climate change, then conducted focus groups to assess how well the system improved judgment about anthropogenic climate change (Schlumpf et al. 2001). A principal result of focus groups was that the designed IS that enabled the integrated assessment shaped beliefs by improving understanding of the risk and uncertainty associated with climate change as well as enhanced discourse about climate change.

Given the small amount of research that has been done to date, combined with the rapid emergence of innovative IS applications in practice, many research questions arise. First, what types of information systems are effective in shaping beliefs about the environment? Candidates include public display systems visualizing real-time eco-information, social media such as online social networking platforms, personal carbon footprint applications informing individuals of their real-time energy use, and online mapping applications with carbon emission overlays. Each of these system types provides a different user experience, different types of information, and may have a different objective. Thus, there are likely different causal mechanisms at play, which leads us to our second question: what causal mechanisms may be at work across the various information system types? These may include individual phenomena such as the triggering of altruism, social phenomena such as peer-pressure, economic phenomena resulting from identification and presentation of the economic consequences of negative externalities, or other mechanisms. In addition, ego centrism may be mitigated by the presentation of "clear and obvious" data via IS (see Shu & Bazerman [Chapter 9] this volume). Third, what is the role (if any) of information systems in exacerbating or attenuating tension that may exist between beliefs derived from society and those espoused by the organization? Agency issues may arise if the personal environmental values of the manager do not align with those of the company (Eisenhardt 1989; Jensen & Meckling 1976). As underscored by Andersson, Shivarajan, & Blau (2005): "With salary and lifestyle on the line employees may toss their values, beliefs, and norms aside." Fourth, what design methods might be used to design effective information systems that inform sustainability beliefs? The emerging fields of sustainable interaction design (Blevis 2007), design thinking (Brown 2008), and design-science research (Gregor & Jones 2007; Hevner, March, & Park 2004; March & Smith 1995; Peffers et al. 2007) may be helpful in this regard.

What of the negative or unintended consequences of how IS might be used to shape beliefs about business and the natural environment? For example, might new forms of greenwashing emerge as well as other forms of purposely misleading information (cf. Markus & Robey 2004; see also Forbes & Jermier [Chapter 30] this volume). Technology is value-laden, so an application intended to inform the public about climate science objectively might just as easily be applied to trick the public into believing a particular point of view over another. IT itself may foster a techno-determinist view in which managers believe that IT can solve all problems, a form of positive illusion (see Shu & Bazerman [Chapter 9] this volume). Finally, there is a general sense of information-overload on the part of business managers: will new messaging around the natural environment break through the cognitive load? (Kollmuss & Agyeman 2002).

How can information systems transform environmental sustainability practices and strategies?

Information systems research has demonstrated important differences in individual reactions to information technologies that affect their adoption. A long line of research has been conducted employing the technology acceptance-model (TAM) as a conceptual foundation. TAM posits that perceived usefulness and perceived ease of use are antecedents to information systems use, mediated by intention to use (Davis 1989; Davis, Bagozzi, & Warshaw 1989). TAM has been extended in a variety of ways, such as by adding personality traits (Devaraj, Easley, & Crant 2008), gender (Gefen & Straub 1997), and control, motivation, and emotion (Venkatesh 2000). Criticism has also been leveled at TAM. For instance, Bagozzi (2007) points out that the link between intention to use and behavior has not been questioned. He proposes an alternative formulation centered on goal-striving, comprising numerous stages that mediate existing linkages in the TAM framework: intention formation, planning, overcoming obstacles, resisting temptations, monitoring progress, readjusting actions, maintaining willpower, and reassessing goals.

Extensions to the TAM model provide a finer-grained view of how individuals in organizations might adopt information systems for sustainability. For example, if an individual in an organization is mandated to use a new carbon management system, perceived usefulness and perceived ease of use may not fully capture the antecedents to use, which may include altruism and beliefs about the environment. Another example involves the use of wikis as a collaborative information system to motivate employees to engage in eco-friendly commuting options such as public transportation. Even if the wiki is poorly designed, those employees with a strong belief system favoring environmental issues may be more inclined to use the information systems relative to those that have no such beliefs, *ceteris paribus*.

Prior IS research has examined the role of IS and information in shaping behavior outside of the environmental context. Shepherd et al. (1995) examine the role of social comparison enabled by electronic brainstorming systems, finding that such comparison reduces loafing. Feedback is another potentially important dynamic. Examination of feedback in the context of decision-making behavior reveals that IS-based feedback can reinforce desired behavior (Hosack 2007). In the consumer behavior literature, Stern (1999) explicates synergistic effects between information and incentives in the formation of environmental behavior: "the effectiveness of incentive programs depends on factors in the personal domain and can be increased markedly by informational interventions" (Stern 1999: 469). Related to this is the suggestion that behavior change results from information-based feedback in the presence of norm activation (see Shu & Bazerman [Chapter 9] this volume). Examples of informational interventions include the possibility that *how* information is explained or communicated may impact the effectiveness of incentives to conserve electricity, the observation that information and incentives serve different purposes (with differing underlying causal mechanisms), and the importance of the credibility of information provided. Stern concludes that price elasticity of demand can be affected by information provided about an energy conservation incentive program.

In contrast to research into IS and sustainability belief formation, there is a large foundation of extant research into IS and sustainability action formation—including theoretical perspectives and empirical analyses—on which to build. Fruitful approaches might extend TAM literature or incorporate findings from consumer behavior and cognitive science that consider information about sustainability programs in the context of behavior change, but do not consider information systems, with studies from IS that focus on systems and behavior change. IS innovation theory foundations, such as situated change (Orlikowski 1996), innovation routines (Pentland & Feldman 2008), IS assimilation (Fichman & Kemerer 1999), and the tri-core IS innovation model (Swanson 1994) might also be fruitfully applied to the sustainability context.

Several questions arise. First, how might TAM approaches (and extensions) be applied to the sustainability context? Insight into why individuals adopt or do not adopt sustainability-oriented IS contributes both to understanding of IS adoption in general, as well as to the development of effective IS for environmental sustainability applications. Second, given the sometimes opposing perceived outcomes of IS for sustainability (e.g. lowers greenhouse gasses but raises costs), how do individuals justify adoption of such systems within organizations? Third, does the form of information communication within an information system affect environmental sustainability behavior? Fourth, how do incentives combined with information provided via information systems modify behavior? Do findings follow directly from prior research about information, or does the presence of IS introduce new mechanisms and phenomena? Finally, how do personal beliefs and organizational values determine sustainability actions within organizations and what is the role of IS?

Unanticipated consequences are also salient in the realm of individual actions within organizations that may or may not promote environmental sustainability. For example, if environmental management systems are well designed, but the desired accompanying routines are not, then the "folly of designing artifacts while hoping for patterns of action," may arise (Pentland & Feldman 2008). Another possibility is the emergence of tension between personal values and organizational values, which may lead to the unintended consequence of organizational inertia. More obviously, information systems that are intended to improve environmental performance may be co-opted for purposes of greenwashing, for example, by creating a green image that is not backed up by action. Finally, might innovative environmental actions enabled by smart phones, such as flash mobs, do more harm than good?

What is the impact of information systems on environmental and economic performance?

Transforming the practice of business and the natural environment via digital business may have significant impacts on the environmental and economic performance of firms. Such effects may span myriad analysis levels and metrics, from organizational culture to market share. Given space constraints, we examine just a few herein, including energy reduction and e-waste.

Based on published data from the US Department of Energy, energy intensity in the US economy declined by 1.6 percent per year for the period 1985–2004 (US DOE 2010). Subtracting the impact of structural shifts in the economy and other non-efficiency factors, the decline of energy intensity attributable to improvements in energy efficiencies accounts for roughly 0.56 percent per year. Might such a decline be in part due to the aggregate actions of individuals in organizations in substituting away from energy-intensive business processes and toward more IT-intensive and lower energy-intensive business processes? Romm (2002) makes the case for IT-enabled efficiencies by citing examples such as supply-chain management software enabling better inventory management (lower physical flows of goods), online retail stores using less energy, and the impact on transportation. He concludes that "[The Internet] appears instead to be driving efficiencies throughout the economy that have resulted in the biggest drop in electricity intensity and energy intensity the nation has seen in decades" (Romm 2002: 152).

Econometric analysis of the association between IT intensity and energy intensity in South Korean firms reveals that IT investment in the service sector and most manufacturing sectors *increases* electricity intensity (Cho, Lee, & Kim 2007). A more nuanced picture emerges in an empirical analysis of the French service sector, with electricity intensity increasing with computers and software, but decreasing with communication devices, controlling for technical progress, prices, and heated area (Collard, Feve, &

Portier 2005). Working papers that follow in the line of these studies underscore growing interest in this topic, such as those examining cross-country datasets (Bernstein & Madlener 2008) and those examining the energy consumed by various types of Internet activities and data servers (Koomey 2007). Clearly, additional research is needed, perhaps formally examining the substitutability of IT for energy using Allen and Morishima indexes, as has been done for the case of IT and other factors of production such as regular capital and labor (Chwelos et al. 2009; Dewan & Min 1997). Regarding greenhouse gas emissions, we could not identify any studies analyzing the association between information systems and GHG emissions.

The IT business value literature provides some insight into fruitful directions. For example, researchers have found that the competitive environment moderates the association between IT and productivity (Melville, Gurbaxani, & Kraemer 2007; Stiroh 1998), that complementary work practices are required to attain value (Bresnahan, Brynjolfsson, & Hitt 2002), and that the financial impacts of productivity-enhancing IT may be competed away in free markets (Hitt & Brynjolfsson 1996). Methodological approaches pertinent to the sustainability context include efficiency frontiers, production functions, and the event study methodology.

A final area involves unanticipated impacts (Markus & Robey 2004). One dimension is the need for new data management procedures and the issues of environmental data privacy and accuracy (Cayzer & Preist 2009). Data accuracy is a significant issue with other forms of data, and there is no reason to believe such issues will not arise in the environmental context (CIO 2010). A second dimension is the proliferation of toxic "e-waste" resulting from rapid technological change leading to short IT product life cycles. Estimates of the total 2005 e-waste in the US (including IT and consumer electronics such as televisions) include 1.9–2.2 million tons of obsolete equipment, 1.5–1.8 million tons disposed, and only 345,000–379,000 tons recycled (19–25 percent of total disposed) (US EPA 2008). Researchers have examined the scope of the problem and potential remedies. In an assessment of the US e-waste problem, Kahhat et al. (2008) propose a market-based innovation: a deposit-refund system to incentivize return collection of e-waste and promote a competitive market for re-use and recycling. Another proposal for alleviating the problem involves placing the burden of responsibility on the manufacturer. The concept has been implemented in Switzerland, providing an opportunity to analyze its strengths and weaknesses (Khetriwal, Kraeuchi, & Widmer 2009). Key issues and areas of concern include system introduction, securing financing, developing a logistics network, and verifying compliance. Economic modeling of such "fee-upon-disposal" versus "fee-upon-sale" approaches reveals differing mechanisms based on slowing new product introductions and thereby decreasing e-waste, versus motivating producers to design for recyclability (Plambeck & Wang 2009). Researchers have also examined the impact of e-waste on those most affected (Schmidt 2006). Overall, e-waste might be framed as an externality that, via effective regulatory or market mechanisms, might also be viewed as an innovation opportunity. Given the operations dimension in this area, collaboration with operations researchers may be productive.

COMPLEXITIES AND CHALLENGES: MINI-CASE OF CARBON MANAGEMENT SYSTEMS

Similar to many large organizations and universities, the University of Michigan (U-M) in 2004 began an annual sustainability reporting effort focusing on measuring and reporting water, waste, and energy use, and computing and reporting greenhouse gas emissions. The reporting effort emerged based on the recommendations of the U-M Environmental Task Force (ETF), which suggested "an effective and efficient system....to manage the data through the reporting life cycle," necessitating "central data compilation, data analysis, conversion to appropriate measurement units, [and] normalization"(UM CSS 2005).

In response to the ETF recommendations, and necessitated by new reporting objectives, the U-M environmental data repository (EDR) was developed. The EDR comprised a set of Excel spreadsheets with specialized macros to enable business units to enter data into customized forms and email completed forms to an administrator who imports the data into a master spreadsheet. The EDR also enabled data to be entered from sources outside the U-M, such as emissions factors from the US Department of Energy (DOE) and Environmental Protection Agency (EPA). Data entry involved a mix of manual and automated processes, and once the data were entered, calculations were performed, such as the computation of total energy consumption. GHG emissions were also calculated based on known emissions factors and converted to user-friendly metrics such as emissions per student. The adoption of the EDR fits the pattern described earlier that begins with automation and efficiency and then shifts to informating and transforming. And U-M is not alone: organizations today tend to rely on spreadsheets to automate carbon emission management (Greenbiz 2010).

Emerging regulation, shifts in consumer demands, and risk arising from the visible and predicted impacts of climate change are significantly increasing environmental information requirements in organizations. The spreadsheet approach may have reached the limits of its usefulness for several reasons. First, it is difficult to audit the data, given that workflow management, for example, tracking data entry using individual logins and timestamps, is not part of spreadsheet functionality. Second, the financial implications of carbon reductions are not embedded in spreadsheet functionality, making it difficult to compute financial impacts of mitigation programs. Third, the process cannot automatically generate reports that conform to external agencies, such as the Carbon Disclosure Project. This means that each new regulatory requirement requires customized macros to generate reports in the required format. Fourth, the use of the spreadsheet approach involves some manual data entry, raising the possibility of data-entry errors.

Aware of the social, economic, and environmental changes ahead driven by climate change, U-M (as with many large organizations) initiated a new strategic initiative in 2010 via a campus-wide Integrated Assessment (IA) to establish goals and targets for sustainability efforts. One potential outcome may be the adoption of a dedicated carbon management software system (CMS) to replace spreadsheets and potentially transform environmental sustainability. CMS fully automate input metrics to the extent possible, whether energy, or miles traveled, etc., and ease manual input where possible. They enable analysis and management of emission sources such as energy use, and translate them to carbon emissions, using built-in and automatically updated emissions factors. They also visually display data in dashboards for internal use, what-if analyses, links to business initiatives, etc. Finally, CMS enable senior executive functionality by tying environmental resource use to financial metrics, and facilitating external reporting and auditing capabilities (Mines 2009). Note that CMS are related to environmental management systems (see Buhr & Gray [Chapter 23] this volume).

Will CMS transform carbon emission management at large companies? Or, will we see large-scale disasters similar to enterprise resource planning software in earlier decades? Success will rely on the adoption and development of effective new information systems, business processes, and work practices. Prior IS research demonstrates the need for significant work practice and business process changes in order to leverage the value of information systems (Melville, Kraemer, & Gurbaxani 2004). How will such changes occur, who is responsible, and is the organization capable of making such changes, without which the effective implementation of CMS is threatened? For example, how will the environmental function within large firms manage the vetting of software and selection of vendors, as well as the ensuing changes to work routines? Given the high rate of IT project failure rooted in people and process issues (Nelson 2007), routines appropriate to the sustainability domain may be particularly difficult to design and enact. Says a former *Fortune 50* IT executive and CFO: "It's usually not the technology that fails, it's the interaction between the technology and the organization itself"(CIO Update 2010).

In summary, this mini-case illustrates several aspects of ES 2.0. First, shifting environmental strategies in organizations are creating new information requirements, which in turn drive the need for better environmental information systems, processes, and work practices. This form of innovation is market driven, as companies perceive the competitive implications of risk exposure and business opportunities. At the same time, regulation such as the UK CRC Energy Efficiency Scheme may add additional pressure to this complex market system, further inducing innovation. Second, designing the proper environmental routines will be as important as choosing the right software system, lest firms fall prey to adopting artifacts when hoping for patterns of action (Pentland & Feldman 2008). Third, adoption of CMS might be employed as greenwash by companies wishing to be perceived as environmentally friendly. Finally, it is unclear how CMS might shift the belief systems of employees, or the extent to which carbon emission may be reduced in practice.

Discussion

Information systems are poised to transform business and the natural environment, suggesting that the era of Environmental Sustainability 2.0 may be upon us. However, decades of IS scholarship suggest that optimism ought to be tempered with caution.

Organizations too often do not comprehend the scale and scope of change required; underestimate the resistance of employees and the complexity of effectively managing data, information, and knowledge; and neglect the need to design new work routines to maximize the effectiveness of new technology artifacts. IS scholarship is therefore needed to create new knowledge in the environmental sustainability context and inform managerial practice.

The belief–action-outcome framework is one way of thinking about the role of IS in the realm of business and the natural environment. In each of the three realms, I examined some of the relevant questions including what we know and what we don't know, taking a critical stance that includes the possibility of negative or unanticipated consequences. The mini-case illustrated the challenges and opportunities facing firms in one particular area: implementing complex new information systems for managing carbon emissions, water, and waste. In this final section, I suggest several areas in urgent need of scholarship to assist managers as they develop new IS-enabled strategies and practices in response to—or in anticipation of— new business realities rooted in environmental sustainability.

First, field and case studies are needed to better understand the triggers, mechanisms, and consequences of IS-enabled organizational change focused on environmental sustainability. We know little about the extent to which the new context, which introduces such phenomena as altruism and new outcome measures such as carbon intensity, alters, reinforces, or perhaps obviates extant concepts and theories. Moreover, enhanced understanding of mechanisms informs management practice, possibly lowering the chances of high failure rates as was seen in former eras, for example enterprise resource planning software.

Second, given fierce debate among the general population about even the most basic environmental facts, measures, and dynamics, studies of the impact of presenting environmental messaging in new forms of online channels, such as online social networks and wikis, have the potential to greatly improve understanding and awareness in the general population. In particular, such modes of communication and "digital peer pressure" within organizations may prove to be a key factor in shifting beliefs of employees within organizations. However, given the potential for unanticipated outcomes, more research is needed to understand what works, in what contexts, and why.

Lastly, increased study of information system issues that lie at the intersection of traditional environmental sustainability topics (e.g. life-cycle analysis) and IS scholarship has great potential to accelerate what we know. For example, cradle-to-cradle and closed loop supply chain tracking (see Abbey & Guide [Chapter 16] this volume) is impossible without sophisticated sensors, databases, and real-time reporting, but few researchers have begun to examine how new forms of IS can enable and transform in this context. Another example is eco-labeling, which might integrate with innovative new camera-phone applications to allow real-time decision-making within retail stores. These and other innovations are likely to benefit from collaboration between IS scholars and other business disciplines.

In conclusion, there is opportunity and risk at the nexus of information systems, business, and the natural environment. An optimistic but critical stance is required by scholars and managers. IS might prove to be a champion in the fight against environmental calamity, reinforce business as usual, or even exacerbate climate change. The future is now being written, and anything is possible.

REFERENCES

Abrahamse, W., Steg, L., Vlek, C. and Rothengatter, T. (2005). "A Review of Intervention Studies Aimed at Household Energy Conservation," *Journal of Enviromental Psychology*, 25(3): 273–91.

Andersson, L., Shivarajan, S. & Blau, G. (2005). "'Enacting Ecological Sustainability in the MNC: A Test of an Adapted Value-Belief-Norm Framework," *Journal of Business Ethics*, 59(3): 295–305.

Avison, D., Gregor, S. & Wilson, D. (2006). "Managerial IT Unconsciousness," *Communications of the ACM*, 49(7): 88–93.

Bagozzi, R. (2007). "The Legacy of the Technology Acceptance Model and a Proposal for a Paradigm Shift," *Journal of the Association for Information Systems*, 8(4): 244–54.

Berkes, F. & Folke, C. (2000). "Linking Social and Ecological Systems for Resilience and Sustainability," in F Berkes & C. Folke (eds), *Linking Social and Ecological Systems*, Cambridge University Press, Cambridge.

Berkhout, P., Muskens, J., & Velthuijsen, J. (2000). "Defining the Rebound Effect," *Energy Policy*, 28(6–7): 425–32.

Bernstein, R. & Madlener, R. (2008). *The Impact of Disaggregated ICT Capital on Electricity Intensity of Production: Econometric Analysis of Major European Industries*. E. ON Energy Research Center, Future Energy Consumer Needs and Behavior.

Blevis, E. (2007). "Sustainable Interaction Design: Invention & Disposal, Renewal & Reuse," in *CHI 2007 Proceedings*, San Jose, California, 503–12.

Boccaletti, G., Loffler, M. & Oppenheim, J. (2008). "How IT Can Cut Carbon Emissions," *McKinsey Quarterly*, 1–5.

Bresnahan, T., Brynjolfsson, E., & Hitt, L. (2002). "Information Technology, Workplace Organization, and the Demand for Skilled Labor: Firm-level Evidence," *Quarterly Journal of Economics*, 117(1): 339–76.

Brown, T. (2008). "Design Thinking," *Harvard Business Review*, June 2008.

Carbon Disclosure Project (2010). website: <https://www.cdproject.net/en-US/Results/Pages/overview.aspx>, viewed 11/14/2010.

Cayzer, S. & Preist, C. (2009). "The Sustainability Hub: An Information Management Tool for Analysis and Decision Making," in *SIGMETRICS '09*, Seattle, WA USA.

Cho, Y., Lee, J. & Kim, T. (2007). "The Impact of ICT Investment and Energy Price on Industrial Electricity Demand: Dynamic Growth Model Approach," *Energy Policy*, 35: 4730–8.

Chwelos, P., Ramirez, R., Kraemer, K. & Melville, N. (2009). "Does Technological Progress Alter the Nature of Information Technology as a Production Input? New Evidence and New Results," *Information Systems Research*, 21(2): 392–408.

CIO (2010). website: <http://www.cio.com/article/591114/Data_Data_Everywhere_But_Not_Enough_Smart_Management>, viewed on 11/16/10.

CIO Update (2010). website: <http://www.cioupdate.com/features/article.php/3866441/Reinventing-IT-Project-Management—Peter-Drucker-Style.htm>, viewed on 11/16/10.

Coleman, J. (1986). "Social Theory, Social Research, and a Theory of Action," *American Journal of Sociology*, 91: 1309–35.

—— (1994). *Foundations of Social Theory*, 2nd edn. Harvard University Press.

Collard, F., Feve, P., & Portier, F. (2005). "Electricity Consumption and ICT in the French Service Sector," *Energy Economics*, 27(2): 541–50.

Davis, F. (1989). "Perceived Usefulness, Perceived Ease of Use, and User Acceptance of Information Technology," *MIS Quarterly*, 13: 319–39.

——, Bagozzi, R.& Warshaw, P. (1989). "User Acceptance of Computer Technology: A Comparison of Two Theoretical Models," *Management Science*, 35: 982–1003.

Devaraj, S., Easley, R., & Crant, J. (2008). "How Does Personality Matter: Relating the Five-Factor Model to Technology Acceptance and Use," *Information System Research*, 19(1): 93–105.

Dewan, S. & Min, C. (1997). "The Substitution of Information Technology for Other Factors of Production: A Firm Level Analysis," *Management Science*, 43(12): 1660–75.

Dittmar, L. (2010). "If You Can't Measure It, You Can't Manage It," *SAP Insider*, Jul-Aug Sep: 1–2.

Dray, J. & Foster, S. (1996). "ISO 14000 and Information Systems: Where's the Link?" *Total Quality Environmental Management*, 5(3): 17–23.

Dumont, J. & Franjeska-Nicole, B. (2008). *Learning about the Environment: The Role of Information Technology in Shaping Attitudes and Developing Solutions*, University of Indianapolis, Indianapolis.

Eisenhardt, K. (1989). "Agency Theory: An Assessment and Review," *Academy of Management Review*, 14(3): 57–74.

Erdmann, L., Lorenz, H., Goodman, J. & Arnfalk, P. (2004). *The Future Impact of ICTs on Environmental Sustainability*, 21384 En, Institute for Prospective Technological Studies, European Commission Joint Research Centre.

Felin, T, & Foss, N. (2006). "Individuals and Organizations: Thoughts on a Micro-foundations Project For Strategic Management and Organizational Analysis," in Ketchen, D. and Bergh, D. (eds), *Research Methodology in Strategy and Management*, Elsevier Ltd., 3: 253–88.

Fichman, R. & Kemerer, C. (1999). "The Illusory Diffusion of Innovation: An Examination of Assimilation Gaps," *Information Systems Research*, 10(3): 255–75.

Fishbein, M, & Azjen, I. (1975). *Belief, Attitude, Intention, and Behavior: An Introduction to Theory and Research*. Addison-Wesley Publishing, Reading, Massachusetts.

Friedman, T. (2007). "The Dawn of E2K in India," *New York Times*, November 7, 2007.

Gefen, D. & Straub, D. (1997). "Gender Differences in the Perception and Use of E-mail: An Extension to the Technology Acceptance Model," *MIS Quarterly*, 21(4): 389–400.

Greenbiz (2010). website: <http://www.greenbiz.com/blog/2010/07/29/its-time-give-spread-sheets-tracking-carbon-emissions?ms=36097>, viewed on 11/16/10.

Greenpeace (2010). website: <http://www.greenpeace.org/international/en/campaigns/climate-change/cool-it/ITs-carbon-footprint/Facebook/?thingstodo>, viewed 11/14/2010.

Gregor, S. & Jones, D. (2007). "The Anatomy of a Design Theory," *Journal of the Association for Information Systems*, 8(5): 1–25.

Heptinstall, J. (2001). "Environmental Information Management Systems at Rhone-Poulenc," in DJ Richards, BR Allenby & D Compton (eds), *Information Systems and the Environment*, National Academy of Engineering, Washington, DC, 87–93.

Hevner, A., March, S. & Park, J. (2004). "Design Science in Information Systems Research," *MIS Quarterly*, 28(1): 75–105.

Hitt, L. & Brynjolfsson, E. (1996). "Productivity, Business Profitability and Consumer Surplus: Three Different Measures of Information Technology Value," *MIS Quarterly*, 20(2): 121–42.

Holmes, T. (2006). "Environmental Awareness Through Eco-Visualization: Combining Art and Technology to Promote Sustainability," in *CHI 2006*, Montreal, Canada.

Hosack, B. (2007). "The Effect of System Feedback and Decision Context on Value-based Decision-making Behavior," *Decision Support Systems*, 43(4): 1605–14.

Howard, S. (2008). *SMART 2020: Enabling the Low Carbon Economy in the Information Age*. The Climate Group.

Jensen, M. & Meckling, W. (1976). "Theory of the Firm: Managerial Behavior, Agency Costs, and Ownership Structure," *Journal of Financial Economics*, 3: 305–60.

Kahhat, R., Kim, J., Xu, M., Allenby, B., Williams, E. & Zhang, P. (2008). "Exploring e-Waste Management Systems in the United States," *Resources, Conservation, and Recycling*, 52: 955–64.

Khetriwal, D., Kraeuchi, P. & Widmer, R. (2009). "Producer Responsibility for E-Waste Management: Key Issues for Consideration—Learning from the Swiss Experience," *Journal of Environmental Management*, 90: 153–65.

Kleindorfer, P. & Snir, E. (2001). "Environmental Information in Supply-Chain Design and Coordination," in Richards, D., Allenby, B and Compton, D. (eds), *Information Systems and the Environment*, National Academy of Engineering, Washington, DC, 115–38.

Kollmuss, A. & Agyeman, J. (2002). "Mind the Gap: Why Do People Act Environmentally and What are the Barriers to Pro-Environmental Behavior?" *Environmental Education Research*, 8(3): 239–60.

Koomey, J. (2007). "Estimating Total Power Consumption by Servers in the U.S. and the World," Palo Alto, CA.

March, T. & Smith, G. (1995). "Design and Natural Science Research on Information Technology," *Decision Support Systems*, 15(4): 251–66.

Markus, M. & Robey, D. (2004). "Why Stuff Happens: Explaining the Unintended Consequences of Using Information Technology," in *The Past and Future of Information Systems*, Elsevier Butterworth-Heinemann, Amsterdam.

Melville, N., Gurbaxani, V. & Kraemer, K. (2007). "The Productivity Impact of Information Technology across Competitive Regimes: The Role of Industry Concentration and Dynamism," *Decision Support Systems*, 43(1): 229–42.

—— Kraemer, K. & Gurbaxani, V. (2004). "Information Technology and Organizational Performance: An Integrative Model of IT Business Value," *MIS Quarterly*, 28(2): 283–322.

—— (2010). "Information Systems Innovation for Environmental Sustainability", *MIS Quarterly*, 34(1): 1–21.

Mines, C. (2009). "Market Overview: The Advent of Enterprise Carbon and Energy Management Systems," Forrester Research.

Morgan, M. & Dowlatabadi, H. (1996). "Learning from Integrated Assessment of Climate Change," *Climatic Change*, 34(3–4): 337–68.

Nelson, R. (2007). "IT Project Management: Infamous Failures, Classic Mistakes, and Best Practices," *MIS Quarterly Executive*, 6(2): 67–78.

Orlikowski, W. (1996). "Improvising Organizational Transformation Over Time: A Situated Change Perspective," *Information Systems Research*, 7(1): 63–92.

Peffers, K., Tuunanen, T., Rothenberger, M. & Chatterjee, S. (2007). "A Design Science Research Methodology for Information Systems Research," *Journal of Management Information Systems*, 24(3): 45–77.

Pentland, B. & Feldman, M. (2008). "Designing Routines: On the Folly of Designing Artifacts While Hoping for Patterns of Action," *Information and Organization*, 18(4): 235–50.

Pereira, A. & O'Connor, M. (1999). "Information and Communication Technology and the Popular Appropriation of Sustainability Problems," *International Journal of Sustainable Development*, 2(3): 411–24.

Plambeck, E. & Wang, Q. (2009). "Effects of E-Waste Regulation on New Product Introduction," *Management Science*, 55(3): 333–47.

Romm, J. (2002). "The Internet and the New Energy Economy," *Resources, Conservation, and Recycling*, 36(3): 197–210.

Rowley, M. (2009). "Why Social Media is Vital to Corporate Social Responsibility," *Mashable— The Social Media Guide*, viewed March 19, 2010: <http://mashable.com/2009/11/06/social-responsibility/>.

SAP (2010). website: <http://www.sapsustainabilityreport.com/performance/carbon-footprint>, viewed 11/14/2010.

Schlumpf, C., Pahl Wostl, C., Schonborn, A., Jaeger, C. and Imboden, D. (2001). "An Information Tool for Citizens to Assess Impacts of Climate Change from a Regional Perspective," *Climatic Change*, 51: 199–241.

Schmidt, C. (2006). "Unfair Trade e-Waste in Africa," *Environmental Health Perspectives*, 114(4): A232–A5.

Seligman, C. & Darley, J. M. (1977). "Feedback as a Means of Decreasing Residential Energy Consumption," *Journal of Applied Psychology*, 62(4): 363–8.

Sen, T., Moore, L., & Hess, T. (2000). "An Organizational Decision Support System for Managing the DOE Hazardous Waste Ceanup Program," *Decision Support Systems*, 29(1): 89–109.

Shaft, T., Ellington, R., Meo, M. and Sharfman, M. (1997). "A Framework for Information Systems in Life-Cycle-Oriented Environmental Management," *Journal of Industrial Ecology*, 1(2): 135–48.

—— Sharfman, M. & Swahn, M. (2002). "Using Interorganizational Information Systems to Support Environmental Management Efforts at ASG," *Journal of Industrial Ecology*, 5(4): 95–115.

Sharma, R. & Yetton, P. (2009). "Estimating the Effect of Common Method Variance: The Method-Method Pair Technique with an Illustration from TAM Research," *MIS Quarterly*, 33/3: x–y.

Shaw, D. and Clarke, I. (1999). "Belief Formation in Ethical Consumer Groups: An Exploratory Study," *Marketing Intelligence & Planning*, 17(2): 109–20.

Shehadi, R., Fayad, W., Karam, D., Sabbagh, K. & Harter, G. (2010). *ICT for a Low-Carbon World: Activism, Innovation, Cooperation*. Booz & Company.

Shepherd, M., Briggs, R., Reinig, B., Yen, J. & Nunamaker, J. (1995). "Invoking Social Comparison to Improve Electronic Brainstorming: Beyond Anonymity," *Journal of Management Information Systems*, 12(3): 155–70.

Sourcemap (2010). website: <http://www.sourcemap.org/>, viewed 11/16/10.

Stern, P. (1999). "Information, Incentives, and Proenvironmental Consumer Behavior," *Journal of Consumer Policy*, 22: 461–78.

Stiroh, K. (1998). "Computers, Productivity, and Input Substitution," *Economic Inquiry*, 36: 175–91.

Swanson, E. (1994). "Information Systems Innovation among Organizations," *Management Science*, 40(9): 1069–88.

UM CSS (2005). website: <http://www.oseh.umich.edu/pdf/Environmental%20Reporting%20(CSS05-11).pdf>, viewed on 11/16/10.

Urban Ecomap (2010). website: <http://ams.urbanecomap.org/?locale=en_US>, viewed 11/16/10.

US DOE (2010). website: <http://www1.eere.energy.gov/ba/pba/intensityindicators/total_ energy.html>, viewed on 11/16/10.

US EPA (2008). *Fact Sheet: Management of Electronic Waste in the United States*, by U.S.EPA, vol. EPA530-F-08-014, viewed April 2010, <http://www.epa.gov/osw/conserve/materials/ ecycling/docs/fact7-08.pdf>.

Van Dam, S., Bakker, C. & van Hal, J. (2010). "Home Energy Monitors: Impact Over the Medium-Term", *Building Research & Information*, 38(5): 458–69.

Venkatesh, V. (2000). "Determinants of Perceived Ease of Use: Integrating Control, Intrinisic Motivation, and Emotion into the Technology Acceptance Model," *Information Systems Research*, 11(4): 342–65.

Watson, R., Boudreau, M. and Chen, A. (2010). "Information Systems and Environmentally Sustainable Development: Energy Informatics and New Directions for the IS Community," *MIS Quarterly*, 34(1): 23–38.

Wong, C., Duzgoren-Aydin, N., Aydin, A. & Wong, M. (2007). "Evidence of Excessive Releases of Metals from Primitive E-waste Processing in Guiyu, China," *Environmental Pollution*, 148(1): 62–72.

Zuboff, S. (1984). *In the Age of the Smart Machine : The Future of Work and Power*. Basic Books, New York.

PART VI

MARKETING

CHAPTER 19

··

FROM GREEN MARKETING TO MARKETING FOR ENVIRONMENTAL SUSTAINABILITY

··

DEBRA L. SCAMMON
AND JENNY MISH

WHILE much marketing practice today relies on established knowledge and theory, marketing as a field is in a state of flux. Like marketing metrics, social media, co-creation of value, and global consumer culture, marketing related to the natural environment extends conventional marketing thought beyond its prior scope. Specifically, it involves value creation, delivery, and communication objectives beyond those that satisfy immediate customer wants and needs. It places marketers in mediating roles between customer satisfaction and firm profitability, and between the customer's needs and the firm's needs for reputation management, long-term viability, and stewardship, all of which involve multiple stakeholders. The pressure on marketers to demonstrate the contribution of their activities to the financial performance of firms has never been greater. This encourages practices that narrow the scope of marketing activities at a time when the need for broad inclusive thinking is increasingly critical.

The following two chapters (see Gershoff & Irwin [Chapter 20] and Devinney [Chapter 21] this volume) discuss the challenges of understanding consumer ambivalence toward green consumption. In this chapter we consider the role of marketing for the natural environment in catalyzing environmentally sustainable consumption. What have scholars learned about green marketing? What challenges do marketers and marketing scholars face in practicing effective marketing for the sustainability of the natural environment? What research is needed to guide successful marketing for environmental sustainability?

We provide an integrative review of four decades of "green" marketing emphasizing potentially catalytic avenues for further investigation. Throughout our review we reference both literature reviews and seminal papers in the field. Our scope is limited to work that specifically addresses *marketing*. We include environmental, ecological, and sustainability-related marketing studies in addition to those using the terms "green" and "social responsibility," but we do not review the cause marketing, social marketing, and corporate social responsibility literatures (for the latter, see Bondy & Matten [Chapter 28] this volume; for marketing reviews see Maignan & Ferrell 2004; Peloza & Shang 2011). Our integrative analysis is intended to increase understanding at a time when the role of marketing in environmental sustainability is far from clear. Ultimately, the greatest research challenges for marketers related to environmental sustainability are those that illuminate the paradigm shift as a cultural transformation.

Past eras of "green marketing"

Interest in environmental issues by marketers has evolved through several distinct phases (Menon & Menon 1997; Kilbourne & Beckman 1998; Peattie 2001). As noted by Hoffman & Bansal ([Chapter 1] this volume), concern about the welfare of the natural environment arose initially in the 1960s and 1970s with media exposés of environmentally damaging business practices. Combined with market research evidencing increased consumer desire to buy "green" products, this spurred marketers to experiment with new products, packaging, and claims related to environmental impacts during the 1980s and 1990s. The field entered the new century with a broader systemic approach to environmental issues which has come to be called "environmental sustainability."

The 1960s and 1970s

Prior to the 1970s, the natural environment did not have a significant impact on the practice of marketing (Menon & Menon 1997). With limited social pressure for attention to environmental concerns, environmentalists put legal pressure on business practices. In response, firms generally adopted defensive strategies, doing as little as possible to meet the letter of regulations. Environmental and business interests appeared to be irreconcilable.

Media coverage of contamination and pollution put the spotlight on a few "dirty" firms and industries thought to cause these problems. Marketers in industries targeted by environmentalists became more aware of reputation risks. New laws and regulations provided mechanisms to address market externalities in targeted industries. Firms directed their efforts toward developing product features to meet new regulations (e.g. emission control devices) rather than trying to develop environmentally-friendly products (e.g. cars that are inherently non-polluting) (Varadarajan & Menon 1988).

Along with a flurry of food cooperatives, a few entrepreneurial "boutique" firms, such as Patagonia, The Body Shop, and Ben & Jerry's, emerged. Such pioneers were small and easy for mainstream marketers to dismiss. However, these entrepreneurs tapped enduring social undercurrents with innovative brand marketing built around ecological values, and eventually came to serve as important examples of values-based strategies for mainstream marketers.

During these early years, scholars such as Feldman (1971), Fisk (1974), and Henion & Kinnear (1976) encouraged marketers to adopt a broader view of their field. They advocated the examination not only of marketing activities that contribute to environmental problems but also those that could help remedy environmental problems (Henion & Kinnear 1976). Fisk alluded to the need to understand the root causes of society's environmental problems, but few scholars explored such issues. Feldman (1971) predicted that due to environmental pressures "marketing is about to undergo a profound change by shifting its emphasis to non-material consumption and societal considerations" (p. 54).

The 1980s and 1990s

During the 1980s and 1990s, environmental disasters continued to amplify public awareness, alerting business leaders to the market significance of a broad set of stakeholders. Environmental groups began working more collaboratively with business and government (Menon & Menon 1997). The UN Brundtland Commission (1987) launched the concept of "sustainable development," allowing companies, governments, and environmentalists to find new common ground.

For the first time, market research began to reveal a potential market for "green" products. Surveys found that a large percentage of US consumers was concerned about the environmental impacts of their purchases, and said that they would pay up to 5 percent more for products in packages that were recyclable or biodegradable (Roper 1990; Mintel 1991). Earth Day 1990 (twenty years after the first Earth Day) "may have been the world's first major green marketing campaign" (Makower 2009, p. 2). Environmental claims for new products, especially in the household, health and beauty, and pet-related categories, increased dramatically between 1988 and 1990, peaked during the early 1990s, and declined modestly through the remainder of the decade (Mayer et al. 2001; Banerjee et al. 1995; Carlson et al. 1993).

Green claims during this period typically emphasized the presence of a single product attribute (such as biodegradable, recyclable, or recycled) or the absence of a negative attribute (such as no fluorocarbons or no phosphates). Many made vague assertions that the product was "natural," "environmentally friendly," or just plain "green." Consumer confusion became a key concern, raising the issue of potential deception. The regulatory environment for green products was uneven, leading firms to push for more consistency (Simon 1992; Scammon & Mayer 1995). In 1992, the US Federal Trade Commission issued comprehensive national guidelines for environmental claims (US Code of Federal Regulations 1992). These "Green Guides" were revised in 1996 and 1998 (US Code of Federal Regulations 1996, 1998) and new updates are expected in 2011.

A number of pioneering eco-labels were launched during this period, such as Blue Angel in Germany, Environmental Choice in Canada, Eco-Mark in Japan, Energy STAR in the US, and Organic and Fair Trade in Europe and North America (Mayer et al. 2001; Sahota et al. 2009). Some of these seals of approval consider multiple dimensions of a brand's environmental performance and are applicable across a wide range of product classes (e.g. Blue Angel). Others relate to a single attribute and apply to a narrower range of products (e.g. Energy STAR). These "third party" certifications provided credibility and support to growing niche markets.

Peattie & Crane (2005) argued that most of the green marketing of the 1990s was neither green nor marketing (see also Devinney [Chapter 21] this volume). By the mid 1990s, "under-performing green products, over-zealous promotional claims, inexact science and inconsistent legislation conspired to discredit the practice of green marketing," leaving consumers "confused and reluctant to engage in green purchasing behavior" (Crane 2000, p. 278). A consumer "backlash" against green marketing emerged (Wong et al. 1996), resulting in a rich "mythology" among marketers about the difficulties of successful green marketing (Peattie & Crane 2005, p. 367).

During the 1990s environmental problems were increasingly reframed as economic problems. Strategies that developed competitive advantages while resolving environmental concerns were viewed positively (Porter & van der Linde 1995). As the 1990s came to a close, cost reduction carried more momentum than the promotion of green products to consumers.

The need for product design for sustainability began to be recognized. Topics such as life cycle design, design for disassembly, and the role of stakeholders in the sustainable design process began to appear (e.g. Polonsky & Ottman 1998). Corporate purchasing of environmental products gradually increased (Drumwright 1994; Polonsky et al. 1998). However, consumers continued to reject products that achieved competitive superiority on a single environmental dimension while compromising performance in other ways. Companies that attempted to charge a "green premium" were discouraged by low cash-register receipts.

Regulations and flat consumer demand curtailed the flagrant excesses of the green marketing boom, and niche markets continued their slow growth. Meanwhile, cause marketing, whereby consumers had opportunities to direct a portion of their dollars to non-profit causes without paying higher prices, was becoming more common. The bases on which marketers measured the impact of their green strategies broadened to include not just financial measures such as brand revenue, market share, and return on investment, but also brand image, customer loyalty, and corporate image (Menon et al. 1999).

Peattie (2001) called the stalemate at the end of the 1990s the "Green Wall." Once the low-hanging fruit had been harvested, more radical changes were needed to produce green innovations, and this was often seen as cost prohibitive. Delivery of environmental performance had turned out to be complex, difficult to assess, and difficult to communicate with credibility. Successful environmental product differentiation required consumer willingness to pay for public goods, credible dissemination of information about environmental product attributes, and defense against imitation (Reinhardt 1998). Rather than being lauded for their efforts, firms that took steps to improve environmental performance were often criticized for their imperfections. As Walley & Whitehead (1994) lamented, "It's Not Easy Being Green."

During the 1990s, a smattering of academic papers addressed managerial issues in environmental marketing. Mendleson & Polonsky (1995) examined the use of strategic alliances to enhance green marketing credibility, Brown & Dacin (1997) looked at consumer responses to socially responsible brand associations, and Menon & Menon (1997) developed an Enviropreneurial Marketing model. A number of handbooks for managers summarized what had been discovered thus far in the realm of environmental marketing (Fuller 1999; Polonsky & Mintu-Wimsatt 1995; Coddington 1993; Ottman 1998).

The 2000s

In the new century, environmental "sustainability" began to take hold. This concept embraces the complexity of interdependence and reframes green marketing from a long-term, global, and inclusive perspective. Many companies began issuing sustainability reports, reflecting increased investor concern about future viability and competitiveness.

Growth rates increased in niche green markets. For example, spurred by the launch of the LEED certification for new buildings in the US in 2000, the green building industry began to flourish. Similarly, the launch of the USDA Organic standard in 2003 galvanized a decentralized undercurrent in the food industry, creating double-digit growth for most of the decade (Organic Trade Association 2010). The coffee market was disrupted by Fair Trade coffee, which came to be widely available at retailers such as Starbucks, Marks & Spencer, and McDonald's. The use of environmental sustainability standards and certifications contributed to public awareness about underlying environmental issues (Conroy 2007). Many of the boutique pioneers, such as Ben & Jerry's, were purchased by conglomerates seeking to learn about sustainable practices.

A new market impetus came from B2B customers who were increasingly demanding environmental information and accountability. During the 2000s, large buyers such as Walmart, Target, and government and institutional purchasers became significant forces through their environmental procurement policies and the sheer volume of products they purchased.

Innovations in product development began to appear. Scholars explored similarities between environmental and conventional new product development processes and identified antecedents to the former (Pujari et al. 2003; 2004). Others identified boundary conditions in which increased regulations could be profitably met by firms through environmental product development (Chen 2001), and factors influencing the market performance of green products (Pujari 2006). By the end of the decade, the growing B2B market began to have ripple effects for mainstream consumers, especially in terms of environmental product strategies (Albino et al. 2009).

Costing and therefore pricing gradually began to incorporate more social and environmental costs, accounting for specific environmental externalities in production, use, and post-use phases. For example, the European Union's RoHS directive took effect in

2006, restricting the use of less costly hazardous materials in electronics products. However, manufacturers such as IBM and HP have preferred to uphold a single set of criteria globally, extending the benefit of this regulation beyond the EU. The higher costs of developing and producing environmental value propositions without sacrificing quality remains a major issue (Dangelico & Pujari 2010).

With the arrival of the Great Recession in 2008, many predicted that the niche markets for sustainability would perish. However, the green retail market grew 41 percent from 2004 to 2009 despite the recession (Mintel 2010). Growth slowed, but many companies continued to invest in environmental sustainability projects, viewing them as points of leverage for future stability and competitive advantage. B2B buyers continued to expect more of their suppliers. Consumers continued to support niche markets. Green consumer services, personal care products, and baby products that avoided harmful ingredients were especially strong growth categories at the end of the decade (Mintel 2010).

Marketers began to look beyond making simplistic claims, but it wasn't obvious which changes could add to environmental sustainability and profits while contributing positively to the lives of their customers. Consumer research during this decade aimed for a more complex understanding of the gap between green attitudes and behavior (see Gershoff & Irwin [Chapter 20] this volume). Some marketing scholars addressed related ethical and macro questions, such as normative principles for responsible marketing (Laczniak & Murphy 2006), market system constraints and opportunities for sustainability (Press & Arnould 2009), and the relationship between financial performance and corporate social performance (Luo & Bhattacharya 2006). Green corporate strategies and green marketing strategies were found to involve different relationships between top management commitment and public concern, regulatory forces, and competitive advantage (Banerjee et al. 2003).

Building socially and environmentally responsible brands and safeguarding brand equity in the face of activist criticism were central concerns for many firms (Conroy 2007; Palazzo & Basu 2007). Brand innovation appeared closely intertwined with trust-building. Some argued that "products with sustainability attributes will only appeal if they are clearly consistent with the values and activities of the company" (World Business Council 2005).

This more holistic approach was also advocated by marketing scholars. Ginsberg & Bloom (2004) argued that marketers should position based on importance of greenness to their target consumers and their ability to differentiate from competitors. They encouraged firms to focus marketing-mix strategies selectively, using price, place, and promotion as well as product to achieve goals. These authors noted that firm strategies are likely to evolve over time, for example by "quietly" implementing changes without making them central to brand identity, or by progressively becoming more green as employees become more committed to underlying values.

Ottman et al. (2006) argued that an exclusive focus on environmental product features is short-sighted, calling it "green marketing myopia." They suggested that marketers must offer both improved environmental quality and customer satisfaction through careful value positioning vis-à-vis benefits such as efficiency and cost effectiveness, health and safety, overall performance, symbolism and status, and convenience. These authors pointed to the importance of accurately calibrating consumer knowledge and establishing product-claim credibility, particularly through the use of consumer-generated information and environmental seals.

Walmart's strategy illustrates the caution that many firms brought to marketing for the natural environment. In spite of changing its brand message from "Everyday Low Prices" to "Save Money. Live Better," the giant retailer pursued its environmental goals primarily via suppliers, increased logistical efficiencies, and employee initiatives, innovating in product, place, and price, rather than in promotion. Only after achieving a number of internal goals did the firm begin to turn strategic attention to the challenge of communicating this value, and thus to the issue of sustainability standards and certifications. Under development is a Product Sustainability Index intended to provide transparent product information to consumers in a simple, easy way. This is a long-term collaborative project with suppliers, other retailers, academics, NGOs, and government officials (<http://walmartstores.com/Sustainability>).

The Walmart example highlights four key insights about marketing for the natural environment. First, reliable metrics are needed in order to translate environmental commitments and activities into customer value. Second, verifiable product standards and certifications help deliver and communicate this value. Third, to be credible, these standards must be developed collaboratively with multiple stakeholders. Fourth, environmental sustainability-related brand value must be rooted in sincere, systemic, and organization-wide commitments.

In summary, the opportunism and reactivity of green marketers in the twentieth century gave way to the beginnings of a more mature and sophisticated approach in the new century. The incorporation of multiple stakeholder perspectives throughout the marketing process, measurement of non-economic impacts as a foundation for offering credible marketing claims supported by third-party certification, and open educational approaches to building globally relevant brands for the future became more common However, major obstacles remain. We turn next to the challenges that marketers currently face in marketing for the natural environment.

CHALLENGES FOR MARKETING
AND THE NATURAL ENVIRONMENT

In the new millennium, marketers must address the complexity of delivering environmentally sound value. Marketing for the natural environment involves value creation, delivery, and communication objectives beyond those that satisfy immediate customer wants and needs. Ultimately, this means that marketers and marketing scholars are facing a major reorientation of the field. In this section, we address this fundamental disciplinary shift. We begin by discussing the definition of marketing, its dominant logic, and the role of the marketing mix, all of which raise unresolved issues. We then address sustainable levels of consumption, and the need for systemic integration in marketing for the natural environment.

Definition of marketing, marketing logic, and marketing mix

A variety of definitions of marketing for the natural environment have been put forward, all recognizing ecosystem needs while highlighting different aspects of marketing (Jones et al. 2008). For example, in defining sustainable marketing, Fuller (1999) focuses on management of the marketing mix, while Belz & Peattie (2009) focus on relationship building. Martin & Schouten (2011) define sustainability marketing with a focus on value creation. These new definitions stand in contrast to the practices of many firms of offering differentiated products that meet the short-term needs and wants of consumers. Smith et al. (2010) characterized this latter practice as "the new marketing myopia," a single-minded focus on the consumer and a failure to see the broader societal context of business decision-making.

The newest American Marketing Association definition of marketing suggests that marketing's goals should be the creation of value for customers, clients, partners, and society at large (<www.marketingpower.com>). This new definition was announced in 2007 after several years of scholarly debate over the boundaries of the field (Gundlach & Wilkie 2010). It broadens the scope of marketing to embrace a systemic societal view and represents a paradigm shift in thought, following Menon et al. (1999).

Given this and other trends, marketing scholars have asked if marketing needs reform (Sheth & Sisodia 2006), what marketing needs to do to "regain its seat at the table" (Webster et al. 2003), and what a new logic for marketing might entail (Gronroos 2007; Vargo & Lusch 2004). In the context of sustainability, the underlying rationale for the field was challenged by Kilbourne (2010), who cited Einstein's recognition that problems cannot be solved by the same thinking that created them. Similarly, Varey (2010) suggested that "a radical new logic for marketing as a social process" is needed for a sustainable society (p. 112).

Service-dominant logic (SDL) represents an emerging market logic that deals with the marketing paradigm shift toward social processes. In a seminal paper, Vargo & Lusch (2004) contrasted service-dominant logic with goods-dominant logic (GDL), noting that both exist concurrently in the marketplace. They suggested that marketing needs to break free from the goods and manufacturing-based model (GDL), and recognize that "organizations, markets, and society are fundamentally concerned with exchange of service—the application of competences (knowledge and skills)" (<http://www.sdlogic.net>). This view "embraces concepts of the *value-in-use* and *co-creation of value* rather than the *value-in-exchange* and *embedded-value* concepts of [GDL]" (ibid.). These authors further suggested that "instead of firms being informed to *market to* customers, they [should] *market with* customers, as well as other value-creation partners in the firm's value network" (ibid.). SDL offers a frame-work for scholars seeking to situate marketing for the natural environment in rela-tion to the dominant market logic, as well as for developing insights about meeting customer needs through less material consumption, and for collaborating with stakeholders.

The usefulness of the marketing mix is also contested. Critics suggest that it is simplis-tic, takes the seller's viewpoint, and overemphasizes the product as compared to the service or use value that is more central to the value proposition (Belz & Peattie 2009; Constantinides 2006, Gronroos 2007). It is argued that the product-based language of the marketing mix fails to recognize the fundamentally dynamic and relational nature of value and thus marketing. Belz & Peattie (2009) proposed an alternative marketing mix specifically for marketing for sustainability, consisting of the four Cs: customer solu-tions, customer cost, convenience, and communications. Here, the focus is on solving customer problems in a co-creative relationship throughout the total consumption process. This viewpoint shifts the emphasis from the firm as a central agent to the rela-tionships between the firm and its customers, and attends to customer wants and needs in terms of convenience in space and time, solutions rather than goods, two-way com-munication, and value for value.

As noted by Shrivastava ([Chapter 35], this volume), everyone in the field is a pioneer during these early years of B&NE. This may be especially true in marketing. Redefining marketing, recognizing the appearance of a new market logic(s), and refining the mar-keting mix are critical to overcoming the crisis of relevance facing marketing for the natural environment. Theory and practice in this area must address the identification and delivery of customer value, including the accurate assessment of the nature and role of marketing in relation to society as a whole.

Sustainable levels of consumption

Although consumption has a place in a sustainable future, unchecked consumption is ultimately unsustainable. The global rate of consumption is rapidly increasing and cur-rently exceeds the Earth's carrying capacity (see Gladwin [Chapter 38] this volume).

Critics of marketing complain that marketing and sustainability are inherently con-tradictory objectives, since the former promotes consumption and the latter calls for responsible use of resources (Jones et al. 2007). In this environment, "reputation and trust may not be sufficient to safeguard a brand. To succeed, marketers must lead the path towards more sustainable consumption" (World Business Council 2008, p. 10). Marketers can guide change toward environmental sustainability, but as Jones et al. (2007) report, marketing teams rarely play strategic roles in driving sustainability agendas.

Indeed, many of the most promising insights and innovative approaches to marketing for the natural environment have come from outside of corporations. For example, New American Dream, an NGO, promotes responsible purchasing programs for organizations and consumers and provides tools to help families keep a focus on meaningfulness as they consume (<www.newdream.org>). McKenzie-Mohr (1999) applied findings from social psychology to the challenge of "fostering sustainable behavior," and his recommendations have been adopted by thousands of government and NGO efforts around the world (<www.cbsm.com>). Assadourian (2010) traced the history of consumerism as the dominant cultural norm and its spread across the globe, arguing that marketing, media, and government are the institutions that have been most responsible. As such, he calls upon these institutions to actively guide the shift to a culture of sustainability.

Marketers in firms seeking to "lead the path towards more sustainable consumption" must overcome deep-seated habits and assumptions that have led to the current global cultural emphasis on material consumption. This includes organizational values and norms that may inhibit accurate assessments of market opportunities for products and especially services that facilitate sustainable lifestyles. Although the marketing function typically encompasses environmental scanning and the development of strategic responses to macro trends, many firms appear to have responded to marketing's identity crisis by moving these critical activities elsewhere within the firm, often to the C-suite.

Systemic integration

To move towards marketing for sustainability, marketing scholarship needs both the micro perspective of marketing management, with its emphasis on managing for profitability, and the macro perspective of macromarketing, with its emphasis on systemic and inclusive relationships. The subdiscipline of macromarketing is concerned with the impact of society on marketing systems and the impact of marketing systems on society (Hunt 2007). Marketing for the natural environment must similarly integrate macro perspectives. Viewing the market as a complex system with a heterogeneous structure recognizes that participants' choices "have consequences far beyond themselves, for better or for worse" (Mittelstaedt et al. 2006, p. 135).

In a twenty-five year review of marketing and the environment, Kilbourne & Beckman (1998) observed that with few exceptions micro perspectives dominated researchers' interests prior to 1995, resulting in an overall "failure to adequately define the environmental problem" (ibid., p. 519). Despite a subsequent increase in emphasis on macro perspectives beginning in 1995, the vast majority of marketing scholarship still remains focused on micro questions without significant attention to contextual implications.

Ultimately, it is the *integration of micro and macro forces into a systemic perspective* that we highlight as a key challenge, echoing Peattie (1999), Crane (2000), and Jones et al. (2007). Marketing managers will always need a strategic emphasis on firms and their customers, even if that emphasis is expanded beyond a short-term profit orientation. However, in a future sustainable global market environment, macro issues, such as ecosystem well-being, must be fully integrated into the development of marketing strategies.

In summary, we have highlighted the definition and framing of marketing, current unsustainable levels of consumption, and a systemic perspective that integrates micro and macro contexts as three key challenges facing marketers and marketing scholars in marketing for the natural environment. We turn now to the research needs of this transition to a systemic perspective and its implications for environmental value propositions.

FUTURE DIRECTIONS IN RESEARCH FOR MARKETING AND THE NATURAL ENVIRONMENT

Opportunities abound for marketing scholars to provide guidance to managers and policymakers on marketing for the natural environment. Research in this area must be framed to carefully consider the macro context in which marketing operates. In this section, we provide specific directions for future work. We first suggest existing theoretical foundations that could be more broadly leveraged to increase scholarly understanding of marketing for the natural environment. We then identify key arenas in which new theories are needed.

Applications of existing theories

Complex systems theory

As shown by Levy & Lichenstein ([Chapter 32] this volume), complex systems theory may be usefully applied as a managerial lens. We suggest that existing marketing theories should be reexamined to determine how they might need to be adapted to accommodate a systems perspective.

Service-dominant logic (SDL) explicitly builds on systems theory (Vargo & Lusch 2010) and may provide a useful framework for examining disciplinary assumptions about the roles and relationships between firms and consumers, policymakers, NGOs, and other firms. For example, the relationship between B2B and B2C demand for environmental sustainability is important to understand. In moving to a long-term perspective, the resource-based theory of the firm might be enlarged to embrace systemic implications by viewing labor and inputs as investment "capital" rather than as expendable ecological and human "resources" (Hawken et al. 1999). The opportunities and threats in an economic downturn might be assessed differently given a longer-term, investment capital perspective. Ethical principles, such as those presented by Laczniak & Murphy (2006), may be useful as diagnostic tools. Especially important will be accounting for externalities which have previously not been included in decisions (Schultz & Holbrook 1999). By integrating new market conditions into a variety of existing theories using concepts from complex system theory, marketing can contribute to creating a society in which sustainability is the norm (Martin & Schouten 2011).

To apply complex systems theory to marketing mix-elements, research that aims to develop customer solutions (as Belz & Peattie [2009] suggest should be a goal) must include a stronger emphasis on collaborative co-creation of services that are needed by customers before and after purchase. As noted by the authors of *Natural Capitalism* (Hawken et al. 1999), "product dematerialization" implies a shift from the sale of goods to the sale of services. Options such as sharing, rental, and reuse should be explored to determine how they might fit into and shape evolving consumer lifestyles. Channel models need to become circular rather than linear to accommodate the new recognition that "all waste is food" (McDonough & Braungart 2002). Localization and other new spatial approaches to production and consumption may be needed to optimize customer convenience.

Research is needed about consumer willingness to pay for these new options. The shift to environmental sustainability represents a systemic adjustment (market correction) with pricing implications. Rather than implicitly suggesting that new options will cost more or that there is some "normal" price that can be assumed for such options, a shift in thinking toward greater complexity is required (Peattie 2010). An environmentally sound alternative might cost less to produce, and a "normal" price established in the minds of consumers might include externality-based cost subsidies.

Marketing communications research is needed to identify ways to make sustainability appear fun, appealing, and simple to adopt. Research is needed about greenwashing, particularly about how firms can make progress without being targeted as hypocrites. Theory is needed to understand the current experience of brand managers who are experimenting with environmental sustainability as a secondary rather than primary brand attribute. Complexity theory offers useful tools for addressing each of these issues.

Stakeholder theory

Another platform for micro-macro integration is stakeholder theory (Bhattacharya & Korschun 2008). Stakeholder relationships provide a bridge between the firm and the larger society. Rather than simply managing these relationships or marketing to these stakeholders, firms can invest in them as assets and collaborate with them to co-create value (Mish & Scammon 2010). We note the need for marketers to include a wider variety of stakeholders in their planning, and to assess the impact of their actions on these stakeholders. Models for balancing and prioritizing stakeholder concerns are also needed, including methods for evaluating the contextual features that may impact prioritization.

To this end, effective methodologies for assessing stakeholder concerns and impact in marketing intelligence and environmental scanning are needed. Participatory action research (PAR), and specifically community action research (CAR), have proven to be invaluable in gaining insights about situational constraints and resources that can be harnessed to deliver value to multiple stakeholders (see Ozanne & Anderson 2010; Ozanne & Saatcioglu 2008). Measurement tools not just for products and services, but also for relevant cultural phenomena, such as consumer backlashes, latent demand, inter-group and community influences are required. Both qualitative and quantitative data will need to be seamlessly integrated in effective marketing for the natural environment.

Quality of life

Research has consistently shown that, beyond a minimum threshold, the accumulation of material goods is not a foundation for high quality of life (e.g. Ryan & Deci 2001; Malhotra 2006; Kahneman et al. 2004). Instead, marketers can turn their attention to delivering quality of life in many forms, such as experiential rewards (Csikszentmihalyi 2000), enhancement of family and other social relationships, supports for health and healthy lifestyles, interactions between consumers and the natural environment, and assistance with challenges such as time, information, and possession overload. Consumer desires for these improvements in well-being represent cultural undercurrents that can be tapped by marketers in much the same way that consumer desires for social status and novelty have long been tapped.

Research that moves beyond value as measured by satisfaction (of immediate) needs to quality of life enhanced through attention to the health of the natural environment is needed. Researchers should explore how marketing for the natural environment relates to the long-term systemic well-being of the natural environment. Consideration should be given to impediments and threats to economic well-being, ecological/environmental well-being, and social/cultural well-being. Scales and other tools that can be used to better understand systemic well-being overall are needed.

Consumer culture theory

The insights of consumer culture theorists (CCT) (e.g. Arnould & Thompson 2005) may be especially important to marketers in navigating the multiple simultaneous constructs operating to create markets as this shift occurs. According to CCT, the meanings held by people about products and consumption are heterogeneous, overlapping, and exist within the socio-historic frame of globalization and market capitalism. Consumer culture is viewed as a social arrangement in which the relationships between lived culture, social resources, and symbolic material resources are mediated through markets (ibid.).

Models are needed to understand how the world's population may come to consume in an environmentally sustainable fashion in the future. This may entail new conceptualizations of wants and needs, consumer responsibility and engagement, and consumer learning about complex systems phenomena.

New theoretical territory

Growth versus sustainable development

Further investigation of the implications of a shift to a sustainability paradigm is essential. In the current marketplace, the nature of value is expanding to include social and environmental forms of value that were previously not part of the value equation (Mish & Glavas 2010). A clear specification of that value is needed as the foundation of credibility for environmental value propositions. Businesses typically focus on growth and measure their marketing success in terms of revenue, market share, and incremental growth over prior periods.

Sustainable marketing means marketing in a sustainable manner, such that all marketing processes are environmentally and socially benign (Martin & Schouten 2011). With this perspective, a shift to marketing for the natural environment will require new conceptualizations of goals and new metrics to measure progress towards them.

The pursuit of an environmentally sustainable future will require a shift to a sustainable development view which prioritizes optimization of a variety of resources above maximization of any one resource. Methods to accurately and fully assess the costs and benefits of firms' actions both to the firm and to its stakeholders are needed. With a sustainable development perspective, externalities must be accounted for, both to achieve sustainability and to endure activist scrutiny. Innovative methods for accurately capturing the full cost of products as they are used throughout their life cycle, including costs incurred by the customer during and after use, are needed. As many firms have discovered, a shift in perspective can reveal market opportunities in places that were previously only perceived in terms of costs, such as transforming waste into new products.

Standards and certifications

To effectively market environmental value, marketers must use standards and certifications in new ways. The challenge of delivering and communicating environmental value with credibility is paramount. Standards and certifications can be pivotal tools for addressing this challenge, but they are not well understood by scholars or managers. At their best, these tools can: 1) meet the information needs of firms, their organizational partners, concerned societal stakeholders, and customers; 2) allow harmonization of practices; and 3) provide much needed credibility and trust in the marketplace. However, theoretical work is needed to guide standards development processes and strategic use of standards by marketers.

Development and adoption processes for standards are extremely challenging. Both processes must involve multiple stakeholder groups, each with their own interests and agendas. At the industry level, the competitive landscape must be considered, since standards can be molded to provide opportunities for firms seeking competitive advantage through differentiation. Vulnerable stakeholders, such as the natural environment, need legitimate representation. Once standards are developed, compliance monitoring is essential to ensure fair competition and to optimize the potential for industry wide improvement. As Mish & Scammon (2010) suggest, "standards can be a way to 'raise the bar' for all competitors" (p. 24).

Research is needed to support marketers' strategic use of standards and certifications. For example, the roles of standards across the marketing mix should be clarified, and the relative strength of brands, marketing claims, and eco-labels in establishing and communicating brand value should be explored.

Summary

Ultimately, the greatest research challenges in marketing for the natural environment may be those that illuminate the paradigm shift as a cultural transformation. Marketing has been a substantial force in the development of consumer culture, and it can be a positive force for its transformation in the future (Assadourian 2010). As Jackson (2009) wrote, "prosperity has vital social and psychological dimensions" (p. 7) that marketers have not yet wholeheartedly aimed to provide in the marketplace. Research is needed to overcome the challenges of communicating and delivering consumer and environmental well-being with the same vigor and skill that marketers have brought to selling consumer products. Scholarly efforts to meet these needs will contribute to an understanding of ways in which marketing can be a proactive force in changing the dominant social paradigm.

Conclusion

In this chapter we have reviewed the historical development of marketing practices related to the natural environment, highlighting many of the seminal works that have appeared in the literature during this evolution. Stepping back from these important contributions, we highlight challenges for marketers in pursuing marketing for the natural environment in the future. These include shifts in thought about marketing as a field, and the challenge of achieving sustainable levels of consumption. We conclude by suggesting ways that researchers can contribute to the development of needed insights about the impacts of marketing for the natural environment on a broad set of stakeholders, and thus produce theories that can better guide marketers and policy makers. A key theme for the future will be the successful integration of micro and macro perspectives into a more systemic view of concern for the natural environment.

References

Albino, V., Balice, A., & Dangelico, R. M. (2009). "Environmental Strategies and Green Product Development: An Overview on Sustainability-Driven Companies," *Business Strategy & the Environment*, 18(2): 83–96.

Arnould, E. J. & Thompson, C. J. (2005). "Consumer Culture Theory (CCT): Twenty Years of Research," *Journal of Consumer Research*, 31(4): 868–882.

Assadourian, E. (2010). "The Rise and Fall of Consumer Cultures," in *State of the World: Transforming Cultures From Consumerism to Sustainability*, Worldwatch Institute Report, New York: WW Norton and Company.

Bannerjee, S., Iyer, E. S., & Kashyap, R. K. (2003). "Corporate Environmentalism: Antecedents and Influence of Industry Type," *Journal of Marketing*, 67(2): 106–122.

Belz, F.-M. & Peattie, K. (2009). *Sustainability Marketing: A Global Perspective*. West Sussex, United Kingdom: John Wiley & Sons, Ltd.

Bhattacharya, C. B. & Korschun, D. (2008). "Stakeholder Marketing: Beyond the Four Ps and the Customer," *Journal of Public Policy & Marketing*, 27: 113–116.

Brown, T. J. & Dacin, P. A. (1997). "The Company and the Product: Corporate Associations and Consumer Product Responses," *The Journal of Marketing*, 61 (Jan.)

Carlson, L., Grove, S. J., & Kangun, N. (1993). "A Content Analysis of Environmental Advertising Claims: A Matrix Method Approach," *Journal of Advertising*, 22(09): 27–39.

Coddington, W. (1993). *Environmental Marketing: Positive Strategies for Reaching the Green Consumer.* New York: McGraw-Hill.

Conroy, M. E. (2007). *Branded: How the 'Certification Revolution' is Transforming Global Corporations.* Gabriola Island, BC: New Society Publishers.

Constantinides, E. (2006). "The Marketing Mix Revisited: Towards the 21st Century Marketing," *Journal of Marketing Management*, 22(04): 407–38.

Crane, A. (2000). "Facing the Backlash: Green Marketing and Strategic Reorientation in the 1990s," *Journal of Strategic Marketing*, 8(09): 277–96.

Csikszentmihalyi, M. (2000). "The Costs and Benefits of Consuming," *Journal of Consumer Research*, 27(09): 267–72.

Dangelico, R. & Pujari, D. (2010). "Mainstreaming Green Product Innovation: Why and how Companies Integrate Environmental Sustainability," *Journal of Business Ethics*, 95(09): 471–86.

Drumwright, M. E. (1994). "Socially Responsible Organizational Buying: Environmental Concern as a Noneconomic Buying Criterion," *The Journal of Marketing*, 58: 1–19.

Feldman, L. P. (1971). "Societal Adaptation: A new Challenge for Marketing" *Journal of Marketing*, 35(3): 54–60.

Fisk, G. (1974). *Marketing and the Ecological Crisis*, New York: Harper and Row.

Fuller, D. A. (1999). *Sustainable Marketing: Managerial-Ecological Issues.* Thousand Oaks, CA: Sage Publications.

Ginsberg, J. M. & Bloom, P. (2004). "Choosing the Right Green Marketing Strategy," *MIT Sloan Management Review*, 79–84.

Gronroos, C. (2007). *In Search of a New Logic for Marketing* New York: John Wiley & Sons.

Gundlach, G. T. & Wilkie, W. L. (2010). "Stakeholder Marketing: Why 'Stakeholder' Was Omitted from the American Marketing Association's Official 2007 Definition of Marketing and Why the Future Is Bright for Stakeholder Marketing," *Journal of Public Policy & Marketing*, 29(1): 89–92.

Hawken, P., Lovins, A., & Lovins, L. H. (1999). *Natural Capitalism.* Boston: Little, Brown, and Company.

Henion, K. E. II & Kinnear, T. C. (1976). *Ecological Marketing*, Chicago: American Marketing Association.

Hunt, S. D. (2007). "A Responsibilities Framework for Marketing as a Professional Discipline," *Journal of Public Policy & Marketing*, 26: 277–83.

Jackson, T. (2009). "Prosperity without Growth? The Transition to a Sustainable Economy," Sustainable Development Commission. Accessed June 15, 2010 from <http://www.sd-commission.org.uk/publications.php?id=915>

Jones, P., Clark-Hill, C., Comfort, D. & Hillier, D. (2008). "Marketing and Sustainability," *Marketing Intelligence & Planning*, 26(2): 123–130.

Kahneman, D., Krueger A. B., Schkade, D., Schwarz, N. & Stone, A. (2004). "Toward National Well-being Accounts," *The American Economic Review*, 94: 429–434.

Kilbourne, W. E. (2010). "Facing the Challenge of Sustainability in a Changing World: An Introduction to the Special Issue," *Journal of Macromarketing*, 30(20): 109–111.

—— & Beckman, S. C. (1998). "Review and Critical Assessment of Research on Marketing and the Environment," *Journal of Marketing Management*, 14: 513–532.

Laczniak, G. R. & Murphy, P. E. (2006). "Normative Perspectives for Ethical and Socially Responsible Marketing," *Journal of Macromarketing*, 26(2): 154–77.

Luo, X. & Bhattacharya, C. B. (2006). "Corporate Social Responsibility, Customer Satisfaction, and Market Value," *Journal of Marketing*, 70(4): 1–18.

McDonough, W. & Braungart, M. (2002). *Cradle to Cradle: Remaking the Way We Make Things*. New York: North Point.

McKenzie-Mohr, D. and Smith, W. (1999). *Fostering Sustainable Behavior*. Gabriola Island, BC: New Society Publishers.

Maignan, I. & Ferrell, O. C. (2004). "Corporate Social Responsibility and Marketing: An Integrative Framework," *Journal of the Academy of Marketing Science*, 32: 3–19.

Makower, J. (2009). *Strategies for the Green Economy: Opportunities and Challenges in the New World of Business*, New York: McGraw Hill.

Malhotra, N. K. (2006). "Consumer Well-being and Quality of Life: An Assessment and Directions for Future Research," *Journal of Macromarketing*, 26(06): 77–80.

Martin, D. M. & Schouten, J. W. (2011). *Sustainable Marketing*, Upper Saddle, River NJ: Prentice Hall.

Mayer, R. N., Lewis, L. A., & Scammon, D. L. (2001). "The Effectiveness of Environmental Marketing Claims," in *Handbook of Marketing & Society*, Paul Bloom and Gregory Gundlach, Editors. Thousand Oaks, CA: Sage Publications, Inc.

Mendleson, N. & Polonsky, M. J. (1995). "Using Strategic Alliances to Develop Credible Green Marketing," *Journal of Consumer Marketing*, 12(06): 4–18.

Menon, J. & Menon, A. (1997). "Enviropreneurial Marketing Strategy: The Emergence of Corporate Environmentalism as Market Strategy," *Journal of Marketing*, 61: 51–67.

——————Chowdhury, J., & Jankovich, J. (1999). "Evolving Paradigm for Environmental Sensitivity in Marketing Programs: A Synthesis of Theory and Practice," *Journal of Marketing Theory and Practice*, 1–15.

Mintel (1991). *The Green Consumer Report*, London: Mintel.

—— (2010). *Green Living—US*, London: Mintel.

Mish, J. & Glavas, A. (2010). "Systemic Transparency as the Key to Marketing and Sustainability: Lessons from Pioneering Firms." *University of Notre Dame Working Paper*.

—— & Scammon, D. L. (2010). "Principle Based Stakeholder Marketing: Insights from Private Triple-Bottom-Line Firms," *Journal of Public Policy & Marketing*, 29(1): 12–26.

Mittelstaedt, J. D., Kilbourne, W. E., & Mittelstaedt, R. A. (2006). "Macromarketing as Agorology: Macromarketing Theory and the Study of the Agora," *Journal of Macromarketing*, 26(2): 131–142.

Organic Trade Association (2010). "Organic Trade Association's 2010 Organic Industry Survey," Organic Trade Association.

Ottman, J. A., Stafford, E. R., & Hartman, C. L. (2006). "Avoiding Green Marketing Myopia: Ways to Improve Consumer Appeal for Environmentally Preferable Products," *Environment*, 48: 22–36.

Palazzo, G., & Basu, K. (2007). "The Ethical Backlash of Corporate Branding," *Journal of Business Ethics*, 73(4): 333–46.

Peattie, K. (1999). "Trappings Versus Substance in the Greening of Marketing Planning," *Journal of Strategic Marketing*, 7(06): 131–48.

—— (2001). "Towards Sustainability: The Third Age of Green Marketing," *Marketing Review*, 2(2): 129–46.

—— (2010). "Green Consumption: Behavior and Norms" *Annual Review of Environment and Resources*, 35: 195–228.

—— & Crane A. (2005). "Green Marketing: Legend, Myth, Farce Or Prophesy?" *Qualitative Market Research: An International Journal*, 8(04): 357–70.

Peloza, J. & Shang, J. (2010). "How Can Corporate Social Responsibility Activities Create Value for Stakeholders: A Systematic Review," *Journal of the Academy of Marketing Science*, 39(1): 117–135.

Polonsky, M. J. & Mintu-Wimsatt, A. T. (1995). *Environmental Marketing: Strategies, Practice, Theory, and Research*. Binghamton, NY: Haworth Press.

—— & Ottman, J. (1998). "Stakeholders' Contribution to the Green New Product Development Process," *Journal of Marketing Management*, 14(07): 533–57.

—— Brooks, H., Henry, P., & Schweizer, C. (1998). "An Exploratory Examination of Environmentally Responsible Straight Rebuy Purchases in Large Australian Organizations," *Journal of Business & Industrial Marketing*, 13: 54–69.

Porter, M. E. & van der Linde, C. (1995). "Toward a New Conception of the Environment-Competitiveness Relationship," *Journal of Economic Perspectives*, 9: 97–118.

Press, M. & Arnould, E. J. (2009). "Constraints on Sustainable Energy Consumption: Market System and Public Policy Challenges and Opportunities," *Journal of Public Policy & Marketing*, 28: 102–13.

Pujari, D. (2006). "Eco-Innovation and New Product Development: Understanding the Influences on Market Performance," *Technovation*, 26(1): 76–85.

—— Peattie, K., & Wright, G. (2004). "Organizational Antecedents of Environmental Responsiveness in Industrial New Product Development," *Industrial Marketing Management*, 33(07): 381–91.

—— —— —— (2003). "Green and Competitive: Influences on Environmental New Product Development Performance," *Journal of Business Research*, 56(8): 657–71.

Reinhardt, F. L. (1998). "Environmental Product Differentiation: Implications for Corporate Strategy," *California Management Review*, 40: 43–73.

Roper Organization (1990). *The Environment: Public Attitudes and Individual Behaviour*, New York: Roper Organization and SC Johnson and Son.

Ryan, R. M. & Deci, E. L. (2001). "On Happiness and Human Potentials: A Review of Research on Hedonic and Eudaimonic Well-being," *Annual Review of Psychology*, 52: 141–66.

Sahota, A., Haumann, B., Givens, H., & Baldwin, C. (2009). "Ecolabeling and Consumer Interest in Sustainable Products," in *Sustainability in the Food Industry*, ed. Cheryl J. Baldwin, Ames, IA: Wiley-Blackwell.

Scammon, D. L. & Mayer, R. N. (1995). "Agency Review of Environmental Marketing Claims: Case-by-Case Decomposition of the Issues," *Journal of Advertising*, 24(2): 33–44.

Schultz, C. J. & Holbrook, M. B. (1999). "Marketing and the Tragedy of the Commons: A Synthesis, Commentary, and Analysis for Action," *Journal of Public Policy & Marketing*, 18: 218–29.

Sheth, J. N. & Sisodia, R. S. (eds), (2006). *Does Marketing Need Reform?* Armonk, NY: M. E. Sharpe.

Simon, F. L. (1992). "Marketing Green Products in the Triad," *Columbia Journal of World Business*, 27: 268–85.

Sirgy, M. J., & Samli, A. C. (eds.), (1995). *New Dimensions in Marketing/Quality-of-Life Research*, Westport, CT: Quorom.

Smith, N. C., Drumwright, M. C., & Gentile, M. C. (2010). "The New Marketing Myopia," *Journal of Public Policy & Marketing*, 29(1): 4–11.

UN (1987). *Our Common Future*, World Commission on Environment and Development, Oxford: Oxford University Press.

US Code Of Federal Regulations (1992, 1996, 1998). "Green Guides." 57 FR 36363, 61 FR 53311, 63 FR 24240.

Varadarajan, P. R. & Menon, A. (1988). "Cause-Related Marketing: A Coalignment of Marketing Strategy and Corporate Philanthropy," *The Journal of Marketing*, 52: 58–74.

Varey, R. J. (2010). "Marketing Means and Ends for a Sustainable Society: A Welfare Agenda for Transformative Change," *Journal of Macromarketing*, 30(2): 112–126.

Vargo, S. L. & Lusch, R. F. (2010). "It's All B2B ...and Beyond: Toward a Systems Perspective of the Market," *Industrial Marketing Management*, (forthcoming).

—— —— (2004). "Evolving to a New Dominant Logic for Marketing, *Journal of Marketing*, 68: 1–17.

Walley, N. & Whitehead, B. (1994). "It's Not Easy being Green," *Harvard Business Review*, 72: 46–51.

Webster, F. E., Malter, A. J., & Ganesan, S. (2003). "Can Marketing Regain its Seat at the Table?" *MSI Reports*, Working Paper Series 29–47.

Wong, V., Turner, W. & Stoneman, P. (1996). "Marketing Strategies and Market Prospects for Environmentally-Friendly Consumer Products," *British Journal of Management*, 7(3): 263–281.

World Business Council For Sustainable Development (2008). "Sustainable Consumption Facts and Trends: From a Business Perspective," 1–40.

—— (2005). "Driving Success: Marketing and Sustainable Development," 1–20

WHY NOT CHOOSE GREEN? CONSUMER DECISION MAKING FOR ENVIRONMENTALLY FRIENDLY PRODUCTS

ANDREW D. GERSHOFF
AND JULIE R. IRWIN

OVER the last decade there has been a marked increase in consumers' interest in products that are considered environmentally friendly or "green". Consumers are saying they would prefer to purchase products that use fewer scarce resources, are non-polluting, and are less harmful to the physical environment and to people (Mackoy, Calantone, & Droge 1995; Luchs, Naylor, Irwin, & Raghunathan 2010). In response, manufacturers and retailers have increased their offerings of products that feature attributes or processes that have less environmental impact. Paradoxically, despite consumers' favorable attitudes and increased availability, sales of these green products often lag behind their less-green competitors (UNEP 2005).

The purpose of this chapter is to better understand this paradox by exploring factors that influence consumers' adoption of green products, with an eye toward (1) understanding why consumers' green interests are not becoming consumers' green behaviors and (2) suggesting marketing solutions that might increase sales of green products. As a part of this collection on business and the environment, this chapter shares a marketing focus with both the other marketing chapters in this volume. Like the Devinney chapter ([Chapter 21] this volume), which examines methods of segmentation, we also highlight how green attitudes are only a part of a more complex decision calculus. However, our aim is to understand psychological factors that influence how individuals make decisions for or against green products. Our approach shares the flavor of Shu & Bazerman ([Chapter 9] this volume), because we also use behavioral explanations to address our primary question (although they focus on managers and policy makers and we focus on consumers). The chapter by Scammon & Mish ([Chapter 19] this volume) more broadly examines the role of marketing in green products by tracing the evolution of green products through time and how they have changed to incorporate objectives of the many stakeholders in the environmental discussion.

In this chapter we highlight notable examples from the body of consumer research on green consuming, and take an in-depth look at four key factors that may lead consumers to forego green options despite their stated intentions to buy them. In the first section, we discuss how consumers evaluate whether a product will actually provide a green benefit, and how they evaluate the costs of achieving those benefits. Next we examine how consumers' emotional reactions play a role in their decisions, and how these emotions can work against their desires to make green choices. Third, we look at contextual elements, such as how the decision is presented to the consumer and how the consumer indicates preference for one product over another. Finally, because consumers' attitudes and behaviors may be shaped by their identities, we examine how identity may be a contributing factor in consumers' failure to be green. Throughout, we suggest that societal and marketplace influences, including prior experiences with green products, retail environments, moral expectations, and marketers' attempts to persuade consumers, are often not consistent with an environment that would optimally facilitate green decisions. Finally, we seek to provide suggestions for improvement on this mismatch, with the goal of increasing green purchasing and consumption.

Evaluating the costs and benefits of going green

We might expect that consumers who say they want to make environmentally friendly purchases, will do so if they perceive the benefits of choosing a green product outweigh the costs. Unfortunately, one reason why consumers may not choose green products is that many factors hinder their ability to accurately evaluate the benefits of green products and the associated costs.

In this section we will consider three areas of particular interest. First is consumers' beliefs that products and behaviors described as green will actually provide any green benefit. The second is consumers' evaluations and inferences about the trade-offs they must make in order to obtain a green benefit. Finally we will consider the way consumers evaluate the costs they bear relative to others in order to receive green benefits.

Consumers don't see green actions leading to green outcomes

The environmental benefit of buying a product with a "green" label is often difficult to observe. For example, there is very little a consumer can do to test a claim that a product is made with recycled raw materials or using an energy-saving production method. As a result, compared to more concrete attributes, such as size or style, attributes that make a product green require that a consumer trust the seller. Attributes such as these, that would require great effort or expertise to evaluate even after using the product, are referred to as "credence attributes" by marketers (Darby & Karini 1973). Compared to other attributes, consumers are more skeptical of credence claims and associate these attributes with greater risk. Thus, for credence attributes, consumers tend to require more information from trusted sources, and tend to rely more on branding and product quality (Ostrom & Iacabucci 1995). For example, Srinivasan & Till (2002) showed that the credence claim of "easily biodegradable" for facial tissues was rated as more likely to be true when it was made by the well-known Kleenex brand than when made by a generic producer.

Unfortunately, even well-known brands' trust has potentially been eroded by over-statements of the benefits of their green products. For example, a recent report by the environmental marketing firm, TerraChoice, charged that 98 percent of commonly purchased green household items misled consumers by making claims with vague terms like 'natural' and 'earth-friendly' that cannot be verified, or by highlighting aspects of products that, although potentially beneficial to the environment in the short run provide little benefit when looked at in the entirety of the product life cycle (Terrachoice 2009). This report has been echoed by thousands of examples in the media, critical of marketers' use of greenwashing tactics.

When consumers are aware of these deceptions, the likelihood of future purchase is greatly diminished. Research exploring consumers' understanding of marketers' intentions suggests that individuals are quite aware of marketers' persuasive intents and have well-developed methods to cope with, and guard against them (Friestad & Wright 1994). Vohs, Baumeister, & Chin (2007) argue that when people enter into an exchange that they hope will turn out fairly but does not, they feel duped, particularly if they believe that greater scrutiny or vigilance might have prevented the unfair outcome. After such an event, people become more vigilant to protect against recurring harm, and may be less likely to repurchase (Harley & Strickland 1986; Broniarczyk & Gershoff 2003).

In addition, consumers may be motivated to rely on, and even overweigh, this mistrust as they make choices. Specifically, the growing notion that marketers may be misleading consumers with green claims may provide those who are more reluctant to make green choices with an excuse to avoid green products altogether. Deciding that a green claim is overstated or false is one way to avoid learning more about the environmental issue, to avoid trading off the issue with other product attributes, and finally a way to avoid buying a more environmentally friendly product (Namkoong & Irwin 2010).

For marketers, finding ways to prove the environmental benefit to customers may be a solution. Research on overcoming consumer reluctance to rely on credence attributes suggests that finding ways to communicate value can have a positive effect. For example, credibility may be improved when marketers not only make environmental claims about their products, but also meet expectations on other more observable attributes. Consumers' beliefs about the relationship between the observable attributes and the unobservable claims have been shown to lead to greater trust of those claims (Grolleau & Caswell 2006). Another option is for marketers to rely on third-party labeling or "eco-seals." These labels effectively relieve consumers of the task of verifying green claims, and make the credence attribute behave like a search attribute. Empirical research on use of such seals, including a 'Dolphin Safe' seal for tuna (Teisl, Roe, & Hicks 2002), and the 'Nordic Swan' seal for paper products (Bjørner, Hansen, & Russell 2004), has shown they can be effective in increasing sales.

Consumers don't think tomorrow's benefit is worth today's cost

Using environmentally friendly products or acting in more environmentally favorable ways often involves trade-offs, either real or expected. For example, a consumer may have to wait more than twenty years before the upfront cost of installing an energy-saving solar electrical system will be offset by utility cost savings (National Renewable Energy Laboratory 2004; Galbraith 2009). More common consumer goods may not require such a large investment in the future, but many still require consumers to either forgo another quality attribute to obtain the "green" one, or to pay more for a green version of the product with the expectation that it will repay this investment via a better future environment.

For consumers, a problem with attributes requiring delayed gratification is that they often fall victim to "hyperbolic discounting" (Loewenstein & Prelec 1992): attributes that provide immediate rewards are valued more than are attributes that provide rewards in the future (i.e. the future is discounted). Even if consumers would actually be happier and feel better about themselves in the future if they chose the "virtue" of the green product over another product that is more harmful to the environment (a "vice"), they often in the moment choose the vice (Read, Loewenstein, & Kalyanaraman 1999). Discussions of intertemporal biases and trade-offs among individuals can be found in Bazerman & Shu ([Chapter 9] this volume) and Tost & Wade-Benzoni ([Chapter 10] this volume).

Consumers assume there's a catch

Even when there are no real trade-offs to be made, consumers may infer them. Many people implicitly believe that the market ensures "no free lunch." Any improvement on an aspect of a product, such as an increase in size, must come with a decrease on another aspect, such as a reduction of quality (Chernev 2007). Apart from generally expecting to give up something to get something, consumers may also make specific inferences about how a green attribute affects a product. For example, Luchs et al. (2010) found that consumers associate firms that care about the environment (in addition to other factors associated with sustainability) with gentleness and gentleness-related attributes, whereas firms that do not care about the environment are more likely to be associated with strength. As a consequence of these associations, having green and sustainable benefits can reduce preference for products in categories (such as automobile tires and hand sanitizers) in which strength is especially valued. On the other hand, in product categories in which gentleness is valued, such as baby shampoo, green and sustainable benefits can increase preferences.

For marketers, understanding consumers' inferences about how green benefits will affect a product's other attributes is important. For example, marketers could leverage consumers' inferences that green products have superior performance in terms of gentleness-related attributes (e.g. safety, healthfulness) by highlighting them where appropriate. Because Luchs et al. found that providing guarantees of strength, such as with taglines reading "guaranteed strong", attenuated negative inferences, marketers of products for which strength is important should be sure to include assurances that the green benefit does not indicate any loss of strength.

Consumers let others bear the costs

Although the costs of selecting green products tend to fall on individual consumers, the benefits tend to be shared. For example, many electric suppliers now have programs that allow consumers to pay a higher rate to have their power produced exclusively from renewable energy sources such as wind or solar. Although these programs reduce the amount of carbon released into the atmosphere, this benefit is enjoyed even by those who purchase less expensive and less environmentally friendly electricity. Free rider effects (Dawes, McTavish, & Shaklee 1977) are thus a potential problem when consumers consider green products and behaviors; consumers may be reluctant to participate if they believe they must bear costs that should be shared, and even if they care deeply about the issue, they may assume that others will act in accordance with their beliefs, allowing them to reap the benefits while others pay the cost.

Research on the evaluation of public goods suggests that consumers do sometimes attempt to free ride, either by offering to pay less than the good is worth to them or by demanding much less to relinquish the good than they would actually require to give it up. These consumers assume others will pay for the good and they will get to benefit from it without paying their "fair share" or experiencing their fair amount of sacrifice. Interestingly, though, consumers do not universally free ride, even in patently economic games exchanging public goods for real money (see Ledyard 1995). In studies of values for environmental goods such as air quality (e.g. Irwin et al. 1993) respondents showed very little free riding. Although there are a number of explanations for this lack of free riding, a primary reason is that consumers' ethical and social beliefs argue against doing so.

We suspect that free riding is similar to other sorts of cheating, in which people might cheat to a point, but are unlikely to completely give into selfish impulses, because doing so threatens their view of themselves as ethical beings (Mazar, Amir, & Ariely 2008). Indeed such reinforcement of existing moral beliefs by having people sign an honor code, write the Ten Commandments, or just think about 'God' has been shown to decrease cheating and increase pro-social behavior (Mazar et al. 2008; Shariff & Norenzayan 2007). Marketers and public policymakers might exploit this finding by including themes that cue morality in advertising and packaging of green products and programs.

THE ROLE OF EMOTION IN ENVIRONMENTAL EVALUATION

Having to trade off pedestrian attributes such as price or quantity for attributes associated with environmental issues such as protecting resources for great grandchildren or keeping life-threatening catastrophe at bay, is likely to induce a great deal of emotion. The emotions that may be generated by these decisions is another reason why consumers who indicate they would buy green products may not do so. In this section we look at two specific aspects of emotion and decision-making. The first is that emotional decisions may be made by attending to the emotional reactions rather than a rational consideration of facts. The second is that the trade-offs necessary to make an optimal decision may become compromised and perhaps even abandoned in order to protect the decision maker from emotional stress.

Consumers' emotions may hinder evaluation of green benefits

In evaluating options and making decisions, people rely on two independent but inter-active systems: a deliberative, analytic, rational system, and a more automatic system in which one's emotions and visceral reactions are more likely to influence the outcome (Chaiken & Trope 1999; Epstein et al. 1996). When evaluating outcomes that involve risk, including environmental risk, consumers are more likely to rely on their emotional system, letting feelings about the possible outcomes influence their evaluation of the risk rather than performing a rational consideration or calculation of actual probabilities (Loewenstein et al. 2001). Researchers have described this as an "affect heuristic," that allows individuals to make judgments that are quick, but which may not be consistent with the decision maker's broader goals, nor with normative standards (Slovic & Peters 2006). As Slovic, Lichtenstein, & Fischhoff (1979) have demonstrated, people respond to risks not solely in terms of the objective possibility for harm, but in terms of other issues such as whether the harm is "dreaded" (involuntary, sudden, frightening risks such as nuclear accidents, or terror attacks) and whether it is considered "catastrophic" (many people are affected at one time, such as with airplane accidents). Unfortunately, environ-mental risks often fall into these categories. For example, effects of global warming are often described as leading to catastrophic flooding, and mass starvation.

Consumers' emotional responses can drive judgments of environmental risks such that they may respond only to their emotional response to the generic issue associated with the risk, but not to obviously normative aspects such as the degree to which the environment is affected. Some striking examples of this are predicted "scope" (Nadler et al. 2001) or "embedding" (Kahneman & Knetsch 1992) effects that show that people are willing to pay similar amounts for vastly different degrees of benefit. For example, when asked to donate money to a charity, participants gave similar amounts whether they were saving many animals or many lakes compared to saving just one animal or just one lake (Kahneman & Knetsch 1992; Diamond & Hausman 1994). Similarly, Irwin & Spira (1997) showed that adding a new unrelated environmental attribute (e.g. recycled content) to a set of possible products (in this case, cars) reduced the impact of a pre-existing environmental attribute (e.g. CO emissions) in respondents' evaluations of the products. Because the attributes both triggered similar emotional responses, respondents tended to group the two attributes together into one attribute in their minds, thus reducing the impact of both of the individual attributes.

Results like those described above suggest that ethical behavior may be largely symbolic. Thus, the slightest pro-environmental behavior may work to signify that the decision maker is being "green". So, for example, installing just one low-energy light bulb may be valued as much as installing a household full, even though environmentally the impacts are very different. Although marketers might be pleased to know that small environmental gestures may sell well despite their small impact, from a prescriptive standpoint, it might be better to avoid these symbolic gestures that do not make much of a difference. Since, as mentioned earlier, eco-labels may be helpful toward increasing purchase of green products, requiring significant environmental improvement before allowing the label would help avoid scope problems.

Consumers may avoid green trade-offs to avoid negative emotions

Another way in which emotion can influence consumer decision-making is by causing consumers to "shut down," refusing to face a trade-off at all. In fact, just the act of considering a trade-off involving an emotional attribute, such as considering trading off safety features in a car in order to get a better radio, can lead to suboptimal choices (Luce, Bettman, & Payne 1997). These suboptimal choices may occur either because decision makers painstakingly focus on one attribute at a time to avoid thinking about the trade-offs, or because they simply avoid the trade-off by avoiding the decision altogether. Frequently this avoidance is accomplished by simply sticking with their status quo (i.e. what they have tended to buy in the past).

In a green marketing context this avoidance of emotional attributes could have the greatest influence on those who care the most about environmental issues. The presence of trade-offs for environmental benefit may cause these consumers the most emotional stress, so they avoid the choice entirely, either by purchasing nothing, or by just repeating past purchases. Indeed, the "taboo" trade-off and protected values literature includes many examples of individuals indicating that there are some trade-offs that simply cannot even be considered, such as trading off saving human lives for money (Tetlock et al. 2000) or trading off endangered forests for cheaper or more beautiful furniture (Irwin & Baron 2001). It is ironic that consumers' emotional reactions may actually lead to less action, not more, because of a closely held environmental value.

Although much of the preceding would suggest that marketers might aim to reduce the emotional reactions to green products in order to increase sales, emotional reactions may be used to marketers' advantage as well. For example, Liu & Aaker (2008) increased the amount of money donated to charities by asking participants to donate their time to a charity prior to asking them to donate money. They argued that asking for time, as opposed to money, changes the way people think about the exchange from a purely economic perspective to a more emotional consideration. As a result, people tend to give both more time and more money. Likewise, Hsee & Rottenstreight (2004) found that using affect-rich examples influenced use of emotional evaluations, and in turn influenced charity donation behaviors. In one study, they presented graphical representations of the exact number of endangered pandas that needed help through consumer donations. When the pandas were represented as simple dots, the amount people gave depended on the number of pandas that needed help. However, when the animals were represented by individual photographs of cute pandas, the donation amounts were less sensitive to the number of pandas to be saved. Further, the amount donated to save just one panda was greater when it was presented in an affect-rich picture compared to an affect poor dot.

Using this information, marketers might develop a number of targeted strategies that could positively influence consumer response. For example, for those products for which an economic evaluation of a trade-off is particularly unfavorable, using an emotional appeal first might move people toward a more emotional consideration of the impact of their actions. For instance when the environmental benefit may be considered relatively small, using an affect rich presentation of the benefit could increase compliance. Conversely, when the environmental benefit cues negative emotions, it may be beneficial to reduce such thinking by presenting information in a way that leads to more rational evaluation of outcomes (Gershoff & Koehler, 2011).

Consumers may willfully ignore information

Although some products highlight and display their green attributes, some do not. In fact, some of the most environmentally friendly products, such as baking soda, vinegar, or lemon juice, often do not tout green aspects at all. The lack of information in the marketplace about many products' green attributes means that consumers must gather the information on their own. Unfortunately, consumers may sometimes intentionally avoid gathering this information in order to avoid negative emotions that are triggered when they consider environmental issues. Ehrich & Irwin (2005) showed that when given the option of finding out whether a set of products was "green" or not (such as whether furniture was made from wood taken from endangered rainforests) before making a purchase decision, many participants, including those who indicated that they cared deeply about the relevant underlying environmental issue (such as rainforest preservation), avoided asking for the available information and remained ignorant about whether the goods were "green" or not. Yet, when participants were given all of the attribute information (and did not have to ask for it) those who cared more about the environmental issue relied more on the green attribute in making their purchase decision. In other words, simply telling consumers whether the goods are green or not (and not making them ask for the information) greatly increased the probability of greener decision making.

For marketers, an implication of this research is that when products contain positive green attributes, these attributes ought to be emphasized in an overt manner, where it will be hard for consumers to miss. If this attribute information is readily available, it appears consumers will use it in making a choice, but the emotional cost may prevent them from pursuing the information if it is more elusive.

CONTEXTUAL INFLUENCES ON GREEN CHOICES

In the previous sections we described how consumers may not choose green products because of the way in which they evaluate green attributes and the role that emotions play in their evaluations. In this section we examine a few contextual factors that might decrease consumers' choice of green products.

Green products may be chosen if consumers reject rather than select options

A recent study (Irwin & Naylor 2009) illustrates how including options versus excluding options from the set of eligible purchases (the consideration set) significantly affects the evaluation of green products. Green products are more likely to be included in the consideration set if the decision process involves excluding unwanted items than if it involves selecting wanted options. For instance, if decision makers put the set of products that they are interested in considering into a bin marked "interested" they will pay less attention to whether the products are "green" than if they put the set of products they are not interested in considering into a bin marked "not interested." It seems that it is more difficult for consumers to admit that they do not want something ethical by explicitly rejecting it than it is for them to simply not include the ethical option as they winnow down a set of potential alternatives. In fact, the work on loss aversion and environmental preference (e.g. Irwin 1994) shows that environmental goods (e.g. radon prevention devices), and policies (e.g. requiring an increase in air quality), tend to be valued much more highly when the decision maker is considering what may be given up versus what may be gained.

Consideration of money may reduce preference for green products

Evaluating environmental improvements as they relate to money may be difficult for many consumers. Indeed in a study of values for environmental versus non-environmental market goods, many respondents indicated that environmental goods "should not have to be valued monetarily" (Irwin 1994). In some cases, people may respond with disgust that a sacred value has been monetized, and this disgust may lead consumers to entirely avoid or reject the consideration (Tetlock et al. 2000; Lichtenstein, Gregory, & Irwin 2007). Alternatively, consumers may adopt a market-based mode of evaluation and simply avoid the implication of their values in the decision.

Joint versus separate evaluation

Decisions among alternatives tend to be made either jointly (A vs B directly compared) or separately (A evaluated, then B evaluated, etc.). It has been shown (Irwin, Lichtenstein, & Slovic 1993; Bazerman, Tenbrunsel, & Wade-Benzoni 1998) that joint evaluations tend to increase focus on "should" attributes such as environmental quality and that separate evaluations increase focus on "want" attributes such as price and quality. In addition, many studies indicate that attributes that are difficult to evaluate, as green attributes often are, will receive more attention in joint versus separate evaluation (Hsee et al. 1999).

Context effects and the marketplace: a problem for green marketers

Unfortunately, much of the research on context effects suggests that the very contexts that tend to be present at the time of purchase may be those that tend to hinder the choice of green products. Retail environments have steadily increased variety, making it more likely that consumers will select just a few alternatives to include in consideration sets, as opposed to selecting alternatives to reject from further consideration. In fact, the shopping cart itself is very similar to the "interested" bin used in Naylor & Irwin's (2009) study. Likewise, retail environments tend to focus on price; all products are clearly priced and the transaction ends at the cash register. Thus, economic evaluations loom large in the consideration of alternatives in the marketplace. Also, very few purchasing contexts will encourage direct comparison of two products with each other: it is more likely that consumers evaluate each product individually. All three of these aspects of retail environments should, research suggests, decrease focus on "green" attributes.

On the other hand, marketers might be able to use these context effects to increase sales of green products. Potentially, an ideal environment would be one that either offers fewer alternatives or provides promotional materials that offer decision strategies or checklists that lead consumers to start with initial sets of products from which they eliminate options. Some retail spaces, such as fair-trade only stores, and companies such as Whole Foods and Patagonia provide these sorts of prescreened products for consumers. Additionally, retailers and manufactures might do more to decrease an economic mindset and/or to facilitate an environmental mindset in retail settings, potentially by providing opportunities to participate in other green activities, such as recycling, or composting, as part of the retail experience. Advertisers could also encourage the sort of head-to-head comparison process that benefits green and other "should" attributes; for example the promotion could single out a competitor and explicitly explain how the promoted product is more environmentally friendly than the competitor's product. These seemingly-minor contextual shifts could have sizable effects on preference for green products.

ENVIRONMENTAL IDENTITY

Personal identities, such as being socially concerned or being a caring person, are representations of one's self as well as one's traits, characteristics, and goals. Identities help individuals guide, organize, and give meaning to their behaviors (Brewer 1991). Each person has numerous personal and social identities: one may consider him or herself to be a parent, a banker, and a handy person. However not all of a person's identities will be salient or relevant at the same time (Oyserman 2009; Tajfel & Turner 1979). Just which identity is salient for an individual at any given time depends on a number of contextual factors (Oyserman 2009; McGuire, McGuire, & Winton 1979). In this section we examine how personal identities may play a role in the decision to purchase green products.

Consumers may not buy green products if appropriate identities are not cued

Salient identities can influence how individuals think about and process information, and can also influence the effectiveness of attempts to change attitudes and behavior (Erikson 1964; Oyserman 2009). For example, in a study by Grinstein & Nisan (2009), compliance with a government-sponsored campaign to save water in Israel was linked to the extent to which a citizen identified with the majority community, and by extension, identified with the government. Thus, Non-Orthodox Jews, whose social identity is closest to that of the Israeli government, showed the greatest reduction in water consumption, while Arab Israelis, whose social identity is less closely tied to the government, had less reduction in their water consumption associated with the campaign.

Although broad ethnic identities are often considered psychologically salient, contextual identity may be more effective for influencing behavior, especially when norms associated with the identity are also presented. For example, Goldstein, Cialdini, & Griskevicius (2008) examined the relationship between consumers' likelihood of re-using towels during a hotel stay and written requests that manipulated the social identity of others who were said to have reused towels. The greatest amount of reuse was found when situation-specific identities were cued. If a guest was told that others who had previously stayed in the exact same room had reused their towels, then compliance was highest, followed by when they were told that the others had merely stayed at the same hotel, with the least compliance for when the others were described simply as "fellow citizens."

In addition to community and situation specific-identity, cuing moral identity may also be particularly effective for motivating consumer decisions that affect the environment.

Recent research argues that many individuals may hold an identity for themselves that is organized around a set of moral traits including being caring, compassionate, fair, and kind (Acquino & Reed 2002). Compared to individuals who have lower importance for moral identity, those with higher moral identity importance have been shown to engage in more volunteering to help others, greater donations to food drives, and more donations to help out-group others (Acquino & Reed 2002; Reed & Acquino 2003). Nyborg, Howarth, & Brekke (2006) take moral identity into account in an economic model of propensity to adopt green products. They conclude that knowledge of others' behavior may influence a consumers' moral motivation to buy green products by increasing the extent to which they see themselves as responsible for doing so. Similarly, support for the importance of moral identity also comes from a study which found that consumers' avoidance of groceries with excessive packaging and purchase of beverages in refillable bottles can be predicted by personal moral beliefs about responsibility to solving waste problems (Thogersen 1999).

In sum, individuals' identities may influence whether or not they choose green products or engage in green behaviors. If identities and norms consistent with making green choices are not salient at the time of the decision, however, green products may not be selected. Marketers and policymakers may consider the influence of identities as they plan their marketing programs. For example, if a program instituted by a government includes expectations of compliance by a minority group, it may be necessary to alter the program to cue the relationship between the minority identity and the desired behavior. Research suggests that as simple a manipulation as using a spokesperson who is also a member of a minority group may achieve this goal (Deshpande & Stayman 1994; Grier & Deshpande 2001). Further, if possible, marketers may seek to provide individually tailored examples of other consumers who follow desired norms, and who also closely mirror the situations of prospective customers. Finally, cuing moral identities may be an effective way to influence consumer behavior toward making green purchases. Bundling may be a way to accomplish this cuing, such as when Dell computer offered to make a donation to plant a tree when consumers purchased certain computer configurations. Research on bundling of charitable donations, including donations to environmental causes, shows that bundling with luxuries results in greater response than does bundling with necessities, because both pleasure and guilt cues are linked to ethical identity (Strahilevitz & Meyers 1998).

Consumers may not purchase green products if others don't see them doing so

Individuals are influenced by their desire to manage or influence others' beliefs about their identities. Thus, although green products often involve some added costs, consumers may choose and use green products as a means to signal their status. For example, Griskevicius, Tybur, & Van den Bergh (2010) manipulated whether or not participants were primed with the importance of seeking status and then, afterwards, gave the participants choices between purchasing green or luxury (but not green) products. If the purchase was made in public then those who were primed for status preferred green products to luxury products more than did those who were not primed. However, when the purchase setting was private, those primed with status were more likely to choose the luxurious options over the green options. This finding suggests that participants were intentionally choosing green products as a signal to others. Bennet & Chakravarti (2009) report very similar findings, such that consumers were likely to value a cell phone company that gave a portion of its proceeds to charity if the product allowed them to display this fact where others could see it.

Marketers and policymakers might assume that making a product easier to obtain, or lowering price, might increase compliance or sales. Yet this research suggests that the degree to which the purchasing is public matters as well. If the desired behaviors are likely to be observed by others, marketers may have greater success if they help consumers signal status to others by marketing the products where others can see, and through branding efforts that reinforce the link between the behavior and the status.

CONSUMERS MAY NOT PURCHASE GREEN PRODUCTS BECAUSE THEY ALREADY HAVE DONE SO

Although cuing moral identity may lead to purchase of green products, it may not lead to repurchase. Research on the psychology of morality suggests that people often use a moral behavior at one moment as a license to behave in a less moral way in the next. Thus, the purchase of a green product at one moment may actually decrease the likelihood of the purchase of a green product in the next.

A number of studies support this notion. Sachdeva, Iliev, & Medin (2009) showed that people were less likely to cooperate with an agreement to reduce factory pollution after just thinking and writing about their positive compared to their negative traits. In a consumer setting, participants who chose products from a store that specialized in green products, compared to a traditional store, were more likely to cheat on an unrelated game that paid cash for performance (Mazar & Zhong 2010). In a similar study, participants either talked about or actually performed a few small environmentally friendly tasks. Those who performed the tasks viewed themselves as more eco-friendly than those who did not. However those who performed the task were also less likely to engage in subsequent, yet more demanding green behavior, compared to those who had not performed the task (Becker-Olsen, Bennett, & Chakravarti 2010).

Making it easy for consumers to make small changes to their lives to help the environment might seem like a good idea to overcome stubborn or habitual behavior. However, the preceding suggests that giving small or simple solutions may backfire, leading consumers to perceive that they have satisfied an obligation to be green with very little impact. As a result, marketers and policymakers should carefully consider the requests made of consumers. Potentially suggesting bundles of activities, such as greening one's entire kitchen or heating system, rather than suggesting individual activities such as purchasing a single green cleaner or window shade, might decrease the likelihood that individuals will perceive they have earned any license to stop being green.

CONCLUSION

The purpose of this chapter was to consider why consumers often forego products, and fail to perform behaviors, that are considered environmentally friendly, given increased consumer interest in making decisions that preserve and protect the environment. We argue that it is a problem of many facets, and we explored four key factors; consumers' trust that the decisions they make will actually lead to the green outcomes they desire, the role of emotions in green choices, contextual elements in the decision environment, and finally the role of salient and desired identities. Of course these areas are not exhaustive of all possible factors that may influence green decision-making, but each sheds light on what may lead consumers away from intended green behaviors.

An overarching issue that appears to apply to almost all of the research outlined here is that there may be the mismatch between the contexts that are ideal for consumers to behave in a green manner and the way our marketplace, especially the retail marketplace, is organized. Opportunistic marketers over-claiming of actual green advantages may contribute to uncertainty about the value of green products (Terrachoice 2009). Sensationalized media reporting may contribute to emotional anxiety about potential catastrophe from environmental disasters (Vasterman, Yzermans, & Dirkzwager 2005). The rise of major discount retailers has shifted consumers' attention toward economic and price based considerations of exchanges, and potentially away from other benefits (van Heerde, Gijsbrechts, & Pauwels 2008). Purchasing involves choosing items (as opposed to rejecting items) in separate evaluations, in a context that is very focused on price. In terms of identity, changes in family structure, work life, and suburban organization, have altered social identities, decreased feelings of belonging and membership, and possibly reduced pro-social behaviors (Putnam 2000). At the least, it is likely that pro-social identities dominate more in arenas such as politics and charitable donations than in the marketplace, which is more likely to emphasize other identities such as success and thrift. Although not insurmountable, there may be much to overcome in order to bring consumers' green behaviors in line with their good intentions. We hope that our analysis in this chapter is a starting point for this endeavor.

We are interested in encouraging future research that takes what we know to be barriers to green consumer behavior and using this knowledge to increase the possibility that a consumer who cares about an environmental issue will express this attitude in what he or she buys. For example, future research might delve more into the assumptions consumers make about green products, especially the fallacious assumptions, as well as testing whether it is possible to correct those assumptions using packaging or third-party labeling. In addition, researchers ought to find ways marketers might lead consumers away from the avoidance mechanisms that cause them to shun emotional and difficult decisions, perhaps by making the decision to go green more enjoyable, easy, and automatic. For example, researchers might follow the approach used by Gershoff & Koehler (2011) in which a series of methods are presented to improve choices for safety products such as vaccines and airbags by reducing emotional impact associated with making these decisions. Alternatively researchers might find ways to reframe green options so that they nudge people toward making better choices (Thaler & Sunstein 2008). Perhaps this might be accomplished by manipulating whether or not a green choice is presented as a default option or whether it is presented as being novel versus being a norm (Johnson and Goldstein 2003; Goldstein et al. 2008). Finally, research is needed into whether there are contexts in which people are especially likely to be green, such as charities, political arenas, or for decisions about their own neighborhoods. Researchers might explore what may be borrowed from those contexts and applied to advertising, point of purchase, or retail design to increase the choice of green products and behaviors.

References

Bazerman M. H., Tenbrunsel A. E., & Wade-Benzoni K. (1998). "Negotiating with Yourself and Losing: Making Decisions with Competing Internal Preferences, *Academy of Management Review*, 23(2): 225–241.

Becker-Olson, K., Bennett A., & Chakravarti, A. (2010). "Self and Social Signaling Explanations for Consumption of CSR-Associated Products," special session presentation at the Society for Consumer Psychology Conference, St Petersburg, FL, February 25–27.

Bennett A. & Chakravarti A. (2009). "The Self And Social Signaling Explanations For Consumption of CSR-Associated Products," Advances in Consumer Research, Vol XXXVI Book Series: *Advances in Consumer Research*, 49–52.

Bjørner, T. B., Lars Gårn Hansen, L. G., & Russell, C. S. (2004). "Environmental Labeling and Consumers' Choice: An Empirical Analysis of the Effect of the Nordic Swan," *Journal of Environmental Economics and Management*, 47(3): 411–434.

Brewer, M. B. (1991). "The Social Self: On Being the Same and Different at the Same Time," *Personality and Social Psychology Bulletin*, 17(5): 475–482.

Broniarczyk, S. M. & Gershoff, A. D. (2003). "The Reciprocal Effects of Brand Equity and Trivial Attributes," *Journal of Marketing Research*, 40: 161–175.

Chaiken, S. & Trope, Y. (1999). *Dual-Process Theories in Social Psychology*. New York, Guilford Press.

Chernev, A. (2007). "Jack of All Trades or Master of One? Product Differentiation and Compensatory Reasoning in Consumer Choice," *Journal of Consumer Research*, 33(4): 430–444.

Darby, M. R. & Karni, E. (1973). "Free Competition and Optimal Amount of Fraud," *Journal of Law and Economics*, 16: 67–86.

Dawes, R., McTavish, J. & Shaklee, H. (1977). "Behavior, Communication, and Assumptions About Other People's Behavior in a Common's Dilemma Situation," *Journal of Personality and Social Psychology*, 35(1): 1–11.

Deshpandé, R. & Stayman, D. (1994). "A Tale of Two Cities: Distinctiveness Theory and Advertising Effectiveness," *Journal of Marketing Research*, 31: 57–64.

Diamond, P. & Hausman, J. (1994). "Contingent Valuation: Is Some Number Better than No Number?" *Journal of Economic Perspectives* 8(4) 45–64.

Ehrich, K. & Irwin, J. R. (2005). "Willful Ignorance in the Request for Product Information," *Journal of Marketing Research*, 42: 266–277.

Epstein, S., Pacini, R., Denes-Raj, V. & Heier, H. (1996). "Individual Differences in Intuitive and Analytical Information Processing," *Journal of Personality and Social Psychology*, 72(2): 390–405.

Erikson, E. H. (1964). *Insight and Responsibility*. New York: Norton.

Friestad, M. & Wright, P. (1994). "The Persuasion Knowledge Model: How People Cope with Persuasion Attempts", *Journal of Consumer Research*, 21(1): 1–31.

Galbraith, K. (2009). "More Sun for Less: Solar Panels Drop in Price," *New York Times*, August 26, 2009.

Gershoff, A. D. & Koehler, J. J. (2011). "Safety First? The Role of Emotion in Betrayal Aversion," *Journal of Consumer Research*, 38: 140–150.

Goldstein, N. J., Cialdini, R. B. & Griskevicius, V. (2008). "A Room with a Viewpoint: Using Social Norms to Motivate Environmental Conservation in Hotels," *Journal of Consumer Research*, 35: 472–482.

Grier, S. A. & Deshpandé R. (2001). "Social Dimensions of Consumer Distinctiveness: The Influence of Social Status on Group Identity and Advertising Persuasion," *Journal of Marketing Research*, 38(2): 216–224.

Grinstein, A. & Nisan, U. (2009) "Demarketing, Minority Groups, and National Attachment," *Journal of Marketing*, 73(2): 105–122.

Griskevicius, V., Tybur, J. M., & Van den Bergh, B. (2010). "Going Green to be Seen: Status, Reputation, and Conspicuous Conservation." *Journal of Personality and Social Psychology*, 98: 392–404.

Grolleau, G. & Caswell, J. A. (2006). "Interaction Between Food Attributes in Markets: The Case of Environmental Labeling," *Journal of Agricultural and Resource Economics*, 31(3): 471–484.

Harley, W. E. & Strickland, B. R. (1986). "Interpersonal Betrayal and Cooperation: Effects on Self-Evaluation and Depression," *Journal of Personality and Social Psychology*, 50: 386–391.

Hsee, C. K. & Rottenstreich, R. (2004). "Music, Pandas and Muggers: On the Affective Psychology of Value," *Journal of Experimental Psychology: General*, 133: 23–30.

—— et al. (1999). Preference Reversals between Joint and Separate Evaluations of Options: A Review and Theoretical Analysis, *Psychological Bulletin*, 125(5): 576–590.

Irwin, J. R. (1994). "Buying/Selling Price Preference Reversals: Preference for Environmental Changes in Buying Versus Selling Modes," *Organizational Behavior and Human Decision Processes*, 60: 431–457.

—— & Baron, J. (2001). "Response Mode Effects and Moral Values, *Organizational Behavior and Human Decision Processes*, 84: 177–197.

—— & Naylor, R. W. (2009). "Ethical Decisions and Response Mode Compatibility: Weighting of Ethical Attributes in Consideration Sets Formed by Excluding Versus Including Product Alternatives," *Journal of Marketing Research*, 46: 234–46.

——, Slovic, P., Lichtenstein, S., & McClelland, G. H. (1993). "Preference Reversals and the Measurement of Environmental Variables." *Journal of Risk and Uncertainty*, 6: 5–18.

—— & Spria J. S. (1997). "Anomalies in the Values for Consumer Goods with Environmental Attributes," *Journal of Consumer Psychology*, 6(4): 339–363.

Johnson, E. J. & Goldstein D. G. (2003). "Do Defaults Save Lives?" *Science*, 302: 1338–1339.

Kahneman, D. & Knetsch, J. L. (1992). "Valuing Public Goods: The Purchase of Moral Satisfaction," *Journal of Environmental Economics and Management*, 22(1): 57–70.

Ledyard, J. O. (1995). *Handbook of Experimental Economics*. Princeton University Press.

Levin, I. P. (1987). "Associative Effects of Information Framing Onhuman Judgments." Paper presented at the annual meeting of the Midwestern Psychological Association, May, Chicago, IL.

—— & Gaeth, G. J. (1988). "Framing of Attribute Information before and after Consuming the Product," *Journal of Consumer Research*, 15: 374–378.

Lichtenstein, S., Gregory, R., & Irwin, J. (2007). "What's Bad is Easy: Taboo Values, Affect, and Cognition," *Judgment and Decision Making*, 2: 169–188.

Liu, W. & Aaker, J. (2008). "The Happiness of Giving: The Time-Ask Effect," *Journal of Consumer Research*, 35(3): 543–557.

Loewenstein, G. F. & Prelec, D. (1992). *Choices Over Time*. New York, Russell Sage Foundation.

—— Weber, E. U., Hsee, C. K. & Welch, N. (2001). "Risk as Feelings," *Psychological Bulletin*, 127(2): 267–286.

Luce, M. F., Bettman, J. R., & Payne, J. W. (1997). "Choice Processing in Emotionally Difficult Decisions," *Journal of Experimental Psychology: Learning, Memory, and Cognition*, 23: 384–405.

Luchs, M. G., Naylor, R. W., Irwin, J. R., & Raghunathan, R. (2010). "The Sustainability Liability: Potential Negative Effectgs of Ethicality on Product Preference," *Journal of Marketing*.

Mackoy, R. D., Calantone, R., & Droge, C. (1995). "Environmental Marketing: Bridging the Divide between the Consumption Culture and Environmentalism," in Polonsky, M. J. and Mintu-Wimsatt, A. T. (eds), *Environmental Marketing*, Binghamton, NY: Haworth, 37–54.

Mazar, N., Amir, O., & Ariely, D. (2008). "The Dishonesty of Honest People: A Theory of Self-Concept Maintenance," *Journal of Marketing Research*, 45(6): 633–644.

—— & Zhong, C. B. (2010). "Do Green Products Make Us Better People?" *Psychological Science*, 21, 2010: 494–498.

McGuire, W. J., McGuire, C. V., & Winton W. (1979). "Effects of Household Gender Composition on the Salience of One's Gender in the Spontaneous Self-Concept," *Journal of Experimental Social Psychology*, 15(1): 77–90.

Nadler, J., Irwin, J. R., Davis, J. H., Au, W. T., Zarnoth, P., Rantilla, A., & Koesterer, K. (2001). "Order Effects in Individual and Group Policy Allocations," *Group Processes and Intergroup Relations*, 4: 99–115.

Namkoong, J. & Irwin J. R. (2010). "Prospective Motivated Reasoning in Charitable Giving: Making Sense of Our Future Behavior and Protecting Our Future Self." *Working Paper*.

National Renewable Energy Laboratory (2004). "PV Facts: What is the Energy Payback for PV?" Available at <http://www.nrel.gov/docs/fy04osti/35489.pdf>

Nyborg, K., Howarth, R. B., & Brekke, K. A. (2006). "Green Consumers and Public Policy On Socially Contingent Moral Motivation," *Resource and Energy Economics*, 28(4): 351–366.

Ostrom, A. & Iacobucci, D. (1995). "Consumer Trade-Offs and the Evaluation of Services," *Journal of Marketing*, 59: 17–28.

Oyserman, D. (2009). "Identity-Based Motivation: Implications for Action Readiness, Procedural-Readiness, and Consumer Behavior," *Journal of Consumer Psychology*, 19(3): 250–260.

Putnam, R. D. (2000). *Bowling Alone: The Collapse and Revival of American Community*. New York: Simon and Schuster.

Read, D., Loewenstein, G., & Kalyanaraman, S. (1999). "Mixing Virtue and Vice: Combining the Immediacy Effect and the Diversification Heuristic," *Journal of Behavioral Decision Making*, 12: 257–273.

Reed, A. & Aquino, K. F. (2003). "Moral Identity and the Expanding Circle of Moral Regard Toward Out-Groups," *Journal of Personality and Social Psychology*, 84(6): 1270–1286.

Rozin, P., Grant, H., Weinberg, S., & Parker, S. (2007). "'Head Versus Heart': Effect of Monetary Frames on Expression of Sympathetic Magical Concerns," *Judgment and Decision Making*, 2(4): 217–224.

Sachdeva, S., Iliev, R., & Medin, D. L. (2009). "Sinning Saints and Saintly Sinners: The Paradox of Moral Self-Regulation," *Psychological Science*, 20(4): 523–528.

Shariff, A. F., Norenzayan, A. (2007). "God Is Watching You: Priming God Concepts Increases Prosocial Behavior in an Anonymous Economic Game," *Psychological Science*, 18(9): 803–809.

Slovic, P., Fischhoff, B., & Lichtenstein, S. (1979). "Rating the Risks," *Environment*, 21(14–20): 36–39.

—— & Peters, E. (2006). "Risk Perception and Affect," *Current Directions in Psychological Science*, 15: 323–325.

Srinivasan, S. S. & Till, B. D. (2002). "Evaluation of Search, Experience, and Credence Attributes: Role of Brand Name and Product Trial," *Journal of Product and Brand Management*, 11(7): 417–431.

Strahilevitz, M. & Meyers, J. G. (1998). "Donations to Charity as Purchase Incentives: How Well They Work May Depend on What You Are Trying to Sell," *Journal of Consumer Research*, 434–446.

Tajfel, H. & Turner, J. C. (1979). "An Integrative Theory of Intergroup Conflict," in W. G. Austin & S. Worchel (eds.), *The Social Psychology of Intergroup Relations*, Monterey, CA: Brooks-Cole.

Teisl, M. F., Roe, B., & Hicks, R. L. (2002). "Can Eco-Labels Tune a Market? Evidence from Dolphin-Safe Labeling," *Journal of Environmental Economics and Management*, 43(3): 339–359.

Terrachoice (2009). "The Seven Sins of Greenwashing: Environmental Claims in Consumer Markets." Available at <http://sinsofgreenwashing.org/findings/greenwashing-report-2009/>

Tetlock, P. E., Kristel, O. V., Elson, S. B., Green, M. C., & Lerner, J. S. (2000). "The Psychology of the Unthinkable: Taboo Trade-Offs, Forbidden Base Rates, and Heretical Counterfactuals," *Journal of Personality and Social Psychology*, 78(5): 853–870.

Thaler, R. H. & Sunstein, C. R. (2008). *Nudge: Improving Decisions about Health, Wealth, and Happiness*, Yale University Press.

Thogersen, J. (1999). "The Ethical Consumer. Moral Norms and Packaging Choice," *Journal of Consumer Policy*, 22: 439–460.

United Nations Environment Programme (UNEP) (2005). *Talk the Walk: Advancing Sustainable Lifestyles through Marketing and Communications*. UN Global Compact and Utopies.

van Heerde, H. J., Gijsbrechts, E., & Pauwels, K. (2008). "Winners and Losers in a Major Price War," *Journal of Marketing Research*, 45(5): 499–518.

Vasterman, P., Yzermans, C. J., & Dirkzwager, A. J. E. (2005). "The Role of the Media and Media Hypes in the Aftermath of Disasters," *Epidemiologic Reviews* 27(1): 107–114.

Vohs, K. D., Baumeister, R. F. & Chin J. (2007). "Feeling Duped: Emotional, Motivational, and Cognitive Aspects of Being Exploited by Others," *Review of General Psychology*, 11(2): 127–141.

....

CHAPTER 21

USING MARKET SEGMENTATION APPROACHES TO UNDERSTAND THE GREEN CONSUMER[1]

....

TIMOTHY M. DEVINNEY

ALTHOUGH there has been considerable academic work focusing on discovering and characterizing the Green Consumer—or more correctly, those espousing "green" attitudes—there is considerably less academic interest in understanding the segment characteristics of consumers with varying degrees and types of environmental concern. The importance of understanding both the heterogeneous nature of ethical and green consumers and the segmentation characteristics can be seen in the following quotation:

> According to LOHAS (2002), which tracks green economic trends, about 30 percent of US adults—more than 63 million consumers—now purchase goods and services with a nod toward the products' health, environmental, social justice and sustainability value. The marketplace, worth $227 billion a year, is expanding at a healthy pace and is projected to reach $1 trillion annually by 2020.

If there was validity in what is being said then we would expect that approximately 30 percent of groceries consumed would be organic, 30 percent of cars bought would be hybrids and 30 percent of coffee drunk would be fair trade. However, none of this is even remotely true.

---

[1] This research has been supported by a grant from the Australian Research Council Discovery Grants Program. The chapter has been improved greatly by the insightful comments of Grahame Dowling, Pratima Bansal, and Andrew Hoffman.

This disconnect between bold statements of attitudes and intention and the reality of everyday consumer behavior brings to the fore the problems with focusing on attitudes as a source of demand prediction or segmentation characterization. For attitudes to matter to consumption there needs to be a line of sight between the attitudes being measured and relevant behaviors. This is rarely the case when it comes to socially-laden "expressed" attitudes that arise in surveys and contextually constrained behavior that occurs in reality. However, this does not mean that green consumers do not exist or that segments with green proclivities cannot be found. What it implies is that we have to take into account: (a) the variations of individual values and attitudes, (b) the validity of the means by which those attitudes and values are measured, (c) the contexts and constraints on the behaviors of relevance (and how they relate to attitudes) and (d) the opportunities that foster values and attitudes to be revealed by behavior.

This chapter concentrates on how we can apply models of market segmentation to the understanding of the varying nature of green consumers. As academic work is limited and the commercial work is of varied quality, purposely biased, or targeted at a very specific organizational need, what follows is more of a primer on thinking rather than a summary of a well-established literature.

The next section outlines two approaches of segmentation and argues that only one of them will be effective when attempting to understand socially laden consumption behavior. This will then be followed by a discussion of how we can think about segmentation from this perspective. We conclude with some managerial prescriptions.

MODELS OF SEGMENTATION

It is important that we get a clear understanding of the meaning and operationalization of market segmentation. In its most basic form, segmentation is about a consumer's sensitivity to the components of a product as revealed in their willingness to purchase either products with more of the desired components or less of the undesired components. It is about characterizing the differential "want" for a product possessing a specific attribute mix at a given price in specific circumstances, or the differential "price" the individual is willing to pay for the same mixture of attributes making up a product. Schlegelmilch, Bohlen, & Diamantopoulos (1996) and Diamantopoulos et al. (2003) provide the most complete overviews of the academic work to date as it applies to the "green" consumer and there are a host of commercial applications that we discuss throughout this chapter.

This differential want can arise for a host of reasons—some rational, some less than rational. First and foremost, it can be a natural reflection of the statement *de gustibus non est disputandum*—there is no accounting for taste. *Different rational individuals* may simply possess *different preferences* that show up in a *different decision model* being used to determine what is purchased. Second, it can arise because individuals are faced with *different situations or contexts* where the cost of revealing a specific desire is different (see Gershoff & Irwin [Chapter 20] this volume). People may desire similar things but these things are either unavailable or available at significantly different costs that ultimately lead to different choices. Third, it can arise because individuals are *differentially sensitive to persuasion* (e.g, advertising, information), social pressures, or other factors related to the purchasing context. Finally, it can arise, as discussed in some detail by Shu & Bazerman (Chapter 9, this volume), because of *cognitive biases*. This differential want can be captured by organizations in many ways, but is fundamentally about differential demand at a price, however that differential demand arises.

It is important to note how the definition of segmentation given here differs subtly but importantly from the commercial market-research definition. For example, in one typical approach, NBC Universal (Banikarim 2010) identifies different segments that include: Alpha-Ecos (deeply committed to green causes), Eco-Centrics (concerned with how green products benefit them personally), Eco-Chics (want the cachet of being seen as green), Economically Ecos (less concerned about green), and Eco-Moms (emphasis on green products for kids). NBC Universal focuses on what people say about "why they purchase" and how that differs between groups, not what they actually do and how that differentiates them from others faced with similar circumstances. Although understanding why peoples' intentions do not translate into actions may be relevant to something like a communications strategy, market segmentation is ultimately about effective characterization and prediction. Segmentation modeling ignores the supposed "why" different people behave differently, unless the "why" provides important insights into actions, which translate into greater profitability, customer satisfaction, or improvement on other dimensions of firm strategy.

Before moving on to a detailed description of two specific approaches to segmentation, it is important to understand the parameters underlying the logic underlying the methods. Our ultimate concern is with what a consumer chooses—for example, a "green" alternative—and how that varies from individual to individual (or segment to segment). This can be related to three major factors: (1) the *external context* in which the purchasing is occurring; (2) the manner or *basis on which the decision* is being made; and (3) the *individual differences* based on individual antecedents, such as values and personality, and observable or fixed covariates, such as gender, age, income, and so on.

Although it might appear obvious that all of these factors matter and that it is appropriate to throw them into the mix, we will discuss why it is critical to understand where these factors stand in the decision-making process of consumers and how we measure them. Standard market-research approaches utilize what is known as an *a priori segmentation* model. This model does not ignore the decision model but views it as something of a black box with an assumed form. It places emphasis on the individual descriptors as predictors of choice with the antecedents acting as the primary drivers. *Behavioral segmentation* concentrates on the decision model and attempts to understand how the model used by people to make decisions differs from individual to individual and situation to situation.

WHAT IS NECESSARY FOR
EFFECTIVE SEGMENTATION?

First, effective segmentation requires heterogeneity of *revealed preferences*. This is a complex issue that can be broken into a number of components that focus on the *preferences* aspect and others that focus on the *revealed* aspects.

We can think of consumers as being fundamentally different in terms of their known preferences. For the moment we will assume that people know their own preferences. For example, some individuals, even in the most ideal circumstances, may simply ignore environmental issues, while others in the direst of circumstances will give environmental issues preference over everything else. This implies that opportunities for segmentation arise when individuals possess different sensitivities to the components of the products available. In the environmental context, individuals may purchase a product because of its green attributes/features, or equally likely, the possession of an attribute by one product and the absence of that or other attributes in the competing product, or a "bad" attribute in a competing product. This can be exemplified by the matrix given in Figure 21.1.

In our simple world there are only two possible products (Product 1 and Product 2) and let us assume that firms can choose to offer either of these but not both. These products can either be green (Green+), neutral (Green Ø), or environmentally damaging

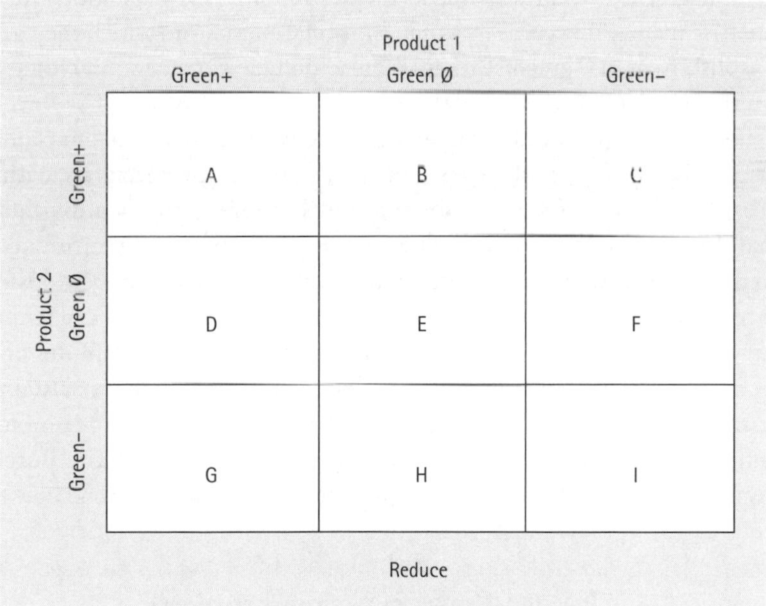

FIGURE 21.1 Stylized Segmentation Patterns

(Green−). It should be obvious that the diagonal cells (A, E, I) provide no opportunities for segmentation on green credentials, which is the heterogeneity argument. If there are no differences in preferences there is no value in segmentation. Among those consumers that care, the segmentation options that are taken up are not immediately clear. For example, if some green consumers exist and others are neutral, then cells B and D are the most obvious, but G and C are also open to exploitation. If, for example, the cost of providing a green product is very high and the latent green segment is small, and remaining people are totally uncaring about the environment, then it may make sense to offer products that are environmentally damaging (meaning the segment pairs are C/G rather than B/D).

This effect would be mitigated if there were a negative customer value impact from being environmentally damaging. In these circumstances, individuals need not be proactively green for the green segment to exist! In this situation individuals want to avoid products with a bad environmental positioning (Green−) but have no positive inclination toward the environment—they will not seek out (Green+) products. The reverse logic implies that the obvious solution is that there is a segment of "neutrals" that will pay something to avoid a bad environmental product, while others continue to purchase the environmentally damaging product; the segmentation pattern would then be F/H. However, even though no one wants a positive environmental outcome, there may be those with a very strong inclination to want to avoid bad environmental outcomes. It is, therefore, possible that this effect will lead one firm to force those with such an inclination to purchase (Green+) products, meaning that the segmentation pattern becomes C/G.[2]

What this discussion implies is that: (a) effective segmentation requires that realistic and actionable preference differences exist; (b) these preference differences can include avoidance of negative attributes as well as the desire for positive attributes; (c) the segments that arise may be more extreme than the preferences from which they derive; and (d) the establishment of a green segment may actually lead to a counter-establishment of an "anti-green" segment.

The last two points (c and d) bring up the issue of the revealed aspects of effective segmentation. In surveys and experiments individuals provided us with "stated" preferences. In the case of surveys these are little more than an individual's guess about what they might do or believe. The responses can be heavily influenced, in the case of environmental or social attributes, by individual biases and the desire to give socially acceptable answers. In the case of experiments, they can vary from laboratory or survey-based experiments—which are more controlled examples of what we might get from a survey—to simulation or field experiments where actual purchasing is occurring. Although less subject to social acceptance bias, experiments can be only weakly related to what the individual might do when actually purchasing a product unless the simulation or field experiment is very close to the context faced

---

[2] Note that this assumes a degree of market power.

by the consumer in the purchasing environment. The revelation of those preferences when consumers go to purchase is influenced by the opportunities in the market that are determined entirely by availability, which is determined entirely by
firms.

Figure 21.2 provides an overview of this issue of stated versus revealed preference,
which will take on importance when we discuss different forms of segmentation and
their validity.

A second requirement for effective segmentation is *survival when contested in a market*. Point (a) is a necessary condition in that segmentation is the result of *both* heterogeneity in the structure of customer preferences *and* the ability of the firm to exploit or
accommodate that heterogeneity more efficiently than its competitors. In other words,
the segments must be sustainable commercially.

The first issue in making segmentation viable for the firm is the reduction in the
economies of scale/scope that arise from offering more variants within a product category than are met by increases in demand for the more specialized product. In other
words, segmentation requires that those receiving more specialized products ascribe
value to the specialization they are receiving so as to cover the costs of lost economies
of scale/scope.

Looking at the offerings of a company like Whole Foods illustrates this last point.
By purchasing at Whole Foods, the consumer is essentially going "fully organic" on
that purchase occasion as the grocer requires strict compliance from its suppliers.
So if I am interested in being a "limited" organic consumer—I want my dairy and
meat products to be organic but can care less about everything else—I face a
dilemma with Whole Foods. Either I spend time shopping at more than one grocer
or I pay a very high price by purchasing some products that (a) do not meet my

	Stated		Revealed
Examples	Focus groups Interviews Surveys	Experiments Simulations	Observation Purchasing Panels
Positives	Simple to implement	Involves tradeoffs Closer to behavior Difficult to "game"	Realistic Linked directly to market behavior
Negatives	Social response bias Speculative Link to behavior limited	Artificial	Costly Limited by market alternatives

FIGURE 21.2 Stated versus Revealed Preference

ideal requirements (they are organic when I do not demand organic) and (b) are priced beyond my reservation price for individual products (but below the reservation price for the bundle of products purchased). This will lead to the ironic outcome that I could become a "revealed" fully organic consumer but only because I am too lazy or find it too costly to spend more time shopping for non-organic alternatives.

This example also shows why it is so difficult to extrapolate from simple sales figures to something that is meaningful from the standpoint of consumer preferences. For example, there has been considerable interest in the dramatically rising sales of fair trade coffee products. However, as Argenti (2004) notes, and Devinney, Auger, & Eckhardt (2010) show through field experiments, this is much more of a market-based availability phenomenon, than a customer demand driven trend. All that can be said based on over-the-counter sales of fair trade coffee is that when it is made available consumers do not actively avoid it when the choice is fair trade or nothing (as it is at many coffee shops today). Similarly, the success or failure of over-the-counter environmental solutions (e.g. energy efficient appliances) may reflect regulatory and standards changes that satisfy specific niche political interests but do not reveal whether consumers truly want to go green. For example, one cannot purchase non-energy efficient light bulbs in Australia because they are banned. Hence, if regulations require, or major manufacturers concentrate on producing, predominantly energy-saving appliances, it is possible that these become the dominant design in the market independent of whether or not they are preferred by consumers.

A second issue is whether the segments are stable in a competitive environment. Going back to Figure 21.1, let us suppose that there was a third firm operating. Firm 1 begins to offer a green product, leaving firms 2 and 3 to decide whether or not they (a) offer a green product, (b) offer a neutral product, or (c) offer an environmentally damaging product.[3] Suppose that consumers have preferences that imply they either want a good environmental product or they don't care. For those that don't care, a neutral or damaging product is the same from a demand perspective. For those demanding a (Green+) product, a neutral product won't do. In these circumstances, the firms have only two choices, either they both offer the damaging product or one offers the damaging product and one offers the (Green+) product. None, however, will offer the neutral product as (a) it is not good enough for the (Green+) segment and (b) it is too costly for the remaining consumers who don't care. Whichever choice these firms make, the result is that they will split one of the segments, thereby reducing its potential profitability and also potentially increasing the price even further than the specialization might originally justify. Whether this outcome is profitable will determine the form and structure of the segments.

[3] This example can be replicated for the case where people don't value the environment positively but want to avoid damaging products.

THE INDIVIDUAL IN SEGMENTATION

The discussion in the prior section showed that preference heterogeneity is a necessary but not sufficient condition for effective segmentation and that heterogeneity can lead to non-obvious outcomes. We have up to this point ignored the source of that heterogeneity—individual preferences—and the different forms that it can take.

The individual comes into segmentation discussions in three basic ways: (a) differences in purchasing proclivity; (b) differences in attribute sensitivity; and (c) variance in preferences. Theoretically, this says that segmentation will arise when individual consumers have different decision models.[4] In the discussion below we will focus on segmentation based on (b) and (c) as it is the most common.

The most obvious aspects of segmentation arise by examining the influence of the attributes of the products in the market and the differential reaction by individual consumers to those offerings. Hence, segmentation becomes a process whereby firms seek to provide products with mixtures of attributes that match most effectively with the types of trade-offs individuals are willing to make (e.g., between power and fuel efficiency in a hybrid automobile).

More pragmatically, the firm is faced with two strategies. One is that they can simply offer a range of products with varying sets of attributes into the market and consumers will naturally pick the one most amenable to them. This is a *natural, or revealed, segmentation* solution. The second is that they target specific consumers based upon the relationship between the sensitivities and the characteristics of the individuals in question. This is a *targeted segmentation* solution. Natural segmentation requires that: (a) consumers understand their preferences to some reasonable degree; (b) the relevant mixture of products is available; and (c) they have sufficient knowledge of the market alternatives to be able to choose appropriately. The targeted segmentation solution is more controlled in that it removes much of the search burden from consumers and allows them to receive information (persuasion) about what is relevant to them.

Segmentation is also influenced by the variance of consumer preferences. What this picks up is the variation in choice that would arise when: (a) individuals actively seek variety; (b) individuals do not have a sense of their own preferences (hence choose in what appears to be a random fashion); and (c) they take into account factors that are not included in the attributes of the available alternatives. In this situation, you have a different source of segmentation that relates differential sensitivity to factors such as: (a) boredom—hence the need for variety; (b) experience—hence the possibility that individuals do not understand their preferences; (c) intangible factors that influence the choices of individuals that cannot easily be captured—such as acting green just to be seen to be acting "good" (e.g. Griskevicius, Tybur, & Van den Bergh 2010); (d) cognitive or other psychological factors

---

[4] In line with Shu & Bazerman (Chapter 10, this volume) we could also add a fourth basis of segmentation founded on the cognitive biases of the individual.

that make choice appear to be random or irrational (e.g. Shu & Bazerman [Chapter 9] this volume); and (e) situational factors unaccounted for in the model.

A PRIORI VERSUS BEHAVIORAL SEGMENTATION

To this point we have focused on providing a logical structure to thinking about individual consumer choice and how the heterogeneity of consumer preferences can lead to opportunities for segmentation. From a more practical standpoint we need to also examine what the basic theoretical structural logic of segmentation entails. There are essentially two models of segmentation utilized today: *a priori segmentation* and *behavioral segmentation*. The vast majority of work on green consumers, both commercial and academic, has been of the a priori variety (Cotte 2009).

A priori segmentation is based on characteristics that can be seen prior to the purchase. A typical a priori model is given in Figure 21.3. Its logic is based upon a premise that there are individual antecedents to purchasing. In the case of the green consumer, these might be "values" as measured on various scales, a stated preference for specific environmental causes, various environmental proclivities, and so on. The main point with a priori models of segmentation is that the firm is seeking to find observable measures that relate to the unobservable drivers. In other words, what motivates a consumer to go green are these unseen values and personal tendencies, for which observable factors such as gender, education, income, location, etc., serve as targetable descriptors, predictors or differentiators.

From a practical standpoint, a priori segmentation traditionally relies on the following process:

(1)   Survey potential and actual consumers on their values, attitudes, and other factors that serve as antecedents;
      (a) Analyze the antecedents to discover general tendencies;
(2)   Survey potential and actual consumers on their observables (e.g. age, gender, past behavior, store preferences, and so on);
(3)   Relate the observables to the antecedents via correlational techniques (e.g. factor and cluster analysis);
(4)   Survey potential and actual consumers on their intention to purchase products of specific types;
      (a) Relate the intention to purchase to the antecedents and observables;
(5)   Validate the intention to purchase with actual purchase activity.

Academic research rarely addresses (5), although in the commercial realm it is generally assumed that there is some relationship since that is where the money is made. However, research on the attitude-behavior gap (e.g. Boulstridge & Carrigan 2000; Carrigan & Attala 2001) implies that the relationship is less predictive than one would desire.

Behavioral segmentation reverses the logic of Figure 21.3. What matters in this case is what people do given the constraints they are facing, not what they intend to do absent those constraints. Also, the antecedents become immaterial as all that matters are the behavioral differences. In other words, there is no strong assumption that antecedents matter (although having an understanding might help to communicate a message to specific target groups).

Figure 21.4 presents a simple behavioral model. Note two major differences with Figure 21.3. First, the available alternatives create an opportunity to purchase that the individual either takes up or not. The choice conditional on availability reveals the consumers differential valuation. From the standpoint of segmentation it is the different choices individuals make when faced with similar or identical alternatives that is important. In the case of experimental approaches, the available alternatives can be constrained to be identical (or from a design standpoint, informationally identical). In the case of market data, the available alternatives need to be sufficiently varied to lead to real opportunities for different choices to be made. However the goal in either case is to get the individual to reveal their preferences in a way that can determine the mental model they are using to make their decision. What then matters is: (a) to what extent are there fundamental differences in the choices made when identical alternatives are available, and (b) whether these differences relate to observable characteristics of the individual and/ or observable patterns in the purchasing of other individuals so that targeted segmentation can be used by the firm.

The simplest example of behavioral segmentation is the "Customers Who Bought This Item Also Bought /…" function seen on websites like Amazon.com. This is just a between-individuals matching exercise that becomes more accurate as more information

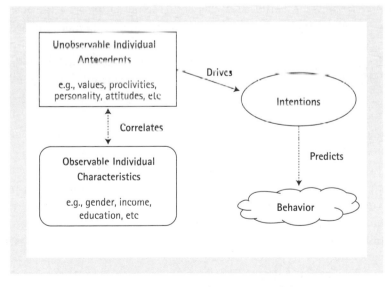

FIGURE 21.3 A Simple a Priori Model

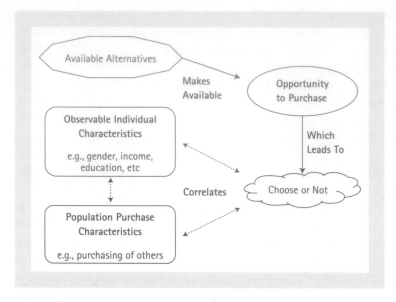

FIGURE 21.4 A Simple Behavioral Model

about more people becomes available. More sophisticated variants also account for individual characteristics so that this becomes "Customers Like You Who Bought This Item Also Bought…." With sufficient data on an individual's purchasing behavior this can become very accurate, with companies like Tesco (UK) and Von's (US) using their massive databases and loyalty programs to engage in very specific behavior-based targeting.

The differences between a priori and behavioral segmentation are quite profound and their implications significant. For example, the notion of "segments of 1" or mass customization can only be based on the logic of behavioral segmentation. A priori segmentation is effectively about characterizing a population, whereas behavioral segmentation is about characterizing individuals who may or may not be similar enough to be represented as a population. We can see this in how the two approaches would create a new green product.

Those following the precepts of a priori segmentation would first try and understand what motivated the green consumer and survey them on their values, interests, and "desire to do good environmentally." One would see questions like "I consider the Earth's environment to be a public good that all should protect", or "I think about my carbon footprint when purchasing" presented on a 1–5 scale ranging over "does not/does represent me well." The responses would then be related to specific individual characteristics and intention to purchase scales. A product would then be developed based on the responses.

A classic a priori approach is the LOHAS Segmentation. LOHAS uses the procedure outlined in Figure 21.3 and in its original formulation came up with four segments—Lifestyle of Health and Sustainability (LOHAS, 19%), Naturalites (15%), Drifters (25%), Conventionals (24%)—with a fifth segment, the Unconcerned (17%), added after 2006.[5] These segments are more general than the ones we saw with NBC Universal in that they are less driven by intention and more by basic attitudinal differences. To some degree they are less operational than NBC Universal's approach and do little more than spread individuals out on a continuum that ranges from:

i don't care under any circumstances ‹   ⸺→It is my #1 priority in life.

In addition, this approach is stifled by the fact that the segments themselves do not align with market trends because they abstract completely from specific market and product contexts. In other words, if an individual is in the "Unconcerned" segment, then they are "unconcerned" about every case in every circumstance. If they are a LOHAS consumer, they are a LOHAS consumer everywhere for everything. The vagueness of this approach was seen in the quotation given at the beginning of this. The problem is not that there might not be information in a priori approaches but that the information is not precise enough to be operationally useful.

Those following the behavioral approach would start by trying to determine what components of the new product were related to "greenness". They would then mock up product alternatives that included both environmental and functional components, as well as brand, price, and other costs, and vary these according to some experimental design. They would then present these to a sample of individuals in some form—such as a discrete choice experiment, simulated shopping environment, or even a real store if this were possible. Information would be collected about the purchase choices as well as about the individuals making the purchases. The process might be repeated and the product refined or there would be similar experiments or tests that include communication, advertising, and distribution campaigns. Those mixtures of characteristics that were demanded by customers and technically feasible and financially viable for the firm would then drive the commercial product developed.

It is difficult to find publicly available market-based commercial examples of behavioral segmentation that relate directly to the green consumer. This is partially due to the fact that behavioral segmentation makes little sense when utilized generally (hence there are no LOHAS or Eco-Moms to discuss). Also, because it puts emphasis on the purchasing context, it is less amenable to breathless press releases espousing universal truths. In addition, those applying the approach normally do not want to make their findings public due to the fact that they reveal quite a lot about their underlying strategies (again because it is so product-class specific). Auger et al. (2010) and Devinney, Auger, & Eckhardt (2010) provide the most complete examples in the academic literature,

---

[5] The percentages refer to percent of the US population. The LOHAS Segmentation can be seen at their website, <http://www.lohas.com>.

one of which is described in the next section. Their work reveals that it is important to avoid focusing on the green consumer alone and to concentrate on building a complete segmentation model that includes all aspects of the individual's purchasing decision calculus, part of which might be green.

APPLYING SEGMENTATION MODELS

As noted, there are a considerable number of studies that attempt to understand the green consumer. Rather than attempt to replicate the reviews given in Scammon & Mish ([Chapter 19], this volume) and Gershoff & Irwin ([Chapter 20], this volume) our focus will be on three areas of application: (1) examples of a priori segmentation; (2) examples of behavioral segmentation; and (3) developing a general way of thinking about applications of segmentation models.

A priori segmentation

We have already provided two well-recognized examples of a priori segmentation, but there are many more, perhaps the largest and most comprehensive being Roper's Green Gauge.[6] However, as we have noted, the difficulty in applying these approaches is the extent to which they reflect actual behavior. This lack of accuracy has led to attempts to understand the mediators and moderators of the relationship between the characterizations of these segments and behavior—to explain the attitude-behavior gap, not by asking whether the basic model is correct, but by trying to find "barriers" that stop people from behaving according to the model.

Often such information is gleaned from surveys, which results in prescriptions that are somewhat bland and generic. For example, McKinsey conducted a survey of over 7,000 consumers to determine why individuals did not buy green. They found five barriers and their solutions (given in parentheses): (a) a lack of awareness of eco-friendly goods (educate consumers); (b) negative perceptions of green products (build better products); (c) distrust of green claims (be honest); (d) higher prices (offer more); and (e) low availability (bring the products to the people). Such insights are not helpful for companies wanting to convert consumers into more effective green consumers. Indeed, if one just ignored the green in this discussion the five barriers could apply to any product or service in any market.

However, keeping these limitations in mind, a priori segmentation can have some value when its limitations are properly understood (Straughan & Robert 1999). How might we do this?

---

[6] The Roper Green Gauge can be viewed in summary form at their website: <http://www.gfkamerica.com/practice_areas/roper_consulting/roper_greengauge/index.en.html>.

A Revised a Priori Segmentation Approach

First, we need a more detailed scientific understanding of the barriers to going green that avoid the vagueness of Bonini & Oppenheim (2008) and incorporate the logic of cognitive science (e.g. Shu & Bazerman [Chapter 9] this volume).We need to know if the barriers are: (a) segment specific; (b) internal to the individuals in the segment(s) or external (e.g. such as might exist if it was related to availability or influenced only women or, in the Shu and Bazerman case, related to individual level cognitive biases); and (c) structural (e.g. as might be the case if it required related market actions, such as investment in ancillary services).

Second, and more importantly, we need to know how these barriers influence behavior. This has two parts. Simply because something appears to be a barrier does not mean that it necessarily influences behavior. For example, it is quite common for individuals to state that they want "more information" about a cause (as we saw in Bonini & Oppenheim). However, the importance of this is in whether or not the individuals will utilize the information in a proactive manner that leads to pro-environmental outcomes. For example, in an unpublished experiment, we gave individuals the opportunity to access information on various social issues relating to the purchasing of products (e.g. environmental standards). However, we purposely manipulated the information (which was in the form of a ten-minute documentary) so that it was "good," "bad," or "neutral" with respect to the issue of relevance. What we discovered was that information rarely changed behavior and that individuals were more likely to remember those facts that were most in line with their pre-experimental positions. In other words, rather than using the information to change behavior, selective aspects of the information were being used to reinforce behavior (and pre-stated beliefs).

Third, how do the segments evolve? Ultimately, if going green is inevitable, we will all be green consumers, and segmentation will lose its relevance. But what this implies is that we need to understand the transition and evolution of the segments. This is not necessarily a natural process and, therefore, of immense strategic importance to firms, NGOs, and policy makers. To date there is no meaningful work being done on exactly how people move across segments although within the marketing literature there is considerable work on the evolution of lifestyle segments.

All of this together provides the semblance of how a strategy can be built on the logic of a priori segmentation. There is, of course, the assumption that the segments that are derived are meaningful. But based on this we can build a logical path based on three necessary, but not sufficient, conditions.

First, the *ideal behaviors underlying the segments must be understood and characterized*. Although a priori segmentation tends not to rely on actual behavior, specific segments must be characterizable based on what is the "best" behavioral outcome for them if they are going to be meaningful.

Second, *the segments must be accessible*. Accessibility means that the behaviors that ideally suit individuals in the segments are identifiable and, if not arising, are not arising because of barriers that can be identified. Accessibility does not necessarily mean that the individuals in the segment must be identifiable, only that they can be reached some-how (e.g. through advertising, product placement, etc.).

Third, *the barriers to ideal behavior must be identified and understood*. In other words, if individuals in a segment are not behaving in a manner that is "ideal", then this must be either because the individuals in the segments are mis-categorized or because barriers are stopping them from purchasing optimally.

Based upon this, firms have a number of strategic options. First, and most obviously, they can attempt to mitigate barriers in some way. For example, companies can lobby for subsidies that reduce the price of green energy options, or they can institute an outright ban (as has been done with incandescent light bulbs in several countries). Note that this does not neces-sarily alter the segments (since it does not change the antecedents). Second, they can do an "end around" the barriers. For example, companies can introduce new products or product packages that take into account the barriers or bypass them completely. Third, companies can attempt to shift individuals between the segments. The first two strategies are aimed at altering the market constraints, while the third is an attempt at changing the psychology and motivation of the individual. It is also why understanding the transition between the seg-ments is important. Hence, if the goal is to make more individuals green consumers, ulti-mately what matters is how they move from one segment to another. For those believing in a priori segmentation, this is the most difficult facet as the segments are themselves, and by definition, reflections of deeper seeded antecedents that are unlikely to be easily altered.

Behavioral segmentation

To illustrate some of the complexities of consumer-decision models, I offer an illustra-tion based on my prior work that may provide guidance to understanding the logic and strategic relevance of behavioral approaches (Auger et al. 2010).

Consumers had to choose amongst a set of product alternatives across two categories, athletic shoes, and AA batteries. The products they chose amongst differed in terms of their: functional attributes (e.g. battery life); social attributes (e.g. mercury/cadmium free); price; brand; and the country in which the product was produced. Based on these experiments we could estimate (1) the sensitivity of product choice to each of the levels of the attributes, both functional and social; (2) the differences in these sensitivities between individuals; and (3) whether these decision models were product specific or not. What makes this study different from a priori approaches is that we: (a) never asked consumers their general opinions of environmental issues; and (b) never asked individ-uals about the specific product attributes directly.

Figure 21.5 represents the archetypal segments that are estimated based on our experi-ment. The horizontal axis presents the importance of the attributes based on their sig-nificance. For simplicity, we have aggregated the functional attributes. What we are interested in showing in this graph is the segmentation and how it varies. The three seg-ments are roughly identifiable as (1) Brand, (2) Price, and (3) Social. Segment (1) is driven by positive and negative brand associations (the other category represents a local brand), positive and negative country of production associations, and the functional attributes

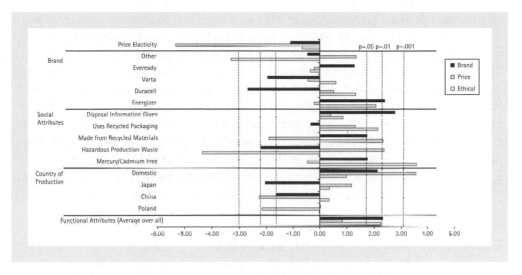

FIGURE 21.5 Segments and Product Feature Sensitivity

of the product. Segment (2) is overwhelming influenced by price and the fact that the product is produced locally, with virtually no effect of the functional attributes. Segment (3) reveals itself to be concerned about the environmental composition of the product and its functional attributes. Brand and price play almost no part in their decisions.

It should be obvious how these results differ from a priori segmentation. The behavioral approach does not focus on describing green segments but determining purchasing segments for which there might be green components that are relevant. There is no a priori assumption that there are green segments out there in the product category to be discovered. There are only differences in purchasing propensities at the individual level. The "greenness" of any consumer is determined by the extent to which that propensity is influence by the presence or absence of the environmental attributes.

There is a lot that is being revealed in these results that can be used strategically and is informative in understanding the individual "greener" consumer. First, there is a strong negative relationship between price sensitivity and social sensitivity, which allows for effective pricing approaches for the different product attribute mixes (including the green attributes). Second, social attributes must be bundled with functional attributes. Those willing to sacrifice functionality will do so for price (segment 2) but not the environment (segment 3). Third, branding plays an odd role, in that those concerned about the environment are not positively brand sensitive (they seem unwilling to pay for branding) but are negatively affected by local branding. Finally, we can see the differential value of different green attributes and how they influence choice. Hazardous product waste and being cadmium/mercury free dominates the other green attributes.

Overall, we can see how organizations can employ behavioral approaches to gaining information about segmentation. *First, they need to understand that searching for the green consumer is not about green but about the consumer.* They should concentrate on models of consumption for which green is a component. A priori segmentation starts with a belief that green is a primary determinant of behavior. It is not. It is just one aspect of a complex decision calculus. Also, to talk about segments of green consumers absent the segmentation based on all other aspects of that calculus will lead to incorrect model and segment specifications and a higher probability of disappointment in the market. This leads to *our second rule, understanding the green consumer requires understanding all aspects of the consumer's decision calculus, from the functional attributes to the circumstances in which purchasing is occurring*. We like to compartmentalize issues into boxes that we can analyze more easily but the reality is that consumers are making complex trade-offs all the time. To understand why someone is a green consumer or not is also asking a question about what else they do or don't care about. When someone chooses not to be a green consumer it may have nothing to do with "barriers" to being green but that the individual has other priorities that imply that they simply do not "do green."

SUMMARY

This chapter highlights the complexity associated with understanding environmentally driven consumption and green consumerism. Much of what we supposedly know about green consumers is, in reality, quite limited due to the fact that we have been investigating a phenomenon that is not well suited to many standard market-research techniques that have been applied. It is also limited by the nascence of the market for true green alternatives to many products in the marketplace.

However, as we have shown, there are research alternatives that allow us to get a better insight into the psyche of the consumer and glean how green they are. What we should learn, to paraphrase Maryam Banikarim (2010), is that there are many shades of green and how green someone appears is due not just to their color but the lighting and other ambient colors around.

Three critical lessons can be drawn from this discussion:

There are very few examples of a day-in-day-out green consumer. In other words, the ubiquity of the LOHAS consumer is, like the ethical consumer, a myth. It is not a representation of widespread behavior but an artifact of survey methodology.

Hence, it follows that,

It is impossible to understand green consumption without a complete understanding of the non-green aspects of particular consumption contexts. In other words, to get at the nuances of green consumers, you need to understand that this is simply a statement about the segmentation of consumers in particular markets and that you are really seeking to understand the nuances of their behavior holistically.

Strategically, this requires having an evolving strategy for green consumerism that digs deeply into the way in which consumers trade off functional and social aspects of their consumption. For some consumers, in some markets, green consumption is very rational. For these consumers green consumption is about the intangible benefits that arise with a different lifestyle. In this case, firms have to understand the intangible benefits and come up with ingenious ways to capture consumers' intangible demands in their products and services.

Overall, what we have emphasized in our discussion is that to understand the consumer, researchers must attempt to understand behavior first and foremost. Values, attitudes, and intentions may be interesting, theoretically, but they prove to be too variable and too subject to bias to get at the essence of actual individual purchasing behavior, which is what segmentation is all about. Segmentation that is effective is segmentation that is sustainable in a market because it is both meaningful to consumers and profitable to firms because it exposes real and relevant trade-offs.

There is no doubt that issues of environmentalism and sustainability are critical to the future of humankind. And it behooves us as researchers to provide policymakers with the most accurate guidance that we can that is based upon the best methodologies we have available. However, environmental science is evolving and the implications of policy choices, or failing to make policy choices, are unclear even to the experts. To then throw into the mix the partially informed, or uninformed, consumer adds a level of complexity that strains the best of theories and methodologies. However, the multifaceted interaction of environmental development and individual decision making opens up real opportunities for discovery.

We can think about the opportunities in three ways as they pertain to the discussion in this chapter and research in this field.

First, in many ways segmentation research to date has been too focused on the individual as a consumer of a product or service, and not as an individual who is part of a social system. This is particularly relevant in the case of environmental concerns, as these are issues embodying externalities, and externalities rarely resonate with individuals as self-interested market consumers. Indeed, externalities to rational consumers are "bad," while green consumerism is attempting to get people to perceive them as "good." Both perspectives are naive. We live in a social milieu where we bestow benefits and costs on one another all the time. Failure to account for the human social context can cause us to miss the critically important social network aspects of consumption, which is potentially critical to the future of green consumerism. I would argue that looking only at the individual benefits of environmental outcomes is a small part of the story, and focusing on segmentation based on these individual benefits will limit our understanding of the importance of making externalities less of a deterrent and more of an incentive to engage in sustainable behavior.

Second, individual environmental concerns are evolving along with the science and the associated technologies, but we know little about how this influences people. How consumers react as the context evolves is unclear, and this presents real opportunities for research into the co-evolution individual preferences and markets. Just asking people what they believe today or how they will act today or tomorrow is not necessarily relevant to how they will act in the future, if that future is very different from the reality of today. However, how they act today may make that future, and we need to understand this.

Finally, ultimately the study of behavior is an investigation of the decision models that lead to choices that lead to behavior. However, we rarely look at the decision models in any detail. This requires that we think more deeply about how we investigate behavior *in situ* and how we can develop new ways of decomposing what people do and why they do what they do. If sustainability is going to be a new model for life it must ultimately lead to different ways of making decisions, not just for the big issues for society but also for the mundane everyday decisions of individuals.

REFERENCES

Argenti, P. A. (2004). "Collaborating with Activists: How Starbucks Works with NGOs," *California Management Review*, 47(1): 91–116.

Auger, P., & Devinney, T. M. (2007). "Do What Consumers Say Matter? The Misalignment of Preferences with Unconstrained Ethical Intentions," *Journal of Business Ethics*, 76(4): 361–383.

—— ——, Louviere, J. J., & Burke, P. F. (2008). "Do Social Product Features Have Value to Consumers?" *International Journal of Research in Marketing*, 25(3): 183–191.

—— —— —— —— (2010). "The Importance of Social Product Attributes in Consumer Purchasing Decisions: A Multi-Country Comparative Study," *International Business Review*, 19(2): 140–159.

Banikarim, M. (2010). "Seeing Shades in Green Consumers," *Adweek* (19 April 2010). <http://www.adweek.com/aw/content_display/community/columns/other-columns/e3i33e34f97cd-beee3ef24db33271b96735>, Accessed 12 June 2010.

Bonini, S., & Oppenheim, J. (2008). "Cultivating the Green Consumer," *Stanford Social Innovation Review*, 6(4): 56–61.

Boulstridge, E., & Carrigan, M. (2000). "Do Consumers Really Care about Corporate Responsibility? Highlighting the Attitude-Behavior Gap," *Journal of Communication Management*, 4(4): 355–368.

Carrigan, M., & Attala A. (2001). "The Myth of the Ethical Consumer-Do Ethics Matter in Purchase Behaviour?" *Journal of Consumer Marketing*, 18(7): 560–577.

Cottee J. (2009). "Socially Conscious Consumers: A Knowledge Project for the RNBS." Unpublished working paper, Ivey Business School.

Devinney, T. M. (2010). "The Consumer, Politics and Everyday Life," *Australasian Marketing Journal*, 18(3): 190–194.

—— Auger, P., & Eckhardt, G. M. (2010). *The Myth of the Ethical Consumer*. Cambridge, UK: Cambridge University Press.

Diamantopoulos, A., Schlegelmilch, B. B., Sinkovics, R. R., & Bohlen, G. M. (2003). "Can Socio-Demographics Still Play a Role in Profiling Green Consumers? A Review of the Evidence and an Empirical Investigation," *Journal of Business Research*, 56(6): 465–480.

Griskevicius, V., Tybur J. M., & Van den Bergh, B. (2010). "Going Green to be Seen: Status, Reputation, and Conspicuous Conservation," *Journal of Personality and Social Psychology*, 98(3): 392–404.

LOHAS (2002). "LOHAS Consumer Research," *LOHAS Weekly Newsletter*, Monday, 10 June 10 2002. Available at <http://www.lohas.com/articles/68495.html>, (last accessed 1 January 2011).

Namkoong, J. & Irwin, J. R. (2010). "Slam the Cause: Reactions to Being Asked to Contribute to a Charity." Working paper.

Schlegelmilch, B. B., Bohlen, G. M., & Diamantopoulos A. (1996). "The Link Between Green Purchasing and Measures of Environmental Consciousness," *European Journal of Marketing*, 30(5): 35–55.

Straughan, R. D., & Roberts, J. A. (1999). "Environmental Segmentation Alternatives: A Look at Green Consumer Behavior in the New Millenium," *Journal of Consumer Marketing*, 16(6): 558–575.

Train, K. (2009). *Discrete Choice Methods with Simulation*, 2nd ed. Cambridge, UK: Cambridge University Press

Wedel, M. & Kamakura, W. A. (2000). *Market Segmentation: Conceptual and Methodological Foundations,* 2nd ed. Boston, MA: Kluwer.

PART VII

ACCOUNTING
AND FINANCE

....

SUSTAINABILITY AND SOCIAL RESPONSIBILITY REPORTING AND THE EMERGENCE OF THE EXTERNAL SOCIAL AUDITS: THE STRUGGLE FOR ACCOUNTABILITY?

....

ROB GRAY
AND IRENE M. HERREMANS

SOCIETY's definition of accountability has broadened to include a diversified set of stake-holders, a rigorous assessment of performance on multiple dimensions, and communication of results in many different formats (Logsdon & Lewellyn 2000). Yet, the business community's definition of accountability has been restricted only to those dimensions that affect financial performance. As all organizations have a range of interactions with society and the natural environment that are not captured in the financial statements alone (see Cho, Patten, & Roberts [Chapter 24] this volume), the organization's stakeholders (see Kassinis [Chapter 5] this volume) may have a desire for—even a right to—information about aspects of its environmental (and social) performance beyond the narrow definition of financial accountability. With the recent formation of the International Integrated Reporting Committee (IIRC) the multi-dimensional definition of accountability is in the process of becoming legitimized by the business community. The IIRC is a joint effort by the IFAC (International Federation of Accountants), the Global Reporting

Initiative (GRI), and The Prince's Accounting for Sustainability Project. It, along with other initiatives, is shifting the major emphasis of reporting from short-term financial performance to the long-term consequences of decision-making by including non-financial indicators of environmental and social, along with financial performance.

This chapter discusses the current state of accountability and how it is evolving to embrace environmental, social, and sustainability accountability, reporting, and disclosure.

Organizations communicate with stakeholders in many ways, including through such vehicles as the financial statements and annual report, advertising, seminars, lobbying, the website, one-off and special reports, and so on. As the vehicles open to organizations have developed, so has the interest of researchers. Particularly, researchers with an interest in organizational accountability have traditionally focused upon statutory and non-statutory disclosures in the annual report (Cho et al. [Chapter 24], this edition; Gray et al. 1995a; 1995b; 1996). However, for the last two decades, our attention has increasingly been drawn to the relatively recent emergence of a new type of report—the "stand-alone." More recently still, we begin to see increasing interest in the corporate use of websites as a medium of disclosure (Patten & Crampton 2004; Lodhia 2005). Whilst a comprehensive examination of organizational accountability would require an analysis of all the media used by an organization (Zeghal & Ahmed 1990) this has rarely been undertaken in the literature. This lacuna arises, in part, because there is a distinct sense that different media are used to talk about different issues—and probably to talk to different constituents. It also arises, in part, because there is significant overlap (even information redundancy) between the material contained in the different media, such that the website, for example, will reproduce and thereby duplicate hard-copy annual reports and stand-alone reports (Freedman & Stagliano 2004). But the research has also limited its attentions for reasons of practicality because the process of collating and synthesizing such a diverse range of media is a daunting task, the value of which is not always apparent (although see, for example, Unerman 2000).

In this chapter we want to explore the actual and potential widening of environmental (and social) accountability to a range of constituents. Whilst Cho, Patten & Roberts ([Chapter 24] this volume) have focused upon the annual report and the process of reporting predominantly to stockholders and financial markets, we draw our interest wider and focus on the (relatively) recent phenomena of both the stand-alone reports and emergence of 'counter-accounting' by civil society.

Stand-alone reports have appeared under many names from 'Environmental Reports,' 'Citizenship Reports,' to even 'Sustainability Reports.'[1] What particularly makes these stand-alone reports remarkable is that they represent a very clear engagement by corporations with the increasingly critical issues of environmental stewardship, social responsibility, and planetary sustainability at a time when society's well-being and the planet

---

[1] The term 'sustainability report' has become the over-riding label of choice and is used widely (if erroneously) to refer generically to reports which provide social, environmental, and/or economic information, and sometimes (again erroneously) interchangeably with CSR.

itself are under unique levels of threat. Indeed, such reporting has every appearance of a voluntary accountability by many of the world's corporations. Such accountability is very clearly needed, but it is not entirely clear that these voluntary reports are actually increasing accountability—as opposed to increasing the appearance of such accountability. So despite a remarkable and impressive growth in forms of voluntary disclosure there has been, perversely it might almost seem, a steady growth in the activities of civil society organizations which have sought to develop independent accounts of corporate activity (generally known as 'external social audits').

A number of initial observation should be made.

First, our brief will necessarily take us broader than business and the natural environment. Any sensible understanding of the natural environment cannot be easily separated from (see Ehrenfeld [Chapter 33] this volume) either an explicit recognition of societal interactions with, and mediation of, that environment, or a recognition of the planetary context of social and environmental sustainability. Therefore, to talk of environmental accountability without a recognition of the societies about whom and to whom the accountability is owed would be facile. Equally, to talk of environmental stewardship with no recognition of planetary (un)sustainability would be, largely, to miss the principal point.

Second, the way in which corporate reporting has developed has blurred any distinctions that might be drawn between social, environmental, and sustainability reporting. Although early reporting related explicitly to environmental reporting, this has not been the case from about the mid 1990s when such voluntary disclosure became entwined with social responsibility and then, eventually, the so-called triple bottom line and sustainability reporting. The distinctions are not helpful in this context of corporate accountability, and we will not maintain them here.

Finally, there are materially different interpretations of corporate reporting behaviour, its progress, and how it might be improved, which depend upon whether one is adopting a business-centred (managerialist, marginalist) perspective or a society/planetary (holistic, radical) perspective. We shall seek to provide evidence and argument in support of, and deriving from, both points of view.

The chapter is organized as follows. We first explore the meaning of the stand-alone report, its recent history, and some of the parameters of this phenomenon. We then examine some conflicting views: different ways in which this remarkable and largely voluntary activity might be evaluated. Then, from a managerial perspective, we identify a number of the challenges which corporations face when undertaking this voluntary reporting. After that, we introduce the use, reliability, and attestation of these stand-alone reports. In the next section, we offer a different view of accountability that focuses less on what the organization might wish to say about itself and more on what civil society, faced with an absence of what it believes to be real accountability, says about it: what 'accounts' those external to the organization might propose and produce. Finally, we tease out a few conclusions and suggest some of the ways in which the relationships between civil society, the market, and the state might be better mediated in the interests of democracy.

THE EMERGENCE OF STAND-ALONE REPORTING

Business' disclosure of data concerning its social and environmental interactions is, for the most part, a voluntary act. Despite the increasing regulation of such disclosure in countries as diverse as Australia, Denmark, France, and Korea (for example) the systematic reporting of social and environmental information is undertaken only partially for legal reasons: voluntary disclosure is undertaken for the business' own (often complex) reasons(see Cho, Patten, & Roberts [Chapter 24] this volume).

The growth of voluntary disclosure in the corporate annual report, the emergence of experimental social and environmental accounts and the growth in employee reporting from the mid-1960s onwards forms the basis for most of the study of social and environmental reporting (AICPA 1977; Estes 1976; Gray et al. 1996). It was only with the emergence of the stand-alone reports in the 1990s that this emphasis began to change.

It is difficult to be certain what brought about this change but the 1980s was perhaps a pivotal decade. The widespread stagnant or low growth, high levels of debt (especially in developing countries), and (perhaps ironically) the surge of neo-liberalism coupled with a range of highly visible industrial disasters (such as Bhopal, Chernobyl and the *Exxon Valdez*) all seem to have played a part in changing expectations: expectations which were perhaps crystallized in the Brundtland Commission (UNWCED 1987).

The first major examples of the stand-alone reports were the environmental reports from companies such as British Airways, Noranda Minerals, and Norsk Hydro in the early 1990s. These first examples were soon joined by a growing range of reports from both large international companies and, increasingly, from a range of smaller organizations. The development of reporting was stimulated and supported by a disparate range of initiatives, including the range of guidance and cajolery from industry, governmental and professional organizations (see, for example, United Nations 1992; International Chamber Of Commerce 1991; *Public Environmental Reporting Initiative (PERI) Guidelines* 1994).

By the mid to late 1990s, the notion of a purely environmental report was giving way to a recognition of the importance of social issues, and we see reports now named as (for example) corporate social responsibility or citizenship reports. This development in turn was overtaken by the affectation to refer to the stand-alone reports as a sustainability report by the turn of the century. Whatever their titles, reports now typically address an interwoven set of social, environmental, and economic issues.

The development of these stand-alone reports has continued to gain pace, and in addition to the plethora of academic studies that they have attracted, their progress has been systematically monitored and assessed by SustainAbility/UNEP (see, for example, 1996; 2002) and KPMG (1997 et seq.). Table 22.1 provides a collation of data taken from KPMG's surveys of the reporting practices of some of the world's larger companies.

The trend in reporting is clearly upwards (although see Norway in 2005 and the USA in 1999), and apart from some return to integrating reporting into the annual report, it

Table 22.1 Trends in reporting by large companies (% of the largest 100 companies producing reports in selected countries)

	1996	1999	2002	2005	2008[2]
Australia	5	15	14	23	37
Brazil	-	-	-	-	56
Canada	-	-	19	41	60
Czech Republic	-	-		-	14
Denmark	8	29	20	22	22
Finland	7	15	32	31	41
France	4	4	21	40	47
Germany	28	38	32	36	n/a
Hungary		-	-	-	25
Italy	-	2	12	31	59
Japan	-	21	72	80	88
Mexico	-	-	-	-	17
Netherlands	20	25	26	29	60
Norway	26	31	30	15	25
Portugal	-	-	-	-	49
Romania		-	-	-	23
South Africa	-	-	-	18	26
South Korea	-		-	-	42
Spain	-	-	-	25	59
Sweden	26	34	26	20	59
Switzerland	-	-	-	-	28
United Kingdom	27	32	49	71	84
United States	44	30	36	32	73
Global 250 companies % (n)	-	35(88)	45(112)	52(129)	79(198)
KPMG Country average % (n)	17(220)	24(267)	23(440)	33(525)	45(990)

Adapted from KPMG (1997, 1999, 2002, 2005, 2008)

looks likely to continue (although see Pallenberg et al. 2006). However, it is important to note that (i) reporting continues to be dominated by the very largest companies (nearly 80% of the Global 250 produce reports whereas less than half of each country's top 100 does so) and (ii) after nearly twenty years of a voluntary initiative, it is still the case that less than half of a country's large companies are likely to report regularly.

Attempts to establish guidelines for voluntary reporting that would be widely accepted and widely adopted met with only limited success until the establishment of

[2] The numbers shown in the table exclude those "sustainability" reports which were integrated with the corporate annual report itself and which, in 2008, KPMG began to capture separately. This understates the reporting by between 1 and 5% in most cases. However a few countries have a significant presence on the annual report. These include Brazil (22%), France (12%), Norway (12%), South Africa (19%) and Switzerland (21%).

Table 22.2 Organizations reporting based upon the Global Reporting Initiative (numbers reporting)

	1999	2002	2005	2008
Australia		7	17	62
Brazil		6	10	71
Canada		6	14	38
Czech Republic			1	1
Denmark		4	2	7
Finland		1	12	14
France		3	12	37
Germany		5	18	39
Hungary		3	4	9
Italy		3	12	40
Japan	1	17	22	61
Mexico			1	10
Netherlands		5	26	39
Norway			5	9
Portugal		1	2	19
Romania			0	0
South Africa	1	10	22	51
South Korea			8	46
Spain		8	62	131
Sweden	2	2	9	23
Switzerland		1	11	29
United Kingdom	1	14	24	46
United States	4	26	37	110
OTHER		18	55	208
Total	9	140	386	1100

Derived from Global Reporting Initiative website Reports List. Sampled 17 February 2010
The countries listed were selected by the authors simply to make Table 22.2 comparable with the KPMG figures in Table 22.1.

the Global Reporting Initiative (GRI). GRI is a multi-stakeholder attempt to establish a framework and generally accepted reporting principles for environmental, social, and sustainability reporting, similar to generally accepted accounting principles for financial reports. The *G3 Guidelines* (the third edition, current at the time of writing) contain principles and guidance on content, quality, and report boundaries. They suggest standard disclosures for an organization's strategic profile, management approach, and performance indicators in an attempt to make reports more standardized and comparable among organizations worldwide. These *Guidelines* are supplemented by sector-specific guidance. Organizations are then invited to comply with the *Guidelines* and to lodge their compliance on the GRI website.[3] Table 22.2 shows the number of organizations that have done this.

The organizations represented in Table 22.2 (which may, possibly, be only the self-declaring tip of the GRI reporting iceberg) are much more diverse than those upon which KPMG focuses. The GRI list includes not just the largest corporations but also (for example) universities, small values-based businesses; social enterprises and non-governmental organizations (NGOs) and covers a much wider range of countries Comparing Tables 22.1 and 22.2 also shows that in some countries (Australia, Brazil, and Spain being the most obvious) it is not the larger companies that dominate stand-alone reporting.

These data allow us to conclude that whilst stand-alone reporting is very diverse, widespread, and growing, it is by no means ubiquitous. Inevitably, that begs the question of whether or not a lack of ubiquity matters. This, in turn, leads us to consider what these reports contain, their reliability, and their importance. In essence, how do we interpret this remarkable, global voluntary phenomenon? This is the task of the next section.

THE EMERGING CONFLICTS

Although this widespread voluntary phenomenon appears to suggest that business *can* voluntarily demonstrate its accountability, its responsibility, and its sustainability, this may be an unreliable inference. (See, for example, Walley & Whitehead 1994; Milne et al. 2009; Milne & Gray 2007; Gray 2006; 2010; Moneva et al. 2006).

Two immediate problems present themselves. First, stand-alone reporting is only undertaken by a minority of organizations. For illustration, there are estimated to be approximately 60,000 multinational corporations in the world; of these, it seems likely that less than 2,000 actually report (ACCA/Corporate Register 2004; UNCTAD 2005; Pallenberg et al. 2006). Second, the reports are usually designed to suggest a positive image of the organization's activities and are essentially one-sided and incomplete, although not without a recognition of challenges and problems. Therefore, the reporting is sometimes superficial and thus not relevant and useful to decision makers. (Figure 22.1 offers a few illustrations of this.)

In general, the stand-alone reports say a lot about what an organization would like the reader to see as its responsibility. What a reader of most stand-alone reports will not learn is the extent to which the corporation is (or is not) satisfying the responsibility and accountability that society(ies) ask of it (Mintzberg 1983; Cooper and Owen 2007). If corporations are not (and perhaps cannot be) environmentally responsible or sustainable, then society really needs to know this. However, the current state of disclosure leaves the various segments of society unable to judge the state of sustainability of many corporations.

---

[3] At the time of writing, GRI has become a major element of a new initiative known as the International Integrated Reporting Committee which is seeking to develop a synthesis of sustainability and financial reporting for all organizations.

Now that some of the world's largest companies have been able to quantify the business case for corporate responsibility and reporting,...... corporate responsibility reporting is building value for companies in many ways **(KPMG, 2008, p4 + p10)**

Two thirds of the world's leading public companies now report formally on sustainability...... (o)f the 79 organizations that use the term 'sustainability' in their CR reporting, only two define what they mean by it in the first instance **(SPADA, 2008, p9 + p3)**

"Being sustainable is **now mandatory** for any 21st Century business" (emphasis in original) *Business and sustainable development (base) conference* London 16–17 March 2010

The *Coca Cola Sustainability Report 2008/2009* mentions sustaining or sustainable 86 times but never defines it/links it to planet or justice. "*We are assessing everything to increase productivity, minimize waste and maximize resources—a clear example of where sustainability goals and business objectives align. (p2) LIVE POSITIVELY™ is our commitment to making a positive difference in the world. Through redesigning the way we work and live, we consider sustainability as part of everything we do. As we act with an eye toward future generations, we will focus on driving business growth and creating a more sustainable world. (p6)*

The *Puma Sustainability Report 2007/2008* mentions sustainability 146 times; it is one of the world's best reports and makes several attempts to link **indirectly** to sustainability via other organizations (SAM, Global Compact, DJSI, which themselves do *not* explain links to sustainability):*This path that PUMA has paved over the past ten years is a testament to the fact that we do not simply talk about sustainable development, we take action. (p5) Sustainability is a given rather than a trend... (p52)*

FIGURE 22.1 Some suggestive statements about sustainability and CSR reporting

The argument is fairly straightforward. The most widely used standard of sustainability reporting is the GRI *Guidelines*. In 2009, 1,290 organizations, a very small proportion of the world's significant organizations, had registered as having produced a report that recognized these *Guidelines*. Of those 1,290 organizations, by no means all fully comply with the GRI Guidelines. Let us be generous and suggest that 1,000 comply fully. The GRI *Guidelines* are a rough approximation of the "Triple Bottom Line" (Elkington 1997, also see Klassen & Vachon [Chapter 15] this volume). All commentators agree that the GRI *Guidelines* are a work in progress and they do not capture the full Triple Bottom Line (Henriques & Richardson 2004). More robust analysis suggests that they do not yet even come close, especially on social indicators (Moneva et al. 2006; Milne & Gray 2002; Gray 2006). Furthermore, the Triple Bottom Line does not—and in all probability cannot—provide guidance on the extent to which an organization is contributing to, or detracting from, the sustainability of social and ecological systems. The Triple Bottom Line, in principle, can represent a first step towards (un)sustainability reporting but it is not sustainability reporting.

Indeed, a priori reasoning would suggest that it is much more likely to be the case that all commercial organizations are actually *un-sustainable*. Therefore, as citizens and researchers, we would be wiser to approach the issues of business and the natural environment with this assumption and work to invite rejection of the contention, as opposed to assuming the corollary and leaving society to try and ascertain whether or not it is true. (See also Gladwin et al. 1995; York et al. 2003; Ehrenfeld, [Chapter 35] this volume).

The crucial point is that the stand-alone report does not provide evidence which might enable a reader to assess an organization's environmental impacts, let alone its contribution to (un)sustainability. The documents are self-evidently valuable from a managerial point of view; the evidence is fairly compelling that they may be misleading from society's (and the planet's) point of view. Why would that be? That is what we address in the next section.

THE EMERGING CHALLENGES

Whilst it is important to understand that there is a range of societal views that might challenge what a corporation claims as its social responsibility and its sustainability, it is equally important to understand how it is that an organization might arrive at a position to make such claims. Only then is it possible to grasp the rationale that drives much current voluntary reporting and, perhaps more relevantly, suggest how those who wish to improve such reporting might seek to engage with it.

Despite the range of theories of voluntary reporting (Gray et al. 2010), when seen through the eyes of the reporting entity, decisions about whether to and what to report seem a little simpler. Putting aside the more consciously cynical attempts by corporations to mislead their relevant publics, reporting has to fit the logic of the organization and sit comfortably in one form or another of a business case. It is a truism therefore to say that such reporting must be (on the whole) managerialist, marginalist, and predominantly in the interests of the organization.

There are then a range of issues that affect how those organizational decisions are translated into reporting practice. We touch on just a few of these here.

Diversity of views and understandings

Corporate social responsibility (CSR) and sustainability remain highly contested terms and ones which are understood differently by different individuals and groups, by different organizations, and by different industries (Wood 1991; Herremans et al. 2009). Notwithstanding Mintzberg's suggestions (1983) about the societal basis of responsibility and notwithstanding the evidential basis of sustainability (species extinction, poverty, water shortages, global climate change, etc), organizations are likely to continue to understand the term differently and articulate cases for reporting accordingly.

So for most organizations, it is not a case of seeking to take the Brundtland definition (for example) and translate that into organizational logics (Herremans et al. 2009), but rather it is a case that the notions implicit in Brundtland are mediated, first through international bodies such as World Business Council for Sustainable Development, The International Chamber of Commerce, and the GRI, and that then the message from these bodies is mediated again into the sense-making and business case for the organization itself (see, for example, Angus-Leppan et al. 2009; Gray & Bebbington 2000). It is little wonder that understandings of sustainability and CSR are thus interpreted in many different ways.

Diversity of responses

Broad-brush explanations of reporting behaviour, although not without empirical support, fail to capture and explain the differences both within and between organizations and how those differences manifest themselves in reporting (see, for example, Buhr 2002; Matten & Moon 2008; Angus-Leppan et al. 2009).

Materiality and information systems

Organizations need information systems to support their reporting, substantiate any claims therein, and to help identify risks and exposures (Buhr & Gray [Chapter 23] this volume). Organizational information systems develop in those areas that the organization considers material, but it is less clear how the organization judges the materiality of the demands of stakeholders for information which, on the face of it, are not cost-effective to collate. Whilst the company will understand the salience of its stakeholders sufficiently, it is not necessarily the case that it will have an equally sufficient grasp on information salience.

Selection and balance

How does the organization select from the very wide range of potential information that it could report? Decisions will have to be made in order to provide a report which the organization judges to be balanced and fair, which reflects the information that is available and perceived as needed, and recognizes that many stakeholders are likely to be sceptical about the report, and so the report must appear to be credible and reliable. Greenwashing is not a charge any organization wants to face but, equally, a company will be reluctant to disclose data that are likely to attract unwanted and unpleasant attention.

Comparability

The most obvious form of guidance for a reporting organization is the GRI. With its increasing development of industry-specific guidelines, GRI offers the organization a sensible and defensible strategy for its reporting choices. However, the organization is also going to be concerned about how its own performance is represented vis-à-vis its competitors and, as the diverse experiences with (for example) accounting for carbon have shown, the corporate world is some way from reliable comparable reports (Kolk et al. 2008). It is in this connection that the views of the users and the role of assurance take on more importance.

Users, assurance, and the stand-alone report

The examination of the extent to which corporate information satisfies the wants and needs of those who use the data has a very long—although perhaps not so glorious—history in accounting and accounting research. Such concerns have extended into the examination of the production of non-financial disclosure in both the corporate annual report and, more recently, the stand-alone report. This line of research might usefully be thought of as having two strands: one concerned with the needs and responses of financial participants (see Cho, Patten, & Roberts [Chapter 24]; and Russo & Minto [Chapter 2] this volume); and one concerned with other stakeholders and their responses to the data (which we address here) (see also Kassinis [Chapter 5] this volume).

The enquiry into the needs and wants of non-financial participants suggests that current voluntary social and environmental disclosure fails to meet the expectation and needs of stakeholders (Deegan & Rankin 1999; O'Dwyer et al. 2005). Broadly speaking, this should not surprise us: voluntary disclosure is primarily designed to meet corporate needs rather than stakeholders' needs: the two sets of needs are rarely entirely aligned. Of perhaps more concern is the finding that social and environmental disclosure also fails to meet the needs of the socially responsible investment community (Freidman & Miles 2001; Solomon & Solomon 2006; Hunt III & Grinnell 2004; Solomon & Darby 2005).

Two of the key lacunae that the literature has identified in the reporting processes—especially concerning the stand-alone report—relate to the extent to which the stakeholders themselves have been involved in the reporting process (typically referred to as stakeholder dialog), and the reliability of the information produced in these reports (typically referred as the assurance issue).

The growth in stakeholder dialog as part of an organization's responsibility and accountability processes has the appearance of a very positive development. However, stakeholder dialog would seem to be more dominated by appearance than by substance (Owen et al. 2000; 2001). It is this, that Cooper & Owen (2007) conclude, is the central (but currently missing) ingredient that might turn a managerialist reporting function into a genuine process of accountability.

In addition to involving the stakeholders, the stand-alone reports need to be something upon which a reader can rely. Such reliability has two principal threads: completeness and trustworthiness. We have already questioned whether the information contained in most sustainability reports can be realistically considered to be either complete or entirely satisfying of users' wants. A similar conclusion is reluctantly reached in the explorations of the quality of assurance.

We have already seen that a sensible organization will ensure that it has a structure, an information system, and decision process in place so that any resultant report is reliable and defensible. In addition, many organizations require that the Board sign off on the report, so that the whole organization is committed to the stand-alone report. These are important internal assurance processes. The usual way to try to add *external* credibility to the report—to convince the readers that the report is balanced and fair—would be to have the report assured in some way. (The analog with the statutory audit of the financial statements is obvious.) The simplest and least expensive way of approaching this process is to ask a number of stakeholders to read and comment upon the report. These comments may then be included in the report, with suggestions for improvements. The more systematic and expensive approach is to employ an independent consultancy or audit firm who will provide an assurance statement about (for example) the reliability, completeness, balance, and accuracy of the report. Increasingly, the investigation that underlies the statement of assurance follows one of the international guidelines such as AA1000 or ISEA 3000 (Leipziger 2010).

The value of such assurance can prove elusive, however. Although the number of reports that contain assurances is rising, still less than 50 percent of reports are assured (KPMG 2008). If assurance is valuable, then over 50 per cent of reports may be considered as deserving some skepticism. However, Ball et al. (2000) and O'Dwyer & Owen (2005) conclude that in many cases, the careful reading of the assurance statement will lead to the conclusion that the existence of an assurance statement in itself may not warrant increased confidence in the accuracy of the information that has been assured. (See also, Henriques & Richardson 2004.) Because the assurance procedures, the qualifications of the assurance providers, and the assurance statements themselves vary considerably from report to report and are not standardized at this time, a user must read an assurance statement carefully to judge the rigor of the assurance and the extent to which it can be relied on.

OFFERING A COUNTER-ACCOUNT: THE EXTERNAL SOCIAL AUDITS

One of the advantages of democratic society is that, to a degree at least, it permits alternative voices to be heard. Whether or not we subscribe to the view that modern Western society is dominated by the voice of the corporation, the plurality of voices is probably a sign of a healthy democracy. The growth in stakeholder consultation suggests the possibility of voices counter to that of the business becoming better heard, or at least that the business voice may become more harmonious with that of civil society. However, it is not obvious that these other voices are, as yet, as ubiquitous on social and environmental accountability and sustainability as perhaps they need to be (see, for example, Owen et al. 2001; Cooper & Owen 2007). It is this (perceived?) absence of a voice for civil society that has led to what are broadly called the external social audits.

The term is used to embrace a bewildering array of accounts—anything, in fact, that involves some body, group, or person independent of the accountable organization producing a story (an account) about that organization. One might think of it as a range of mechanisms by which bodies dissatisfied with corporate voluntary accountability seek to impose the accountability they require. The actual vehicles used may be simply ad hoc and comprise such things as newspaper reports, citizen protest reports, and campaigning documents from NGOs. Or these counter accounts might equally comprise investigations by bodies as diverse as governmental committees, statutory agencies, or academics.

The more interesting audits (at least in the present context) tend to be the more system-atic, in-depth and wide-ranging investigations carried out over a period of time and sometimes on a continuing basis.

The approach to these audits was probably pioneered by the consumer movement in the USA, but many of the standards were set in the 1970s by organizations such as Social Audit Ltd (Medawar 1976) and The Council on Economic Priorities (CEP 1977), as well as by early environmental pressure groups and representatives of the labor movement (see, for example, Harte & Owen 1987; Gray et al. 1996; Geddes 1991). External social audits are now ubiquitous and, for example, are now a major tool of the NGOs (see, for example, Greenpeace 1985; Christian Aid 2005). They are an essential part of the information sources for the socially responsible investment movement (Global Witness 2005), and a major source of reputational risk for organizations (Deegan & Blomquist 2006).

The diversity and range of potential external social audits is enormous (Gray & Bebbington 2001: 279; Gray et al. 1996, [Chapter 9]; Geddes 1991). We will very briefly review three broad themes here: monitoring organizations, the one-off report, and counter-accounting.

Monitoring organizations

Monitoring organizations are perhaps most apparent in the consumer movement where the assessment of product quality, value for money, safety, and so forth can range from specialist journals and websites through to accreditation bodies like Fairtrade or the Forest Stewardship Council. However, such organizations are by no means restricted to consumer issues, and every business will be fully aware of many government, quasi-government, and independent bodies that monitor business performance in everything from environmental pollution through human rights abuses to health and safety matters. But perhaps one of the most important developments—for accountability at least—has been the growth of organizations which provide various indices and rankings and which have emerged, largely, in response to the needs of socially responsible investment movements. These indices and rankings cover such matters as reputation (e.g. Most Admired rankings), sustainability performance (e.g. the Dow Jones Sustainability (sic) Index), and social responsibility performance (e.g. FTSE KLD Social Index). These sources have made enormous inroads as they are relatively simple and relatively easily accessible. And herein lies the dangers of such indices (Fowler & Hope 2007) in that it is fairly unlikely that a simple measure can capture successfully a complex and elusive quality (the experience with financial profit is a case in point), and they are used too frequently by researchers who, delighted by the data, appear to forget that these are (often very crude) *proxies* for the variable of interest. Consequently incorrect inferences are far too often drawn (see, for example, Gray 2006).

These monitoring processes have societal value in that they are one of the ways in which a balancing view is offered to counter the view which business might prefer to communicate (Medawar 1976; Stephenson 1973). The processes have the intention of keeping the firm honest. (And, of course, we should not forget that if businesses were capable of complete and honest self-reporting, such activities as these might well be unnecessary.) However, *and it is a very important caveat*, any sensible citizen (and that hopefully includes researchers) will check the provenance and focus of any monitoring: if it is a market-based index or monitoring and evaluation process directed towards business, then one should always exercise a healthy skepticism as to its reliability as an independent mechanism of accountability.

Providing reports only after a crisis

Whilst monitoring is part of normal business practice, the possibility of providing a report only once can always challenge a business' strategy, reputation, and perception. If a business has a problem of which it is unaware (poor management) or is seeking to hide (poor judgment), then providing a report only once becomes a distinct possibility. Corporations such as Shell, BP, Nike, Gap, Nestle, Coca Cola, and WalMart can all attest to this experience.[4] The reports vary massively in terms of their depth and trustworthiness but, in their appeal to civil society, they speak loudly of the accountability of unaccountable organizations.

Counter-accounting

The final, and perhaps most diverse, category we touch upon here is that of counter-accounting: in essence, accounts that offer a directly different and challenging story from that offered by the business itself. The process of counter-accounting is undertaken by individuals and organizations (academics or NGOs, for example) who are quite independent of the accountable organization. They produce 'accounts' from a wide variety of sources of information, including company or industry watchdog data and other publicly available sources (the Internet, journalism, and disaffected stakeholders would be amongst the most common), and then (on occasions) combine this with the company's own sustainability information. The result provides a different, contrasting and possibly more comprehensive or balanced view of the business' activities. We see this in Adams (2004) where she offers counter statements to many of the claims made by her case study company. A similar strategy is suggested by Gallhofer et al. (2006) with the Internet offering possibilities for emancipatory accounts. Gibson et al. (2001) offer a slightly different approach, suggesting the construction of two accounts: (a) the 'silent account', using only the corporation's own information; and (b) the 'shadow account', using public

---

[4] Examples are available at: <http://www.st-andrews.ac.uk/~csearweb/aptopractice/ext-aud-examples.html>.

information to counter the claims in the silent account. This approach seeks a systematic exposure of the issues of bias and unreliability in reporting.[5]

All of these approaches have—at least superficially—the common goal of improving accountability and allowing other voices to speak alongside the views that the businesses wish to present to the state and civil society. And in many cases it is the non-financial stakeholders who have driven this external social audit agenda. However, there is an irony in that the most established of the external social audits have become institutionalized as a service to support financial participants. Whether it be the monitoring agencies like Ethical Investment Research Services (EIRIS), *Environmental Finance,* and Pension Investment Research Consultants (PIRC), the indices such as Dow Jones Sustainability Index (DJSI), and FTSE 4Good of the UK, or possibly even the Global Compact itself, all support the burgeoning socially responsible investment movement. In doing so they seek (whether successfully or not is a moot point) to gain convergence between the societal and the managerial preferences for accountability around social, environmental and sustainability issues (Owen 1990).

The way forward

Society has experienced a sea-change as it has slowly woken up to the environmental (and social) catastrophes that its current ways of organization seem to be creating—or at least exacerbating. Not surprisingly, business has similarly experienced major changes in its relationships with the environment, communities, and stakeholders. The development of the voluntary stand-alone report, the stimulus of the GRI and emergence of monitoring, and the external social audits are all part of that change.

There are two major imponderables lying at the heart of our discussion here. The first is the question of whether or not organizations should be accountable. And if so how and to whom? Corporate accountability to its financial participants has been long accepted: the acceptance of the *principle* of accountability to non-financial stakeholders appears now to be more widespread. It is the practice of that accountability that is interpreted differently by corporations and their stakeholders, in some instances, and therefore results in considerable variance in quality and quantity of reporting. Researchers are needed to urgently explore why there is a difference between what society needs and what the organization can accommodate, and how this gap may be closed through a greater communication and understanding. A slow and gradual path towards full social and environmental accountability—probably through complete Triple Bottom Line accounts (Spence & Gray 2008)—is a tantalizing and exciting prospect —not least because it just might bring organizations' conceptions of responsibility and sustainability more into line with those needed by society.

[5] This is also available on the CSEAR website at <http://www.st-andrews.ac.uk/~csearweb/aptopractice/silentacc.html>.

However, the introduction of sustainability changes everything: the evidence is pretty unequivocal that long slow paths are not an option (see Ehrenfeld [Chapter 33] this volume). Pretty radical change is needed—and soon. At the heart of our discussion, then, lies the second imponderable: where do businesses sit on the sustainability issue? Many businesses and business-related organizations claim, directly, or by implication, to be sustainable or, at least, to be on the path towards sustainable development (Milne et al. 2006). The growth of sustainability reports might suggest that this view is substantiated—but these reports offer no obvious evidence that any business is contributing to (as opposed to detracting from) a sustainable world as understood by Brundtland. This failure looks like a major limitation of sustainability reports. If the financial markets were unable to assess the financial performance of a corporation from its financial statements, this would be entirely unacceptable. Why might it be acceptable with sustainability reports? Only when most major organizations are required to produce complete, competent, and complex statements about their social, environmental, and sustainability performance, will society be in a position to judge the extent to which (if at all) organizations are performing to the highest standards of social and environmental stewardship and are being truthful with their claims to probity and propriety.

The role of the researcher is critical: not least because so much research seems content to ignore the wider data, ignore the wider context, and accept a business-as-usual scenario as beyond consideration (Milne et al. 2009). What this chapter has tried to show is that there is an infinitude of very important questions needing urgent answers about the whole relationship between business, financial markets, the natural environment, society, and sustainability. Little extant research has addressed these relationships seriously and prefers, so it would seem, to unquestionably accept poor and misleading proxies in the pursuit of more and more refined answers to less and less interesting questions. If, as the data suggest, we should express some equivocation about the way in which business and business organizations articulate the business-society-environment relationship, the most important task for any researcher is to investigate whether these crucial claims are true. If they are not, society and the planet are in a very dangerous place indeed.

REFERENCES

ACCA/Corporate Register (2004). *Towards Transparency: Progress on Global Sustainability Reporting 2004*. London: ACCA.

Adams, C. (2004). "The Ethical, Social and Environmental Reporting-Performance Portrayal Gap," *Accounting, Auditing and Accountability Journal* 17(5): 731–757.

American Institute Of Certified Public Accountants (1977). *The Measurement of Corporate Social Performance*. New York: AICPA.

Angus-Leppan, T., Metcalf, L., & Benn, S. (2009). "Leadership Styles and CSR Practice: An Examination of Sensemaking, Institutional Drivers and CSR Leadership," *Journal of Business Ethics* 93: 189–213.

Ball, A., Owen, D. L. & Gray, R. H. (2000). "External Transparency or Internal Capture? The Role of Third Party Statements in Adding Value to Corporate Environmental Reports," *Business Strategy and the Environment* 9(1): 1–23.

Buhr, N. (2002). "A Structuration View on the Initiation of Environmental Reports," *Critical Perspectives on Accounting* 13(1): 17–38.

Christian Aid (2005). *The Shirt off their Backs: How Tax Policies Fleece the Poor*, September. Available at <http://wwwchristianaid.org.uk/indepth/509tax/index.htm>

Cooper, S. M. & Owen, D. L. (2007). "Corporate Social Reporting and Stakeholder Accountability: The Missing Link," *Accounting Organizations and Society* 32: 649–667.

Council On Economic Priorities (1977). *The Pollution Audit: A Guide to 50 Industrials for Responsible Investors*. New York: CEP.

Deegan, C. & Blomquist, C. (2006). "Stakeholder Influence on Corporate Reporting: An Exploration of the Interaction between WWF-Australia and the Australian Minerals Industry," *Accounting Organizations and Society* 31(4–5): 343–372.

—— & Rankin M. (1999). "The Environmental Reporting Expectations Gap. Australian Evidence," *British Accounting Review* 31(3): 313–346.

Elkington, J. (1997). *Cannibals with Forks: The Triple Bottom Line of 21st Century Business*. Oxford: Capstone Publishing.

Estes, R. W. (1976). *Corporate Social Accounting*. New York: Wiley.

Fowler, S. J. & Hope, C. (2007). "A Critical Review of Sustainable Business Indices and their Impact," *Journal of Business Ethics* 76: 243–252.

Freedman, M. & Stagliano, A. J. (2004). "Environmental Reporting and the Resurrection of Social Accounting," *Advances in Public Interest Accounting* 10: 131–144.

Friedman, A. L. & Miles, S. (2001). "Socially Responsible Investment and Corporate Social and Environmental Reporting in the UK: An Exploratory Study," *British Accounting Review* 33(4): 523–548.

Galllhofer, S., Haslam, J., Monk, E. & Roberts, C. (2006). "Emancipatory Potential of On-Line Reporting: The Case of Counter Accounting," *Accounting Auditing and Accountability Journal* 19(5): 681–718.

Geddes, M. (1991). "The Social Audit Movement," in D. L. Owen (ed.) *Green Reporting*, London: Chapman Hall, 215–241.

Gibson, K., Gray, R., Laing, Y. & Dey, C. (2001). *The Silent Accounts Project: Draft Silent and Shadow Accounts Tesco plc 1999–2000*, Glasgow: CSEAR. Available at <www.st-andrews.ac.uk/management/csear>

Gladwin, T. N., Kennelly, J. J., & Krause, T.-S. (1995). "Shifting Paradigms for Sustainable Development: Implications for Management Theory and Research," *Academy of Management Review* 20(4): 874–907.

Global Witness (2005). *Extracting Transparency: The Need for an IFRS for the Extractive Industries*, London: Global Witness Ltd.

Gray, R. H. (2006). "Does Sustainability Reporting Improve Corporate Behaviour? Wrong Question? Right Time?" *Accounting and Business Research (International Policy Forum)* 2006: 65–88.

—— (2010). "Is Accounting For Sustainability Actually Accounting For Sustainability…and How Would We Know? An Exploration of Narratives of Organisations and the Planet," *Accounting, Organizations and Society* 35(1): 47–62.

—— & Bebbington, K. J. (2000). "Environmental Accounting, Managerialism and Sustainability: Is the Planet Safe in the Hands of Business and Accounting?" *Advances in Environmental Accounting and Management* 1: 1–44.

——— ———(2001). *Accounting for the Environment*, 2nd edition. London: Sage.

Gray, R. H., Kouhy, R., & Lavers, S. (1995a). "Corporate Social and Environmental Reporting: A Review of the Literature and a Longitudinal Study of UK Disclosure," *Accounting, Auditing and Accountability Journal* 8(2): 47–77.

——— ——— ———(1995b). "Constructing a Research Database of Social and Environmental Reporting by UK Companies: A Methodological Note," *Accounting, Auditing and Accountability Journal* 8(2): 78–101.

Gray, R. H., Owen, D. L., & Adams, C. (1996). *Accounting and Accountability: Changes and Challenges in Corporate Social and Environmental Reporting*. London: Prentice Hall.

Gray, R. H., Owen, D. L. & Adams, C. (2010). "Some Theories for Social Accounting? A Review Essay and Tentative Pedagogic Categorisation of Theorisations around Social Accounting," *Advances in Environmental Accounting and Management* 4: 1–54.

Greenpeace (1985). *Whiter Than White?* London: Greenpeace.

Harte, G. & Owen, D. L. (1987). "Fighting De-Industrialisation: The Role of Local Government Social Audits," *Accounting, Organizations and Society* 12(2): 123–142.

Henriques, A. & Richardson, J. (2004). *The Triple Bottom Line: Does it Add Up?* London: Earthscan.

Herremans, I. R., Akathaporn, P., & Mcinness, M. (1993). "An Investigation of Corporate Social Responsibility Reputation and Economic Performance," *Accounting Organizations and Society* 18(7–8): 587–604.

Herremans, I. M., Herschovis, M. S., & Bertels, S. (2009). "Leaders and Laggards: The Influence of Competing Logics on Corporate Environmental Action," *Journal of Business Ethics* 89: 449–472.

Hunt III, H. G. & Grinnell, D. J. (2004). "Financial Analysts' Views of the Value of Environmental Information," *Advances in Environmental Accounting and Management*(ed.) M. Freedman and B. Jaggi, Volume 2, Oxford: Elsevier, 101–120.

International Chamber Of Commerce (1991). *Business Charter for Sustainable Development*. Paris: ICC.

Kolk, A., Levy, D., and Pinkse, J. (2008). "Corporate Responses in an Emerging Climate Regime: The Institutionalization and Commensuration of Carbon Disclosure," *European Accounting Review* 17(4): 719–745.

KPMG (1997). *Environmental Reporting.* Copenhagen: KPMG.

———(1999). *KPMG International Survey of Environmental Reporting 1999*. Amsterdam: KPMG/WIMM.

———(2002). *KPMG 4th International Survey of Corporate Sustainability Reporting*, Amsterdam: KPMG/WIMM.

———(2005). *KPMG International Survey of Corporate Responsibility 2005*. Amsterdam: KPMG International.

———(2008). *KPMG International Survey of Corporate Responsibility Reporting 2008*. Amsterdam: KPMG International.

Leipziger, D. (2010). *The Corporate Responsibility Code Book*, revised second edition. Sheffield: Greenleaf.

Lodhia, S. K. (2005). "Legitimacy Motives for World Wide Web (WWW) Environmental Reporting: An Exploratory Study into Present Practices in the Australian Minerals Industry," *Journal of Accounting and Finance* 4: 1–16.

Logsdon, J. M., & Lewellyn, P. G. (2000). "Expanding Accountability to Stakeholders: Trends and Predictions," Business and Society Review, 105(4): 419–435.

Matten, D. & Moon, J. (2008). "'Implicit' and 'Explicit' CSR: A Conceptual Framework for a Comparative Understanding of Corporate Social Responsibility," *Academy of Management Review* 33(2): 404–424.

Medawar C. (1976). "The Social Audit: A Political View," *Accounting, Organizations and Society* 1(4): 389–394.

Milne M. J., Kearins, K. N. & Walton, S. (2006). "Creating Adventures in Wonderland? The Journey Metaphor and Environmental Sustainability," *Organization* 13(6): 801–839.

Milne, M. & Gray, R. (2002), "Sustainability Reporting: Who's Kidding Whom?" *Chartered Accountants Journal of New Zealand* 81(6): 66–70.

——— ———(2007). "Future Prospects for Corporate Sustainability Reporting," in J. Unerman, J. Bebbington, and B. O'dwyer (2007). (eds) *Sustainability Accounting and Accountability*, London: Routledge, 184–208.

Milne, M. J., Tregidga, H. M., & Walton, S. (2009). "Words Not Actions! The Ideological Role of Sustainable Development Reporting," *Accounting Auditing and Accountability Journal*, 22(8): 1211–1257.

Mintzberg, H. (1983). "The Case for Corporate Social Responsibility," *The Journal of Business Strategy* 4(2): 3–15.

Moneva, J. M., Archel, P., & Correa, C. (2006). "GRI and the Camouflaging of Corporate Unsustainability," *Accounting Forum* 30(2): 121–137.

O'Dwyer, B. & Owen, D. L. (2005). "Assurance Statement Practice in Environmental, Social and Sustainability Reporting: A Critical Evaluation," *British Accounting Review* 37(2): 205–230.

—— Unerman, J. & Hession, E. (2005). "User Needs in Sustainability Reporting: Perspectives of Stakeholders in Ireland," *European Accounting Review* 14(4): 759–787.

Owen, D. L. (1990). "Towards a Theory of Social Investment: A Review Essay," *Accounting, Organizations and Society* 15(3): 249–266.

—— Swift, T., Bowerman, M. & Humphreys, C. (2000). "The New Social Audits: Accountability, Managerial Capture or the Agenda of Social Champions?" *European Accounting Review* 9(1): 81–98.

—— —— & Hunt, K. (2001). "Questioning the Role of Stakeholder Engagement in Social and Ethical Accounting, Auditing and Reporting," *Accounting Forum* 25(3): 264–282.

Palenberg, M., Reinicke, W., & Witte, J. M. (2006). *Trends in Non-Financial Reporting*. Berlin. Global Public Policy Institute.

Patten, D. M. & Crampton, W. (2004). "Legitimacy and the Internet: An Examination of Corporate Web Page Environmental Disclosures," *Advances in Environmental Accounting and Management* (ed.) M. Freedman and B. Jaggi, Volume 2, Oxford: Elsevier, 31–57.

Solomon J. & Darby, L. (2005). "Is Private Social, Ethical and Environmental Reporting Mythicizing or Demythologizing Reality?"*Accounting Forum* 29(1): 27–47.

Solomon J. F. & Solomon, A. (2006). "Private Social, Ethical and Environmental Disclosure," *Accounting, Auditing and Accountability Journal* 19(4): 564–591.

SPADA (2008). *Environmental Reporting: Trends in FTSE 100 Sustainability Reports*, London: SPADA.

Spence, C. & Gray, R. (2008). *Social and Environmental Reporting and the Business Case*. London: ACCA.

Stephenson, L. (1973). "Prying Open Corporations: Tighter than Clams," *Business and Society Review*, Winter, 66–73.

SustainAbility/UNEP (1996). *Engaging Stakeholders: The Benchmark Survey*, London/Paris: Sustainability/UNEP.

—— (2002). *Trust Us: The 2002 Global Reporters Survey of Corporate Sustainability Reporting*. London: SustainAbility/UNEP.

Unerman, J. (2000). "Reflections on Quantification in Corporate Social Reporting Content Analysis," *Accounting, Auditing and Accountability Journal* 13(5): 667–680.

United Nations (1992). *Environmental Disclosures: International Survey of Corporate Reporting Practices*, Report of the Secretary General, 13 January (E/C.10/AC/1992/3), New York: UN.

United Nations Conference On Trade And Development (2005). *World Investment Report 2005*. New York: United Nations.

United Nations World Commission On Environment And Development (1987). *Our Common Future (The Brundtland Report)*. Oxford: OUP.

Walley, N. and Whitehead, B. (1994). "It's Not Easy Being Green," *Harvard Business Review* May/June, 46–52.

Wood, D. (1991). "Corporate Social Performance Revisited," *Academy of Management Review*, 16(4): 691–718.

York, R., Rosa, E. A. and Dietz, T. (2003). "Footprints on the Earth: The Environmental Consequences of Modernity," *American Sociological Review*, 68(2): 279–300.

Zeghal, D. &. Ahmed, S. A. (1990). "Comparison of Social Responsibility Information Disclosure Media Used by Canadian Firms," *Accounting, Auditing and Accountability Journal* 3(1): 38–53.

CHAPTER 23

ENVIRONMENTAL MANAGEMENT, MEASUREMENT, AND ACCOUNTING: INFORMATION FOR DECISION AND CONTROL?

NOLA BUHR
AND ROB GRAY

It only takes a few moments with the index of this book to appreciate the range and complexities of the interactions between business and the natural environment. All organizations, to a greater or lesser extent, draw their resources from that environment and return their wastes and emissions to it. More subtly, but no less crucially, the very principles of business (however we choose to define them) profoundly affect how we as individuals and societies perceive and negotiate our relationships with each other and with the planet and the natural world—of which (whether we remember this or not) we are so much a part. Whilst there are many, substantive, arguments around the extent to which modern business *can* operate in a manner that harmonizes with the natural environment (Bakan 2004), such concerns (however legitimate) will not detain us overmuch in this chapter. We will ignore such matters as to whether or not the natural environment can (or should) be managed. We will take management of the natural environment by business organizations as a given, and devote this chapter to how this might be aided by environmental management systems and environmental management accounting. Nevertheless, at the end of the chapter we turn to the question about future prospects for the relationship between business and the natural environment and what this means for researchers.

Environmental management systems are one type of system used to control business activities. To be well-functioning, all management systems must incorporate a range of business disciplines, such as strategy, human resources, and accounting. However, the "control" function in business has typically been the purview of the accounting discipline (albeit drawing on other areas), and has been directed towards financial control.[1] Because the basic elements are the same, regardless of the purpose, we begin with a brief overview of management control systems in general, and then move on to environmental management systems in particular. We look at the need these systems have for information and the kinds of information that these systems can generate.

Much of this information falls under our definition of environmental management accounting, which we broadly describe as the production of financial and non-financial information for the use of an organization's management in its decision and control activities relating to the business and environment interface. This is contrasted with the production of information for external, stakeholder use (see Cho, Patten, & Roberts [Chapter 24]; and Gray & Herremans [Chapter 22] this volume). As we will delineate, environmental management accounting information can be produced in the context of a management system or in isolation.

This chapter will seek to be informative, descriptive, *and* critical. Our purpose is to point out that management control systems can support, oppose, or ignore environmental management issues. Why that should be and to what extent this is inevitable, is one matter we will explore here. We also look at some of the emerging possibilities in environmental management accounting that organizations could apply—but currently do not do so. We wish to offer a realistic appraisal of some of the genuinely positive implications that well-understood environmental management systems and environmental management accounting offer the organization. However, we are also very aware that a great deal of assertive kitsch exists in this area, and we would like to offer some critical appraisal of such claims. Therefore, we will include discussion on the business case for environmental management and possibilities for the future. See Russo & Minto ([Chapter 2] this volume) for a much more developed discussion of the business case, and whether or not it "pays" to be green. In our judgment, it is essential to demonstrate where the very real limitations of environmental stewardship lie, and why there must always be very real conflicts between the traditional pursuit of financial goals and the very highest standards of environmental probity.

This chapter is organized as follows. Following a brief exploration of management control systems, we introduce the nature and detail of environmental management systems. Then, a section is provided that examines how the environmental management systems and the organization's management control systems might (or might not) be brought into harmony. A key element in this process is the management accounting systems and, particularly, the range of techniques commonly referred to as environmental management accounting. These are reviewed in the next section. Then, we step away

---

[1] It must be noted that the accounting function does not have the same degree of involvement with environmental management systems as with financial systems. This is due in large part to the fundamental disjoint between a healthy environment and the pursuit of profit, a topic we discuss later in this chapter.

from the simple managerialism of the rest of the chapter and explore the business case and the win-win opportunities—and their limitations. This brings us to the point of recognizing that financial success and environmental stewardship are not necessarily in harmony either: a matter explored in a little more detail when we briefly examine the relationship between environmental management systems, environmental management accounting, and the natural environment. Finally, we provide some summary comments as well as three possible outcomes for our present relationship with the natural environment and what those outcomes mean for researchers.

MANAGEMENT CONTROL SYSTEMS

Environmental management is, essentially, about control. And, environmental management systems are essentially management control systems that have been adapted to focus on environmental issues. Such a perspective requires that we start our exploration of environmental information with a clear (if simple) view of management and management control.

Anthony (1965: 245) suggests, albeit somewhat functionally, that management control "is the process of assuring that resources are obtained and used effectively and efficiently in the accomplishment of an organization's objectives." Knights & Willmott (2007: 146) suggest that control means "the mechanism of exploitation," whilst Grey (2005: 56) concludes that "management is really about control." So whilst we may engage in subtle conjectures around the nature of organization, control, and objectives, at the heart of the notion we have some purposive activity undertaken principally by management. Merchant (1985) is more direct and argues that control revolves around influencing human behaviour and dealing with three control problems: individual lack of direction, motivational problems, and personal limitations—not least because, of course, people are sometimes unwilling or unable to act in the organization's best interest (however, that is understood). So, Merchant (pages 4–5) argues, "Controls are necessary to guard against the possibilities that people will do something the organization does not want them to do or fail to do something that they should do."

Control and controls do not function in isolation but rather in packages of control (Sundin et al. 2009) or, more conventionally, in systems of control. Management control systems have been defined by Simons (1995: 5) as "the formal, information-based routines and procedures managers use to maintain or alter patterns in organizational activities." Two components of this definition merit stressing: "formal" and "information-based." Because these systems are formal, they officially consume organizational resources and direct organizational attention. Because these systems are information-based, financial and non-financial information is produced for the purpose of making decisions, monitoring the achievement of plans and goals, communicating corporate strategy internally, supporting organizational learning, and producing external reporting.

Whilst much of the early control literature takes strategy as being separable from control (Merchant 1985), Simons (1995) develops an approach to control that takes a broader definition and establishes linkages between accounting, control, and strategy through a number of control systems. These control systems include belief systems, boundary systems, diagnostic systems, and interactive systems. For example, Simons advocates the establishment and use of belief systems to communicate values and inspire organizational commitment. Consequently, management control is now understood—not as something sought through a single monolithic system—but rather as an ideal pursued through the interaction of a number of controls-based systems. The integrity of the information used within these systems is also critical and, as Simons notes, relies upon (what is commonly referred to as) the internal control system. According to the Committee of Sponsoring Organizations (1994), internal control can be defined as "a process, effected by an entity's people, designed to accomplish specified objectives."[2] These objectives can be thought of as relating to three broad functions:

- Operations (effective and efficient use of the entity's resources);
- Financial reporting (preparation of reliable published financial statements); and
- Compliance (the entity's compliance with applicable laws and regulations).

To facilitate these three functions, it is necessary for information to be generated from internal and external sources in order to manage business operations, develop financial statements, and ensure the entity is complying with applicable laws.

Environmental management systems and management accounting systems are particular examples of management control systems, and it is to these that we now turn.

ENVIRONMENTAL MANAGEMENT SYSTEMS

Environmental management systems are control systems that focus on environmental issues and can be defined as: "the organizational structure, responsibilities, practices, procedures, processes and resources for determining and implementing environmental policy" (Netherwood 1996). Whilst such systems may develop at the whim of the organization's management it is much more typical that they are developed in line with established voluntary guidelines, most commonly the European Union Eco-management and Audit Scheme (EMAS) and/or the International Organization for Standardization ISO 14000 series.[3] (See King, Prado, & Rivera [Chapter 6]; and Baron & Lyon [Chapter 7] in this volume for an in-depth discussion of self-regulation systems.)

[2] The Committee of Sponsoring Organizations of the Treadway Commission (COSO 1994) sets out a framework for internal control which has become the standard in most of North America. This definition comes from COSO (page 13). In the UK, the Turnbull Report (Institute of Chartered Accountants in England and Wales 1999) which is focused on listed companies is a comparable counterpart to the COSO report.

[3] One other early standard was the British Standards Institution (BSI) BS7750 although this is now subsumed within ISO14001.

These systems have common elements (Schaltegger & Burritt 2000: 379–80):

- Goal-setting;
- Information management;
- Support for decision-making, organization or planning of environmental management programmes;
- Steering, implementation, and control;
- Communication; and
- Internal and external auditing and/or review.

It is the systematic weaving of these elements into the fabric of the organization and, especially, into the fabric of its management (and accounting) control systems that will determine the extent to which environmental matters are substantially addressed by the firm. Although there are a variety of voluntary guidelines, the ISO 14000 series has emerged as the dominant set of standards for environmental management systems. This is due in part to the take-up by large US companies and, in part, to the explicitly voluntary nature of the system. Importantly, ISO is focused on environmental *management* rather than environmental *performance* and it contains no requirement for either disclosure or rigorous verification. Krut & Gleckman (1998) argue that it is the less demanding nature of the standard and its dilution of best practice that has ensured both its popularity in business and its unpopularity with critics and NGOs. However, there is some evidence that some (albeit low) level of environmental management really is better than no environmental management at all (Potoski & Prakash 2005).

It is essential to note that the installation of an environmental management system requires no specification of organizational goals, nor does it imply how the organization should fulfill requirements of an environmental management system standard accreditation. Organizational certification need not mean a great deal if one takes a broad view of environmental management.

ENVIRONMENTAL MANAGEMENT SYSTEMS AND MANAGEMENT CONTROL SYSTEMS: HARMONY, CONFLICT, OR NOT TALKING TO EACH OTHER?

If control systems are to serve any purpose beyond the ceremonial or symbolic, they must be used and usable. If they are going to work in harmony, the various control systems, environmental and otherwise, must also be integrated and capable of talking to each other. It is critical to have linkages between the systems and, indeed, to ensure that the different systems can actually point in the same direction. Bluntly put, performance and decision-making will respond to—and be in pursuit of—the dominant control system. This is typically the system(s) responsible for measuring profitability. In the event of conflict—whether to choose, for example, a more benign environmental option or an apparently cheaper financial option—of course the financial option wins.

Inevitably, the level of integration between the environmental management systems and management control systems depends upon the strategy and objectives of the organization, and the status of the environment therein (for a discussion of environmental strategy, see Delmas & Toffel [Chapter 13] this volume). The starting point—and indeed a crucial factor—will be the issue of how the organization actually defines and recognizes environmental issues. After all, the dominance of a financial and market orientation in most businesses means that the "environment" has no role at all unless it is either represented in costs and prices or is likely to influence the behaviour and attitudes of stakeholders. So the way in which an organization scans for environmental issues will be central to how it responds to them, and whether or not they become integrated. With crude scanning, an organization will limit environmental issues to environmental legislation or possibly industry best practices. A more advanced scanning will include upstream and downstream supply-chain impacts. The most sophisticated will recognize and seek to understand externalities. The extent to which the organization sees the environment as being a part of operations will determine the extent to which environmental issues are included in, or integrated with, operational management systems.

Epstein (1996: xxvii) addresses (what he calls) "corporate environmental integration" which comprises ten elements that include: environmental strategy; information systems; internal auditing systems; costing systems; and capital budgeting systems, among others. He advocates the integration of environmental management with, not only the organizational strategy, the product design, and performance evaluation systems but, crucially, also the management accounting system. However, like other early authors, he is equivocal about this point. He says (1996: 87):

> Is a link necessary? No. Is it desirable? In most cases, yes! Integrating the physical data and cost data related to wastes and other environmental impacts into the management accounting and reporting systems gives decision makers more complete information with which to make improved decisions.

Putting environmental strategy aside, and assuming that the link between environmental management systems and management control systems is seen as necessary, conventional management accounting systems and practices still have limitations that make it difficult to collect and utilize environment-related data (International Federation of Accountants 2005: 26–29). These limitations lead to missing, inaccurate, and misinterpreted information and, consequently, sub-optimal decision-making. As we shall see below, a key function of an environmental management system is to help the organization exploit win-win opportunities; to help it develop mechanisms for exploring longer-term cases where the organization's objectives and the environment are in harmony and, perhaps most importantly, to identify those circumstances where they are not. Limitations to management accounting are therefore important and can arise in a number of ways:

- Communication/links between accounting and other departments are often not well developed. Different departments have different goals and perspectives and tend to focus on "their" piece of operations without linking with other departments. A holistic perspective of operations and communication is necessary to address this.
- Environment-related cost information is often "hidden" in overhead accounts. Overhead accounts are a way to accumulate costs, such as electricity and waste disposal, that are difficult to assign to products.
- Materials use, flow, and cost information often are not tracked adequately. Data systems need to be established for ongoing materials flow management.
- Many types of environment-related cost information are not found in the accounting records. Accounting typically is historically focused rather than future focused. Yet, poor environmental performance has future financial impacts such as fines, lost customers, and lost reputation (to say nothing of social and environmental impacts).
- Investment decisions are often made on the basis of incomplete information. Although accurate and complete information will never be available, it is something that managers should strive for in decision-making. For example, information is needed to answer the question: "What impact would implementation of the Kyoto Protocol have on capital investment in equipment versus investment in permits?".

These sorts of limitations emerge from research findings time and time again (see, for example, Bebbington et al. 1994; Gray & Bebbington 2001; Schaltegger & Burritt 2000; Epstein 1996; Ditz et al. 1995; Durden 2008). Indeed, there seems to be a consistent message that, regardless of whether environmental management can or cannot deliver the levels of environmental stewardship that society needs (see later), businesses as a whole seem incapable of exploiting even those aspects of environmental management systems that will support and enhance their business. Why this should be, remains a matter of some controversy (see, for example, Bansal & Roth 2000; Young & Tilley 2006; Henri & Journeault 2010)

ENVIRONMENTAL MANAGEMENT ACCOUNTING TECHNIQUES

One attempt to close the gap between the management accounting system and the environmental management system has focused on the development of variations in, and adjustment of, the management accounting craft itself so that it can explicitly recognize environmental factors (Bennett & James 1998).[4] One would typically expect environmental

---

[4] In the interests of completeness, it is worth emphasizing here that our current discussion is both organization-centred (we are ignoring a wider societal point of view) and shareholder centred (in that wider accountability to society and the environment is being ignored). We will redress this lacuna briefly towards the end of the chapter.

management accounting techniques to be part of an environmental management system, but this need not necessarily be the case. Especially when an organization is at an experimental stage with environmental measurement, it is quite possible to find environmental management accounting techniques operating in isolation.

Management accounting is sufficiently established that its definition is widely accepted as "an organization's development of both non-monetary and monetary information to support both routine and strategic decision-making by internal managers" (International Federation of Accountants 2005: 16). However, the field of environmental management accounting is new enough that there are no agreed definitions for what the field comprises. Indeed the breadth of the definitions reflects the ways in which the environment can be seen either as a fundamental aspect of business or as an add-on. From the UN we have:

> the identification, collection, estimation, analysis, internal reporting, and use of physical flow information (i.e., materials, water, and energy flows), environmental cost information, and other monetary information for both conventional and environmental decision-making within an organization.
>
> (United Nations Division for Sustainable Development 2002: 11)

From the International Federation of Accountants (IFAC) (2005: 19) we have:

> the management of environmental and economic performance through the development and implementation of appropriate environment-related accounting systems and practices. While this may include reporting and auditing in some companies, environmental management accounting typically involves life-cycle costing, full-cost accounting, benefits assessment, and strategic planning for environmental management.

Although there remain inevitable tensions between those accountants who eschew all non-financial data and those environmental managers who barely trust accountants (see, for example, Gray & Bebbington 2001), most established research in the field would want to embrace both the focus on the nature of the information (provided by the UN) and the emphasis on a systems approach (provided by the International Federation of Accountants).

For our purposes, we have classified environmental management accounting techniques into three categories:

- Operational and capital budgeting;
- Costing and measuring; and
- Monitoring.

Operational and capital budgeting

Gray & Bebbington (2001) suggest that it is with the integration of environmental issues into standard operational and capital budgeting procedures that businesses signal their seriousness about environmental issues. At its simplest, the operational budget is the means whereby an organization identifies its key areas of income and expenditure and then specifies its expectations of individuals, groups, and units. We tend to know it best as the amount a cost centre has to spend, for example. This specification then has two crude but important effects. First, it signals where activity is expected and at what level: What can we spend on X? How many staff do we want in Y? How much of Z is needed? If the environment doesn't feature here, whether it be costs for safety, accident prevention, environmental management staff, remediation, recycling, labeling, etc., then it comes as no surprise that it is likely to be ignored. Equally, the second effect of the budget is to feed into the performance appraisal system (see also below on monitoring). If managers, employees, and units are not appraised for their environmental performance, there is unlikely to be any conscious environmental performance (Gray & Bebbington 2001).

The capital budget—also sometimes called investment appraisal—has even greater structural impact. This is where the decisions are taken on new products, processes, and plant and equipment. Such decisions will determine the environmental performance of units and businesses for the continuing life of the investment (see, for example, Ditz et al. 1995). In essence, there is a range of ways in which environmental criteria—and not necessarily financially quantified environmental criteria—can be integrated into investment rules and procedures. (Two of the most straightforward are the pre-screening of future choices to ensure compliance with environmental policy, or the setting of environmental "hurdles" over which all future investment must pass.) At the same time, the more sophisticated businesses recognize that there are many 'soft' numbers in an investment decision, and this recognition allows many of the potential environmental costs and benefits to be integrated within the decision criteria (see, for example, International Federation of Accountants 1998; Society of Management Accountants of Canada 1997). The 'soft' numbers would include incorporating future environmental costs into today's decisions. Future environmental costs relate to possible changes to environmental legislation and marketplace demands. This approach to capital budgeting forces a long-term perspective into investment appraisal decisions.

Costing and measuring

There is a plethora of costing and measuring techniques for environmental management accounting. The more popular techniques (which inevitably focus upon internalized, privately incurred costs rather than any imputed costs or measurement of external social and public costs) include the following.

Activity-based costing

Traditional methods of product and service costing tend to allocate overhead items on an arbitrary and simplistic basis. Activity-based costing results in (what is claimed to be) more meaningful cost information by identifying cost drivers that cause the costs to be incurred in the first place. This reduces the amounts that are arbitrarily assigned, and leads to a better understanding of what costs are attached to what products and services. By incorporating environmental costs into this costing methodology it would be possible, for example, to allocate the costs of treating toxic waste to the product that creates the waste (see Ditz et al. 1995, for example).

Quality costing

Quality costing is part of a total quality management system (TQM) or a total quality environmental management system (TQEM), as it is known once the focus is on environmental issues. This approach to costing includes four types of costs: (i) the costs of preventing the defects; (ii) appraisal (i.e. monitoring and detection) costs to ensure that defects are detected; (iii) internal failure costs which are defects/problems that occur before the product leaves the organization; and (iv) external failure costs which are defects/problems that occur after products have left the organization.

Product/service costing

Taking a more simplistic approach than activity based costing or quality costing, organizations can examine the costs of products and services from various environment-related perspectives, such as energy consumption, transportation, wastes, and emissions. This information can then be used strategically to encourage or discourage certain inputs, activities, and outputs. For example, using Tetra Pak packaging for wine saves costs and enables the organization to make claims of "sustainability."[5]

Physical flow/eco-balance analysis

Physical flow analysis is a non-financial quantification of organizational resource usage and outputs. It is a crucial first-step in the identification of environmental impacts and of the various activities, products, and substances that will need controlling. The more serious the business's environmental intent, the greater the range of things to be identified and controlled (see, for example, Schaltegger & Burritt 2000; and especially, Jasch 2009). Obviously, to effectively manage environmental impacts of waste, effluents, and emissions, for example, it is essential that the organization monitor the physical flow of these contaminants. Of course, this monitoring process is critical for those contaminants that are actually regulated, and whose regulation is linked with government sanction.[6]

Eco-efficiency indicators

Eco-efficiency indicators are designed to measure such things as energy and material intensity. They are expressed in non-financial ratios, for example, energy consumed by

---

[5] Tetra Pak cartons use 92% less packaging and 54% less energy, create 80% less greenhouse gases, and require 35–40% fewer trucks than delivering the same amount of wine in glass bottles (Tetra Pak 2010).
[6] In the US, organizations are required to report contaminants in accordance with the Toxic Release Inventory (TRI) managed by the EPA (Environmental Protection Agency). In Canada, the government has implemented a similar scheme known as the National Pollutant Release Inventory (NPRI).

the company divided by unit of output. Ideally, then, these indicators are used as benchmarks to improve the efficiency of resource usage. The efficiency losses and gains can be linked to costs borne or saved by the business.[7]

Going beyond the internalized, privately incurred costs, there are a number of costing mechanisms that take a broader view of an organization's environmental impact and incorporate social costs and public costs. In short, these mechanisms include externalities and are known by a variety of terms: full-cost accounting, life cycle (cradle to grave) costing, and cost-benefit analysis. We discuss these further in a subsequent section.

Monitoring

The third segment of our brief review of management accounting techniques brings us to monitoring. Monitoring has been central to much that we have discussed above, but its role in performance measurement and appraisal is the most important. In this brief section we will only focus upon environmental auditing and the balanced scorecard.

Environmental auditing

The term "environmental auditing" is used to represent a range of activities that organizations use for monitoring environmental performance (see for example, Gray & Bebbington 2001). These activities include, but are not limited to, the following.

- Environmental impact assessment—These assessments focus on the identification of the environmental impacts of a specific proposed project such as a new road or a new mine. Activity in this area is largely driven by environmental legislation and that will determine what aspects are included in the assessment. Regulated environmental impact assessments typically require the organization to consult with the affected community.
- Supplier audit—Such audits relate to the quality and environmental impacts of products and services used as inputs. This is necessary if the downstream organization is making claims about the "greenness" of its products and services or is taking a strategic focus on supply-chain management issues. This may also take the form of ethical audits of upstream suppliers in the areas of health and safety.
- Operational compliance—Operational compliance audits relate to whether the organization is in compliance with applicable laws, regulations, and/or company policies.
- Systems assessment—This refers to activities undertaken to ensure that an organization's environmental management system is functioning as designed.

---

[7] For more on costing and measurement see, for example, Bennett & James (1998); Ditz et al. (1995); EPA (1995, 1996); Epstein (1996); and Gray & Bebbington (2001).

Internal reporting through the balanced scorecard

For the environmental management (and accounting) system to operate successfully and to integrate with the rest of the control systems requires integrated information from carefully integrated monitoring systems. This recognition has encouraged the development of a range of newer processes. The balanced scorecard is perhaps the most popular of these. The balance scorecard was developed in the 1990s (Kaplan & Norton 1996) as a new approach to performance measurement. It is seen as a way to link strategy with management activities and includes four perspectives: the financial perspective, the customer perspective, the internal process perspective, and the learning and growth perspective. Environmental aspects can be integrated into this mechanism provided they are already part of the explicit organizational strategy (Schaltegger & Burritt 2000).

THE BUSINESS CASE: EXPLORING THE LIMITS OF WIN-WIN

We now step away from the managerialist perspective motivating the discussion thus far and adopt a more critical approach beginning with an analysis of the business case. Given the constraints under which business operates, the best we can perhaps hope for is that organizations recognize and manage environmental issues to the extent that environmental management (including pollution prevention) pays. That is, business will manage environmental issues to the extent that to do so affords win-win opportunities to the business and/or to do so fits within the business case.

An environmental management system and its role in business (see, for example, Brady 2005) is founded (at least initially) on the principle that what is good for business is good for the environment. This is what Walley & Whitehead (1994) refer to as the win-win opportunities: saving energy benefits both environment and business; reducing waste ditto. The first role of the environmental management system is, without question, to tease out these opportunities and encourage their exploitation. What savings they bring and the extent to which they are economically worth pursuing directly involves the accountants and the accounting system. Thus if it is going to cost $100,000 to eliminate a particular waste but the savings to the firm from doing so is only $50,000, the business is going to struggle to make a business case for its adoption. Environmental managers struggle with these problems all the time and, making the accountants more environment-savvy, or the environmental manager more financially literate, seems to be the only way of solving this potential conundrum.

As long as win-win opportunities exist, the development and integration of environmental management systems and management control systems is a clear imperative. But there are two problems that flow from such an apparently simple assertion. First, how are these win-win opportunities to be identified: is the costing always that simple?

Clearly, if one is contemplating a quantification of all social and environmental impacts, including externalities, the answer is no. The second problem is whether or not the pursuits of environmental probity and financial success are in harmony or in conflict.

The "business case" looks a lot like an open-and-shut case. However, it is far from such a thing. We have already seen that there is a range of factors that any good management team will take into account when seeking to articulate strategy, locate the firm and/or make decisions. Risk, reputation, freedom, relationships with governments and stakeholders, and so on, are all essential to the organization's continued success—but few of them can be easily expressed in simple financial terms. Indeed, Spence & Gray (2008) found that the business case was a subtle and flexible idea that varied considerably from firm to firm. So much so, that as long as an option could be expressed in recognisable terms and language to the business, it was, by definition, within the business case. Consequently, good environmental management recognizes that the value of an environmental initiative depends exclusively on one's ability to provide a convincing articulation of it. This finding runs through both Gray et al. (1995) and Levy (1997), where examples of "environmental champions" pushing an issue outside its obvious parameters, persuades an organization to recognize a previously unrecognized business case.

Reading much of the business press and many business and "sustainability" texts would lead one to conclude that, with the right "environmental champion", the limits to the business case are almost boundless. For example, Willis & Desjardins (2001: 18) suggest that it is important for corporations to go beyond compliance with laws and regulations because good environmental management is linked with the creation of shareholder value. They assert that, in the long term, this will provide benefits that are positive and far-reaching. Leadership in environmental matters, they say, can be a source of market advantage that can result in increased sales and lower cost of capital. Also, such a reputation for leadership may enhance organizational relations with regulatory bodies or the organization's ability to influence public policy. Little convincing evidence is offered to support these assertions.

There are clearly limits to any business case—no matter how well argued. There are, inevitably, environmental initiatives that a corporation is *not* going to undertake regardless of its environmental benefit: zero emissions, avoidance of new non-renewable raw materials, transport only by non-fossil fuels, no impact on habitat, etc. are simply not current business options.

Despite the very considerable advances in environmental management over the last twenty years or so, planetary degradation has continued and, as far as any evidence suggests, no organization in its pursuit of eco-efficiency has succeed in improving its eco-effectiveness (Gray 2006a; Young & Tilley 2006). In essence, there is a remaining and critical question—can organizations (with or without environmental management) deliver sustainability in the form of long-term health of the planet and everyone on it? That is the issue for the next section.

THE RELATIONSHIP BETWEEN ENVIRONMENTAL MANAGEMENT SYSTEMS, ENVIRONMENTAL MANAGEMENT ACCOUNTING, AND ENVIRONMENTAL SUSTAINABILITY

Can environmental management systems and environmental management accounting lead business into the promised land of environmental sustainability? The answer is "no", but the reasons might seem a little obscure—and are certainly unpopular with business writers.

First, the art of environmental management accounting (and yes it is more of an art than a science) is wrought with problems. We provide just a few of them by way of illustration. Environmental management accounting rarely extends to the whole supply chain (cradle to grave) or the whole of society (Bennett & James 1998: 31). Taking a "whole of society" point of view would require organizations to grapple with externalities that impact all stakeholders, perhaps even those as yet unborn. Then, there are geographic, global space issues. In accounting for costs, where does one draw the boundaries around the acid rain damage caused by a particular business? And, there are the issues of time. Laws are continually changing and what was once acceptable behaviour becomes an illegal activity with costs that the firm must bear. The Love Canal is a case in point here (Rubenstein 1991). Finally, there are issues like global warming that encompass the whole of society, all of the globe and the future of the human species.

Nevertheless, despite these difficulties, accountants have developed more inclusive costing methodologies that are primarily known as full-cost accounting. They differ from the environmental accounting techniques discussed above in that they include a monetization of externalities. Bebbington et al. (2001) describe how full-cost accounting includes: (1) the usual direct and indirect costs; (2) hidden costs such as regulatory, monitoring, and safety costs; (3) liability costs including fines and future clean-up costs; (4) less tangible costs such as the loss or gain of goodwill arising from a project, and the impact of changing stakeholder attitudes; and (5) costs to ensure that a project has zero environmental effect.

The challenges of full-cost accounting can be illustrated by examining its employment in a life cycle, "cradle to grave", analysis. Going upstream this includes identifying raw materials and analyzing the energy consumed and the ecological impacts of producing the raw materials. Downstream this includes the consumer's use and final disposition of the item. Identifying the scope of the analysis can become exceedingly complex. For example, upstream products also have a life cycle and the inputs to energy generation should, theoretically be included in the analysis. The difficulty comes in that, while it is necessary to draw boundaries to avoid an infinite regress, the act of drawing such boundaries renders the analysis less than complete or comprehensive.

Presuming that the scope and impacts can be identified, the next step is to monetize the external costs. The International Federation of Accountants (2005: 52) identifies four approaches for estimating externalities: (1) the avoidance cost approach which uses the capital expenditure cost of prevention as a proxy for the monetary value of the damage; (2) the damage cost approach which uses scientific and economic valuations to determine how much an individual would pay to prevent environmental damage; (3) the restoration cost approach which estimates the cost to restore a damaged site to its original state; and (4) the direct monetization of emissions which uses a trading price or treatment fees charged by a treatment facility using the best available technology.

In short, full-cost accounting is considerably more demanding than (the already demanding) environmental accounting and even more subjective.

Second, environmental management systems are centred on eco-efficiency: using resources more carefully in the production of goods and services. (This is sometimes, misleadingly thought of as "doing more with less.") An environmental management system guides the business to manage its environmental resources, it has nothing to say about how much environmental resources should be used or whether or not the business should be growing and increasing its "ecological footprint" (Wackernagel & Rees 1996). At best, an environmental management system will lead to slow improvements which, in some distant and sunlit future, will produce ecological businesses which can claim (realistically) to be environmentally sustainable. There are also two problems with this "best scenario" picture. The first is that the rates of eco-efficiency are nowhere near enough to counter the rise in ecological footprints (York et al. 2003; Polimeni et al. 2008). The second problem is that, if all the data is to be believed, there really isn't that much time in which to swing business into line with sustainability (Meadows et al. 2004). Indeed, we may have as little as five years (Hamilton 2010).

SUMMARY COMMENTS, POSSIBLE OUTCOMES, AND IMPLICATIONS FOR RESEARCHERS

This chapter has outlined the role that systems and measurement play in environmental management, and the relationship (or not) between the environmental management systems and the profit-oriented management control systems of the organization. Whilst environmental management accounting and environmental management systems have a great deal to offer organizations and eco-efficiency, the astute reader will have noted, we believe that, as they are now practiced, they have little ability to significantly change the way we consume resources and befoul the Earth.

Despite (for example) Schaltegger & Wagner's *Managing the Business Case for Sustainability* (2006), there is no case for business leading to environmental sustainability. Despite (for example) Bennett et al.'s *Sustainable Measures* (1999), there are no such measures that are currently commensurate with business financial success. Put simply, the case against these assertions is clear and rests on (at least) three simple ideas: (i) environmental sustainability cannot be applied at the corporate level (any ecological textbook would make this clear, but see also Milne & Gray 2007); (ii) there is no evidence offered (that we can find anyway) in which the performance of business organizations is shown to be commensurate with a more environmentally sustainable planet and a sustainable means of organization (see, for example, Gray 2006b)—the assertions are just that, assertions; and (iii) the *prima facie* case is that planetary destruction and social injustice are as likely to be the result of the very successes of international financial capitalism as they are to be the result of anything else (Gray 2010; Levy 1997).

Society's needs and business practice are not always and necessarily in harmony. Any such suggestion that they are, is actually ludicrous, and no matter how good our design of an environmental management system, and no matter how well integrated it is with the management control system and accounting, it will not, does not, and cannot deliver a more environmentally sustainable business. (Or if it can, would somebody please let us in on the secret?)

Whether you agree with this position or not, there are only three possible outcomes to our present relationship with the natural environment.

1. Carry on as we have in the last decade and fool ourselves that our tweaking will make a difference.
2. Radically change the way we live (and by the way, this will need to be led by civil society, not the corporation) and do it quickly enough to make a difference.
3. Carpe diem and go have a beer, knowing that the human species, like most species, has a finite time in this world.

What do these outcomes mean for researchers? If you believe that our tweaking will make a difference, then it is important to research the use of environmental management systems and environmental management accounting, whether externalities are incorporated or not. If you believe that the human species is doomed (and there are many academics such as Hamilton (2010) who do), then you still may want to do this if only to delay the inevitable. The goal will be to get business to change as much as possible as soon as possible to slow down the destruction. Or, you can let the profit motive be your guide and research environmental management systems and environmental management accounting to determine where it does "pay" to be green and exploit those opportunities.

Thus, despite our pessimism (or perhaps it is just realism) we have an abiding belief in the importance of understanding humanity's relationship with the natural environment and the role that environmental management accounting and environmental management systems can play in that relationship.

REFERENCES

Anthony, R. N. (1965). *Management Accounting Principles.*Homewood, IL: Richard D. Irwin, Inc.
Bakan, J. (2004). *The Corporation: The Pathological Pursuit of Profit and Power.*Toronto: Penguin Canada.

Bansal, P. & Roth, K.   (2000). "Why Companies Go Green: A Model of Ecological Responsiveness," *Academy of Management Journal*, 43(4): 717–736.

Bebbington, J., Gray, R., Hibbitt, C. & Kirk, E. (2001). *Full Cost Accounting: An Agenda for Action*. London: ACCA.

Bebbington, K. J., Gray, R. H. Thomson, I. & Walters, D. (1994). "Accountants' Attitudes and Environmentally-Sensitive Accounting," *Accounting and Business Research*, 24(94): 109–120.

Bennett, M. & James, P. (eds.) (1998). *The Green Bottom Line: Environmental Accounting for Management*. Sheffield: Greenleaf.

—— ——with Klinkers, L. (eds.) (1999). *Sustainable Measures: Evaluation and Reporting of Environmental and Social Performance*. Sheffield: Greenleaf.

Brady, J. (ed.) (2005). *Environmental Management in Organizations: The IEMA Handbook*, London: Earthscan.

Committee of Sponsoring Organizations of the Treadway Commission (1994). *Internal Control—Integrated Framework*. Vol. 1.

Ditz, D., Ranganathan, J. & Banks, R. D. (1995). *Green Ledgers: Case Studies in Corporate Environmental Accounting*. Baltimore, MD: World Resources Institute.

Durden, C. (2008). "Towards a Socially Responsible Management Control System," *Accounting Auditing and Accountability Journal*, 21(5): 671–694.

Environmental Protection Agency (1995). *Environmental Accounting Case Studies: Green Accounting at AT&T*. Washington, DC: EPA.

—— (1996). *Environmental Accounting Case Studies: Full Cost Accounting for Decision Making at Ontario Hydro*. Washington, DC: EPA.

Epstein, M. J. (1996). *Measuring Corporate Environmental Performance: Best Practices for Costing and Managing an Effective Environmental Strategy*. Montvale, NJ: The IMA Foundation for Applied Research, Inc.

Gray, R. (2006a). "Social, Environmental, and Sustainability Reporting and Organisational Value Creation? Whose Value? Whose Creation?" *Accounting, Auditing and Accountability Journal*, 19(3): 319–348.

—— (2006b). "Does Sustainability Reporting Improve Corporate Behaviour? Wrong Question? Right Time?" *Accounting and Business Research (International Policy Forum)*, 65–88.

—— (2010). "Is Accounting For Sustainability Actually Accounting For Sustainability…and How Would We Know? An Exploration of Narratives of Organisations and the Planet," *Accounting, Organizations and Society*, 35(1): 47–62.

—— & Bebbington, K. J. (2001). *Accounting for the Environment* (2nd edn). London: Sage.

Gray, R. H., Bebbington, K. J., Walters, D. & Thomson, I. (1995). "The Greening of Enterprise: An Exploration of the (non) Role of Environmental Accounting and Environmental Accountants in Organisational Change," *Critical Perspectives on Accounting*, 6(3): 211–239.

Grey, C. (2005). *A Very Short, Fairly Interesting and Reasonably Cheap Book About Studying Organizations*. London: Sage.

Hamilton, C. (2010). *Requiem for a Species: Why We Resist the Truth About Climate Change*. London: Earthscan.

Henri, J.-F. & Journeault, M. (2010). "Eco-control: The Influence of Management Control Systems on Environmental and Economic Performance," *Accounting Organizations and Society*, 35(1): 63–80.

Institute of Chartered Accountants in England & Wales (1999). *Internal Control: Guidance for Directors on the Combine Code* (Turnbull Report). London: The Institute of Chartered Accountants in England and Wales.

International Federation of Accountants (1998). *Environmental Management in Organizations: The Role of Management Accounting* Study # 6. New York: IFAC.

—— (2005). *Environmental Management Accounting.* New York: IFAC.

Jasch, C. (2009). *Environmental and Material Flow Cost Accounting.* Milton Keynes: Springer Science.

Kaplan, R. S. & Norton, D. P. (1996). *The Balanced Scorecard: Translating Strategy into Action.* Boston: Harvard Business School.

Knights, D. & Willmott, H. (2007). *Introducing Organizational Behaviour and Management.* London: Thomson Learning.

Krut, R. & Gleckman, H. (1998). *ISO 14001: A Missed Opportunity for Sustainable Global Industrial Development.* London: Earthscan.

Levy, D. L. (1997). "Environmental Management as Political Sustainability," *Organization and Environment,* 10(2): 126–147.

Meadows, D. H., Randers, J. & Meadows, D. L. (2004). *The Limits to Growth: The 30-year Update.* London: Earthscan.

Merchant, K. A. (1985). *Control in Business* Organizations. Cambridge, MA: Ballinger Publishing Company.

Milne, M. & Gray, R. H. (2007). "Future Prospects for Corporate Sustainability Reporting," in J. Unerman, J. Bebbington, & B. O'Dwyer (2007) (eds.), *Sustainability Accounting and Accountability,* London: Routledge, 184–208.

Netherwood, A. (1996). "Environmental Management Systems," in R. Welford (ed.), *Corporate Environmental Management: Systems and Strategies.* London: Earthscan, 35–58.

Polimeni, J. M., Mayumi, K., Giampietro, M. & Alcott, B. (2008). *The Jevons Paradox and the Myth of Resource Efficiency Improvements.* London: Earthscan.

Potoski, M. & Prakash, A. (2005). "Covenants with Weak Swords: ISO14001 and Facilities Environmental Organization," *Journal of Policy Analysis and Management,* 24(4): 745–769.

Rubenstein, D. B. (1991). "Lessons of Love," *CA Magazine.* March, 34–41.

Schaltegger, S. & Burritt, R. (2000). *Contemporary Environmental Accounting: Issues, Concepts and Practices.* Sheffield: Greenleaf.

—— & Wagner, M. (2006). *Managing the Business Case for Sustainability.* Sheffield: Greenleaf.

Simons, R. (1995). *Levers of Control: How Managers use Innovative Control Systems to Drive Strategic Renewal.* Boston: Harvard Business School Press.

Society of Management Accountants of Canada (1997). *Accounting for the Sustainable Development: A Business Perspective.* Hamilton, ON: The Society of Management Accountants of Canada.

Spence, C. & Gray, R. (2008). *Social and Environmental Reporting and the Business Case.* London: ACCA.

Sundin, H., Granlund, M. & Brown, D. (2009). "Balancing Multiple Competing Objectives with a Balanced Scorecard," *European Accounting Review,* 1–44.

Tetra Pak, (2010). *"Vintage goes Modern".* Available at <http://www.tetrapak.com/us/packaging/food_categories/wine/Pages/default.aspx>, accessed on 24 March 2010.

United Nations Division for Sustainable Development (2002). *Environmental Management Accounting: Policies and Linkages.* New York: United Nations.

Wackernagel, M. & Rees, W. (1996). *Our Ecological Footprint: Reducing Human Impact on the Earth.* Gabriola Island, BC: New Society Publishers.

Walley, N. & Whitehead, B. (1994). "It's Not Easy Being Green," *Harvard Business Review* May/June:46–52.

Willis, A. & Desjardins, J. (2001). *Environmental Performance: Measuring and Managing What Matters*. Toronto: CICA.

York, R., Rosa, E. A. & Dietz, T. (2003). "Footprints on the Earth: The Environmental Consequences of Modernity," *American Sociological Review* 68(2): 279–300.

Young, W. & Tilley, F. (2006). "Can Business Move Beyond Efficiency? The Shift Toward Effectiveness and Equity in the Corporate Sustainability Debate," *Business Strategy and the Environment* 15: 402–415.

CHAPTER 24

CORPORATE ENVIRONMENTAL FINANCIAL REPORTING AND FINANCIAL MARKETS

CHARLES H. CHO,
DENNIS M. PATTEN,
AND ROBIN W. ROBERTS

CORPORATE environmental financial reporting is broadly defined as the set of information items related to a company's past, current and future environmental management activities and performance (adapted from Berthelot, Cormier, & Magnan 2003). A corporation's reporting of its environment-related actions may be mandated by financial regulation, such as the disclosure of environmental liabilities on a corporation's balance sheet, or voluntary, such as the reporting of recycling activities in the management discussion and analysis section of a corporation's annual report. In both cases the precise nature and extent of a corporation's environmental financial reporting reflects strategic decisions that are made by corporate management (Aerts, Cormeir & Magnan 2008). Corporate environmental financial reporting should be viewed as an integral part of a firm's overall approach to disclosure and reporting, which is "endogenously driven by both financial markets' and public interest considerations" (Aerts et al. 2008: 643). It should also be noted that financial reporting refers to the provision of information to users external to the firm. The provision of information to internal members of the company is referred to as managerial accounting, and that aspect of environmental accounting research is discussed in Gray & Herremans ([Chapter 22] this volume). Another aspect of environmental accounting research is the examination of financial market reaction in relation to environmental performance as discussed later in this chapter and also in Bauer & Derwall ([Chapter 25] this volume).

Financial market participants rely on corporate disclosure and reporting to provide information that is important to investment decision-making. Because financial reporting is a strategic exercise, corporations carefully craft mandatory and voluntary disclosures and reports to meet regulatory requirements and market informational expectations while also managing the process to their best advantage. Some streams of accounting research argue that by making accurate disclosures corporations reduce "information risk" and facilitate a more accurate pricing of their stock (Graham, Harvey, & Rajgopal 2005). Others argue that corporations use disclosure and reporting more to provide a corporation with social legitimacy and to manage financial markets' and other stakeholders' impressions of corporate performance than to provide accurate, unbiased information (Merkl-Davies & Brennan 2007).

Given that a corporation's environmental disclosures that are provided within its financial reports are used by financial market participants to assess risk and perfor- mance, both of these rationales for reporting are used in environmental financial report- ing research. As a matter of fact, the literature on the determinants of corporate environmental disclosure and reporting and its associated regulatory and market con- sequences is extensive (see Berthelot et al. 2003). A rather consistent theme across cor- porate environmental financial reporting research is the disconnect between increasing societal concern for the environment and an increasing demand for corporate environ- mental disclosure, and the limited amount of meaningful disclosure and reporting that corporations provide (Solomon & Lewis 2002). Even more recent studies of alternative corporate disclosure platforms, such as stand-alone sustainability reports and internet reporting, found a disappointing lack of breadth and depth in voluntary corporate envi- ronmental reporting (Milne, Tregidga, & Walton 2009; Cho & Roberts 2010).

The purpose of our chapter is to discuss two specific questions regarding corporate environmental financial reporting and financial markets. The questions are:

1. Why do corporations disclose environmental information in their financial reports?

And,

2. Do capital markets value corporate environmental information?

Without a doubt, these questions are open to interpretation and can generate a wide range of responses. The responses offered by economists (e.g. Graham et al. 2005) will be quite different from those offered by critical accounting researchers (e.g. Milne et al. 2009). Given this theoretical eclecticism (Sil 2000) found in social and environmental accounting research, it is not possible to present a complete review of how prior work has investigated these two research questions. Thus, we use this chapter to introduce the most common theoretical approaches used by accounting researchers to tackle these issues, and review related empirical findings. Our review will help new researchers to the field gain an understanding of the key considerations associated with these streams of research. We refer you to Gray, Owen, & Adams (2010) for a comprehensive review of theories relevant to social and environmental accounting.

The remainder of the chapter is organized as follows. First we examine why corporations make environmental disclosures in their financial reports, focusing on two major theories utilized in related accounting research. Second, we discuss how economic theories of stock-market behavior are used to assess whether the market values corporate environmental information contained in financial reports. In the final section, we relate these two streams of research to newer, potentially productive avenues of research related to environmental financial reporting and financial markets.

CORPORATE ENVIRONMENTAL DISCLOSURE IN FINANCIAL REPORTS

Corporate disclosure of environmental information is often at least partially driven by the existence of reporting regulations. In the US, for example, the Securities and Exchange Commission (SEC) integrated all existing disclosure requirements under federal securities laws into a comprehensive disclosure system, Regulation S-K (Johnson 1993). Three sections of the Regulation—Item 101 (Description of Business), Item 103 (Legal Proceedings) and Item 303 (Management's Discussion and Analysis of Financial Condition and Results of Operations)—are particularly relevant to environmental disclosure. As summarized by Johnson (1993: 119):

> Item 101 requires a general description of the business and specific disclosure of the material effects that compliance with environmental laws may have on the capital expenditures, earnings, and competitive position of the registrant. Disclosures include material estimated capital expenditures for the current and succeeding fiscal years and for any further periods in which those expenditures may be material, including costs of bringing an entity into compliance with environmental regulations.

Johnson (1993: 119) further notes that

> Item 103 requires disclosure of pending or contemplated administrative or judicial proceedings, including those arising under environmental laws that (a) are material, or (b) the claim for which exceeds 10 percent of the registrant's current assets, or (c) a governmental authority is a party to and for which sanctions will be greater than $100,000.

Finally, Item 303 of the Regulation requires companies to disclose in their Management's Discussion and Analysis section "information on any environmental matters that could materially affect company operations or finances." It seems clear that the environmental disclosure requirements identified by the SEC in Regulation S-K focus on giving investors financial information that may be relevant in assessing how environmental regulations and requirements have led to existing obligations, and have impacted, or will likely affect financial position, spending, and profitability (Cho & Patten 2008).

Other pronouncements from the SEC, including Financial Reporting Release (FRR) No. 36, issued in 1989, and Staff Accounting Bulletin (SAB) No. 92, issued in 1993, offer examples and/or guidance on environmental disclosure, but are limited to issues related to remediation exposures. Further, both the American Institute of Certified Public

Accountants (AICPA) and the Financial Accounting Standards Board (FASB) also issued pronouncements with implications for the disclosure of environmental information, most notably the AICPA's Statement of Position (SOP) 96–1.

In spite of the regulatory guidance discussed above, studies of financial report environmental disclosure by US companies (e.g. Cho & Patten 2008; Freedman & Stagliano 1998; Gamble, Hsu, Kite, & Radtke 1995) consistently report that, while there is considerable variation in the extent of environmental disclosure across firms and across time, the overall level and depth of information provided tends to be, at best, very limited (Cho & Patten 2008).[1]

In continental Europe, notably France and Spain, comparable trends in the promulgation and application have been observed. For example, the 2001 Nouvelles Régulations Economiques (NRE-New Economic Regulations) Bill in France mandates all publicly listed French companies to include within their annual reports information related to the social and environmental impacts of their activity, but does not appear to be effective: an independent report was commissioned by the French government to critically assess the application of the NRE law requirements by French companies in 2003, the first year of application and found that the average compliance rate was only 35 percent (Delbard 2008). Similarly, in Spain, despite the environmental disclosure standard obligation issued through the Plan General de Contabilidad (PGC—General Accounting Plan) for electric utilities (RD 437–98), research results demonstrate a very low compliance level, with about 80 percent of companies not providing any environmental information (Larrinaga, Carrasco, Correa, Llena, & Moneva 2002).

Finally, Owen, Shaw & Cooper (2005) investigated the potential role of mandatory reporting requirements in the UK. Their analysis of the Operating and Financial Review (OFR) requirement's evolution shows that, while the OFR has been considered by regulators as a suitable platform for social and environmental information disclosure, the purpose of, and audience for, such disclosure has become narrower (i.e. shareholder-dominated rather than widened to other non-financial stakeholders). Other issues raised in the study included the problem caused by the lack of specific reporting guidance from either the government or the Accounting Standards Board, and the informal nature (as opposed to full documentation) of the policies for determining 'necessity to report' decisions. Overall, there are some limits as to the potential for the OFR requirement in the UK to be a "catalyst" for improved social and environmental disclosure. Such disclosures appear to be driven primarily by financial risks, and the usefulness of the OFR requirement is questionable, given the lack of clear reporting guidance (Owen et al. 2005).

Overall, research into the extent of corporate environmental disclosure demonstrates that, while a number of environmental disclosure regulations are in place, problems with oversight, monitoring, and enforcement by the agencies responsible for implementation has led to relatively low levels of environmental disclosure in corporate financial reports.

---

[1] In spite of this body of research, the US Governmental Accountability Office (GAO), based on a review of corporate environmental disclosure requested by the US Congress, concluded "little is known about the extent to which companies are disclosing environmental information in their filings with [the SEC]" (Government Accountability Office 2004: 4).

Driven partially by the low level of disclosure, but more so by its variation across companies, research attempted to identify what motivates differing disclosure choices and whether environmental information impacts market participants. Before reviewing these veins of research, however, we discuss the issues associated with measuring the extent of disclosure.

Environmental disclosure measurement

Methods used to measure financial report environmental disclosures, particularly those of a qualitative or narrative nature, have generated substantial debate among researchers. This has primarily been due to a lack of consistency across studies regarding the way corporate financial reports' content has been analyzed, leading to associated measurement reliability issues (Milne & Adler 1999; Unerman 2000). This debate is important because content analysis is a "research technique for making replicable and valid inferences from data according to their context" (Krippendorff 1980: 21). Milne & Adler (1999) argue that prior environmental accounting research shows "unevenness in regard to dealing with matters of reliability and replicability" (238). While some studies report the use of multiple coders and explain their coding rules to address inter-rater reliability issues (see, e.g. Hackston & Milne 1996; Gray, Kouhy, & Lavers 1995b), others provide little or no explanation of how those issues are addressed and how the coded data can thus be considered reliable (see, e.g. Freedman & Jaggi 1986; Neu, Warsame, & Pedwell 1998; Trotman & Bradley 1981). Milne & Adler (1999) stress that careful explanation of how content is analyzed is necessary to allow readers to assess whether similar pieces of information get coded in a consistent fashion.

Al-Tuwaijri, Christensen, & Hughes (2004) and Smith & Taffler (2000) distinguish disclosure measurement techniques for environmental disclosure content analysis into two distinctive groups. The first group uses a disclosure-scoring measure index derived from pure *content analysis* or a "meaning oriented" (subjective) analysis (Smith & Taffler 2000: 627). With this technique, the examination focuses primarily on the underlying themes or topics themselves that are textually present in the disclosures of interest. Researchers identify a certain number of environmental issues of interest to determine whether or not such topics are addressed or discussed by corporate managers in their environmental disclosures. Accordingly, a scoring index categorizing those themes is designed, and researchers assess the presence or the absence of each identified item in the disclosures using a "yes/no" (or 1, 0) coding methodology. After their quantification, an aggregate score is determined for each firm in the sample, generally labeled as the disclosure score variable (see, e.g. Barth, McNichols, & Wilson 1997; Cho & Patten 2007; Cho, Patten, & Roberts 2006; Ingram & Frazier 1980; Patten & Trompeter 2003). Recent studies have modified the traditional content analysis scoring method. For example, different levels or weights are assigned according to whether the disclosure contained monetary, quantitative, or qualitative terms (see, e.g. Choi 1999; Al-Tuwaijri et al. 2004; Wiseman 1982), or whether the disclosures were descriptive, vague, or immaterial (see, e.g. Hughes, Anderson, & Golden 2001).

The second approach measures the *quantity* of environmental disclosures, which relates to what Smith & Taffler (2000: 627) refer to as "form oriented" (objective) analysis. This has been generating discussion among researchers about what is the optimal "unit of analysis" (see, e.g. Milne & Adler 1999). Disclosures have been measured by counting the number of words (see, e.g. Deegan & Rankin 1996; Neu et al. 1998), number of sentences (see, e.g. Buhr 1998; Hackston & Milne 1996; Tsang 1998), or number of pages (see, e.g. Guthrie & Parker 1989; Patten 1992; 1995). The disclosure measure may also be calculated as the percentage of pages (see, e.g. Gray, Kouhy & Lavers 1995a, O'Dwyer & Gray 1998) or the percentage of total disclosures[2] (see Trotman & Bradley 1981). This count method solely focuses on the extent of disclosures. After a thorough review of different units of analysis, Milne & Adler (1999: 243) prescribe using sentence counts for both coding and measurement because they offer "complete, reliable and meaningful data for further analysis."

While both the themes ("what") and the amount ("how much") of disclosures are important for firm managers and accounting-report users, some measurement concerns related to validity and reliability seem to persist. For the "meaning oriented" (subjective) analysis (Smith & Taffler 2000: 627), the problem seems to relate to the intrinsic human subjectivity when coding the narratives or determining the absence or the presence of sought themes (Krippendorff 1980). This need for the researchers' judgment can cause some inherent reliability issues, even with the use of several coders. That is, even where inter-coder ratings are consistent, a question of how well the content item truly reflects underlying attributes can still be a problem. As to the "form oriented" (objective) analysis (Smith & Taffler 2000: 627), solely focusing on the amount of environmental disclosure in a given accounting report can be misleading. For instance, if companies provide a large quantity of environmental information expressed in a language that is biased, the validity of this disclosure measurement may be questionable. Aligned with this line of thought, Cho, Roberts, & Patten (2010) recently conducted an investigation to determine whether biased language and verbal tone is present in corporations' environmental disclosures, and found, as predicted, that worse environmental performing firms' disclosures exhibit significantly more optimism and significantly less certainty than those of their better performing counterparts. They conclude that "the language and verbal tone used in corporate environmental disclosures, in addition to their thematic content, must be considered when investigating the relation between corporate disclosure and performance" (Cho, Roberts, & Patten 2010: 432).

Motivations to disclose environmental information

Given the variance in corporate environmental disclosure noted above, it is perhaps not surprising that a substantial body of research (e.g. Al-Tuwaijri et al. 2004; Cho & Patten

[2] The percentage of pages is computed as the number of pages (or fractions of pages) dedicated to discussions about social and environmental issues over the total number of pages of the report analyzed. Similarly, the percentage of total disclosures is determined by the total amount of social and environmental disclosures (on a line-by-line or sentence-by-sentence basis) over the total amount of discussions on all issues.

2007; Fekrat, Inclan, & Petroni 1996; Freedman & Wasley 1990; Hughes et al. 2001; Hughes, Sander, & Reier 2000; Ingram & Frazier 1980; Patten 2002; Wiseman 1982) examines the dynamics of corporate environmental disclosure in financial reports. However, the question of what motivates corporations to provide what is considered largely non-mandated environmental information to their various stakeholders remains unresolved.

Two primary competing, but not necessarily mutually exclusive, theories have been developed to offer explanations for the corporate choice to disclose discretionary environmental information. Each theory relates disclosure choice to firm environmental performance, but they argue opposite relations. One theory is labeled *voluntary disclosure theory* and is based on neo-classical economics (see, e.g. Dye 1985; Verrecchia 1983). In applying voluntary disclosure theory to environmental disclosure and reporting, proponents posit that firms with better environmental performance are motivated to use disclosure to signal their superior strategy to investors and other relevant stakeholders (Bewley & Li 2000; Li, Richardson, & Thornton 1997). Disclosure is needed because many important aspects of a proactive environmental strategy are unobservable (Clarkson, Li, Richardson, & Vasvari 2008). In addition, these good environmental performers have an incentive to focus on "objective, 'hard' measures that cannot be easily mimicked by poor environmental performers" (Clarkson et al. 2008: 309). Thus, from the voluntary disclosure theory perspective, companies disclose environmental information to signal their proactive strategy and relatively superior environmental performance. The disclosures help provide clarity and understanding to capital market participants regarding a corporation's environmental performance, reduce any associated information risk, and become reflected in the calculation of that firm's cost of capital (Graham et al. 2005). Bewley & Li (2000), Al-Tuwaijri et al. (2004), and Clarkson et al. (2008) all provide evidence of a positive association between corporate environmental performance and the extent of corporate environmental disclosure.

A second theoretical approach to environmental financial reporting research is labeled *legitimacy theory*. It is a socio-political theory (Gray et al. 1995a) that is rooted in the notion that a corporation has a legitimate right to exist only as long as it fulfills its social contract with broader society (Mathews 1993). Corporations are viewed as legitimate if they pursue socially acceptable goals in a socially acceptable manner. Given this normative quality, performance and economic efficiency alone appear to be insufficient to obtain or maintain legitimate status (Epstein & Votaw 1978). Thus, legitimacy is not defined by economic viability, or achievement, or adherence to law. Legitimacy theory sees economic viability as only one aspect of legitimacy, and legality is theoretically an enforcer, not a creator, of changes in social values (Chen & Roberts 2010; Deegan 2002; Lindblom 1994). In addition, whether the activities of a corporation are legitimate depends upon the audiences who observe them (Suchman 1995).

Proponents of legitimacy theory (see, e.g. Cho 2009; Deegan 2002; Deegan & Gordon 1996; Milne & Patten 2002; Patten 2002) suggest that because firms with poorer environmental records face greater social and political pressures and threats, corporations have an incentive to use environmental disclosure as a mitigating tool in order to: (1) educate and inform relevant publics about (actual) changes in their performance, (2) change perceptions about their performance, (3) deflect attention from the issue of concern by highlighting other accomplishments, and/or (4) seek to change public expectations of their performance (Lindblom 1994). Deegan & Rankin (1996), Patten (2002), and Cho & Patten (2007), among other studies, present evidence supporting a negative relation between environmental performance and corporate environmental disclosure. The conflicting results across the legitimacy and voluntary disclosure theory studies remain unresolved.

Recently, environmental accounting researchers have used an application of legitimacy theory to develop and test hypotheses regarding corporate environmental financial reporting. These studies view a corporation's environmental disclosure decision as determined primarily by its desire to engage in *impression management* (Neu et al. 1998; Merkl Davies & Brennan 2007). Cho et al. (2010) adapted the Merkl-Davies & Brennan (2007) impression-management framework to structure an approach for examining the degree of impression-management techniques present in corporations' environmental financial reporting disclosures. Under this framework, corporations are expected to engage in concealment and attribution behaviors that help present their environmental activities as favorably as possible. Concealment activities include highlighting positive news and obfuscating negative news. Attribution activities allow the corporation to take credit for positive environmental achievements and mitigate blame for any poor environmental performance. Both concealment and attribution activities produce corporate environmental disclosures that use biased and uncertain language to portray the corporation's environmental record as favorably as possible.

ENVIRONMENTAL REPORTING AND MARKET VALUATION

A substantial body of empirical accounting research investigates the extent to which capital markets value social and environmental information. These studies tend to focus primarily on environmental performance and disclosure (although a few exceptions are discussed below) and can be roughly divided into (1) studies relying on market valuation models to assess the extent to which environmental information, typically not firm-provided, is captured by the market, (2) examinations of the stock-market reaction to events associated with social or environmental disclosure, and (3) experimental investigations of the role environmental disclosures play in investor decisions.[3] We discuss each of these areas in more detail below.

---

[3] A substantial body of research in the management domain also investigates the relation between environmental performance and various aspects of financial performance (see Russo & Minto [chapter 2] this volume).

Market valuation research

One of the primary questions addressed in accounting research related specifically to environmental issues is whether the market appears to value information related to potential exposures across the environmental domain. As noted by Hughes (2000: 210), costs likely to be incurred in the future to address environmental performance concerns often fail to meet SFAS No. 5 requirements that they be "reasonably estimable," and as such are usually not recognized in financial statement presentations. However, because these costs can be substantial, they could be expected to impact firm value. Relying on models controlling for the impacts of the book value of assets and liabilities, a limited number of studies examine whether differences in the market value of equity are related to future environmental cost exposures. Representative of this line of investigation, Barth & McNichols (1994) examine the extent to which publicly available information on companies' exposures to investigations under the Comprehensive Environmental Response, Compensation and Liability Act of 1980, commonly referred to as Superfund, allows the market to capture unrecognized liabilities for affected firms. Based on a variety of environmental cost proxies drawn primarily from Environmental Protection Agency (EPA) Records of Decisions, Barth & McNichols find evidence that market prices reflect environmental liabilities substantially in excess of amounts already accrued by their sample of firms.

Similar to Barth & McNichols (1994), Hughes (2000) examines whether nonfinancial pollution measures are captured in market value as an exposure to future liabilities. More specifically, Hughes argues that pollution performance information is more relevant for companies facing specific regulatory exposures, and finds that differences in sulfur dioxide emissions as reported by the Department of Energy for publicly traded utility companies targeted for reduction goals under the 1990 Clean Air Act Amendments (CAAA) are associated with differences in the market value of those firms. Higher levels of pollution appear to have led to more negative market valuations, evidence suggesting the market captures the environmental exposures for the affected firms. Hughes also reports that the sensitivity of the pollution data's impact on market value varies as the general level of regulatory oversight changes. In contrast, Hughes finds no evidence of market valuation effects for emissions information for utilities not targeted under the CAAA.

In a final market valuation study, Clarkson, Li, & Richardson (2004) use two different measures of corporate environmental performance compiled by the EPA (toxic chemical releases and Biological Oxygen Demand discharges) to partition their sample of pulp and paper companies into high-polluting and low-polluting sub-samples. Consistent with both Barth & McNichols (1994) and Hughes (2000), Clarkson et al. (2004) find the market assesses a statistically significant unbooked liability for the high polluting firms. Clarkson et al. also report the market appears to positively value corporate environmental capital expenditures, but only for firms classified as low polluters. The authors attribute this effect to perceived benefits of overcompliance in the environmental domain.

In general, Barth & McNichols (1994), Hughes (2000), and Clarkson et al. (2004) all present evidence suggesting the market captures environmental performance information made available through non-company sources, and values exposures to the potential future costs negatively. From a different perspective, two recent studies, Murray, Sinclair, Power, & Gray (2006) and Jones, Frost, Loftus, &Van der Laan (2007) attempt to identify whether differences in social and environmental disclosure have longer-term market valuation effects. Murray et al. (2006), utilizing a sample of firms from the UK, report no significant short-term associations between disclosure and market valuation, but they do find that over a nine-year period, higher levels of disclosure appear to correlate with higher market valuation. Jones et al. (2007) on the other hand, report that disclosure for their sample of Australian companies appears to be negatively, but only weakly, associated with longer-term market valuation effects.

Market reaction studies

In contrast to the small number of studies relying on market valuation models, a considerable body of accounting research has used market model methods[4] to investigate the impact of social and/or environmental information on changes in market returns. Most of these studies focus either on the reaction to the release of disclosure through companies' financial reports, or the indirect value of disclosures at the time of other social-cost-inducing events. Results of investigations in the former area have been mixed, whereas findings from the latter group of studies consistently document that disclosure appears to mitigate the extent of negative market effects for affected companies. We discuss each of these respective streams in more detail below.

Most of the early studies of the market reaction to corporate environmental disclosures relied on information compiled in the Ernst & Ernst (1973 et seq.) surveys of corporate social responsibility disclosure to identify sample companies and their choice to disclose. Belkaoui (1976), for example, used a monthly return model to test for differences in market reaction to the issuance of annual reports for a sample of fifty firms identified by Ernst & Ernst as having pollution control disclosures, versus a control group of non-disclosing companies. Belkaoui reports a positive, but temporary reaction favoring the disclosing firms. Ingram (1978), using a broader sample and disclosure across both social and environmental areas, finds no significant market reaction for his sample of disclosing companies overall, although, controlling for the sign of unexpected earnings and partitioning across industry subsets did indicate some limited positive effects. Anderson & Frankle (1980), also relying on a broad sample of companies drawn from the Ernst & Ernst surveys and controlling for differences in firm-specific market risk, report significant positive market reactions for disclosing companies vis-à-vis non-disclosing counterparts, but primarily only for the month preceding annual report releases. One exception to the reliance on Ernst & Ernst survey firms is Freedman & Jaggi's (1986) investigation of the market reaction to annual report pollution disclosures by a sample of companies from four environmentally sensitive industries (chemicals, steel, pulp and paper, and oil). Using a monthly returns model, Freedman & Jaggi find no

[4] See Watts & Zimmerman (1986: 33–35) for an overview of market model methods.

significant differences in market reaction across companies classified as extensive or minimal disclosers.

In contrast to the mixed findings summarized above, studies of the mitigating effect of prior CSR disclosure at times of social-cost-inducing events consistently indicate a significant positive association with market impact. For example, Blacconiere & Patten (1994) investigate the market reaction for a sample of US chemical firms at the time of Union Carbide's disastrous Bhopal, India chemical leak (Union Carbide was not included in the sample). The authors report that while the overall intra-industry market reaction was significantly negative, the extent of prior environmental disclosure in test firms' 10-K reports served to mitigate the extent of the reaction. Similar results are reported by Blacconiere & Northcut (1997) for reactions to Congressional debates over Superfund legislation, Patten & Nance (1998) for market reactions to the *Exxon Valdez* oil spill, Freedman & Stagliano (1991) for reactions to changes in occupational safety cotton-dust regulations, and Freedman & Patten (2004) for market reactions to the Clean Air Act Amendments of 1990. Blacconiere & Patten (1994: 363) suggest such mitigating effects may be due to market participants viewing more extensive disclosure as a signal that firms are in a better position for dealing with increased social and political exposures arising from the social-cost inducing events.

Experimental investigations

Supplementing the market-based research into the value of social and environmental information, a number of recent studies also investigate the impact of these disclosures using experimental designs. Chan & Milne (1999), for example, examine whether disclosure of positive or negative environmental information influences investment decisions for a sample of accountants and investment analysts. They report negative disclosures lead to decreased investment choice, but positive environmental information has little impact. In contrast, Holm & Rikhardsson (2008) find positive environmental performance disclosure positively influences investment choice across both differing investment time horizons and the experience level of the investor. Milne & Patten (2002) report evidence of the legitimating impact of disclosure in that positive environmental disclosures were found to mitigate the impacts of negative environmental performance information. Finally, Milne & Chan (1999), using social rather than environmental disclosures, find that the information has little impact on investment decisions.

CONCLUSIONS AND FUTURE DIRECTIONS

Researchers interested in environmental financial reporting can see from our review that environmental financial reporting, much like other types of corporate reporting, is investigated through a number of different theoretical lenses that adopt appropriate, yet different, methodological approaches. Research to date almost always adopts either some variant of a voluntary disclosure perspective or a legitimacy perspective to ground its theoretical basis for analysis. The theoretical perspective drives a study's research questions as well as the types of policy implications that follow from its empirical findings. Regardless of the theoretical and methodological approach used, we continue to struggle with ways to empirically examine the relationship between environmental performance and environmental disclosure effectively. Conflicting findings force us to conclude that this issue remains unresolved and continually worthy of study. Given the tentative findings of disclosure research, we are also left unsure of how to best measure the quality of environmental disclosure. In short, there is much research left to be done.

We agree with Sil (2000) that theoretical eclecticism is healthy in the social sciences, and that researchers should continue to explore environmental financial reporting from a variety of theoretical vantage points. That said, we offer some suggestions that we believe can move the field forward in our understanding of why corporations undertake environmental financial reporting and how financial markets react to these types of regulatory mandated and voluntary disclosures.

Gray et al. (2010: 6) point out that "theory is a tricky thing" and that "theory is, at its simplest, a conception of the relationship between things." This conception, however, is often complicated by a multitude of relationships among market actors, regulators, and other stakeholders. Prior research in environmental financial reporting has shown this to be the case. Corporations may use environmental financial reporting to provide useful information to regulators and market participants even though the information contains a significant degree of positive bias. Policy recommendations by Solomon & Lewis (2002) appear to reconcile these inconsistencies by pointing out that corporations may use environmental financial reporting to meet regulatory, information dissemination, and educational objectives. Future research can be performed to help us better understand the manner in which corporations weigh the importance of these objectives and operationalize their reporting strategies.

Aerts et al. (2008) offer a way to integrate these conflicting theoretical perspectives by focusing on the information dynamics that underlie managerial decisions to report environmental activities. Their analysis takes into account both the market information demands described in voluntary disclosure theory and management incentives for manipulation of disclosures that are forwarded by legitimacy and impression management theories. Their empirical results support the notion that both motivations can be operating in the market simultaneously. Future research needs to acknowledge the complexities inherent in environmental financial reporting decisions and model the complexities in a way that treats disclosure as both informative and persuasive.

Recent trends in environmental disclosure and reporting practices (Buhr 2007), suggest a largely increasing number of stand-alone reports, which include social, environmental, and economic/financial information reflecting what Elkington (1997) refers to as triple bottom line reporting (Milne & Gray 2007). The issuance of such sustainability-type reports has now become almost standard among the world's largest corporations—KPMG International reports in its 2008 survey of sustainability reporting, for example, that nearly 80 percent of the Global 250 companies now issue such reports (KPMG International 2008: 13).[5] The Global Reporting Initiative (GRI) attempts to provide voluntary guidance for corporations that generate stand-alone reports. Despite this growing trend of stand-alone sustainability reporting, no official, regulatory (or other authoritative body) guidance has been issued for this matter in the US. Corporations' increasing use of stand-alone and internet corporate environmental reporting further complicates the research process because recent research shows that media disclosure type affects what disclosures are made and the manner in which the market responds (Aerts et al. 2008). A corporation's overall environmental strategy may change in response to market or public pressures, thus changing the role of environmental reporting in financial reports. Through the reviews and suggestions we have forwarded in this chapter, we hope to spur new and innovative ways to investigate why corporations make environmental disclosures in their financial reports and to what extent the market values the information contained there.

REFERENCES

Aerts, W., Cormier, D., & Magnan, M. (2008). "Corporate Environmental Disclosure, Financial Markets and the Media: An International Perspective," *Ecological Economics*, 64: 643–659.

Al-Tuwaijri, S. A., Christensen, T., & Hughes, K. E. (2004). "The Relations among Environmental Disclosure, Environmental Performance, and Economic Performance: A Simultaneous Approach," *Accounting, Organizations and Society*, 29(5–6): 447–471.

Anderson, J. C. & Frankle, A. W. (1980). "Voluntary Social Reporting: An Iso-Beta Portfolio Analysis," *The Accounting Review*, 55(3): 467–479.

Barth, M. E. & McNichols, M. F. (1994). "Estimation and Market Valuation of Environmental Liabilities Relating to Superfund Sites," *Journal of Accounting Research*, 32(3): 177–209.

—— & Wilson, P. (1997). "Factors Influencing Firms' Disclosures about Environmental Liabilities," *Review of Accounting Studies*, 2: 35–64.

Belkaoui, A. (1976). "The Impact of the Disclosure of the Environmental Effects of Organizational Behavior on the Market," *Financial Management*, Winter, 26–31.

Berthelot, S., Cormier, D., & Magnan, M. (2003). "Environmental Disclosure Research: Review and Synthesis," *Journal of Accounting Literature*, 22: 1–44.

Bewley, K. & Li, Y. (2000). "Disclosure of Environmental Information by Canadian Manufacturing Companies: A Voluntary Disclosure Perspective," *Advances in Environmental Accounting and Management*, 1: 201–226.

Blacconiere, W. G. & Patten, D. M. (1994). "Environmental Disclosure, Regulatory Costs, and Changes in Firm Value." *Journal of Accounting and Economics*, 18: 357–377.

---

[5] While the rise in stand-alone sustainability reporting is potentially a positive trend, many critics of the sustainability accounting trend see the reports as little more than public relations tools (Unerman, Bebbington, & O'Dwyer 2007).

Blacconiere, W. G. & Northcut, W. D. (1997). "Environmental Information and Market Reactions to Environmental Legislation." *Journal of Accounting, Auditing, and Finance*, 12(2): 149–178.

Buhr, N. (2007). "Histories of and Rationales for Sustainability Reporting," in J. Unerman, J. Bebbington, and B. O'dwyer (eds.), *Sustainability Accounting and Accountability*. London: Routledge, 57–69.

—— (1998). "Environmental Performance, Legislation and Annual Report Disclosure: The Case of Acid Rain and Falconbridge," *Accounting, Auditing and Accountability Journal*, 11(2): 163–190.

Chan, C. C. C. & Milne, M. J. (1999). "Investor Reactions to Corporate Environmental Saints and Sinners: An Experimental Analysis," *Accounting and Business Research*, 29(4): 265–279.

Chen, J. & Roberts, R. W. (2010). "Towards a More Integrated Understanding of the Organizations-Society Relationship: Implications for Social and Environmental Accounting Research," *Journal of Business Ethics*, forthcoming.

Cho, C. H. (2009). "Legitimation Strategies Used in Response to Environmental Disaster: A French Case Study of Total S.A.'s Erika and AZF Incidents," *European Accounting Review*, 18(1): 33–62.

—— & Patten, D. M. (2007). "The Role of Environmental Disclosures as Tools of Legitimacy: A Research Note," *Accounting, Organizations and Society*, 32(7–8): 639–647.

—— —— (2008). "Did the GAO Get It Right? Another look at Corporate Environmental Disclosure," *Social and Environmental Accountability Journal*, 28(1): 21–32.

—— —— & Roberts, R. W. (2006). "Corporate Political Strategy: An Examination of the Relation between Political Expenditures, Environmental Performance, and Environmental Disclosure," *Journal of Business Ethics*, 67(2): 139–154.

—— —— (2010). "Environmental Reporting on the Internet by America's Toxic 100: Legitimacy and Self-Presentation," *International Journal of Accounting Information Systems*, 11(1): 1–16.

—— —— & Patten, D. M. (2010). "The Language of U.S. Corporate Environmental Disclosure," *Accounting, Organizations and Society*, 35(4): 431–443.

Choi, J. (1999). "An Investigation of the Initial Voluntary Environmental Disclosures Made in Korean Semi-Annual Financial Reports," *Pacific Accounting Review*, 11(1): 75–102.

Clarkson, P. M., Li, Y., & Richardson, G. D. (2004). "The Market Valuation of Environmental Capital Expenditures by Pulp and Paper Companies," *The Accounting Review*, 79(2). 329–353.

—— —— —— & Vasvari, F. P. (2008). "Revisiting the Relation between Environmental Performance and Environmental Disclosure: An Empirical Analysis," *Accounting, Organizations and Society*, 33(4–5): 303–327.

Deegan, C. (2002). "The Legitimising Effect of Social and Environmental Disclosures: A Theoretical Foundation," *Accounting, Auditing and Accountability Journal*, 15(2): 282–311.

—— & Gordon, B. (1996). "A Study of the Environmental Disclosure Practices of Australian Corporations," *Accounting and Business Research*, 26(3): 187–199.

—— & Rankin, M. (1996). "Do Australian Companies Report Environmental News Objectively? An Analysis of Environmental Disclosures by Firms Prosecuted Successfully the Environmental Protection Authority," *Accounting, Auditing and Accountability Journal*, 9(2): 50–67.

Delbard, O. (2008). "CSR Legislation in France and the European Regulatory Paradox: An Analysis of EU CSR Policy and Sustainability Reporting Practice," *Corporate Governance*, 8(4): 397–405.

Dye, R. A. (1985). "Disclosure of Non-Proprietary Information," *Journal of Accounting Research*, 23(2): 123–145.

Elkington, J. (1997). *Cannibals with Forks: The Triple Bottom Line of 21st Century Business.* Oxford, UK: Capstone Publishing.

Epstein, E.M and Votaw, D. (eds) (1978). *Rationality, Legitimacy, and Responsibility: Search for New Directions in Business and Society.* Goodyear Publishing Co., Santa Monica, CA, 116–130.

Ernst & Ernst (1973 *et seq.*). *Social Responsibility Disclosure.* Cleveland, OH: Ernst & Ernst.

Fekrat, M. A., Inclan, I. & Petroni, D. (1996). "Corporate Environmental Disclosures: Competitive Disclosure Hypothesis Using 1991 Annual Report Data," *The International Journal of Accounting*, 31: 175–195.

Freedman, M. & Jaggi, B. (1986). "An Analysis of the Impact of Corporate Pollution Disclosures Included in Annual Financial Statements on Investors' Decisions," *Advances in Public Interest Accounting*, 1: 193–212.

—— & Patten, D. M. (2004). "Evidence on the Pernicious Effect of Financial Report Environmental Disclosure," *Accounting Forum*, 28(1): 27–41.

—— & Stagliano, A. J. (1991). "Regulators and Economic Benefits: The Case of Occupational Health Standards," *Advances in Public Interest Accounting*, 4: 131–142.

—— (1998). "Political Pressure and Environmental Disclosure: The Case of EPA and the Superfund," *Research on Accounting Ethics*, 4: 211–224.

—— & Wasley, C. (1990). "The Association between Environmental Performance and Environmental Disclosure in Annual Reports and 10Ks," *Advances in Public Interest Accounting*, 2: 183–193.

Gamble, G. O., Hsu, K., Kite, D., & Radtke, R. R. (1995). "Environmental Disclosures in Annual Reports and 10Ks: An Examination," *Accounting Horizons*, 9(3): 34–54.

Government Accountability Office (2004). *Environmental Disclosure - SEC Should Explore Ways to Improve Tracking and Transparency of Information.* Washington, D.C.: GAO.

Graham, J. R., Harvey, C. R., & Rajgopal, S. (2005). "The Economic Implications of Corporate Financial Reporting". *Journal of Accounting and Economics*, 40: 3–73.

Gray, R., Kouhy, R. & Lavers, S. (1995a). "Corporate Social and Environmental Reporting: A Review of the Literature and a Longitudinal Study of UK Disclosure," *Accounting, Auditing and Accountability Journal*, 8(2): 47–77.

—— —— —— (1995b). "Methodological Themes: Constructing a Research Database of Social and Environmental Reporting by UK Companies," *Accounting, Auditing and Accountability Journal*, 8(2): 78–101.

—— Owen, D. & Adams, C. (2010). "Some Theory for Social Accounting? A Review Essay and a Tentative Exploration of Categorisation of Theorisations Around Social Accounting," *Advances in Environmental Accounting and Management*, 4: 1–54.

Guthrie, J. & Parker, L. D. (1989). "Corporate Social Reporting: A Rebuttal of Legitimacy Theory," *Accounting and Business Research*, 19(76): 342–356.

Hackston, D. & Milne, M. J. (1996). "Some Determinants of Social and Environmental Disclosures in New Zealand Companies," *Accounting, Auditing and Accountability Journal*, 9(1): 77–108.

Holm, C. & Rikhardsson, P. (2008). "Experienced and Novice Investors: Does Environmental Information Influence Investment Allocation Decisions?" *European Accounting Review*, 17(3): 537–557.

Hughes II, K. E. (2000). "The Value Relevance of Nonfinancial Measures of Air Pollution in the Electric Utility Industry," *The Accounting Review*, 75(2): 209–228.

Hughes, S. B., Anderson, A., & Golden, S. (2001). "Corporate Environmental Disclosures: Are they Useful in Determining Environmental Performance?" *Journal of Accounting and Public Policy* 20(3): 217–240.

Hughes, S. B., Sander, J. F., & Reier, J. C. (2000). "Do Environmental Disclosures in U.S. Annual Reports Differ by Environmental Performance?" *Advances in Environmental Accounting and Management*, 1: 141–161.

Ingram, R. W. (1978). "An Investigation of the Information Content of (Certain) Social Responsibility Disclosures'," *Journal of Accounting Research*, 16(2): 270–285.

—— & Frazier, K. B. (1980). "Environmental Performance and Corporate Disclosure," *Journal of Accounting Research*, 18(2): 614–622.

Johnson, L. T. (1993). "Research on Environmental Reporting," *Accounting Horizons*, 7(3): 118–123.

Jones, S., Frost, G., Loftus, J., & Van Der Laan, S. (2007). "An Empirical Investigation of the Market Returns and Financial Performance of Entities Engaged in Sustainability Reporting," *Australian Accounting Review*, 17(1): 78–87.

KPMG International (2008). *KPMG International Survey of Corporate Responsibility Reporting*. Amstelveen, The Netherlands: KPMG International.

Krippendorff, K. (1980). *Content Analysis: An Introductory to its Methodology*. London, UK: Sage.

Larrinaga, C., Carrasco, F., Correa, C., Llnea, F., & Moneva, J. M. (2002). "Accountability and Accounting Regulation: The Case of the Spanish Disclosure Standard," *European Accounting Review*, 11(4): 723–740.

Li, Y., Richardson, G. D., & Thornton, D. (1997). "Corporate Disclosure of Environmental Information: Theory and Evidence," *Contemporary Accounting Research*, 14(3): 435–474.

Lindblom, C. K. (1994). "The Implications of Organizational Legitimacy for Corporate Social Performance and Disclosure," Paper presented at the Critical Perspectives on Accounting Conference, New York, NY.

Mathews, M. R. (1993). *Socially Responsible Accounting*. London, UK: Chapman Hall.

Merkl-Davies, D. M. & Brennan, N. M. (2007). "Discretionary Disclosure Strategies in Corporate Narratives: Incremental Information or Impression Management?" *Journal of Accounting Literature*, 26: 116–194.

Milne, M. J. & Adler, R. W. (1999). "Exploring the Reliability of Social and Environmental Disclosures Content Analysis," *Accounting, Auditing and Accountability Journal*, 12(2): 237–256.

—— & Chan, C. C. C. (1999). "Narrative Corporate Social Disclosures: How Much of a Difference Do They Make to Investment Decision-Making?" *British Accounting Review*, 31: 439–457.

—— & Gray, R. (2007). "Future Prospects for Corporate Sustainability Reporting," in J. Unerman, J. Bebbington, and B. O'Dwyer (eds.), *Sustainability Accounting and Accountability*. New York, NY: Routledge, 184–207.

—— & Patten, D. M. (2002). "Securing Organizational Legitimacy: An Experimental Decision Case Examining the Impact of Environmental Disclosures," *Accounting, Auditing and Accountability Journal*, 15(3): 372–405.

Milne, M. J., Tregidga, H., & Walton, S. (2009). "Words not Actions! The Ideological Role of Sustainable Development Reporting," *Accounting, Auditing and Accountability Journal*, 22(8): 1211–1257.

Murray, A., Sinclair, D., Power, D., & Gray, R. (2006). "Do Financial Markets Care about Social and Environmental Disclosure? Further Evidence and Exploration from the UK," *Accounting, Auditing and Accountability Journal*, 19(2): 228–255.

Neu, D., Warsame, H., & Pedwell, K. (1998). "Managing Public Impressions: Environmental Disclosures in Annual Reports," *Accounting, Organizations and Society*, 23(3): 265–82.

O'Dwyer, B. & Gray, R. H. (1998). "Corporate Social Reporting in the Republic of Ireland: A Longitudinal Study," *Irish Accounting Review*, 5(2): 1–34.

Owen, D., Shaw, K., & Cooper, S. (2005). "The Operating and Financial Review – A Catalyst for Improved Social and Environmental Disclosure?" *ACCA Research Report No. 89.*

Patten, D. M. (1992). "Intra-Industry Environmental Disclosures in Response to the Alaskan Oil Spill: A Note on Legitimacy Theory," *Accounting, Organizations and Society*, 17(5): 471–475.

—— (1995). "Variability in Social Disclosure: A Legitimacy-Based Analysis," *Advances in Public Interest Accounting*, 6: 273–285.

—— (2002). "The Relation between Environmental Performance and Environmental Disclosure: A Research Note," *Accounting, Organizations and Society*, 27(8): 763–773.

—— & Nance, J. R. (1998). "Regulatory Cost Effects in a Good News Environment: The Intra-Industry Reaction to the Alaskan Oil Spill," *Journal of Accounting and Public Policy*, 17: 409–429.

—— & Trompeter, G. (2003). "Corporate Responses to Political Costs: An Examination of the Relation between Environmental Disclosure and Earnings Management," *Journal of Accounting and Public Policy*, 22(1): 83–94.

Sil, R. (2000). "The Foundations of Eclecticism: The Epistemological Status of Agency, Culture, and Structure in Social Theory," *Journal of Theoretical Politics*, 12(3): 353–387.

Smith, M. & Taffler, R. (2000). "The Chairman's Statement: A Content Analysis of Discretionary Narrative Disclosures," *Accounting, Auditing and Accountability Journal*, 13(5): 624–646.

Solomon, A. & Lewis, L. (2002). "Incentives and Disincentives for Corporate Environmental Disclosure," *Business Strategy and the Environment*, 11: 154–169.

Suchman, M. C. (1995). "Managing Legitimacy: Strategic and Institutional Approaches," *Academy of Management Review*, 20(3): 571–610.

Trotman, K. T. & Bradley, G. W. (1981). "Associations between Social Responsibility Disclosure and Characteristics of Companies," *Accounting, Organizations and Society*, 6(4): 355–362.

Tsang, E. W. K. (1998). "A Longitudinal Study of Corporate Social Reporting in Singapore: The Case of the Banking, Food and Beverages and Hotel Industries," *Accounting, Auditing and Accountability Journal*, 11(5): 624–635.

Unerman, J. (2000). "Reflections on Quantification in Corporate Social Reporting Content Analysis," *Accounting, Auditing and Accountability Journal*, 13(5): 667–680.

—— Bebbington, J. & O'Dwyer, B. (2007). "Introduction to Sustainability Accounting and Accountability," in J. Unerman, J. Bebbington, and B. O'Dwyer (eds.), *Sustainability Accounting and Accountability*. New York, NY: Routledge, 1–16.

Verrecchia, R. (1983). "Discretionary Disclosure," *Journal of Accounting and Economics* 5: 179–194.

Watts, R. & Zimmerman, J. (1986). *Positive Accounting Theory*. Edgewood Cliffs, NJ: Prentice Hall.

Wiseman, J. (1982). "An Evaluation of Environmental Disclosures Made in Corporate Annual Reports," *Accounting, Organizations and Society*, 17(1): 53–63.

CHAPTER 25

....

VALUES-DRIVEN AND PROFIT-SEEKING DIMENSIONS OF ENVIRONMENTALLY RESPONSIBLE INVESTING

....

ROB BAUER
AND JEROEN DERWALL

CORPORATE environmental responsibility is no longer below the radar screens of the investment community. Some of the world's largest institutional asset managers, for example, those at CalPERS in the US, Universities Superannuation Scheme in the UK, and APG in the Netherlands, are expressing their commitment to investing in companies that are environmentally and socially responsible. Estimates by the Social Investment Forum (2005) suggest that, in the US, assets managed in an environmentally and/or socially responsible way cover more than 10 percent of the entire stock market. According to Eurosif (2008), socially responsible assets under management have reached €2.665 trillion as of 2008 in Europe, as much as 17.5 percent of the asset management industry.

However, these estimates mask ongoing debates about a tension between environmental and financial goals, which hamper a full integration of environmental information according to many institutional investors. A great deal of the tension revolves around the idea that environmentally responsible investing is a *values-driven* investment approach, that is, not financially motivated but rooted in non-pecuniary motivations such as personal values and societal concerns.[1] Institutional investors worry that pursuing goals

---

[1] We borrow the terms "values-driven" and "profit-seeking" from Derwall, Koedijk, & Ter Horst (2010), who explain them in detail. The term "values-driven" is used here to refer to non-pecuniary motives for making investment decisions.

other than maximizing risk-adjusted return conflicts with their fiduciary responsibilities. In the US, for example, many states have adopted the Uniform Prudent Investor Act, in which Section 2b states that "a trustee's investment and management decisions respecting individual assets must be evaluated not in isolation but in the context of the trust portfolio as a whole and as a part of an overall investment strategy having risk and return objectives reasonably suited to the trust."[2] Therefore, unless the terms of the trust specify a preference for non-pecuniary objectives, a fiduciary cannot easily integrate a values-driven investment style if it implies sacrificing return (Bollen 2007). Although regulation concerning fiduciary duties is more lenient outside the US, institutional investors lack a proper understanding of how they can serve different pecuniary and non-pecuniary needs among clients and beneficiaries.

The trade-off between values and financial performance explains why recent adopters of SRI suggest that environmentally responsible investing is feasible as long as it comes in a *profit-seeking* form that is geared to earning superior returns. For example, many institutional investors are signatories of the Principles for Responsible Investment (PRI). According to PRI, "environmental, social and corporate governance (ESG) issues can affect the performance of investment portfolios and therefore must be given appropriate consideration by investors if they are to fulfill their fiduciary (or equivalent) duty."[3]

All these developments have intensified the confusion about what environmentally responsible investing entails, and which needs of investors it serves. Nevertheless, understanding values-driven versus profit-seeking motives behind environmentally responsible investing is useful for several reasons.

To begin with, values-driven environmental investors form a challenge to conventional theories about the functioning of financial markets, the behavior of asset prices, and the goals of fiduciary managers, which assume that investors are a rather homogenous group of wealth-maximizing agents. In a world with values-driven motives among certain investors, financial markets may be segmented, values can influence asset prices, and fiduciaries may not cater optimally to all beneficiaries by delivering risk-adjusted return on investment alone. Furthermore, because of their potential effect on firms' stock prices, values-driven investors can theoretically influence firms' ability to attract new capital, which gives them a mechanism to induce better corporate behavior.

In contrast, environmental investors with a profit-seeking mindset may pursue an entirely different approach to environmental investing and have different expectations about the relevance of corporate environmental performance in financial markets. Like mainstream investors (and unlike values-driven investors), their aim is to beat the market, but unlike mainstream investors, they believe that environmental information enriches their investment skills. Their decision to invest environmentally responsibly leans on the

---

[2] Moreover, Section 5 of the Act says that "no form of so-called social investing is consistent with the duty of loyalty if the investment activity entails sacrificing the interests of trust beneficiaries—for example, by accepting below-market returns—in favor of the interests of the persons supposedly benefited by pursuing the particular social cause." <http://www.law.upenn.edu/bll/ulc/fnact99/1990s/upia94.pdf>.

[3] See <www.unpri.org/about/>.

belief that firms increase their (discounted) future cash flow through better environmental performance, and that this relation is underestimated by the financial market.

Little is known about which of these views is borne out in reality, despite the fact that each view has different implications for asset prices, the management of investment portfolios, and the environmentally responsible behavior of companies. Following the market segmentation theory of Derwall, Koedijk, & Ter Horst (2010), we ask whether these views are truly mutually exclusive or whether environmentally responsible investing attracts *both* values-driven and profit-seeking investors. To further explore this idea in this chapter, we synthesize theoretical studies on environmentally responsible investing, empirical studies on investor behavior, and evidence on the returns of environmentally screened investments.

Based on these studies, we consecutively answer several important questions in this chapter. What do theories about values-driven and profit-seeking environmental investing say about investors' preferences, their effects on financial markets, and investment returns? Are environmentally responsible investors values-driven or profit-seeking in reality? Which theory of environmentally responsible investing finds support in evidence on the performance of environmentally responsible investment portfolios? Finally, we discuss the implications of the values-driven and profit-seeking movements for practitioners and researchers.

Theoretical background

The values-driven environmentally responsible investor

Investors may choose to hold certain assets for reasons unrelated to expected future cash flow and risk. Some of these types of investors can be thought of as "values-driven" investors, who weigh pecuniary benefits against non-pecuniary utility that can be derived from their investments.

Multi-attribute utility theory provides a way to model preferences when investors may care about more than just return and risk. Inspired by Bollen (2007), we could describe investors who are willing to sacrifice return for utility from the environmental responsibility features of investments by using a multi-attribute utility function:

$$U = w(\mu - \theta\sigma^2) + (1-w)G$$

where μ and σ^2 are, respectively, the expected return and the variance of return on investors' portfolios, $0 \leq w \leq 1$, and G is an indicator variable that equals one if the investment satisfies the investors' demand for "environmental responsibility", and zero otherwise. The assumption is that preferences are conform an additive utility function, in which utility (U) derived from the "environmentally responsible" feature of the investment is separable from, and substitutable for, the utility derived from return and risk (Bollen 2007).

While such a utility function is suitable for describing the trade-off that values-driven investors make, why they care about non-pecuniary aspects of environmentally responsible investments is not entirely clear. Researchers suggest that several factors may explain non-pecuniary motives behind investment decisions. Examples are societal norms (e.g. Hong & Kacperczyk 2009), political values (Hong & Kostovetsky 2009), "affect" (Statman, Fisher, & Anginer 2008), and religion (for example, Kurtz 2008).

One implication of values-driven environmentally responsible investors is that they may pose a challenge to conventional financial models on the pricing of financial assets, which relate expected return to, for example, market risk under the capital asset pricing theory (CAPM) of Sharpe (1964) and Lintner (1965). When such investors come in large numbers, they will create a shortage of demand for environmentally irresponsible assets and excess demand for responsible assets that can cause stock prices to deviate from those in a market without such investors. Consequently, theoretically, values-driven investors can influence the functioning of financial markets, and ultimately persuade firms to be environmentally more responsible.

Specifically, these investors can theoretically drive up the cost of capital of environmentally controversial firms and drive down the cost of capital of responsible firms. Here, the effect of corporate environmental performance on the cost of capital materializes through at least two economic channels. First, a stock boycott by environmentally responsible investors limits the risk-sharing opportunities of those invested in environmentally controversial firms (Heinkel, Kraus, & Zechner 2001). Because of their inability to share risks with environmentally responsible investors, shareholders of controversial companies command compensation for holding more shares of environmentally controversial firms than they would if the market were free of boycotts.

Second, because values-driven investors can cause segmented capital markets and the CAPM may not hold, idiosyncratic (firm-specific) risk may become a relevant economic channel through which corporate environmental performance influences the cost of capital. Litigation risk is one example of a risk related to corporate environmental responsibility that can be diversified away according to conventional financial market theory, but which can be priced in a segmented market.

Angel & Rivoli (1997) formulate the relation between investor boycotts of controversial stocks and firms' capital costs using an equilibrium model from Merton (1987). In their model, a controversial stock has a higher cost of capital as the fraction of investors excluding the stock gets larger, all else equal. Here, the increase in cost of capital for firm i is given by:

$$\lambda_i = \delta \sigma_i^2 x_i \frac{(1-q_i)}{q_i}$$

where δ is the coefficient of aggregate risk aversion, σ_i^2 represents idiosyncratic risk for stock i, and x_i is the market value of the firm relative to aggregate market value, and $(1-q_i)$ is the fraction of investors (relative to the total number of investors in the market) unwilling to hold stocks of firm i.

Equation (2) illustrates why financial markets can theoretically encourage firms to be environmentally more responsible. A higher cost of capital due to stock boycotts by values-driven environmental investors may ultimately push firms into better environmental responsibility. At some point, environmentally weak companies are better off by reforming to better environmental performance, as soon as the cost of capital increase exceeds the cost of reforming.

Standard finance theory relates a firm's stock price to the firm's expected future cash flows to shareholders discounted at the cost of equity capital. If environmentally controversial stocks have higher capital costs because they are shunned by certain investors then these stocks trade at relatively lower prices compared to stocks of more responsible (but otherwise equal) firms. These lower prices set the stage for higher returns in the future.[4] Following Derwall et al. (2010) we formalize this predicted relationship by referring to the "shunned-stock hypothesis":

> Expected stock returns are higher for firms that are more environmentally controversial, all else equal.

Environmentally responsible investors that are values-driven may pay for their non-pecuniary preferences in the form of a relatively lower financial return, but they may derive non-pecuniary utility from the environmental attribute of their investment portfolios to compensate for this loss.

Whether values-driven investors can influence asset prices and corporate behavior crucially depends on whether they come in large numbers. According to the theoretical model of Heinkel et al. (2001), environmentally responsible investors can influence firms' capital costs as soon as they represent a significant percentage of the financial market. They also estimate that the effect on capital costs is material enough to influence corporate behavior if the proportion of environmentally responsible investors is about 20 percent. This implies that the 10 to 17.5 percent of total assets that are currently invested according to environmental and/or social criteria are not sufficient to encourage controversial firms to change environmental policy, despite a potentially higher cost of capital for those firms. Ultimately, the effect of values-driven investors on capital costs and stock returns are empirical questions that we address throughout this chapter.

The profit-seeking environmentally responsible investor

The idea that environmentally responsible investing is a values-driven exercise that involves weighing non-pecuniary considerations against return is unacceptable to some types of investors. Their main concern is that the trade-off creates a tension with fiduciary responsibilities, which are often believed to exclude an explicit willingness to sacrifice

---

[4] The cost of capital is equal to the expected return to investors who supply the capital.

return to beneficiaries. These hesitant attitudes towards environmentally responsible investing explain why recent waves within the SRI movement advocate a "profit-seeking" variant that is geared to earning superior returns, or "doing well while doing good" (Hamilton, Jo, & Statman 1993).

Profit-seeking environmentally responsible investors aim to "beat the market" by delivering superior long-term risk-adjusted return, or "abnormal" return, just like conventional investors. These investors believe that using information about firms' environmental performance helps to achieve that objective. Specifically, these investors believe that corporate environmental performance is relevant for firms' fundamental value but the value-relevance of corporate environmental responsibility is not yet properly understood by the financial market.

For the profit-seeking view towards environmentally responsible investing to hold, two conditions must be met. The first condition is that, all else equal, firms' (discounted) future cash flows should be influenced by environmental performance. The question of whether environmental performance is positively associated with firms' future cash flow has been the subject of considerable debate. Skeptics have contended that environmental management comes at a cost (e.g. Walley & Whitehead 1994), whereas others see economic gains, such as a superior resource efficiency, that outweigh these costs (Porter & Van Der Linde 1995). The relation between environmental performance and proxies for cash flow as well other performance measures is reviewed in Griffin & Mahon (1997) and Margolis, Elfenbein, & Walsh (2007). The conclusion that we derive from the literature so far is that environmental practices can lead to higher profitability.[5] However, several studies conclude that firms achieve a competitive edge only through proactive forms of environmental management. A plausible rationale is that basic compliance with environment-related regulation does not yield competitive advantages to the firm because compliance affects all industry-peers almost equally. But in line with the "resource-based view" (e.g. Wernerfelt 1984), environmental management can be shaped in a way such that it becomes a valuable asset that is unique to the firm and not easily replicated by competitors (see, e.g. Hart & Ahuja 1996; Russo & Fouts 1997). This shaping requires more proactive forms of environmental management, such as "eco-efficiency" (e.g. Dowell, Hart, & Yeung 2000).

The second condition inherent in the profit-seeking view is that stock prices do not reflect all of the value-relevant information related to firms' environmental performance. Superior profits that firms generate through environmental management are a source of *abnormal* stock return to the extent that they are unexpected by the financial market. Environmentally responsible investors with a profit-seeking mindset can earn abnormal returns only when the financial market systematically underestimates the degree to which corporate environmental performance enhances firms' future cash flows, or overestimate associated costs. The goal that profit-seeking investors pursue builds on the "errors-in-expectations" hypothesis (Derwall et al. 2010).

---

[5] See, for example, Russo & Fouts (1997), Waddock & Graves (1997), Dowell et al. (2000), King & Lenox (2002), and Guenster, Derwall, Baner, & Koedijk (2010).

Stock returns are higher for firms that are more environmentally responsible, all else equal.

This hypothesis contrasts with the view of efficient capital markets, in which stock prices quickly incorporate all new value-relevant information about firms' environmental management. Admittedly, the idea that markets are not in equilibrium because investors are slow to recognize firms' future cash flows is difficult to reconcile with conventional economic logic, at least in the long run. Nevertheless, there are some reasons to expect that the market may fail to fully value some environmental information properly.

First, as pointed out by Cho, Patten, & Roberts ([Chapter 24] this volume), information about value-relevant environmental performance is not easily available via standard corporate reports or other sources. Because of these shortcomings, investors may lack the tools that are needed to evaluate the entire spectrum of environmental management practices and assess their effects on firm value. Second, pro-active environmental management is costly at the outset, and the economic gains that it generates, if any, are likely to materialize slowly. Underdeveloped accounting conventions may hamper a proper judgment on the added value of environmental performance, especially intangible value. Scholars have written extensively on complications associated with measuring firms' long-term value creation potential under current accounting conventions (e.g. Lev & Schwartz 1971; Damodaran 2002).

All these arguments suggest that investors in the financial market could be surprised about the value-relevance of certain information about corporate environmental performance.

MOTIVES AMONG ENVIRONMENTALLY RESPONSIBLE INVESTORS

A crucial question in the discussion about different forms of environmentally responsible investment is: why do investors care about corporate environmental performance in the formation of investment decisions? Are environmental investment preferences based on values-driven or profit-seeking motivations? As we explain later in more detail, this profiling and segmentation is critical to understanding the ways through which environmental investments influence the functioning of financial markets, as well as the ways through which fiduciaries can cater to different types of environmental investors.

Although it is unavoidably difficult to understand the breadth of motivations behind investors' trading decisions, the field has gradually uncovered that the values-driven versus profit-seeking dimension is relevant for distinguishing environmental investment preferences among both individual and institutional investors. Table 25.1 summarizes the results of studies that report on interviews, surveys, and conjoint experiments involving individuals that were conducted to investigate whether investors are willing to sacrifice return in exchange for the non-pecuniary benefits derived from environmentally and socially responsible investments.

Table 25.1 Values-driven and profit-seeking dimensions of environmental investing: studies on individual investors

Study	Sample	Summary
Panel A: Evidence suggesting a values-driven motive to environmentally responsible investing		
Beal & Goyen (1998)	825 shareholders of ethical firm	Investment decisions are more motivated by environmental features than by investment return.
Williams (2007)	Responders from Globescan survey	SRI may be driven more by attitudes towards firms' environmental/social goals than by financial return. Demographics hardly explain SRI. CSR-active consumers are more likely to invest socially responsible.
Owen & Qian (2008)	1055 investors	Non-financial considerations in addition to financial considerations explain decisions to invest responsibly. People who purchase environmentally friendly products as consumers are also more likely to invest responsibly.
Haigh (2008)	382 fund investors	Intention to hold SRI funds is positively related to information accuracy, SRI approaches, and portfolio listings. These issues rank higher than funds' expenses and historical return
Panel B: Evidence of profit-seeking / against values-driven motive to environmentally responsible investing		
Rosen et al. (1991)	1493 investors in 2 SRI funds	Social investors most often expressed concerns for environmental and labor issues, and largely agree that SRI should perform as well as other investments.
Lewis & Webley (1994)	UK residents and students	Although environmentally conscious attitudes enhance positive attitude to SRI, investors seem unwilling to forego additional return that conventional investments might earn.
Vyvyan et al. (2007)	318 employees and members of 2 Australian organizations	Investors with environmentally most active attitudes rate environmental fund attributes as highly important and return as moderately important. But according to actual investment preferences, most investors are concerned with return.
Panel C: Detecting both values-driven and profit-seeking segments		
Bauer & Smeets (2010)	Client database of 2 Dutch social responsible banks	Produces a segmentation of clients. One segment obtains non-pecuniary benefits by investing in funds that apply environmental and social screens. At the other end, a segment mainly invests based on funds' past return, which suggests a focus or pecuniary benefits.

On the one hand, there is evidence that investors assign importance to the environmental implications of their investment for reasons unrelated to financial performance, consistent with them being values-driven. For example, in a survey conducted by Beal & Goyen (1998) shareholders of an ethical company in Australia responded that financial considerations were not the primary motivation for investing in the ethical company. Important motivations were the firm's role in the conservation of animals, plants, and ecosystems, and the firms' ethical profile. More recently, Owen & Qian (2008) concluded, based on a large survey across the US, that non-financial motives play an important role in investors' decision to purchase SRI products. They found that consumers' environmental concerns particularly influence investment choices.

On the other hand, there is also evidence that many individuals see financial performance as the primary goal of environmental and other socially responsible investments, consistent with them being profit-seeking investors. For example, the survey of Rosen, Sandler, & Shani (1991) among mutual fund investors suggests that these investors expect socially responsible investments to pay off as well as other types of investments. In addition, even when investors' attitudes to environmentally responsible investing point to values-driven motives, their actual investment preferences may reveal that financial return is their principal concern (e.g. Vyvyan, Ng, & Brimble 2007).

Although it seems that most studies disagree about investors' motivations, researchers have begun to reconcile earlier evidence by acknowledging that environmentally responsible investors may have different motives. For example, Bauer & Smeets (2010) find, using conjoint analysis, that the clientele of two environmentally and socially responsible banks can be segmented based on pecuniary and non-pecuniary dimensions. At one end of this dimension is a segment that derives much non-pecuniary benefit through SRI funds, and which largely ignores past performance and fund fees when selecting funds. At the other end, a large subset of the SRI clientele predominantly invests based on past return, which suggests a focus on pecuniary benefit.

An alternative body of research investigates drivers of environmentally and socially responsible investing among institutional investors by focusing on patterns in the ownership structure of companies. Table 25.2 summarizes these studies, which point out that various dimensions of corporate social responsibility explain differences in ownership across various types of institutions. Specifically, higher scores on environmental performance and other CSR issues have been found to be positively related to pension fund ownership, but less related to ownership by mutual funds and investment banks.

One explanation for this pattern in support of a profit-seeking motive is that firms' investments in environmental management are investments that pay off mainly in the long run, and therefore predominantly attract investors with a long-term perspective, such as pension funds (e.g. Johnson & Greening 1999; Cox, Brammer, & Millington 2004; Neubaum & Zahra 2006). However, an alternative explanation that is consistent with a values-driven motive is that public pension funds shun environmentally controversial stocks because pension funds are more vulnerable to public scrutiny and societal norms compared to other types of institutional investors. Hong & Kacperczyk (2009) offer a similar norms-based explanation for pension funds' avoidance of tobacco, alcohol, and gambling stocks.

Mutual funds have been a recent laboratory for proving that political values affect environmental investment preferences. Based on the holdings and donations of US mutual fund managers, Hong & Kostovetsky (2009) find that managers who donate to Democrats underweight in socially controversial stocks and tilt more towards environmentally and socially responsible stocks compared to those who donate to Republicans. Although SRI funds are typically run by Democrats, they show that the effect of political values on fund holdings holds for both SRI funds and non-SRI funds. The authors remain cautious about attributing this effect exclusively to non-pecuniary motivations.

These studies altogether suggest that investors who care about the environmental performance of their investments form a heterogeneous group. Recent research concludes that values-driven and profit-seeking investors co-exist (e.g. Bauer & Smeets 2010; Derwall et al. 2010). The natural follow-up question is which of these views dominates in the explanation of the returns on stocks of environmentally responsible and less responsible companies, with the net effect ultimately being an empirical question.

CORPORATE ENVIRONMENTAL PERFORMANCE AND INVESTOR RETURNS

We now survey empirical studies on the long-run returns of environmentally responsible and less responsible stock portfolios. All of the studies we discuss have been methodologically quite consistent. The studies construct various hypothetical investment portfolios that differ in environmental responsibility and evaluate the post-formation returns of the portfolios using a performance attribution model. The main objective of this exercise is to find out whether environmentally responsible investment portfolios have earned an average return that differs from that of less responsible investments, controlling for other factors that determine the portfolios' returns. The environmental profile of the portfolios is determined prior to portfolio formation, by ranking all available stocks on an environmental performance measure, which is often collected from a research firm that specializes in assessing corporate environmental performance. As soon as new performance measures are released and become available to investors, portfolios are rebalanced to represent the updated information.

Essential in the attribution of portfolios' returns to environmental performance is a well-specified performance attribution model. It is by now well known that a host of risks and investment styles unrelated to environmentally responsible investing are important in explaining return differences across different portfolios. Failure to correct for these multiple effects may bias the estimation of return that is attributable to the environmental attribute of the portfolio. The research that we discuss has largely reached consensus about which measure is most suitable for performance evaluation.

Table 25.2 Environmental performance, institutional ownership, and mutual fund holdings

Study	Sample	Summary
Johnson & Greening (1999)	286 US firms, 1993	Performances concerning"product quality" (including environmental performance) and "people" relate positively to ownership by pension funds, but are not affected by investment bank and mutual fund ownership.
Cox et al. (2004)	541 UK firms, 2002	Environmental performance (and"employee" and "community" dimensions of CSR) are positively related to ownership by "long-term" institutions and not (or negatively) related to ownership by "short-term" investors.
Neubaum & Zahra (2006)	357 US firms, 1995 & 383 firms, 2000	A composite CSR measure (including environmental performance) is positively related to pension fund ownership but is negatively related to investment bank and mutual fund ownership.
Hong & Kostovetsky (2009)	488 US mutual funds, 1992–2006	Democratic fund managers tilt towards firms with positive environmental and social features and avoid controversial stocks.

The three-factor alpha based on the Fama & French (1993) model and Carhart's (1997) four-factor alpha, which we describe below, are measures that most studies use to compare the performance of environmentally responsible portfolios with those of less responsible portfolios. These models take the following form and are usually estimated through regressions, using monthly returns on the portfolios and the independent variables:

$$R_{i,t} - R_f = \alpha_i + \beta_{0,i}(R_{m,t} - R_f) + \beta_{1,i}SMB_t + \beta_{2,i}HML_t + \varepsilon_{i,t}$$
$$R_{i,t} - R_f = \alpha_i + \beta_{0,i}(R_{m,t} - R_f) + \beta_{1,i}SMB_t + \beta_{2,i}HML_t + \beta_{3,i}MOM_t + \varepsilon_{i,t}$$

where
$R_{i,t}$ is the return on an environmentally responsible (or less responsible) equity portfolio. $R_{m,t} - R_f$ is the return on a value-weighted portfolio that represents the overall market return in excess of a risk-free rate of return. Portfolios that are more vulnerable to this factor have a higher systematic risk ("beta"), and high-beta stocks should deliver a higher return in the long run. SMB_t is the return difference between a small cap portfolio and a large cap portfolio: small stocks have historically outperformed large capitalization stocks. HML_t is the return difference between a "value" portfolio (with a high book/

market value ratio) and a growth (low book/market value) portfolio: value stocks have historically outperformed growth stocks. MOM_t is the return difference between a portfolio of past twelve month winners and a portfolio of past twelve-month losers: momentum strategies that buy return winners and sell short losers have delivered positive risk-adjusted returns.[6]

Correcting for exposure to these factors is important because environmentally screened portfolios are known to display tilts towards SMB, HML, and MOM. The Fama-French (1993) three-factor alpha (α_i in equation 3) and the Carhart (1997) four-factor alpha (α_i in equation 4) are the intercepts from these regressions, and represent the average abnormal (or risk-adjusted) portfolio return. Academic studies interpret alpha along several lines. One interpretation of alpha is that the portfolio compensates investors for exposure to a risk premium that is not properly captured by the variables in the three- and four-factor models. The alternative interpretation is that the portfolio comprises stocks that are "mispriced" by the market, such that its returns are different from those predicted by a market-equilibrium model.

In a world with a significant number of values driven environmental investors, we would expect that environmentally controversial stocks earn positive alpha, or that responsible stocks earn negative alpha, because values-driven trades affect stock prices. By contrast, profit-seeking environmental investors expect that environmentally responsible stocks are undervalued and therefore produce positive alpha.

Whether one of these predictions holds, or dominates, in reality is an empirical question that has attracted the attention of recent studies. These studies are summarized in Table 25.3.[7] The first evidence revolved around the performance of investment portfolios formed based on firms' eco-efficiency. Derwall, Guenster, Bauer & Koedijk (2005) evaluated equity portfolios based on eco-efficiency scores collected from Innovest Strategic Value Advisors. They report that a best-of-sector portfolio that contained the top 30 percent of US stocks with highest eco-efficiency scores relative to industry peers delivered a four-factor alpha of 4.15 percent per year over the period 1995–2003. In contrast, a portfolio of firms with lowest scores produced a negative but non-significant alpha of –1.8 percent.

Subsequent studies contribute by testing portfolios that are formed based on alternative environmental responsibility criteria. For example, Kempf & Osthoff (2007) used various responsibility indicators from Kinder, Lydenberg, & Domini (KLD) to form US portfolios that score high and low on responsibility. They found that some environmentally high-ranked portfolios earned a higher four-factor alpha than did their lowest ranked counterparts over the period 1991–2004. An interesting pattern emerges from their analysis of firms for which KLD reports "controversies", and those for which KLD reports "strengths." A portfolio comprising companies with "strengths"

---

[6] Fama & French (1993) and Carhart (1997) provide further details on the construction of the factor-mimicking portfolios and the performance evaluation model.

[7] Other studies measure these alphas for *mutual funds* that apply environmental investment criteria. Because these are SRI funds that adopt environmental screens in conjunction with other CSR criteria, they are not reviewed in this chapter. Bauer, Koedijk, & Otten (2005), Bauer, Derwall, & Otten (2007), and Renneboog, Ter Horst, & Zhang (2008) are examples.

earned a 3.6 percent annualized abnormal return, while a portfolio formed based on "weaknesses" earned a statistically non-significant alpha of 0.6 percent. Other ranking procedures, such as a best-of-sector ranking on environmental performance, resulted in performance differences between the best- and worst-scoring portfolios that were generally positive but statistically not always significant.

Outside the US, there is less conclusive evidence about the performance of environmentally responsible investments, and the studies that document it experience small-sample problems. Vermeir, Van de Velde & Corten (2005) used company ratings from French CSR rating firm Vigeo to examine three-factor alphas of portfolios that comprise stocks from the European Monetary Union (EMU) area. They concluded that various high-rated portfolios, including an environmentally responsible portfolio, have performed better than low-rated portfolios over the period 2000–2004, but not significantly so. Brammer, Brooks, & Pavelin (2006) studied the association between social responsibility measures and stock returns for firms in the United Kingdom. Using information from EIRIS, they formed portfolios based on various social responsibility criteria, and subsequently examined risk-adjusted returns. Concerning environmental issues, a high-ranked portfolio outperformed its low-ranked counterpart, by about 3.5 percent on an annualized basis.

Taken as a whole, it appears that positive long-term abnormal returns, if any, were earned by portfolios composed of firms that display relatively strong environmental performance. By contrast, portfolios composed of firms with relatively weak or controversial environmental performance did not earn an abnormal return.

It is interesting to note that these results on long-term performance appear to display a consistency with studies on stock market reactions immediately following news events about firms' environmental performance. Event studies, which we do not discuss in detail here, hint that the financial market is less attentive to positive corporate environmental responsibility practices than to negative issues. Hamilton (1995) and Klassen & Mclaughlin (1996) found that firms' stock prices change in reaction to news about environmental performance. But Klassen & Mclaughlin (1996) additionally suggest that positive returns after positive news are smaller than negative returns after negative news. Why these investors react significantly to negative news is a question that is addressed in Karpoff, Lott, & Wehrly (2005). They estimate that the decline in firms' market value subsequent to their environmental violations is equivalent to the size of the legal penalty imposed.[8] Taken together, the results of these studies could imply that investors fully anticipate the negative effects of poor environmental performance on firms' future cash flows, but not fully the potentially positive effects associated with strong environmental performance. Finding that long-term abnormal returns are positive for stocks with environmental strengths and less significant for stocks with environmental weaknesses is consistent with this idea.

---

[8] We note that firms may experience a relatively weaker decline in stock return after negative events when they have a good track record on environmental disclosure. See Cho et al. in Chapter 24 for a discussion.

Table 25.3 Long-run performance of stock portfolios formed based on environmental performance

Study	Scope / Period	Environmental rating data	Portfolio selection criterion	Alpha high-ranked portfolio	Alpha low-ranked portfolio
Derwall et al. (2005)	US 1995–2003	Innovest	Best vs. worst of sector eco-efficiency	4.15%*	–1.81%
Kempf & Osthoff (2007)	US 1991–2004	KLD	Environmental strength vs. controversy portfolio	3.60%*	0.59%
Vermeir et al. (2005)	Europe 2000–2004	Vigeo	Best versus worst of sector ratings	1.03%	0.12%
Brammer et al. (2006)	UK 2002–2005	EIRIS	Best versus worst environmental score	18.59%	15.14%

Annualized alphas are derived from monthly returns and based on numbers reported in the referenced studies.

Note: Vermeir et al. (2005) report three-factor alphas whereas other studies report four-factor alphas. Brammer et al. (2006) evaluate $R_{i,t}$ instead of $R_{i,t} - R_f$. * indicates alpha is statistically significant at conventional levels

The results altogether support the errors-in-expectations hypothesis underlying the profit-seeking view towards environmentally responsible investing. A dominant effect of values-driven environmental investors on asset prices, as is predicted by the shunned stock hypothesis, finds currently little support in these empirical studies. One explanation for this observation is that, in aggregate, the number of values-driven investors that adopts environmental investment criteria is not yet large enough to affect stock prices.[9]

IMPLICATIONS FOR PRACTITIONERS AND RESEARCHERS

The distinction between values-driven and profit-seeking environmental investors yields a number of interesting practical implications that deserve closer attention by practitioners and scholars.

First, the earlier discussed evidence on investment performance teaches us that profit-seeking investors, both environmental and mainstream investors, can benefit from screening companies along positive environmental performance measures. It turns out that firms that display strengths or best-of-sector environmental performance have delivered attractive risk-adjusted returns, at least in the US market. Future research should examine whether these results carry over to other markets, based on long-run returns data.

Second, the environmental investment domain has so far not explicitly recognized that both values-driven and profit-seeking motives among investors shape environmentally responsible investment decisions. The observation that there is heterogeneity in pecuniary and non-pecuniary preferences among environmental investors calls for a rethinking of environmentally and socially responsible investment practices. One question that logically arises is whether environmentally responsible investing should be used as a sole term for describing investment practices performed by a group with heterogeneous motives (Derwall et al. 2010).

Third, economic logic teaches us thatsupport for the errors-in-expectations hypothesis concerning environmentally responsible investing will diminish over time, whereas the shunned-stock hypothesis may find more support in the future. Profit-seeking investors cannot exploit the financial market's misunderstanding of information about firms' future cash flows permanently, because investors eventually learn about their mistakes, and prices will be restored to fundamental value (see, e.g., Core, Guay, & Rusticus 2006; Derwall et al. 2010). In contrast, it stands to reason that values-driven investor segments are likely to grow because of people's growing concerns about global warming and sustainable development.

---

[9] Consistent with this conclusion, Derwall et al. (2010) suggest that predominantly the prices of "sin" stocks (such as those from tobacco, alcohol, and gambling industries) are currently affected by values-driven investors.

As a result, the role of values in financial markets may become much more significant in the long run, and unavoidable in the discussion about optimal investment policy.

In fact, the growing emphasis on serving values can be witnessed from mutual fund families, which increasingly realize that their products should not cater to a homogenous clientele group that is only served by maximum risk-adjusted return. Rather, mutual fund companies appear to maximize the level and stability of their funds' cash flows through a market segmentation strategy aimed at competing, based on both performance and non-performance aspects of their investment vehicles (see, e.g. Massa 2003). Furthermore, the proliferation of funds that cater to specific segments may benefit the brand value of the fund family, which in turn may generate positive "spillover" (money flows) to a wider range of funds within the family. Bollen (2007) and some follow-up studies provide evidence that mutual funds that integrate environmental and other social responsibility issues form a tool to cater to values-driven segments of the investor population. Specifically, socially responsible mutual funds enjoy lower cash flow volatility and weaker outflow after negative financial performance compared to non-SRI funds, which suggests that investors choose to be more loyal to SRI funds because of some non-pecuniary benefits. Thus, while product differentiation may require each individual fund manager to limit investment scope and constrain investment skills, it enriches fund families' opportunities' to deliver alternative investment vehicles.

For several institutional investors, however, tailoring to a heterogeneous group of individuals is much more complicated. A substantial number of endowment funds, pension funds, and foundations are managed by fiduciaries who act based on guidelines that prioritize achieving superior investment returns. The critical assumption here is that preferences of the beneficiaries fully revolve around financial pay-off, despite our suggestion that not all participants share this goal. Even when this assumption is relaxed and trustees integrate environmental values into investment policy, the question arises whether these values match those of the beneficiaries. This problem is particularly delicate in cases where pension funds aim to serve the aggregate rather than different segments, and in cases where beneficiaries are not free in choosing a different pension fund.

These concerns are also relevant to regulators and legislators. They could play an important role in encouraging large institutions to invest in recognition of different environmental preferences among their clientele. Some governments have already enacted legislation that allows beneficiaries to select portfolios that best match their pecuniary and non-pecuniary preferences. An interesting example is Australia's Superannuation Legislation Amendment Act, which grants employees more rights in determining how their compulsory contributions are managed (see Richardson 2010 for examples).

All these unresolved issues illustrate the need for more research into the pecuniary and non-pecuniary motives and goals that investors have in mind when they choose environmentally responsible investments. There is a clear appetite for segmentation and investor profiling methods that are better than those seen so far (see Gershoff & Irwin [Chapter 20]; and Devinney [Chapter 21] this volume, for valuable suggestions in the context of consumers). An important question here is how segmentation of environmentally responsible investors based on their pecuniary and non-pecuniary motivations translates into specific investment rules and subsequent evaluation of financial *and* environmental performance of the investment decision. Another important question is whether pecuniary and non-pecuniary goals among environmentally responsible investors change over time. What these developments will imply for financial markets and optimal investments policy are interesting questions for further research.

CONCLUSION

Studies illustrate that investors differ regarding the pecuniary and non-pecuniary benefits that they intend to derive from SRI. Knowing their heterogeneous motives and preferences is important for understanding investors' influence on financial markets, optimal investment policy, and corporate behavior. Following this reasoning, we examine whether environmentally responsible investing is a concept that attracts a heterogeneous group of investors. Based on a synthesis of various literatures, we conclude that environmentally responsible investing attracts *both* values-driven investors and profit-seeking investors, consistent with the investor segmentation suggested by Derwall et al. (2010).

Theory predicts that values-driven environmental investors drive up the cost of capital (expected return) of environmentally controversial companies, drive down the cost of capital of responsible companies, and sacrifice return for non-pecuniary benefits. Profit-seeking environmental investors expect to earn superior risk-adjusted returns because the market is slow in recognizing the relation between corporate environmental performance and firms' future cash flows. Assuming that the two alternative views do not pertain to different forms of environmental investing, a natural question that follows is which of these views holds, or dominates. Empirical evidence suggests that environmentally responsible investments have not delivered inferior risk-adjusted returns. Rather, stocks of environmentally responsible companies have earned positive abnormal returns in the US market.

Although studies up to this point suggest that it is possible to achieve positive abnormal returns through environmental investment, the growing evidence that non-pecuniary characteristics matter to values-driven investors creates new challenges for investment policy and regulation. Research that explains how fiduciaries can adequately meet the various non-pecuniary needs of investors is still in an early stage. This chapter lays some groundwork for research in the future.

REFERENCES

Angel, J. J., & Rivoli, P. (1997). "Does Ethical Investing Impose a Cost upon the Firm? A Theoretical Perspective". *Journal of Investing*, 6(4): 57–61.

Bauer, R., Derwall, J., & Otten, R. (2007). "The Ethical Mutual Fund Performance Debate: New Evidence from Canada". *Journal of Business Ethics*, 70(2): 111–124.

—— Koedijk, K., & Otten, R. (2005). "International Evidence on Ethical Mutual Fund Performance and Investment Style," *Journal of Banking and Finance*, 29(7): 1751–1767.

—— & Smeets, P. (2010). "Social Values and Mutual Fund Clientele." Working Paper, European Centre for Corporate Engagement.

Beal, D. & Goyen, M. (1998). "Putting Your Money Where Your Mouth Is. A Profile of Ethical Investor," *Financial Services Review*, 7(2): 129–143.

Bollen, N. (2007). "Mutual Fund Attributes and Investor Behavior," *Journal of Financial and Quantitative Analysis*, 42(3): 683–708.

Brammer, S., Brooks, C., & Pavelin, S. (2006). "Corporate Social Performance and Stock Returns: UK Evidence from Disaggregate Measures," *Financial Management*, 35(3): 97–116.

Carhart, M. M. (1997). "On the Persistence in Mutual Fund Performanc." *Journal of Finance*, 52(1): 57–82.

Core, J., Guay, W., & Rusticus, T. (2006). "Does Weak Governance Cause Weak Stock Returns? An Investigation of Operating Performance and Investors' Expectations," *Journal of Finance*, 62(1): 655–687.

Cox, P., Brammer, S., & Millington, A. (2004). "An Empirical Examination of Institutional Investor Preferences for Corporate Social Performance," *Journal of Business Ethics*, 52: 27–43.

Damodaran, A. (2002). *Investment Valuation*. Wiley, 2nd edition.

Derwall, J., Guenster, N., Bauer, R., & Koedijk, K. (2005). "The Eco-Efficiency Premium Puzzle," *Financial Analysts Journal*, 61(2): 51–63.

—— Koedijk, K., & Ter Horst, J. (2010). "A Tale of Values-Driven and Profit-Seeking Social Investors." Working Paper, Tilburg Sustainability Center, Tilburg University.

Devinney, T. M. (2010). "Using Market Segmentation to Understand the Green Consumer," in P. Bansal and A. Hoffman (eds), *Oxford Handbook of Business and the Environment*, Oxford: Oxford University Press.

Dowell, G. A., Hart, S., & Yeung, B. (2000). "Do Corporate Global Environmental Standards Create or Destroy Market Value?" *Management Science*, 46(8): 1059–1074.

Eurosif (2008). "European SRI study 2008." Available at <http://www.eurosif.org>

Fama, E. F. & French, K. R. (1993). "Common Risk Factors in the Returns on Stocks and Bond," *Journal of Financial Economics*, 33(1): 3–56.

Gershoff, A. D. & Irwin, J. D. (2011). "Why Not Choose Green? Consumer Decision Making for Environmentally Friendly Products," in P. Bansal and A. Hoffman (eds), *Oxford Handbook of Business and the Natural Environment*, Oxford: Oxford University Press.

Griffin, J. J. & Mahon, J. F. (1997). "The Corporate Social Performance and Corporate Financial Performance Debate. Twenty-Five Years of Incomparable Research," *Business & Society*, 36(1): 5–31.

Guenster, N. Derwell, J., Bauer, R., & Koedijk, K. (2009). "The Economic Value of Corporate Eco-Efficiency," *European Financial Management*, forthcoming.

Haigh, M. (2010). "What Counts in Social Managed Investments: Evidence from an International Survey," *Advances in Public Interest Accounting*, 13: 35–62.

Hamilton, J. T. (1995). "Pollution as News: Media and Stock Market Reactions to the Toxics Release Inventory Data," *Journal of Environmental Economics and Management*, 28(1): 98–113.

Hamilton, S., Jo, H., & Statman, M. (1993). "Doing Well While Doing Good? The Investment Performance of Socially Responsible Mutual Funds," *Financial Analysts Journal*, 49(6): 62–66.

Hart, S. L. & Ahuja, G. (1996). "Does It Pay To Be Green? An Empirical Examination of the Relationship between Emission Reduction and Firm Performance," *Business Strategy and the Environment*, 5(1): 30–37.

Heinkel, R., Kraus., R., & Zechner, J. (2001). "The Effect of Green Investment on Corporate Behavior," *Journal of Financial and Quantitative Analysis*, 36(4): 431–449.

Hong, H. & Kacperczyk, M. (2009). "The Price of Sin: the Effects of Social Norms on Markets," *Journal of Financial Economics*, 93(1): 5–36.

—— & Kostovetsky, L. (2009). "Values and Finance," Working Paper, Princeton University.

Johnson, R. A. & Greening, D. W. (1999). "The Effects of Corporate Governance and Institutional Ownership Types on Corporate Social Performanc," *Academy of Management Journal*, 42(5): 564–576.

Karpoff, J. M., Lott, Jr., J. E., & Wehrly, E. W. (2005). "The Reputational Penalties forEnviron-mental Violations: Empirical Evidence," *Journal of Law and Economics*, 48(2): 653–675.

Kempf, A. & Osthoff, P. (2007). "The Effect of Socially Responsible Investing on Financial Performance," *European Financial Management*, 13(5): 908–922.

King, A. & Lenox, M. (2002). "Exploring the Locus of Profitable Pollution Reduction," *Management Science*, 48(2): 289–299.

Klassen, R. D. & Mclaughlin, C. P. (1996). "The Impact of Environmental Management on Firm Performance," *Management Science*, 42(8): 1199–1214.

Kurtz, L. (2008). "Socially Responsible Investment and Shareholder Activism," in Crane, A., Mcwilliams, A., Matten, D., Moon, J., and Siegel, D. (eds.), *The Oxford Handbook of Corporate Social Responsibility*, Oxford University Press, 249–280.

Lev, B. & Schwartz, A. (1971). "On the Use of the Economic Concept of Human Capital in Financial Statements," *Accounting Review*, 46(1): 103–112.

Lewis, A. & Webley, P. (1994). "Social and Ethical Investing: Beliefs, Preferences and the Willingness to Sacrifice Financial Return," in Lewis, A. and Warneryd, K-E. (eds.), *Ethics and Economic Affairs*, Routledge, London, 171–182.

Lintner, J. (1965). "The Valuation of Risk Assets and the Selection of Risky Investments in Stock Portfolios and Capital Budgets," *Review of Economics and Statistics*, 47(1): 13–37.

Margolis, J. D., Elfenbein, H. A., & Walsh, J. P. (2007). "Does it Pay to Be good? A Meta-Analysis and Redirection of Research on the Relationship Between Corporate Social and Financial Performance." Working Paper, Harvard University.

Massa, M. (2003). "How do Family Strategies affect Fund Performance? When Performance-Maximization is not the only Game in Town," *Journal of Financial Economics*, 67(2): 249–304.

Merton, R. C. (1987). "A Simple Model of Capital Market Equilibrium with Incomplete Information," *Journal of Finance*, 42(3): 483–510.

Neubaum, D. O. and Zahra, S. A. (2006). "Institutional Ownership and Corporate Social Performance: The Moderating Effects of Investment Horizon, Activism, and Coordination," *Journal of Management*, 32(1): 108–131.

Owen, A. L. and Qian, Y. (2008). "Determinants of Socially Responsible Investment Decisions." Working Paper, Hamilton College.

Porter, M. E. and Van Der Linde, C. (1995). "Green and Competitive. Ending the Stalemate," *Harvard Business Review*, 73(5): 120–135.

Renneboog, L., Ter Horst, J., & Zhang, C. (2008). "The Price of Ethics: Evidence from Socially Responsible Mutual Funds," *Journal of Corporate Finance*, 14(3): 302–322.

Richardson, B. (2010). "From Fiduciary Duties to Fiduciary Relationships for Socially Responsible Investment," PRI Academic Conference 2010 Paper.

Rosen, B. N., Sandler, D., & Shani, D. (1991). "Social Issues and Socially Responsible Investment Behavior: A Preliminary Empirical Investigation," *Journal of Consumer Affairs*, 25(2): 221–234.

Russo, M. V. & Fouts, P. A. (1997). "A Resource-Based Perspective on Corporate Environmental Performance and Profitability," *Academy of Management Journal*, 40(3): 534–559.

SIF (2005). "2005 Report on Socially Responsible Investing Trends in the United States," US Social Investment Forum, Available at <http://www.socialinvest.org>

Sharpe, W. F. (1964). "Capital Asset Prices: A Theory of Market Equilibrium under Conditions of Risk," *Journal of Finance*, 19(3): 425–442.

Shane, P. B. & Spicer, B. H. (1983). "Market Response to Environmental Information Produced Outside the Firm," *Accounting Review*, 58(3): 521–285.

Statman, M., Fisher, K., & Anginer, D. (2008). "Affect in a Behavioral Asset-Pricing Model," *Financial Analysts Journal*, 64(2): 20–29.

Vermeir, W., Van De Velde, E., & Corten, F. (2005). "Sustainable and Responsible Performance," *Journal of Investing*, 14(3): 94–100.

Vyvyan, V., Ng, C., & Brimble, M. (2007). "Socially Responsible Investing: the Green Attitudes and Grey Choices of Australian Investors," *Corporate Governance: an International Review*, 15(2): 370–281.

Waddock, S. A. & Graves, S. B. (1997). "The Corporate Social Performance-Financial Performance Link," *Strategic Management Journal*, 18(4): 303–319.

Walley, N. & Whitehead, B. (1994). "It's Not Easy Being Green," *Harvard Business Review*, 72(3): 46–52.

Wernerfelt, B. (1984). "The Resource-Based View of the Firm," *Strategic Management Journal*, 5(2): 171–180.

Williams, G. (2007). "Some Determinants of the Socially Responsible Investment Decision: A Cross-County Study," *Journal of Behavioral Finance*, 8(1): 43–57.

CHAPTER 26

···

ENVIRONMENTAL RISKS AND FINANCIAL MARKETS: A TWO-WAY STREET[1]

···

JEAN-LOUIS BERTRAND AND
BERNARD SINCLAIR-DESGAGNÉ

IN the corporate world, risks are random adverse events that might bring down an annual or seasonal business plan and entail losses in revenue, profitability, or the net valuation of assets. Company managers have a basic choice when it comes to risks. They can decide that some are either "strategic," in which case shareholders will demand additional returns for bearing them, or "non-strategic," in which case shareholders, creditors, and other stakeholders will expect such risks to be transferred or mitigated. Over time, companies have learned to deal with the non-strategic market risks associated with foreign exchange, interest rates, or commodity prices. They routinely make forecasts of market outcomes, which they include at inception in budget preparation. They regularly turn to banks, insurers, and financial engineers to hedge such risks when necessary, often using over-the-counter forward contracts or options. They must finally ensure that corporate reports explain what those risks are and imply for the company, in order to obey current regulations.[2]

A similar approach now holds increasingly for environmental risks, as such risks are ever more accurately captured in financial markets. Through corporate reports, rating agencies, the business press, and financial networks, environmental information currently spreads more and more rapidly across investors, thereby fostering efficient risk-

---

[1] We wish to thank the editors of this Handbook, Tima Bansal and Andy Hoffman, for suggestions and comments which greatly helped improving the content and format of this chapter. All errors and shortcomings are of course ours.

[2] See, for instance, International Accounting Standards such as IAS32 39, IFRS 7, or IFRS 9.

sharing and financial innovation. This chapter constitutes a brief introduction to this recent development. The following two sections successively sketch the dual role financial markets play in (1) transmitting environmental information and (2) providing instruments companies can use to manage environmental risks. We next pay extra attention to the latter, since the former is already exhaustively and competently covered in this Handbook (see Bauer & Derwall [Chapter 25]; Cho, Patten, & Roberts [Chapter 24]; and Gray & Herremans [Chapter 22] in this volume). For a broader introduction to the whole area of environmental risk management, the interested reader may turn to Sinclair-Desgagné (2001, 2005). The fourth section of this chapter considers at greater length one specific financial instrument—weather derivatives—which seems particularly relevant in coping with the consequences of climate change and associated weather variations; it discusses the impact of weather volatility on companies and economies as a whole, and provides an assessment of the new market for weather derivatives. Valuable research issues are raised as we proceed and in the concluding section.

Conveying environmental information (and incentives)

Financial markets tend to pass on three main pieces of environmental information: the economic impact of exogenous *extreme events such as hurricanes or tornadoes and other non-catastrophic weather events* (rainfall, snowfall, changes in temperatures, etc.), company *disclosures* about environmental risks, and the business effect of *news* such as oil spills or class actions. After providing some historical background, this section will review the current literature which considers how markets—stock markets in particular—react to these different outcomes. It will also show that financial statements as they exist today do not necessarily provide all the information that users need in order to make economic and investment decisions.

Weather events

In the nineteenth century, Eduard Brückner (1862–1927), an Austrian geographer and climatologist was one of the first scientists to work on the impact of climate variability on politics and economics. Like other contemporaneous geographers or economists, such as Tooke, Huntington, Beveridge, or Heckscher, he believed that climate cycles played an important role in economic cycles through their influence on harvest levels and therefore crop prices (Brückner 2000). He thereby preceded Labrousse (1895–1988), who considered that harvests and their underlying weather variables were the key determining factors of crop prices and rural employment levels, which in turn affected urban revenues (Pfister 1988). Labrousse's statistical work is still a standard reference today, but Stanley Jevons (1835–1882) is known to have been the first econo-mist to build a model showing the relationship between climate and economic cycles. Moreover, Jevons (1875) found out that the estimated sunspot cycle of 10.45 years cor-related almost perfectly with the time length between two economic crises, which he calculated to be 10.43 years based on crop prices (1878). His "sunspot theory" asserted that sunspots impacted vintages and harvests, and therefore the price of food and raw materials and the state of the money market. Garcia-Mata & Shaffner (1934) later denied causality between sunspots and economics, but they cited Moore (1914, 1923) and his work on precipitation cycles in the United States, which coincided with the eight-year economic cycles measured between 1881 and 1921. In 1929, Humphreys linked volcanic and solar activities to Earth temperature. This work was then used by Garcia-Mata & Shaffner to correlate New York and London stock market indices and solar activity.

Attempts to measure the effects of climate are still being pursued, of course. There is, for instance, a large literature on the consequences of natural disasters for the economy at large (Popp 2006) and insurance and finance more specifically (see, e.g. Kunreuther 1998, Froot 1999, and OECD 2003, and the references therein).[3] A recurrent conclusion is that the frequency and overall human, material, and financial costs of events like hur-ricanes, cyclones, tornadoes, etc. have grown significantly over the past decades (trigger-ing a wave of financial innovations we will briefly talk about in the next section). The impact of disasters on the stock market, however, will differ across sectors, depending on each sector's respective exposure. In a careful study focusing on Australian capital mar-kets, Worthington & Valadkhani (2005) found, for example, that consumer discretion-ary, financial services (notably insurance) and materials were the sectors most adversely affected by disasters.

Corporate environmental disclosures

The content and financial impact of corporate disclosures is another classical subject in the finance and accounting literature (see, e.g. the respective surveys by Verrechia 2001 and Dye 2001). Corporate disclosures now increasingly include data on how a company is doing with respect to the environment (see Epstein 1996, and this Handbook's Chapter 23 by Cho, Patten, & Roberts). Pressure naturally comes from worried investors and employees, but also from regulators. The literature now offers analyses of the managerial (oftentimes strategic) motives for making environmental disclosures (Sinclair-Desgagné & Gozlan 2003; Dasgupta et al. 2007; Lyon & Kim 2010; and Bauer & Derwall's Chapter 25 in this volume) and of their linkages with financial markets (Arts et al. 2008).

[3] Recent accounts on how markets react to mild (yet significant) weather distortions, such as abnormal temperatures or precipitations, will be covered in the subsection 'Defining weather risks' later in this chapter.

When it comes to climate and weather risks, corporate environmental disclosures are still deficient in several respects, however. A five-year (2004–2008) study of the disclosure of weather information by SBF 120 NYSE/Euronext-traded companies recently showed that one report in six referred to weather conditions in the Management Commentary section of the annual report to explain company performance (Bertrand 2010). In the food and beverage sector, 80 percent of firms mentioned the weather; other figures were 71 percent among utilities, 43 percent in construction and 25 percent in the tourism and leisure sector. The study revealed, moreover, that three out of five companies that brought up the weather did *not* provide any information on its financial consequences nor on their risk management policy towards weather risks, while only one in four had a dedicated paragraph and clear explanation about such risks. Overall it can be said that company managers make an opportunistic use of weather conditions, as references to weather generally seem to only justify disappointing financial performance. Another recent study of weather risks disclosures by European utilities reported that nine in ten annual reports contained some reference to the weather, but only one in three disclosed weather as a risk and a mere one in ten described weather risks clearly.[4] Disclosure quality also varied over the years: there was significantly more information in 2007 than in 2008, which can be explained by the mild spring of 2007 that had a negative impact on most utilities sales, while the weather in 2008 was more favourable to the utility sector.

This situation might now change rapidly, following the US Securities and Exchange Commission (SEC) release of its new *Guidance Regarding Disclosure Related to Climate Change* in February 2010. Weather risks can no longer be ignored by shareholders and other financial stakeholders, or be misused by company executives. As SEC Chairman Mary Schapiro declared when the Guidance was issued:

> under our traditional framework the company must evaluate the impact [...] on the company's liquidity, capital resources, or results of operations, and disclose to shareholders when that potential impact will be material. [...] if something has a material impact on a company then it is something that needs to be disclosed [...], whether those risks are due to increased competition or severe weather.

News about environmental incidents

Finally, it is expected that financial markets will respond somehow negatively to news about environmental incidents such as lawsuits and accidental pollutions. Using a sample of forty-seven events involving Canadian firms between 1982 and 1991, Lanoie & Laplante (1994), for example, observed that Canadian shareholders react unfavorably to the announcement of suit settlements, but not to the announcement of lawsuits.[5] More

---

[4] Institute for Accounting, Controlling and Auditing of the University of St. Gallen and Celsius Pro Ltd, "Disclosure of weather risks of European utilities," White Paper, published in January 2010.

[5] Interestingly, this is contrary to what happens with American shareholders. Lanoie & Laplante (1994) infer that "These results yield support to the view that the enforcement of environmental regulations has generally been more severe in the United States than in Canada."

recently, Capelle-Blancard & Laguna (2010) found that petrochemical firms experience a drop of 1.3 percent in market value in the two days following a chemical disaster. Over six months after a toxic release happened, the total loss amounted to as much as 12 percent; this delayed reaction suggests that investors in stock markets may not fully and immediately grasp environmental risks, but may end up asking for a premium as their perception of riskiness grows.

This ability of financial markets to convey environmental information has led several researchers and policymakers to inquire whether they can provide incentives to firms to deal better with environmental risks (see, e.g. Tietenberg & Wheeler 2001). In support of this view, Lanoie et al. (1998), for instance, conclude that the evidence drawn from American and Canadian studies indicates that capital markets do indeed react to the release of information, and that large polluters are affected more significantly from such releases than smaller polluters. The phenomenon apparently holds in emerging countries as well (see, e.g. Ruiz-Tagle 2006, in a study that took place in Chile).

How those incentives materialize will depend, of course, on the available means, which now rely in a partial but increasingly important way on financial management.

HEDGING AGAINST ENVIRONMENTAL RISKS (NOTABLY CLIMATE AND WEATHER)

Environmental risks can be classified into five categories. *Regulatory, reputation* and *litigation* risks arise from poor regulatory compliance or irresponsible behavior. On the other hand, *physical* and *weather* risks refer to external occurrences—such as earthquakes and storms—a company cannot prevent. According to a KPMG (2008) study of fifty corporate reports addressing the business risks and economic impacts of climate change, regulatory risks are the most commonly cited by companies, followed by physical risks.

Table 26.1 shows the main instruments a company can use to cope with environmental risks. All have evolved considerably in recent years, and three are specifically meant to deal with the consequences of climate change: tradable emissions permits, catastrophe bonds, and weather derivatives.

The idea of trading emissions permits (or cap and trade) dates back to Coase (1960)'s seminal article. It is now implemented to efficiently limit the releases of several major pollutants, such as SO_2 (sulphur dioxide, which comes out of coal-burning electricity plants and is largely responsible for acid rain) and greenhouse gases. At this point, there is a wealth of research, data, and experience that can be called upon to analyze or design markets for emissions (see, e.g. Hansjürgens 2005 and the enclosed references). Most current discussions and remaining disagreements have to do with how to make initial allocations (should permits initially be auctioned or allocated for free?), who is allowed to trade (only certain large polluters or other stakeholders as well?), and how well cap

Table 26.1 Environmental business risks and financial remedies

Type	Description	Financial remedy
Regulatory	Government intervention at the international, regional, national or local levels to preserve the environment (limit GHG emissions) or natural resources (tariffs on fossil energies, incentives or targets on renewable energies)	Mandatory disclosures; Emission permits (when they exist, such as in the E.U. Emission Trading Scheme)
Reputation	Decrease in consumer confidence and brand value; destruction of intangible asset value	Voluntary disclosures; Ethical investments
Litigation	Procedural lawsuits granted by law or regulation; claims against individual companies for damages to the environment; actions from shareholders for not taking account of disclosing climate-change risks	Liability insurance
Physical	Hazards due to the impact of weather-related hazards such as storms, hurricanes, cyclones, typhoons, hailstorms, snowstorms which result in physical damage or prevent regular business from taking place	Natural disaster insurance; Catastrophic bonds
Weather	Variations in climate variables such as temperatures, precipitation, wind which have an impact on a company's sales, production and/or profits	Disclosures (voluntary or mandatory); Catastrophic bonds; *Weather derivatives*

and trade schemes regulate pollution compared with other policy instruments (such as taxes or voluntary approaches). Somewhat less understood so far are the nature and size of transaction costs and the role of intermediaries (such as carbon brokers) in determining these costs.

The first catastrophe bonds (or cat-bonds) were introduced in 1994, most market participants being insurance and reinsurance companies. Catastrophes being by definition low-probability events involving a large number of *simultaneous* individual losses, it was indeed appropriate to complement standard insurance contracts with this new financial instrument. Theoretical support for this proposition was notably provided by Graciela Chichilnisky, who summarizes the argument as follows (Chichilnisky 2006: 7):

> Correlated risks are hedged through securities by taking advantage of *negative* correlations. For example, most earthquakes in California are followed by a boom in the construction industry. Therefore appropriate securities can be created by investing in the construction industry. This has clear implications for hedging catastrophic hurricane risks. The rebuilding efforts in New Orleans following Katrina will involve hundreds of billions of dollars in local and federal funds and in private donations throughout the nation. By carefully structuring insurance and security contracts, the Katrina victims could therefore be compensated for their financial losses through the negative correlation between the catastrophe and the value created by rebuilding efforts.

Risk-linked securities transactions have since become common (see, e.g. the excellent account on the subject by Andersen 2002); total cat-bond issuance is now estimated at around US$ 8 billion, and it is growing.

Perhaps unfortunately, such a successful outcome has so far not been the case for weather derivatives, which the upcoming section will now discuss extensively.

THE INCIPIENT MARKET FOR
WEATHER DERIVATIVES

Hedging against adverse weather is certainly not new. Claudius (Roman emperor AD 41 to 54), for example, used to offer financial protection against bad weather to merchants travelling back and forth the Mediterranean Sea with shiploads of wheat (Goetzmann & Rouwenhorst 2005). In the seventeenth century, the rice futures market was created to protect farmers from bad weather conditions, and Lloyds of London introduced an insurance (called "pluvius insurance") to protect its customers against precipitations. In the middle of the nineteenth century, Lloyds is also said to have created the very first weather derivative, thanks to an underlying index based on cumulated precipitation (Roberts 2002).

The rest of this section will now successively define weather risks, show how these risks matter for business firms and the economy as a whole, explain weather derivatives, and discuss the current and future state of the present market for these financial products.

Defining weather risks

Climate change risks span three distinct timescales: hours to days, months to seasons, and decades to centuries (Dutton 2002a).

Decades to centuries relate to long cycles of glacial and warmer periods which have historically determined human migrations, agricultural productivity, and economic prosperity. It has now become an urgent issue since there is a risk human activities may significantly alter the climate with some known consequences on the atmosphere and mostly unknown consequences on the economic landscape.

At the other end, hours to days relate to extreme events. They are low probability, high impact risks and have been the primary focus of governments and the private sector as they take lives and cost large sums of money. The United States alone has endured ninety-six weather disasters over the last thirty years (1980–2009), with overall damages exceeding one billion dollars each and a total cost (using a GNP inflation index) of seven hundred billion dollars (NCDC, WHO);[6] it is estimated that extreme events have caused about 30,000 deaths in the US between 1990 and 2006 (Goklany 2007) and about 600,000 deaths globally in the 1990s (WHO fact sheet 2005).

Days to months and seasons, finally, have to do with variations and deviations from normal climate. We refer to them as *weather risks*. Weather risks are thus *non-catastrophic weather events* which have a *financial impact on company sales or profits*. They relate to any measurable (and eventually tradable) variation to a definable benchmark such as changes in temperature, rainfall, snowfall or even wind speed (Brockett et al. 2005; Bertrand and Buchar 2009). Weather risks mostly affect volume indicators: if the winter is warmer than usual, energy consumption is lower irrespective of the price of this energy. They are high-probability low-impact events, although their economic consequences can be quite significant as we will see later. According to WMO, weather risks are likely to weigh even more on the economy as disturbances in temperature, precipitation, etc. might increase in magnitude due to climate change.

Quantifying weather risks

W. Daley, the US Secretary of Commerce in the Clinton administration, once stated in front of the US Congress that 25 percent of GDP and 80 percent of US companies were weather-sensitive. Meanwhile, the United Nations have put the weather-sensitive

---

[6] NCDC: National Climatic Data Centre; WHO: World Health Organization.

proportion of world GDP at 17 percent, the Deutsche Bank estimates that weather risks affect four-fifths of the World economy (Auer 2003), and ABN-Amro Bank shows that weather risks matter for between 20 and 30 percent of industrial production in Europe and 35 percent of that in the United States (Triana 2006).

Some industry sectors are of course more sensitive to weather than others. Dutton (2002b) pinpoints agriculture, energy, construction, transportation, tourism and leisure, and retail as the most weather-sensitive sectors (the upshot being that one-third of U.S. GDP turns out to be weather-sensitive). Changnon (1999) estimates that the mild winter due to El Niño was directly responsible for an additional 5.6 billion dollars in US retail sales.

Larsen (2006) has developed a methodology based on the sensitivity to temperatures and precipitations of eleven activity sectors in the US and concluded that at least 16.2 percent of the US economy was exposed to weather risks (2006). In 2008, WeatherBill extended Larsen's work to the rest of the world and published a study which ranked sixty-eight countries based on their exposure to weather. This study shows in fact that as much as 23 percent of the United States GDP was weather-sensitive (i.e. 2.6 trillion dollars); percentages are 33 per cent, 45 per cent and 37 per cent for Japan, China, and Germany respectively. Other studies by Météo France have concluded that changes in weather variables explained up to 90 percent of electricity consumption, 80 percent of beer consumption, 45 percent of textile sales, and a high share of selected food products (Marteau et al. 2004).

At the microeconomic level, Roll (1984) was a pioneer when he studied the influence of weather on the return of the Frozen Concentrated Orange Juice (FCOJ) future contract.[7] FCOJ was an ideal candidate, as the production of oranges was restricted to a small geographical area, and weather was about the only variable which could explain price movements. Roll found that unexpected weather ("weather surprises") was a key explanatory factor for the price of the FCOJ future, although it only explained a small portion of the financial performance. Roll's conclusions were later reinforced by Boudoukh et al. (2007) who focused on freezing temperatures.

More recently, Bertrand (2010) studied the weather-sensitivity of quarterly reported sales for a selection of companies listed on the Paris stock exchange. Since companies are not systematically required to publish the geographical distribution of their sales, the analysis is limited to those fifty-eight companies for which information is available. To grasp the influence of weather conditions, Bertrand measured the correlation between changes in quarterly sales for each company and changes in temperatures, sunlight hours, humidity, and precipitation levels; each company was therefore a point in a five-dimension space (each company being characterized by five correlation figures). He then kept those companies for which correlations were statistically significant and projected the five-dimension points onto the two-dimension principal plane using Principal Component Analysis. The two-dimension principal plane which

---

[7] See also Doll (1971) on weather and corn, and Fleming et al. (2006) on soybeans, wheat and corn.

retains 87.9 percent of the information contained in the initial five dimensions is displayed in Figure 26.1. The horizontal axis is mainly related to temperatures and explains 67 percent of the overall correlation information whilst the vertical axis which is mostly related to precipitation explains 20.6 percent. From Figure 26.1, we see that *Bricorama*'s sales, for instance, are positively correlated to high temperatures but are not very sensitive to sunny or wet conditions. At the other end of the horizontal axis, we see that the sales of *Cie Parisienne de Chauffage*, an energy company, are positively correlated with cold temperatures. *Malteries Franco-Belge*, a beer company, has some sensitivity to warm temperatures but is highly positively impacted by sunny conditions.

The merit of Figure 26.1 is to plot and characterize companies according to their weather exposure. For the purpose of this chapter, it demonstrates that weather conditions affect company sales and activity sectors in different ways and with different intensities. It confirms, for example, the existence of a positive correlation between the energy sector's performance and cold temperatures (*Electricité de Strasbourg* and *Cie Parisienne de Chauffage*). The DIY sector is at the other end of the weather spectrum (*Mr Bricolage* and *Bricorama*). It is also worth noticing that the textile sector's (*Etam*) exposure is the opposite of that of the beverage sector (*Malterie Franco-Belge*).

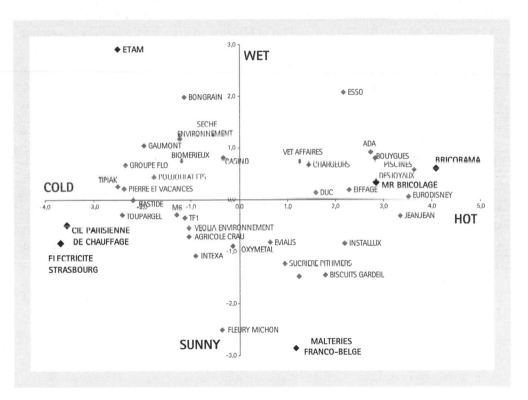

FIGURE 26.1 Weather-sensitivity display of a selection of Paris-listed companies

Bertrand (2010) did the same type of analysis to compare quarterly sales and abnormal weather changes (i.e. warmer than usual, wetter than usual, etc.). This further confirmed that *weather is a specific risk*: not all companies are affected the same way, even when they operate in the same industry (such as, for instance, *Groupe Pierre et Vacances* and *ClubMed* in leisure and tourism, and *VM Matériaux* and *Mr Bricolage* in DIY).

Weather conditions do not just affect sales volumes. They can also influence business profitability. Roustant (2003) investigates the impact of exceptionally favourable weather conditions on the profitability of four companies (in the beverage, leisure, and energy sectors), and shows that it was possible to link favorable weather conditions to increased returns.

To test the impact of weather on the financial performance of listed companies, Bertrand (2010) analyzed weekly returns of a selection of stocks on the Paris exchange. Arbitrage Pricing Theory (APT) models were used to explain weekly returns, with economic, financial, and weather explanatory variables over a period of 473 weeks.[8] After running a partial least-square (PLS) regression, results were consistent with classical finance theory. The most important explanatory variable of a single stock return was the market itself. Accumulated weather conditions, however, could account for a significant portion of returns on some stocks; on some occasions, they could matter even more than the economic factors altogether. Two examples can illustrate this finding—one in the food and beverage business (*Danone*), and one in the textile industry (*Etam*). Economic variables introduced in the absence of weather variables explained 72 percent of returns for *Danone* and 86 percent of returns for *Etam*. When weather variables (cumulative three-month indices) were put in, the percentage of *Danone*'s returns explained by economic variables dropped to 27 percent whilst weather accounted for 46 percent; in the case of *Etam*, the percentage of returns explained by economic variables dropped to 37 percent and weather explained close to 50 percent of financial performance.

Bertrand (2010) finally used Capital Asset Pricing Models (CAPM) to calculate weather-beta coefficients for a selection of weather-sensitive stocks, thereby showing that it was possible, by selecting the appropriate stocks, to either create weather-exclusively-dependent portfolios of stocks or neutralize portfolios from the effects of the weather. To confirm the *specific* character of weather risks, the same models were run on the Paris stock indices themselves (CAC 40, SBF 120, SBF 250) and showed no weather-sensitivity at the 1 percent, 5 percent or 10 percent levels. This further confirmed that weather-sensitivity is a *specific* risk which can be eliminated through diversification.

In sum, while the above works end up measuring different things in different ways, they altogether concur that weather risks have a major impact on firms and the overall economy.

[8] For a comprehensive description of Multi-Index and APT models, see for instance Elton et al. (2007). The economic explanatory variables used in our models were the returns of the Paris stock index SBF 120, currency rates, commodity prices, inflation, and yield curve. Weather variables were cumulative temperatures, precipitations, humidity levels, and sunlight reports over 1, 2, and 3 months.

Corporate weather-risk management

The previous results demonstrate one important fact: weather can be a *material* risk.[9] Literally, the direction the wind is blowing can boost or damage company results. Shareholders may thus demand to be told when they are bearing weather risks, so they can distinguish apart performance that is weather-related from performance that is related to management skills and decisions.

A company that wishes to manage weather risk properly may find it sufficient to integrate weather information in operational management by creating appropriate weather-specific indicators to be used in the company ERM system (exactly the same way other financial indicators, such as foreign exchange or interest rates, are used). As an illustration, METNEXT, which helps companies measure their sensitivity to weather, and NIELSEN have together designed weather-sensitive indicators for hundreds of product families (ice-cream, soup, cheese, water, etc.), which can be used by manufacturers, distributors, supermarkets and advertisers to optimize their business activity. If the volatility of sales or earnings due to changes in weather conditions is deemed to be too high, taking appropriate financial cover is the only way to transfer some of the risk away.

The basic weather instrument is a *swap* (OTC) or a *future* (exchange-cleared), which is equivalent to a traditional forward contract.[10] It is characterized by its amount, maturity date (generally less than six months), and the tick value. *Options* are also available. They give the right to the buyer to buy or sell an underlying future or an underlying weather index, in which case the option is cash-settled.

Weather derivatives

Weather derivatives look like any traditional derivative instrument, except that the underlying commodity is a weather index. A weather index is, for instance, an average temperature or cumulated precipitations figure measured at a stated location during an explicit period (Dischel & Barrieu 2002). Filippi & Retaureau (2009) provide an accurate and complete overview of the topic, together with a nice and thoughtful application.

The most frequently used weather indices are temperature-based. Since weather derivatives were initially created for the needs of the energy sector, a useful weather index had to respond to the specific traits of this sector: in the winter, every drop of one degree below the comfort temperature of 18°C generates additional energy consumption. The larger the fall in temperature, the more energy is required. Hence, the "degree-day" was introduced. If no energy is required on one given day, the value of the

---

[9] Information is material if its omission or misstatement could influence the decisions that users (of annual reports) make on the basis of [a company's] financial information.

[10] That is, a commitment to exchange a defined quantity of a good or a product at a future date at a price agreed upon at the time the transaction is done.

"degree-day" for that day is zero. Otherwise, it is the positive difference between actual and comfort temperatures. Degree-days are accumulated over months or seasons, and serve as underlying indices for most exchange-cleared weather derivatives. Heating degree-days (cooling degree-days) reflect the amount of energy required to heat (cool) homes or businesses in the winter (in the summer). Contracts using HDD and CDD indices are available on the Chicago Mercantile Exchange (CME) for some thirty cities in the US, ten in Europe, and six in Australia and the Asia Pacific.[11]

Weather derivatives can be standard exchange-cleared or OTC instruments. Weather derivatives are cash-settled and the cash settlement is calculated from the value of a unit (tick) of the weather index, as agreed upon by the parties to the trade. Unlike traditional market indices, however, weather indices cannot be bought, sold, borrowed, or stored. It is then impossible to create a portfolio with the underlying commodity and replicate the behaviour of the derivative instrument. The upshot is that weather-derivatives markets are incomplete (Davis 2001) and classical derivative valuation methods, such as Black & Scholes or Cox, Ross, & Rubinstein, do not work (Dischel 1998; Geman 1999; Cao & Wei 2000; Moreno 2000; 2003; Young & Zariphopoulou 2002; Geman & Leonardi 2005). Fortunately, there are ways to price derivatives in incomplete markets.

Brocket (2005) reviews a number of valuation methods for weather derivatives.[12] They can be summarized in four categories: *actuarial*, traditional methods using a *replication* of the underlying weather index using weather swaps (Jewson & Zervos 2005) or energy derivatives (Geman 1999), *equilibrium* models (Richards et al. 2004), and *utility functions*. In practice, since end-users tend to keep hedging instruments in their books until expiry, the valuation of the hedge is done against the average expected value of the underlying weather index (Cao & Wei 1998; 2005; Laurent & Roustant 2003; Brix, Jewson, & Ziehmann 2002; Campbell & Diebold 2004; Alaton, Djehiche, & Stillberger 2002; Brody, Syroka, & Zervos 2002; Richards, Manfredo, & Sanders 2004). There may not be one single universally accepted way to price weather derivatives, but corporate risk managers (and shareholders!) should know that hedging instruments do exist and can be used to cover weather exposure.

A slow beginning

According to most literature reviews of weather derivatives, the first weather financial transaction (as we know them today) took place in the United States at the end of the nineties, after the deregulation of the US energy sector and an unusually warm winter

---

[11] The list of cities and contracts specifications can be obtained from the Chicago Mercantile Exchange (CME) Group.

[12] That is: super-replication (El Karoui & Quenez 1995), quadratic approaches (Follmer & Sondermann 1986; Schweizer 1988; 1991; Bouleau & Lamberton 1989; Duffie & Richardson 1991), quantile hedging and shortfall minimization (Cvitanic 1998; Follmer & Leukert 1999; 2000), marginal utility approach (Davis 1998), and indifference pricing (Hodges & Neuberger 1989; Davis, Panas, & Zariphopoulou 1993).

caused by El Niño. This deregulation meant that energy companies could no longer transfer additional production or distribution costs to their customers as they used to through Weather Normalization Adjustment systems (Cooper 2004). Their shareholders realized quickly that electricity consumption (and therefore profits) was very dependent on temperature and pressured management to find ways to secure profits and lower the volatility of returns. Weather derivatives and weather risk management were born. The first transaction to be widely advertised took place in 1997 between Enron and Koch Industries.[13] Enron rapidly emerged as the leader in the new weather derivatives market and was soon followed by companies in the reinsurance sector such as AIG, American Re, or Swiss Re (Nichols 2005). In Europe, the first transaction took place in 1998 between Enron and Scottish Hydro Electric.

The first exchange-cleared contracts were launched by the CME in the summer of 1999. Traded volumes remained relatively low for some years, and the collapse of Enron in 2001 did not help. Enron's staff quickly redeployed elsewhere in the industry and, in June 2006, the Weather Risk Management Association (WRMA) announced that the notional value of weather-risk contracts had grown almost fivefold, from $9.7 billion to $45.2 billion.

Relative to the stakes (trillions of dollars), however, the volume of weather hedging seems quite low (by comparison, daily foreign exchange turnover was in excess of 3.2 trillion dollars at the same time). After ten years, the weather-derivatives market is still in its infancy. The post-financial crisis figures published by WRMA indicated an annual volume of only $15 billion in 2009. CME statistics show that the drop in weather contracts between August 2007 and August 2009 was 46 percent, while the volume on other CME products only dropped by 14 percent over the same period. Curiously, this happened at a time when getting ready to mitigate the consequences of climate change had never been so important.

In a study with three associations of European treasurers (in France, Belgium, and Luxemburg), Bertrand (2008) selected 130 companies outside the energy sector which were active in risk management and extensively used derivatives. The objective was to understand if weather risks were identified and quantified, and to explore the reasons why an active treasury organization did not use weather derivatives when weather risks mattered. The study shows that 67 percent of respondents considered that weather risks significantly affected their company's sales and profits, but 79 percent of companies had never analyzed and quantified the financial impact of these risks and 85 percent had no intention to do so in the foreseeable future. Stated explanations ran as follows. *Nine in ten CFOs thought that their competitors had not analyzed weather risks.* Other factors were the lack of disclosure framework and accounting rules (22%), the absence of relevant hedging instruments (16%), and insufficient in-house skills (9%). Interestingly, one in two treasurers who had not analyzed weather risks thought nevertheless that their financial impact would be negligible (for those who had, the financial consequences of

---

[13] In 1996, Aquila and Continental Edison had entered a transaction to protect the latter against a drop in temperature in August. The same year, another transaction had involved Enron and Florida Power and Light.

weather risks could exceed those of other market risks). A study of small and medium-size companies produced similar results (Bertrand 2010).

Things might be changing, however. CME and Storm Exchange presented the results of a US study on 205 finance executives during the Risk and Insurance Management Annual Conference in San Diego (2008). Eighty-two percent of senior finance and risk management executives thought they might have to change their business models over the long term to cope with climate change and weather volatility, 59 percent said their company's exposure to risks stemming from weather volatility meant that the impact on their financial performance could be significant (38 percent) or severe (21 percent) and that they needed protection from it. On the other hand, 51 percent of respondents said that their company was not well prepared to deal with the day-to-day economic risks stemming from the weather, while the only industry that seemed to have made the effort to analyze its exposure to weather risks was the energy sector. In February 2010, the US Securities Exchange Commission observed that "some business leaders are increasingly recognizing the current and potential effects on their companies' performance and operations, both positive and negative, which are associated with climate change."[14]

CONCLUSION

This chapter briefly looked at the relationship between environmental risk management and financial markets. Its main message is that this is a two-way street. On the one hand, capital markets convey valuable information about environmental events and good or bad managerial practices; on the other hand, they can often be harnessed to hedge environmental risks, using new financial instruments such as weather derivatives.

Research clearly suggests that environmental events, in particular weather turbulences that may result from climate change, could have a significant financial impact on business and the economy. Yet, investors and financial managers show rather low awareness when it comes to mitigating the risk of adverse weather conditions using amended operational management and/or new financial products. Additional research should now be performed to understand this phenomenon and see what can be done about it. Readers wanting to reflect more about this, or about any of the topics presented above, may turn to some of the quoted articles. If many end up doing so then this chapter will have fulfilled its purpose.

REFERENCES

Aerts, W., Cormier, D., & Magnan, M. (2008). "Corporate Environmental Disclosure, Financial Markets and the Media: An International Perspective," *Ecological Economics* 64(3): 643–659.

---

[14] Commission Guidance Regarding Disclosure Related to Climate Change, 2 February 2010.

Alaton, P., Djehiche, B., & Stillberger, D. (2002). "On Modelling and Pricing Weather Derivatives," *Applied Mathematical Finance* 9(1): 1–20.

Andersen, T. (2002). "Innovative Financial Instruments for Natural Disaster Risk Management," Inter-American Development Bank – Sustainable Development Department Technical Paper Series.

Auer, J. (2003). "Weather Derivatives Heading for Sunny Times," Deutsche Bank Research, Frankfurt Voice, 25 February, 8 pages.

Barrieu, P. & El Karoui, N. (2004). "Présentation générale des dérivés climatiques," *Actes de la Société Française de Statistique*, 29 January.

Bertrand, J.-L. (2008). "Les entreprises européennes face à la gestion des risques météorologiques," in *Économies et Sociétés*, Série *Économie de l'Entreprise*, K 18(6–7): 1225–1249.

—— (2010). "La Gestion des Risques Météorologiques en Entreprise," Unpublished doctoral dissertation.

—— & Bachar, K. (2009). "La valeur d'une entreprise peut-elle être sensible à la météo? Une étude empirique du marché français," *Management & Avenir* 28: 56–72.

Boissonnade, A., Heitkemper, L. & Whitehead, D. (2002). "Weather Data: Cleaning and Enhancement," *Climate Risk and the Weather Market*, Risk Books, 73–93.

Boudoukh, J., Richardson, M., Yuqing, S. & Whitelaw, R. (2007). "Do Asset Prices Reflect Fundamentals: Freshly Squeezed Evidence From the OJ Market," *Journal of Financial Economics* 83(2): 397–412.

Bouleau, N., & Lamberton, D. (1989). "Residual Risks and Hedging Strategies in Markovian Markets," *Stochastic Processes and Their Applications* 33: 131–150.

Brix, A., Jewson, S. & Ziehmann, C. (2002). "Weather Derivative Modelling and Valuation: a Statistical Perspective," in *Climate Risk and the Weather Market*, ed. S. Dischel, Risk Books, London, 127–150.

Brockett, P., Wang, M. & Yang, C. (2005). "Weather Derivatives and Weather Risk Management," *Risk Management and Insurance Review* 8(1): 127–140.

Brody, D. C., Syroka, J. & Zervos, M. (2002). "Dynamical Pricing of Weather Derivatives," *Quantitative Finance* 2: 189–198.

Brückner, E. (2000). "The Sources and Consequences of Climate Change and Climate Variability in Historical Times," in N. Stehr and H. Von Storch (eds.), Kluwer Academic Publisher.

Campbell, S. D., & Diebold, F. X. (2004). "Weather Forecasting for Weather Derivatives," CFS Working Paper.

Cao, M. & Wei, J. (1998). "Pricing Weather Derivatives: An Equilibrium Approach," Mimeo.

—— —— (2000). "Pricing the Weather," *Risk Magazine*, 67–70.

—— —— (2005). "Stock Market Returns: A Note on Temperature Anomaly," *Journal of Banking and Finance* 29: 1559–1573.

Capelle-Blanchard, G. & Laguna, M. A. (2010). "How Does the Stock Market Respond to Chemical Disasters?" *Journal of Environmental Economics and Management* 59: 192–205.

Chang, S.-C., Chen, S.-S., Chou, R. & Lin, Y.-H. (2008). "Weather and Intraday Patterns in Stock Returns and Trading Activity," *Journal of Banking and Finance* 32: 1754–1766.

Changnon, S. A. (1999). "Impact of 1997–98 El Niño Generated Weather in the United States," *Bulletin of the American Meteorological Society*, 1819–1827.

Chichilnisky, G. (2006). "Catastrophic Risks: The Need for New Tools, Financial Instruments and Institutions," Mimeo, Columbia University.

Coase, R. H. (1960). "The Problem of Social Cost," *Journal of Law and Economics*, vol. 3: 1–44.

Cooper, V. (2004). "Mitigating Your Weather Exposure," *Electric Light and Power*, January issue.

Cvitanic, J. (1998). "Minimizing Expected Loss of Hedging in Incomplete and Constrained Markets," Preprint, Columbia University.

Dasgupta, S., Wang, H. & Wheeler, D. (2007). "Disclosure Strategies for Pollution Control," in *The International Yearbook of Environmental and Resources Economics* (eds.) H. Folmer and T. Tietenberg, Edward Elgar.

Davis, M. (1998). "Option Prices in Incomplete Markets," In *Mathematics of Derivative Securities*, Cambridge University Press.

—— (2001). "Pricing Weather Derivatives by Marginal Value," *Quantitative Finance* 1(3): 305–308.

—— Panas, V. & Zariphopoulou, T. (1993). "European Option Pricing with Transaction Costs," *SIAM Journal on Control and Optimization* 31: 470–493.

Dischel, R. (1998). "Black-Scholes Won't Do," *Weather Risk Supplement to the Risk Magazine*, October issue.

—— & Barrieu, P. (2002). "Financial Weather Contracts and Their Application in Risk Management," in *Climate Risk and the Weather Market* (ed.) R. S. Dischel, Risk Books, London, 25–41.

Doll, J. (1971). "Obtaining Preliminary Bayesian Estimates of the Value of a Weather Forecast," *American Journal of Agricultural Economics* 53: 651–655.

Duffie, D. & Richardson, H. (1991). "Mean-Variance Hedging in Continuous Time," *Annals of Applied Probability* 1: 1–15.

Dutton, J. A. (2002a). "The Weather in Weather Risk," in *Climate Risk and the Weather Market* (ed.) S. Dischel, Risk Books, London, 185–211.

—— (2002b). "Opportunities and Priorities in a New Era for Weather and Climate Services," *Bulletin of the American Meteorological Society* 83(9): 1303–1311.

Dye, R. A. (2001). "An Evaluation of 'Essays on Disclosure' and the Disclosure Literature in Accounting," *Journal of Accounting and Economics* 32(1–3), 181–235.

El Karoui, N., Quenez, M. C. (1995). "Dynamic Programming and Pricing of Contingent Claims in Incomplete Market," *SIAM Journal of Control and Optimization*, 29–66.

Elton, E. et al. (2006). *Modern Portfolio Theory and Investment Analysis*. 7th edition, Ed. Wiley, 752 pages.

Epstein, M. J. (1996). *Measuring Corporate Environmental Performance: Best Practices for Costing ang Managing and Effective Environmental Strategy*, Irwin.

Filippi, A. & Retaureau, C. (2009). "Weather Derivatives Structuring and Pricing: Application to the Maple Syrup Industry in Québec," Mimeo, École polytechnique, downloadable at <http://%20www.enseignement.polytechnique.fr/economie/chaire-business-economics/RetaureauFilippirapportcomplet.pdf>

Fleming, J., Kirby, C., & Ostdiek, B. (2006). "Information, Trading, and Volatility: Evidence from Weather-Sensitive Markets," *The Journal of Finance*, vol. LXI, No. 6: 2899–2930.

Föllmer, H. & Leukert, P. (1999). "Quantile Hedging", *Finance and Stochastics*, 3: 251–273.

—— —— (2000). "Efficient Hedging: Cost versus Shortfall Risk," *Finance and Stochastics*, 4: 117–146.

Föllmer, H. & Sondermann, D. (1986). "Hedging of Non-redundant Contingent Claims," in W. Hildenbrand and A. Mas-Colell (eds.) *Contributions to Mathematical Economics*, 205–223.

Froot, K. A., (ed.) (1999). *The Financing of Catastrophe Risk*, National Bureau of Economic Research Project Report.

Garcia-Mata, C. & Shaffner, F., (1934). "Solar and Economic Relationships: A Preliminary Report," *The Quarterly Journal of Economics,* Vol. 49(1): 1–51.

Geman H. (1999). "The Bermuda Triangle: Weather, Electricity and Insurance Derivatives," in *Insurance and Weather Derivatives: From Exotic Options to Exotic Underlyings* (ed.) H. Geman, 197–203.

—— & Leonardi, M. P. (2005). "Alternative Approaches to Weather Derivatives Pricing," *Managerial Finance* 31(6): 46–72.

Goetzmann, W. & Rouwenhorst, G. (2005). *The Origins of Value: The Financial Innovations that Created Modern Capital Markets.* Oxford University Press.

Goklany, I. M. (2007). "Deaths and Death Rates due to Extreme Weather Events: Global and U.S. Trends," *International Policy Press* (a division of International Policy Network). Available online at <http://www.csccc.info/reports/report_23.pdf>

Hansjürgens, B. (ed.) (2005). *Emissions Trading for Climate Policy: US and European Perspectives.* Cambridge University Press.

Hirschleifer, D. & Shumway, T. (2003). "Good Day Sunshine: Stock Returns and the Weather," *Journal of Finance* LVIII(3): 1009–1032.

Hodges, S. & Neuberger, A. (1989). "Optimal Replication of Contingent Claims under Transaction Costs," *Review of Futures Markets,* 8: 222–239.

Intergovernmental Panel on Climate Change (2001). *Climate Change 2001: Impacts, Adaptation, and Vulnerability,* Cambridge University Press.

Jacobsen, B. & Marquering, W. (2008). "Is It the Weather?," *Journal of Banking and Finance* 32: 526–540.

Jevons, W. S. (1875). "The Periodicity of Commercial Crises and its Physical Explanation," in *Investigations in Currency and Finance,* Macmillan: London, 334–342.

—— (1884). "The Solar Period and the Price of Corn," in *Investigations in Currency and Finance,* Macmillan, London, 194–205.

—— & Zervos, M. (2005). "No-Arbitrage Pricing of Weather Derivatives in the Presence of a Liquid Swap Market." Working paper, 1–13.

Jewson, S., Ziehmann, C. and Brix, A. (2002). "Use of Meteorological Forecasts in Weather Derivative Pricing," In *Climate Risk and the Weather Market* (ed.) S. Dischel, Risk Books, London, 169–183.

Kamstra, M., Kramer, L. & Levi, M. (2003). "Winter Blues: A SAD Stock Market Cycle," *American Economic Review* 93(1): 324–343.

—— (2008). "Is It the Weather: Comment," *Journal of Banking and Finance* 33: 578–582.

KPMG (2008). "Climate Changes Your Business: KPMG's Review of the Business Risks and Economic Impacts at Sector Level," 76 pages.

Kunreuther, H. & R. J. Roth, R. J. (eds.), (1998). *Paying the Price: The status and role of insurance against natural disasters in the United States,* John Henry Press.

Lanoie, P. & Laplante, B. (1994). "The Market Response to Environmental Incidents in Canada: a Theoretical and Empirical Analysis", *Southern Economic Journal* 60(3): 657–672.

—— —— & Roy, M. (1998). "Can Capital Markets Create Incentives for Pollution Control?" *Ecological Economics* 26(1): 31–41.

Larsen, P. (2006). "An Evaluation of the Sensitivity of US Economic Sectors to Weather," Master's Thesis, Cornell University.

Laurent, J.-P. & Roustant, O. (2003). "Weather Derivatives and the Stock Market: A Risk Assessment." Working paper, AFFI.

Lettre, J. (2000). "Weather Risk Management Solutions: Weather Insurance, Weather Derivatives." November research paper, Rivier College.

Llewellyn, J. (2007). *The Business of Climate Change*. Report prepared for Lehman Brothers.

Lyon, T. P. & Kim, Eun-Hee (2010). "Strategic Environmental Disclosure: Evidence from the DOE's Voluntary Greenhouse Gas Registry," *Journal of Environmental Economics and Management*, forthcoming.

MacMichael, A. & Woodruff, R. (2004). 'Climate Change and Risk to Health,' *BMJ* 329: 1416–1417.

Marteau, D., Carle, J. Fourneaux, S., Holz R. & Moreno, M. (2004). *La Gestion du Risque Climatique*. Economica, Paris.

Meehl, G. A., Zwiers, F., Evans, J., Knuston, T., Mearns, L. & Whetton, P. (2000). "Trends in Extreme Weather and Climate Events: Issues Related to Modelling Extremes in Projections of Future Climate Change," *Bulletin of the American Meteorological Society* 81: 427–436.

Moore, H. (1914). *Economic Cycles, Their Law and Cause*. Ed. Macmillan co.: New York.

Moreno, M. (2000). "Riding the Temp," FOW, Special Supplement Weather Derivatives, December.

—— (2003). "Weather Derivatives Hedging and Swap Illiquidity," *WRMA*, June.

Müller, A. & M. Grandi (2000). "Weather Derivatives: A Risk Management Tool for Weather Sensitive Industries," *The Geneva Papers on Risk and Insurance* 25(2): 273–297.

Nichols, M. (2005). "Confounding the Forecast", *Environmental Finance* , 16 February NOAA (National Oceanic and Atmospheric Administration), US Department of Commerce, Economic Statistucs for NOAA, 4th edition.

Organization for Economic Cooperation and Development (OECD) (2003). "Catastrophic Risks and Insurance." Papers and proceedings of the conference on "Policy Issues in Insurance."

Pardo, A. & Valor, E. (2003). "Spanish Stock Returns: Where is the Weather Effect?," *European Financial Management* 9(1): 117–126.

Patz, J. (2004). "Climate change: Health Impacts May Be Abrupt as Well as Long-Term," *BMJ* 328: 1269–70.

Pfister, C. (1988). "Fluctuations climatiques et prix céréaliers en Europe du XVIe au XXe siècle", *Annales. Histoire, Sciences Sociales*, 43ème année, No. 1 (Janvier–Février), 25–53.

Popp, A. (2006). "The Effects of Natural Disasters on Long –Run growth," in *Major Themes in Economics*, Spring 2006.

Richards, T., Manfredo, M. & Sanders, D. (2004). "Pricing Weather Derivatives," *American Journal of Agricultural Economics* 8(4): 59–86.

Roberts, J. (2002). "Weather Risk Management in the Alternative Risk Transfer Market," *Climate Risk and the Weather Market* (ed.) S. Dischel, Risk Books, London, 215–229.

Roll, R. (1984). "Orange Juice and Weather," *American Economic Review* 74: 861–880.

Roustant, O. (2003). "Produits dérivés climatiques: aspects économétriques et financiers," Unpublished doctoral dissertation.

Ruiz-Tagle, M. T. (2006). "How Do Capital Markets Respond to Environmental News?" Discussion paper no. 22-2006, Department of Land Economy, University of Cambridge.

Saunders, E. M. J. (1993). "Stock Prices and Wall Street Weather," *American Economic Review* 83: 1337–1345.

Schweitzer, M. (1988). *Hedging of Options in a General Semimartingale Model*. Dissertation ETHZ no. 8615, Zurich.

—— (1991). "Option Hedging for Semimartingales," *Stochastic Processes and Their Applications* 37: 339–363.

Sinclair-Desgagné, B. (ed.) (2005). *Corporate Strategies for Managing Environmental Risks*, in The International Library of Environmental Economics and Policy, Volume XX, Ashgate Publishing Limited, 2005.

—— (2001). "Environmental Risk Management and the Business Firm," in *The International Yearbook of Environmental and Resource Economics 2000/2001: A Survey of Current Issues*, H. Folmer and T. Tietenberg (eds.), Edward Elgar, June 2001.

—— & Gozlan, E. (2003). "A Theory of Environmental Risk Disclosure," *Journal of Environmental Economics and Management* 45: 377–393.

Tietenberg, T. & Wheeler, D. (2001). "Empowering the Community: Information Strategies for Pollution Control," in *Frontiers of Environmenal Economics* (eds.) H. Folmer, H. L. Gabel, S. Gerking, and A. Rose, Edward Elgar.

Triana, P. (2006). "Are You covered?" *European Business Forum*, Autumn issue, 50–55.

Trombley, M. (1997). "Stock Prices and Wall Street Weather: Additional Evidence," *Quarterly Journal of Business and Economics* 36: 11–22.

Tufan, E. & Hamarat, B. (2004). "Do Cloudy Days Affect Stock Exchange Returns: Evidence from Istanbul Stock Exchange," *Journal of Naval Science and Engineering* 2: 177–126.

Verrechia, R. E. (2001). "Essays on Disclosure," *Journal of Accounting and Economics* 32(1–3): 97–180.

WeatherBill (2008). "Global Weather Sensitivity: A Comparative Study," Report downloadable on <http://www.weatherbill.com/learn/research/>

Worthington, A, & Valadkhani, A. (2005). "Catastrophic Shocks and Capital Markets: A Comparative Analysis by Disaster and Sector," *Global Economic Review* 34(3): 331–344.

Young, V. & Zariphopoulou, T. (2002). "Pricing Dynamic Insurance Risks Using the Principle of Equivalent Utility," *Scandinavian Actuarial Journal* 4: 246–79.

Zeng, L. (2000). "Pricing Weather Derivatives," *Journal of Risk & Finance* 1(3): 72–78.

....

CHAPTER 27

CORPORATE DECISION-MAKING, NET PRESENT VALUE, AND THE ENVIRONMENT

....

BRYAN R. ROUTLEDGE

A large fraction of economic activity takes place in corporations. Obvious to anyone interested in environmental issues, much of this activity has direct and large environmental consequences. The goal of this chapter is to illuminate how decision-making—at least the business school finance perspective—occurs. As we explore this topic, we can understand where and how environmental consequences show up in this decision-making process.

The central feature of modern corporations is the separation of ownership and management. Corporations are owned by many disperse and heterogeneous shareholders. However, the long-term strategic and the day-to-day decision-making about resource allocation, including resources with environmental consideration, is delegated to management (e.g. the CEO). The gains from separating ownership from management include the liquidity of financial markets, the diversification benefits from portfolios that span thousands of companies, and the investment of specialized skill professional managers. A downside of this arrangement is that aligning everyone's interests is challenging. Mix in environmental issues, and aligning everyone's interests does not become any easier.

In economics, any delegation of decision-making creates an "agency" problem. With the separation of ownership and management, an obvious agency relationship to consider is that of managerial incentives. This agency structure with the CEO as the agent of the shareholders is much studied in finance. How can shareholders motivate the CEO to focus on shareholder interests? Executive pay contracts and other oversight mechanisms are designed to mitigate against perquisite consumption (e.g. corporate jets), inappropriate risk-taking, empire building (e.g. ill-advised takeovers) and other conflict of interests, while offering incentives for the CEO to work hard. This is a challenging problem. However, in my view, when thinking about the environmental consequences of decisions, there is a deeper, more important, and less studied problem: Just what are "shareholder interests"? More specifically, are shareholders unified in their goals and objectives for the corporation? What happens when they are not?

Think of any decision with important environmental consequences. It would be unusual if it were simple. Even if we are focusing only on the cash flow implication of environmental decisions, it is still not simple. Characterizing the random variable representing just cash flow implications of an environmental consequence is hard. Fines and lawsuits that might result from an oil spill, for example, are highly uncertain. They are often the low probability events with big outcomes and few observations to ground estimation. Not only is this the sort of setting where cognitive biases are prevalent, it is also a natural setting for disagreement. More generally, of course, environmental policy involves a non-trival trade-off of costs and benefits, with different people drawing different conclusions. Some differences of opinion come from data that is non-intuitive or hard to access (think of the scientific knowledge needed to do or understand an environmental study). Other differences of opinions come from decisions having different impacts on different people (electric cars might reduce smog but increase production of chemicals used to make batteries). Or more basically, differences stem from differences in tastes and preferences (do you prefer a city park, golf course, or swimming pool?)

The goal of this chapter is to provide some background on shareholder unanimity and governance in general and specific to issues related to environmental impact. How do modern corporations choose projects, given a shareholder base that is diverse in preference and opinion? The issues are both deeply fundamental and practical. As you might expect, there is much that is open and unresolved. The plan is to start with Net Present Value ("NPV"). NPV or Value-Based Management is the cornerstone of corporate finance. Resource allocation (broad use of the term resource but think "capital budgeting") happens inside corporations intermediated with financial and goods markets. The basic idea is that, all shareholders, with differing views and preferences, agree that more wealth is better than less. Therefore a manager working for the shareholders need only focus on increasing wealth. This is directly implemented by calculating the NPV, the value of the cash flows relative to their cost. If the NPV is positive, the activity is a good one. The reason all shareholders agree on wealth is that differences of opinion and taste can be expressed in the goods and/or financial market—take your wealth and buy and/or save as it suites you.

Shareholder unanimity with the delegation of decision-making to managers with the NPV rule is a foundational issue in finance. It ties closely to Pareto optimality and the efficiency of a market-based economy. But, the NPV rule is practical. The "NPV rule" has a profound impact on the day-to-day management of almost every corporation. Business planning and action at every corporation will mostly likely (almost certainly, for the larger ones) involve an a NPV calculation.[1] Moreover, it turns out that finance professors (and text books etc.) happen to be very good at teaching NPV. It is something that students almost

---

[1] See Graham and Harvey (2001).

universally cling to as axiomatic. They do not always get the details of the calculation right, but they stick to the NPV principle. This is less true for other parts of a corporate finance curriculum. The ubiquity of NPV is worth noting. If your objective, as say an advocate for an environmental policy, is to change corporate behavior, you will need to speak in "NPV."

An NPV rule that unifies shareholders' diverse beliefs and preferences is impressive. It does, as you would expect, rely on a set of assumptions. We will look at these details more closely and focus in on the assumptions whose violation makes environmental policy nettlesome. Specifically, we will start with a simple example to illustrate how and why the NPV rule works. The stripped-down example will illustrate the assumptions underlying NPV and how they can and cannot reflect environmental concerns. Stepping out of the theoretical setting of NPV makes delegating decision-making ambiguous and hard. We will take a look at how things might work—and the vast sea of open questions—in the corporate governance of voting, corporate control, and manager-shareholder agency. These issues are, as you would expect, large and more general than environmental, so we will try to hone in on the issues that are more specific to the environmental setting.

FOUNDATIONS OF NPV

To see how and why managers and shareholders focus on NPV or wealth, we can work through a simple example. To help see how the example generalizes, a little notation for the model is helpful. If you prefer, you can jump down to the example without missing the argument that follows.

Most resource allocation decisions are both intertemporal and uncertain. We can think of time as discrete, with dates $t = 0, 1, 2, \ldots$. Uncertainty is represented by a sequence of random events. At each $t > 0$, an event z_t is drawn from a finite set Z, following an initial event z_0. One particular sequence of events is a history or path. The t-period history of events is denoted by $z^t = (z_0, z_1, \ldots, z_t)$. The set of all possible possible t-histories by Z^t. The evolution of events and histories is conceptually illustrated by an event tree, with each branch representing an event and each node a history or state.[2] Environments like this, involving time and uncertainty, are the starting point for most of finance. A typical person in such a setting has preferences over payoffs $c(z^t)$ for each possible history. For the time being, think of these payoffs as monetary (or, more carefully as a single numeraire good). We will see in a minute, that this is a central assumption we want to relax to consider environmental policy. Imposing a little structure on preferences, we can capture the preferences with a scalar-valued utility function, say $U(\{c(z^t)\})$ (the curly brackets remind us that preferences are over payoffs on the whole tree). There are two key assumptions on preferences. First, as mentioned, preferences depend only on payoffs. We revisit this

---

[2] Although it is not central to our topic, most of the tree-like structure is to allow an easy description of conditional probabilities. The alternative way this structure is described is with a set of terminal states and a filtration (sigma algebra).

shortly. Second, preferences are monotonic in that more is better than less. Think of two payoffs that are identical everywhere on the tree except at one node; we prefer the larger one. Of course, most decisions are not that obvious. A typical capital budgeting project at a corporation involves less payoff now in exchange for more (and risky) payoff later. This is the source of potential difference of opinion. Shareholders, with different preferences reflected in U, view trade-offs differently.

Preferences, captured by U, aggregate the time and risk embedded in the consumption stream. For concreteness, think of the utility function that is a simple linear aggregation of the time and risk dimensions. That is, we impose time additivity and expected utility structure

$$U(\{c(z_t)\}) = \sum_{t=0} \beta^t \sum_{z^t \in Z^t} p(z^t)u[c(z^t)] = E_0 \sum_{t=0} \beta^t u(c_t), \qquad (1)$$

where $0 < \beta < 1$. $p(z^t)$ is the probability of history z^t (and E_0 is the expectation operator), and u is a period/state utility function. These preferences are parsimonious: behavior over time and across states depends solely on the discount factor β, the probabilities p, and the function u. Note that the function u is not time or state dependent. Its curvature captures risk aversion. In this setting, we can think of different shareholders as having different discount rates ("patience") or curvature in the function u (a property that defines "risk aversion").[3]

Here is an example:

> *Example 1:* ABC Co. can spend $1,975,000 on Project X. The result will be to increase cash flows ("profits") by $2,328,900 next year if the economy is booming and $1,896,700 next year if the economy is in a recession. Probability of booming is 50%. One-year US Treasury Bill costs $98.00 now and pays $100.00 in one year. S&P 500 Index costs $1,110.69 now and in one year will be $1000.00 or $1400.00

This example is simple on several dimensions. First, the decision has implications for payoffs only at two dates, let's call them $t = 0, 1$. Uncertainty is also simple here as there are only two outcomes at date 1, $z_1 = z_b$ "boom" or $z_1 = z_r$ "recession". Both outcomes are equally likely.[4]

The project and the financial assets are just payoffs (cash-flows). The project, although highly stylized, captures the main aspects of capital budgeting. Cash is spent now $c(z_0) = -1975$ in exchange for future cash flows that are risky $c(z_b) = 2328.9$ or $c(z_r) = 1896.7$. Is this a good idea? It is easy to imagine a shareholder who is patient and not particularly risk averse and this project is attractive (think of a youngster saving for far-off retirement). It is also the case that a quite reasonable investor would be the opposite and this project is unattractive (think of a retiree living off savings). The bigger problem for the manager of ABC Co. is that he might have both types of investors as shareholders. How can differing views be resolved?

In the example there are two financial assets (all we need at the moment). The first asset is a risk-free bond with payoffs that are constant across the two outcomes $b(z_b) = b(z_r) =$

---

[3] For a more general explanation on modeling preferences, see Backus, Routledge, & Zin (2005).
[4] With just two dates and two outcomes, there the tree has just two paths $Z^1 = \{(z_0, z_b), (z_0, z_r)\}$. This is more notation than we need.

100. The price of this asset is 98.00. We can write this as the current payoff as $b(z_0) = -98$— if you buy a bond your cash is smaller by 98 today and larger by 100 at $t = 1$. The payoff on a broad portfolio of stocks (if you have run across the CAPM before, think "market portfolio") is risky in that its payoffs are not constant at date $t = 1$. Here we have $d(z_b) = 1000$ and $d(z_r) = 1400$. The current price of this asset, like the bond, we can think of as an outflow $d(z_0) = -1110.69$. Are either of these assets attractive to an individual? Again it depends on an individual's preference. The optimal amount of savings (how much of these assets to buy) and the optimal mix (the portfolio or asset allocation between stocks and bonds) will depend on individual preferences of patience and individual risk aversion.

It might be helpful to pause for a moment and ask where all these numbers might come from. First, the cash flows attached to the project—the initial cost and the subsequent risky cash flows—come from business analysis. Forecasting cash flows from sales and costs is not a trivial task. For any sizable project, it will involve many hours of work from many different parts of the organization. When we consider the environmental impacts below, we will think of them as a random variable that comes from analogous analysis (business, technological, environmental, etc.). In particular, the details of the project are not particular to "finance." Our example is overly simplistic here in that there are only two possible outcomes (states) for our project. This is an easy assumption to relax if we want to model cash flows with more sophisticated distributions (e.g. a normal distribution characterized by first and second moments). The financial information in the example is a bit easier to come by. Much of the information is simply "prices" that we can observe in real-time in financial markets. The state-contingent payoffs come from a financial model that we calibrate with past data.[5]

We can combine these financial assets into a portfolio. Table 27.1 lists the cash flows for a portfolio with an arbitrary number of bonds (y) and stocks (x). Notice that the portfolio cash flows are linear functions of the number of stocks and bonds you buy (or sell) and yield cash flow implications of $a(z_0)$ now and $a(z_r)$ and $a(z_b)$ at $t = 1$. That feature comes from ignoring transaction costs of buying and selling stocks (a relatively mild assumption given our objective to evaluate capital spending projects, and quite unrelated to the broader question of environmental impacts). For simplicity, x and y are real valued (ignore the fact that "shares" are bought in discrete units) and can be "negative" (you can sell stocks and sell bonds, if you like).

Back to our example: ABC Co. can spend $1,975,000 on Project X. Should it do so? We can calculate the NPV of the project by using the financial prices (and model) to determine the value of the project. In particular, we can find a portfolio that duplicates the cash flows on the project and, hence, informs us about the value of the project.

---

[5] The return on the bond is a risk-free 2%—something we can observe currently. The expected return on the stock, estimated from historic data, is 6% above the bond (called the equity risk premium) with a standard deviation of this return of about 18% per year. $d(z_b)$ and $d(z_r)$ are the solution to two equations. One for the mean return: $0.5 \log(d(z_b)/1110.69) + 0.5 \log(d(z_b)/1110.69) = 0.02 + 0.06$. And one for the variance: $0.5 (\log(d(z_b)/1110.69)-0.08)^2 + 0.5 (\log(d(z_b)/1110.69) - 0.08)^2 = 0.18^2$. I rounded a bit to make the calculations that follow a bit less tedious. If you are more familiar with discounting cash flows at the opportunity cost of capital, you can simply calculate returns based on these values to reach the same conclusion.

Table 27.1 Portfolios of Stock and Bonds

	$t = 0$ z_0 "now"	$t = 1$ $z_1 = r$ "recession"	$t = 1$ $z_1 = b$ "boom"
Buy y bonds	−98.00y	100y	100y
Buy x stocks	−1110.69x	1000x	1400x
Portfolio	= −1110.69x−98.00y = $a(z_0)$	= 1000x + 100y = $a(z_r)$	= 1400x + 100y = $a(z_b)$

Take a look at Table 27.2. The cash flows of the project are on the first line. The bottom line is the cash flows of a portfolio that just happens to have identical period one cash flows as Project X. We of course picked this portfolio to have exactly this property (by solving two linear equations). The reason this portfolio is interesting is that it tells the value of the cash flows for Project X. The NPV is calculated as value minus cost which in this case is $25,000 (= $2,000,000−$1,975,000). One way to state this: Project X "buys" a portfolio of 8.163 bonds and 1.080 stocks for 1,975,000. This is cheap relative to the value of $2,000,000, so the project is a good one and increases the wealth of shareholders by $25,000. Any shareholder who prefers more wealth to less (the monotonicity assumption we discussed above) views this project as a good idea the ABC Co. should invest in. In particular, even shareholders with different views on patience or risk aversion all arrive at the same conclusion about this project. They are unanimous. Why? Shareholders that do not like the risk characteristics of the project's cash flows need only adjust their personal portfolio. The project is similar to (exactly) a portfolio of stocks and bonds. If that portfolio does not suit you, sell some stock and buy some bonds. Adjustments to your portfolio do not change your current wealth level. For example, sell $50 in stock and buy $50 in bonds. Current wealth level is unchanged (ignoring transaction costs). Of course, the risk characteristics of your future cash flows has changed and, if you have done things right, better suit your risk preference.

Table 27.2 Project X and Similar Portfolios of Stock and Bonds

	($'000's)		
	$t = 0$ z_0 "now"	$t = 1$ $z_1 = r$ "recession"	$t = 1$ $z_1 = b$ "boom"
Project X	−1,9750	1,8967	2,3289
Buy y = 8.163 bonds	−8000	8163	8163
Buy x = 1.080 stocks	−1,2000	1,0804	1,5126
Portfolio	−2,0000	1,8967	2,3289

FURTHER READING

The basic concept of NPV dates back to Fisher (1930). However, coherent general equilibrium analysis of the topic is Arrow (1964) and Debreu (1959). For an understanding of how information is formally conveyed by prices to capital budgeting decisions, see Radner (1979).

ENVIRONMENTAL IMPLICATIONS

The NPV rule is a central foundation of finance and modern corporations. But does this setting consider environmental and other non-cash implications of projects or operations? The short answer is no and it makes life complicated. We can use our Project X example to see how/when/why things get more complicated. Let's add a few more details.

> *Example 2:* ABC Co. can spend $1,975,000 on Project X. The result will be to increase cash flows ("profits") by $2,328,900 next year if the economy is booming and $1,896,700 next year if the economy is in a recession. Probability of booming is 50%. [a] Building the project reduces green space in the city. [b] Air emissions increase in proportion with activity and cash flow.

This example is simple on several dimensions. Like our model of cash flows, the characterization of environmental impacts is not trivial and, usually, requires a fair bit of engineering and environmental economics expertise. However, we will take this analysis as given and again focus on the issue of shareholder unanimity. Can we summarize all the heterogeneous shareholders' views on these effects along one dimension analogous to the way NPV does for cash flow and wealth?

MONETARY

Let's start with shareholders "from out of town", with preferences defined only over the numeraire consumption good (money) as in equation (1). This scenario is (mostly) straightforward. What is relevant to the shareholders is the cash flow implications of the environmental effects. For example, a regulatory charge for use of the green space (item [a]) will directly reduce the NPV of the project. A government fee that reflects the environmental value of the land will efficiently (socially) allocate the land. If the fee is above $25,000, then Project X is a negative NPV proposition, and shareholders would be in agreement that the project should not go forward.

It is of course not easy nor without controversy for a regulator to determine the monetary value of an environmental resource. In particular, it assumes that there is a unique

Table 27.3 Air Quality Costs of Project X and Similar Portfolios of Stock and Bonds

	($'000's)		
	$t = 0$	$t = 1$	$t = 1$
	z_0	$z_1 = r$	$z_1 = b$
	"now"	"recession"	"boom"
Air quality costs		18,967	23,289
Buy $y = 0.08163$ bonds	−80	8,163	8,163
Buy $x = 0.11080$ stocks	−120	10,804	15,126
Portfolio	−200	18,967	23,289

value that can be agreed upon. We will come back to that. However, conditional on the environmental valuation, the policy implementation is straightforward. Perhaps this is obvious, but there is nothing necessarily "anti-environmental" in wealth maximization and the NPV rule. Environmental activism, in this simple example, that focuses on the cost of the green space charged by a regulator, is effective.

Next, consider the environmental effects that occur in the future and are stochastic. We will stick with our assumption that we can appropriately summarize the costs in financial terms. In the example, the project has pollution levels that are proportional to the cash flows. For concreteness, let's think of the monetary costs of this future pollution as 1 percent of the cash flows. That is $c(z_b) = 23.3$ or $c(z_r) = 19.0$. It is only a matter of simplicity that these cash flows are proportional. The key distinction from green space (item [a]) is that these cash flows are in the future and are stochastic. Using the same logic (and algebra) as above, if we all (you, me, shareholders) agree that the cash flows of $c(z_b) = 23.3$ or $c(z_r) = 19.0$ capture the environmental cost, then date-zero value ("present value") of these costs is $20 thousand. The value of the project to ABC Co. is $20 thousand less.[6] Table 27.3 has the details. The details are similar to Table 27.2 since we assumed the costs were proportional. However, the idea is more general. The financial implications for ABC Co. and its shareholders can be summarized by the value of the cash flows. For $20 thousand now, a shareholder could purchase the portfolio in Table 27.3 as "insurance" that would perfectly offset the additional cost. Since this cost is the same for all shareholders, all shareholders agree on the cost of this environmental impact.

In this setting, we can also say something a bit stronger. It is not just the shareholders who place a (present) value on these costs at $20 thousand. It is everyone. Conditional on us (you, me, shareholders, non-shareholders, regulators) agreeing that the state-contingent environmental impact is captured by $c(z_b) = 23.3$ or $c(z_r) = 19.0$ (a condition we will get back to in a moment), we all agree on the $20 thousand current value. That might

---

[6] Implicit in the "linear" valuation model implied by no-aribtrage is that we can look at cash flows incrementally. That is; we can value the net cash flows or value each component's cash flows and add the value at the end.

be a bit surprising. It implies "discounting" is appropriate. The environmental costs that happen in the future have less weight today (smaller present value). It also implies a (unique) adjustment for risk. Rather than focus on the worst-case scenario or the expected cost, the (present) value of the cost is calculated from the same financial prices and risk premiums as the original value of the project. The reasoning is the same as with the green-space (item [a]). A regulator could charge ABC Co. a fee in period one that depended on the degree of pollution (namely, $c(z_b) = 23.3$ or $c(z_r) = 19.0$). Alternatively, it could charge a fee at date zero (now) of $20 thousand. With the $20 thousand, it could buy a portfolio (see Table 27.3) that would exactly offset the cost in either event in period one. Either choice has an identical effect on the government and on the company. Again, the NPV rule is consistent with environmental concerns. Given environmental resources are priced correctly now and at states in the future, the NPV calculation summarizes the prices coherently, uniquely, and in a way we can all unanimously agree on.

NON-MONETARY

Financial markets take financial cash flows and, given the mild assumption of "no arbitrage," summarize them with a unique value. Given cash flows, we all agree on operating and investment decisions of a company. The difficulty—and the difficulty that financial markets and finance will not resolve—is that projects have effects that are not always easily boiled down to just cash flows. In the previous section, we assumed that the environmental impact of the green space (item [a]) and state-contingent future costs of air emissions (item [b]) had impacts we could all agree on. In particular, we assumed they were summarized in terms of cash flow (dollars).

Let's revisit the assumption that shareholders "from out of town" have preferences defined only over cash flow. Instead let's mix in a few "local" shareholders that occasionally walk the dog on the green space that may be the home of Project X. You can see, immediately, how shareholder unanimity may be lost. The original Project X (before we addressed the environmental impacts) increased shareholder wealth by $25,000. A shareholder from "out of town" is better off by her share of the $25,000. Since this is positive, Project X is viewed favorably. It is not so simple for a "local" shareholder. She is better off by her share of the $25,000. But, is this enough to compensate her for the lost green space? Maybe or maybe not. It depends on the relative (to money) value of the green space to her. This is a matter of preferences where there is no reason to expect different individuals would view the trade-off similarly. We all prefer more money to less and we all prefer more green space to less. However, the rate at which we might trade one for the other differs across people. And the differences need not just be based on "use"— the term preference here we can take to be quite literal.

Formally, we need to revisit equation (1) that assumed shareholder preferences were defined solely over the unidimensional good $c(z_t)$ we called "cash flow." A general model would, instead, think of a vector of N goods $c(z_t)$ (with a similar time and state dependence). "Goods" typically include the food we eat and stuff we consume, but can also include things we think of as environmental (green spaces, clean water, pristine mountains, etc.). An individual's preferences rank different bundles of consumption. With some structure on the preferences, we can find a utility function that will capture the ranking.[7] For concreteness, let's keep things simple and think about just two goods. m will denote consumption of a composite commodity. Since this is the stuff we buy with money, think of this as money which is directly linked to the NPV calculations we did before. Positive NPV leave you with more money. Good e denotes the (unidimensional) environmental good like green space. Here is a simple functional form to capture the trade-off:

$$u(m,e) = \left((1-\eta)m^{\gamma} + \eta e^{\gamma}\right)^{1/\gamma} \tag{2}$$

The $\eta > 0$ parameter is a scaling that puts the two goods m and e into an equivalent scale. The key preference parameter that will define a persons trade-off between money and the environment goods is γ [8]

To see how the trade-offs differ, here are two extremes. Think of a person characterized by $\gamma = 1$. This implies $u(m,e) = (1-\eta)m + \eta e$. Here, "money" and the "environment" are substitutes—in fact, perfectly linear substitutes. The trade-off between money and the environment is simply one of quantities (up to the scaling parameter η). If the shareholder's share of Project X's NPV is large enough to compensate for the lost green space, the project is viewed positively. At the other extreme, let $\gamma<1$. This might seem odd, but if you take the limit carefully, you end up with $u(m,e) = \min(m,e)$. Here, money and environment are complements. An extra dollar does not increase happiness unless it comes with an extra unit of the environmental good.[9] In our example, Project X offers more money (NPV) at the expense of lost green space. This is a decrease e and an increase in m. Given the preferences, the decrease is much more biting, and the shareholder will not approve the project. Heterogeneity of preferences about environment is a source of shareholder conflict. However, it is not just the heterogeneity. It is the heterogeneity coupled with the familiar characteristics of environmental resources of non-exclusion and externalities.

What is special about the "environment" in this example? Just why do preferences for good e warrant special attention? Implicitly we have corporations make their profits and distribute them to shareholders as money.[10] Suppose, and this is an exaggeration, that corporations paid shareholders with "goods" (a basket of groceries, airline tickets, etc.). How would our analysis in, say, Table 27.2 change? In theory, not much changes. Project X

---

[7] The combination of multiple goods and a stochastic dynamic setting requires a bit of care in characterizing a coherent utility function. For example, the definition and meaning of "risk aversion" is no longer obvious with multiple goods. The subtleties are not central to the issues we are addressing here. Even more generally, general equilibrium also requires a bit of care in this setting as non-uniqueness, non-existance can show up.

[8] Usually we restrict $\gamma \leq 1$. In the case of $\gamma=0$, preferences are $u(m,e)=\exp(1-\eta)\log m+\eta\log e$.

[9] Preferences with this property are lexiographic.

[10] Ignore for a moment the area of corporate finance that deals with capital structure and payout policy. These are largely unrelated to our topic.

delivers a basket of goods at period one that is contingent on the state; $c(z_b)$ or $c(z_r)$. Now our first step in the analysis would be to sell the basket of goods at the (perhaps state contingent) prevailing prices. Using the cash we net from this step, the NPV analysis follows as before. Practically, of course, the transaction cost of selling a basket of goods (or selling and buying to adjust to a basket we like) is large. However, in theory, the price of a good in a competitive market is the same for all shareholders, so the conversion of any basket of good into money is the same for all shareholders. Hence, the composition of the basket of goods does not cause shareholders to disagree. In fact, this is just a roundabout way of describing what a business analyst would do when evaluating a project. The first step, recall, in project analysis was assessing the activities to determine cash flows—effectively selling the basket of goods that represents the project's activities.

The difficulty caused by an environmental good comes from the fact that there is not a "price" at which it trades. Green space and air pollution are examples of goods that are non-exclusion or externalities. This is not specific to finance but is central to environmental economics more generally. Green space is a good that is "non-excludable" in that many can benefit without having to pay an admission fee. As a result, the "free rider" problem will lead to the under-provision of green space. Government regulation and/or community organization is typically required to resolve public provision (a government that provides parks funded by taxes or a homeowner association that charges a condo-fee for common-area maintenance are the canonical examples). Air pollution is an example of an externality. The direct cost of the pollution is not borne directly and/or completely by the shareholders. In both cases, the benefit or cost is not measured by cash flows and the NPV rule falters. Our example Project X has cash flows and environmental effects. Using the common financial market, we agree on the value of the cash flows. But we disagree on the value (or utility) of the non-cash flow items. This is a vexing problem, but we will look at some potential solutions next.

VOTING, TAKEOVERS, AND CORPORATE GOVERNANCE

The "simple" solution to public good and externality is regulation that has the effect of adjusting cash flows to properly reflect the social value. But, as you would expect, the reason this is not a simple solution is that there is often no agreement on the value of public goods or externalities. For much of the political economy literature, this is the central question. Two mechanisms that are commonly explored (and used in practice) are "voting" and "matching." Voting as a choice mechanism is well known by all. Its difficulties are also well known. For issues that are relatively simple and one-dimentional, voting works well. But for issues that are complex and hard to understand (think of differentially informed voters) or not unidimensional (think of a two-party system and long platforms) then voting works less well. Matching, often called Tiebout competition in this setting, addresses that individuals can self-sort into (more) homogenous groups. Some cities have higher taxes and nicer parks. Others have lower taxes and fewer parks. Individuals move to where they are happiest. If moving is not relatively costly and the source of the heterogeneity is not too much larger than the choice of communities, things work pretty well. One example of these models that is extensively studied is in school choice (e.g. house prices by school district). Political economy is a large research area in economics. Whether or not these ideas and models are helpful in thinking about corporation finance with environmental impacts is open. As a start, we can look at these two ideas in the corporate setting.

Most corporations have in place a voting mechanism that is one-share one-vote with a majority rule. This is different from political settings since votes can be bought or sold. Since votes are attached to shares, buying and selling votes is directly related to buying and selling the cash flows. That is, you cannot accumulate a lot of votes in our ABC Co. without increasing your monetary investment in a company.

Let's take a look at this in the context of our Project X example at ABC Co. The cash flows have a monetary value, the NPV, of $25,000. The environmental impacts on the green space ([a]) and pollution ([b]) have no monetary implications but, to differing degrees, affect shareholders. Suppose, we put the project to a vote.[11]

If a majority of the shareholders prefer the green space, then the project is not approved. That seems sensible and reasonable. Here is the problem: The cash value of Project X is $25,000. The value of the company is $25,000 lower that it could be with the project (with corresponding lower share value). If you were a shareholder who voted in favor of the project or just an outsider looking to make a profit, you have the opportunity to acquire shares at the lower share price. You could even buy enough of them at the lower price to change the outcome of the vote. Once the vote changes to accept Project X, the value of the shares jumps up to reflect the $25,000 in NPV. This might strike you as odd. Previously, the majority of shareholders rejected Project X, why would they sell their shares? This you will recognize as a version of a "free-rider problem." With shareholders with small holdings, individually, selling a share will not change control of the company. This is a well-studied problem in the market for cooperate control. Grossman & Hart (1980) show how what is individually rational for a shareholder can be collectively sub-optimal. Understanding how this applies to issues of the environment is quite open.

You might ask if trading shares can swing things the opposite way. Here, suppose a majority of the shareholders prefer Project X over the green space. Again, that seems a sensible and reasonable outcome of a vote. Could shareholders who have a strong preference for the green space purchase shares to reverse the Project X decision? If collectively, a subset of shareholders (or outside investors) place a value on the green space

[11] That would be unusual, of course, in part because corporate voting on specific items is rather tedious and expensive. Proxy contest, or attempting to sway your fellow shareholders, are particularly expensive if the disagreement is substantial and campaigning spending and legal bills rack up. Furthermore, in this simple setting since we will abstract from the complexities of agenda-setting or strategic voting. Here, assume people simply vote according to their preference.

above $25,000 they could buy enough shares to change the vote. It would be expensive for the shareholders since they would, perhaps, pay a price for the shares that reflected the value of the project they intend to cancel. But, again, there is a free-rider problem. An even better outcome for me is for you and others to purchase the (expensive) shares and cancel the Project X. If this happens, I get the benefit of the green space without having to expend any resources. This, of course, mirrors the free-rider problem that governments or community associations attempt to solve. Is an analogous organization that focuses on purchasing shares to change corporate behavior, such as a socially responsible investment fund, feasible? In principal, yes. In practice, it is difficult since influencing large corporations and projects with large environmental impact requires a sizable commitment of resources.

FURTHER READING

There are not many research papers that I know of that might offer some guidance. The place to start is with DeMarzo (1993) that looks at voting equilibria. Linking up the theory of local externalities along the lines of Tiebot (1956) with the voting in DeMarzo (1993) seems a fruitful approach. See Ross, S. & J Yinger (1999) for an overview of voting and mobility as it relates to local public goods and schools. The idea of the "free rider" problem in corporate governance more generally begins with the Grossman & Hart (1980) paper. That paper is specific to takeovers but the idea applies more generally.

MANAGERIAL AGENCY

So far, we have focused on how financial markets can and cannot reconcile competing shareholder objectives. The shareholder objectives, that the NPV rule captures, are left to be implemented by management. Aligning the interests of management and the CEO is also not an easy problem. Finance and, in particular, corporate finance research has looked at this incentive problem in detail with both theory and empirical research. The basic ingredients include performance pay where performance is a noisy measure of managerial input (say, "effort") and an equity-like share in the corporation (e.g. stock options). Since managerial input is not perfectly measured, the induced outcome is usually not ideal. Oversight from a board of directors, regulation, and takeovers typically help mitigate the adverse effects of contracting by shifting managerial focus to the longer term ("career effects").

What difficulties arise when we add in the environmental concerns over project selection? Suppose (for simplicity) we had shareholders who uniformly viewed the value of the green space in Project X above the $25,000 NPV and therefore prefered to pass on this project. However, a CEO with the usual incentive package that focusses on financially measured performance, such as a share price, will accept the value-increasing project.

There are a couple of possible remedies. First, we can adjust the performance measure to include items not directly measured by typical financial measurements such as stock price or earnings. Sometimes such broad measures are called the "balanced scorecard" approach. This is hard to make work in practice. In our simple example, we would need some way to measure green space that reflects the shareholder opinion of its value. Were this the only decision the corporation makes, the measurement is feasible. However, calibrating a measure for complicated decentralized decision-making is difficult. Moreover, giving managers "fuzzy" objectives generally makes incentives less powerful, since the CEO can emphasize the objective they find easier to meet (see Dewatripont et al. 1999). A second approach is to impose "constraints" on decision-making. For example, in the context of Project X, the company's management might simply be prohibited from accepting projects that reduce green space. This has the advantage that shareholders need not characterize the trade-off between money (NPV) and green space. The disadvantage is that it might lead to foregoing a project that, for shareholders, is attractive (suppose the NPV of Project X was double or ten times higher). Third, CEOs and managers, like shareholders, have preferences over both money and non-monetary items like environmental impact. One solution to the agency issue over green space in Project X is to hire like-minded managers. If the CEO's trade-off between money and green space is roughly in line with shareholders, then "simple" (simpler) monetary incentives are sufficient. The difficulty here, of course, is that CEO preferences are not observed and must be elicited in an interview or through some self-selection mechanism (e.g. a screening equilibrium).[12]

FURTHER READING

The managerial agency problem is the subject of a huge volume of theoretical and empirical work in economics and finance (As a pointer, see Aggarwal (2008) and others in the two-volume set). More specifically, Dewatripont, Jewitt, & Tirole (1999) look at the managerial agency problem in a setting with multiple corporate objectives.

FINAL THOUGHTS

The Net Present Value "rule" is pervasive in modern corporations. It is a tool that almost every MBA student will learn and use. This is not without good reason. Aligning the diverse preferences of shareholders to facilitate the separation of ownership and control

---

[12] Moral hazard and screening in models of principal and agent are closely related. The distinction between the two is that a moral hazard problem is where the action (i.e. work) cannot be observed by the principal and a screening problem where the type (i.e. preference) cannot be observed by the principal.

is central to the modern economy. There are two implications (at least that I see) for a researcher interested in environmental issues. First, cash flows are central. The NPV rule, using financial markets, sensibly aggregates cash flows to calculate value. Therefore a direct way to confront corporations with environmental concerns is with their cash flow implications. These cash flow implications can be immediate, future, or future and uncertain. As long as the cash flows reflect sensible environmental policy (not easy, I understand), corporate decision-making will internalize them properly. Second, environmental policy is not always easy to characterize in terms of cash flows. As a result, we cannot count on shareholder unanimity. A deeper understanding of what corporations do, and ought to do, in this setting is needed. Do voting mechanisms lead to sensible outcomes? Do we need a dominant shareholder to impose stability in voting? Can corporate charters be effectively designed to allow for sensible deliberation of complex environmental issues? There are lots of open and challenging questions here .

References

Aggarwal, R. K. (2008). 'Executive Compensation and Incentives', in Espen B. Eckbo (ed.) *Handbook of Corporate Finance: Empirical Corporate Finance*, Volume 2, Elsevier: Amsterdam, 17: 497–538.

Arrow, K. (1964). 'The Role of Securities in the Optimal Allocation of Risk-Bearing', *Review of Economic Studies*, 31: 1407–1416.

—— (1970). *Essays in The Theory of Risk-Bearing*, North Holland, Amsterdam.

Backus, D. K., Routledge, B. R., and Zin, S. E. (2005). 'Exotic Preferences for Macroeconomists', in Mark Gertler and Kenneth Rogoff (eds.) *NBER Macroeconomics Annual 2004*, vol. 19, MIT Press: Cambridge, MA.

Debreu, G. (1959). *The Theory of Value*, Yale University Press: New Haven CT.

DeMarzo, P. M. (1993). 'Majority Voting and Corporate Control: The Rule of the Dominant Shareholder', *The Review of Economic Studies*, 60: 713–734.

Dewatripont, M., Jewitt, I., and Tirole, J. (1999). 'The Economics of Career Concerns, Part II: Application to Missions and Accountability of Government Agencies', *The Review of Economic Studies*, 66: 199–217.

Fisher, I (1930). *Theory of Interest: AS Determined by Impatience to Spend Income and Opportunity to Invest it*, Augstum M. Kelley: Cliffton.

Graham, J. R. and Harvey, C. (2001). 'The Theory and Practice of Corporate Finance: Evidence from the Field', *Journal of Financial Economics*, 60: 187–243.

Grossman, S. J. and Hart, O. D. (1980). 'Takeover Bids, The Free-Rider Problem, and the Theory of the Corporation', *The Bell Journal of Economics*, 11: 42–64.

Radner, R. (1979). 'Rational Expectations Equilibrium: Generic Existence and the Information Revealed by Prices', *Econometrica*, 47: 655–678.

Ross, S. and Yinger, J. (1999). 'Sorting and voting: A review of the literature on urban public finance', in Paul Cheshire and Edwin S. Mills, (eds.), *Handbook of Regional and Urban Economics*, Elsevier, Volume 3, Applied Urban Economics 2001–2060.

Tiebout, C. (1956). 'A Pure Theory of Local Expenditures', *The Journal of Political Economy*, 64: 416–424.

PART VIII

EMERGENT AND ASSOCIATED PERSPECTIVES

CHAPTER 28

....

THE RELEVANCE OF THE NATURAL ENVIRONMENT FOR CORPORATE SOCIAL RESPONSIBILITY RESEARCH

....

KRISTA BONDY AND DIRK MATTEN

CORPORATE social responsibility (CSR) is a sub-discipline of management that has gained prominence in academic debate and business practice over the last two decades. It seeks to answer fundamental questions about what a business is; its basic purposes; how it relates to other sectors within society; and how it shapes and is influenced by each sector; and investigates the nature and quality of these relationships. Although using 'social' in the label, CSR includes social, environmental, ethical, economic, and political aspects of the business relationship with society.

The central challenge for CSR lies in realigning the inherent economic goals of business with the wider interests of society. In doing so, it challenges existing theories of the firm that conceptualize business as a purely economic actor, and suggests that business may also occupy social, ecological, or political roles within society. The CSR debate also increasingly raises questions about whether micro forms of governance, such as organizational codes, are effective in regulating the relationship between business and society, highlighting the need for more consistent, macro forms of social regulation (Matten & Moon 2008). As such, CSR contributes to our understanding of business and the natural environment (B&NE) in many ways.

This chapter will first adumbrate CSR from the specific angle of this Handbook, then focus on different theoretical strands in the CSR literature that are particularly relevant in investigating the relationship between B&NE. We will then provide a brief overview over some core areas of empirical CSR research, highlighting specific links to the environment. Finally, we raise a few key questions in moving our knowledge on CSR forward in light of its relationship to environmental issues.

WHAT IS CSR?

Social and environmental concerns regarding business were made explicit long before terms such as CSR and B&NE were used. The first official recording of the term 'CSR' is commonly credited to Howard Bowen in 1953, who defined it according to the obligations of businessmen to make decisions in line with the 'objectives and values of society' (Carroll 2008: 25). In the 1960s and 1970s, this was interpreted business meeting its societal obligations through philanthropic activity rather than as changes to operational practices (e.g. Frederick 2006).

Today, CSR is sometimes referred to as a 'cluster concept' (Matten & Moon 2008), often used synonymously with other terms (such as corporate responsibility, corporate citizenship, corporate social leadership, corporate social accountability, responsible business, etc.). As Lockett et al. have argued in a study of the CSR literature over a ten-year period, 'CSR knowledge could best be described as in a *continuing state of emergence*. While the field appears well established ... it is not characterized by the domination of a particular theoretical approach, assumptions and method', as it were, 'a field without paradigm' (Lockett et al. 2006: 133). We would therefore contend that rather than being a well-defined concept, CSR is more a field of scholarship, using a multiplicity of conceptual lenses and theoretical approaches (van Oosterhout & Heugens 2008). Nevertheless a broader analysis of the literature and emerging practice of CSR would suggest six core characteristics (Crane et al. 2007: 7–9):

1. CSR focuses on voluntary activities of business;
2. CSR is concerned with internalizing or managing externalities;
3. CSR has a multiple stakeholder orientation;
4. CSR attempts an alignment of societal, environmental, and economic responsibilities;
5. CSR emerges with a fairly common set of practices and values;
6. CSR goes beyond mere philanthropy.

CSR first became conceptually linked to the environment through the Bruntdland Commission's definition of sustainable development: "meeting the needs of present generations without compromising the ability of future generations to meet their own needs" (World Commission On Environment And Development 1987). Mostly driven by the practitioner's discourse following the Rio Conference in 1992, sustainable development (SD) has been conceptualized as a 'triple bottom line' for business, including ecological, economic and social goals (Elkington 1997). This overlap has caused many companies, most notably in Europe, to use both terms interchangeably (Crane & Matten 2010: 32). In academia the overlap is recognized conceptually but much of the empirical research still occurs along disciplinary lines (Seager 2008). This is, however, starting to change as academics and practitioners begin to explicitly highlight the need for both social and environmental aspects in their work (Montiel 2008; Moon 2007; Topal et al. 2009). Therefore, despite its relative vagueness (Norman & MacDonald 2004), the central contribution of the SD concept to the CSR debate is the appreciation of the trade-offs between social and environmental responsibilities of business.

Leaving definitional questions at this rather broad stage, we now turn to how different theoretical streams in the CSR field shape, explain, and help to predict issues related to the interaction of business and the natural environment.

CSR THEORY AND THE ENVIRONMENT

Generally, CSR theories are organized along a continuum from instrumental to values-based (e.g. Garriga & Melé 2004; Windsor 2006), with instrumental approaches focusing on CSR solely as a tool for improving the profitability of the organization, while values-based approaches conceptualize CSR as a moral imperative for business (see also Post [Chapter 29] this volume). This continuum provides the backdrop for discussing four groups of CSR theories with specific implications for the environment: instrumental, economic, network, and political approaches. Our focus will be less on instrumental or economic approaches (see Russo & Minto [Chapter 2] this volume) rather than on broader social and political explanations of the role business plays in social and ecological systems.

Instrumental theories

Instrumental theories justify CSR by demonstrating the link to traditional business imperatives. In most cases, the environment is treated as a set of resources which—if used more efficiently or innovatively—leads to cost savings or other types of competitive advantages (McWilliams & Siegel 2001). Therefore, environmental and social resources are protected to the extent that they help improve competitive positions and business success (e.g. Kurucz et al. 2008; Schaltegger & Wagner 2006).

Often referred to as the 'business case', substantial parts of the CSR literature emphasize direct and indirect financial benefits associated with voluntary CSR. For instance, CSR improves competitive advantage (e.g. Burke & Logsdon 1996; Husted & Allen 2000; Porter & Kramer 2002), through, for instance, improving reputation (e.g. Fombrun 2005); reducing risks of litigation and social pressure (e.g. Zadek 2004); or creating niche market opportunities such as 'ethical' or 'green' products (e.g. Shaw & Clarke 1999). In this perspective, where CSR helps reduce costs or generates new revenue, it is valued, but as resource for increased profitability.

Supporting this instrumental approach to CSR is the work on corporate social performance (CSP) (Carroll 1979; Swanson 1995; Wood 1991). This literature seeks to prove a business case for CSR by quantifying the direction and strength of the relationship between social/environmental and financial performance (Griffin & Mahon 1997). Although the subject of debate for over thirty years, recent meta-analyses agree on an overall small but positive relationship mediated by a range of factors (Margolis et al. 2007; Orlitzky et al. 2003; Wu 2006). CSR activity is thus justified on financial grounds and tolerated where it contributes to the financial performance of the organization.

Instrumental approaches to CSR and B&NE—particularly popular in the practitioner literature (e.g. Willard 2007)—take a rather narrow view of the nature of the firm and the role it plays in society. CSR is seen as a resource to support organizations and their goal of maximizing profits. It is a legitimate investment equal to the degree with which it is an effective tool for achieving improved financial performance. CSR is therefore enacted at the micro level of society where agents within organizations identify and engage in specific social and environmental initiatives that support financial performance.

Economic theories

Economic theories treat CSR and B&NE as under-valued or excluded resources in the broader economy. To become a legitimate cost of production, and thus properly valued within the economic system, they must be converted from societal goods to types of capital. In other words, they must be internalized and adequately priced.

Economic approaches conceptualize different forms of capital. Financial (cash and investments), physical (infrastructure, land, equipment), and to some extent human (workforce and organizational culture) are traditionally included in the price of production. However, many aspects of social and natural systems are excluded from these categories. Reframing them as social (e.g. societal license to operate; Nahapiet & Ghoshal 1998) and natural capital (e.g. ecosystem services such as cleaning air; Lovins et al. 1999), translates them into the categories of the economic system. But it is only through valuing these services in monetary terms that they can be empirically included within the economy (Costanza et al. 1997; Daly 1998). Through re-framing social and natural systems as forms of capital and assigning them monetary value, they can be internalized into the economic system and included into the costs of production. Consequently, products and services more accurately reflect actual resources used and are priced according to their impact on social and natural systems.

In some ways then, instrumental and economic theories of CSR approach social and environmental issues in similar ways. Social and natural systems have value in as much as they can be quantified in monetary terms and therefore can be included in cost/benefit calculations of organizations and their agents (Chiesura & de Groot 2003). Reframing CSR issues as additional types of capital supports a relatively unchallenged view of the firm, the economic system, and the goals of business within society. However, economic theories differ from instrumental ones in two important areas: emphasis and level. The focus of CSR within instrumental theories is to help firms improve their competitive positions. Within economic theories, it is the attempt to internalize a broader range of social and environmental 'services' for the production of goods and services. While both perspectives reframe CSR issues to fit within the existing rationale, one does so to enhance profits, while the other aims at benefiting social and natural systems. The theories also differ in the level at which they are applied. While both focus on micro-level voluntary practices, instrumental theories focus on organizations, while economic theories focus on wider economic systems. Economic theories, therefore, maintain the existing logic of business and the theory of the firm, but extend the range of legitimate inputs.

Network theories

Network theories challenge the notion of business and its role in society. In general terms, this broad group of theories investigates CSR through the relationships between economic actors and their surroundings. In some cases, they present a modest challenge to a theory of the firm, such as the vast body of work on stakeholder theory (e.g. Donaldson & Preston 1995; Freeman 1984; Phillips et al. 2003), while in other cases the challenge is more substantive, such as ecocentrism (Gladwin et al. 1995; Purser et al. 1995; Starik & Rands 1995). Common to this approach is a recognition that business is more firmly embedded within social and natural systems than core organizational theories, such as agency theory, suggests. Business is part of a much larger societal network in which each party has responsibility for itself and its relationships with others in their spatial and operational networks. Business logics must therefore be reoriented to recognize and integrate them. Of the many CSR theories based on network approaches, there are three that are specifically pertinent to the B&NE relationship: stakeholder theory; ecofeminism, and sustaincentrism.

Stakeholder theory and the environment

Stakeholder theory focuses on the firm's interaction with groups that can affect, or are affected by the achievement of organizational objectives (Freeman 1984). Deferring to Kassinis ([Chapter 5] this volume) for the main arguments, we would here reiterate the aspect of representativeness: some stakeholders have more ability to voice their concerns and participate in corporate activities than others (e.g. Mitchell et al. 1997). This is particularly serious for the environment because it cannot represent itself (Phillips & Reichart 2000; Starik 1995). It is instead represented by proxy through different human stakeholders. Thus, environmental issues are represented only where they are sufficiently valued by humans who are prepared to pursue them.

Given these limits of stakeholder theory, Driscoll & Starik (2004) attempt to redefine the stakeholder concept to allow for the inclusion of environmental issues. They do so by redefining the three core concepts affecting representativeness (power, legitimacy and urgency, see Mitchell et al. 1997), and adding 'proximity' as a fourth. Proximity refers mainly to physical proximity, where stakeholders are deemed legitimate due to their spatial closeness to the business (i.e. a river system into which effluent is released, a forest adjacent to a facility, or a community in which a company operates). Being 'next door' becomes a sufficient condition for attaining necessary legitimacy. In this way, proximity reshapes the stakeholder model to explicitly include environmental considerations even if not represented by humans, and as such places business back into its broader context.

Ecofeminism

In a similar vein, ecofeminism seeks to reemphasize the role of the firm in its wider societal context by focusing on the context in which ethical frames are created and practiced (e.g. Borgerson 2007; Brennan 1999; Derry 2002). 'The primary belief of ecofeminism is that the domination of women (as studied in traditional feminism) parallels the domination of nature, and that this mutual domination has led to environmental destruction by the controlling patriarchal society' (Dobscha 1993: 36–37). This approach seeks to make transparent the systems of dominance that are inherent in taken-for-granted beliefs about business and the environment. For instance, Dobscha (1993) challenges the notion that people make exclusively rational decisions around the environment. She suggests that our emotions, feelings, and passion towards the environment significantly influence how we make decisions on environmental issues. By focusing on rational solutions to environmental problems (such as providing more information), society ignores much of what is required to encourage change. McMahon (1997) supports this critique by highlighting that traditional economic theory and the model of living promoted by traditional economists ignores its socially and environmentally destructive consequences.

By maintaining existing social frames and ignoring underlying power structures (see also Banerjee [Chapter 31] this volume), many theories of the firm contribute to the oppression and destruction of social and environmental systems by modifying 'reality' (Borgerson 2007). Perpetuating these frames further entrenches the logics of business, with the result that 'corporate capitalism is one of the driving forces of the momentous changes currently reworking humanity into a global monoculture and vigorously transforming bioregions' (Crittenden 2000: 52). Ecofeminism argues for a revolutionary shift in the business paradigm to redress these issues at a broad societal level.

Sustaincentrism

Coined by Tom Gladwin and co-authors (1995), the concept of 'sustaincentrism' starts from the position that business is embedded within social and natural systems and is a major contributor to social and environmental problems. It is therefore responsible, not only to recognize these problems, but to make fundamental, systemic changes required to mitigate them (e.g. Bansal & Roth 2000; Jennings & Zandbergen 1995). The literature seems to focus on two aspects, first a reorientation of the firm towards its ecological environment (ecocentrism), and second a reorientation towards its social environment ('socialcentrism'). Ecocentrism highlights four common aspects (e.g. Purser et al. 1995; Shrivastava 1995; Whiteman & Cooper 2000):

- A relative agreement on fundamental principles of ecology such as conservation and system limits;
- A rejection of current 'environmental management' approaches because they support the existing, destructive paradigm;
- A belief that business and ecological principles are not mutually exclusive;
- A focus on organizations as core actors responsible for change.

In a similar vein, the 'socialcentrism' literature highlights the systemic embeddedness of business in society and social systems at multiple levels (e.g. Aguilera et al. 2007). The core challenge, this school of thought would argue, is not just to recognize individual links between firms and specific stakeholder groups (Key 1999) but rather to embrace the complex and systemic interactions between business and its social environment (Stern & Barley 1996; Walsh et al. 2003). One of the more prominent approaches to take this further in the CSR literature is integrative social contract theory (ISCT) (Donaldson & Dunfee 1994; 1999). In essence, ISCT suggests that business has a broader responsibility to society because of its membership in an implicit contract. Like all others in society, firms have implicitly consented to rules, practices, and institutions that are mutually beneficial to all parties and form the basis for a contract of interaction. Thus firms have a contractual obligation to uphold the conditions of this agreement. It is assumed these contracts are governed by 'hypernorms' or universal principles which apply to all human condition (most notably universal human rights), and create the initial conditions for micronorms or context-based norms developed in smaller groups such as nations or communities. Ecological considerations in this context are just part of a larger, systemic embeddedness of business through a multi-level web of implicit contracts with societal actors.

To sum it up, network theories relocate business within a broader social network and thus challenge the narrow focus of instrumental and economic theories on economic activities of the firm as separate from, and largely ignorant of, their impact on social and natural systems. All approaches discussed so far, however, share a focus on largely micro-level actors as agents of change, who must adapt their frames and practices towards a paradigm that is more relevant for the role business plays in society.

Political theories of CSR

As a relative recent newcomer to the debate, political theories question this domain by investigating the political nature of CSR (Detomasi 2008; Scherer & Palazzo 2007; Scherer et al. 2009). This stream of work is based on the insight that in fact much of what corporations do, or are expected to do, in terms of responsibility towards wider society invades a space which in most liberal democracies fell traditionally into the sphere of political actors, most notably either governments or individuals in their roles as citizens (Matten

& Crane 2005; Moon et al. 2005). Corporations becoming involved in providing health-care, education or—in the B&NE context—designing voluntary measures for greenhouse gas reduction turns them into political actors who 'are increasingly part of the authoritative allocation of values and resources' in society (Crane et al. 2008a: 1). This debate has chiefly taken place under the label of 'corporate citizenship' (Scherer & Palazzo 2008) and explores new roles and responsibilities of business in such an alleged political role. It resounds with the debate on B&NE in a number of ways, most pronounced around the concepts of 'new corporate environmentalism' (NCE) and ecological citizenship.

New corporate environmentalism

More recently, Jermier and co-authors (2006) have suggested the conceptual framework of 'new corporate environmentalism' (NCE), which is defined 'as rhetoric concerning the central role of business in achieving both economic growth and ecological rationality and as a guide for management that emphasizes voluntary, proactive control of environmental impacts that exceed or go beyond environmental laws and regulatory compliance' (Jermier et al. 2006: 618). One of the key contributions of this work lies in exposing the fundamentally political nature of NCE. Corporations are at the core of shaping—some would even argue 'hijacking' (Welford 1997)—the debate on environmental protection (see also Forbes & Jermier [Chapter 30] this volume). Their voluntary engagement in (or sometimes obstruction of, or even disengagement from) environmentally friendly management practices locates them deeply into the broader public debate on a host of normative and highly political processes in societies both local and global. Looking at the rather technical nature of much of the literature on corporate greening, Jermier et al. (2006: 640) thus conclude that 'developing a fuller appreciation of the political content and meaning of the NCE and avoiding reduction of it to technical issues' is indeed one of the key contemporary challenges in the field. Business has a significant opportunity to shape and influence social and environmental issues for itself and other institutions (see also Roome [Chapter 34] this volume). It is therefore a powerful actor in the shaping of society-wide conceptions of 'environment' by influencing both macro level political debate and micro level business decision making. Even firms accused of greenwashing can be argued to move the debate forward by showing symbolic support for environmental rhetoric (Pulver 2007; Forbes & Jermier [Chapter 30] this volume). Thus, whether symbolic or substantive, business' contribution to green politics redefines and broadens the role of business in society.

Ecological citizenship

Ecological citizenship challenges the notion of a territorial citizenship based on individual rights. Instead, it emphasizes formal (collective rights and responsibilities) and substantive (participation and identity) aspects of citizenship that transcend traditional geographic boundaries (e.g. Delanty 1997; Dobson 2003; Saiz 2005). It therefore shifts the primary political membership of an individual away from her nation-state, to one that focuses instead on the natural environment and other forms of community (Crane et al. 2008b). An emphasis on participation means that membership is extended to include such groups as non-humans and future generations (Dobson 2003). By reforming notions of citizenship to focus on broad communities linked by rights, duties, participation and identity with social and natural systems, ecological citizenship becomes a foundation for interactions between members.

The key implication for the debate on B&NE hints at a change in how to conceptualize the relevant 'community' for business. Such a notion of community can include the local, physical surroundings of a business or it can focus on the widest set of stakeholders potentially affected by a business' impact on the natural environment, including future generations. Such broad notions of 'community', while clear conceptually, are problematic in application. To address this, Dobson (2003) suggests that the community to which a member is obligated is based on the 'ecological footprint' as a measure of an actor's (i.e. a firm or individual) impact on the limited natural resources in a given community (Wackernagel & Rees 1996). Because certain actors (firms in particular) use more resources than others, this asymmetrical use results in asymmetrical obligations to other members within the community. Business therefore, as asymmetrical user of resources, has broader obligations within its community. Compared to network theories, political theories focus at the macro level, recognizing the fact that business *does* play a political role in society and advancing a new paradigm for business through changes in sociopolitical structures such as citizenship.

In summary, instrumental, economic, network and political theories of CSR seek to realign business with social and natural systems. Instrumental and economic theories largely support existing theories of business where the social and environmental issues are redefined and become tools for supporting the existing paradigm. Network and political theories seek not only to reorient specific practices or ideas, but to challenge the fundamental concept of business by extending and shifting the emphasis of its role in society. Although some theories have implications for macro levels within society, they typically focus on changes at the micro level, conducted by organizations and their agents. There is also some question as to whether these theories can deliver the realignment of business with social and environmental issues. While some approaches contest the underlying philosophy of the dominant business paradigm, they offer only partial solutions. CSR, then, is still in need of robust theory that realigns broader societal goals with narrow business interests. Network and political theories are a substantial step forward and could form a solid foundation upon which a new theory of the firm could be conceived.

ENVIRONMENTAL ISSUES AS DRIVERS OF THE CSR AGENDA

Although there exists a vast body of literature investigating the relationship between business and the natural environment, it is highly debatable which aspects of this literature comfortably sit within the CSR field. In fact, it is rather arbitrary to draw the line between clear CSR issues and environmental issues, as the broad scope of CSR would make environmental issues nearly always part of the CSR agenda by dint of their societal relevance. In this section then we will attempt to identify core areas of overlap between the two fields; that is, where environmental issues have been crucial to the wider debate on CSR, and vice versa, where CSR has predominantly focused on and been driven by environmental issues. These areas have been chosen because they also highlight key questions within the CSR field.

One of the core questions is how to institutionalize a CSR theory of the firm and associated practices within business. In other words, how can CSR move from a voluntary, ad-hoc set of attitudes and practices, to a fundamental aspect of macro sociopolitical institutions? One answer to this has been through self-regulation (see also King, Prado, & Rivera [Chapter 6] this volume), often in the form of standardized management systems, also referred to as industrial metastandards (Uzumeri 1997).

Industrial metastandards, the environment and CSR

As far as management systems are concerned it is conspicuous that these have first and foremost occurred with a predominant focus on the environment. One of the first, the British Standard for Environmental Management (BS7750), was introduced in 1992 (Bohoris & O'Mahony 1994), followed by the EU Eco-Management and Audit Scheme (EMAS) in 1993 (Glachant et al. 2002). Both of these were somewhat obliterated by the ISO 14000 series in 1995 (Ghisellini & Thruston 2005), which quickly gained a predominant momentum globally (Corbett & Kirsch 2001). It is only within the last couple of years that a similar standard has been debated with regard to CSR and the ISO 26000 Standard on Social Responsibility which has come into effect in 2011 (Sandberg 2006; Schwartz & Tilling 2009). Although not certification-based, codes of practice/ethics/ conduct as popular CSR instruments can also arguably be traced back to environmental issues (Bondy et al. 2006). Most notably one of the first industry codes, the Responsible Care Program of the global chemical industry, was set up to address concerns over poor environmental practices of this sector (King & Lenox 2000).

Both types of initiatives focus on standardizing different aspects of social and environmental issues with the goal of embedding these within organizations. The purpose of certified initiatives is to standardize the process by which social and environmental issues are managed (Thompson 2002). For non-certified initiatives the purpose is to standardize specific issues for consistent management across broad operational territories (Bondy et al. 2008). In either case, standardization is believed to result in more consistent and effective governance of social and environmental issues, and to thus further embed them within firms (e.g. Paine et al. 2005; Sethi 2003; Williams 2001).

The literature on environmental management systems offers other substantive insights for understanding CSR governance. Topics include the effective design of management systems focused on non-market issues (e.g. Kirkland & Thompson 1999; Rondinelli & Vastag 2000; Russo & Harrison 2005), alternative forms of regulation (e.g. Stenzel 1999), impacts of best practice performance (e.g. Christmann 2000), the integration of individual and business level perspectives to improve sustainability and sustainable consumption (e.g. Amine 2003), or how to effectively measure (e.g. Figge et al. 2002) and report on social and environmental issues (e.g. Donnelly et al. 2008). But the question remains whether the B&NE literature, mostly supporting the existing business paradigm (Purser et al. 1995), can provide the kinds of insights into CSR governance necessary to effect a fundamental realignment of business and societal goals. In other words, can standardization of issues and governance processes support paradigmatic changes to the role of business in society? Whether and to what degree this is possible is still of much debate in the literature, and forms one of the open questions within the field.

CSR and the environment in comparative perspective

Since early research into CSR was chiefly conducted in a North-American context (Carroll 1979; Davis 1960; Sethi 1975), another line of CSR research has been comparative studies, aimed at understanding the global variations of this management idea over the last two decades (Matten & Moon 2008; Williams & Aguilera 2008). This perspective casts an interesting light on the relationship with, and the role of, environmental issues for the wider CSR debate.

As Carroll (2008) argues in his historical overview over CSR, the agenda in North America was chiefly set by CSR as corporate philanthropy and community involvement, followed by issues of equal opportunity in the 1970s and ethical issues in the narrow sense (such as corruption or discrimination). Environmental issues entered the agenda relatively late. This is mirrored by the academic debate on the issues. While there is a long history of CSR-related journals, such as *Business & Society* (founded 1960) or *Business and Society Review* (1972), journals focusing on B&NE issues, such as *Organization & Environment* (1987) or *Journal of Industrial Ecology* (1993) were set up much later and are dedicated to more specific issues rather than just broadly B&NE. It took the mainstream of the academic debate until 1995 to accept the relevance of the B&NE topic, if the first special issue/section on the topic in *Academy of Management Review* in 1995 is anything to go by.

In Europe, the situation is rather different. CSR as an explicit management concept came into fashion in the 1990s, underpinned by implicit business responsibilities to society in the set-up of societal institutions that govern business behavior (Matten & Moon 2008). It was only in 2001, that the first European academic journals on CSR were set up (*Corporate Governance: The International Journal of Business in Society* and *Journal of Corporate Citizenship*). However, B&NE, as a largely independent field of business practice and academic investigation had already emerged during the 1980s. Journals such as *Business Strategy and the Environment* (1992), *Journal of Cleaner Production* (1993) or *Ecomanagement and Auditing* (1993) were among the first journals to address the B&NE interface. Conspicuously, the range of the journals was never quite focused just on the environment, and many issues of a more generic (North American) CSR agenda gradually entered the debate. This general trend, that the debate on CSR (as an explicit management concept) in Europe emerged from the B&NE field is reflected by the fact that the first proper CSR journal, *CSR and Environmental Management*, turned out to be a renaming of *Ecomanagement and Auditing* in 2001. It might be fair to say that the contemporary debate on CSR in Europe is largely a sequel to earlier debates on B&NE, often under the label of SD. This is probably nowhere better reflected than in the title of the EU Commissions' central policy document on CSR, which just equates CSR with SD (Commission Of The European Communities 2002). This latter observation provides an interesting backdrop for some final remarks.

CSR AND THE NATURAL ENVIRONMENT: CONVERGING AGENDAS

While the fields of CSR and B&NE have developed into academic areas of inquiry independently from each other, it is clear that there is significant overlap and a common purpose. Even a cursory look at the core issues in both fields, such as the debate on business and climate change (e.g. Begg et al. 2005; Hoffman 2005; Levy & Kolk 2002), illustrates the overlap and convergence of both literatures. While clearly an environmental issue, a quick glance at many CSR websites of large multinational corporations (MNCs) is enough to see that business responses to climate change are seen as part of their wider CSR or sustainability commitments. They tend to portray it as one of many overlapping issues that have both social and environmental implications, to which they bear some responsibility. A similar situation can be seen with regard to other contemporary environmental issues, such as water management or biodiversity. Addressing these issues is not just a question of solving an environmental problem. Rather they raise questions, not only around business responsibility for global justice or its role in private and public governance, but also more narrowly evoke classic CSR tools, such as voluntary commitments and industry agreements, stakeholder consultation, human rights management or reporting and auditing. Addressing these environmental issues from a CSR perspective, nearly always involves a careful consideration of the trade-offs between environmental, social, and economic responsibilities of the firm. It is therefore to no surprise that CSR has so willingly adopted the language of SD or the 'triple bottom line' (Norman & MacDonald 2004).

CSR and B&NE also share a common purpose. Both fields search for new conceptualizations of business that incorporate wider goals of society and recognize limits of social and natural systems. Thus, both offer alternative theories of the firm and recommend actions to embed and realign business with these goals. However, there is a need for further integration of both social and environmental considerations within each literature, as current conceptualization often favors one set of issues over another. There is also need for extension or new alternatives to these perspectives to better address a broader scope, from micro level actors to macro level institutions operating across geographical territories. Thus, new theoretical conceptualizations of business must be both multi-level and multi-disciplinary to adequately capture the complexity and inter-connectedness of relevant phenomena. From there, research also needs to address how to institutionalize these alternative paradigms for business at multiple levels, in particular addressing the embeddedness of CSR within socio-political institutions. Those debates in both the CSR and B&NE literatures will not only share common concerns with regard to practical or instrumental questions (such as standardization), but also more strategic and normative concerns about the role of business in society (including ecological aspects) in general. Addressing social responsibilities does inevitably include the relevance of environmental concerns for society and—vice versa—the big environmental challenges for business cannot be discussed without considering their implications for wider society. The resulting question about the purpose and responsibilities of business and new theoretical conceptualizations of what a business is for, then, inevitably suggest a further convergence of the CSR and B&NE literatures.

References

Aguilera, R. V., Rupp, D., Williams, C. A. & Ganapathi, J. (2007). "Putting the S Back in Corporate Social Responsibility: A Multi-Level Theory of Social Change in Organizations," *Academy of Management Review*, 32(3): 836–863.

Amine, L. S. (2003). "An Integrated Micro- and Macrolevel Discussion of Global Green Issues: It Isn't Easy Being Green". *Journal of International Management*, 9(4): 373–393.

Bansal, P. & Roth, K. (2000). 'Why Companies go Green: A Model of Ecological Responsiveness," *Academy of Management Journal* 43(4): 717–736.

Begg, K., Van Der Woerd, F. & Levy, D. L. (eds.) (2005). *The Business of Climate Change. Corporate Responses to Kyoto*. Sheffield: Greenleaf.

Bohoris, G. A. & O'Mahony, E. (1994). "BS7750, BS5750 and the EC's Eco Management and Audit Scheme," *Industrial Management & Data Systems*, 94(2): 3–6.

Bondy, K., Matten, D., & Moon, J. (2006). "Codes of Conduct as a Tool for Sustainable Governance in Multinational Corporations," in Benn, S. and Dunphy, D. (eds.), *Corporate Governance and Sustainability: Challenges for Theory and Practice*, London: Routledge, 165–186.

————— (2008). "Multinational Corporation Codes of Conduct: Governance Tools for Corporate Social Responsibility?" *Corporate Governance: An International Review*, 16 (4): 294–311.

Borgerson, J. L. (2007). "On the Harmony of Feminist Ethics and Business Ethics," *Business and Society Review*, 112(4): 477–509.

Brennan, S. (1999). "Recent Work in Feminist Ethics," *Ethics*, 109(4): 858–893.

Burke, L. & Logsdon, J. M. (1996). "How Corporate Social Responsibility Pays Off," *Long Range Planning*, 29(4): 495–502.

Carroll, A. B. (1979). "A Three Dimensional Model of Corporate Social Performance". *Academy of Management Review*, 4: 497–505.

———— (2008). "A History of Corporate Social Responsibility: Concepts and Practices," in Crane, A., Mcwilliams, A., Matten, D., Moon, J. and Siegel, D. (eds), *The Oxford Handbook of CSR*. Oxford: Oxford University Press, 19–46.

Chiesura, A. & Groot, R. (2003). "Critical Natural Capital: A Socio-Cultural Perspective". *Ecological Economics*, 44: 219–231.

Christmann, P. (2000). "Effects of 'Best Practices' on Environmental Management on Cost Advantage: The Role of Complementary Assets". *Academy of Management Journal*, 43(4): 663–680.

Commission Of The European Communities (2002). *Communication from the Commission concerning corporate social responsibility: A business contribution to sustainable development.* Brussels: EU Commission.

Corbett, C. J. & Kirsch, D. A. (2001). "International Diffusion of ISO 14000 Certification," *Production and Operations Management*, 10(3): 327–342.

Costanza, R., d'Arge, R., de Groot, R., Farber, S., Grasso, M., Hannon, B., Naeem, S., Limburg, K., Paruelo, J., O'Neill, R., Raskin, R., Sutton, P. & van de Belt, M. (1997). "The Value of the World's Ecosystem Services and Natural Capital," *Nature*, 387: 253–260.

Crane, A. & Matten, D. (2010). *Business Ethics. Managing Corporate Citizenship and Sustainability in the Age of Globalization.* Oxford: Oxford University Press.

——— & Moon, J. (2008a). *Corporations and Citizenship.* Cambridge: Cambridge University Press.

——— (2008b). "Ecological Citizenship and the Corporation: Politicizing the New Corporate Environmentalism," *Organization & Environment*, 21(4): 371–389.

Crane, A., Matten, D., & Spence, L. (2007). *Corporate Social Responsibility: Readings and Cases in Global Context.* London: Routledge.

Crittenden, C. (2000). "Ecofeminism Meets Business: A Comparison of Ecofeminist, Corporate and Free Market Ideologies". *Journal of Business Ethics*, 24: 51–63.

Daly, H. E. (1998). "The Return of Lauderdale's Paradox," *Ecological Economics*, 25: 21–23.

Davis, K. (1960). "Can Business Afford to Ignore Corporate Social Responsibilities?" *California Management Review*, 2: 70–76.

Delanty, G. (1997). "Models of Citizenship: Defining European Identity and Citizenship," *Citizenship Studies*, 1(3): 285–303.

Derry, R. (2002). "Feminist Theory and Business Ethics," in Frederick, R. (ed). *A Companion to Business Ethics*, Oxford: Blackwell Publishing, 81–87.

Detomasi, D. A. (2008). "The Political Roots of Corporate Social Responsibility," *Journal of Business Ethics*, 82: 807–819.

Dobscha, S. (1993). "Women and the Environment: Applying Ecofeminism to Environmentally-Related Consumption," *Advances in Consumer Research*, 20: 36–40.

Dobson, A. (2003). *Citizenship and the Environment.* Oxford: Oxford University Press.

Donaldson, T. & Dunfee, T. W. (1994). "Toward a Unified Conception of Business Ethics: Integrative Social Contracts Theory," *Academy of Management Review*, 19: 252–284.

—— (1999). *Ties that Bind : A Social Contracts Approach to Business Ethics.* Boston, Mass.: Harvard Business School Press.

—— & Preston, L. E. (1995). "The Stakeholder Theory of the Corporation: Concepts, Evidence, and Implications," *Academy of Management Review*, 20(1): 65–91.

Donnelly, A., Prendergast, T. & Hanusch, M. (2008). "Examining Quality of Environmental Objectives, Targets and Indicators in Environmental Reports Prepared for Strategic Environmental Assessment," *Journal of Environmental Assessment Policy and Management*, 10(4): 381–401.

Driscoll, C. & Starik, M. (2004). "The Primordial Stakeholder: Advancing the Conceptual Consideration of Stakeholder Status for Natural Environment," *Journal of Business Ethics*, 49(1): 55–73.

Elkington, J. (1997). *Cannibals with Forks: The Triple Bottom Line of 21st Century Business.* Oxford, UK: Capstone Publishing Ltd.

Figge, F., Hahn, T., Schaltegger, S. & Wagner, M. (2002). "The Sustainability Balanced Scorecard: Linking Sustainability Management to Business Strategy," *Business Strategy and the Environment,* 11: 269–284.

Fombrun, C. (2005). "Building Corporate Reputation through CSR Initiatives: Evolving Standards," *Corporate Reputation Review,* 8(1): 7–11.

Frederick, W. (2006). *Corporation be Good: The Story of Corporate Social Responsibility.* Indianapolis, US: Dog Ear Publishing.

Freeman, R. E. (1984). *Strategic Management. A Stakeholder Approach.* Boston: Pitman.

Garriga, E. & Melé, D. (2004). "Corporate Social Responsibility Theories: Mapping the Territory," *Journal of Business Ethics,* 53(1–2): 51–71.

Ghisellini, A. & Thruston, D. (2005). "Decision Traps in ISO 14001 Implementation Process: Case Study Results from Illinois Certified Companies," *Journal of Cleaner Production,* 13: 763–777.

Glachant, M., Schucht, S., Bultmann, A. & Watzold, F. (2002). "Companies' Participation in EMAS: The Influence of the Public Regulator," *Business Strategy and the Environment,* 11: 254–266.

Gladwin, T. N., Kennelly, J. J. & Krause, T. S. (1995). "Shifting Paradigms for Sustainable Development: Implications for Management Theory and Research," *Academy of Management Review,* 20(4): 874–907.

Griffin, J. J. & Mahon, J. F. (1997). "The Corporate Social Performance and Corporate Financial Performance Debate: Twenty-five Years of Incomparable Research," *Business & Society,* 36(1): 5–31.

Hoffman, A. J. (2005). "Climate Change Strategy: The Business Logic Behind Voluntary Greenhouse Gas Reductions," *California Management Review,* 47(3): 21–46.

Husted, B. W. & Allen, D. B. (2000). "Is it Ethical to Use Ethics as Strategy?" *Journal of Business Ethics,* 27(1–2): 21–31.

Jennings, P. D. & Zandbergen, P. A. (1995). "Ecologically Sustainable Organizations: An Institutional Approach," *Academy of Management Review,* 20(4): 1015–1052.

Jermier, J. M., Forbes, L. C., Benn, S. & Orsato, R. J. (2006). "The New Corporate Environmentalism and Green Politics," in Clegg, S., Hardy, C., Lawrence, T. and Nord, W. R. (eds.), *The SAGE Handbook of Organization Studies,* London: Sage, 618–650.

Key, S. (1999). "Toward a New Theory of the Firm: A Critique of Stakeholder 'Theory,'" *Management Decision,* 37(4): 317–328.

King, A. A. & Lenox, M. J. (2000). "Industry Self Regulation Without Sanctions: The Chemical Industry's Responsible Care Program," *Academy of Management Journal,* 43(4): 698–716.

Kirkland, L.-H. & Thompson, D. (1999). "Challenges in Designing, Implementing and Operating an Environmental Management System," *Business Strategy and the Environment,* 8: 128–143.

Kurucz, E., Colbert, B. & Wheeler, D. (2008). "The Business Case for Corporate Social Responsibility," in Crane, A., McWilliams, A., Matten, D., Moon, J. and Siegel, D. (eds.), *The Oxford Handbook of CSR.* Oxford: Oxford University Press, 83–112.

Levy, D. L. & Kolk, A. (2002). "Strategic Responses to Global Climate Change: Conflicting Pressures on Multinationals in the Oil Industry," *Business and Politics,* 3(2): 275–300.

Lockett, A., Moon, J. & Visser, W. (2006). "Corporate Social Responsibility in Management Research: Focus, Nature, Salience, and Sources of Influence," *Journal of Management Studies,* 43(1): 115–136.

Lovins, A. B., Lovins, L. H. & Hawken, P. (1999). "A Road Map for Natural Capitalism," *Harvard Business Review* (May-June), 145–158.

Margolis, J., Elfenbein, H., & Walsh, J. (2007). "Does it Pay to be Good? A Meta-Analysis and Redirection of Research on the Relationship between Corporate Social and Financial Performance," *Academy of Management*. Philadelphia, PA.

Matten, D. & Crane, A. (2005). "Corporate Citizenship: Toward an Extended Theoretical Conceptualization," *Academy of Management Review*, 30(1): 166–179.

—— & Moon, J. (2008). "'Implicit' and 'Explicit' CSR: A Conceptual Framework for a Comparative Understanding of Corporate Social Responsibility," *Academy of Management Review*, 33(2): 404–424.

McMahon, M. (1997). "From the Ground up: Ecofeminism and Ecological Economics," *Ecological Economics*, 20: 163–173.

McWilliams, A. & Siegel, D. (2001). "Corporate Social Responsibility: A Theory of the Firm Perspective," *Academy of Management Review*, 26(1): 117–127.

Mitchell, R. K., Agle, B. R. & Wood, D. J. (1997). "Toward a Theory of Stakeholder Identification and Salience: Defining the Principle of Who and What Really Counts," *Academy of Management Review*, 22(4): 853–886.

Montiel, I. (2008). "Corporate Social Responsibility and Corporate Sustainability: Separate Pasts, Common Futures," *Organization & Environment*, 21: 245–269.

Moon, J. (2007). "The Contribution of Corporate Social Responsibility to Sustainable Development," *Sustainable Development*, 15: 296–306.

—— Crane, A., & Matten, D. (2005). "Can Corporations be Citizens? Corporate Citizenship as a Metaphor for Business Participation in Society," *Business Ethics Quarterly*, 15(3): 427–451.

Nahapiet, J. & Ghoshal, S. (1998). 'Social Capital, Intellectual Capital, and the Organisational Advantage," *Academy of Management Review*, 23: 242–266.

Norman, W. & MacDonald, C. (2004). "Getting to the Bottom of 'Triple Bottom Line,'" *Business Ethics Quarterly*, 14(2): 243–262.

Orlitzky, M., Schmidt, F. L. & Rynes, S. L. (2003). "Corporate Social and Financial Performance: A Meta-Analysis," *Organization Studies*, 24(3): 403–441.

Paine, L., Deshpande, R., Margolis, J. & Bettcher, K. E. (2005). "Up to Code: Does Your Company's Conduct Meet World-Class Standards?" *Harvard Business Review*, December, 122–133.

Phillips, R., Freeman, R. E., & Wicks, A. C. (2003). "What stakeholder theory is not," *Business Ethics Quarterly*, 13(4): 479–502.

—— & Reichart, J. (2000). "The Environment as a Stakeholder? A Fairness-Based Approach," *Journal of Business Ethics*, 23(2): 185–197.

Porter, M. E. and Kramer, M. R. (2002). "The Competitve Advantage of Corporate Philanthropy," *Harvard Business Review*, 80(12): 56–69.

Pulver, S. (2007). "Making Sense of Corporate Environmentalism: An Environmental Contestation Approach to Analysing the Causes and Consequences of Climate Change Policy Split in the Oil Industry," *Organization & Environment*, 20(1): 44–83.

Purser, R., Park, C., & Montuori, A. (1995). "Limits to Anthropocentrism: Toward an Ecocentric Organisation Paradigm?" *Academy of Management Review*, 20(4): 1053–1089.

Rondinelli, D. & Vastag, G. (2000). 'Panacea, Common Sense, or just a Label? The Value of ISO 14001 Environmental Management Systems," *European Management Journal*, 18(5): 499–510.

Russo, M. & Harrison, N. (2005). "Organizational Design and Environmental Performance: Clues from the Electronics Industry," *Academy of Management Journal*, 48(4): 582–593.

Saiz, A. V. (2005). "Globalisation, Cosmopolitanism and Ecological Citizenship," *Environmental Politics*, 14(2): 163–178.

Sandberg, K. (2006). "Groundwork Laid for ISO 26000," *Business and the Environment*, 17(1): 14.

Schaltegger, S. & Wagner, M. (eds.) (2006). *Managing the Business Case for Sustainability*. Sheffield, UK: Greenleaf Publishing.

Scherer, A. G. & Palazzo, G. (2007). "Toward a Political Conception of Corporate Responsibility: Business and Society seen from a Habermasian Perspective," *Academy of Management Review*, 32(4): 1096–1120.

———— (eds.) (2008). *Handbook of Research on Global Corporate Citizenship*. Cheltenham: Edward Elgar.

———— & Matten, D. (2009). "The Changing Role of Business in a Global Society: New Challenges and Responsibilities," *Business Ethics Quarterly*, 19(3): 327–347.

Schwartz, B. & Tilling, K. (2009). "'ISO-lating' Corporate Social Responsibility in the Organizational Context: A Dissenting Interpretation of ISO 26000," *Corporate Social Responsibility and Environmental Management*, 16: 289–299.

Seager, T. (2008). "The Sustainability Spectrum and the Sciences of Sustainability," *Business Strategy and the Environment*, 17: 444–453.

Sethi, S. P. (1975). "Dimensions of Corporate Social Performance: An Analytical Framework," *California Management Review*, 17(3): 58–64.

—— (2003). *Setting Global Standards: Guidelines for Creating Codes of Conduct in Multinational Corporations*. Hoboken, NJ: J. Wiley.

Shaw, D. & Clarke, I. (1999). "Belief Formation in Ethical Consumer Groups: An Exploratory Study," *Marketing Intelligence & Planning*, 17(2): 109–119.

Shrivastava, P. (1995). "Ecocentric Management for a Risk Society," *Academy of Management Review*, 20(1): 118–137.

Starik, M. (1995). "Should Trees have Managerial Standing? Toward Stakeholder Status For Non-Human Nature," *Journal of Business Ethics*, 14: 207–217.

—— & Rands, G. P. (1995). "Weaving an Integrated Web: Multilevel and Multisystem Perspectives of Ecologically Sustainable Organizations," *Academy of Management Review*, 20(4): 908–935.

Stenzel, P. L. (1999). "Can the ISO 14000 Series Environmental Management Standards Provide a Viable Alternative to Government Regulation?" *American Business Law Journal*, 37: 238–298.

Stern, R. N. & Barley, S. R. (1996). "Organizations and Social Systems: Organization Theory's Neglected Mandate," *Administrative Science Quarterly*, 41: 146–162.

Swanson, D. L. (1995). "Addressing a Theoretical Problem by Reorienting the Corporate Social Performance Model," *Academy of Management Review*, 20(1): 43–64.

Thompson, D. (ed) (2002). *Tools for Environmental Management: A Practical Introduction and Guide*. Gabriola Island, BC: New Society Publishers.

Topal, R. S., Ongen, A. & Filho, W. L. (2009). "An Analysis of Corporate Social Responsibility and its Usefulness in Catalysing Ecosystem Sustainability," *International Journal of Environment and Sustainable Development*, 8(2): 173–189.

Uzumeri, M. V. (1997). 'ISO 9000 and Other Metastandards: Principles for Management Practice?'. *Academy of Management Executive*, 11(1): 21–36.

Van Oosterhout, J. H. & Heugens, P. P. M. A. R. (2008). 'Much Ado About Nothing: A Conceptual Critique of CSR," in Crane, A., McWilliams, A., Matten, D., Moon, J. and Siegel, D. (eds.), *The Oxford Handbook of Corporate Social Responsibility*. Oxford: Oxford University Press, 197–223.

Wackernagel, M. & Rees, W. (1996). *Our Ecological Footprint: Reducing Human Impact on the Earth*. Gabriola, British Columbia: New Society Publishers.

Walsh, J. P., Weber, K. & Margolis, J. D. (2003). "Social Issues in Management: Our Lost Cause Found," *Journal of Management*, 29: 859–882.

Welford, R. J. (1997). *Hijacking Environmentalism: Corporate Responses to Sustainable Development*. London: Routledge.

Whiteman, G. & Cooper, W. H. (2000). "Ecological Embeddedness," *Academy of Management Journal*, 43(6): 1265–1282.

Willard, B. (2007). *The Business Case for Sustainabilty*. Vancouver: New Society Publishers.

Williams, C. A. & Aguilera, R. V. (2008). "Corporate Social Responsibility in a Comparative Perspective," in Crane, A., McWilliams, A., Matten, D., Moon, J. and Siegel, D. (eds.). *The Oxford Handbook of CSR*. Oxford: Oxford University Press, 452–472.

Williams, O. F. (ed.) (2001). *Global Codes of Conduct*. Chicago, IL: University of Notre Dame Press.

Windsor, D. (2006). "Corporate Social Responsibility: Three Key Approaches," *Journal of Management Studies*, 43(1): 93–114.

Wood, D. J. (1991). "Corporate Social Performance Revisited," *Academy of Management Review*, 16: 691–718.

World Commission On Environment And Development (1987). *Our Common Future*. NY: Oxford University Press.

Wu, M.-L. (2006). "Corporate Social Performance, Corporate Financial Performance, and Firm Size: A Meta-Analysis," *The Journal of American Academy of Business, Cambridge*, 8(1): 163–171.

Zadek, S. (2004). "The Path to Corporate Responsibility," *Harvard Business Review*, 82: 125–132.

CHAPTER 29

BUSINESS, SOCIETY, AND THE ENVIRONMENT

JAMES E. POST

BUSINESS cannot operate apart from the rest of society. Indeed, commerce is an integral dimension of society and has been so for many centuries. Since the nineteenth century, however, there has been a growing emphasis on limiting, or reversing, the many negative externalities caused by industrial practice. The interaction of economy, politics, and culture regarding the environment has attracted the attention of social scientists for centuries. In the world of practice, this has been a never-ending story of challenge, conflict, and changing public policy. For scholars, however, this dynamic has inspired an analysis of the fundamental relationship between management and society. This chapter focuses on how the relationship between business, society and the environment has evolved, with each system affecting the others. I trace the effort to shift from a traditional "dominion of nature" paradigm toward a radically different "sustainability" paradigm. Effecting this change requires a new definition and understanding of the role of the corporation in society. The features of this new model are proposed.

MODELS OF MANAGEMENT AND SOCIETY

In *Private Management and Public Policy* (1975), Preston & Post employed a systems perspective to analyze the relationship between management and society. Market exchange and public policy were defined as the two processes through which economic and social interests are reconciled in a democratic society. In the pure market contract model, it is assumed that every actor in society gets what they need through exchange relationships with others. In contrast, the Marxian analysis of capitalist production inevitably points to the exploitation of labor—and in the context of this book, exploitation of natural resources—as the source of "surplus value" (i.e. profit). The continuous pressure to generate profits produces a new stock of capital that is used, in turn, to add to the capacity for more exploitation. For as Marx wrote, *"Accumulate, accumulate! That is Moses and the prophets!"* (quoted in Preston & Post 1975: 21). Economic power becomes political power, and the system of exchange transactions breaks down because of excessive power or elitist decision-making, both of which constitute "market failures." The existence of these failures gives rise to "exploitation" or "technocratic" systems, emphasizing the Marxian or Galbraithian tendencies originally defined by those authors (Galbraith 1967). Empirical evidence confirms that reality supports each theory to some extent, but that none of these theories explains all facts. We concluded that the appropriate model for understanding the business–society relationship in modern times is one that recognizes the interpenetrating effects of business and societal systems on one another. The business system shapes society, as the social system shapes business. This interpenetration happens through the market, the public policy process, and the acceptance of changing values in the larger social milieu (Preston & Post 1975).

The interdependence of business and society, while self-evident to many observers, is neither universally understood nor wholly accepted. History provides many examples of enterprises that operated with disregard for the side effects and consequences of their behavior. In theory, the rich and the powerful are not exempt from legal and ethical norms of society; in practice, the story differs.

With respect to natural resources and the environment, many industries have behaved as if they were empowered to operate apart from legal or moral restraint. At various times, the agricultural, petroleum, chemical, forestry, and biotechnology industries—to name but a few—have engaged in behavior that imposed damages, costs, and risks on citizens and communities in disregard of conventional ethical and legal rules. The cumulative impact on property and human life is incalculable, but few communities have escaped such externalities.

The business and society perspective complements that of corporate social responsibility—which asks the questions "to whom" and "for what" is the corporation responsible—and stakeholder theory, which is a response to those questions. (See Kassinis [Chapter 5] and Bondy & Matten [Chapter 28] this volume.) Rather, the business and society perspective is a macro viewpoint, focusing on the evolutionary interaction of economic, political, and cultural forces in national and global society.

Our thesis is simple: The study of business in contemporary society poses questions about how business relates—and *should* relate—to the natural environment, uses resources that all beings share, and internalizes costs that have so often been externalized to society in the past. Answering those questions begins with an understanding of how we have evolved since the Industrial Revolution.

A HISTORY OF THE BUSINESS, SOCIETY AND ENVIRONMENT RELATIONSHIP

Looking over several centuries, it is evident that individuals, firms, and industries have taken advantage of natural resources such as coal, petroleum, iron ore, timber, water, and land to meet their needs for energy and raw materials by employing a "rule of capture" rationale (i.e. whoever first exercises dominion over the resource is entitled to enjoy its use and benefits). From the hunter-gatherer societies whose members exercised dominion through hunting and fishing, to the industrial age when organization and scale enabled widespread economic activity, the *dominion of nature* has been a core reality of the human relationship with the natural environment. In some measure, the entire history of business, society, and the environment for the last 100 years has been a challenge to the "dominion of nature" paradigm. As discussed below, growing numbers of people have challenged the *dominion of nature paradigm* with alternative ideas and actions. From industrial hygiene to modern pollution control systems and futuristic global codes of practice, the environmental movement has sought to redefine the relationship between business, society, and the environment away from exploitation. But it has been a long, slow journey toward sustainability.

Four axial themes in environmental history

Within this history, four themes shape our understanding of how business, society, and the environment have evolved over time. These axial themes form a structure of understanding about the complex relationship between critical dimensions of life that are drawn together as business and society interact with the environment. Through this lens, we can see the interplay of economics, technology, moral values, and institutional action.

The first two themes (technology and economics) explain what can be considered the "drivers" of human use of environmental resources. These are forces that have propelled humans to use natural resources more expansively for centuries. The second two themes (public policy and ethics) are the sources of ideas and actions to "constrain" the use of those resources. Together, these four "axial" themes form a structure for understanding and analyzing this history. Let us briefly consider each of the axial themes.

Technology and science drive resource consumption. Science and technology form a powerful force that has driven consumption of natural resources to increasingly high levels. The development of machinery to enable massive harvesting of timber, deep-water drilling for oil, and vast mining operations exemplifies the "exploitation" or *dominion of nature* model suggested above. Business has used advances in chemistry, biology, and other physical sciences to capture the productivity potential of natural resources. Of course, science has also illuminated environmental harms, risks, and damage, and offered what appears to be "solutions" to such problems, but over several centuries technology's primary role has been a productivity driver.

Economic incentives fuel the use and abuse of natural resources. The second axial theme is the role of the economic marketplace. For centuries, the incentives of the market have led humans to pursue commercial progress. Coupled with scientific knowledge, economics has provided an incentive for widespread use, and abuse, of all manner of natural resources. But markets fail, and a body of scholarship has steadily grown to address the causes and consequences of market failures (see Baron & Lyon [Chapter 7] this volume). Many failures have involved environmental externalities; once again, history is replete with examples of damage to nature due to a misunderstanding of market signals. More recently, the market has been harnessed on occasion to promote environmental goals through policies that incentivize environmentally benign or environmentally friendly action.

Law and Public Policy provide vital constraints on commercial use. Law and public policy form the third axial theme in the evolutionary story. Law and public policy often constrain commercial use of natural resources. Public policy is often the preferred (or only) solution to market failures and, hence, pivotal to challenging rampant or unguided destruction of natural resources throughout history (see Coglianese & Anderson [Chapter 8] this volume). Today, government involvement extends from the local, state, and federal levels to an expanding system of international environmental governance. This trend seems likely to continue as the "logic of collective action" (Olson 1965) becomes clearer and more compelling.

Sustainability concerns are driven by moral, ethical reasoning. The fourth axial theme is the growing recognition that what is at stake as we confront environmental issues is a test of human values, morality, and ethics. In the past fifty years, business has often been confronted by individuals and communities who have framed and voiced their concerns in moral, ethical, and human rights terms. The language of the environmental movement has often been cloaked in normative language—what "ought" to happen—and pursued as an ethical, moral, or religious imperative. This is not new, for many of the movements to promote social welfare for children, health and hygiene for those in poverty, and assistance for vulnerable people without food, water, and shelter, have been defined in "environmental justice" terms. Moral conscience is critical to the modern debates about natural resource use and environmental impacts.

Taken together, the interplay of science, markets, public policy, and ethical reasoning helps us understand the way business and society interpenetrate and influence one another in relation to the environment. As illustrated in Figure 29.1, these four themes enable us to understand the dynamic ebb and flow of environmental history as it has touched business and society in recent centuries.

Challenging the 'dominion of nature' paradigm

The history of environmental awareness and activism stretches back more than 500 years. The process of challenging what was once accepted as "natural" dates to the

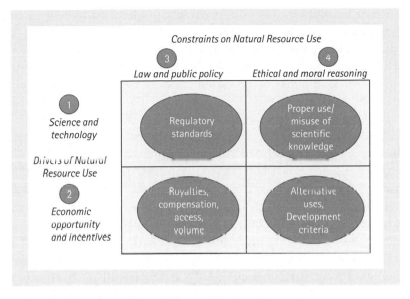

FIGURE 29.1 Axial Themes in Environmental History

Plague, which devastated Europe in the 1200s and stimulated early efforts to create a public health system. Water pollution problems were recognized as a problem in communities where population density produced dangerously unsanitary conditions. Rudimentary sanitation was enforced by local communities. The destruction of natural resources was also widespread. Forestry practices in Germany, France, and England left large tracts denuded and forced a shift to coal. Knowledge of soil conservation spread slowly, although cultures in China, Peru, and India understood the impact of soil erosion and used terracing, crop rotation, and natural fertilizer to prevent it. This "pre-history" also saw early efforts to understand and prevent occupational diseases.

By the 1700s, the Age of Enlightenment emphasized the power of reason as an anti dote to superstition. The era produced noteworthy efforts to safeguard human health, reflecting enlightenment philosophy that held that the individual citizen was valuable and that wretched conditions were not inevitable. But it was Thomas Malthus' argument that grain supplies, which increase at arithmetic rates, will run out as population increases at geometric rates, that remains most notable, for it established the idea that the Earth has limitations associated with "carrying capacity." As populations expand, argued Malthus, natural systems will be tested, with inevitable and tragic consequences. Hundreds of years later, that proposition is still being tested.

Of course, there were early warning signs of the health and environmental catastrophe that would soon take place on a much larger scale. The Enlightenment was an era of new technologies, some of which produced new types of pollution. Coal burning created tars that contaminated waterways, vulcanized rubber discharged noxious chemicals into streams and rivers, coal smoke choked the air in cities, and chemical factories operated without regard to those living downwind (Brimblecomb 1988). As the Industrial Revolution took hold, economic progress became synonymous with environmental degradation. Throughout the nineteenth century, living conditions deteriorated as cities grew, water quality worsened, and smog killed residents of large cities like London. Pressure mounted to change these conditions. In 1843, the House of Commons Select Committee on Smoke Nuisance recommended that all manufacturers be removed to a distance of five or six miles from the city center. The measure was ultimately defeated, but a new idea had emerged in public policy debate: industrial activity should be located apart from population centers.

Public health epidemics afflicted cities and prompted scientists and medical practitioners to action. John Snow, a London physician, traced a deadly cholera epidemic to a contaminated water pump in 1855. Water pollution often carried diseases such as cholera, but it was not until the 1880s that clean water was viewed as a vital public necessity. (As modern crises in Haiti and other nations show, problems such as cholera persist to the present.) The nineteenth century also signaled early efforts to conserve wilderness areas in the United States by using government (law and public policy) to say, in effect, "off limits." As often occurs, public awareness followed tragedy. Following the California gold rush in 1849, settlement of the Sierra Nevada mountain range began. In 1851, an enormous tree called "Mother of the Forest," measuring more than 300 feet in height and 92 feet in circumference, was felled. Public outrage grew as news of the cutting spread to San Francisco and other major cities. Ultimately, the controversy led to calls for a system of state or federal parks. There was a public sentiment that certain treasures of nature, such as giant sequoias, needed to be preserved even if "economic progress" was temporarily slowed.

These initiatives were isolated and sporadic, but gained force as the nineteenth century ended and the evils of polluted cities, industries, and impoverished communities generated fledgling social movements. These movements—especially conservation and preservation efforts—drew significant support from the wealthy as well as the poor and uneducated. Associations and societies such as the Boone and Crockett Club (founded in 1887 by future president, Theodore Roosevelt, and named after frontiersmen Daniel Boone and Davy Crockett) were formed and played an important role in the environmental crusades of the twentieth century.

Leading environmentalists such as John Muir also emerged. Muir's campaign to save Yosemite from commercial exploitation, and his numerous letters, newspaper columns, and magazine articles formed a foundation of ideas that shaped national parks in the early twentieth century.

The early twentieth century was a hotbed of reform activism in the United States. Working conditions, housing, adulterated food, sanitation, polluting industries, and political corruption all became targets for reform. President Theodore Roosevelt enlisted passionate advocates to implement his expansive vision of a better society. Foremost was Gifford Pinchot, who generated ideas about conservation of public lands and putting forests to "wise use." But others, such as John Muir, were strongly opposed to "wise use" and fought for outright preservation of unspoiled wilderness areas, foreshadowing debates that continue to the present. Roosevelt walked the political tightrope, holding together his coalition of nature lovers while moving environmental policy through—or around—the US Congress (Brinckley 2009).

The Progressive era was dominated by social movements led by such notables as Jane Addams (Hull House), Florence Kelly, and Alice Hamilton. New organizations advocated causes including environmental conservation. Among the new groups was the Sierra Club, which championed natural preservation and conservation, and by the early 1900s, the National Audubon Society, which became an effective advocate for birds, habitat, and conservation. Through these entities, the "dominion of nature" philosophy was challenged across the nation, dispute by dispute, one controversy after another. To a progressive like Roosevelt, respect for nature was part of how America defined (or ought to define) "progress." It was an uphill battle.

The legal system played an important role in adjudicating controversies and legitimizing the legal ideas of various state and federal legislators. In 1872, for example, the so-called "public trust doctrine" was certified by the US Supreme Court in the case of *Martin v. Wadell*. The *Martin* decision established that wildlife belonged to the people (the *state*), although conservation was not yet fully a part of the American identity.

Public policy also became a pathway to protect wildlife populations. The widespread destruction of buffalo, waterfowl, and other wild game species decimated America's wildlife to support commercial demand for "food, feathers, and trophies." In response, dedicated hunters and anglers from New York to Montana pushed for the nation's first game laws, restricting the numbers and methods of take for wildlife. Laws were established to sustain healthy wildlife populations, and conservation-minded leaders emerged to challenge how Americans viewed wildlife. Enforcement systems followed.

When Theodore Roosevelt, an avid outdoorsman and hunter, became president in 1901, conservation became part of the nation's agenda. Roosevelt's conservation ethic was part of a life-long desire to explore, enjoy, and write about the wonders of nature. The environment never had a more vigorous advocate in the White House than it had in Theodore Roosevelt (Brinckley 2009). Roosevelt articulated his conservation philosophy in speeches, interviews, and writings. He wrote,

> Above all, we should realize that the effort toward this end is essentially a democratic movement. It is…in our power…to preserve large tracts of wilderness…and to preserve the game…for the benefit all lovers of nature, and to give reasonable opportunities for the exercise of the skill of the hunter, whether he is or is not a man of means…It is foolish to regard proper game laws as undemocratic. On the contrary, they are essentially in the interests of the people as a whole, because it is only through their enactment and enforcement that the people can preserve the game and prevent its becoming purely the property of the rich. The man of small means is dependent solely upon wise and well-executed game laws for his enjoyment of the sturdy pleasure of the chase. (Quoted at National Wildlife Federation website, <www.nwf. org>, accessed 22 April, 2010).

Roosevelt vigorously pursued environmental goals: National parks, monuments, and preserves were created and more than a quarter million square miles of land were protected from development and exploitation. Roosevelt was not a model of democratic process, but he was a champion for environmental causes, and his passion inspired others, making the first decade of the twentieth century a "golden era" for environmental advocacy. The Roosevelt era was followed by a period of environmental backsliding and by the early 1930s, poor farming practices produced a "Dust Bowl" across great swaths of the nation. Coupled with the economic hardship of the Great Depression, the nation shifted focus away from natural resources and toward her unemployed population.

The 1930s produced two notable developments. First, the federal government joined employment and environmental goals through programs to improve national parks and related public works. From the Hoover Dam to the Civilian Conservation Corps, the nation's environmental infrastructure received a massive injection of resources. Second, the conservation movement became organized, and focused on advocating critical environmental goals. The formation of the General Wildlife Federation (later named the National Wildlife Federation (NWF)) in 1936 brought together an estimated 36,000 local and regional organizations as a coherent voice for fish, game, and wildlife protection. From the outset, the NWF lobbied for congressional action on a variety of environmental and conservation objectives.

Prosperity and social consciousness were not a smooth mixture during the high-octane economy of the 1920s. New actors were created such as the National Coast Anti-Pollution League, formed by municipal officers from East Coast communities from Atlantic City to Maine. Their concern focused on the oil and sewage pollution in coastal waters which were affecting tourism, an economically important industry. The League succeeded in getting an international oil-dumping treaty passed by the US Congress in 1924. The *"dominion of nature"* was challenged by economic arguments as well as conservation (public trust) arguments. A pragmatic, utilitarian strain of thinking joined conservation and preservationist arguments as reasons to weigh costs and consequences before allowing more exploitation of nature to occur.

The externalities of industrial activity were becoming clearer and more scientifically established. Once again, the environmental battleground was public health. Alice Hamilton led a losing crusade to ban leaded gasoline, which ultimately became the standard fuel for most of the world. But other cases of industrial harm successfully stirred the public imagination. Hamilton publicized the "Radium Girls," a group of young women who were dying of radiation-induced cancer due to exposure in the workplace. Crusading journalist Walter Lippmann worked with Hamilton to bring their case to public attention. The publicity and campaign succeeded in getting medical care and some compensation for their families.

Science and commerce found expression in the "chemurgy" movement, a populist and scientific cause. Agricultural interests pressed for expanded use of farm products, including the replacement of petroleum with alcohol. The movement attracted successful businessmen to the ideas. Henry Ford sought to make cars and fuels from agricultural products, especially soybeans which Ford successfully used for gearshift knobs and horn buttons. George Washington Carver, an early contributor, developed industrial uses (e.g. paints, dyes, glues) for peanuts, sweet potatoes, and other crops to diversify the cotton-dominated industry of the South. During World War II, many efforts were made to employ farm products as substitutes for scare natural resources, most notably syn-

1

thetic rubber in place of scarce natural rubber for tires. Chemurgy faded as a political movement, but never lost its industrial appeal. Indeed, it has twenty-first century descendants in the biotechnology companies that are using agricultural feedstocks to make plastics, paints, textile fibers, and other products now derived from oil.

Industrial chemistry, which focused on managing industrial waste and creating methods of using apparently worthless products, or enhancing the value of seemingly worthless items, also flourished. As Pierre Desrochers has written, these "Victorian pioneers of corporate sustainability" argued that profitability and a cleaner environment went hand-in-hand (Desrochers 2009: 704). Attention to industrial by-products produced innovations for manufacturers and their customers, and minimized environmental problems. The early movement was supported by the British Society for the Encouragement of Arts, Manufactures and Commerce, which promoted creation of by-products from polluting industrial waste (Desrochers 2009: 703). By the end of the nineteenth century, however, the scale of industrial enterprise dwarfed the achievements of the industrial waste management movement. Still, an important line of scientific knowledge and thought was established that became a precursor for developments a half-century later. As suggested in Figure 29.2, the *"dominion of nature"* premises that were the underpinnings of economic exploitation of the environment throughout history were now being challenged by a new set of ideas. While limited in their immediate effects, the idea that nature and its bounty had to be protected, conserved, and valued formed the premises of a new paradigm that would gain strength, momentum, and a new name—*"sustainable development"*—in the second half of the twentieth century.

The modern environmental movement

The post-World War II era marked the beginning of modern environmental awareness (for more history of this period, see Weber & Soderstrom [Chapter 14] this volume).

FIGURE 29.2 Two Paradigms

War is devastating to the natural environment and wide swaths of Europe and Asia were left with chemical waste from explosives, petroleum residues, and contaminated water supplies; widespread destruction of buildings and contamination of agricultural soil were common by-products. Restoration of natural habitat and productive land space required extensive reclamation efforts. The continental United States was spared major environmental damage, but suffered the consequences of major military facilities where millions of soldiers received training in live fire exercises and toxic landfills proliferated.

The "moral voice" of environmental policy emerged with the publication of forester Aldo Leopold's famous *Sand County Almanac* shortly after his death in 1948. Leopold made a compelling case for expanding the sense of human responsibility for each other and for the earth. Through his writings, Leopold contributed a treasure trove of stimulating ideas about the relationship between humans and the environment. His writing contributed to the ethical discourse about human beings in relation to the environment between 1948 and the 1960s. The "marketplace of ideas" would expand greatly in postwar America. The popularity of Leopold's work foreshadowed the tremendous response yet to come to other environmental treatises (e.g., Rachel Carson's *Silent Spring*).

Meanwhile, evidence mounted that air quality was deteriorating as deadly smog events occurred in Donorra, PA (1948), London (1952, 1956), New York (1953), and Los Angeles (1954). The public realized that air pollution was a new crisis. In 1955, the first international air pollution conference was held. Two years later, an increasing CO_2 buildup in the Earth's atmosphere was one of the surprising conclusions of Scripps Oceanographic Institute scientists working on International Geophysical Year projects (1957).

The modern environmental movement was forged in the social and political turbulence of the 1960s and 1970s. Rachel Carson's *Silent Spring* (1962) struck a responsive chord with a public that worried about the effects of chemicals on food, animals, birds, and children. A few years later this call to action was made more vivid by the "burning river" of oil and chemicals that ignited in the Cuyahoga River in Cleveland, Ohio (June 22, 1969). Flames soared five stories high; pictures of the conflagration circulated across the US and many foreign countries. The Cuyahoga became the visible answer to the question of "what does pollution look like?" It looked like a burning river.

Three developments shaped the new public policy context. First, the nation's political leadership embraced protection of the environment. Republican President Richard M. Nixon recognized the political power of the movement and sought to harness it by taking a front row position on the issues. Presidential endorsement provided mainstream legitimacy.

Second, events drew crowds to celebrate the Earth and advocate protection and restoration. Earth Day (22 April, 1970) was a political event whose success surprised its most optimistic organizers. Twenty million men, women, and children participated; the unity of such a coalition was unprecedented. The environment became a citizens' movement with political clout.

Third, the environmental movement inspired innovative Americans to offer practical steps, solutions, and systems at every turn. The environmental movement has always been about ideas + action: *"What can I do?"* has been central to every meeting, rally, and event. This remains true more than forty years after the original Earth Day event.

The 1970s produced a public awakening and a series of monumental policy actions. Three pieces of federal legislation—the Clear Air Act, Clean Water Act, and the Endangered Species Act—provided an essential framework for modern environmental regulation, policy, and practice. President Nixon used his State of the Union address to offer several memorable rhetorical lines: "(W)e must make peace with nature"…we must begin "making reparations" for the damage done to the environment. The movement embraced the message, if not the messenger. As environmental activist Stewart Udall said of the environmental movement: "it enlarged the conservation movement to (include) the planet itself" (American Experience 2009). The creation of the Environmental Protection Agency in 1970 was another landmark. For the first time in history, a federal agency had been created for the explicit purpose of guiding the nation's efforts to tackle the problems of air and water pollution. "Pollution prevention" became the strategic concept guiding EPA activities, providing focus to an entity with vast responsibility but limited financial and human resources.

What has been described as a "decade of awakening and cleanup" began with the birth of the Environmental Protection Agency and ended with the Appropriate Community Technology demonstration on the Washington Mall in 1979. During the 1970s, air pollution was dramatically cut through use of catalytic converters on new cars that used unleaded gasoline. But the predicted "pollution free car" proved to be a false hope. Water pollution decreased through a massive sewage treatment expansion program, and rivers which once functioned as sewers began a gradual restoration. Still, the "national pollution discharge elimination system" failed to actually eliminate discharges. Toxic chemicals became a serious threat. Corporations like Allied Chemical, manufacturer of Kepone, were exposed as polluters that had put the public at risk for profit. The nation discovered more toxic sites, including Love Canal (Niagara Falls, New York) and Valley of the Drums (Louisville, Kentucky). These examples eventually led to new laws, including the much-heralded "Super Fund" law in 1980.

The greatest public crisis of the decade occurred in 1979 when the nuclear power plant at Three Mile Island (PA) released radiation into the atmosphere. The accident at TMI effectively guaranteed that no nuclear plant would be approved for decades to come. Once again, the fallacy of the *dominion of nature* paradigm was exposed. Industrial disasters became an increasingly important theme in the environmental debate. Three Mile Island gave meaning to "meltdown" and made vivid the risks that communities faced from nuclear as well as chemical facilities. (In time, this would extend to biotechnological and magnetic risks factors as well.) The media began to link industrial hazards to human health and to the fate of communities. A "risk management paradigm" was introduced in the 1980s by EPA Administrator William Ruckelshaus. Society could not expect a risk-free way of life, Ruckelshaus argued, but it could insist on careful risk assessment, evaluation, and risk management. This seemed a "balanced" course between the costs of environmental protection and the benefits of resource use.

Environmental disasters at home and abroad curbed the Reagan Administration's efforts to roll back regulations. In 1984, the Union Carbide plant in Bhopal, India, suffered an industrial accident that immediately killed thousands of citizens, and whose long-term effects have allegedly accounted for the deaths of more than 100,000 people. In the Ukraine, the Chernobyl nuclear reactor exploded, causing deaths and radiation leaks that spread worldwide. Such disasters put science and technology on the defensive. When the Challenger space shuttle exploded, killing its crew of astronauts, the accident was blamed on the failure of "O" rings. But the cause was ultimately traceable to an organizational culture that minimized risks in the name of mission. To many observers, this accident symbolized excessive risk tolerance in industry and the scientific community. The emerging ethos seemed to be "safety first." In 1989, the Exxon Valdez oil tanker ran aground in Prince William Sound, Alaska, spilling millions of barrels of crude oil into pristine waters, killing untold numbers of fish, seabirds, and mammals. This accident was attributable to human failure: an inebriated sea captain allowed an unqualified seaman to steer the ship through the dangerous Prince William Sound passageway. It was also the nation's costliest environmental clean-up, with Exxon liable for nearly $3 billion of damages. Once again, the public confronted the high environmental costs of economic activity.

A more hopeful note was struck when an international accord was reached to address ozone depletion through the creation of the Montreal Protocol in 1987. The accord created a precedent-setting plan of international action that even US President Ronald Reagan and Britain's Prime Minister, Margaret Thatcher, signed despite their antipathy to international regulation. The Montreal Protocol reflected a scientific consensus that global environmental problems transcended the borders of sovereign nations, and a political consensus that intergovernmental collective action was required at the global level. The dangers of environmental advocacy were underscored by conflict on the high seas over whaling, industrial fishing fleets, oil production, and nuclear testing. In 1985, a Greenpeace ship—the Rainbow Warrior—was bombed in New Zealand. The ship had been used to confront "environmental terrorists" and the bombing was seen as an act of retaliation. The bombing provoked international outcry and was a reminder of other situations when protectors of the environment were assaulted or killed.

By the 1990s, the *dominion of nature* mindset had been widely challenged, but not reversed. The events of the 1970s and 1980s had called for new ways of doing business. In the marketplace of ideas—and ultimately in the political arena—it became clear that there was an imperative to create "win-win" outcomes. The 1970s and 1980s had demonstrated that "win-lose" thinking could quickly deteriorate into "lose-lose" outcomes. Business responded to this challenge with imagination. By the 1990s, environmental lessons about pollution prevention, waste reduction, recycling, and green design were widely shared. The economic market for environmental technologies, products, and services expanded. Improved environmental health and safety systems were implemented in many industries. These were "win-win" outcomes.

International environmental issues commanded growing attention during this period. In 1987, the Single Act of Europe amended the Treaty of Rome to provide an explicit legal basis for pan-European regulations. By the early 1990s, the need for harmonized EU environmental standards was recognized, and in 1993 the Maastrict Treaty officially made environmental issues a key EU policy area. Trans-boundary pollution is of serious concern in European nations, reflecting serious toxic spills along the Rhine, Danube, and other major rivers. In many respects, Europeans have provided strong public support for environmental policy and regulation. European environmental consciousness was stirred in 1995 when Shell was challenged regarding its plans to sink the Brent Spar oil rig in the North Sea. Greenpeace members seized control of the rig and an international campaign was directed at Shell, including a European consumer boycott. The company was further challenged by the international community when it was deemed complicit in the Nigerian government's execution of journalist and environmentalist Ken Saro-Wiwa who documented environmental and human rights abuses taking place in the oil-rich delta region where Shell operated. Although Shell denied the charges, and publicly sought Saro-Wiwa's release, critics deemed Shell's behavior a human rights disaster. The twin crises ultimately caused Shell senior management to reassess its way of doing business and to develop a host of new stakeholder-engagement policies and practices.

Global environmental awareness was building throughout this period. The Persian Gulf War became an environmental disaster when Saddam Hussein ordered the burning of thousands of oil wells. The images of burning oil fields were shown around the world. Another international cause of note involved worldwide protest at the construction of China's Three Gorges Dam project. This project, along with the burning of the Amazon rainforest, became visible examples of the globalization of environmental concerns during the 1990s. (For a discussion of the Amazon rainforest debate in the 1990s see Buchholz, Marcus, & Post 1992.)

Business schools were notoriously slow to introduce environmental issues to the curriculum. But in the 1990s, with industry support, a few business schools focused on ways in which environmental issues intersected the economic and strategic interests of companies. The National Wildlife Federation and its Corporate Conservation Council fostered dialog between environmental leaders and senior executives of member companies on "common ground" topics, such as recycling, habitat conservation, and conservation of natural resources. In 1990, the NWF/CCC also sponsored the development of the first environmental curriculum in American business schools and the creation of pilot undergraduate and MBA courses in three American universities. Other schools soon joined the effort, and the field of environmental management grew quickly. The AACSB accrediting agency sponsored meetings, and the *Wall Street Journal* reported that within one year, more than 150 business schools were offering courses on business and the environment.

The *dominion of nature* paradigm was being broadly challenged by the end of the 1990s. The premise of air and water as "free goods" was no longer accepted. Economists and regulators focused on the proper pricing of environmental externalities and the creation of markets for trading emission rights. Economics and technology had both shifted from exploiting nature to preserving nature. The concept of sustainability began to take root in industry, government, and society, and the millennium provided a unique opportunity to focus public attention on the sustainability agenda.

SUSTAINABILITY AND THE NEW MILLENNIUM

The new millennium provided a focal point for efforts to document, assess, and project the future of the planet's natural environment. Notably, the Millennium Development Goals Project placed vital environmental goals in a framework of other human goals. Eight goals were defined:

1. Eradicate extreme poverty and hunger.
2. Achieve universal primary education.
3. Promote gender equality and empower women.
4. Reduce child mortality.
5. Improve maternal health.
6. Combat HIV/AIDS, malaria, and other diseases.
7. Ensure environmental sustainability.
8. Develop a global partnership for development.

The international community (governments, NGOs, and other institutions) mobilized support and resources for programs to achieve these goals. The lasting effect may be the framework itself, for it highlights the structural elements that must be in place if the twenty-first century is to be the era in which the new paradigm of sustainability and human progress takes root. The interdependency of business and society—and the inability of governments to address environmental problems alone—led UN Secretary-General Kofi Annan in 1996 to call for the creation of a global partnership, or "compact," between leading businesses and the United Nations. The UN Global Compact was created to define an ethical and moral framework of responsible business principles and practices that would respect human rights, the environment, and labor rights. Ten principles of responsible business conduct were developed, including three that bear directly on the environment. The three core environmental principles are:

- Global Compact Principle 7: "Businesses should support a precautionary approach to environmental challenges."
- Global Compact Principle 8: "Businesses should undertake initiatives to promote greater environmental responsibility."
- Global Compact Principle 9: "Businesses should encourage the development and diffusion of environmentally friendly technologies."

By 2010, more than 8,000 organizations, from all continents, had signed the Global Compact, committing to its principles and reporting requirements. The Millennium

Development Goals and the UN Global Compact signify global environmental awareness and action at the highest political level. Scientific research has created awareness of what is at stake in curbing greenhouse gas emissions and preserving biodiversity. Intergovernmental cooperation has taken place on a host of other environmental issues, and private actions by companies, NGOs, and citizens are growing in number and significance. Sustainability remains an elusive goal, but the global business community has become an integral participant in efforts to address the environmental and development agenda. The UN Global Compact and Millennium Goals represent important steps to harmonize the behavior of corporations with the "high principles" embodied in these documents. These documents, and the processes that created them, provided an unparalleled opportunity to focus on the moral dimensions of how humans use the earth's resources. At their best, the companies that have made public commitments to these principles are creating "best practice" models of how business and the environment can operate in a more harmonious relationship.

But is this enough? The *dominion of nature* paradigm has prevailed since the Industrial Revolution, enlisting economics, technological innovation, and the power of government to pursue "progress" in materialistic terms. In the twenty-first century, the four great axial themes that have shaped how business and society relate to the environment—economics, technology, public policy, and moral thought—are turning in the direction of sustainability. But to achieve that goal requires that we transform the institutions of the old order. Foremost among these is the corporation itself.

The number of signatories to the Global Compact or other codes remains small relative to the total number of economic enterprises. And there are geographic, industry, and resource settings where ecological impacts have barely been addressed. The adaptive stakeholder model falls short of harmonizing economic activities with environmental consequences and risks. What is required is a "transformative" model that places environmental effects at the center of all economic, technological, and political considerations (see also Hart [Chapter 3] this volume). In such a model, the license to operate, the license to compete, and the license to innovate would form three distinct decision contexts in which the full array of environmental consequences can be evaluated in operational decision-making (Sachs et al. 2011). What is needed is a redefinition of the corporation for the twenty-first century (see also Elkington & Love [Chapter 36] this volume).

REDEFINING THE CORPORATION

The corporation has evolved as a legal form and an economic entity for more than three centuries. Among the noteworthy changes is the shift from narrow to general purpose charters, public accountability, global business operations, and expanded liability. These changes have greatly expanded corporate rights to participate in the economic and political life of nations. In Europe, Asia, Latin America, and other centers of corporate power, similar expansion of responsibilities and rights make clear the dynamic and global character of corporate existence.

There is reason to think we will see further evolution of the "stakeholder corporation" (see Kassinis [Chapter 5] this volume) as an incrementally more accountable enterprise. But there is a need to ask the more radical question: *How would a corporation be designed to seamlessly integrate social and financial purpose?* This question has been addressed by Corporation 20/20, an international, multi-stakeholder initiative. Its goal is to develop and share corporate designs in which social purpose moves from the periphery to the heart of the organization (<www.corporation20/20.org>). The Corporation20/20 process has produced six principles of corporate design to guide the creation of such corporations in the twenty-first century. These are,

1. The purpose of the corporation is to harness private interests to serve the public interest.
2. Corporations shall accrue fair returns for shareholders, but not at the expense of the legitimate interests of other stakeholders.
3. Corporations shall operate sustainably, meeting the needs of the present generation without compromising the ability of future generations to meet their needs.
4. Corporations shall distribute their wealth equitably among those who contribute to its creation.
5. Corporations shall be governed in a manner that is participatory, transparent, ethical, and accountable.
6. Corporations shall not infringe on the right of natural persons to govern themselves, nor infringe on other universal human rights.

Two of these principles—#1 and #5—are of special relevance to issues involving natural resource use and environmental impact. The purpose of the corporation (#1) has long been thought a "given." In truth, the purpose of the corporation may be the most contestable proposition of all. As the principals write, "The question of corporate purpose is seldom asked yet lies at the heart of societal expectations, contemporary corporate conduct and prospects for innovative corporate designs in the coming decades. The common wisdom that used to divide the world into the Anglo-Saxon shareholder-oriented approach and the Continental Europe stakeholder-oriented approach is overly simplistic and should not be accepted at face value. New developments in US state charter law open new possibilities for repurposing the corporation" (www.corporation2020.org).

The other relevant principle is Principle #5 dealing with governance. As C20/20 principals write, "corporations (must) be governed in a manner that is participatory, transparent, ethical and accountable." Accountability is a pivotal concept, evolving as societal expectations of business change in response to twenty-first century circumstances. Accountability is manifested in governance, stakeholder relations, and the organization's commitment to transparency and ethical conduct. What norms should corporations be held to? What are the leading examples of organizations whose practices provide a glimpse of the frontier in corporate accountability? These are questions for scholars and practitioners. The next phase in the process of business evolution is toward a corporation that no longer seeks to be, and is actively prevented from becoming, an "externalizing machine" (Monks & Minow 2008).

The natural environment and a global population of 6 billion people cannot bear the externalizing consequences of corporate disregard for the environment. Environmental damage has now reached proportions unknown in human history. For these reasons, scholars must search for new ways to harness the power of the corporation to public purposes. Neither the ends nor means are adequate to the task. Corporations do not voluntarily "do the right thing" very often, if at all, in the absence of economic incentives. And economic incentives sometimes create perverse, anti-social results. Regulation counts for very little when enforcement of standards and rules is lax or ineffectual.

What are the moral values and principles to shape the organizations of the future? If we begin with the assumption that each living person has a basic right to exist on Earth, then service to all humanity must be a guiding criterion. If we include the rights of other species, as well, we further constrain permissible activity. That people and other species have interests in common suggests that much more effort must be invested in optimizing survival strategies. Our thinking must venture beyond Garrett Hardin's "Tragedy of the Commons." But the number and complexity of moral dilemmas grows quickly, and the debate over which values should shape the conversation expands.

It is clear that the narrow, private-purpose corporation is a poor fit with the realities of the twenty-first century. If it concentrates only on economic growth, business cannot adequately adjust to the other demands of modern life. A public-purpose corporation has more potential to adjust, but only if its governance and accountability mechanisms ensure—at minimum—that all relevant stakeholders interests are taken into account.

New models are needed. A stakeholder-owned enterprise could be one such option, though it must sacrifice "market efficiency" for "social effectiveness" if it is to place the environment in a position of prominence. Based on the needs of the future, the structure and governance of the corporate form need to reflect four characteristics:

- The organization must be a participatory entity. Those who are affected by its operations must have a voice in the decisions.
- Transparency and disclosure of operating results must be assured.
- Ethical principles of decision-making must be communicated, including a clear statement of the values, principles, and norms to be followed.
- Accountability for resources used, results achieved, and unintended consequences. This should include, but not be limited to, regular reporting of economic, environmental, and social equity information.

This agenda requires elaboration and refinement. It is the kind of scholarly work that addresses not only what is, but what can be.

LOOKING AHEAD

This paper has offered an evolutionary view of the relationship between business, society, and the environment as interpenetrating social systems. As these systems have evolved, both the drivers of natural resource use and the constraints on the use of resources have become more sophisticated. Today, the adaptive stakeholder corporation is no longer an adequate model. A "transformative" or redefined corporation is required with a public purpose and new principles of governance and accountability (see Ehrenfeld [Chapter 33] this volume).

Business and society share a common destiny with regard to the environment. If human beings are unable to rebalance business activity and environmental consequences, future generations will bear a heavy burden in terms of the quality of life. Worst case scenarios abound for unchecked industrial activity.

The challenges are as daunting as any in human history. But the history of environmental action, from the earliest days of basic public health campaigns to the present is one of science, economics, politics, and ethical thought interacting to shape a new consciousness. Environmental issues are prominent in the economic marketplace, public policy arena, and the marketplace of ideas (i.e. the "public square"). Although opinion polls suggest shifting priorities, there is little reason to believe that interest in the environment will diminish for long. Global scientific communities, governments, NGOs, and millions of citizen voices are now joined in conversation through the Internet and other forms of communication. These voices are stating an unmistakable truth: The moral and practical mandate to preserve and protect nature rests with every person, organization, and public institution. For hundreds of years, humans believed in the *dominion of nature*. Today, the *dominion of nature* paradigm is being replaced by a *sustainability paradigm*. The ideas are clear, but progress is uneven. Nevertheless, science, public policy, and moral thought all suggest that achieving sustainability is the ultimate environmental challenge for business and society in the twenty-first century.

REFERENCES

American Experience (2009). *Earth Days* (A Robert Stone film). *The American Experience*, PBS, April.

Brimblecomb, P. (1988). *The Big Smoke*. London: Routledge.

Brinckley, D. (2009). *The Wilderness Warrior: Theodore Roosevelt and the Crusade for America*. New York: Harper.

Buchholz, R., Marcus, A. & Post, J. (1992). *Managing Environmental Issues: A Casebook*. Prentice-Hall.

Carson, R. (1962). *Silent Spring*. NY: Houghton Mifflin.

Cohen, M. (1984). *The Pathless Way: John Muir and American Wilderness*. Madison, WI: University of Wisconsin Press.

—— (1988). *History of the Sierra Club.* San Francisco, CA: Sierra Club Books.

Desrochers, P. (2009). "Victorian Pioneers of Corporate Sustainability," *Business History Review* 83(4): 703–729.

Galbraith, J. (1967). *The New Industrial State.* Boston: Houghton Mifflin.

Gore, A. (1993). *Earth in the Balance: Ecology and the Human Spirit.* N.Y : Plume

Gottlieb, R. (2005). *Forcing the Spring: The Transformation of the American Environmental Movement.* Washington, DC: Island Press.

Hayes, D. (1977). *Rays of Hope: The Transition to a Post-Petroleum World.* Worldwatch / W.W.Norton.

Markham, A. (1994). *A Brief History of Pollution.* New York: St. Martin's Press.

McKibben, B. (1989). *The End of Nature.* New York: Random House.

Melosi, M. (ed.) (1980). *Pollution and Reform in American Cities, 1870–1930.* Austin: University of Texas Press.

Monks, R. & Minow, N. (2008). *Corporate Governance,* 4th ed , John Wiley & Sons.

Muir, J. (1991). *Our National Parks.* San Francisco CA: Sierra Club Books.

Mumford, L. (1961). *The City in History.* NY: Harcourt, Brace & World.

Olson, M. (1965). *The Logic of Collective Action: Public Goods and the Theory of Groups.* Cambridge, MA: Harvard University Press.

Preston, L. E. and Post, J. E. (1975). *Private Management and Public Policy: The Principle of Public Responsibility.* Englewood Cliffs, NJ: Prentice Hall.

Post, J. E., Preston, L. E. & Sachs, S. (2002). *Redefining the Corporation: Organizational Wealth and Stakeholder Management.* Stanford, CA: Stanford University Press.

Rosner, D. & Markowitz, G. (1989). *Dying for Work: Workers Safety and Health in Twentieth Century America.* Bloomington, Ind.: Indiana University Press.

Sachs, S. et. al. (2011). *Stakeholders Matter.* Cambridge, Cambridge University Press.

Schell, J. (1982). *The Fate of the Earth.* New York : Knopf.

Shabecoff, P. (1993). *A Fierce Green Fire: The American Environmental Movement.* NY: Hill and Wang.

Sicherman, B. (1984). *Alice Hamilton: A Life in Letters.* Cambridge, Mass.: Harvard University Press.

Udall, S. (1988) *The Quiet Crisis and the Next Generation.* Salt Lake City: Gibbs-Smith.

CHAPTER 30

THE NEW CORPORATE ENVIRONMENTALISM AND THE SYMBOLIC MANAGEMENT OF ORGANIZATIONAL CULTURE

LINDA C. FORBES AND JOHN M. JERMIER

It has been nearly forty years since business scholars and economists began calling attention to the negative environmental implications of unbridled growth and imagining alternatives to the status quo of the growth imperative (e.g. Meadows et al. 1972; Schumacher 1973). Growth in population, the scale of production, energy consumption, and the commodification of life have increasingly impacted the natural environment in each successive decade, resulting in what some knowledgeable observers contend are unprecedented environmental threats and challenges (Speth 2008). Through the decades, the environmental movement has energized and channeled some resistance to unbridled growth and environmental degradation, dragging business and industry, government, consumers, and other institutions into greater awareness of environmental problems and occasionally into greater protection or restoration of the environment. Recently, however, business has attempted to fashion a new role for itself in relation to the environment—a role that positions it as leader of the contemporary environmental movement. The argument often made in support of this new role is that business should take the lead because it has more resources and more access to environmentally relevant matters than other institutions. We refer to this new way of understanding the role of business as "the New Corporate Environmentalism" (Jermier et al. 2006) and address it in this chapter through the lens of organizational culture (see Howard-Grenville & Bertels [Chapter 11] this volume) and symbolic organizational theory.

The reason we focus this chapter on organizational culture is because we believe a cultural perspective can provide a more radical and comprehensive understanding of greening business and other organizations than has been produced by business schol-ars guided by the reformist paradigm (see Egri & Pinfield 1996). Early research that launched the scholarly field of organizations and the natural environment advocated comprehensive approaches to greening, approaches rooted in radical ecological thought while still engaging the practice of business (Callenbach et al. 1993; Gladwin 1993; Shrivastava 1994; 1995; Egri & Pinfield 1996). Often, it was asserted that greening would be best accomplished through new forms of management and organizing built around ecologically sensitive cultural assumptions, norms and practices. In this chap-ter, we return to this fundamental insight and make the argument that, especially in the age of corporate greenwashing (Athanasiou 1996), it is necessary to take a compre-hensive approach to assessing organizations and their greening efforts in order to sep-arate genuine improvements from mere claims about progress. This entails theorizing and examining both the *symbol* and the *substance* of organizational greening initiatives.

In the next section, we present theoretical material on greening organizational culture that is helpful in understanding the response of contemporary business to environmen-tal problems. We then examine several cultural manifestations of organizational green-ing, and in the last section we draw some conclusions about using symbolic organizational theory to understand the greening of contemporary business.

ORGANIZATIONAL CULTURE AND SYMBOLIC ORGANIZATIONAL THEORY

Business is a powerful institution that will play a central role in our future—whether that future is an era of sustainability or an age of reacting to accelerating ecological decline (Assadourian 2010b: 84).

The 2010 edition of the *State of the World Report*, produced by the authoritative Worldwatch Institute, focuses attention on the need for cultural change to confront envi-ronmental problems (Starke & Mastney 2010). The chapters in that volume document how deep cultural entrenchment of many major institutions contributes to the unsus-tainable path of human development (e.g. consumer culture, the commercialization of children's lives, conventional design and building, government capture, media program-ming, human resource systems, and organizational culture). It is significant that many citizens are exposed to at least degrees of anti-ecological business practices during half their waking hours while serving as employees in the workplace itself. Of course the cul-tural programming does not end there. What is often not recognized is the degree to which various industries have shaped cultural assumptions, norms, and practices through their products and services. Examples that have global environmental impacts include the success of the $60-billion dollar bottled-water industry that has convinced people that bottled water at 240 to 10,000 times the cost is "healthier, tastier and more fashionable than publicly supplied water" despite numerous studies finding evidence to the contrary; a $120-billion dollar fast-food industry that has helped "transform dietary norms"; and a deep dependence on disposable paper products that has "cultivated the belief that these products provide convenience and hygiene" to the extent that in many places in the world they are seen as a "necessity" (Assadourian 2010a: 14).

The new corporate environmentalism

Contemporary organizations, however, are under pressure from a variety of stake-holders to become better corporate citizens and to make pro-environmental contributions. Similar to the way Hackman & Wageman (1995: 309) framed Total Quality Management as "something of a social movement," a similar phenomenon is unfolding when it comes to corporate environmental management. A New Corporate Environmentalism (NCE) has emerged that "combines a specific voluntary leadership role for the corporate sector in environmental policy-making with the powerful symbolism of using comprehensive, 'rational' management approaches to address the environment" (Jermier et al. 2006: 627). More precisely, the NCE is defined as "*rhetoric* concerning the central role of business in achieving both economic growth and ecological rationality and as a *guide* for management that emphasizes voluntary, proactive control of environmental impacts in ways that exceed or go beyond environmental laws and regulatory compliance." Importantly, the theme of voluntary corporate environmentalism places emphasis on *self-regulation*, which aims to situate control of environmental impacts in the hands of individual corporations, value-chain requirements, industry and trade associations, third-party commercial certification, sectoral guidelines and covenants, government incentive programs and other alliances, rather than government regulatory agencies (cf. Andrews 1998, also Baron & Lyon [Chapter 7] and King, Prado, & Rivera [Chapter 6] this volume). The NCE is most directly relevant to business organizations but, to some degree, it puts pressure on all contemporary organizations and their leaders. It is described as *rhetoric* in that it offers a coherent set of ideas that are advanced by oratorical and literary skill with the intention of influencing political discourse on the environment. The NCE's clarion call is to alert business to respond to, and control, the impact of production on the environment (Jermier et al., 2006).

  We refer to this form of corporate environmentalism as "*new*" because only in the last decade or so has it developed into a "relatively coherent and widely circulated set of ideas [that] emerged specifying a new set of leadership responsibilities for business in relation to the natural environment and identifying a variety of techniques for enhancing corporate environmental performance" (Jermier et al. 2006: 628). The rhetoric of corporate environmentalism has shifted, positioning business in a leadership role concerning the environment. The shift is underscored by a promise of "win-win" wherein economic "gains for business do not necessarily have to be losses for the environment and…vice versa" (Holliday, Schmidheiny, & Watts 2002: 16; see also, Schmidheiny 1992; Hawken, Lovins, & Lovins 1999).

We also refer to the NCE as a *guide* for management because it provides practical ideas for thinking and action. It provides ideas that are "bite sized chunks of objectives, action plans and measurable results" (Holliday et al. 2002: 139). At the center is environmental management involving voluntary, self-regulatory approaches to environmental protection that go beyond compliance with legal requirements (Jermier et al. 2006; see also Carraro & Leveque 1999; Morelli 1999; Reinhardt 2000; Gunningham, Kagan, & Thornton 2003; Lyon & Maxwell 2004). Other elements include eco-efficiency gains through technological innovation, waste reduction and cleaner production systems, the elaboration of eco-sensitive mission statements and codes of conduct, eco-inspired stories and rituals, and other cultural elements. Importantly, the NCE stance on protecting the natural environment has contributed to moving the environment from a fringe issue to a strategic one in many organizations and industries.

Increasingly, business leaders are being pressed by various stakeholders to take responsibility for the state of environmental degradation as well as meet expectations for developing restorative measures. The NCE social movement is so compelling that it approaches the status of an *imperative* whereby organizations are required to exhibit at least *symbolic* pro-environmental gestures. That is, they may not be required to demonstrate environmental progress materially (in part because measurement in this domain of performance presently is still difficult), but they must create some symbols that reflect positively on their environmental orientation and their willingness to participate in the environmental movement. We do not, however, want to leave the impression that we see business leaders in a totally reactive mode when it comes to environmentalism. Many business leaders see themselves as environmental leaders and seek to play a large role in environmental policy-making (e.g. Anderson 1998).

Symbolic organizational theory

We have found that a cultural studies approach for the analysis of the NCE is constructive for a number of reasons. The most obvious is that many scholars have advanced the idea that organizational culture is *the essential ingredient* in generating successful environmental performance (e.g. Callenbach et al. 1993; Halme 1996; Petts et al. 1999; Jermier et al. 2006; Esty & Winston 2006). Equally importantly, in the age of corporate greenwashing (Athanasiou 1996), it is necessary to take a comprehensive approach to assessing organizations and their greening efforts in order to separate genuine improvements from mere claims of progress.

To be more precise, the cultural studies approach we adopt for our analysis is symbolic organizational theory (SymOT), a framework with roots in symbolic anthropology and high relevance when it comes to theorizing and examining both the *symbol* and the *substance* of organizational greening initiatives. Given that the NCE includes a range of phenomena that are rich in rhetorical content and also imbued with material significance, we think SymOT is especially apt for analyzing the NCE.

SymOT treats organizational culture as a root metaphor not a variable. From this perspective, culture is not something that an organization has, but something that it is (Smircich 1983). Organizations are expressive forms that are studied in terms of their symbolic and material components (e.g. Geertz 1973; Jermier et al. 1991). Symbols are routinely read, interpreted, and deciphered. Each symbol has meaning though some are "*mere symbols*," a concept we use to refer to material and other tangible phenomena that distract or mislead by intentionally presenting an image that does not accurately represent environmental costs and benefits. It camouflages what is actually going on in a field of action, obscuring the negatives while trumpeting the positives.

According to SymOT, organizations are symbol-processing systems. In such systems, human action, values, beliefs, and attitudes are socially constructed, sustained, challenged and sometimes changed (Pondy & Mitroff 1979; Smircich 1983; Jones 1996). Symbolic organizational theorists are interested in "the levels of shared meanings and symbolism in all aspects of organizational life"…and, they also seek to understand uncertainty, incoherence, contradiction, and variation (Alvesson 1998: 87; Martin 2002).

In Jacobs (1969) classic study of symbolic bureaucracy, the public impressions of a social welfare agency were compared with its behind-the-scenes operations (see Forbes & Jermier 2002). While the agency appeared to possess all of the elements of an ideal-type bureaucracy, each feature was routinely circumvented through "unofficial changes" in order to meet organizational goals (e.g. clearing cases) while overloaded case managers maintained decorum and served clients. Jacobs' findings suggested that "it is possible for an organization to conform little or not at all to the conditions of bureaucracy, while maintaining an image of complete adherence to bureaucratic ideals" (Jacobs 1969: 414). This ethnographic work and that of a number of other studies have illustrated how the formal structure of an organization "can be a device that camouflages what actually goes on in the organization from an external public" (Forbes & Jermier 2002: 205), and more generally the proposition that organizations develop forms of "symbolic reassurance to achieve legitimacy from their influential constituents" (Mizruchi & Fein 1999: 656; see also Meyer & Rowan 1977).

The green ceremonial façade and greenwashing

A key concept from SymOT is the ceremonial *façade* or artificial or false front that in the case of formal organizations is fashioned to create a favorable impression. A wide variety of an official culture's elements can be crafted without much concern as to how they will practically enable or hinder an organization's need for efficiency (e.g. goals, mission statements, programs, products, technologies and reporting systems, formal structure). These cultural manifestations may be constructed to signal to relevant external (and internal) stakeholders that society's expectations are being met. Regarding current responses of business to the environment, the NCE is the way to understand much of what is driving cultural movement and change. On its face, the NCE appears to be a positive force for change toward increasing environmental protection, but a number of scholars express serious concerns about the prevalence of *greenwashing*. Greenwashing is a superficial corporate environmentalism that is all style and no substance, basically giving lip service to some or all "greened" cultural elements (Greer & Bruno 1996; Tokar 1997; Beder 2002; Bruno & Karliner 2002; Ramus & Monteil 2006). Greenwashing is a sophisticated form of symbolic management. Explained within the context of SymOT, greenwashing is a *green ceremonial façade*. It focuses attention on one or a small number of highly visible green criteria and neglects all others (Jermier & Forbes 2003). A green ceremonial façade "greens" the organization in its surface appearance, but it likely has little to do with actual environmental performance (Forbes & Jermier 2002).

Through the concept of the green ceremonial façade, a more realistic appraisal can be launched because, according to SymOT, the central tendency of all organizations involves construction of a ceremonial façade and other symbolic management activities. When it comes to corporate greening, it is wise to begin assessment by probing the façade and then move systematically across other cultural manifestations to arrive at a comprehensive picture. Our approach to organizational greening is described well by Hoffman's assertion: "there is no such thing as a 'green company'. The best one can do is describe the progression of how companies are 'going green'" (Hoffman 2001: 14).

ORGANIZATIONAL CULTURAL MANIFESTATIONS

In this section of the chapter, we sketch eight cultural manifestations that are essential to conducting a symbolic analysis of organizational greening activities. While no common definition of the green organization has emerged, organizational scholars tend to agree that a wide range of factors need to be considered in assessing various approaches to organizational greening. Each factor discussed below is a key element of the NCE and has tremendous symbolic significance as well as material effects that must be assessed. Using the SymOT perspective, it is important to recognize that all cultural manifestations contain both symbolic and substantive elements.

Mission statements

The centerpiece of an organization's official culture (assumptions, beliefs, and material symbols endorsed by leadership and crafted for the general public and stakeholders) is the mission statement (Jermier et al. 1991). Mission statements include a vision of a desired future and aspiring values. Often, they are filled with extreme and lofty language. For example: "The Coca-Cola Company exists to benefit and refresh everyone it touches. The basic proposition of our business is simple, solid, and timeless. When we bring refreshment, value, joy and fun to our stakeholders, then we successfully nurture and protect our brands, particularly Coca-Cola. That is the key to fulfilling our ultimate obligation to provide consistently attractive returns to the owners of our business" (Abraham 2007: 40). The company's values are explicitly espoused and they appear to be crafted to include all and offend none. They convey the organization's higher purposes and represent its idealized face. Instructively for our purposes, however, this type of language assumes consensus among stakeholders and benefits for all. Of course Coca-Cola does not even hint at controversial issues such as groundwater exploitation and indigenous community displacement (see Shiva 2002).

The issue that has intrigued organizational researchers for years and that runs through this section on cultural manifestations is what lies behind the official culture. As espoused values, mission statements signal abstract goals that can cajole stakeholders, solidifying the green façade in most cases but driving higher employee motivation in others. Alternatively, they can spawn new environmental performance standards that Esty & Winston (2006: 209) refer to as "stretch goals"—clear, specific, far-reaching objectives that can lead to genuine advances.

Organizational structure

In early responses to environmental regulation and other similar pressures, organizations created specialized roles, positions, and departments designed to deal with greening issues (Hoffman 2001). Often, these structural elements were combined initially with worker health and safety, legal affairs, and public relations subunits, and then expanded into more specialized units. Designation of a role, position or department devoted to greening issues has obvious symbolic significance, but an even greater symbolic meaning can be attached to a broader structural arrangement—the formal environmental management system. For example, with the advent and popularization of ISO 14000 standards, guidelines for designing and implementing a formal environmental management system that can be externally certified by a third party are now widely available. With over 188,000 separate certifications (see International Organization For Standardization 2008), the ISO 14001 system appears to be quickly becoming the standard for separating environmentally responsible organizations from those seen as laggards. Yet, the ISO 14001 environmental management system is rife with symbolism, and it is not at all clear from research that this structural approach to greening is closely associated with higher environmental performance (see Hillary 2000; Russo & Harrison 2005). The same argument could be made about the popular Eco-Management and Audit Scheme (EMAS) except that it requires more rigorous outcome assessment, making it more difficult to operate at the level of mere symbols.

The built environment and transportation

Green building and transportation are two emerging areas in organizational research. Their environmental impacts are substantial and, when combined, staggering. Buildings in the US, for example, account for 39 percent of total energy use, 12 percent of total water consumption, 68 percent of total electricity consumption and 38 percent of carbon dioxide emissions (USGBC; see <http://www.usgbc.org>, see also Hoffman & Henn 2008). The transportation sector accounts for roughly 30 percent of US greenhouse gas emissions (Friedman 2009). With the greening of buildings and transportation come many operational advantages, including greater efficiency, the minimization of environmental impacts, and reductions in the use of non-renewable resources. Improvements in these sectors provide healthier environments for communities. In the case of green buildings, productivity increases, as does learning in schools (www.usgbc.org).

A variety of certification programs in both green building and transportation have been, or are in the process of being, developed. The symbolism embodied in high-visibility buildings and many modes of transportation provide powerful opportunities to showcase greening efforts. Building a green corporate headquarters (see Smith 2003) or adding a fleet of hybrid cars sends a strong message to internal and external stakeholders. These powerful messages can also serve as greenwashing façades when they correspond little with behind-the-scenes or overall operations (i.e. broader environmental performance criteria).

Environmental technology

A major part of any organizational culture is the range of equipment, techniques, information, and processes through which inputs are transformed into outputs—the organization's technologies. Technological change often signals much more than engineering logic in that it represents commitments to new directions and has broad implications for organizing. When an organization implements environmental technologies that reduce manufacturing emissions, minimize energy and resource consumption, or enhance the recyclability and harmlessness of products (cf. Lenox & Ehrenfeld 1997), a statement is made that has symbolic importance. Some technological changes involve design for the environment principles and have obvious environmental impacts, such as office furniture manufacturer Herman Miller's process that burns scrap fabric to heat their facilities. Other processes are more embedded but still have symbolic significance, such as 3M's decision to forego sizable revenues in the short run to change their technology for manufacturing yellow sticky notes. A market emerged for the notes that involved vertical surfaces (e.g. computer screens) but a stronger adhesive was required to ensure a quality product, which in turn required the use of volatile organic compounds. 3M reportedly stuck with their pledge not to develop new products that depended on dangerous industrial solvents and spent six years creating an adhesive that worked without VOC-based solvents. Surprisingly, the new solvent saved money but, more importantly,

3M was able to signal to relevant stakeholders that it was serious about its pledge to reduce its toxic footprint (Esty & Winston 2006).

Partnerships with environmental stakeholders

There are a wide range of environmental stakeholders that can symbolize a culture of environmental concern when partnerships are established. Partnerships between business and, for example, government agencies, local community groups, industry allies, and NGOs can produce tangible environmental benefits and can also create tremendous symbolic leverage. While the state of the art in collaborations between business and environmental NGOs hardly guarantees mutual compatibility and success when they establish partnerships, there are numerous examples in the popular press (e.g. Deutsch 2006) and business literature (Yaziji & Doh 2009) suggesting win-win outcomes. To illustrate, we turn to an unlikely partnership between banana producer and distributor Chiquita and the Rainforest Alliance. Despite a contentious beginning when the Rainforest Alliance wrote a set of standards for growing environmentally friendly bananas which were rejected by the industry, today this partnership can be described as "multifaceted and deeply entrenched" (Esty & Winston 2006: 183). It is credited with enhancing farm productivity and profits as well as producing notable environmental results, including reductions in the use of plastic, pesticides, herbicides, and other hazardous substances (Esty & Winston 2006). In addition, through symbolic management, this exercise that began as an experiment seems to have at least partially transformed Chiquita from a social and environmental villain to a more respectable corporate actor.

Human resources

Human resource management (HRM): "focuses on what can be broadly described as the human side of the enterprise: recruitment, training, staffing, career planning and development, compensation, and labour relations" (Alvesson & Kärreman 2007: 711). When viewed as a functional tool, HRM's strategic role in greening efforts is crucial. It impacts from the early stages of employment via recruitment goals and strategies that find the "right" people through to the extensive reinforcement of policies and acceptable practices. HRM can also be viewed as a symbolic manifestation of culture. It can serve as a powerful meaning-making device that can support *or undermine* a sustainability orientation. Some of the effects of HRM are mediated through communication and other structural mechanisms (e.g. incentive systems). These mechanisms articulate and propagate shared understandings in order to instruct about what it means to be "green" and also establish goals that inspire and motivate in the service of green initiatives. Thus, HRM's role can be viewed as that of symbolic manager—expressing basic values and assumptions concerning greening efforts through corporate policies and a myriad of other mechanisms (see Berg 1986).

Stories and rituals

Martin (2002: 47) describes stories and rituals as cultural forms that are part of the esoterica of organizations. They become important when people interpret their meanings. As with other manifestations of culture, they can be viewed as functional mechanisms of organizational control or as symbols that reflect superficial and sometimes deeper assumptions. To illustrate, we turn to what is likely the most frequently repeated story advocating greener business practices—Ray Anderson's tale of redemption (Anderson 1998). During a reflective few days, while CEO of Interface Carpets and while preparing to give a talk to a task force responding to customer questions about the environment, Anderson convicted himself as a "plunderer of the earth." His revelation led him to vow to make Interface's culture more eco-friendly. He has since become a highly symbolic presence through his own volition and through the frequent retelling of his conversion story to a wide array of audiences (businesses, educational institutions, conferences, and the popular press). The impact of Anderson's story has been profound as it has focused the attention of Interface employees and many others in the industry and world of business on environmental goals.

Rituals are like dramas: well-defined scripts repetitively carried out in a social context (Martin 2002). Norm Thompson Outfitters, a progressive retail clothing firm seeking to create a "shared mental model" about sustainability, developed a four-hour, multi-media, interactive, training session that is a mandatory part of employee orientation (Smith 2003). It thus serves functionally as an initiation ritual. It is symbolically rich as an expression of environmental values but, like Anderson's conversion story, it is one piece of a complex organizational mosaic that needs to be carefully interpreted.

Sustainability reporting

Producing and distributing sustainability reports is an organizational cultural phenomenon that has gained importance during the past two decades (see Gray & Herremans [Chapter 22] this volume). According to the tax, auditing, and management consulting firm, KPMG, about 52 percent of Fortune 500 firms produce sustainability or corporate social responsibility reports, and the number exceeds two-thirds if we count firms that discuss these topics in their annual reports. Some scholars contend that we are witnessing the beginning of a new movement in corporate accountability, one that can only become more important in the years ahead (Epstein 2008). Perhaps more than any other cultural manifestation, sustainability reporting is replete with potential for both legitimate greening and devious greenwashing. Space does not permit us to describe all the relevant angles in this arena, but the main point we want to emphasize is that sustainability reports vary widely in the domains and depth of disclosures and in the degree to which the reports are audited and certified by legitimate independent, external agencies. It should be clear that if the report is not externally assessed, in light of the tremendous pressure on organizations to establish and meet challenging sustainability goals, it will likely contain data lacking measurement rigor, and information that is misleading or even fraudulent. Perhaps more than any other area of symbolic management, sustainability reporting presents an interpretive challenge for even a relatively sophisticated stakeholder.

MERE SYMBOLS? ANALYZING THE GREENING OF ORGANIZATIONAL CULTURE

Leaders who see business taking on a more ambitious role when it comes to environmental problems must accept the fact that stakeholders expect ever higher levels of transparency and are developing better methods for detecting merely symbolic gestures when it comes to greening organizational culture. Building an organizational culture of environmental concern is one of the greatest challenges facing contemporary business and, as we have shown, it requires radical and comprehensive approaches that instill green values throughout the organization. It requires greening at both the surface level and at deeper levels in the realm of values and basic assumptions, and it requires greening throughout the organization's various components. Some organizations, such as BP, seem to succeed in grafting highly visible, cost-effective green initiatives on an otherwise monolithic culture characterized by what many critics regard as the single-minded pursuit of profit (see Leopold 2010; National Academy of Engineering and National Research Council of the National Academies 2010). This sets them up for calls of hypocrisy and harsh criticism from environmentalists (e.g. Ridgeway 2010).

We use the SymOT lens to interpret organizational greening because it focuses attention, first, on the green ceremonial façade typically constructed in the age of greenwashing and, second, on the deeper meaning material symbols convey to external and internal stakeholders. Each of the eight cultural manifestations we identified and sketched has the potential to represent superficial and even fraudulent greening activity but also the potential to represent environmental stewardship that can support claims of genuine progress. We do not think all contemporary approaches to organizational greening should be completely dismissed as mere empty symbols— epiphenomena that mislead and distract from shameful practices. Some organizational greening initiatives that begin with seemingly superficial symbols, such as the plans and policy statements of ISO 14001 or the LEED certified corporate headquarter buildings, might lead to further steps along the pathway to ecocentric organizing. Once an organization and its leaders commit publically to a green initiative, even if it is relatively minor, at a minimum they create higher stakeholder expectations and open the door for greater scrutiny. A turning point is established that can result in merely buttressing the green ceremonial façade or conceivably launching in the direction of ecocentric change.

FUTURE RESEARCH ON CORPORATE ENVIRONMENTALISM AND SYMBOLIC MANAGEMENT

Research on organizational symbolism and symbolic management has come a long way since Dandridge, Mitroff, & Joyce (1980) published an article whose purpose was "conceptual exploration of an unresearched topic" (p. 81). Dandridge et al. (1980) called for multi-method studies aimed at uncovering the "deep structure of organizations" (p. 82). One rapidly growing domain of symbolic management (and the deep structure associated with it) involves voluntary environmental initiatives launched by corporations and other enterprises—initiatives aimed at institutionalizing self-regulatory schemes and other partnerships forged to manage environmental impacts. We refer to this rapidly expanding field as the NCE and see many opportunities in this field to sort out what are merely greenwashing and other symbolic responses from more genuine attempts to respond to pressure designed to eliminate pollution and waste. Contemporary corporate environmentalism provides an arena for the study of symbolic organizational processes that is at least as rich as civil rights laws governing the workplace (e.g. Edelman 1992) or long-term incentive plans for executives and other aspects of corporate governance (e.g. Westphal & Zajac 1998). The rapid expansion of the NCE as an empirical referent combined with important developments in studying artifacts (see Rafaeli & Pratt 2006), sets the stage for more incisive empirical analysis that can extend SymOT. Strong steps in this direction have recently been taken by organizational scholars investigating US firms that joined voluntary climate protection agreements (Delmas & Montes-Sancho 2010) and voluntary reports of US Clean Air Act violations and future violations as impacted by government regulatory surveillance (Short & Toffel 2010; see also Delmas & Toffel [Chapter 13] this volume). These studies and others cited above demonstrate that SymOT can benefit from research that relies on positivist epistemology and quantitative analysis as well as the interpretive methods that marked the anthropological origins of this approach to organizational analysis.

REFERENCES

Abraham, J. (2007). *101 Mission Statements From Top Companies*. Berkeley, CA: Ten Speed Press.

Alvesson, M. (1998). "The Business Concept as a Symbol," *International Studies of Management and Organizations*, 28(3): 86–108.

—— & Kärreman, D. (2007). "Unraveling HRM: Identity, Ceremony, and Control in a Management Consulting Firm," *Organization Science*, 18(4): 711–723.

Anderson, R. C. (1998). *Mid-Course Correction: Toward a Sustainable Enterprise*. White River Junction, VT: Chelsea Green.

Andrews, R. N. L. (1998). "Environmental Regulation and Business 'Self-Regulation,'" *Policy Sciences*, 31: 177–197.

Assadourian, E. (2010a). "The Rise and Fall of Consumer Cultures," in L. Starke & L. Mastny (eds.), *2010 State of the World: Transforming Cultures*, New York, NY: W.W. Norton & Company, 3–20.

—— (2010b). "Business and Economy: Management Priorities," in L. Starke & L. Mastny (eds.), *2010 State of the World: Transforming Cultures*, New York, NY: W.W. Norton & Company, 83–84.

Athanasiou, T. (1996). "The Age of Greenwashing," *Capitalism, Nature, Socialism*, 7: 1–36.

Beder, S. (2002). *Global Spin: The Corporate Assault on Environmentalism, Revised edition*. White River Junction, VT: Chelsea Green.

Berg, P. (1986). "Symbolic Management of Human Resources," *Human Resources Management*, 25(4): 557–579.

Bruno, K. & Karliner, J. (2002). *earthsummit.biz: The Corporate Takeover of Sustainable development*. Oakland, CA: Food First Books.

Callenbach, E., Capra, F., Goldman, L., Lutz, R., & Marburg, S. (1993). *Ecomanagement*. San Francisco, CA: Berrett Koehler.

Carraro, C. & Leveque, F. (eds.) (1999). *Voluntary Approaches in Environmental Policy*. Dordrecht: Kluwer Publishers.

Carson, R. (1962). *Silent Spring*. Boston, MA: Houghton Mifflin.

Dandridge, T. C., Mitroff, I., & Joyce, W. F. (1980). "Organizational Symbolism: A Topic to Expand Organizational Analysis," *Academy of Management Review*, 5: 77–82.

Delmas, M. & Montes-Sancho, M. (2010). "Voluntary Agreements to Improve Environmental Quality: Symbolic and Substantive Cooperation," *Strategic Management Journal*, 31: 576–601.

Deutsch, C. H. (2006). "The New Black; Companies and Critics Try Collaboration," *New York Times*. Retrieved from <http://nytimes.com>

Edelman, L. B. (1992). "Legal Ambiguity and Symbolic Structures: Organizational Mediation of Civil Rights Law," *American Journal of Sociology*, 97: 1531–1576.

Egri, C. P. & Pinfield, L. T. (1996). "Organizations and the Biosphere: Ecologies and Environments," in S. R. Clegg, C. Hardy, and W. R. Nord (eds.), *Handbook of Organization Studies*, London: Sage Publications, 459–483.

Epstein, M. J. (2008). *Making Sustainability Work*. San Francisco, CA: Berrett- Koehler.

Esty, D. C. & Winston, A. S. (2006). *Green to Gold: How Smart Companies Use Environmental Strategy to Innovate, Create Value, and Build Competitive Advantage*. New Haven, CT: Yale UP.

Forbes, L. C. & Jermier, J. M. (2002). "The Institutionalization of Voluntary Organizational Greening and the Ideals of Environmentalism: Lessons about Official Culture from Symbolic Organization Theory," in A. Hoffman and M. Ventresca (eds.), *Organizations, Policy and the Natural Environment: Institutional and Strategic Perspectives*, Stanford, CA: Stanford UP, 194–213.

Friedman, T. L. (2009). *Hot, Flat and Crowded: Why We Need a Green Revolution—and How it Can Renew America, Release 2.0*. New York: Piador/Farrar, Straus and Giroux.

Geertz, C. (1973). *The Interpretation of Cultures: Selected Essays*. New York, NY: Basic Books.

Gibbs, L. M. (1982). *Love Canal: My Story*. Albany, NY: SUNY UP.

Gladwin, T. N. (1993). "The Meaning of Greening: A Plea for Organizational Theory," in K. Fischer & J. Schot (eds.), *Environmental Strategies for Industry*, Washington, DC: Island Press, 37–61.

Greer, J. & Bruno, K. (1996). *Greenwash: The Reality behind Corporate Environmentalism*. New York: Apex Press.

Gunningham, N., Kagan, R. A., & Thornton, D. (2003). *Shades of Green: Business, Regulation, and Environment*. Stanford, CA: Stanford UP.

Halme, M. (1996). "Shifting Environmental Management Paradigms in Two Finnish Paper Facilities: A Broader View of Institutional Theory," *Business Strategy and the Environment*, 5: 94–105.

Hackman, J. R. & Wageman, R. (1995). "Total Quality Management: Empirical, Conceptual, and Practical Issues," *Administrative Science Quarterly*, 40: 309–342.

Hawken, P., Lovins, A., & Lovins, L. H. (1999). *Natural Capitalism: Creating the Next Industrial Revolution*. Boston, MA: Little Brown and Company.

Hillary, R. (ed.) (2000). *ISO 14001: Case Studies and Practical Experiences*. Sheffleld, UK: Greenleaf Publishing.

Hoffman, A. J. (2001). *From Heresy to Dogma: An Institutional History of Corporate Environmentalism (Expanded Edition)*. Stanford, CA: Stanford UP.

Hoffman, A. & Henn, R. (2008). "Overcoming the Social and Psychological Barriers to Green Building," *Organization & Environment*, 21(4): 390–419.

Holliday, C. O., Jr., Schmidheiny, S., & Watts, P. (2002). *Walking the Talk: The Business Case for Sustainable Development*. San Francisco, CA: Greenleaf.

Intergovernmental Panel On Climate Change (IPCC) (2007). *Climate Change 2007: Synthesis Report*. Geneva.

International Organization For Standardization (2008). *The ISO Survey—2008*. <www.iso.org/iso/survey2008.pdf>

Jacobs, J. (1969). "Symbolic Bureaucracy: A Case Study of a Social Welfare Agency," *Social Forces*, 47: 413–422.

Jermier, J. M. & Forbes, L. C. (2003). "Greening Organizations: Critical Issues," in M. Alvesson & H. Willmott (eds.), *Studying Management Critically*, London: Sage Publications, 157–176.

—— Forbes, L. C., Benn, S. & Orsato, R. J. (2006). "The New Corporate Environmentalism and Green Politics," in S. R. Clegg, C. Hardy, T. B. Lawrence & W. Nord (eds.), *The Sage Handbook of Organization Studies*, 2nd edition, London: Sage Publications, 618–650.

—— Slocum, J. W. Jr., Fry, L. W., & Gaines, J. (1991). "Organizational Subcultures in a Soft Bureaucracy: Resistance Behind the Myth and Façade of an Official Culture," *Organization Science*, 2: 170–194.

Jones, M. O. (1996). *Studying Organizational Symbolism: What, How, Why?* Thousand Oaks, CA: Sage.

Lenox, M. & Ehrenfeld, J. (1997). "Organizing for Effective Environmental Design," *Business Strategy and the Environment*, 6: 187–196.

Leopold, J. (2010). "BP Risks More Massive Disasters in the Gulf," *Truthout/Report*. Retrieved from http://oildisaster.com/2010/05/02/whistleblower bp risks-more-massive-catastrophes-in-gulf/

Lyon, T. P. & Maxwell, J. W. (2004). *Corporate Environmentalism and Public Policy*. Cambridge: Cambridge UP.

McKibben, B. (1989). *The End of Nature*. New York, NY: Random House.

Marshall, R. S. & Brown, D. (2003). "The Strategy of Sustainability: A Systems Perspective on Environmental Initiatives," *California Management Review* 46(1): 101–126.

Martin, J. (2002). *Organizational Culture: Mapping the Terrain*. Thousand Oaks, CA: Sage.

Meadows, D. H., Meadows, D. L., Randers, J., & Behrens, W. W. III. (1972). *The Limits to Growth; A Report for the Club of Rome's Project on the Predicament of Mankind*. New York, NY: New American Library.

Meyer, J. W. & Rowan, B. (1977). "Institutionalized Organizations: Formal Structure as Myth and Ceremony," *American Journal of Sociology*, 83, 340–363.

Mizruchi, M. S. & Fein, L. C. (1999). "The Social Construction of Organizational Knowledge: A Study of the Uses of Coercive, Mimetic, and Normative Isomorphism," *Administrative Science Quarterly*, 44: 653–683.

Morelli, J. (1999). *Voluntary Environmental Management: The Inevitable Future*. Boca Raton, FL: Lewis Publishers.

National Academy of Engineering and National Research Council of the National Academies (2010). "Interim Report on the Causes of the *Deepwater Horizon* Oil Rig Blowout and Ways to Prevent Such Events." Retrieved from <http://www.nationalacademies.org/includes/DH_Interim_Report_final.pdf>

Petts, J., Herd, A., Gerrard, S., & Horne, C. (1999). "The Climate and Culture of Environmental Compliance within SMEs," *Business Strategy and the Environment*, 8: 14–30.

Pondy, L. R. & Mitroff, I. I. (1979). "Beyond Open System Models of Organization," *Research in Organizational Behavior*, 1: 3–39.

Rafaeli, A. & Pratt, M. G. (eds.) (2006). *Artifacts and Organizations: Beyond Mere Symbolism*. Mahwah, New Jersey: Erlbaum Publishers.

Ramus, C. A. & Montiel, I. (2006). "When are Corporate Environmental Policies a Form of 'Greenwashing?'" *Business & Society*, 44: 377–414.

Rasanen, K., Merilaninen, S., & Lovio, R. (1995). "Pioneering Descriptions of Corporate Greening: Notes and Doubts about the Emerging Discussion," *Business Strategy and the Environment*, 3: 9–16.

Reinhardt, F. (2000). *Down to Earth: Applying Business Principles to Environmental Management*. Boston, MA: Harvard Business School.

Ridgeway, J. (2010). "BP's Slick Greenwashing," *Mother Jones Online*. Retrieved from <http://motherjones.com/mojo/2010/05/bp-coated-sludge-after-years-greenwashing>

Russo, M. V. & Harrison, N. S. (2005). "Organizational Design and Environmental Performance," *Academy of Management Journal*, 48: 582–593.

Schmidheiny, S. (1992). *Changing Course: A Global Perspective on Development and the Environment*. Cambridge, MA: MIT Press.

Schumacher, E. F. (1973). *Small is Beautiful: A Study of Economics as if People Mattered*. London: Blond and Briggs.

Shiva, V. (2002). *Water Wars: Privatization, Pollution and Profit*. Cambridge, MA: South End Press.

Short, J. L. & Toffel, M. W. (2010). "Making Self-Regulation More Than Merely Symbolic: The Critical Role of the Legal Environment," *Administrative Science Quarterly*, 55: 361–396.

Shrivastava, P. (1995). "The Role of Corporations in Achieving Ecological Sustainability," *Academy of Management Review*, 20: 936–960.

—— (1994). "Castrated Environment: Greening Organizational Studies," *Organization Studies*, 15: 705–726.

Smircich, L. 1983 "Concepts of Culture and Organizational Analysis," *Administrative Science Quarterly*, 8: 339–358.

Smith, D. (2003). "Engaging in Change Management," in S. Waage (ed.), *Ants, Galileo and Gandhi: Designing the Future of Business*, Sheffield, UK: Greenleaf, 93–108.

Speth, J. G. (2008). *The Bridge at the Edge of the World: Capitalism, the Environment, and Crossing from Crisis to Sustainability*. New Haven, CT: Yale UP.

Starke, L. & Mastny, L. (eds.) (2010). *2010 State of the World: Transforming Cultures from Consumerism to Sustainability*. New York, NY: W.W. Norton & Company.

Tokar, B. (1997). *Earth for Sale: Reclaiming Ecology in the Age of Corporate Greenwash*. Boston, MA: South End Press.

Westphal, J. D. & Zajac, E. J. (1998). The Symbolic Management of Stockholders: Corporate Governance Reforms and Shareholder Reactions, *Administrative Science Quarterly*, 43: 127–153.

Yaziji, M. & Doh, J. (2009). *NGOs and Corporations*. Cambridge: Cambridge UP.

CHAPTER 31

CRITICAL PERSPECTIVES ON BUSINESS AND THE NATURAL ENVIRONMENT

SUBHABRATA BOBBY BANERJEE

In this chapter I describe some critical perspectives on business and the natural environment. The emerging field of critical management studies (CMS) offers unique and important ways to study how business deals with environmental issues. The chapter is structured as follows: I begin the chapter with a brief introduction to CMS and discuss the intellectual and philosophical traditions that inform this field. Issues of power and domination are addressed in CMS in ways that are profoundly different from mainstream organization studies and offer distinctive ways of theorizing environmental issues. In the next section I summarize the key themes of research on business and the natural environment. Almost all of the research on organizational approaches to environmental issues takes a functionalist approach that privileges organizational rather than environmental goals and there are serious limitations of such a win-win approach to environmental issues. I conclude the chapter by outlining a critical research agenda for the study of business and the natural environment.

A variety of philosophical and theoretical strands weave the network of debates that is CMS. Perspectives from critical theory developed by Horkheimer, Adorno, and Habermas from the Frankfurt School inform some formulations of CMS, particularly in its critique of instrumental reason, consumerism, and the positivist bias in social science research and technocracy (Scherer 2009). The notion that knowledge cannot be separated from human interests and that there is no such thing as value-free or neutral science marked a radical departure from conventional theories in organization and management research. Scholars employed perspectives from critical theory to show how organizational structures serve as modes of domination and control while proposing alternate modes of organizing and governance arrangements that are deemed to be less oppressive and more emancipatory (Willmott 1993; Scherer & Palazzo 2007).

Key questions that would emerge from a CMS perspective would focus, not on just explaining contemporary arrangements in organizations and the political economy, but on asking how that particular arrangement came about and exposing power relations that prevent alternate forms of organization. Such a perspective would challenge mainstream research preoccupations with profitability and shareholder value and, rather than ask questions about how to enhance profitability and shareholder value, it would ask questions about how particular profits were created and attempt to identify the social and environmental costs associated with generating profit, or explain how certain segments of society become disenfranchised as a result (Banerjee 2010). Thus, in the context of organizations and the natural environment a critical approach would critique mainstream environmental management or strategy research because it leaves the fundamental assumptions of the profit paradigm unchallenged. As we shall see later, particular constructions of the "environment" and "nature" emerge when environmental issues are framed from the conventional economic paradigm. A critical approach would go beyond searching for economic efficiencies through environmental improvements, but rather highlight its boundary conditions while exploring possibilities of alternate economic and organizational arrangements that could arise from an environmental perspective.

THE EMERGENCE OF CRITICAL MANAGEMENT STUDIES

The discussion that follows on key developments and writings on CMS is by no means exhaustive. Instead, I provide a fairly selective reading of what I think are the key themes of CMS. What began as a fairly fragmented field of research involving a handful of scholars has now evolved into a sub-discipline along with the accompanying institutional structures and processes. Critical Management Studies, which began as an Interest Group, is now a full-fledged division in the Academy of Management with its allocated quota of professional development workshops and competitive paper sessions at annual meetings. A biennial CMS conference has been held since 1999. The 2009 CMS conference held at Warwick Business School in the UK comprised twenty-five streams involving a wide range of topics such as critical perspectives on strategy, globalization, international business, diversity, feminism, race theory, human resource management, marketing, accounting, postcolonialism, sexuality, gender, postmodernism, and environmentalism. Obviously there is much to be critical of in organization and management studies. It will be useful to explore exactly what CMS is critical of, and what alternative worldviews, epistemologies, theories, methodologies, and ways of organizing and managing emerge from such a critique.

The domain statement of the CMS Division in the Academy of Management provides some insights:

> CMS serves as a forum within the Academy for the expression of views critical of established management practices and the established social order. Our premise is that structural features of contemporary society, such as the profit imperative, patriarchy, racial inequality, and ecological irresponsibility often turn organizations into instruments of domination and exploitation. Driven by a shared desire to change this situation, we aim in our research, teaching, and practice to develop critical interpretations of management and society and to generate radical alternatives. Our critique seeks to connect the practical shortcomings in management and individual managers to the demands of a socially divisive and ecologically destructive system within which managers work. (CMS 2010)

Thus, the underlying assumption and the starting point of a critique is the "structural features of contemporary society" that result in "domination and exploitation". What makes management and organization studies the focus of critique is the "profit imperative," which, leaving any "social" or "stakeholder" issues aside for the moment, is the fundamental basis of the modern corporation. CMS challenges the fundamental normative assumptions of management and organization theory and practice—that managerial notions of efficiency are universally desirable, and that pursuing profit motives can only lead to positive outcomes for the workforce and for society. Instead, employing a critical perspective can reveal the hidden structures of oppression in management. Such a perspective would enable us to see organizations and management practices as a contested terrain of power relations. The goal then is to transform existing power relations in organizations with a view to building less oppressive workplaces that do not harm social and environmental welfare.

Such a broad and general critique invites theoretical pluralism from conventional neo-Marxist analyses, labor process theory, and the Frankfurt School of critical theory to postmodernism, poststructuralism, deconstruction, postcolonialism, cultural studies, feminism, queer theory, and psychoanalysis (Fournier & Grey 2000). There is not, and indeed some might argue can never be, an overarching critical management "theory"—rather theoretical developments in CMS can be seen as a connected network of debates with different, sometimes contradictory, political and epistemological stances. While acknowledging the theoretical diversity that informs CMS, Fournier & Grey (2000) nevertheless attempt to describe its boundaries by focusing on aspects relating to performativity, denaturalization, and reflexivity.

Fournier & Grey (2000: 17) argue that performativity is at the root of conventional management studies where efficiency is paramount, and all knowledge and truth is directed at promoting efficiency or the "production of maximum output for minimum input." CMS rejects this quest for performativity and instead advocates a non-performative or even anti-performative approach to the study of management and organizations. Performativity can also be accompanied by exploitation, manipulation, surveillance, subordination, and disempowerment (Burrell 1997), and a critical management perspective would show how knowledge operating in the guise of performative knowledge produces these negative outcomes.

Denaturalization involves exposing irrationalities, "unnaturalness", and power relations behind constructions of rationality (Alvesson et al. 2009). Thus, a denaturalizing organizational inquiry challenges the stability, rationality, and "naturalness" of existing organizational and social relations and attempts to inscribe what has been written out of management theory (Fournier & Grey 2000). Reflexivity marks the third boundary condition between critical and non-critical approaches—positivist epistemologies and methodologies are rarely challenged in mainstream accounts of management, and a reflexive approach would explicitly acknowledge and scrutinize these assumptions with a view to highlighting the limitations of received knowledge. What truths are acknowl edged and what truths are denied is an integral part of the reflexive process. A critical perspective would not just seek new answers to questions but also ask why certain kinds of questions demand answers while others do not, whose interests are included or excluded in the universal quest for knowledge, and why particular approaches to knowledge production are selected over others (Grice & Humphries 1997).

However, Fournier & Gray's boundary conditions of CMS have not gone unchallenged. Critics argue that the preoccupation with philosophical arguments about ontol ogy and epistemology ignore the political realities of the workplace and the material (as opposed to "socially constructed") challenges faced by workers in organizations (Thompson 2004). Rejecting the notion of efficiency as being exploitative, patriarchal, Eurocentric, colonial, capitalistic, hierarchical, and performative is fine, but a theoretical critique must also provide alternate ways of being and knowing while remaining self-reflexive about the knowledge it produces. Otherwise there is a danger that CMS can lapse into cynical management studies or, as Burrell (1993) eloquently puts it, the intellectual equivalent of "pissing in the streets".

Rather than embrace non-performativity or anti-performativity, Spicer et al. (2009) call for an affirmative or critical performativity that calls for performative engagement as an integral part of CMS. Only by engaging with practice and critical dialog and performing pragmatic interventions that challenge oppressive organizational and social relations can CMS hope to create alternatives to existing forms of domination and subordination that its critical scrutiny has revealed. Such a performative stance would be affirmative (not just negative), involve an ethics and duty of care, while also being pragmatic in locating specific organizational practices and spaces that require intervention, as well as identifying alternatives and potentialities along with a critical analysis of the normative criteria used to assess alternative practices (Spicer et al. 2009).

To illustrate some of the perhaps more abstract notions of CMS it may be useful to look at land and resource conflicts between Indigenous communities and extractive industries, such as mining and oil drilling. A mainstream "stakeholder" approach would advocate consultation, dialog, compensation, and resettlement of affected communities so that resource extraction can proceed in a socially and environmentally responsible way (see Bondy & Matten [Chapter 28] this volume). However, such an approach disavows the vastly unequal power relations that underlie "stakeholder engagement" strategies of powerful multinational corporations as well as the colonial relations of power that continue to operate in North-South economic and political interactions.

Indigenous modes of being and relationships with the land are inherently incommensurable with the economic paradigm of resource extraction, and no amount of "stakeholder dialog" can reconcile these fundamental differences unless there is an explicit analysis of power relations that either enable local communities to say no to particular forms of "development", or empower multinational corporations backed by nation states to extract resources from Indigenous lands (Banerjee 2000; 2003).

A critical approach would examine how discursive constructions of "development", "modernity", and "progress" create particular relations and structures of power in the political economy that allow certain forms of development to occur while disallowing others. The separation of economic, social, ecological, and political spheres is also typical of "Western" ways of seeing and organizing the world, and despite its universalistic claims does not reflect the lived reality of a majority of the world's population. For example, the transformation of nature into the "environment" as required by "development" has produced disempowering consequences for millions of people in the Third World because it obscures the social, economic, and political dislocations that result (Banerjee 2000; 2003; 2008). Critical performativity would go beyond exposing oppressive conditions of power and focus on pragmatic interventions such as protecting indigenous land rights, and legal mechanisms to protect indigenous cultural rights and social arrangements.

What impact has CMS had on management and organization theory and on managerial practice? If the quality of research is judged by its relevance and impact then I would argue that, despite its growth and increasing institutionalization in recent years, both the relevance and impact of CMS on managerial practice or public policy has been negligible. While it may have created a new space for academic publishing careers there is a danger that CMS can become an insular sub-discipline in organization and management studies, content to critique the research that appears in mainstream journals, while remaining secure in its philosophical and theoretical comfort zones. Since this Handbook focuses on research on business and the natural environment (B&NE) it will be interesting to see what impact, if any, perspectives from CMS have had on B&NE-related research, as I will discuss in the next section.

RESEARCH ON BUSINESS AND THE NATURAL ENVIRONMENT: A CRITICAL ANALYSIS

Environmental issues entered the corporate agenda in the late 1960s and early 1970s when the first environmental legislation was enacted in the US and Europe. Environmental issues also began to enter the academic literature around the same time, and environmental issues began to be theorized as part of a corporation's responsibility to society. The oil crisis of the 1970s, and mounting evidence of the environmental and health dangers caused by pollution, the indiscriminate use of pesticides, and the dumping of toxic waste, saw a rise in public environmental concern, accompanied by the introduction of environmental legislation. Academic research in the business disciplines, particularly in management, accounting, and marketing began to focus on issues such as energy conservation, ecological responsibility (of both consumers and business firms), and corporate social responsibility. The environmental movement that began in Europe and the United States in the 1960s and 1970s was very much a grass-roots movement that saw the emergence of several green NGOs who directed their attention at the environmental impacts of "big business." However, a decade-long hiatus followed in the 1980s, and environmental issues returned to the corporate agenda in the 1990s, albeit in a different form.

While social responsibility and morality arguments continued to be used as normative justifications for corporate environmentalism there was a strategic shift in theory and practice from the 1990s. Environmental issues became "strategic" because they had the potential to impact the financial performance of firms due to escalating costs of pollution control, environmental liability for damage caused by a firm's products and processes, stricter environmental legislation, and increased consumer awareness of environmental issues (Banerjee et al. 2003). The 1990s saw a minor explosion of articles dealing with corporate greening in the management literature. Much of this literature attempted to incorporate notions of sustainable development into corporate strategy (see for example, the 2000 special issue on the "management of organizations in the natural environment" in *Academy of Management Journal*, the 1995 special issue on "ecologically sustainable organizations" in the *Academy of Management Review*, or the 1992 special issue on "strategic management of the environment" in *Long Range Planning*) and discusses the emergence of corporate environmentalism and organizational processes of environmental management.

In the Academy of Management, this renewed interest in the natural environment was recognized by the emergence of Organization and Natural Environment (ONE) as a field of research, first by the creation of ONE as an interest group in 1994 which was then further legitimized when it was granted the status of a separate division in the Academy. According to the domain statement of the Organization and Natural Environment Division of the Academy of Management the division promotes

> research, theories and practices regarding relationships of organizations and the natural environment. Major topics include: ecological sustainability, environmental philosophies and strategies, ecological performance, environmental entrepreneurship, environmental product and service industries, pollution control and prevention, waste minimization, industrial ecology, total quality environmental management, environmental auditing and information systems, managing human resources for sustainability, ecological crisis management, natural resources and systems management, protection and restoration, interactions of systems management, interactions of environmental stakeholders, environmental policies, environmental attitudes and decision making, and international/comparative dimensions of these topics. As the natural environment is integral in all individual, organizational and societal activity, the interest group encourages holistic, integrative, and interdisciplinary analysis.

It promotes joint exploration of these topics with all other disciplines and Academy units. (ONE 2010)

Apart from a couple of references to "environmental philosophies" and "holistic, integrative and interdisciplinary analysis", the dominant theme of the domain statement is about "managing" environmental issues. So it should not come as a surprise that the "joint exploration" of the majority of research has focused on the strategic implications of the natural environment for organizational survival and growth. Thus, the focus is on "eco-efficiency" and its accompanying economic benefits arising from reduced energy bills, waste and pollution prevention (Banerjee 2001); or ways to enhance competitive advantage through cost leadership and product differentiation (Bansal & Roth 2000; Kallio & Nordberg 2006); or "managing" stakeholders and the regulatory environment in an attempt to circumvent or anticipate legislation (Banerjee 2007; Banerjee & Bonnefous 2010). Although several studies focused on "environmental outcomes" (Bansal & Gao 2006), the underlying assumption was that these outcomes would lead to enhanced financial or economic outcomes for the corporation. This "win-win" approach to environmental research is the fundamental basis of mainstream B&NE related research. Much of this research is silent on explaining what happens when "good" environmental outcomes lead to "bad" financial or economic outcomes, how managers and firms negotiate these trade-offs, or whether "environmental outcomes" are sustained over a period of time (Banerjee 2007: 2010).

While environmental issues have the potential to transform theory and practice in organizations and management there is still a long way to go. In contemplating the future of B&NE-related research, Shrivastava & Hart (1994: 607) commented:

> Environmentalism will be one of the most potent forces of economic, social, and political change in this decade. By the year 2000, organizations and organization theory will need to transform themselves dramatically to accommodate environmental concerns. Despite the rise of environmentalism over the past two decades, organizations and organizational theorists have failed to adequately address environmental concerns.

While there is no consensus on how "adequately addressing environmental concerns" is to be assessed, there is certainly no evidence to suggest that organizations and organization theory have "transformed themselves dramatically to address environmental concerns." In fact, some researchers would argue the contrary: that organizations and organization theory has dramatically transformed nature itself into an "environmental issue" that can be managed, leveraged and manipulated to meet organizational outcomes (Banerjee 2003; 2007; Levy 1997; Newton & Harte 1997; Shrivastava 1994; Welford 1997). While business firms can no longer ignore environmental issues and most large corporations today have environmental management policies in place, the dominant paradigm is still business-as-usual, tinged perhaps with some green credentials. A critical approach would analyze power dynamics in the political economy as well as in the Academy to understand the reasons why such a transformation has not occurred, as well as the role of interest groups that actively prevented the transition to a green economy.

So what impact has B&NE-related research had on the mainstream management and organization literature? What new insights have been developed, and in what ways if any has the natural environment influenced organization theory and practice? Recent reviews of the state of B&NE-related research suggest the impact has been marginal at best. For instance, Kallio & Nordberg (2006) argue that the so-called greening of the field has not led to any fundamental shifts or redirection of research in management (see also Gladwin [Chapter 38] this volume for further critique). Much of this research continues to be informed by managerial and functional perspectives and lacks critical self-reflection. In its eagerness to portray itself as a "legitimate" topic for business, B&NE-related research has not led to any new theoretical frameworks, but rather has focused on the incremental development of dominant theories of organizations, such as resource-based views of the firm or stakeholder theories of the firm (see also Ehrenfeld [Chapter 33] this volume for related argument). The literature has very few "paradigm level" arguments that challenge dominant views of organizations and provide alternative philosophical and theoretical perspectives (Bansal & Gao 2006; Jermier et al. 2006). There was some attempt at paradigm level theorizing in the mid 1990s, where the basic premise was that that attention to the natural environment is lacking in the literature, and in cases where environmental issues have been addressed, the underlying paradigm is anthropocentric where ecological principles are either subsumed or disassociated with the economic paradigm (Purser et al. 1995). For instance, Gladwin et al. (1995) discuss the "technocentric" paradigm with its key assumptions of limitless growth and reliance on science and technology to solve environmental problems. This is contrasted with the "ecocentric" paradigm, which has a different view of nature, and recognizes there are limits to the growth and carrying capacity of the planet. They argue that a "sustaincentric" paradigm has the capability to synthesize the opposing positions of the other two paradigms, and that sustainable development represents a compromise between unbridled growth and no growth. However, even these somewhat critical attempts at framing environmental issues did not account for a sophisticated analysis of power dynamics in the political economy that would enable such a paradigm shift. Moreover, both the impact and scope of B&NE related research appear to be minimal: B&NE-related research accounted for less than 1 percent of journal space in the organization and management studies literature once special issues on the topic are discounted (Bansal & Gao 2006).

A more revealing finding is that the ecological aspects of the natural environment are subservient to conventional perspectives that sustain the primacy of the economic growth model. What B&NE-related research has succeeded in doing is to add the prefix "sustainable" to mainstream accounts of organization theory that continue to privilege growth, production, and consumption. Bansal & Gao (2006) and Kallio & Nordberg (2006) are in agreement that B&NE-related research has not generated the "big questions" one would expect of a strong theoretical framework. Rather, the natural environment has become subsumed under the competitive environment and political economy of business, whereby nature becomes a "bundle of resources" and environmental management becomes a "strategic capability" or "core competence" consistent with mainstream theories of organizations. Even critiques of B&NE-related research are based on the mainstream: Gladwin (1993) in his "plea for organizational theory" to become greener claimed that B&NE-related research lacked, among other things, "precise definitions, causal directionality; empirically testable propositions, and validated general models" (Kallio & Nordberg 2006: 443), and lamented that B&NE scholars did not always "distance themselves from advocacy and ideology" (Gladwin 1993: 43). There have been scores of empirical studies since then that have produced empirically tested hypotheses and measures of environmentalism, but CMS scholars would argue that such assessments of theoretical "rigor" highlight the lack of self-reflexivity and critical perspectives in B&NE-related research, apart from its functionalist and positivist epistemological and ontological assumptions. More accurate measures, empirically testable propositions and sophisticated analytical techniques can generate sound statistical models, but are silent on the "advocacy and ideology" that informs how the natural environment is framed in economic, strategic, and competitive terms. A critical perspective would examine the material, discursive, and institutional power relations that require B&NE scholars to refrain from advocacy and ideology while accepting the normative assumptions of the dominant economic paradigm as one that does not advocate any ideology.

A quick perusal of some of the chapters in this very Handbook shows the discursive framing of environmental issues. For instance, the chapters on competitive strategy and marketing in the context for B&NE research review a range of studies where the basic theoretical approach is to extend existing theoretical concepts from competitive strategy, theories of the firm, market segmentation, and consumer behavior, in an attempt to integrate environmental issues. With few exceptions most studies attempt to make a business case for environmental issues: at the enterprise and corporate level, a green image can yield reputational benefits, at the competitive strategic level, energy efficiencies and product differentiation can lead to competitive advantage and financial benefits, and at the functional level, segmenting markets and producing green products can increase market share and revenues. The main aim is to "fit" the environment into the business model rather than the other way around. This is not to say that products that have a lower environmental impact should not be encouraged but rather to identify the limits of win-win situations. More importantly, the limits to growth and consumption are barely acknowledged—simply prefixing growth and consumption with "sustainable" is not particularly useful. Much of the green consumption literature focuses on trade-offs between environmental improvement and prices that consumers are willing to pay. Even if green products are cheaper, it does not mean they are environmentally sustainable—for instance, in the rapidly growing economies of India and China, manufacturing a super fuel efficient car that is also much cheaper means that while emissions intensity per unit of output is reduced overall, emissions will increase as more people are able to afford cars.

Attempts to "define" what sustainability means for business highlight the discursive power of knowledge in organization studies, and the corporate and institutional capture of sustainability. For instance, the World Business Council for Sustainable Development (WBCSD), a powerful lobby group consisting of CEOs of more than 200 multinational corporations, in developing their "vision of sustainable development," claimed that one of the goals of sustainable development was "to maintain entrepreneurial freedom through voluntary initiatives rather than regulatory coercion" (Schmidheiny 1992: 84). Such an assertion contradicts probably the only consistent finding of research on corporate environmentalism: that government regulation is the most important predictor of corporate environmental performance (Banerjee et al. 2003). Not to be outdone by the WBSCD, the Dow Jones Sustainability Group defined a sustainable corporation as one "that aims at increasing long-term shareholder value by integrating economic, environmental and social growth opportunities into its corporate and business strategies" (Dow Jones Sustainability Group Index 2010).

In a similar vein, Zadek (2001: 9) defined a "civil corporation" as one that builds "social and environmental objectives into its core business by effectively developing its internal values and competencies." These opportunities are to be pursued "within the limits imposed by the tenets of private enterprise," thus reinforcing the narrow focus on win-win approaches to environmental issues. Thus, environmental and social issues can only be conceptualized as "growth opportunities" for business. The assumption is that if they do not provide growth opportunities, business firms should not pursue environmental and social initiatives, which is hardly the "dramatic transformation" that some B&NE scholarship is needed in organizations, even assuming that B&NE is focused around environmental sustainability and not on social, cultural, or political sustainability. Rather, the business-as-usual approach appears to prevail: as Robert Shapiro, the former CEO of the multinational corporation Monsanto, puts it, far from being a soft issue grounded in emotion or ethics, sustainable development involves "cold, rational business logic" (Magretta 1997: 81). It is precisely the "cold, rational" logic of business that needs to be deconstructed if we are to develop radical visions of sustainability that do not privilege narrow economic interests of powerful corporations. It seems extremely unlikely that a "cold, rational business logic" will lead to a complete "moral transformation within the corporation" (Crane 2000: 673) that some scholars claim is needed to meet the challenges of sustainability. Critical management has a crucial role to play in such deconstructions and reconstructions.

Pollution prevention and product stewardship may be the "win-win" environmental strategic capabilities that firms can develop, but it is doubtful if these strategies can address the broader goals of economic, environmental, and social sustainability. If, for example, a "sustainable development" strategy reflects a true "natural-resource-based view of the firm" then there needs to be an effort to "sever the negative links between environment and economic activity in the developing countries of the South" (Hart 1995: 996). Given that much of the global political economy is based on sourcing raw materials from the Third World, it is difficult to see how current theoretical developments in Business Policy and Strategy, or Organization Management and Theory, or even Organizations and the Natural Environment, can even begin to address a problem of this scale and magnitude. Despite calls for a "fundamental revision of organization studies concepts and theories" (Shrivastava 1994) there are no explanations as to how this will occur. Fundamental changes in organizations cannot occur unless there are corresponding shifts in the larger political economy and fundamental questions regarding the role of a corporation and its license to operate in society are addressed.

Recent debates surrounding the failure of global climate change negotiations have demonstrated the power of the business lobby in setting the global environmental agenda: the preferred strategy of large corporations to address climate change was political lobbying to prevent mandatory emissions reductions rather than any "dramatic transformation" of their business models (Bumpus & Liverman 2008; Levy & Egan 2003). While concepts like eco-efficiency, life-cycle assessment, design for environment, and total quality environmental management may enable business firms to develop strategic capabilities to understand and perhaps reduce their environmental impact, current research suggests that even these environmental initiatives are assessed by their economic benefit to the firm, and only the ones that can deliver economic benefits are implemented (Banerjee 2001; Banerjee & Bonnefous 2010). An exclusive focus on win-win situations does not reflect a paradigm shift but rather the capture of sustainability discourses by an economic, not ecological rationality. If the global environmental crisis requires developing an "economy of restoration" whereby the political economy is structured around conservation rather than depletion of resources as Hawken (1994: 11) suggests, then the uncomfortable silence that prevails in organization studies around the environmental destruction and social dislocations caused by capitalist modes of production and consumption must be broken. Perhaps, this is where CMS can play a role. The so-called "greening of business" should not be confused with sustainable development—rather it is the task of the critical researcher to expose how ecological rationalities and moralities are manipulated in organizations and organization research to consolidate business interests. And for it to be relevant and have an impact, such a critique must also provide alternate avenues for research and practice. I will conclude this chapter by outlining a critical research agenda for research on organizations and the natural environment.

TOWARDS A CRITICAL RESEARCH AGENDA FOR B&NE RESEARCH

So what would be the key elements of a critical research agenda based on an analysis of power relations? I discuss five themes for future B&NE research that depart from the mainstream: *paradigmatic research* that attempts to re-conceptualize relations between business and the environment (as opposed to including the "environment" as another resource to be managed); empirical research that describes the *limits of green management*; a *critical political economic approach* that analyzes power relations between market, state, and civil society actors; *global environmental governance* that aims to promote ecological democracy and more participatory forms of decision-making; and *critical engagement* with communities, institutions, and political constituencies.

Critical paradigmatic research

A critical perspective on B&NE research would go beyond identifying technical solutions to environmental problems. As Shellenberger & Nordhaus (2004) point out, framing the environment as an object that has to be managed allows only certain types of problems to be articulated and limits solutions to the narrowly defined problem. Thus, global warming can be "solved" by technological fixes such as pollution control, vehicle fuel economy, and carbon trading, while leaving the fundamentals of the current political economy intact. Such an approach does not address the political, social, and cultural challenges posed by global environmental problems, and more importantly precludes any forms of grass-roots organizing and resistance. Framing global warming as a problem of "too much carbon in the atmosphere" (Shellenberger & Nordhaus 2004), obscures the unequal use of the atmosphere among localities, regions, and countries, as well as the unequal distribution of resources to deal with the problem. Better technologies may well reduce pollution but cannot address the fundamental problems of resource distribution and equity that are also "environmental problems". The global environmental crisis cannot be solved by a privatization of the atmosphere and trading the right to pollute.

Critical perspectives on environmentalism at the paradigmatic level go beyond the reductive nature of a technological approach and focus instead on the social, cultural and political aspects of scientific and technological systems in an attempt to promote a "public ecology" and a democratization of the environmental movement (Luke 2005). If climate change is a form of market failure, then market-based solutions will tend to focus on reducing corporate costs of compliance with regulation and promote private forms of governance, rather than search for more effective forms of public regulation and democratic governance.

The limits of green management

Identifying the limits of "win-win" approaches to environmental issues is one area where CMS research can contribute. There is some evidence to suggest that the cost savings resulting from environmental improvements may be leveling off, and the initial high-return/low investment period of environmental improvement appears to have ended as corporate environmental strategies hit the "green wall" (Piasecki et al. 1999). How these limits can be overcome requires research at institutional, industry, organizational, and managerial levels, and a critical perspective will enable us to see not only how institutional and discursive power creates norms that define "acceptable" environmental limits but perhaps point to ways of organizing that can change the normative framework of decision-making (Banerjee 2010). More research is needed to understand the long-term effects of a particular environmental initiative. Most research has focused on the win-win cases of environmentalism. Once the low-hanging fruit of energy efficiencies, waste reduction, and recycling are picked, companies are confronted with environmental initiatives that no longer provide immediate economic and financial benefits (Banerjee & Bonnefous 2010). How do managers' negotiate trade-offs in a win-lose situation? What are the decision-making criteria that are used? How are these communicated to external and internal stakeholders?

A critical political economic approach

The problem with any normative prescriptions on why organizations should become greener lies perhaps in the level of analysis. The organization of the political economy around notions of competition, production, consumption, and economic growth poses significant structural constraints that limit any fundamental shift to environmentalism at the organizational level. Creating an "economy of restoration" requires interventions, not only at the organizational level, but at institutional, societal, political economy, as well as individual levels. A critical perspective on B&NE research would examine the structures and processes that discursively produce external environmental constraints, and how these constraints determine organizational responses. The critique should allow us to broaden the debate to include the political economy and alternative approaches to addressing environmental problems, something that the current "environmental management" discourse fails to address (Levy 1997).

Ultimately any reconciliation between economic, environmental, and social interests is a political task because it involves structures and processes of power. A critical perspective on ONE research would locate power as the central unit of analysis in theorizing the complex interactions between society, economy, and the polity. Power dynamics have shaped the global environmental movement, from the institutional power of supranational institutions like the World Bank and International Monetary Fund, the economic power of industrialized countries and their multinational corporations, to the discursive power of an "environmental-economic paradigm" that creates and circulates particular notions of "nature," the "environment," and "biological diversity" (Mcafee 1999). Discursive power in the political economy produces a form of corporate rationality that isolates the economic in a particular way and is reflected in the development policies of institutions like the World Bank, World Trade Organizations, and International Monetary Fund, as well as the corporate strategies of business firms. This role is legitimated by promoting an ideology that social progress can be achieved only by global competitiveness through the production and consumption of goods and services. The rules generated by discourse thus become "natural" rules or norms. Thus, definitions of "progress," "development," and "corporate citizenship" become truth effects that obscure the power relationships that govern the definitional process (Foucault 1980).

A critical approach would not merely seek to explain the existing relationships between the economy, society, and polity but analyze how the current order was created and the structures and processes that enable its maintenance. Policy debates about environmental preservation, biodiversity, and planetary carrying capacity have more to do with the preservation of a particular social order than the preservation of nature (Harvey 1996). Thus, a critical approach to business and the natural environment is ultimately an analysis of social change, an attempt to re-embed the social and the ecological in the political economy with the possibility of identifying alternate power-sharing arrangements.

Global environmental governance

Emerging research that focuses on the political and "citizenship" role of firms also provide the basis of a critique of B&NE-related research (Scherer & Palazzo 2007). The assumption is that in a globalizing world the role of the state has changed, perhaps even weakened, as market actors play an increasing role in societal governance. Making explicit the political role of corporations in their engagement with market, state and civil society actors can be seen as a form of "ecological citizenship" that goes beyond conventional environmental management approaches (Crane et al. 2008). If corporations are to carry out activities once the purview of governments, then there is a need to examine the processes and outcomes of corporate involvement in political and social domains. Understanding the social role of corporations through the lens of corporate citizenship raises important normative questions, such as the ability of corporations to deliver citizenship rights more efficiently than state or public actors, the desirability of the outcomes produced, and the motivations of corporations to enter the realm of citizenship rights (Van Oosterhout 2005).

In the context of international trade agreements and environmental policy, more democratic forms of decision-making could see the inclusion of more non-state and non-corporate actors. This can be achieved either through a political process where civil society organizations demand to be included, or through a process of "deliberate democracy" where corporations (and governments) voluntarily engage with civil society actors to enhance the legitimacy of economic, social, and environmental policies. Such a process may enable a more "democratic control on the public use of corporate power" (Scherer & Palazzo 2007). However, while participatory dialog may increase transparency of corporate decisions, it not clear how corporate participation in deliberate democracy can give non-corporate actors "democratic control" over corporate actions. The problem of unequal power dynamics between state, corporate, and civil society actors remains. Open dialog between conflicting interests may manufacture an uneasy form of consent, and perhaps offer better transparency, but it still does not address how accountability can be established and enforced in the context of deliberate democracy. Public–private partnerships may represent a more participatory approach to development, but the rules governing these partnerships tend to be framed by business through structural and discursive power relations (Fuchs & Lederer 2007). As Mouffe (2000: 14) argues, if relations of power are constitutive of the social, then the "main question for democratic politics is not how to eliminate power but how to constitute forms of power more compatible with democratic values."

Critical engagement

Finally, if CMS must have an impact on B&NE-related research, a significant departure from conventional modes of theorizing is needed. Ultimately the relevance and impact of a critical research agenda on environmental issues will be judged on how policy and practice can be changed. Rather than "distance themselves from advocacy and ideology" (Gladwin 1993: 43), critical researchers need to engage with market, state, and civil society actors with a view to promoting more participatory forms of decision-making, while remaining self-reflexive about the limitations of the alternatives they propose. Social movements like the World Social Forum and other coalitions for social and environmental welfare have called for wide-ranging institutional reform in order to address global poverty, labor conditions, climate change, environmental destruction, and biodiversity conservation. At the corporate level, these groups have called for more corporate accountability and democratic control over powerful transnational corporations. For instance, Friends of the Earth, an international environmental NGO, proposed a Framework Convention on Corporate Accountability at the Johannesburg Earth Summit (Bruno & Karliner 2002). Governments and corporations, not surprisingly, largely ignored the proposal. Key elements of the proposal include:

- Mandatory corporate reporting requirements on environmental and social impacts. Process for prior consultation with affected communities including environmental and social impact assessment and complete access to information.
- Extended liability to directors for corporate breaches of environmental and social laws and corporate liability for breeches of international laws and agreements.
- Rights of redress for citizens, including access for affected people anywhere in the world to pursue litigation, provisions for stakeholders to legally challenge corporate decisions and legal aid mechanisms to provide public funds to support such challenges.
- Community rights to resources, including indigenous peoples' rights over common property such as forests, fisheries and minerals.
- Veto rights over developmental projects and against displacement and rights to compensation for resources expropriated by corporations.
- Sanctions against corporations for breaching these duties including suspending stock exchange listing, fines and (in extreme cases) revoking the corporation's charter or withdrawal of limited liability status.

Critical perspectives on research on organizations and the natural environment require not only multidisciplinary approaches but also a plurality of epistemological, ontological, theoretical, and methodological perspectives. Instead of seeking more answers to the same questions, CMS asks different questions. For instance, a critical research agenda for B&NE-related research could explore the following questions:

- How do structural and discursive arrangements in the political economy shape organizational environmental strategies?
- How do managerial subjectivities shape corporate responses to environmental issues?
- What are the forms of resistance employed by environmental activists and civil society actors and how successful are their efforts?
- How do managers negotiate trade-offs between environmental impact and economic benefits? How does the structural and discursive positioning of the "environment" shape the range of organizational responses?
- What political strategies do corporations use to influence environmental policy-making?
- How do firms make problematic stakeholders behave in ways that do not adversely impact their economic bottom line?
- What strategies do corporations use to silence problematic stakeholders or delegitimize their claims?
- How do powerful corporate and institutional interests sustain their dominant position in the political economy? What strategies do they use to manage resistance?

To conclude this chapter I pose a provocative question: does environmental sustainability have a future? Or have we reached the limits of greening business, and further efforts will be purely incremental? Any radical shift in discourses of sustainability needs to squarely confront the power of the "sustainable development industry" led by big business that has successfully controlled the debate by deploying notions of eco-modernisn and eco-efficiency (Springett 2003). More than forty years of B&NE research has failed to ask the "big" questions but focused almost entirely on environmental instrumentalism. Instead of asking the question how do we make economic growth environmentally and socially sustainable CMS would ask: how do we make a low environmental impact lifestyle, reduced consumption, and standard of living among wealthier populations economically sustainable? Critical management research in the B&NE area must go beyond the organization or the corporation as the unit of analysis and focus its attention on the political economy drawing on transdisciplinary perspectives from environmental sociology (Catton & Dunlap 1980), anthropology (Escobar 1995) and ecological economics (Daly 1999; Martinez-alicr 1987). A critical perspective must describe the limits of current approaches to addressing environmental problems, identify strategies and actors to overcome these limits, propose alternative normative criteria for decision-making, and provide directions for future research, while retaining a strong self-reflexivity at all times.

References

Alvesson, M., Bridgman, T. & Willmott. H. (2009). "Introduction," in M. Alvesson, T. Bridgman, & H. Willmott (eds.), *The Oxford Handbook of Critical Management Studies*. Oxford: Oxford University Press.

Banerjee, S. B. (2000). "Whose Land is it Anyway? National Interest, Indigenous Stakeholders and Colonial Discourses: The Case of the Jabiluka Uranium Mine," *Organization & Environment*, 13(1): 3–38.

—— (2001). "Managerial Perceptions of Corporate Environmentalism: Interpretations from Industry and Strategic Implications for Organizations," *Journal of Management Studies*, 38(4): 489–513.

—— (2003). "Who Sustains Whose Development? Sustainable Development and the Reinvention of Nature," *Organization Studies*, 24(1): 143–180.

—— (2007). *Corporate Social Responsibility: The Good, the Bad and the Ugly*. Cheltenham: Edward Elgar.

—— (2008). "Necrocapitalism," *Organization Studies*, 29(12): 1541–1563.

—— (2010). "Governing the Global Corporation: A Critical Perspective," *Business Ethics Quarterly*, 20(2): 265–274.

—— & Bonnefous, A. (2010). "Stakeholder Management and Sustainability Strategies in the French Nuclear Industry," *Business Strategy and the Environment*, 20(2) 124–140.

—— Iyer, E. S. & Kashyap, R. K. (2003). "Corporate Environmentalism: Antecedents and Influence of Industry Type," *Journal of Marketing*, 67(2): 106–122.

Bansal, P. & Roth, K. (2000). "Why Companies go Green: A Model of Ecological Responsiveness," *Academy of Management Journal*, 43: 717–736. 29

—— & Gao, J. (2006). "Building the Future by Looking to the Past: Examining Research Published on Organizations and the Environment," *Organization & Environment*, 19(4): 458–478.

Bruno, K. & Karliner, J. (2002). "Marching to Johannesburg," *Corpwatch*. Available at <http://www.corpwatch.org/article.php?id=3588>. Accessed 31 October 2010.

Bumpus, A. G. & Liverman, D. (2008). "Accumulation by Decarbonisation and the Governance of Carbon Offsets," *Economic Geography*, 84(2): 127–55.

Burrell, G. (1993). "Eco and the Bunnymen," in J. Hassard and M. Parker (eds.), *Postmodernism and Organizations*, London: Sage, 71–82.

—— (1997). *Pandemonium: Towards a Retro-Organization Theory*. London: Sage.

Catton, W. Jr. & Dunlap, R. E. (1980)."A New Ecological Paradigm for Post-Exuberant Society," *American Behavioral Scientist*, 24(1): 15–47.

CMS (2010). Critical Management Studies Domain Statement. Available at <http://www.aomonline.org/aom.asp?ID=18&page_ID=57#cms>. Accessed 31 October 2010.

Crane, A. (2000). "Corporate Greening as Amoralization," *Organization Studies*, 21(4): 673–696.

—— Matten, D. & Moon, J. (2008). "Ecological Citizenship and the Corporation: Politicizing the New Corporate Environmentalism," *Organization & Environment*, 21(4): 371–389.

Daly, H. E. (1999). *Ecological Economics and the Ecology of Economics: Essays in Criticism*. Sheffield: Edward Elgar.

Dow Jones Sustainability Group Index (2010). <http://www.sustainability-index.com/>. Accessed 31 October 2010. 30

Escobar, A. (1995). *Encountering Development. The Making and Unmaking of the Third. World*. Princeton: Princeton University Press,

Foucault, M. (1980). *Power/Knowledge: Selected Interviews and Other Writings, 1972–1977*. New York: Pantheon Books.

Fournier, V. & Grey, C. (2000). "At the Critical Moment: Conditions and Prospects for Critical Management Studies," *Human Relations*, 53(1): 7–32.

Fuchs, D. and Lederer, M. M. L. (2007). "The Power of Business," *Business and Politics*, 9(3): 1–17.

Gladwin, T. N. (1993). "The Meaning of Greening: A Plea for Organizational Theory," in K. Fischer and J. Schot (eds.), *Environmental Strategies for Industry: International Perspectives on Research Needs and Policy Implications*, Washington, DC: Island Press, 37–61.

—— Kennelly, J. J., & Krause, T. S. (1995). "Shifting Paradigms for Sustainable Development: Implications for Management Theory and Research," *Academy of Management Review*, 20: 874–907.

Grice, S. & Humphries, M. (1997). "Critical Management Studies in Postmodernity: Oxymorons in Outer Space?" *Journal of Organizational Change Management*, 10: 412–25.

Hart, S. L. (1995). "A Natural Resource-Based View of the Firm," *Academy of Management Review*, 20(4): 986–1014.

Harvey, D. (1996). *Justice, Nature and the Geography of Difference*. Oxford. Blackwell Publishers Ltd.

Hawken, P. (1994). *The Ecology of Commerce: A Declaration of Sustainability*. London: Phoenix.

Jermier, J., Forbes, L. C., Benn, S., & Orsato, R. J. (2006). "The New Corporate Environmentalism and Green Politics," in S. Clegg, C. Hardy and W. Nord (eds.), *Handbook of Organization Studies*, London: Sage.

Kallio, T. J. & Nordberg, P. (2006). "The Evolution of Organizations and Natural Environment Discourse: Some Critical Remarks," *Organization & Environment*, 19(4): 439–457.

Levy, D. L. (1997). "Environmental Management as Political Sustainability," *Organization & Environment*, 10: 126–147.

—— and Egan, D. (2003). "A Neo-Gramscian Approach to Corporate Political Strategy: Conflict and Accommodation in the Climate Change Negotiations," *Journal of Management Studies*, 40: 803–30.

Luke, T. (2005). "The Death of Environmentalism or the Advent of Public Ecology?" *Organization & Environment*, 18: 489–494.

Mcafee, K. (1999). "Selling Nature to Save it? Biodiversity and Green Developmentalism," *Environment and Planning D*17(2): 133–154.

Magretta, J. (1997). "Growth Through Global Sustainability; An Interview with Monsanto's CEO, Robert B. Shapiro," *Harvard Business Review*, January/February, 79–88.

Martinez-alier, J. (1987). *Ecological Economics: Economics, Environment and Society*. Oxford: Blackwell.

Mouffe, C. (2000). *Deliberate Democracy or Agnostic Pluralism*. Vienna: Institute for Advanced Studies.

Newton, T. J. & Harte, G. (1997). "Green Business: Technicist Kitsch?" *Journal of Management Studies*, 34: 75–98.

ONE (2010). Organizations and the Natural Environment Domain Statement. Available at <http://www.aomonline.org/aom.asp?ID=18&page_ID=57#one>. Accessed 31 October 2010.

Van Oosterhout, J. (2005). "Corporate Citizenship: An Idea Whose Time Has Not Yet Come," *Academy of Management Review*. 30(4): 677–684.

Piasecki, B. W., Fletcher, K. A. & Mendelson, F. J. (1999). *Environmental Management and Business Strategy: Leadership Skills for the 21st Century*. New York: John Wiley.

Purser, R. E., Park, C., & Montuori, A (1995). "Limits to Anthropocentrism: Toward an Ecocentric Organization Paradigm?" *Academy of Management Review*, 20: 1053–1089.

Scherer, A. G. (2009). "Critical Theory and its Contribution to Critical Management Studies," in M. Alvesson, T. Bridgman and H. Willmott (eds.), *The Oxford Handbook of Critical Management Studies*, Oxford: Oxford University Press.

—— & Palazzo, G. (2007). "Towards a Political Conception of Corporate Responsibility: Business and Society from a Habermasian Perspective," *Academy of Management Review*, 32: 1096–1120.

Schmidheiny, S. (1992). *Changing Course: A Global Business Perspective on Development and the Environment*. Cambridge: MIT Press.

Shellenberger, M. & Nordhaus, T. (2004). "The Death of Environmentalism." Available at <http://www.thebreakthrough.org/PDF/Death_of_Environmentalism.pdf>. Accessed 31 October 2010.

Shrivastava, P. (1994). "CASTRATED Environment: GREENING Organizational Studies," *Organization Studies*, 15: 705–726.

—— & Hart, S. (1994). "Greening Organizations—2000," *International Journal of Public Administration*, 17: 607–635.

Spicer, A., Alvesson, M. & Kärreman, D. (2009). "Critical Performativity: The Unfinished Business of Critical Management Studies," *Human Relations*, 62(4): 537–560.

Springett, D. (2003). "Business Conceptions of Sustainable Development: A Perspective from Critical Theory," *Business Strategy and the Environment*, 12(2): 71–86.

Thompson, P. (2004). "Brands, Boundaries and Bandwagons: A Critical Reflection on Critical Management Studies," in S. Fleetwood and S. Ackroyd (eds.), *Critical Realism in Action in Organization and Management Studies*. London: Routledge, 54–70.

Welford, R. J. (1997). *Hijacking Environmentalism: Corporate Responses to Sustainable Development*. London: Earthscan.

Willmott, H. (1993). "Strength is Ignorance, Slavery is Freedom: Managing Culture in Modern Organizations," *Journal of Management Studies*, 30: 515–552.

Zadek, S. (2001). *The Civil Corporation: The New Economy of Corporate Citizenship*. London: Earthscan Publications.

CHAPTER 32

APPROACHING BUSINESS AND THE ENVIRONMENT WITH COMPLEXITY THEORY

DAVID L. LEVY AND BENYAMIN B. LICHTENSTEIN

THE failure to establish an international agreement on climate change at Copenhagen in December 2009 highlights the challenge of managing complex problems at the interface of business and the natural environment (B&NE). Despite the broad consensus on the need for coordinated global action, Copenhagen represented a failure of collective action—and a triumph of inertia—as industries and countries struggled to reconcile narrow conceptions of economic interest with global demands for aggressive action. This unfortunate outcome can be understood in the context of the larger "sociotechnical system" within which business and policymakers are operating: a complex dynamic system comprising economic, technological, social, political, and ecological elements, generating complex interactions and unforeseen outcomes.

Yet even as recriminations were flying at Copenhagen, some welcomed the opportunity to move beyond a centralized, top down model of global climate governance. Instead, they embraced the opportunity for businesses, non-governmental organizations (NGOs), and governmental agencies to experiment with a plethora of innovative approaches to reducing emissions, which offer new opportunities for learning and creative solutions (Hoffmann 2011). Complexity theory provides a grounded theoretical basis for this more optimistic perspective by explaining how networked actors can display adaptive learning and emergent self-organization.

In this chapter we examine the contribution of complexity theory to our understanding of B&NE, with a particular focus on climate change as an illustrative and representative example. We use the term "complexity" to refer to a group of concepts derived from systems theory, including complex dynamic systems theory, chaos, and emergence, among other disciplines. These provide insight into systemic tendencies towards patterned behavior, frozen inertia, and sometimes extreme instability. At a macro level, complexity theory explains why systems are often hard to comprehend and forecast, let alone manage and control. Yet complexity also offers micro-level tools and concepts to help innovative organizations improve sustainability through local initiatives of loosely networked agents (Senge et al. 2008). The field thus offers insights for steering systems toward sustainable transitions and enhancing resilience, without the hubris of complete control (Smith, Stirling, & Berkhout 2005).

The existing literature on B&NE mostly focuses on the organizational level, where managers have authority and responsibility. While this literature is valuable, as exemplified in this Handbook, the narrow focus can obscure an appreciation of the emergent properties and holistic functioning of the broader sociotechnical system. Some (see Ehrenfeld [Chapter 33]; and Roome [Chapter 34] this volume) emphasize that sustainability is only meaningful as a concept at the system level. Even if firms embrace good environmental practice, the aggregate impact of our global production and consumption creates an unsustainable environmental trajectory for the planet and the businesses it sustains. Others (see Banerjee [Chapter 31]; and Gladwin [Chapter 38] this volume) link this dangerous inertia to the wider capitalist system in which business is embedded.

Complexity theory provides a link between macro-level analysis of systems and micro-level understanding of organizational initiatives that might contribute toward potential solutions. This presents a critically important research agenda for understanding and potentially overcoming the disjuncture between the beehive of corporate sustainability efforts and the deteriorating state of the planet. Complexity offers new ways of addressing environmental impacts at the system level, such as supply chains (see Klassen & Vachon [Chapter 15] this volume) and geographic industrial ecologies (see Lifset & Boons [Chapter 17] this volume). Yet many questions remain if complexity theory is to be of practical use. What combination of top-down management and bottom-up initiatives is appropriate? How can points of leverage and influence be identified? What structural changes are needed to systems of finance, corporate governance, and energy pricing? What interventions might facilitate local initiatives and their coalescence into more sustainable production systems?

COMPLEX SYSTEMS AND THE ENVIRONMENT

Complexity theory offers a conceptual framework that incorporates the essential unpredictability of economic and environmental systems with the emergence of distinctive and contingently stable patterns (Anderson et al. 1999; Ormerod 1998). Complexity was originally developed through advances in non-linear mathematics (Thom 1975), thermodynamics (Prigogine & Glansdorf 1971), and computational sciences (Simon 1962). These ideas were quickly adapted to social systems (Ulrich & Probst 1984) and during the 1990s interest exploded in relation to management and organizations (Ashmos & Huber 1987; Kiel & Elliott 1996; Levy 1994; Merry 1995). Complexity theory goes beyond systems perspectives through advances in deterministic chaos theory (Lorenz 1963), power-law phenomena (Andriani & McKelvey 2009) and computational methodologies (Kauffman 1993; Davis, Eisenhardt, & Bingham 2007).

Complexity theory recognizes that economic and environmental systems comprise a multitude of agents, from individuals to large organizations, with distinctive properties at each level. The economy, for example, comprises individual consumers and workers, firms, markets, industries, and national economies. While all these levels are interdependent, higher-level aggregations exhibit "emergent" properties that cannot easily be reduced to the interaction of lower levels (Holland 1998). Macroeconomics, for example, relies on constructs and theories that differ from those relating to individual firms and consumers. Some core properties of complex systems are shown in Table 32.1.

Understanding complexity has been a long-standing concern of organization theory (Simon 1962). It offers insights into the emergence of patterned structure and order in higher-level systems, such as the Earth's climate, economic organizations and social institutions, but also provides methods for finding fundamental relationships and simplicity behind complex phenomena. Complexity helps explain how systems can evolve in unexpected ways, exhibiting dramatic instability (Rudolph & Repenning 2002) and even collapse (McKelvey 1999). The weather, the global climate, and the economy are complex systems that exhibit such chaotic behavior (Brock, Hsieh, & LeBaron 1991).

Chaos theory, a core science of complexity, explores systems in which the recursive application of non-linear functions gives rise to highly complex yet patterned behavior. Chaotic systems have several notable characteristics. First, they are unpredictable in the longer term, even though they are driven by deterministic rules. Weather conditions, for example, evolve due to well-understood interactions among variables such as humidity, air pressure, and temperature; however, the non-linear nature of these interactions makes it impossible to predict the long-term evolution of the weather system. The trajectory of chaotic systems such as these is highly dependent on initial starting conditions: the proverbial butterfly could theoretically cause perturbations that are amplified through successive interactions and reverberate throughout the entire weather system.

An important corollary is that, although chaotic systems never return to the same precise state, the outcomes have predictable boundaries that generate well-known

Table 32.1 Features of complex dynamic systems

1. Complex systems comprise a large number of dynamically interacting elements.
2. Interactions are rich and any element can influence any other.
3. Interactions are non-linear and typically short-range.
4. There are positive and negative feedback loops of interactions.
5. Complex systems are open systems, often under conditions far from equilibrium.
6. Complex systems are path dependent.
7. Individual elements are typically ignorant of the behavior of the whole system.

patterns (Dooley & Van De Ven 1999). Hurricanes emerge in late summer, though we never know their exact timing, path, or strength. Industries exhibit typical patterns of growth and maturity, yet evolve in unpredictable ways. These patterns are shaped by "strange attractors," structural features of systems that constrain and mold their evolution. The patterns reflect macro-level emergent properties: hurricanes, economic recessions, and social movements exhibit system-wide patterns that are distinct from the properties of the components from which these systems emerge.

Another important feature of complex systems is that change can be endogenous; under certain conditions interactions can cascade into systemic transformation (Cheng & Van De Ven 1996). For example, an ecological system in which a rapidly expanding population exhausts a slowly replenishing food supply will produce the classic "overshoot and collapse" outcome (May 1976). Similarly, a stock market collapse can be caused by positive feedback mechanisms affecting investor confidence, liquidity constraints, and computer driven trading. Moreover, systems do not necessarily recover their original pattern after a collapse; rather, they can shift to a new pattern around a different attractor. The economy can become mired in a self-perpetuating depression, and the climate can become locked in an ice age. Crucially, these critical thresholds are hard to predict. Some relatively large perturbations might peter out while smaller ones can propagate into larger-scale shifts. Despite this unpredictability, however, the pattern of sudden shifts, from earthquakes to stock market crashes, tends to follow a power law (Andriani & McKelvey 2009), such that the frequency of large-scale events is inversely related to their magnitude. These features of chaotic systems provide an important basis for understanding the links between the economy and the environment.

Economy and environment dynamic linkages

On the surface, business and the natural environment are very different types of systems. Business is a social system driven by human agents who make choices regarding their consumption and investment. The climate, by contrast, is primarily a physical and biological system driven by the dynamics of solar radiation, the carbon cycle, ice cover and ocean currents. These systems operate on vastly different timescales, with recessions occurring every decade or so, while ice ages occur about every 100,000 years. Yet from the perspective of complexity, these systems are interlinked elements of a larger sociotechnical system. Business is directly dependent on the climate in a number of sectors such as agriculture and tourism, and for clean energy sources like hydroelectric and wind power. Business also depends on a reliable flow of seemingly low-cost natural resources, including water and fossil fuels. Likewise, the carbon emissions that drive climate change are a function of economic growth, technological choices, and corporate governance structures.

At a deeper level, business and climate are both complex dynamic systems, with simultaneous tendencies toward stability and collapse. Both are susceptible to fundamental problems of governance: limits to comprehension, prediction, and control. The recent financial crisis illustrates the difficulties in anticipating and responding to an imminent economic meltdown. As the ice-caps quite literally melt down, the problems of collective action regarding climate change are becoming acute.

The economy-environment linkages have long been understood by environmentalists who argued that the Earth's natural support systems cannot withstand infinite economic and population growth. At some point, growth would be constrained by the lack of natural resources and the inability of the oceans and air to absorb our waste. The Club of Rome's early efforts at system dynamics modeling highlighted these Limits to Growth, and the authors forecast that the system was headed for "overshoot and collapse" (Meadows, Randers, & Meadows 2004). The core insights of the Limits to Growth thesis are borne out by current rates of depletion of fossil fuel, water, forests, arable land, and even species.

These dynamics and interdependencies have become increasingly visible in recent years. In the years leading up to 2008, rapid economic growth in emerging markets drove a dramatic rise in oil, food, and other commodity prices, a trend that was reinforced by financial speculators eager to ride the lucrative wave, until oil prices peaked at nearly $140 a barrel. These high prices spurred substantial investment in alternative energy sources, but also provided at least one of the triggers for the severe recession that began in fall 2008. The recession led to sharp cuts in oil prices and clean energy investment, while also reducing greenhouse gas emissions in the US by about 10 percent in 2008 and 2009, reversing the long term growth trend (EIA 2010). The recession in turn led governments to provide huge fiscal stimulus packages with some clean energy components, yet the ensuing deficits appear to have sapped the resources and political will for assertive longer-term action on emissions. Traditional linear economic models are inadequate to describe these dynamic relationships (Ormerod 1998).

The structure and character of complex dynamic systems raise important questions for governance of both the economy and the environment. Most central is the question of whether complex systems can be understood, their behavior predicted, and their outcomes managed and controlled. These questions are particularly acute for business environment systems such as climate change that present the potential for major threats to our well-being. In the next section, we examine some of the features of the business interface with the climate system that present challenges for timely and effective governance.

SYSTEMIC CHALLENGES TO CLIMATE GOVERNANCE

Perhaps the most serious challenge for effective climate governance is overcoming the inertia of our fossil fuel based economy. Unruh (2000: 817) has used the term *carbon lock-in* to refer to the "interlocking technological, institutional and social forces... that perpetuate fossil fuel-based infrastructures in spite of their known environmental externalities and the apparent existence of cost-neutral, or even cost-effective, remedies."

Carbon-intense technologies become locked in due to economies of scale, network economies, and path dependency (Arthur 1994), and the longevity of assets such as power plants and airports. Complementarities between system components are an important source of inertia (Geels 2004). Electric cars, for example, face hurdles related to the absence of a battery-charging network and the historical dearth of investment in battery technology compared to internal combustion engines.

As significant as technological lock-in, however, is that "carbon lock-in arises from systemic interactions among technologies and institutions" (Unruh 2000: 818). Institutions such as unions, government agencies, and professional bodies generate standards, rules, norms, and routines that stabilize and co-evolve with the dominant technologies. The automobile, for example, is intimately connected to our patterns of work and leisure. Levy & Rothenberg (2002) have suggested that US automobile manu-facturers were reluctant to examine lower emission technologies because of conserva-tive managerial mindsets which eschew the idea that consumers might actually embrace smaller cars or clean diesel engines. On the political level, incumbent businesses with vested interests forge powerful coalitions to perpetuate the status quo. Unruh argues (2000: 825) that "The highway lobby is still recognized today as one of the most powerful interest groups in US fiscal policy." It is this inertia in the energy system that constitutes "perverse resilience" (Gallopín 2006), a highly stable subsystem that threatens the stabil-ity of both the global climate and economy. The challenge is to break this inertia into components that include understanding and simulating complex systems, recognizing a crisis, and determining how to intervene in the system.

Challenges to understanding and simulating complex systems

Effective governance presumes an ability to understand a system, forecast its develop-ment, and intervene with some confidence regarding the outcomes. Complex dynamic systems present challenges to all three elements of the managerial process. The social world is populated by cognizant, emotional agents whose behavior is essentially unpre-dictable at the individual level (Stacey 1996: 187). Even when system function is well understood at the micro-level, forecasting system behavior at the macro-level remains problematic. Simulation models are frequently employed to represent complex systems, because they can better account for iterative and non-linear interactions over time. Weather forecasts, for example, rely on computer simulations that model the atmosphere as a grid whose elements interact in well-defined physical relationships. With a given set of starting conditions, a computer can generate a forecast that is reasonably accurate for about the next five days, and better than random guessing for about ten.

Simulations, however, are always simplified, and thus imperfect, representations of reality. First, the fixed-step, finite resolution of computation misses the continuous dynamics at the molecular level exhibited in natural and social systems. Second, starting conditions are not known with perfect accuracy. Third, the specification of relationships does not capture some more subtle feedbacks, for example, regarding clouds and the ocean-land atmospheric interface. Weather forecasters have attempted to improve accuracy by employing faster supercomputers to tackle models with finer temporal and spatial resolution, but the improvement is marginal, because errors in model specification and starting conditions are magnified through iterative calculations.

Although climate modeling has made remarkable progress and provides a good fit with the historical record, models do not yet reliably incorporate longer-term shifts in ocean circulation, ice and forest cover, and other factors that make the climate chaotic on longer time scales. Neither do they capture interactions with political and economic systems in a detailed way, beyond some broad scenarios. As a result, we can speculate about positive feedback effects that could lead to collapsing ice caps and runaway warming, but it is very difficult to predict if and when we might pass the critical thresholds.

Recognizing a crisis

The dynamics of complex systems make it hard to recognize the approach of critical thresholds and to take timely action to avoid crises. First, it is hard to differentiate between "normal" fluctuations and more drastic transformations. Hurricane Katrina did not raise many alarms regarding climate change, nor did most observers take the collapse of Bear Stearns as a signal of the onset of the global financial crisis. It is only in retrospect, in conjunction with other data, that we are able to see broader patterns and put such events in context. Moreover, complex systems often have regions which appear relatively calm, even while structural pressures are building up. Prior to the financial crisis in October 2008, data on corporate profits and employment gave little cause for concern, even as rising debt and inflated housing prices generated disequilibrium tensions. Similarly, the climate appears relatively stable to casual observers, despite rapidly rising greenhouse gas concentrations.

Fundamentally, the recognition that a crisis demands action is a social and political process. Mass media play a critical role in framing events within a broader narrative context, a role which has been especially evident in the case of climate change (Boykoff, Goodman, & Curtis 2010). Defining a situation as a crisis usually entails allocation of responsibility and demands for redress. However, energy-intense industries and high-emission countries have tried to minimize concern about climate change, presumably because mitigation measures could adversely impact them. Moreover, there are organizational and psychological barriers against recognizing a crisis. We are biased to ignore warnings about catastrophe, and to presume that what appeared to work yesterday will continue tomorrow (Kahneman, Slovic, & Tversky 1982). Within organizations responsible for complex systems, such as the space shuttle or nuclear power plants, intense organizational pressures frequently silence the expression of valid concerns about risks. These pressures arise from power hierarchies, budgetary pressures, and masculine organizational cultures that deride concerns of risk as weakness (Perrow 1989; Vaughan 1996).

Even once an impending crisis has been acknowledged and a need for active intervention recognized, several major impediments to effective action are well explained by complexity theory. The following section explores the difficulties of intervening in complex dynamic systems, including problems of collective action, unintended consequences, and inherent limitations on effective management.

Challenges to effective intervention in complex systems

Intervention in sociotechnical systems entails coordinated action by large numbers of actors, raising the problem of collective action. Hardin's (1968) "Tragedy of the Commons" describes the tendency toward inaction in the face of the overuse of a common resource, such as the atmosphere, when private actors can free-ride and have little incentive to change their behavior. Various societal institutions have evolved to address such collective action problems (Ostrom 1990), but large-scale systemic crises require costly measures that demand an often lengthy process to build consensus.

In part, such delays and disagreements reflect differences in technical understandings of complex systems. Action on climate change, for example, has been delayed while various parties argue over the best course of action: cap-and-trade versus carbon taxes, nuclear power versus renewable energy. Yet these differences are also deeply political, reflecting the asymmetric ways in which actors perceive that a crisis and remedial action will affect them. The fiercest proponents of action on climate change are the low-lying countries likely to be swamped by rising sea levels. In contrast, the countries and sectors who strongly oppose action tend to be heavily dependent on fossil fuels. Some rich countries might be willing to pay 1–2 percent of GDP to cut emissions, but developing countries demand massive transfusions of capital if they are to transition from cheap fossil fuels. The failure to reach agreement in Copenhagen was largely due to these deep divisions.

Problems of collective action are exacerbated by the need to coordinate multiple forms of intervention in complex dynamic systems. Neither a carbon tax nor a single technological breakthrough will, by itself, solve the climate problem, a point made by Jones (2009) in his system dynamics model of the evolution of the solar industry. Intervention in complex systems is also hindered by the likelihood of undesired and unanticipated consequences. Raising vehicle fuel economy standards reduces the cost of travel per mile, encouraging more car travel. Incentives to raise production of biofuels could raise food prices, and perhaps encourage clearcutting forests.

These uncertainties have led some to suggest that complex systems are essentially unmanageable. Perrow's (1989) study of the nuclear accident at Three Mile Island concluded that catastrophic accidents were "normal" in the context of highly complex socio-technical systems. Even the most carefully designed systems, Perrow argued, could not always prevent occasional human or technological failures from cascading into major disasters. The explosion and massive oil leak from BP's oil well in spring 2010 highlights the challenge of anticipating every potential eventuality, especially when regulators and managers are under pressure to overlook risks to meet deadlines and profit targets.

ENVIRONMENTAL ACTION IN COMPLEX SYSTEMS

Despite the failure to reach agreement at Copenhagen, some observers point optimisti-
cally to the multitude of climate- and energy-related initiatives at local and regional
levels being undertaken by cities, state agencies, companies, and NGOs, often in the
form of public-private collaborations (Ostrom 2009a). "Far from lacking climate governance in the face of multilateral deadlock, the world is rather awash in governance
initiatives shaping how individuals, communities, provinces, regions, corporations, and
nation-states respond to climate change" (Hoffmann 2011: 3). For instance, the ICLEI
Climate Program is a network of more than 500 cities and local governments dedicated
to local action on sustainability and climate change (Betsill & Bulkeley 2004). In
Berkeley, California, the Property Assessed Clean Energy (PACE) model was developed
to finance the up-front cost of residential renewable energy and efficiency investments,
with repayment through an assessment on property taxes. This solves the problem facing homeowners who lack the requisite financing or are uncertain when they might
move home.

In the business world, companies are developing low-carbon products and services,
engaging in collaborations with NGOs and government, and forging alliances such as
the US Climate Action Partnership to push for more aggressive action on climate
(Hoffman 2006; Pinkse & Kolk 2009). GE's Ecomagination program has doubled its
investment in R&D for environmental products to $1.5 billion, and Citigroup has com-
mitted to a $50 billion "green" initiative that includes investments in clean energy and
reducing its global carbon footprint. Perhaps more impressive are initiatives to redesign
supply chains, markets, and entire industries. For example, the USGBC's LEED building
certification system has helped generate a $12 billion green construction industry, lead-
ing to long-term efficiencies in materials and energy utilization (Senge et al. 2008).

This rise of local initiatives contradicts conventional theories of collective-action
which predict that "no one will change behavior and reduce their energy use unless an
external authority imposes enforceable rules that change the incentives faced by those
involved. This is why many analysts call for a change in institutions at the global level"
(Ostrom 2009b: 7). In contrast, Ostrom shows how actors often have local incentives
that do *not* depend on coordinated action: "Even without major taxes imposed on energy
at a national level, however, families that decide to invest in better insulation and more
efficient furnaces and other appliances, to join a carpool whenever feasible, and to take
other energy-conserving actions can save funds over the long run" (Ostrom 2009b: 15).
Similarly, cities can enjoy the co-benefits of reducing fossil fuel use, such as cleaner air
and improved public health. Ostrom emphasizes that cooperation can emerge within
networks of actors when sufficient trust, social capital, leadership, and communication
are present, encouraging expectations of reciprocity and mutual learning. She concludes
that "many groups in the field have self-organized to develop solutions to common-pool
resource problems at a small to medium scale" (Ostrom 2009b: 10). Ostrom's allusion to

self-organization within a "polycentric order" suggests an awareness of the potential for effective approaches to emerge "bottom-up" from networks of actors.

The theory of emergence provides understanding of how dynamic systems generate order (Lichtenstein & Plowman 2009; McKelvey 2004) and exhibit "self-organization" (Holland 1998). In this section, we apply this theory to the emergence of business responses to climate change, with models drawn from a range of perspectives including order-creation in complex adaptive systems, far-from-equilibrium conditions that give rise to new opportunities and markets, the critical role of local experiments and learning in emergent systems, and a growing literature on self-organization in supply chains.

Far-from-equilibrium conditions

Many complexity researchers have argued that far-from-equilibrium conditions—pushing systems beyond their normal range of activity—is a key factor driving emergence (Meyer, Gaba, & Colwell 2005). Climate change, for example, creates pressures from consumers, activists, competitors, and regulators for change; similarly, resource scarcity is a force for innovation. Perhaps the leading scholarship in this area has been done by Chiles and colleagues (2010) who have developed a "radical subjectivist" approach to show how the uncertainty facing entrepreneurs leads to market *divergence*, a process stronger than equilibrium-based *convergence* towards imitation. Divergence increases heterogeneity, the driver for innovation, experimentation, and co-evolution (Lewin & Volberda 1999).

The rise of the clean energy sector reflects a slow but persistent system-wide emergence of technologies, regulations, and demand patterns that catalyze the creation and expansion of businesses growing in sheltered market niches. For example, as technologies around solar power develop, business and policy entrepreneurs have identified practices and models that overcome market, technological, and political lock-in. The market begins to "self-organize" as venture capitalists, entrepreneurs, consumers, and regulators interact in a network and create self-sustaining norms, rules, practices, and institutions. Over time, expectations and interactions lead to loosely coordinated self-organization of the market, and the emergence of new technologies and business models. "Thus, entrainment of entrepreneurs' activity/thought patterns in competitive entrepreneurial markets may spontaneously create a far-from-equilibrium market order that is both heterogeneous and coherent" (Chiles et al. 2010: 39). Shai Agassi's Better Place project to create a national replaceable battery infrastructure for pure electric vehicles illustrates how an entrepreneur can mobilize other actors to transform markets and overcome systemic obstacles in infrastructure and scale.

Experimentation for emergence

Studies of the order-creation process show that far-from-equilibrium systems tend to generate local experiments aimed at creating a solution to the internal tension (Prigogine

& Stengers 1984; Lichtenstein 2000). These experiments are more intentional and solu-tion-oriented than the random variation exhibited in Darwinian evolutionary proc-esses; they tend to "bubble up" in organizations (Fuller, Warren, & Argyle 2008) or market regions (Chiles et al. 2010) as an adaptive response to these conditions, and the more successful experiments can grow by replication and attracting more resources.

Sustainability experiments have emerged in a variety of industries with a high utilization of natural resources. A special issue of the Journal of Cleaner Production (Jegatheesan et al. 2009) highlighted experiments for transitioning from resource-intensive manufacturing toward innovative approaches that reduce energy and mate-rial sources, such as producing biopolymer-based plastics without petroleum. These experiments and others like them are focused within individual industries, but can be linked into broader production systems.

Business initiatives for sustainability interact dialectically with government experi-ments, not only responding to regulatory pressures, but also creating the political space for policy development. Hoffman & Eidelman (2009: 2) describe the profusion of cli-mate governance experiments in terms of self-organization: "Governance is about mak-ing rules above, below, and between established political authorities. Experimentation implies innovation and trial and error with new forms of governance." They classify fifty-eight unique experiments, each of which intentionally aims to influence awareness and behavior at various levels. These classifications include *Networks* like the Evangelical Climate Initiative, *Infrastructure Builders* like ICLEI and the American Carbon Registry; *Voluntary Actors* such as the e8 Network of Expertise for the Global Environment; and *Accountable Actors*, such as WWF's Climate Savers.

Hoffman & Eidelman (2009: 2) suggest that "While individual experiments arise for idiosyncratic reasons, experimentation is a broader, patterned process driving signifi-cant innovation." They describe a process in which political agents are "adaptive actors embedded in a co-evolutionary or mutually constitutive relationship with their govern-ance context", so that "There is constant feedback between actors' beliefs, interests, and actions.... Without centralized planning, the experimental initiatives may form a sys-tem of governance where networking, a combination of competition and cooperation, the emergence of communities of practice, and the development of redundancy in the system are likely (Hoffman & Eidelman 2009: 13).

Between Collapse and Emergence

We have presented two very different perspectives on business and the natural environ-ment. The pessimistic macro-view, informed by system dynamics and chaos theory, sug-gests that environmental externalities and collective action failures are leading to a "tragedy of the commons." The inherent difficulties in understanding and controlling chaotic systems can turn us into unwitting accomplices in the ineluctably unfolding "overshoot and collapse" of natural ecosystems and the businesses embedded within them. However, complexity theory also presents a more optimistic micro-level view of system-wide order emerging from self-organized solutions in local contexts. Between these poles, a number of approaches exist which suggest that a limited degree of prediction and managerial intervention is not only possible but necessary to steer our economic and environmental systems away from catastrophe. Here we take a brief look at several approaches including systems dynamics modeling, and the development of sustainable supply chains and ecodistricts.

Many types of complex systems are sufficiently tractable that computational models can provide a degree of forecasting and planning. Global climate models are increasingly able to reproduce the historical record as well as regional features such as the El Nino phenomenon. Likewise, systems dynamics models (Forrester 1971; Sterman 1989) can portray cyclical and chaotic behavior, as well as tendencies toward stability or collapse, providing tools for better understanding threshold effects, unexpected outcomes, and likely responses to intervention (Warren 2004). Using these tools, Jones (2009) found that a sequenced combination of policies such as incentives, information, and research support is much more effective in inducing systemic shifts in an industry than reliance on a single tool such as subsidies.

In contrast to modeling approaches that aspire for prediction and control by autonomous agents standing "outside" the system, an emerging environmental literature on managing sociotechnical transitions draws from complexity to emphasize the limited yet tangible power of managers who are inextricably embedded *within* systems. Managers can *steer* the path of a system, rather than precisely determine outcomes (Garud & Karnoe 2003). At the same time, actors within the system have differential interests and power, resulting in potential conflicts over the direction in which to steer. This insight prompted Smith & Sterling (2006: 1) to suggest, "In short, we need to move from a view of 'steering as management' to an understanding of 'steering as politics.'"

Environmentally favorable new technologies and practices often face hurdles because initially they exhibit relatively poor technical and economic performance, as well as being incongruous with existing infrastructure, interests, incumbent firms, and regulations (Geels 2004; Meadowcroft 2005). Thus, the transitions approach points to the importance of "strategic niche management," encouraging new models to emerge in niches that are protected from the dominant market regime, and the subsequent diffusion and hybridization of innovations into the mainstream in a co-evolutionary process (Kemp, Schot, & Hoogma 1998; Raven 2007).

Likewise, sustainable supply-chain management and industrial ecology represent efforts to improve environmental performance at the system rather than firm level. As Lifset & Boons ([Chapter 17] this volume) state, "A central premise of industrial ecology is that environmental problems and remedies should be viewed from a systems perspective." Klassen & Vachon ([Chapter 15] this volume) similarly argue that organizations can only thrive sustainably when they consider the supply chain as a whole. More specifically, research into supply chains has shown that agents can organize themselves in ways that increase efficiency and improve environmental performance (Choi, Dooley, & Rungtusanatham 2001). Across numerous studies, supply chains have been shown to exhibit self-organization and improve the sustainability of the entire network through adaptive innovation and stronger connections among local firms, suppliers, and customers (Lichtenstein, in press; Pathak et al. 2007; Varga et al. 2009)

A similar process of self-organization across economic entities is at the core of industrial ecology (Ehrenfeld 2009) and eco-industrial parks (Rosenthal & Cote 1998). Based on an operational analogy between ecological habitats and industrial regions, the idea is that one or more of the outputs ("waste") from one business, such as lumberyard scraps, can become the inputs for another business, such as a paper factory. Successful eco-industrial parks have been set up throughout the world, where each participating firm helps identify and transfer resources that other firms can utilize in their production process (Spiegelman 2003). These adaptive network organizations often connect a wide range of industries, as Klassen & Vachon (Chapter 15) show for the Kalundborg case.

Complexity theory, as well as empirical studies, suggests that adaptive self-organization of supply chains requires particular conditions. According to the NK Landscape models (Kauffman 1993), when a system contains agents who are rigidly connected with a very high degree of interdependence, the computational ecology can "freeze up"—what McKelvey (1999) called a "complexity catastrophe": the system becomes highly inflexible and unable to adapt. Loose networks, in which autonomy is balanced with interdependence, facilitate adaptive experimentation as well as diffusion of the more successful innovations. Complexity research employing agent-based models also points to the value of integrating bottom-up efforts with top-down guidance and structure. Empirical evidence from these models suggests that self-organizing of autonomous agents can create only minimal degrees of order (McKelvey & Lichtenstein 2007), whereas modern organizations are necessarily composed of seven or eight hierarchical levels (Jacques 1989).

CONCLUSIONS AND FUTURE DIRECTIONS

Complexity approaches contain a core tension between two perspectives on the dynamic interactions between business and natural environment. A macro-level systems perspective emphasizes structural inertia, misaligned incentives, and failures of collective action. It therefore offers a pessimistic view that we are headed toward environmental overshoot and collapse, with dire consequences for business and society. A more micro-level perspective, however, suggests that under certain conditions, networked actors will engage in a multitude of local initiatives and experimentation, leading to systemic learning and adaptation. A related tension exists in the complexity field between those with confidence that the scientific method can be applied to the development of sophisticated theory and modeling tools, enabling systems to be modeled and controlled, and those who think that complex systems are essentially beyond human management. These tensions are linked, because it is the same characteristics that make complex dynamic systems unpredictable that can facilitate self-organization and emergent order.

Within the context of B&NE, our review suggests the need for a complementarity of local experiments and macro-level governance. Locally designed initiatives have considerable energy and creativity, but in order to grow and scale, they require coordination and a favorable context. In the climate case, this implies economic incentives and political pressures for change, national regulations, and international agreements. Together, these provide some predictability, an alignment of expectations across sectors and geographic boundaries, and coordination mechanisms to generate consensus around goals.

Even with the failure to reach formal agreement at Copenhagen, a consensus around the 2 degrees Celsius ceiling for global warming emerged out of the debates leading up to the international climate conference in 2009, and now serves as a loose policy coordinating mechanism. However, macro-level processes on their own cannot provide the embedded leadership necessary to solve local sustainability challenges, as this requires local initiatives, expertise and participation by businesses and other organizations in specific industries and geographic regions. Thus, progress requires a combination of action at the local level, with coordinated leadership at higher levels.

Ecodistricts and sustainable supply chains illustrate this combination of top-down management and bottom-up self-organization. Regional initiatives for mixed industrial zoning, economic incentives, and integrated infrastructure are often required to initiate the process. Likewise, life-cycle analyses can help identify resource synergies among partner firms. The linkages among the firms, however, need to be enacted by system agents rather than through external forces, in order to generate firm-level commitment and continued innovation.

Opportunities exist here for research into the appropriate form and combination of top-down governance and bottom-up experimentation. While complexity theory has produced some general insights into the conditions needed for self-organization, these are difficult to apply and operationalize in particular circumstances, such as supply chains and local climate governance experiments. Moreover, the sustainable supply chain and industrial ecology literatures are overly reliant on material and energy flows, while neglecting the social, political, and economic structures in which these systems are embedded.

This integrative perspective on bottom-up initiatives and top-down control represents a new and important understanding of complex systems. The notion that self-organization is feasible only in the absence of top-down hierarchical control reflects an inaccurate but popular understanding of complexity science that has generated a faddish wave of organizational consultants invoking complexity in a metaphorical, even mystical manner. Implicit in this approach is a free-market ideology that celebrates individual initiatives and frowns on governmental guidance. Further research can explore the degree, pace, and effectiveness of local environmental initiatives, in the context of complementary dynamics of wider, more structured coordination. If these local initiatives need protection within strategic niches, research is needed into the means of doing so without stifling the active diffusion of successful innovations into the larger system.

The development of modeling tools to represent the complexities of business-environment interactions offers substantial potential for future research. Even as we recognize that limitations on long-term forecasting in complex systems, models that are well specified with realistic structures and parameters promise to generate insights into our current environmental and economic trajectory, critical thresholds, and future dangers, as well as points of leverage and intervention. A more modest goal, which is increasingly embraced by systems dynamics researchers, is to develop models using visual representations in an interactive, collaborative manner with decision-makers. These models draw on the collective expertise of professionals in a range of locations across system to capture the core dynamics and interactions at play. The purpose is not just to develop useful models, but more importantly, to encourage participants to develop an understanding of complex systems and forge consensus about likely outcomes and potential interventions. The current polarization and paralysis regarding climate change highlights the need for a broader awareness of the character and behavior complex systems at the interface of business and the environment.

REFERENCES

Anderson, P., Meyer, A., Eisenhardt, K., Carley, K., & Pettigrew, A. (1999). "Introduction to the Special Issue: Application of Complexity Theory to Organization Science," *Organization Science*, 10(3): 233–236.

Andriani, P. & McKelvey, B. (2009). "From Gaussian to Paretian Thinking: Causes and Implications of Power Laws in Organizations," *Organization Science*, 20: 1053–1071.

Arthur, W. B. (1994). *Increasing Returns and Path Dependence in the Economy*. Ann Arbor, MI: University of Michigan Press.

Ashmos, D. & Huber, G. (1987). "The System Paradigm in Organization Theory: Correcting the Record and Suggesting the Future," *Academy of Management Review*, 12: 607–621.

Betsill, M. M. & Bulkeley, H. (2004). "Transnational Networks and Global Environmental Governance: The Cities for Climate Protection Program," *International Studies Quarterly*, 48(2): 471–493.

Boykoff, M. T. (2007). "From Convergence to Contention: United States Mass Media Representations of Anthropogenic Climate Change Science," *Transactions of the Institute of British Geographers*, 32: 477–489.

——— Goodman, M. K., & Curtis, I. (2010). "Cultural Politics of Climate Change: Interactions in Everyday Spaces," in M. T. Boykoff (ed.), *The Politics of Climate Change*, 140, New York: Routledge.

Brock, W. A., Hsieh, D. A., & LeBaron, B. (1991). *Nonlinear Dynamics, Chaos, and Instability: Statistical Theory and Economic Evidence*. Cambridge, MA: M.I.T. Press.

Cheng, Y. & Van De Ven, A. (1996). "The Innovation Journey: Order out of Chaos?" *Organization Science*, 6: 593–614.

Chiles, T., Tuggle, C. S., McMullen, J., Bierman, L., & Greening, D. (2010). "Dynamic Creation: Elaborating a Radical Austrian Approach to Entrepreneurship," *Organization Studies*, 31(1): 7–46.

Choi, T., Dooley, K., & Rungtusanatham, M. (2001). "Supply Networks and Complex Adaptive Systems: Control vs. Emergence," *Journal of Operations Management*, 19: 351–366.

Davis, J., Eisenhardt, K., & Bingham, C. (2007). "Developing Theory through Simulation Methods," *Academy of Management Review*, 32: 480–499.

Dooley, K., & Van De Ven, A. (1999). "Explaining Complex Organizational Dynamics," *Organization Science*, 10(3): 358–372.

Ehrenfeld, J. (2009). *Sustainability by Design*. New Haven: Yale University Press.

EIA, U. (2010). *U.S. Carbon Dioxide Emissions in 2009: A Retrospective Review*. US Energy Information Administration.

Forrester, J. W. (1971). "Counter-Intuitive Behavior of Social Systems," *Theory and Decision*, 2(2): 109–140.

Fuller, T., Warren, L., & Argyle, P. (2008). "Sustaining Entrepreneurial Business: A Complexity Perspective on Processes that Produce Emergent Practice," *International Entrepreneurship Management Journal*, 4: 1–17.

Gallopín, G. (2006). "Linkages between Vulnerability, Resilience, and Adaptive Capacity," *Global Environmental Change*, 16(3): 293–303.

Garud, R., & Karnøe, P. (2003). "Bricolage Versus Breakthrough: Distributed and Embedded Agency in Technology Entrepreneurship," *Research Policy*, 32: 277–301.

Geels, F. W. (2004). "From Sectoral Systems of Innovation to Socio-Technical Systems: Insights about Dynamics and Change from Sociology and Institutional Theory," *Research Policy*, 33: 897–920.

Hardin, G. (1968). "The Tragedy of the Commons," *Science*, 162: 1243–1248.

Hoffman, A. J. (2006). *Getting Ahead of the Curve: Corporate Strategies that Address Climate Change*. Washington DC: The Pew Center on Global Climate Change.

Hoffmann, M. (2011). *Climate Governance at the Crossroads: Experimenting with a Global Response after Kyoto*. Oxford: Oxford University Press.

—— & Edelman, G. (2009). "Experimenting with Climate Governance." Working Paper, University of Toronto.

Holland, J. (1998). *Emergence: From Chaos to Order*. Cambridge, MA: Perseus Books.

Jacques, E. (1989). *Requisite Organization*. London: Carson & Hall.

Jegatheesan, V., Liow, J. L., Shu, L., Kim, S. H., & Visvanathan, C. (2009). "The Need for Global Coordination in Sustainable Development," *Journal of Cleaner Production*, 17: 637–643.

Jones, C. (2009). "The Renewable Energy Industry in Massachusetts as a Complex System: Developing a Shared Understanding for Policy Making," Ph.D. Dissertation, University of Massachusetts, Boston.

Kahneman, D., Slovic, P., & Tversky, A. (eds.) (1982). *Judgment under Uncertainty: Heuristics and Biases*. New York: Cambridge University Press.

Kauffman, S. (1993). *The Origins of Order*. New York, NY: Oxford University Press.

Kemp, R., Schot, J., & Hoogma, R. (1998). Regime Shifts to Sustainability through Processes of Niche Formation: The Approach of Strategic Niche Management *Technology Analysis & Strategic Management*, 10(2): 175–198.

Kiel, D., & Elliott, E. (eds.) (1996). *Chaos Theory in the Social Sciences: Foundations and Applications*. Ann Arbor, MI: Universtiy of Michigan Press.

Levy, D. L. (1997). "Lean Production in an International Supply Chain," *Sloan Management Review*, 38(2): 94–102.

—— (1994). "Chaos Theory and Strategy: Theory, Application, and Managerial Implications," *Strategic Management Journal*, 15: 167–178.

—— & Rothenberg, S. (2002). "Heterogeneity and Change in Environmental Strategy: Technological and Political Responses to Climate Change in the Automobile Industry," in A. Hoffman, & M. Ventresca (eds.), *Organizations, Policy and the Natural Environment: Institutional and Strategic Perspectives*, Stanford: Stanford University Press, 173–193.

Levy, D. & Scully, M. (2007). "The Institutional Entrepreneur as Modern Prince: The Strategic Face of Power in Contested Fields," *Organization Studies*, 28(7): 971–991.

Lewin, A. & Volberda, H. (1999). "Prolegomena on Coevolution: A Framework for Research on Strategy and New Organizational Forms," *Organization Science*, 10: 519–534.

Lichtenstein, B. (2000). "Self-Organized Transitions: A Pattern Amid the "Chaos" of Transformative Change," *Academy of Management Executive*, 14(4): 128–141.

——— (forthcoming). "Leverage Points for Sustainability Entrepreneuring: A Multi-level Framework of Passion in Action," *Advances in Entrepreneurship, Firm Emergence and Growth*, Volume 13: *Social and Sustainable Entrepreneurship*. edited by Tom Lumpkin & Jerome Katz.

——— & Plowman, D. (2009). "The Leadership of Emergence: A Complex Systems Leadership Theory of Emergence at Successive Organizational Levels," *The Leadership Quarterly*, 20. 617–630.

Lorenz, E. (1963). "Deterministic Nonperiodic Flow," *Journal of the Atmospheric Sciences*, 20: 130–141.

McKelvey, B. (1999). "Avoiding Complexity Catastrophe in Coevolutionary Pockets: Strategies for Rugged Landscapes," *Organization Science*, 10(3): 294–321.

——— (2004). "Toward a Complexity Science of Entrepreneurship," *Journal of Business Venturing*, 19: 313–341.

——— & Lichtenstein, B. (2007) "Leadership in the Four Stages of Emergence," in J. Hazy, J. Goldstein, & B. Lichtenstein (eds.), *Complex Systems Leadership Theory*. Boston: ISCE Publishing, 93 108.

Maguire, S., McKelvey, B., Mirabeau, L., & Oztas, N. (2006) "Complexity Science and Organization Studies," in S. Clegg, C. Hardy, W. Nord, & T. Lawrence (eds.), *Handbook of Organization Studies*, 2nd edition, 165–214. London, UK: SAGE.

Meadowcroft, J. (2005). "Environmental Political Economy, Technological Transitions, and the State," *New Political Economy*, 10(4): 479–498.

Meadows, D., Randers, J., & Meadows, D. L. (2004). *Limits to Growth: The 30-Year Update*. White River Jct., VT Chelsea Green.

Merry, U. (1995). "Coping with Uncertainty: Insights from the New Sciences of Chaos, Self-Organization, and Complexity," Westport, CT: Praeger.

Meyer, A., Gaba, V., & Colwell, K. (2005). "Organizing far from Equilibrium: Nonlinear Change in Organizational Fields," *Organization Science*, 16: 456–473.

Ormerod, P. (1998). *Butterfly Economics. A New General Theory of Social and Economic Behavior*. NY: Pantheon.

Ostrom, E. (1990). *Governing the Commons: The Evolution of Institutions for Collective Action*. Cambridge: Cambridge University Press.

——— (2009a). "A General Framework for Analyzing Sustainability of Social-Ecological Systems," *Science*, #325, 419.

——— (2009b). "A Polycentric Approach for Coping with Climate Change." *World Bank – Policy Research Working Paper #5095*.

Pathak, S., Day, J., Nair, A., Sawaya, W., & Kristal, M. (2007). "Complexity and Adaptivity in Supply Networks: Building Supply Network Theory Using a Complex Adaptive Systems Perspective," *Decision Sciences*, 38: 547–580.

Perrow, C. (1989). *Normal Accidents*. Oxford: Oxford University Press.

Pinkse, J., & Kolk, A. (2009). *International Business and Global Climate Change*. London: Routledge.

Prigogine, I. & Glansdorff, P. (1971). *Thermodynamic Theory of Structure, Stability, and Fluctuations*. New York: Wiley & Sons.

——— & Stengers, I. (1984). *Order out of Chaos*. New York, NY: Bantam Books.

Raven, R. (2007). "Niche Accumulation and Hybridisation Strategies in Transition Processes towards a Sustainable Energy System: An Assessment of Differences and Pitfalls," *Energy Policy*, 35(4): 2390–2400.

Rosenthal, E. C. & Cote, R. P. (1998). "Designing Eco-Industrial Parks: A Synthesis of Some Experiences," *Journal of Cleaner Production*, 6: 181–188.

Rosser, J. B. (1991). *From Catastrophe to Chaos: A General Theory of Economic Discontinuities*. Boston, MA: Kluwer Academic Publishers.

Rudolph, J., & Repenning, N. (2002). "Disaster Dynamics: Understanding the Role of Quantity in Organizational Collapse," *Administrative Science Quarterly*, 47: 1–30.

Schieve, W. & Allen, P. (eds.) (1982). *Self-Organization and Dissapative Structures: Applications in the Physical and Social Sciences*. Austin, TX: University of Texas Press.

Schwark, F. (2009). "Influence Factors for Scenario Analysis for New Environmental Technologies: The Case for Biopolymer Technology," *Journal of Cleaner Production*, 17: 644–652.

——— (2009). "Influence Factors for Scenario Analysis for New Environmental Technologies: The Case for Biopolymer Technology," *Journal of Cleaner Production*, 17: 644–652.

Simon, H. (1962). "The Architecture of Complexity," *Proceedings of the American Philosophical Society*, 106(6): 467–482.

Smith, A., Stirling, A., & Berkhout, F. (2005). "The Governance of Sustainable Socio-Technical Transitions," *Research Policy*, 34: 1491–1510.

——— (2006). *Moving Inside or Outside? Positioning the Governance of Sociotechnical Systems. SPRU Electronic Working Paper Series*.

Spiegelman, J. (2003). "Beyond the Food Web: Connections to a Deeper Industrial Ecology," *Journal of Industrial Ecology*, 7(1): 17–23.

Stacey, R. (1996). "Emerging Strategies for a Chaotic Environment," *Long Range Planning*, 29(2): 182–189.

Sterman, J. D. (1989). "Deterministic Chaos in an Experimental Economic System," *Journal of Economic Behavior and Organization* 12: 1–28.

Thom, R. (1975). *Structural Stability and Morphogenesis*. Reading, MA: Addison-Wesley.

Ulrich, H., & Probst, J. B. (eds.) (1984). *Self-Organization and Management of Social Systems*. Berlin: Springer-Verlag.

Unruh, G. C. (2000). "Understanding Carbon Lock-In," *Energy Policy*, 28(12): 817–830.

Varga, L., Allen, P., Strathern, M., Rose-Anderssen, C., Baldwin, J., & Ridgway, K. (2009). "Sustainable Supply Networks: A Complex Systems Perspective," *Emergence: Complexity and Organization*, 11(3): 16–36.

Vaughan, D. (1996). *The Challenger Launch Decision*. Chicago: The University of Chicago Press.

Veiga, L., & Magrini, A. (2009). "Eco-Industrial Park Development in Rio de Janeiro, Brazil: A Tool for Sustainable Development," *Journal of Cleaner Production*, 17: 653–661.

Warren, K. (2004). "Why has Feedback Systems Thinking Struggled to Influence Strategy and Policy Formulation? Suggestive Evidence, Explanations and Solutions," *Systems Research and Behavioral Science* 21(4): 331–350.

PART IX

··

FUTURE
PERSPECTIVES

··

CHAPTER 33

BEYOND THE BRAVE NEW WORLD: BUSINESS FOR SUSTAINABILITY

JOHN R. EHRENFELD

THIS Handbook is a reflection on the historical development of research linking the business enterprise with its effects on the environment. This connection has broadened in the past decade beyond the health of the environment to include concerns related to conditions of human well-being. Since I believe, as do others (Willard 2002; Werbach 2009), that sustainability is already becoming central to business strategy formation and implementation, this chapter will emphasize this new reality.

It was not always so. The MIT program on Technology Business, and Environment, which I started in the early 1990s, was one of the earliest programs to explicitly explore the nexus between business and the environment. The key papers being published at that time started to mention a new strategic phase beyond mere compliance with regulations (Hoffman & Ehrenfeld 1998; Hunt & Auster 1990; Roome 1992). The Roome paper appeared in the first issue of *Business, Strategy, and Environment*, the publication of which underscored this subject as a serious academic topic. Joining the two words, business and environment, was still verboten in virtually all business schools. It is worth noting that the MIT program was housed in the School of Engineering, not the Sloan School of Management. It took another decade for graduating doctoral students to enter the academic job market without disguising their interests in the environment. By 2010, the situation had completely changed. Business schools without courses in the field and businesses without "greening" or "sustainable" somewhere in their portfolios are rare.

The institutionalization process moved forward with the formation of the Greening of Industry Network, a loose international alliance of academic, government, and industry participants. This network provided a critical step in the development of the field, serving as an important convening mechanism. Some years later, the Academy of Management, after dragging its heels, supported the formation of the Interest Group: Organization and the Natural Environment (ONE). It is a different story now, some twenty years later. The overall theme of the 2009 Academy meeting was "Greening Management Matters," and ONE, elevated to Division status, played a major role in organizing the meeting. The descriptor, greening, has persisted, and is generally taken to refer to the wide range of activities coming under the broad rubric of "business and the environment."

My personal trail in the field ended formally when I retired from MIT in 2000. By the time I left MIT, the "greening" label had started to morph into "sustainability," but with little clarity as to what the new label meant. The 1987 Brundtland Report defined sustainable development as "development that meets the needs of the present without compromising the ability of future generations to meet their own needs" (WCED 1987: 8). Implicit in this definition was an understanding that the global economy was despoiling the Earth and creating gross inequities in the way resources were shared. Translated into business language, slogans like the triple bottom line (economy, environment, equity) or the 3Ps (people planet, profit) quickly entered the strategy of virtually every major corporation in the developed world. Eco-efficiency—producing more value with less environmental impact—became the central environmental strategy of world business (Desimone & Popoff 1997).

Virtually all of these strategies centered on doing less bad while maintaining a healthy bottom line. All assumed that the Earth's natural resources were limitless, and that efficient production and consumption would suffice to support the continuous economic growth policies driving the industrialized world. Symptoms of climate change, collapsing fisheries, and other stresses on the environment began to raise questions about the efficacy of strategies resting on sustainable development. Growing inequality and symptoms of social dysfunction raised similar concerns. Corporate social responsibility (see Matten & Bondy [Chapter 28] this volume) was added to the category of business and environment. The greening label was slowly being replaced by sustainability, but with little agreement as to what that label meant and how business strategies needed to incorporate it. The replacement process has accelerated and gone global. In 2010, a scan of the Internet turns up more than ten times the number of business-related items under "sustainable" than under "greening."

The present and near future of business and the environment is carefully circumscribed by the many chapters in this Handbook. Looking beyond, I believe that business will be shaped by a different sense of the term "sustainability"—a sense that reflects our growing understanding of the role of business in our complex, highly interconnected, and finite world. Further, given that no present society has solved the conundrum of maintaining the well-being of all its citizens and the Earth, sustainability will take on an aspirational, forward-pulling core meaning, rather than one focused on repair and remedy. I define sustainability as "the possibility that human and other life will flourish on the planet forever" (Ehrenfeld 2008: 6). Further, it is important to recognize the distinction between *reducing unsustainability* and *creating sustainability*. Virtually everything that business has done in the name of environmental management, greening, eco-efficiency, sustainable development, or, as the term is mistakenly used, sustainability, fits only under the first rubric—reducing unsustainability.

The last item in the list, sustainability, is categorically different from the first four, particularly from sustainable development. Sustainability carries no intrinsic meaning or value. It describes the persistence of some output from a system, for example, continuous yield from a fishery or the emergence of beauty from a painting. Without naming the output or emergent quality, the term is meaningless, and as such tends to be mystifying or confusing. The lack of reference to some quantity or quality produces confusion, disappointment, and illusory expectations about the state of the world.

I have adopted flourishing as the normative quality. Flourishing has broad cross-cultural understanding and use. It subsumes other norms, such as justice or freedom. Flourishing provides a vision for the future, and, like justice or freedom, is an emergent property of the global socio/economic/technological/environmental (or natural) system. Sustainability is not the property, per se, but, rather, the possibility that the property will continue to emerge over extended periods. It is flourishing or another similar quality, not sustainability, per se, that should be understood and explicitly chosen as the societal goal and the target of business strategy.

These distinctions are currently poorly understood and are used indiscriminately in business-speak. There is no such thing as a sustainable business, sustainable washing detergent, or sustainable brand. Sustainable X, the adjectival use of the cognate, to sustain, is always about the referent, never about sustainability. Often seen in the advertising of many products, the term "environmentally friendly" is, at best, misleading. Virtually nothing that normal businesses do creates a positive effect on the environment. If business, as an institution, is to become a principal driving force toward reaching a flourishing world, as it claims it will, it must get this story straight.

A DIFFERENT FUTURE FOR BUSINESS

Eco-efficiency and all its variants deal largely with the symptoms of unsustainability, not its root causes. These lie deep in the culture of affluent, industrial societies (Ehrenfeld 2008). To go beyond the remedial capabilities of greening, business must find ways to interact directly with beliefs and values, and nudge them toward a new set consistent with flourishing.

Business has a dichotomous choice on the road to sustainability (see Figure 33.1). It can follow one of greening, eco-efficiency, triple bottom line, or any similar framework that is built around the reduction of unsustainability, or it can adopt sustainability strategies designed to produce flourishing. It may be able do both, but the distinctions between these two must be clearly understood. Some synergy may be possible, but these two paths are largely non-overlapping. The rest of this Handbook primarily addresses reducing unsustainability (greening). The other path—creating sustainability—is the focus of this chapter. Once the idea of greening becomes embedded in firms' strategies and their customers' expectations, businesses can fall back on whatever general strategic models are then in vogue. Competitive success under a

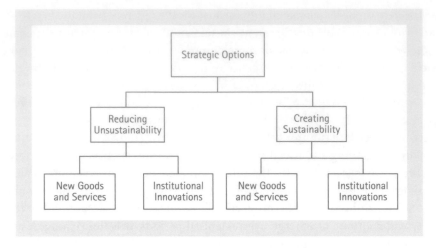

FIGURE 33.1 Alternate sustainability strategic pathways

green strategy can be sought with the same assortment of tools and models that apply to business-as-usual.

The more promising long-range opportunities for firms that accept the criticality of creating sustainability lie in the alternate pathway. This choice poses a huge challenge. The offerings and operations of these firms must not only produce a different kind of customer satisfaction, they must also employ a positive strategy to change the culture inside and outside of the firm (see Hart [Chapter 37] this volume). Deliberately changing culture inside a firm is not new, although experience teaches that such change is difficult (Schein 1984). Deliberately changing the outside culture in which the firm is embedded is a new challenge and departs from traditional models that define roles for business within a political economy. Taking on culture change is about as far as one can get from Milton Friedman's (1970) famous assertion that, "The social responsibility of business is to increase its profits."

The standard business model views the firm as making offers of goods and/or services in the market. Competitive success depends on the value (willingness-to-pay) that customers attribute to these goods and services relative to their ability to pay, and to substitutable offers by competitors (Porter 1980). The values of the customers and of the society at large are generally taken as exogenous. Innovations in products and business practices may change those beliefs and values, but such change usually comes after the fact, rather than through conscious efforts to produce the change. The quest, except for in rare cases, is to introduce offerings into a culture that is already poised to accept them.

Greening strategies, again with few exceptions, reflect existing customer preference profiles. There is little to distinguish them from other general competitive strategies designed to capture some segment of a broad market. Exceptions to this may appear in firms where strong normative aspirations of the sole proprietor or strong controlling interest can depart from some standard competitive model. Patagonia, wholly owned by

Yvon Chouinard, could choose not to grow and to add high-priced organic cotton goods to its catalog almost wholly at the direction of Chouinard (Pongtratic 2007). Similarly, Ray Anderson, the founder and still dominating figure at Interface Carpet, could lead his industry on what he called a sustainability path (Anderson 1998; Dean 2007).

As this Handbook illustrates throughout, greening strategies and operations have become quite commonplace. Systems thinking enters through tools and processes based on product life cycles, industrial ecology, and life-cycle management (Ayres & Ayres 2002). This framing is important in making offerings green, but falls short of contributing to sustainability. This kind of limited systems thinking may lead away from appreciating the complex global system. The tools in all of these systems-oriented disciplines are bounded by the ambit of products or service under analysis, but sustainability emerges from the larger world in which these artifacts appear. Few systems tools that incorporate human or social concerns in that larger systems sense have been developed. Using the standard tools may leave the engineer, designer, or manager believing that the analysis is complete.

The most important sustainability beliefs are that 1) the world operates as a complex, not mechanistic, system, and 2) human beings operate out of a bundle of care, not needs (Ehrenfeld 2008). Failure to accept complexity creates the illusion that conventional analysis mirrors reality. Action based on the models is virtually always going to differ from our model's predictions. Often, the difference is of no significant consequence, but concern over environment and unsustainability in general, tells us that the failures of representation cannot be ignored. The use of the standard economistic human behavior model in market research, system design, or organizational design is also likely to produce incomplete and unsatisfactory results in the context of flourishing.

Sustainability, in the first decade of the twenty-first century, requires actions that will contribute to culture change that leads away from the beliefs that are the root of the problem and toward new ones that are aligned with key relationships responsible for the emergence of flourishing. Gladwin, Newburry et al. (1997) describe a constellation of beliefs and norms that cohere with systemic behavior that is likely to produce flourishing (as contrasted with the present unsustainable world), and offers a starting point for designing change toward sustainability. Items in their lists include communitarian over individualistic, holistic over reductionist, organic over mechanistic, and sufficiency over efficiency. Their taxonomy can be derived from the two more basic beliefs described above: complexity as the model for understanding large living systems, and an ontology of human being based on care, not need (Ehrenfeld 2008).

The institution called "business" has a very special role in modern societies with respect to sustainability and to the culture change needed to create it. Business is the largest and most powerful global institution in terms of financial power, exceeding the historically dominant role of governments. It is the largest employer and, with assistance from academia and governments, the major source of technological innovation. Business is now a global institution matching the scale of the largest set of unsustainable symptoms. Business, more that any other major institution, is focused on innovation and change.

POSITIONING SUSTAINABILITY STRATEGIES

No handbook dealing with business strategy would be complete without including a 2-by-2 matrix. Following the dichotomous presentation in Figure 33.1, the appropriate graph would look like Figure 33.2 with greening or reduction in unsustainability versus sustainability. Strategies would be located horizontally depending on the degree of greenness (some measure of the relative intensity of impacts), and vertically depending on the culture change potential. The greenness position would be located by a life-cycle impact assessment or equivalent procedure. Such evaluation systems are becoming more universal. Walmart, for example, intends to develop a numerical index for all the products they sell.

This matrix depicts the relative positions of a variety of broad strategies. Localization—building small-scale economic infrastructure—interrupts the invisibility of standard market distribution systems and raises consciousness of the value of community (Marglin 2008; Seyfang 2009). Following the precautionary principle introduces complexity to the cultural surround (O'Riordan & Cameron 1996). Participatory planning, design, and decision-making processes raise the value of local knowledge and may root out wasteful practices. Eco-efficiency as a general strategy

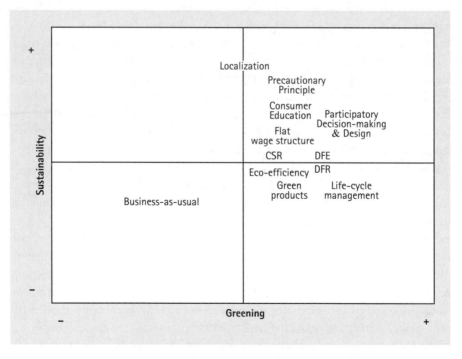

FIGURE 33.2 Strategic sustainability matrix

will fit somewhere along the x-axis, depending on the efficacy of the particular product or process, but will do little for sustainability. All of the purely green strategies have
a tendency to create a false sense of security, reinforcing the status quo and moving the
system away from sustainability. The positions of the items on the figures are approxi-
mate, serving only to illustrate how this could be used.

Figure 33.3 illustrates how market positioning might be similarly analyzed. Items in
the upper-right quadrant can contribute both to lessening of impact and instilling
new values. The examples in this diagram would fit a firm exploring strategies for
mobility. Not all would be realistic for every firm: it would be strange to find Toyotas
thinking about walking shoes. If this presentation had been available in the 1930s,
however, General Motors might have hesitated before buying up the rights of way
for many public transportation systems (Slater 1997). This simplistic format starkly
exposes the trade-off between reducing unsustainability and increasing sustainability,
and, as such, can be very useful in making sustainability concerns explicit and under-
standable in [virtually all] firms that have been confusing the two distinctions. The
availability of procedures for characterizing the attributes of each option is currently
rudimentary, but nevertheless, this format can be very useful in sorting among potential market initiatives.

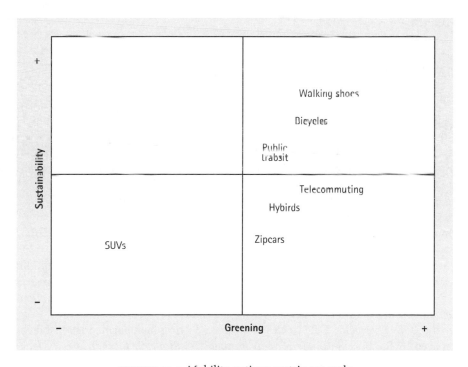

FIGURE 33.3 Mobility options matrix example

CONCLUSION

Sustainability, not greening, is the more important strategic challenge to the business world. Environmental programs have been in place for four decades or more, and are now institutionalized in most companies of any significant size. The focus continues to shift from the impacts of processes to the whole life-cycle, especially where major effects come in the use stage. As industrialization and growth of consumption spreads to the rapidly expanding economies of China, India, Brazil, and other nations, the lessons learned from the United States and Europe, exemplified in this Handbook, can make corporate initiatives more effective.

Sustainability is more than merely a larger and more complicated version of greening, and to address it with the same strategic framework and same practices will not be effective. Sustainability exists in a new paradigm, where the fundamental beliefs that underlie the place, role, and practices of business are no longer capable of producing what is wanted without unintended consequences that more than negate the positive outcomes. As business has become more powerful, changing its ways becomes equivalently more problematic. But change it must, otherwise this great institution will be unable to provision the world. F. Scott Fitzgerald foresaw the challenge of living in the old greening world at the same time as taking on the challenge of sustainability when he wrote in *The Great Gatsby*, "The test of a first-rate intelligence is the ability to hold two opposed ideas in the mind at the same time, and still retain the ability to function."

REFERENCES

Anderson, R. C. (1998). *Mid-Course Correction*. Atlanta, GA, The Peregrinzilla Press.

Ayres, R. U. & Ayres, L. W. (eds.) (2002). *Handbook of Industrial Ecology*. Northampton, MA: Edward Elgar Publishing, Inc.

Dean, C. (2007). "Executive on a Mission: Saving the Planet," *New York Times*, May 22.

Desimone, L. D. & Popoff, F. (1997). *Eco-efficiency: The Business Link to Sustainable Development*. Cambridge, MA, MIT Press.

Ehrenfeld, J. (2008). *Sustainability by Design: A Subversive Strategy for Transforming Our Consumer Culture*. New Haven, CT, Yale University Press.

Friedman, M. (1970). "The Social Responsibility of Business is to Increase its Profits," *The New York Times Magazine*.

Gladwin, T., Newburry, W. E. & Reiskin, E. D. (1997). "Why is the Northern Elite Mind Biased Against Community, the Environment, and a Sustainable Future," in Wade-benzoni, K. A. (ed.) *Environment, Ethics, and Behavior: The Psychology of Environmental Valuation and Degradation*, San Francisco: The New Lexington Press.

Hoffman, A. & Ehrenfeld, J. R. (1998). "Corporate Environmentalism, Sustainability, and Management Studies," in Roome, N. (ed.) *Sustainability Strategies for Industry: The Future of Corporate Practice*, Washington: Island Press.

Hunt, C. & Auster, E. (1990). "Proactive Environmental Management: Avoiding the Toxic Trap," *Sloan Management Review*, 31: 7–18.

Marglin, S. (2008). *The Dismal Science: How Thinking Like an Economist Undermines Community*. Cambridge, MA, Harvard University Press.

O'Riordan, T. & Cameron, J. (eds.) (1996). *Interpreting the Precautionary Principle*. London: Earthscan.

Pongtratic, M. (2007). *Greening the Supply Chain: A Case Analysis of Patagonia*; IR/PS CSR Case # 07–22. San Diego, CA: Graduate School of International Relations And Pacific Studies, University of California, San Diego.

Porter, M. E. (1980). *Competitive Strategy*. New York, Free Press.

Roome, N (1992), "Developing Environmental Management Systems," *Business, Strategy and Environment*, 1: 11–24.

Schein, E. H. (1984). "Coming to a New Awareness of Organizational Culture," *Sloan Management Review*, 25: 3–16.

Seyfang, G. (2009). *The New Economics of Sustainable Consumption: Seeds of Change*. London, Palgrave MacMillan.

Slater, C. (1997). "General Motors and the Demise of Streetcars," *Transportation Quarterly*, 51: 45–66.

WCED. (1987). *Our Common Future*. Oxford, Oxford University Press.

Werbach, A. (2009). *Strategy for Sustainability: A Business Manifesto*. Boston, Harvard Business Press.

Willard, B. (2002). *The Sustainability Advantage*. Gabriola Island, B. C., New Society Publishers.

CHAPTER 34

....

LOOKING BACK, THINKING FORWARD: DISTINGUISHING BETWEEN WEAK AND STRONG SUSTAINABILITY

....

NIGEL ROOME

THIS Handbook illustrates the complex and multi-faceted relationship between business and the natural environment understood by scholars and practiced by managers and business. It shows that the natural environment represents a transversal phenomenon cutting across management functions and the theories of management scholars. The natural environment intrudes on business strategy, organizational design and business models, finance and accounting, product development, production, logistics, marketing and sales, as well as the company's relationships with other economic, social, and political actors.

But this chapter characterizes two distinct perspectives in the field of business and environment—weak and strong sustainability—that have been overlooked in most of the previous chapters of this Handbook. While similar skills and organizational capabilities underpin weak and strong sustainability, the key difference between the two approaches centers on their orientation to the process of integration.

Weak sustainability sets out to bring environmental concerns into the framework provided by the structures and systems of business. Its origins go back to a linkage between environment and business that emerged with the advent of the modern environmental movement from the mid 1960s onwards, that was a reaction to a series of events including Seveso (1976), Love Canal (1978), Bhopal (1984), Exxon-Valdez (1989), Ozone depletion (1985) and the Montreal Protocol (1987), and the Brent Spar (1993/4). They gave rise to many aspects of the managerial practices that make up 'corporate environmental management,' such as Responsible Care$^{(TM)}$, ISO 14001 and Design for the Environment protocols. They contributed to the demand for environmental reporting, that began in Europe and the USA in 1989.

In contrast, *strong sustainability* seeks to integrate the company into environmental or socio-ecological systems, so that the patterns of production and consumption to which the company contributes are within the capacity of the Planet to sustain. Currently it is estimated that we exceed the capacity of the planet by at least 25 percent (World Wildlife Fund 2006). The objectives of fitting business into the capacities of the planet owes its origins to ideas found in the report of the Club of Rome (Meadows, Meadows, & Randers 1972), the Stockholm Conference on the Human Environment (Stockholm 1974) the Brundtland Commission Report (United Nations 1987) and Agenda 21 (United Nations 1992).

The issues that drive strong sustainability are qualitatively different from the issues that drove weak sustainability. They lead management on a trajectory that addresses issues such as the global diffusion of the 'patterns of production and consumption' found in advanced economics which are seen as unsustainable if replicated on a global scale. They suggest a search for new pathways for development that are needed if the benefits of economic and social development are to be maintained without compromising the ability to maintain that level of development into the future (United Nations 1992). On the whole, strong sustainability is a more complex and exacting process, less amenable to the control of a single company and its managers. It represents a form of social and organizational learning, based on innovation and change that involves many actors in multi-actor, collaborative processes.

This is conceptually and paradigmatically different from much of the traditional business theory and practice which is presented in the chapters in this Handbook. The majority of the chapters are centered on extending the existing paradigm of business theory and practice, a paradigm that has been responsible for contributing to the environmental issues that business and society continue to face.

AN APPLICATION OF STRONG SUSTAINABILITY: ONTARIO HYDRO

Few businesses have shown the authenticity of response that is required under strong sustainability. Ontario Hydro, the power corporation in Ontario, offers an exception even though that approach did not endure (Roome & Bergin 2006). Ontario Hydro's strategy for sustainable energy development and use defined in 1992 was developed under the influence of Maurice Strong, who became Hydro's CEO and Chairman immediately after completing his work as Secretary-General of the Earth Summit. Strong had worked with Jim MacNeill and David Runnalls on the Brundtland Report (United Nations 1987), the design of the Earth Summit and the drafting of Agenda 21 (United Nations 1992).

MacNeill and Runnalls were asked to support the development of the strategy at Ontario Hydro as few people understood the concept and approach of sustainable development at that time better than they did. They made use of processes similar to those deployed at the Earth Summit, based on the ideas of Eric Trist and others on socio-ecological systems change (Trist 1983; Tavistock Anthology 1990, 1993, 1997). In terms of content, the ambition of Ontario Hydro's strategy was not the goal of organizational sustainability. Rather the ambition was to contribute to a more sustainable approach to the overall system of energy development and use in the Province of Ontario of which Ontario Hydro was a lead contributor. This required leadership in innovation as well as collaboration with many other actors. The elements of the strategy were cross referenced against the principles of Agenda 21.

Aside from examples such as Ontario Hydro—weak and strong sustainability have invariably been confused and conflated. This has occurred because few scholars and practitioners appreciate the source ideas and thinking that are the basis of strong sustainability as set out in original definitions of sustainable development described in the Brundtland Report (United Nations 1987) and Agenda 21 (United Nations 1992). This lack of clarity has hampered progress, fogging an appreciation of the challenges, ambition and responses that make up the true goals and process of sustainable development. The need to disentangle these two concepts has become more critical as globalization has accelerated the move toward ever more unsustainable outcomes of development (World Wildlife Federation 2006).

To that end, this chapter explores the distinction between corporate environmental management or 'weak sustainability' and the business contribution to sustainable development or 'strong sustainability'. It begins by clarifying the different ways of framing the two concepts. It then examines in more detail what it means for a business to build capacity for weak and for strong sustainability. The chapter ends with a brief statement on the implications for future research and education that stem from these distinctions.

WEAK AND STRONG SUSTAINABILITY

Table 34.1 elaborates six frames that distinguish 'weak' and 'strong' sustainability as distinctive paradigms. The mental frame describes how the integration of business and environment is configured; the decision frame determines the information relevant to choices; the organizational/institutional frame determines the actors that are most deeply engaged in change; the time frame specifies the time horizon for choice; the values frame contains the values needed to make and mediate choice; and, finally, the change/innovation frame concerns the issues subject to innovation and change.

Weak and strong sustainability represent progressive ideas, applying new concepts such as supply-chain management and product stewardship and embedding them in organizational practices (Roome 1994) in ways that go beyond simple technological cooperation and innovation. Weak sustainability involves incremental change, whereas

Table 34.1 Conceptual frames for weak and strong sustainability

'Weak sustainability'	Frames	'Strong sustainability'
Business and economics as dominant systems with environmental impacts brought into control	Mental Frame	Business and economics embedded in, and dependent on, environmental and social systems
Accommodate environmental values in business systems	Decision Frame	Evaluate the environmental and social outcomes of economic choices made in business systems and seek to integrate business into its environmental context
Company and its supply chain	Organizational/Institutional Frame	Economic, institutional, social, and environmental systems and networks that shape patterns of production and consumption
Determined by the life of products/services, and technologies	Time Frame	Intergenerational
Utilitarian with some attention to product stewardship	Values Frame	Utilitarian + stewardship limited by principles of anticipation and precaution: inclusiveness, justice, equity
The company and its supply chain, technology, processes, products, and services driven by technological innovation	Change/Innovation Frame	Limitless—up to reinvent organizations, institutions, and society driven by management innovation

Adapted from Roome, N. (ed.) 1998. Sustainability strategies for industry: The future of corporate strategy. Island Press: Washington DC.

strong sustainability is more radical in orientation, constituting a new paradigm based on systems thinking and organizational and social innovation.

A NEW PARADIGM FOR STRONG SUSTAINABILITY

Management scholars are divided in their view on the capacity for managerial and organizational change implied by sustainability. 'Pessimistic/critical' and 'optimistic/ promotional' views are held. Some chapters in this Handbook (see Banerjee [Chapter 31] and Gladwin [Chapter 38] this volume) offer a critical view of the ability of companies like Wal-Mart, General Electric, and Shell to accomplish the changes needed to contribute to sustainable development. Other chapters (see Elkington & Love [Chapter 36] and Hart [Chapter 37] this volume) show a belief in the capacity of organizations to match the challenge of sustainable development (see also Hart 2005). The latter two draw on the same examples that the former two reject. Surely both cannot be right, unless of course they are talking about different forms of sustainability. In other words, the capacity to match the difficult challenge of sustainable development depends on whether these authors see the ambition for sustainability (weak or strong) as requiring the adoption of an expanded current paradigm or a new paradigm (see also Ehrenfeld [Chapter 33] this volume). For my part, the fact that so few authors in this Handbook appear to discriminate between weak and strong sustainability and their paradigmatic roots some twenty years after the Brundtland Commission Report leads me to the view that paradigm change embodied in strong sustainability will be extremely difficult to foster in business research, management education, and business practice. Even so, the contrasting views held by chapters in this Handbook support the need for managers to operationalize systems approaches to change, and to effect integration through organizational learning, innovation development, and change management. In weak sustainability these ideas are operationalized from within the company, whereas in strong sustainability they are operationalized by companies within the system of other actors through which a company's current and future products and services are used.

These key ideas are introduced in Figure 34.1 which shows three stylized positions that companies can adopt. The compliance position is characteristic of companies that meet legal obligations toward environmental issues. The pro-active position describes companies that deploy organizational learning to understand the relationship between the company and its environment, to develop responses, and to organize those responses into more integrated management structures and systems.

The third position in the diagram describes companies that seek competitiveness within the framework of environmental sustainability. Learning for sustainability moves beyond an organizational activity to a social and organizational activity. It obliges the managers of a focal company to participate with other actors in society and the economy in defining what a future sustainable system of mobility, nutrition, or health might look like. It is possible for a company to lead that process, but more likely the company would be a collaborative partner. This is not the kind of stakeholder engagement that is normally understood as part of weak sustainability. Instead, the activity of organizational and social learning involves the participation by companies in different types of multi-actor platform. These platforms provide mechanisms through which actors—including companies—can envision more sustainable systems (European Commission 2001). Central to the work of these platforms and the advancement of sustainable development more broadly is the idea of a systemic view based on 'systems thinking' (Roome 1994; see also Levy & Lichtenstein [Chapter 32] and Lifset & Boons [Chapter 17] this volume).

Systems thinking

Strong sustainability requires new ways to appreciate the complex relationships and connections between the parts of a system and the function of the whole (Ackoff 1999) built on new capacities for organizational learning and change (Senge 1994; Checkland 1981). Systems thinking predisposes managers to the contributions and ideas of others and promotes the participative approach to change that drives strong sustainability.

This leads to a focus on corporate responsibility, or more critically responsible management and leadership (see also Bondy & Matten [Chapter 28] this volume), as crucial to thinking beyond the choices and actions of business alone. Sustainable development

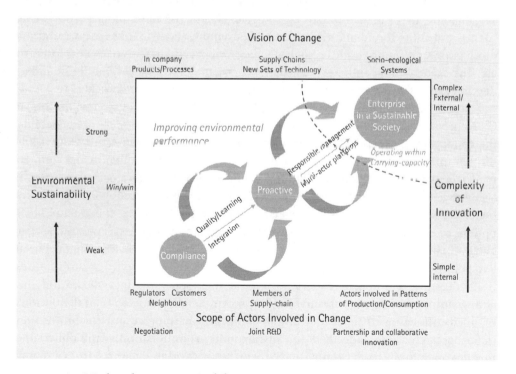

FIGURE 34.1 Weak and strong sustainability

Adapted from Roome (2004)

involves many actors in society in concerted processes of change (United Nations 1987). Companies contribute to the sustainability of the production and consumption systems of which they are part, and to the sustainability of a bioregion or nation in which they operate. A company, indeed any organization, is not, in this view, a proper unit of analysis for understanding strong sustainability as an economic or social project. As shown in Figure 34.1, strong sustainability involves the work of many actors to produce a socio-ecological system in which production and consumption are within the carrying capacity of the planet. This is shown as the area to the north-east of the dotted line.

The axes of Figure 34.1 represent the four central dimensions that delineate weak and strong sustainability. The strength of sustainability is shown on the left-hand vertical axis. The vision of change is shown as the top horizontal axis. The actors involved in the move toward sustainability are shown on the lower horizontal axis. And, the degree of innovation is found on the right-hand vertical axis. Weak and strong sustainability are differentiated by their approach to integration, the ambition of the vision of change, the complexity of the innovation and the extent of collaboration among social, political, and economic actors.

For example, compliance companies work with a limited set of actors to produce incremental innovations that lead to product or process improvements. The proactive position involves the deployment of learning or quality processes that enable integration of environmental considerations with business processes, linked by product sets or supply chains in concerted change. The position in the north-east corner elevates strong sustainability to the level of the socio-ecological system, combining social sub-systems such as nutrition, communications, energy, household services, and transport, and the production-consumption and ecological/environment systems within which they operate. The capacity to learn how to collaborate across organizational boundaries and to develop and deliver a common vision is at a premium in strong sustainability.

The emphasis on multi-actor processes is built upon the foundational work of Chevalier and Cartwright (1966) and Trist (Tavistock Anthology 1990, 1993, 1997) on the resolution of meta-problems or change in socio-ecological systems. These ideas directly informed the thinking of those who wrote the Brundtland Report and contributed to the design of the Earth Summit. In this approach, diverse actors must work together to understand the nature of the issues found in complex problem sets, identify better configurations of what the problem set might be like in the future, search for options or pathways to get from the present to an agreed and desired future, and review and evaluate the consequences from those options on economic, environmental, social, and political conditions of the actors involved.

Readers might note that the organizational and social learning, innovation and change implied by strong sustainability are more socially complex than the notions of open innovation that recent authors claim as a new paradigm for innovation (Chesborough 2003). Indeed, strong sustainability is understood as the most open form of open innovation (Roome 2001), necessarily involving many actors in social, institutional, organizational, and managerial innovation, not just technological innovation.

Organizational leadership and innovation

Companies that have embedded strong sustainability into their business models under-stand corporate responsibility as a form of organizational leadership and managerial innovation (Roome & Jonker 2006). Similar processes are embodied within The Natural Step. They begin with a vision for the organization, which is developed through new concepts that provide shape and direction to new practices advanced through collaboration from across the company (see <http://www.naturalstep.org/the-system-conditions>). Organizational leadership involves shared and distributed leadership spanning the company and other actors (D'Amato & Roome 2009). This is constructed around specific beliefs, practices, and roles that include the value of participation and learning, and a sense that problems and change are challenges and opportunity. Practices include a high level of consistency between words and actions, and commitment to responsibility, learning and change throughout all levels of the company. The progressive adoption of responsibility for strong sustainability is fostered by roles that support change through the generation and operationalization of new concepts, such as stewardship These concepts are translated into action through the work of concept sponsors, networkers, and change agents, who in turn are supported by resource gatekeepers and the ideas of those working across the organization. These beliefs, practices, roles, and processes are rarely deployed by organizations engaged in weak sustainability but form the core of strong sustainability.

FUTURE RESEARCH

The ideas discussed above should not be new to anyone who has worked with organizations striving to integrate sustainable development as an agenda for fundamental change. Unfortunately, such examples are not widespread and their limited impact will not likely reverse the extent to which our way of life and use of planetary resources exceeds the carrying capacity of the planet. Regrettably progress has not matched the challenge called out long ago by reports such as the *Limits to Growth* (Meadows, Meadows, & Randers 1972) or the Brundtland Commission (United Nations 1987). Weak sustainability is not sufficient to bring about the transition to a sustainable future. More radical change is required, as was envisioned by the Brundtland Report (United Nations 1987).

Since strong sustainability represents a new paradigm, there is need to revisit much of current business research and education which is formulated in the paradigm that has created the problems that we now have to address. Research and education at business schools must become more focused on systems thinking and organizational and social learning, rather than focusing narrowly on considerations for agency theory, individual corporate success, and the imperative of economic growth over considerations for ecological and social sustainability (Khurana 2007, see also Banerjee [Chapter 31] this volume).

Such a shift would necessarily involve scholars engaging in open-ended change processes, where praxis is more critical than theorizing, and practical outcomes are as valued as academic publications. Furthermore, dominant theories within the old paradigm of weak sustainability are seen as offering little contribution to the future, whereas strong sustainability emphasizes the development of new considerations for radical rather than incremental change. Business scholars must bring the many facets of strong sustainability into the classroom in order to develop relevant skills that will aid students in their future role as agents of change, not as agents of an unsustainable status quo.

References

Ackoff, R., (1999). *Ackoff's Best: His Classic Writings on Management*. Chichester: Wiley.

Carson, R., (1962). *Silent Spring*. Boston: Houghton Mifflin Co.

Checkland, P. (1981). *Systems Thinking, Systems Practice*. Chichester: Wiley.

Chesborough, H. (2003). *Open Innovation: The New Imperative for Creating and Profiting from Technology*. Boston: Mass.: Harvard Business School Press.

Chevalier, M. & Cartwright, T. (1966). '*Towards an Action Framework for the Control of Pollution*', In National Conference on Pollution and our Environment. Ottawa: Canadian Council of Resource Ministers, paper D 30–1.

D'Amato, A. & Roome, N. (2009). "Toward an Integrated Model of Leadership for Corporate Responsibility and Sustainable Development: A Process Model of CR Beyond Management Innovation," *Corporate Governance: The International Journal of Business and Society*, 9(4): 421–43.

European Commission (2001). "Sustainable Production: Challenges and Objectives for EU Research Policy," *Report of the Expert Group on Competitive and Sustainable Production and Related Services*, European Commission, DG XII (Research).

Hart, S. (2005). *Capitalism at the Crossroads: The Unlimited Business Opportunities in Solving the World's Most Difficult Problems*. Upper Saddle River: New Jersey: Wharton School Publishing.

Khurana, R. (2007). *From Higher Aims to Hired Hands: The Social Transformation of American Business Schools and the Unfulfilled Promise of Management as a Profession*. Princeton, NJ: Princeton University Press.

Meadows, D., Meadows D, & Randers, J. (1972). *The Limits to Growth*. New York: Universe Books.

Roome, N. (1992). "Developing Business Environmental Strategies", *Business Strategy and the Environment*, 1(1): 11–24.

—— (1994). *Taking Responsibility: Promoting Sustainable Practice through Higher Education Curricula—Management And Business*. London: Pluto Press.

—— (ed.) (1998). *Sustainability Strategies for Industry: The Future of Corporate Strategy*. Washington DC: Island Press.

—— (2001). *Metatextual Organisations: Innovation and Adaptation for Global Change*, Inaugural address, Erasmus Center for Sustainable Development and Management: Erasmus University, Rotterdam.

—— (2004). "Innovation, Global Change and New Capitalism: A Fuzzy Context for Business and the Environment," *Human Ecology Review*, 11(3): 277–279.

—— & Jonker, J. (2006). "The Enterprise Strategies of European Leaders in Corporate [Social] Responsibility," in *The Challenge of Organising and Implementing CSR* (eds.) Jan Jonker and Marco De Witte, London: Palgrave.

—— & Bergin, R. (2006). "Sustainable Development in an Industrial Enterprise: The Case of Ontario Hydro," *Business Process Management Journal*, 12(6): 696–721.

Senge, P. (1994). *The Fifth Discipline: The Art and Practice of Organizational Learning.*New York: Doubleday Currency.

Stockholm (1974). *Report of the United Nations Conference on the Human Environment.* <http://www.unep.org/Documents.Multilingual/Default.asp?documentid=97>

Tavistock Anthology (1990/1993/1997). *The Social Engagement of Social Science a Tavistock Anthology*, vol 1, 1990, vol 2, 1993, vol 3, 1997, London: Tavistock Institute.

Trist, E. (1983). "Referent Organizations and the Development of Inter-Organizational Domains," *Human Relations*, 36: 269–284.

United Nations (1987). *Report of the World Commission on Environment and Development.* General Assembly Resolution 42/187, 11 December 1987.

—— (1992). *Agenda 21*, http://www.un.org/esa/dsd/agenda21/res_agenda21_01.shtml

Van Kleef, H. & Roome, N. (2007). "Developing Capabilities and Competence for Sustainable Business Management as Innovation: A Research Agenda," *Journal of Cleaner Production*, 15(1): 38–51.

World Wildlife Fund (2006). *Living Planet Report*. Gland: Switzerland: WWF.

....

CHAPTER 35

ENTERPRISE SUSTAINABILITY 2.0: AESTHETICS OF SUSTAINABILITY

....

PAUL SHRIVASTAVA

THE practical challenges of managing business–nature relationships, and the need for awareness and information on environmental management has grown exponentially. A great deal of information is now available on key environmental management problems of global climate change, environmental resource depletion, energy production and use, and sustainable development of business enterprise (Bansal & Roth 2000; Gladwin 1996; Sharma & Starik 2002; Hoffman 2000; Russo 2010; Stead & Stead 1996). Despite the explosion of knowledge in this area, environmental problems and conditions continue to worsen.

Past research on business sustainability has largely regarded the management of "external" spaces (land, air, water, people) in an ecologically sensible manner. Researchers have pursued a broad agenda of understanding and developing ecological efficiencies in production and distribution of goods and services throughout the value chain (see Gladwin [Chapter 38] this volume). This focus was necessary, and was in fact essential for the early evolution of the field. It still holds potential for scientific contributions to our understanding of business sustainability.

However, a better cognitive understanding of business sustainability has not led to more sustainable consumption and production behaviors. So we need to ask the questions "what will it take to change our behavior individually and collectively?" What kind or awareness and knowledge of environmental issues do we need to make businesses sustainable? How can we change quickly enough to mitigate carbon accumulation in our atmosphere, and the impending global climate changes, within the short time frames we have available to address them (IPCC 2007).

In the remainder of this paper I make some observations about repositioning the research on enterprise sustainability in a new direction. In addition to its past focus on *external spaces*, I also suggest focusing on *internal spaces* of the human mind and emotions. Internal focus includes gaining deeper sensory (bodily) awareness of nature, gaining emotional experience of nature and understanding the connections between external environment and internal psychological identity formation processes. I call this Sustainability 2.0. It is concerned with developing an emotional and passionate relationship to nature, as a prelude to making "improvements" to it. Instead of treating nature as yet another subject for scientific study, to be studied along siloed disciplinary lines, it seeks a more holistic consideration of the environment and human–nature relations.

WHY SUSTAINABILITY 2.0?

The main sources of unsustainability are human and organizational behaviors. Behavioral and organizational changes are necessary to achieve global sustainability. In the twenty-first century the key challenge is not human survival against forces of nature. We possess sufficient financial, natural, knowledge, and technology resources to provide for human populations. How we use these resources is based on human choices that we make everyday in the ways we produce, distribute, and consume goods and services. To become sustainable we need to change our consumption, corporate, institutional, social, and political behaviors (see Ehrenfeld [Chapter 33] this volume).

Behavioral change is driven by emotional connection between subject and object. Intellectual or cognitive understanding alone is not sufficient to evoke change. Deeper (scientific) intellectual understanding may improve the long-term quality of our decisions and changes, but it does not trigger behavioral changes. Therefore, to provoke changes in lifestyle towards sustainable living, and to give impetus to organizational changes, sustainability researchers need to include emotional understanding of sustainability challenges into their agenda (Csikszentmihalyi 2003).

This necessary behavioral shift is accentuated with the state of urgency in the climate system. Such transformation does not come through incremental piecemeal policy solutions. It will require a change in consciousness; a fundamental emotional change in human-nature relationships. We need radical re-imagination and deep emotional transformation that reconnects us to nature in more enduring and benign ways. Sustainability 2.0 is a call to that radical transformation, starting with personal and organizational behaviors.

Focusing on emotional transformation opens up possibilities of using a particular human capability that has been largely ignored in discussions of sustainability and climate change. It is the human capacity for art. Throughout history the arts have served as repositories of human emotional life. They have helped human societies live through difficult times, deal with great human problems, survive great threats by acting as emotional salve, giving meaning, creating beauty, healing, and revealing truth. Arts under the control of sovereigns and churches, and in the past few centuries under more secular benefactors, have always served to educate, and change behaviors. Some scholars, such as the philosopher Denis Dutton have even claimed that arts are a human instinct and serve evolutionary functions (Dutton 2009).

The arts fuel passion for excelling, and in times of major cultural disruptions they serve as salve and healing mechanisms. Sustainability 2.0 seeks to parlay the power of the arts/aesthetics and bring it to bear to address one of the foremost challenges of our time. By using art-based methods of inquiry and action, and aesthetic truths and insights, Sustainability 2.0 augments the largely scientific tool repertoire that humans have for addressing sustainability challenges.

It may seem disjointed in this Handbook to propose Sustainability 2.0 as an appeal for emotional engagement with sustainability. Some of the other chapters in this section ("Future Perspectives") call for a broadening of "business and the environment" to include the social sphere when we consider the term sustainability. They imply that we need to include many social stakeholders in our approach to sustainability. These papers are not incompatible with my position. To be more social and inclusive we need to better understand ourselves, our emotional and sensory selves. That self-awareness permits deeper connections with others and nature. Social and emotional engagement with sustainability are complementary to each other.

WHAT IS ENTERPRISE SUSTAINABILITY 2.0?

Sustainability 2.0 refers to an approach and an orientation to emotionally knowing the natural environment and our personal and organizational relationship to it. It refers to an embodied and experientially felt understanding of human and organizational relationships to nature. It entails holistic embodied awareness of ecosystems, a passion for sustainable living, acknowledging personal responsibility for eco action, and collaborative and cooperative problem-solving (see Post [Chapter 29] this volume).

By applying this idea to business and other enterprises, I am advocating research and best practices that emanate not only from intellectual cognitive understanding of environmental problems, but by integrating cognitive with emotional experience of these problems. This call for emotional understanding may at first seem contradictory to the norms and ideals of science. Emotions are subjective, and have historically been in the realm of the arts. Therefore, a large challenge is finding ways of melding artistic sensibilities and aesthetic inquiry with scientific pursuit of objectivity and rigorous measurement to create both rationally sound and emotionally compelling solutions.

Let me briefly unpack these ideas in three sub-sections below arguing 1) that businesses have emotional infrastructures that are central to their long-term success; 2) that enterprise sustainability in the form of long-term intergenerational-global prosperity, requires a holistic, comprehensive, and inclusive approach offered by embodied understanding of human–nature relationships and the environmental and social challenges they spawn; and 3) that art as repository human emotions, and aesthetic inquiry as a way of revealing truth can be valuable aids in understanding and relating to nature in passionate ways. Sustainability 2.0 seeks holistic experiential understanding of nature to develop a deep passionate commitment to nature and making the right choices at individual and organizational levels.

The emotional infrastructure of enterprises

For the past century "scientific management" has been obsessed with the objective, technological, and rational side of organizations and organizing. The human side of organizing began to be acknowledged in the 1960s. However, conceptions of the human role in organizing were framed within the "machine," "systems," or "socio-technical systems" metaphors of organization. The goal was to understand how humans can be perfected into machine-like behaviors, with consistent, reliable, and predictable outputs. This "industrial era" mentality of viewing humans as labor, as assets, or human resources, instead of holistic social, emotional beings has stymied our ability to fully appreciate the emotional side of organizing.

Organizations possess an emotional infrastructure that determines their mood, work climate, and performance capacities (Barsade & Gibson 2007; Fineman 2003). Employees have emotional lives that interact with, and impact, a variety of organizational decisions. Emotional skills and assets are as important for organizational success as the material, technological, and financial skills. Emotions play a pivotal role in some areas of work, such as building trust, engaging in negotiation, establishing credibility, and exercising judgment. While significant aspects of emotional skills are already part of individual personalities, such skills can also be developed and nurtured. Emotional self-expression can make employees more committed and productive members of the organization. The growing literature and practice in "emotional intelligence" is witness to the possibilities for understanding and developing organizational emotional infrastructures (Cameron, Dutton, & Quinn 2003; Goleman 1995).

Embodied understanding of sustainability

Deep understanding of sustainability requires experiencing it in an embodied way. Embodiment philosophy defines relationships between substance and intentions. Under this approach, the human body is not a vessel but the being itself, where mind and spirit are expressions of the body. Thus, body and mind are the same being. They are bound by a single process, which also binds family and language, dissolving the subjective/objective distinction. The mind extends beyond the body and family, to its environment, community, species and the planet (Bateson 1980). The human mind and thoughts are a function of the brain and physiology. Universal psychological processes can be understood only in the context of their history, culture, ecology, community, habitus, and locale (Csordas 1990; Neidenthal et al. 2005; Sampson 1996). Embodied learning rejects the subjective/objective dichotomy, in favor of holistic experiential understanding. In this view, understanding sustainability issues is, therefore, not just a scientific challenge, but also a physical challenge and a spiritual challenge.

Different and critical insights can come from an exploration of embodied, practical knowledge. In particular, the embodied knowledge that can be generated through artistic and aesthetic inquiry into organizations and socio-technical systems offers new keys to understanding enterprise sustainability (Bourdieu & Wacquant 1992). I suggest that art-based, 'aesthetic' process techniques can be used to generate qualitatively different understandings of the firm's environmental and social risk profiles and develop more resilient ways of coping with crises (Shrivastava & Statler 2010).

Aesthetics of sustainable enterprise

Art and aesthetics are vehicles for accessing emotions and passion. Visual, media and performing arts have historically served to access, examine, and engage human emotions in an embodied way. Some art forms, such as music and dance, are particularly appropriate vehicles for emotional and passionate engagement. Art-making methods use sensory skills and physical activities to create and test emotions.

Aesthetics is a form of inquiry, a way of knowing beauty and grace. Aesthetic experiences provide managers with occasions to a) expand their sense perceptions, b) exercise judgment based on embodied and holistic understanding of natural and human systems, and c) reflect on those perceptions and judgments collectively with colleagues to achieve socially responsible and sustainable outcomes (Shrivastava & Statler 2010).

Sustainability aesthetic acknowledges and valorizes the grace and beauty of nature and its capacity to inspire and motivate humans. Throughout history from the Rock Art of hunting-gathering societies to modern sustainable/environmental art movements of contemporary arts, nature has been both subject and muse of artists. It has led to the creation of objects, fabricated environments, performances cued on nature's values of beauty, and harmony, and balance. It asks different and radical questions about human-nature relationships to destabilize corporate and politically "normalized" views of nature. It provokes thinking about what we humans are doing to nature (Fowkes & Fowkes 2006; Grande 1994; Kagan & Kirchberg 2008).

Enterprise Sustainability 2.0 evokes a sustainable organizational aesthetic. It is about having a vision of the enterprise as a mediator between human needs and the natural world. It is about understanding and accepting our place within a natural order, and using that sense of place to inform organizational mission and commitments. It is about designing products and production systems, logistics and human resources with a sustainability aesthetic. These designs need to go beyond form and function values, beyond consideration of economic productivity, and consequent social welfare, to concerns about human happiness, grace and beauty. Sustainable enterprises conceive of people as whole people, and not as eight hours of labor each day; nor a customer as a certain dollar value each year, or an investor as a certain appetite for funding.

An example of application of the arts to sustainability is the area of "sustainable design" (SD) (also known as environmental design, environmentally sustainable design, environmentally-conscious design, etc.). It is an approach to designing products, services, and the fabricated environment to improve their economic, social, and ecological performance. The goal is to eliminate negative environmental impacts through holistic mindful design. SD emphasizes renewable resources, minimal eco-footprint, cradle-to-cradle design, and organically connecting people with their environments.

Applications of SD include everything from small objects for everyday use (safety pins), to large machines (automobiles), to entire buildings, cities, and the Earth's physical surface. It is a philosophy that is being applied in architecture, landscape, lighting, urban planning, engineering, graphic design, advertising, fashion, industrial design, and interior design.

If sustainability is going to be something more than just a way of "branding" art, we need to understand the radical potential of sustainable arts proposed by Felix Guattari (1989), and his very useful differentiation of the three mental spheres of human subjectivities. Guattari describes the three interrelated ecological 'registers'— the natural environment, the social environment, and the level of mental ecology.

The first, environmental register considers the material burden of artworks and art practices on the natural world. Materials used and wastes created in producing, transporting, and installing arts and crafts could be potentially damaging to natural ecosystems.

The second, Guattari register is the social dimension or the social nexus around the production and use of the work. It raises concerns about the power implications of art. Art works express power and status of individuals and organizations and in relationships. The social implications of sustainable art include ethical implication of art projects, potential empowerment/ disempowerment of specific groups, objectification of living subjects, and the exploitation of artists/crafts-persons.

The most interesting contribution of Guattari in understanding the change potential of sustainable art is his suggestion to use the working methods of artists to understand the influences on "domain of the mental ecology of everyday life." Art offers an antidote to the mental and emotional pollution of commercialism, which eventually lead to the toxification of air, land, water, and the excessive consumption of carbon.

IN LIEU OF A CONCLUSION

The purpose of this article is to broaden our horizon of enterprise sustainability research and think about it in more creative and comprehensive ways. I do not have definitive conclusions to offer. So let me end with some thoughts about three promising new approaches that are implied by Enterprise Sustainability 2.0.

What should be studied? What is interesting?

Traditional approaches to sustainability (Sustainability 1.0) focus predominantly on the aspects of production. Its main concerns are with managing products, materials, and production systems in more efficient ways. In contrast, Sustainability 2.0 focuses on the aspects of consumption. Researchers need to better understand the nature of human desire, sufficiency in consumption, relationship of consumption to self-actualization/ happiness, material versus spiritual consuming, and the role of frugality. How do desire and consumption shape self-identity? We need to develop consumption approaches that will work for a world population of 9 billion. Blindly transferring consumption desires and practices and creating consumer societies across the globe is not sustainable.

In addition, Sustainability 2.0 invites a focus on distributive justice. It asks questions of fairness, equity, and balance in the distribution of ecological and financial goods and services (see Ehrenfeld [Chapter 33] this volume). It invokes ethical roots of aesthetics to make these moral questions a central concern of sustainable enterprises.

Methods for studying

Scientific inquiry has been the predominant mode of inquiry in the past. Sustainability 2.0 offers aesthetical ways of knowing and art-based methods of learning. It calls for a reflective critique of the traditional assumptions about organizational sustainability, and consideration of new ways to improve it. Organizations and nature are both experienced primarily through the body, with our senses. Most current research on sustainable enterprise is cognitive, and linguistically and culturally mediated. It is based on the epistemologies and corresponding methodologies of science. While science offers important methods, and a 200-year tradition of methodology, it is not the only way of knowing across human cultures and time (Lakoff & Johnson 1999). New and important insights can come from an exploration of embodied, experiential, and practical knowledge. Embodied knowledge can be generated through artistic and aesthetic inquiry. Art-based, 'aesthetic' process techniques can be used to generate qualitatively different understandings of sustainability (Taylor & Hansen 2005). Artistic standards of truth and beauty versus scientific standards of objectivity, verifiability, and generalizability are both needed for holistic approaches to sustainable enterprise.

SUSTAINABLE ENTERPRISE PRACTICES

Traditional sustainability concerns are committed to providing benefits of organizations to all stakeholders (customers, employees, business associates, suppliers, the public, communities, government). This is clearly a great improvement over mainstream business approaches that focus on benefits to investors. But even the stakeholder orientation of traditional sustainability research could use reinvention. For example, organizations should be required to produce complete, competent, and complex statements about their social, environmental, and sustainability performance (see Gray & Herremans [Chapter 22] this volume). Some debates are already underway on who should be considered as a legitimate stakeholder of organizations. Sustainability 2.0 invites more categories of stakeholders into consideration. Nature is a stakeholder, as are animals. Future generations are important stakeholders in virtually any definition of sustainability, but they are rarely considered in organizational decisions (see Roome [Chapter 34] this volume). Finally, there is virtual silence on the question of how many generations into the future we should consider.

To sum up, let me say that Sustainability 2.0 is an invitation to look at the less examined but essential emotional and embodied aspects of sustaining humans on Earth. Arts as a repository of emotions can serve as a vehicle for infusing passion for sustainability into enterprises. In our rush to achieve a scientific understanding of sustainability challenges, we have ignored what art has to offer in changing human and organizational behaviors towards sustainability. Melding art with science can provide a more holistic approach to sustainability.

REFERENCES

Bansal, P. & Roth, K. (2000). "Why Companies Go Green: A Model of Ecological Responsiveness," *Academy of Management Journal*, 43(4): 717–736.

Barbican Art Gallery (2009). *Radical Nature: Art and Architecture for a Changing Planet 1969–2009*, Barbican Art Gallery: London.

Barsade, S. & Gibson, D. (2007). "Why does Affect Matter in Organizations," *Academy of Management Perspectives*, 21(1): 36–59.

Bateson, G. (1980). *Steps to an Ecology of Mind*. New York: Bantam Books.

Bourdieu, P. & Wacquant, L. (1992). *An Invitation to Sociology*. Chicago, IL: University of Chicago Press.

Cameron, K., J. Dutton & Quinn, R. (2003). *Positive Organizational Scholarship: Foundations of a New Discipline*. Barrett-Koehler Publishers, San Fransisco.

Csikszentmihalyi, M. (2003). *Good Business. Leadership, flow and the Making of Meaning*. New York: Penguin Viking.

Csordas, T. (1990). "Embodiment as a paradigm for anthropology," *Ethos*, 18(1): 5–47.

Dutton, D. (2009). *The Art Instinct: Beauty, Pleasure and Human Evolution*, New York: Oxford University Press.

Fineman, S. (2003). *Understanding Emotion at Work*. Thousand Oaks, CA: Sage Publication.

Fowkes, M. & Fowkes, R. (2006). "Principles of Sustainability in Contemporary Art," *Praesens: Central European Contemporary Art Review*, 1: 5–12.

Gladwin, T. (1996). "Toward Eco-Moral Development of The Academy of Management (Letter)," *The Academy of Management Review*, 21(4): 912–914.

Goleman, D. (1995). *Emotional Intelligence: Why it Can Matter More than IQ*. New York: Bantam Books.

Grande, J. (1994). *Balance: Art and Nature*. Montreal: Blackrose Publisher.

Guatari, F. (2000). *The Three Ecologies*. Full translation by Ian Pindar and Paul Sutton, London: The Athlone Press, 2000.

Hoffman, A. (2000). *Competitive Environmental Strategy: A Guide To The Changing Business Landscape*. Washington, DC: Island Press.

IPCC (Intergovernmental Panel on Climate Change) (2007). *Fourth Synthesis Report*. Geneva: IPCC.

Kagan, S. & Kirchberg, V. (2008). *Sustainability: A New Frontier for the Arts and Cultures*. Frankfurt am Main: VAS-Verlag für Akademische Schriften.

Lakoff, G. & Johnson, M. (1999). *Philosophy in the Flesh: The Embodied Mind and Its Challenge to Western Thought*. New York: Harper Collins Publishers.

Neidenthal, P., France, F., Barsalou, L. W., Winkielman, P., Krauthgruver, S. & Ric, F. (2005). "Embodiment in Attitudes, Social Perception, and Emotion," *Personality and Social Psychology Review*, 9(3): 184–211.

Russo, M. (2010). *Companies on a Mission: Entrepreneurial Strategies for Growing Sustainably, Responsibly, and Profitably*. Palo Alto, CA: Stanford Business Books.

Sampson, E. (1996). "Establishing Embodiment in Psychology," *Theory and Psychology*, 6(4): 601–624.

Sharma, S. & Starik, M. (eds.) (2002). *Research in Corporate Sustainability: The Evolving Theory and Practice of Organisations in the Natural Environment*. Cheltenham, UK and Northampton, MA, US: Edward Elgar.

Shrivastava, P. (2010). "Pedagogy of Managing Sustainably with Passion," *Academy of Management Learning and Education*, 9(3): 443–455.

—— & Statler, M. (2010). "Aesthetics of Resilience" (in French), *Telescope*, 16(2): 115–130.

Stead, E. & Stead, J. (1996). *Management for a Small Planet: Strategic Decision Making and the Environment*, 2nd edition, California: Sage Publications.

Taylor, S. & Hansen, H. (2005). "Finding Form: Looking at the Field of Organizational Aesthetics," *Journal of Management Studies*, 42(6): 1211–1231.

....

CHAPTER 36

TOMORROW'S C-SUITE
AGENDA

....

JOHN ELKINGTON AND CHARMIAN LOVE

As they push their way into the market mainstream, the corporate responsibility, social innovation, shared value, and sustainability agendas are demanding growing involvement from senior business leaders (Elkington 1997; see Bondy & Matten [Chapter 28] this volume). But how best to capture the complex mix of risks and opportunities that awaits the senior leadership teams that guide a company's strategy—the corporate chief executives from the C-Suite and Boards—over the next decade? What are the drivers for change—and what are the greatest barriers to progress?

And how to say something new and useful after thirty-five chapters by leading experts on business strategy, non-market strategies, organizational theory and behavior, marketing, accounting and finance, and a range of different emergent and future perspectives? The key conclusion, having read much of the earlier sections of this Handbook, is that the environmental and wider sustainability agendas now touch upon a very broad—and still expanding—spectrum of business, financial, and market interests and activities, from supply chains to company valuation. This is a good sign, as messages that have been stifled on the fringes for decades now become stronger and more mainstream. But the fundamental questions remain: How do we push this forward at the necessary speed—and in the right direction?

On the basis of the management literature, you might be inclined to think that the job is almost done. Recent surveys suggest a growing engagement with environmental and sustainability issues by Boards and C-Suites, including that launched in 2010 by Accenture for the UN Global Compact. No less than 96 percent of the CEOs surveyed thought that sustainability issues should be fully integrated into the strategy and operations of a company—up from 72 percent in 2007. But we suspect that there is a good deal of bluff involved (see Forbes & Jermier [Chapter 30] this volume). So we will use the metaphor of poker to explore how different members of the C-Suite consider these trends. Early in 2010, we tested our line of argument for this chapter in a series of blogs for *Fast Company*, as follows:

Anyone who has tried to engage Boards and C-Suites on environmental, sustainability and related issues in recent decades knows that this has been—and generally remains—a hard sell. But progress is being made: let's work through each of the seven areas listed above.

CAPITALISM AS A HIGH-STAKES POKER GAME

When American soldiers invaded Iraq they carried a deck of playing cards with the faces of Saddam Hussein's government and high-ranking Ba'ath party members. The idea: to help them identify the "most wanted" players in the old regime. Now, as sustainability activists and professionals are drawn into the corporate world as stakeholders and as strategy consultants, we thought it might help to have a deck of cards identifying key players in today's C-Suite—the rarefied realm of business decision-makers like CEOs, CFOs and COOs, all of whom have the word 'Chief' in their title.

It's something of a cliché to describe capitalism as a high-stakes poker game—but in what follows we will take the metaphor at face value; though this metaphor isn't virgin territory. "Poker is a microcosm of all we admire and disdain about capitalism and democracy," wrote poker columnist Lou Krieger, enthusiastically. "It can be rough-hewn or polished, warm or cold, charitable and caring, or hard and impersonal, fickle and elusive, but ultimately it is fair, and right, and just" (Krieger 2000).

Really? Think of the fallout from recent market excesses or our increasingly unstable climate. Such externalities have fuelled the explosion in recent decades of high-octane social and environmental movements, dedicated to alerting policy-makers, investors, and business leaders to areas where capitalism disrupts lives, communities, or ecosystems. These movements have included campaigns against abuses in such areas as consumer safety, environment, aid, human rights, and corruption.

Most people in the C-Suite remain blind to such trends, but there's a revolution building—focusing on shifting market mindsets, behaviors, cultures and, ultimately, paradigms. In related work we did for McKinsey, we distinguished between changes impacting these four areas and, at least in relation to environment and sustainability, we would have to conclude that while we have made progress in changing C-Suite mindsets, we are struggling to change the underlying behaviors (witness the BP *Deepwater Horizon* disaster), generally because we have failed to change key elements of the corporate and wider market cultures—and because we are still working within the old "take, make, waste" paradigm (Elkington 2010).

Whatever the rhetoric, too many Boards and C-Suites still have little sense of how challenges like climate change will impact their business models. Traditionally, there has been a sort of holy C-Suite trinity—the Chief Executive Officer, Chief Financial Officer and Chief Operating Officer. They preside over a growing deck of other 'Chiefs', among them Chief Marketing Officers, Chief Innovation Officers, Chief Technology Officers, and Chief Sustainability Officers, to name but a few. Each then cascades to a wider world of Vice-Presidents and lesser denominations, whose role involves implementing the directives flowing from the top table.

The growing complexity of the business environment, coupled with job title inflation, has driven the proliferation of C-Suite titles and reporting lines, which strikes us as unsustainable. Ultimately, we expect to see a consolidation, with fewer, more complex, and better-integrated portfolios. This process has already begun, as corporations restructured through the downturn.

THE STAKES: PLAYING FOR THE ULTIMATE POT

Venture onto the top floor of many corporate headquarters and the silence, the deference, and the sense that the air is thinner can be disconcerting. Most Boards and C-Suites live in reality bubbles, which may—or may not—reflect existing or emergent realities. Exxon CEO Lee Raymond famously presided over the 'God Pod'—the bubble within which his executive office operated with near divine powers. Trying to engage C-Suite leaders on wider environmental, social, or governance issues can be a Sisyphean task, if indeed you can even get through the door.

Of course, the incoming future may be hard to spot if your radar screens are tuned to the business-as-usual frequency. There's a critical lesson for top management in Pablo Picasso's observation that, "I am always doing that which I cannot do in order that I may learn how to do it." As C-Suite thinking morphs from citizenship to an increasingly strategic assessment of risks and opportunities, that's also likely to be good advice for business leaders.

Transformative change generally comes from the margins of the existing system, not from incumbents. Bill Hewlett and Dave Packard effectively co-founded Silicon Valley from a nano-garage. Still, some incumbent leaders can see elements of the future coming, particularly business leaders. Earlier in 2010, for example, twenty-nine global CEOs launched the latest study from the World Business Council on Sustainable Development (WBCSD), called *Vision 2050* (WBCSD 2010). Rather than slumping into post-Copenhagen gloom, they set out an optimistic vision of how a dangerously expanded population could enjoy health, food, shelter, energy, mobility, education, and other basics of life by mid century.

What WBCSD is calling for is "a radical transformation of global markets, governance and infrastructure, and a re-thinking of our ideas of growth and progress." To make all of this possible, corporate Boards and C-Suites are going to have to work out how to effectively work together towards shared goals—and how to incorporate the costs of externalities, starting with carbon, ecosystem services, and water, into the structure of the marketplace. They have to work out how to double agricultural output without increasing the amount of land or water used. And, among many other things, they have to halve carbon emissions worldwide (based on 2005 levels) by 2050.

Happily, history suggests, the bigger the stakes, the greater the risks the best leaders are willing to take. So, as the cards are dealt, a question likely to be on everyone's minds is: How big is this pot—or market reward—going to be? The WBCSD CEOs conclude that new opportunities will be created for business to thrive and grow with a shift toward sustainability, with trillions of dollars being invested in infrastructure, technology, and human services.

PLAYING KINGS: THE CEO AND PRESIDENT

Apart from Aces, who will drop from our sleeves in the last section, Kings are the highest-ranking cards in the poker deck. For us, the Kings of the C-Suite are the Chief Executive Officers (CEOs). Where companies like General Electric, DuPont, Interface or Wal-Mart Stores lead on sustainability challenges, it's usually because of the CEO. Sometimes they do so because their industry is exposed to issues like climate change, as in the case of DuPont or Duke Energy; sometimes because of a perceived new opportunity space (think GE); and sometimes they act—as with Interface and Wal-Mart—because their CEO has had some sort of Eureka! moment.

With Wal-Mart's former CEO Lee Scott, the epiphany came as Hurricane Katrina wiped out many of his stores, whereas for Interface founder Ray Anderson, his "spear in the chest" moment came while reading Paul Hawken's book *The Ecology of Commerce*. His famous remarks at the US Embassy in London sent shockwaves through his company: "I had a revelation about what industry is doing to our planet. I stood convicted as a plunderer of the earth. In the future, people like me will go to jail."

Leaders like Scott and Anderson were dealt the wildest of wild cards—they could not have planned or prepared for their Eureka! moments—but they were quick to spot the long-term implications for their business models. Happily, they're not as unusual as they once were. You see this in the survey data. Social and environmental concerns are not a top-tier issue for most CEOs, according to BusinessWeek Research Services—in a study for SAS. That said, although "still in its adolescence," says BWRS, "sustainability is being recognized by innovative executives for the opportunity it offers; more than half of executives [focused] on sustainability throughout 2009. Additionally, in the last 12 months, half of organizations have increased their focus on sustainability, while two in five have kept their emphasis on sustainability the same" (BWRS 2010).

Happily, a small—but significant—minority of CEOs is now challenging the shareholder-value obsession. "I do not work for the shareholder, to be honest," was the way that Unilever CEO Paul Polman put it early in 2010, in the *Financial Times*. "I work for the consumer, the customer. I'm not driven and I don't drive this business model by driving shareholder value." That would have been heresy even a year or two before. But now even Jack Welch, former CEO of General Electric and for two decades the arch-priest of shareholder value, has declared, taken to its literal conclusion, that shareholder value is the dumbest idea in the world.

You could also say that his attacks on those who wanted GE to clean up its environmental act during his tenure were pretty dumb, too. Thankfully his successor, Jeffrey Immelt, took a different line—with his courageous 2004 playing of a real wild card, Ecomagination. Thanks to sustained investment in new products designed to solve environmental challenges, GE's revenues in this area grew from $6 billion in 2004 to $17 billion in 2008 and were projected to reach $25 billion in 2010. At a recent event, when discussing cost issues related to clean energy, he noted that "coal was considered expensive when it was replacing the wood stove."

PLAYING QUEENS: THE CFO AND CIO

Fan your cards and it's nice to see Queens, which rank third in the poker deck, after Aces and Kings. For us, the Queens in today's C-Suites are the CFOs, or Chief Financial Officers, sometimes supported by Chief Investment Officers (CIOs) and Chief Accounting Officers (CAOs).

Even at the best of times, it's hard not to feel sorry for CFOs, caught between the proverbial rock of CEO enthusiasms and the hard place of financial market judgments. In the teeth of a global downturn, they deserve even more respect. But, in the past, most CFOs have been a real pain, routinely shooting down CEOs and other C-Suite colleagues who wanted to engage the sustainability agenda. Poll CFOs and other senior executives today, however, and it's clear that the landscape is shifting. A study of 175 CFOs and other senior executives conducted in 2008 by CFO Research with global commercial real estate and money management firm Jones Lang LaSalle (CFO Research 2008), found that more than half believed their companies are "very likely" or "somewhat likely" to increase revenue, cut operating costs, improve investor returns and shareholder value, and improve employee retention through sustainability programs. The most often cited benefits were reduced risk ("very" or "somewhat" likely to produce benefits at 78 percent of companies), enhanced brand and reputation (77 percent), customer retention (72 percent), and improved employee health and productivity (68 percent).

The top objectives in corporate sustainability were regulatory compliance (ranked as a high priority for 61 percent and a mid-level priority for 26 percent of respondents), improving energy efficiency, reducing greenhouse gas emissions (a high priority for 47 percent, mid-level for 32 percent), and reducing the environmental impact of operations (45 percent and 32 percent). These objectives are dynamic, and likely to become more so, underscoring the need for future CFOs to engage proactively.

The greatest barriers include the inability to measure the effects of sustainability on shareholder value (ranked among the top three challenges by 46 percent of respondents), inability to document the effects on financial performance (37 percent), and a lack of standard decision-making frameworks that consider environmental factors (36 percent). Perhaps surprisingly, the least significant challenge was organizational resistance, ranked among the top three barriers by just 20 percent of respondents.

Playing Jacks: the COO AND CPO

Lowest-ranked of the so-called 'face cards' is the Jack, or Knave. For us, the Jacks of today's C-Suites are the COOs, or Chief Operating Officers, and the CPOs, or Chief Procurement Officers. The latter—or their equivalents—have become increasingly important, as companies have had to learn how to knit together and operate complex supply global chains. Winning hands in today's markets critically depend on market-sensitive, well-connected and agile Jacks—able to juggle different priorities, deadlines and cultural sensitivities.

As the sustainability agenda has moved from the periphery to the mainstream, businesses of many types have woken up to the need to transform their operations—and, in some cases, their business models—to better integrate sustainability initiatives across the enterprise. When Accenture reviewed the relevant issues for COOs, it identified the following key areas of interest: revenue growth from new products and services, cost reduction and efficiency improvements, better risk management, and brand and reputation enhancement.

Ultimately, Accenture concluded, "sustainability is an engine that can drive high performance. Further, the building blocks of high performance—market focus and position, distinctive capabilities and performance anatomy—can be used to create business opportunities and lasting value, for your stakeholders and for society at large."

Being a COO in a world of radically greater market transparency, with supplier relationships stretched across regions and markets with very different priorities in terms of accountability and sustainability, will be the sort of challenge that makes or breaks C-Suite contenders. Happily, however, even if COOs aren't CSOs themselves, growing numbers can now turn to a new breed of C-Suite professionals whose brief it is to track this wider world.

Playing tens: the CLO, CRO and CSO

Beyond the 'face cards' covered earlier, the most powerful cards are the Tens. For us, the 10s of today's C-Suite are the growing array of senior people who work to maintain and build the brand and corporate reputation. They include CMOs, or Chief Marketing

Officers, CLOs, or Chief Legal Officers, CROs, or Chief Responsibility Officers, and CSOs, or Chief Sustainability Officers.

Sometimes these people take over responsibilities that previously rested –often by default—with COOs and facility managers. More typically, CSOs try hard to guide and support, not override other C-Suite functions. More positively, the shift of this agenda to the C-Suite often signals that a company takes these issues seriously.

As long ago as 2005, most of the 150 largest companies in the world had a sustainability officer with the rank of Vice President or higher. As to their portfolios, a recent survey by *Corporate Responsibility* magazine listed the following tasks as typical: business ethics, communications, compliance and governance, environment, international affairs, politics and legislation, social responsibility and socially responsible investing. None of them exactly trivial tasks.

As it becomes clearer that we are heading into an era of creative destruction, there are two obvious questions. First, we should ask whether CLOs, CROs and even CSOs are up to the task of disrupting their companies' current mindsets and business models. While they can certainly be important catalysts, our sense is that real change will come from elsewhere, as it generally does, from the edges of the system. And that's where we're headed in this chapter's final section. Second, and a question for all C-Suite aspirants, should sustainability elements be built into all top management training?

PLAYING ACES: GOING FOR THE C-SUITE FLUSH

Aces are fascinating cards, scoring high or low, depending on circumstances. Here they stand for the potentially breakthrough individuals, teams, business models and technologies that can help C-Suites to drive transformational change—and future-proof their businesses. Crucially, they can be insiders or outsiders to the company. And there are new ways of finding, grooming, and deploying such talent. At least that's the hope of those who employ the growing armies of CTOs (Chief Technology Officers), CIOs (Chief Innovation Officers) and, the new kids on the block, CCOs (Chief Creativity Officers).

Tomorrow's corporate Aces will know how to play the wild cards that have proved so disruptive for earlier generations of CEOs and senior executives—and they will know how to source suitably disruptive solutions, whether from customers, competitors, NGOs, public agencies, or social and environmental entrepreneurs.

Business issues that were once the preserve of specialist magazines and newsletters and then exploded out into the business innovation media, are now routinely surfacing in the mainstream management media, for example the *Harvard Business Review*. 'Why Sustainability is Now the Key Driver of Innovation' was the title of one major HBR article last year, co-authored by the late C. K. Prahalad and his colleagues Ram Nidumolu and M. R. Rangaswami.

And their conclusion? "Executives behave as though they have to choose between the largely social benefits of developing sustainable products or processes and the financial costs of doing so," they argued. "But that's simply not true. Our research shows that sustainability is a mother lode of organizational and technological innovations that yield both bottom-line and top-line returns. In fact, because those are the goals of corporate innovation, we find that smart companies now treat sustainability as innovation's new frontier."

It's easy to become obsessed with Aces, however, to the detriment of the wider team and culture. Increasingly, corporate intrapreneurs and changemakers can be found across the business spectrum, even if their own management too often fails to recognize their worth and potential. It's time to find and support these people, whether inside or outside today's C-Suite, and inside or outside the corporation, and to work with them to create new forms of capitalism fit for the new century.

REFERENCES

Accenture & United Nations Global Compact (2010). *A New Era of Sustainability: UN Global Compact-Accenture CEO Study 2010.*

BWRS (BusinessWeek Research Services) (2010). *Emerging Green Intelligence: Business Analytics and Corporate Sustainability.*

CFO (2008). *The Role of Finance in Environmental Efforts* (March). Available at <http://www.cfo.com/whitepapers/index.cfm/displaywhitepaper/13010943>

Elkington, J. (1997). *Cannibals with Forks: The Triple Bottom Line of 21st Century Business.* New York: Capstone/John Wiley.

—— & Love, C. (2010). "Wild Cards for Tomorrow's C-Suite", online blog series, <http://www.fastcompany.com/tag/john-elkington>

—— (2010). "A New Paradigm For Change, McKinsey & Company", online <http://whatmatters.mckinseydigital.com/social_entrepreneurs/a-new-paradigm-for-change>

Financial Times (4 April 2010) <http://www.ft.com/cms/s/0/72d68b60-4009-11df-8d23-00144 feabdc0,dwp_uuid=1d202fd8-c061-11dd-9559-000077b07658.html>

Hawken, P. (1994). *The Ecology of Commerce: A Declaration of Sustainability.* HarperBusiness; 1st Collins Business Ed edition, New York.

Krieger, L. & Harroch, R. D. (2000). *Poker for Dummies*: IDG Books.

My Hero Project: *Ray Anderson* (1998). <http://www.myhero.com/go/hero.asp?hero=r_anderson>

Nidumolu, R., Prajalad, C. K. & Rangaswami, M. R. (2009). *Why Sustainability Is Now the Key Driver of Innovation*, Harvard Business Review.<http://hbr.org/2009/09/why-sustainability-is-now-the-key-driver-of-innovation/ar/1>

WBCSD (World Business Council for Sustainable Development) (2010). *Vision 2050: The New Agenda for Business.* Switzerland: WBCSD.

CHAPTER 37

....

THE
TIIIRD-GENERATION
CORPORATION

....

STUART L. HART

MARKETS and commerce are as old as our species. As John McMillan points out in his wonderful book, *Reinventing the Bazaar*, the urge to engage in "business" seems to be part of the human DNA. Indeed, throughout recorded history, humans have traded with each other and engaged in exchange relationships for mutual benefit. "Markets" and "bazaars" have flourished for thousands of years. The invention of money only accelerated this phenomenon, and made it easier to exchange value (MacMillan 2002).

The "corporation," however, is a much more recent social invention dating back only about 500 years, to the age of discovery. The concept of "capitalism" is even more recent, rising to prominence in the mid nineteenth century (Braudel 1992). There have been two main stages in the evolution of the corporation, with the third just now emerging (see Figure 37.1). The "chartered" corporation was born during the Renaissance as an instrument of colonial conquest and subjugation. Over-reach, greed, and corruption led to its ultimate demise. The second-generation "industrial" corporation arose in the nineteenth century, was granted personhood in post-Civil War America, and ignited the explosion of "capitalism" in the late nineteenth and twentieth centuries.

Once again, however, over-reach, greed, and corruption appear to have infected the corporate world. And with mounting environmental destruction and growing social inequity, we now begin to see the contours of a third generation of corporation emerging for the twenty-first century—the "sustainable" corporation. With this third generation of corporation, we may also be witnessing the beginnings of a new more "inclusive" brand of capitalism. After a review of the first two corporate generations, I devote the balance of this chapter to considering the prospects for the third-generation corporation, including the important research questions relevant to this emerging domain.

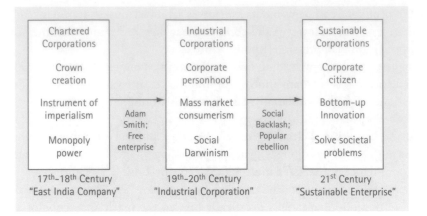

FIGURE 37.1 Three generations of corporations

CORPORATE GENEOLOGY

Beginning in the 1200s, the feudal system began to give way to renewed enterprise and commerce in the towns and cities of Europe. Indeed, "burghers" thrived and "merchants" set sail to take advantage of the vast resources of other territories during the 1300s and 1400s. The aristocracy, however, was virtually handcuffed since its wealth was tied up in the massive landholdings it had accumulated during the Feudal era. By "enclosing" and selling land (and thereby uprooting rural peasants and forcing them into the wage labor market), the ruling aristocracy, in consort with the most successful merchants, forged a new investment vehicle—the corporation. Through limited partnerships which provided for passive participation, the nobility finally had a means for expanding investment beyond their own landholdings (Rushkoff 2009).

The first-generation corporations were thus "trading companies" chartered by monarchs for reasons that had very little to do with exchanging value or carrying out market transactions. Through the ingenious use of limited liability and joint stock ownership, kings could empower those merchants most loyal to them with permanent monopoly control over specific colonial territories and industries. In exchange for granting legally enforceable monopolies, monarchs reaped profits far exceeding the worth of any cash investment they could have made (Robins 2006).

The 1500s and 1600s saw the formation of dozens of large trading companies such as England's Merchant Adventurers, Holland's United East India Company, and France's Companie des Indes. North America was colonized by trading companies such as the Virginia Company and the Hudson's Bay Company (Nace 2005). The corporation that truly changed the world, however, was the British East India Company, founded in 1600: It pioneered the shareholder model of corporate ownership and built the foundations for modern business administration that continue to this day. With a single-minded pursuit of profit, the company and its executives achieved market dominance in Asia for more than 200 years. However, the company also shocked many with the scale of its excesses and human oppression (Robins 2006).

By the late 1700s, many leading figures of the time condemned the practices of the chartered corporations. Adam Smith, Edmund Burke, and Karl Marx were all united in their critique—for quite different reasons—of this domineering, oppressive form of commerce. For Adam Smith, the corporation was one of the great enemies of the "free" market, and his writings clearly reflected this view. Indeed, the American Revolution itself was less a revolt by colonists against Britain than by small businessmen against the market dominance of chartered multinational corporations (Zinn 2003).

To ensure that corporations did not come to dominate "life, liberty, and the pursuit of happiness," the founding fathers drastically limited the reach and scope of corporate power in newly independent America. Corporations could only be chartered by states (not the Federal government), were required to demonstrate a specific public purpose other than making money (such as building a bridge), and were allowed to exist only for a specified period of time. Just like Adam Smith, the founding fathers detested big corporations, and envisioned a "free enterprise" system populated by small-scale firms and farmers, unencumbered by large, remotely run monopolies (Korten 1999).

By the early nineteenth century, chartered corporations were in their waning days. However, there was a new form of corporation emerging—the industrial corporation—which would greatly surpass its predecessor in terms of size, scope, and global impact. It is noteworthy, however, that very few people at the time saw this coming. Neither Adam Smith nor Karl Marx, for example, foresaw the reemergence of the corporation as a dominant institution: Both were influenced mainly by the situation in Britain where virtually all the giant chartered corporations had collapsed and the English industrial revolution was flourishing under quite simple institutional forms, such as family-owned enterprises, partnerships, and unincorporated companies (Rushkoff 2009).

In America, the corporation had experienced a revival, but through the first half of the nineteenth century, the state charter system had functioned to prevent the emergence of large corporations like the East India Company in England. Beginning in the 1850s, however, lobbyists for the newly emerging railroad corporations began exacting concessions from state legislatures. First, the Pennsylvania Railroad convinced the Pennsylvania State Legislature to relax the long-standing prohibition of one corporation owning stock in another. After the Civil War, Union war hero Tom Scott was able to use this exception to pursue his vision of a nationwide railway system. Through the use of a "holding company" structure, Scott was able to purchase a controlling interest in several smaller railroad companies, especially those in the south and the west (Nace 2005).

Scott emerged as the key power broker in determining the outcome of the disputed 1876 presidential election involving Rutherford B. Hayes and Samuel Tilden. In what has come to be known as the Compromise of 1877, Republican Hayes was selected as President by a special commission of Supreme Court justices and congressmen. In exchange for the votes of the southern electors—and tacit approval of Scott's plan to consolidate the southern railways—Hayes agreed to withdraw the remaining Federal troops from the South, which enabled the old southern establishment to reestablish itself and opened the door to the "Jim Crow" system of sharecropping and black disenfranchisement (Painter 1987).

Over the next thirty years, through a series of court decisions, the legal restrictions on corporations were steadily eliminated. By the turn of the century, incorporation had become a perfunctory act, life-span limits had been removed, corporations were free to acquire other companies, and they could expand to other states as they saw fit. But perhaps most significantly, through a quirk in Supreme Court reporting of the *Santa Clara County v. Southern Pacific Railway Company* decision of 1886, corporations were granted the rights of "personhood." Under the Fourteenth Amendment to the US Constitution, written to guarantee the rights of citizenship to former slaves, corporate lawyers were able to apply the phrase "person" to include companies as well. This gave corporations the same rights to "due process" and "equal protection" as any other American citizen (Nace 2005).

These and other changes opened the door to the "Gilded Age" and the emergence of the giant railroad, steel, oil, and financial trusts led by "robber barons" such as Jay Gould, Andrew Carnegie, John Rockefeller, and J. P. Morgan (Morris 2005). Much like the first-generation chartered corporations, these giant trusts were built to restrict competition and take advantage of monopoly power. The tycoons of the Gilded Age, however, were able to exploit the Social Darwinism that was rampant at the time to convince people that they were simply the "winners" in a Darwinian struggle for survival (Trachtenberg 2007). The result was the rapid emergence of the second-generation industrial corporate form and the creation of the mass market, consumer economy. Indeed, it was during the second half of the nieteenth century and early part of the twentieth century that most of the iconic corporations still in existence today were born—General Electric, Ford Motor Company, and Proctor & Gamble—to name just a few.

Economic historian Karl Polanyi labelled this period "The Great Transformation" (Polanyi 1944). Prior to the nineteenth century, economic activity had been "embedded" in the larger society, subordinated to politics, religion, and social relations. However, with the emergence of the "capitalist" system of the late nineteenth century, the economy became increasingly "disembedded," with society subordinated to the interests of the market. This led inevitably to social backlash and popular rebellion—what Polanyi called the "double movement"—to protect society from the excesses of the market. It is no coincidence, therefore, that the labor movement, the transcendentalists, the communist movement, and the anarchists all find their origins during this period. Riots, strikes, bombings, and assassinations became commonplace.

The labor and conservation reforms instituted by Theodore Roosevelt and the "progressives" in the early twentieth century can therefore be seen as necessary palliative measures to enable the capitalist system to continue to function; they addressed the most egregious excesses, but did not institute any fundamental structural changes to the system. World War I served to distract the industrialized world from these fundamental problems. The result was the return to excess after the war with the "Roaring 20s" followed by the collapse of the system in 1929 and the Great Depression (Hofstadter 1955).

Fifteen more years of depression and another world war followed. Significant reforms under Franklin Delano Roosevelt redressed some of the fundamental imbalances associated with the Gilded Age. But with the return to prosperity after World War II, the US was now the dominant economic force in the world. And American corporations were seen as the key to her success: "What's good for GM is good for America" was the slogan of the times. Friedrich Hayek was a tireless promoter of market liberalism in the US and directly inspired influential followers like Milton Friedman, Margaret Thatcher, and Ronald Reagan (see Hayek 1944).

However, as we will see, the unresolved problems associated with the industrial corporate model would reassert themselves in the 1960s. Growing concerns over environmental pollution, social injustice, and, ultimately, global poverty and inequity would foreshadow the rise of the third-generation "sustainable" corporation.

THE RISE OF THE THIRD GENERATION CORPORATION

Just as the first-generation chartered corporations generated a backlash which ultimately brought them to their knees, so today, second-generation industrial corporations are experiencing the same resistance and may be reaching the end of their era of dominance. Indeed, I believe that we are now forty plus years into the next "great transformation" which began during the 1960s environmental revolution. Fifty years from now, our progeny will look back on this time much as we now reflect on the rise of the industrial corporate model in the nineteenth century. I will not review the transformational path of the past forty years, as this has been done very well by recent authors (Hart 2010; Hoffman 2001). I will, however, seek to illuminate the significant differences between the out-going second and emerging third-generation corporate forms (see Table 37.1). Each of these features is discussed in more depth below, along with the relevant research questions for each.

Table 37.1 Comparing corporate models

• Industrial Corporation	• Sustainable Corporation
– Incremental; continuous improvement	– Disruptive; change the rules of the game
– Centralized; driven by economies of scale	– Distributed; exploits diseconomies of scale
– Disembedded; tramples existing socio-cultural traditions	– Embedded; builds on native traditions and knowledge
– Extrinsic; motivated by fear or money	– Intrinsic: motivated by meaning and purpose
– Extractive; practices zero-sum thinking	– Inclusive; shatters trade-offs among stakeholders

Behaving as a disrupter

Given that clean technologies are almost always "disruptive" to existing second-generation corporate strategies, moving to an environmentally sustainable form of enterprise
means *learning to think—and act—like a disrupter* (Christensen 1997). It means launching small-scale experiments with next-generation clean technologies and growing them
from the ground up, rather than continued dependence on large-scale solutions imposed
from the top down (Hart 2011). Industrial corporations concentrated on limiting competition and protecting their established positions as incumbents; third-generation corporations will instead focus their energies on creating the future rather than
consolidating control over what already exists.

Some key research questions for the future, therefore, include: What proportion of
corporate activity should be focused on "exploiting" current markets and technologies
versus "exploring" new ones (see Ehrenfeld [Chapter 33] this volume)? How do the skills
associated with "eco-efficiency" differ from those for disruptive clean technology commercialization? Do existing industrial corporations have the capacity to behave disrup-
tively, or will they necessarily cede the field to entrepreneurial start-ups (see Lenox &
York [Chapter 4] this volume)?

Scaling distributed solutions

The industrial corporate model was based on a high fixed-cost, capital-intensive business model, centered around large-scale centralized production. Over the past few decades, however, the conventional wisdom that "bigger is better" has begun to come under
fire. Distributed generation of energy, point-of-use water treatment, and point-of-care
health technologies actually display *diseconomies* of scale—the smaller, the *more* cost-
effective. As a result, third-generation corporations adopting these strategies and technologies hold the potential to creatively destroy existing hierarchies; bypass corrupt
governments and regimes, and usher in an entirely new age of capitalism that brings
widely distributed benefits to the entire human community of 6.7 billion people (Hart
2010). The "base of the pyramid"—the four billion poor earning less than four dollars
per day—may turn out to be the ideal place to incubate these distributed technologies of
tomorrow, since they do not compete against an existing, centralized infrastructure
(Hart & Christensen 2002).

Some key research questions for the future, therefore, include: Can industrial corporations premised on economies of scale shift their focus to small-scale, distributed strategies? Will new formal systems, metrics, and measures be necessary to enable this shift
to occur? Will corporations based in the emerging markets of the developing world be
more likely to make the "leap" to distributed technologies and business models compared to large incumbent firms from the West?

Embedding business back into society

Unlike their industrial predecessors, third-generation corporations are developing fully contextualized solutions to real problems in ways that respect local culture and natural diversity. This means engaging in *"deep* dialog" with local communities to co-create businesses that are truly *"embedded"* in the local context. Such companies will come to view the communities they serve as partners and colleagues, rather than merely as "consumers." This mindset shift requires the development of a new, "native capability" to complement competencies in global efficiency, local responsiveness, and learning-transfer that most corporations already possess (Simanis & Hart 2009).

Some key research questions for the future, therefore, include: What is the best way for industrial corporations to acquire this new capability? Can such "on-the-ground" skills be taught or is it necessary to "learn-by-doing"? Are there current employees who can rise to this challenge or is it necessary to look outside of the existing corporation to find people and organizations with the requisite motivation and skill set? How do we create incentives for people to step up to this challenge without derailing their careers?

Making meaning through purpose

There is a persistent myth that the ultimate purpose of business is to maximize profit for the investors. However, the maximization of profit is not a purpose; instead, it is an outcome. Indeed, it is now becoming clear that the best way to maximize profits over the long term is to *not* make them the primary goal (Mackey 2009). Profits are like happiness: a by-product of other things like having a strong sense of purpose, meaningful work, and deep relationships. Those who focus obsessively on their own happiness are usually narcissists—and end up miserable. Third-generation corporations, therefore, understand that you make money by doing good things rather than the other way around. First, you make meaning through purpose, then the money follows (Mourkogiannis 2006)

Some key research questions for the future, therefore, include: What is required to generate a strong sense of purpose within a corporation? Can purpose be "dictated" from the top-down, or must it also emerge from the collective aspirations of the people in the organization? How can the management of "human resources" be re-conceptualized to include the development of the whole person? Do corporations driven by a strong social purpose outperform those with more conventional financial or business missions and goals?

Shattering trade-offs through inclusive capitalism

Truth be told, there is no inherent conflict between financial and societal performance. Third-generation corporations therefore consciously seek to overthrow the tyranny of the "trade-off" mentality. The key is learning to jointly optimize the needs and desires of all stakeholders, rather than elevating one stakeholder above all others (Freeman 1984). Paradoxically, such companies can evolve competitively superior strategies that produce superior financial returns—the definition of a truly sustainable enterprise (Sisodia, Sheth, & Wolfe 2007). The lesson: "hit and run" players like predatory lenders and Ponzi scheme artists can make lots of money in the short term by ignoring or even damaging some of their stakeholders. But eventually the negative feedback loops catch up on them. Sustainable enterprises—those interested in flourishing for the long term—learn to delight all their stakeholders.

Some key research questions for the future, therefore, include: Can stakeholders be effectively included in the development of corporate strategy? Is it possible to connect stakeholders' interests together so that they become mutually reinforcing rather than competing interests? How should a firm measure "stakeholder value" which would include the *total* value created for all the stakeholders by the company? Do firms that create more stakeholder value consistently outperform others on purely financial grounds?

Conclusion

While many today instinctively turn to government for solutions, the third-generation corporation may turn out to be our best hope for a "sustainable" future—economically, socially, and environmentally. Increasingly, corporations are *global* in scope, making them ideally suited to address trans-boundary problems and international challenges. It is not by happenstance, for example, that some multinational companies have led initiatives to address climate change (e.g. the US Climate Action Partnership), loss of marine fisheries (e.g. the Marine Stewardship Council), and sustainable development (e.g. the World Business Council for Sustainable Development).

Even more significantly, third-generation corporations may be better positioned than governments to understand—and respond to—emerging societal needs. Not the broad and abstract "public interest" trumpeted by enlightenment thinkers, but rather the fine-grained, on-the-ground, "micro" interests of actual individuals, families, and communities (human and natural). Getting "close to the customer" is, after all, the stock and trade of the corporate world.

The profit motive can *accelerate* (not inhibit) the transformation toward global sustainability, with civil society, governments, and multilateral agencies all playing crucial roles as collaborators and watchdogs. Through thousands (or even millions) of business-led initiatives, we can innovate our way into tomorrow's "clean" technology, and welcome the four billion poor at the "base of the pyramid" into the global economy.

Unfortunately, research on the emergence of the third generation "sustainable" corporation has only begun to scratch the surface: To date, most peer-reviewed work has focused on the eco-efficiency agenda, which is focused more on incremental improvement to the industrial model than to transformative change. Why? Because there are large-scale databases to be analyzed which enable sophisticated, quantitative, hypothesis-testing work. What is really needed at this point, however, is more prospective, action-research work which pushes the state of the art. As I argued over a decade ago, we need to move "beyond greening" (Hart 1997). A similar call can be found in the other chapters in the final section of this volume.

Indeed, as clean technology and base of the pyramid strategies gather momentum in the world, the opportunities to advance management theory have never been greater. Each provides important pieces to the sustainable enterprise puzzle: the promise of "next-generation" technologies with dramatically lower environmental impacts, and innovative new ways to reach and include all of humanity in the capitalist dream.

REFERENCES

Braudel, F. (1992). *The Wheels of Commerce*. Berkeley, CA: University of California Press.

Christensen, C. (1997). *The Innovator's Dilemma*. Boston, MA: Harvard Business School Publishing.

Freeman, E. (1984). *Strategic Management: A Stakeholder Approach*. Marchfield, MA: Pittman Publishing.

Hart, S. L. (1997). "Beyond Greening: Strategies for a Sustainable World," *Harvard Business Review*, January/February, 66–76.

—— (2010). *Capitalism at the Crossroads*, 3rd edition. Upper Saddle River, NJ: Wharton School Publishing.

—— (2011). "Taking the Green Leap," in T. London and S. L. Hart (eds.), *Next Generation Business Strategies for the Base of the Pyramid*, Upper Saddle River, NJ: Wharton School Publishing.

——& Christensen, C. (2002). "The Great Leap: Driving Innovation from the Base of the Pyramid," *Sloan Management Review*, 44(1): 51–56.

Hayek, F. A. (1944). *The Road to Serfdom*. Chicago, IL: University of Chicago Press.

Hoffman, A. (2001). *From Heresy to Dogma*. Palo Alto, CA: Stanford University Press.

Hofstadter, R. (1955). *The Age of Reform*. New York: Vintage Books.

Korten, D. (1999). *The Post-Corporate World*. San Francisco: Berrett-Koehler.

Mackey, J. (2009). "Creating a New Paradigm for Business," in M. Strong (ed.), *Be the Solution: How Entrepreneurs and Conscious Capitalists Can Solve All the World's Problems*, Hoboken, NJ: John Wiley & Sons.

Macmillan, J. (2002). *Reinventing the Bazaar: A Natural History of Markets*. New York: W.W. Norton.

Morris, C. (2005). *The Tycoons*. New York: Owl Books.

Mourkogiannis, N. (2006). *Purpose: The Starting Point of Great Companies*. New York: Palgrave-Macmillan.

Nace, T. (2005). *Gangs of America: The Rise of Corporate Power and the Disabling of Democracy*. San Francisco: Berrett-Koehler.

Painter, N. I. (1987). *Standing at Armageddon*. New York, W. W. Norton.

Polanyi, K. (1944). *The Great Transformation*. Boston, MA: Beacon Press.

Robins, N. (2006). *The Corporation that Changed the World: How the East India Company Shaped the Modern Multinational*. Hyderabad: Orient Longman.

Rushkoff, D. (2009). *Life Inc: How the World Became a Corporation and How to Take it Back*. New York: Random House.

Simanis, E. & Hart, S. (2009). "Innovation from the inside-out," *Sloan Management Review*, Summer: 77–86.

Sisodia, R., Sheth, J., & Wolfe, D. (2007). *Firms of Endearment*. Upper Saddle River, NJ: Wharton School Publishing.

Trachtenberg, A. (2007). *The Incorporation of America*. New York: Hill and Wang.

Zinn, H. (2003). *A People's History of the United States*. New York: HarperCollins.

CHAPTER 38

....

CAPITALISM CRITIQUE: SYSTEMIC LIMITS ON BUSINESS HARMONY WITH NATURE

....

THOMAS N. GLADWIN

They go on in a strange paradox, decided only to be undecided, resolved to be irresolute, adamant for drift, solid for fluidity, all-powerful to be impotent...Owing to past neglect, in the face of the plainest warnings, we have entered upon a period of danger. The era of procrastination, of half-measures, of soothing and baffling expedience of delays, is coming to its close. In its place we are entering a period of consequences...We cannot avoid this period, we are in it now.

Winston Churchill, 12 November 1936

How is it that after almost fifty years of "modern environmentalism" we get Paul Hawken, one of the leading gurus of the Business and the Natural Environment (hereafter B&NE) field, concluding that "every living system [on earth] is declining and the rate of decline is accelerating. Kind of a mind-boggling situation—but not one peer-reviewed paper published in the last thirty years can refute that statement" (Hawken 2009: 1). The past half-century has been marked by an exponential explosion of environmental knowledge, technology, regulation, education, awareness, and organizations. But none of this has served to diminish the flow of terrifying scientific warnings about the fate of the planet.

The United Nations *Millennium Ecosystem Assessment*, for example, concluded that nearly two-thirds of the ecosystem services which support life have been degraded or used unsustainably over the past fifty years and warned that the ability of the planet's ecosystems to sustain future generations could no longer be taken for granted (2005). The *Global Environment Outlook GEO-4* report of the United Nations Environment

Programme (2007) similarly documented persistent, systematic and intractable destruction of natural systems gravely putting humanity at risk. Scientists assembled by the Stockholm Resilience Center concluded that humanity has exceeded safe "planetary boundaries" for maintaining the Earth's capacity for self-regulation with regard to atmospheric concentrations of CO_2, biodiversity loss, and nitrogen/phosphorous inputs to the biosphere and oceans, triggering risks of abrupt and irreversible environmental change (Rockstrom et al. 2009). The World Wildlife Fund for Nature has calculated that humanity is now exploiting nature's bioproductive resources and producing CO_2 emissions at a rate 50 percent faster than what nature can regenerate and reabsorb (2010). Most of this overshoot is traceable to the growth of energy and matter throughput in high-income capitalist nations.

THE STATE OF THE B&NE FIELD

As indicated in the literature reviews provided in this Handbook, the B&NE field has yet to substantively acknowledge the magnitude, severity, persistence, complexity, exponential acceleration or the transformational urgency of the global environmental crisis (for exceptions see chapters in sections VIII and IX this volume). Why might this be? Is the field disconnected from environmental science? Is it addicted to reductionism, positivism, empiricism, relativism, rationalism, and objectivism as the only basis of knowledge generation? Has it been seduced by traditional economics into believing that efficient resource allocation is the only goal that really matters, and that issues of equitable distribution and optimal scale of throughput relative to carrying capacity can be safely ignored? Has the field conveniently shunted aside messy moral and ethical concerns?

Part of the B&NE field's blindness to absolute losses of natural life-support capacity lies in its apparent satisfaction with measuring corporate environmental performance in terms of reduced "loadings" placed onto nature, without assessment of the consequences of those loads on the health, integrity, and resilience of the affected systems. This is especially prevalent in the field of industrial ecology (see Lifset & Boons [Chapter 17] and the critique offered by Buhr & Gray [Chapter 23] this volume). Corporate environmental excellence has come to mean doing "less bad" relative to the past or to competitors, often normalized as a percent of output or sales (see Ehrenfeld [Chapter 33] and Roome [Chapter 34] this volume for a critique of "greening" as only contributing to the reduction of unsustainability rather than creating genuine sustainability). The field has not endeavored to appraise corporate behavior using absolute norms, rules or standards of ecological sustainability such as those promulgated in the field of ecological economics (see Daly & Farley 2004).

Another possible reason for neglecting how bad things are, and might get, is that the field appears to revel in forces favoring positive change, however marginal the results. It is much less concerned with the forces resisting change or the ineffectuality of pro-environment forces in genuinely changing corporate behaviors. Why is it that the environment is not a top-tier issue for most CEOs, or that 70 percent of large companies are not actively seeking to invest in sustainability and embed it in their business practices (see Elkington & Love [Chapter 36] this volume)? Why are 90 percent of US assets in the stock markets not owned or influenced by socially responsible investors (see Bauer & Derwall [Chapter 25] this volume)? Why is there a virtual absence of environmental information in conventional management account- ing systems, and why are only 3 percent of the world's multinational companies engaged in social and environmental reporting (see Buhr & Gray [Chapter 23] this volume)? Why is it virtually impossible to determine from the reports that do get pro- duced whether the firms are, or are not, contributing to ecological sustainability and/ or social justice (see Gray & Herremans [Chapter 22] this volume)? Why are there extraordinarily low levels of environmental disclosure in corporate financial reports (see Cho, Patten, & Roberts [Chapter 24] this volume)? Why have investors and ana- lysts so far not penalized companies for ignoring climate risks (see Bertrand & Sinclair-Desgagne [Chapter 26] this volume)? Why are there so few truly green con- sumers (see Devinney [Chapter 21] and Gershoff & Irwin [Chapter 20] this volume)? Why is there so much greenwashing (see Forbes & Jermier [Chapter 30] and Scammon & Mish [Chapter 19] this volume)? Why is there no business or financial case for sus- tainability (see Buhr & Gray [Chapter 23] and Russo & Minto [Chapter 2] this vol- ume)? The authors make note of these dismal facts (which collectively tell us that environmental pressures have so far had only a very limited impact in changing the reality of the business world and financial/consumer markets) but generally do not seek to examine them, typically quickly returning to efforts to explain marginal posi- tive deviance instead of overwhelming negative resistance.

Curtis White notes that "there is a fundamental question that environmentalists are not very good at asking, let alone answering: Why is this, the destruction of the natural world, happening?" (2009: 1). The B&NE field, I believe, stands guilty of the same offense. A few chapters (namely Lounsbury, Fairclough, & Lee [Chapter 12], Buhr & Gray [Chapter 23] and Banerjee [Chapter 31] this volume) show how the field is begin- ning to dig below the surface in search of the hard-to-observe systemic causes generat- ing disharmony between business and nature. These efforts help to discover root rather than symptomatic causes, systemic instead of piecemeal diagnoses, and curative as opposed to palliative solutions. Working above the surface looks for superficial answers within the current system; probing below the surface searches instead for transforma- tional changes needed for constructing entirely new and more functional systems. Philosopher Ken Wilber tells us that discovering new therapies for the world's problems will arise only when we are willing to "shift perspectives, deepen our perception, often against a great deal of resistance, to embrace the deeper and wider context" (1995: 73).

The remainder of this chapter asks members of the B&NE field to consider whether market-based capitalism might chiefly be responsible for the global environment crisis and the dominant "dark" forces resisting solutions to this crisis. The emphasis is particu- larly on the Anglo-Saxon form of capitalism, characterized relatively by unfettered mar- ket transactions, publicly traded companies, high institutional ownership, and the drive for shareholder rather than stakeholder value creation. This will not be a comfortable intellectual journey, as the conventional B&NE field explicitly or implicitly accepts capitalism as "the only game in town" to make sense of business–environment relations. But what if modern capitalism is fundamentally, genetically, and irreparably driven by a mutually reinforcing set of obligatory rules, operating instructions and survival imperatives that preordain ecological destruction (see Mander 1991 and Bakan 2004 for seminal work on this thesis)?

The excesses, flaws, failures, contradictions, and instabilities of capitalism, in all of its forms, have been a playground for socialist, luddite, marxist, and religious criticism for many decades. Criticism on ecological grounds can be traced back to the start of modern environmentalism (e.g. Rachel Carson's indictment of DDT and the chemical industry in her book *Silent Spring* of 1962). Marxist scholars have claimed that capitalism makes social evolution hopelessly incompatible with ecological evolution (Bookchin 1980); creates a vulnerable planet (Foster 1999); and is the real "enemy of nature" (Kovel 2002). Mainstream environmentalists see contemporary capitalism as "a financially profitable, non-sustainable aberration in human development" (Hawken, Lovins, & Lovins 1999: 5); as "incompatible with anything vaguely resembling sustainability" (Porritt 2005: 67); and fundamentally "incapable of sustaining the environment" (Speth 2008: 63).

The B&NE field has constructed its theories, formulated its hypotheses, gathered its data, and offered its assessments within the confines of contemporary free-market capitalism. The logics of capitalism ubiquitously infiltrate, frame, enclose and constrict all of the tacit assumptions in which the field is drenched. The field's judgments are made according to capitalist metrics (e.g. profitability, competitive advantage, revenue growth) rather than ecological criteria of sustainability or ethical criteria of justice. The buy-in to capitalism as the only context for sense making has biased the field, I believe, toward vast underestimation of the magnitude of externalities and other market failures, inertial forces working against sustainability, corporate control of the institutions attempting to shape environmental behavior, and the consequences of current behaviors on the welfare of future generations, the currently deprived, and the rest of nature. The capitalist lock-in has also led to a gross overestimation of the potentials for environmental entrepreneurship and green consumerism, the capacities for decoupling and technological fixes, and the gains derivable from unregulated voluntary approaches and market-based environmentalism. Let's consider six contentions as to why capitalism might represent the ultimate cause of ecological destruction and resistance to change on behalf of a sustainable future.

Contention 1: capitalism commands growth of throughput

Economic historians appear united in capitalism's "consuming passion" for growth. William Baumol suggests that "the capitalist economy can usefully be viewed as a machine whose primary product is economic growth. Indeed, its effectiveness in this role is unparalleled" (2002: 1). The orthodoxy of growth contends that it will stabilize population by inducing a demographic transition, alleviate poverty via job creation and "trickle-down" effects, reduce inequality through a "rising tide that lifts all boats," and improve the environment by raising incomes and thus the means for clean-up, etc. Evidence in support of these "articles of faith" is quite mixed. Nonetheless, virtually all institutions (e.g. workers, consumers, public agencies, nonprofits, investors, etc.) have co-evolved to be dependent on the capitalist growth machine. This establishes the predicament of growth at the system level being environmentally unsustainable, but de-growth being socially and economically disruptive and painful (see Jackson 2009).

At the firm level, there is a near universal consensus on the capitalist "grow or die" imperative which Mander has described as "inexorable, unabatable and voracious" (1996: 322). Growth is variously needed to counter falling rates of profit; to sustain profitability (which in turn is needed to sustain growth); to realize cost-lowering economies of scale; to support innovative activity; to invest in new plant, equipment and inventory; to forestall the threat of new entrants entering markets; to justify the growth of top management compensation; to avoid threats of bankruptcy; to provide investors with expected rates of return; to pay the interest on debt; and to continually increase anticipated profits on which share prices, market capitalizations, and dividends depend. Paul Hawken argues that businesses "need to grow more quickly than ever before, due to the integration of capital markets and globalization; they are punished, even bankrupted, if they do not" (2007: 134).

The growth imperative of capitalism, endorsed by governments and consumers, drove world consumption of goods and services from $4.9 trillion in 1960 to $30.5 trillion in 2006 (both figures in 2008 dollars), resulting in a tripling of consumption expenditures per person over this time period (Assadourian 2010: 4). While this tripling was accompanied by significant reductions in resource and energy consumption per unit of GDP in high-income nations via dematerialization and substitution, all evidence indicates that throughput growth greatly exceeded the efficiency gains (see Speth 2008). Decoupling energy and matter throughput from economic growth as the planetary pathway to sustainability may thus be a myth: "simplistic assumptions that capitalism's propensity for efficiency will allow us to stabilize the climate or protect against resource scarcity are nothing short of delusional. Those who promote decoupling as an escape route from the dilemma of growth need to take a closer look at the historical evidence and at the basic arithmetic of growth" (Jackson 2009: 57).

Perhaps the greatest dilemma of our time is that, although the planet has billions of people living in poverty who want and need to consume more, and another two billion joining the human population by 2050, current levels of consumption may already exceed natural carrying capacity. The World Wildlife Fund for Nature claims that humanity's consumption of renewable ecological services surpassed the Earth's capacity to regenerate them in the mid 1980s, pushing humanity into a state of overshoot (WWF 2010). More than 80 percent of the world's people are now living in nations that are using more biocapacity than the ecosystems within their borders can produce. More than half of American renewable resource consumption, for example, now depends on the importation of goods and services generated from biocapacity elsewhere in the world, the harvesting of resources at home faster than rates of regeneration, and exportation of greenhouse gases into the global atmosphere (WWF 2010). The most capitalist economies of our world are the ones most living beyond their means.

Murray Bookchin (1990: 93–94), the father of libertarian socialist and ecological thought, warned that "to speak of 'limits to growth' under a capitalistic market economy is as meaningless as to speak of limits under a warrior society...Capitalism can no more be 'persuaded' to limit growth than a human being can be 'persuaded' to stop breathing. Attempts to 'green' capitalism, to make it 'ecological', are doomed by the very nature of the system of endless growth."

Contention 2: capitalism commands externalization of costs and risks

Businessman Robert Monks characterized the corporation as "an externalizing machine, in the same way that a shark is a killing machine...There isn't any question of malevolence or of will; the enterprise has within it, and the shark has within it, those characteristics that enable it to do that for which it was designed" (as quoted in Bakan 2004: 70). This compulsion for maximizing negative externalities or spillover effects in order to minimize operating costs is central to the capitalist mandates of increasing efficiency and profits, especially in the face of intense competition. As William Grieder (2003: 39) explains: "the logic of capitalism is ingeniously supple and complete, self-sustaining and forward-looking. Except for one large incapacity: As a matter of principle, it cannot take society's interests into account. The company's balance sheet has no way to recognize costs that are not its own, no reason or method to calculate the future liabilities it causes but someone else will have to pay. The incentives, in fact, run hard in the opposite direction. The firm will be rewarded with greater returns and higher stock prices if it manages to externalize its true operating costs."

Theories on the propensity of firms and industries to externalize their environmental and social costs are disparate and undeveloped. We would expect higher levels of cost and risk externalization to correlate positively with "gain-seeking" motivations (Kapp 1950) and the intensity of competitive pressures. Higher gain seeking might be motivated by falling profits, loss of market share, falling stock prices, entry of new competitors, consumer desire for lower prices, etc. Greater opportunities for cost externalization might be afforded by dynamic complexity, separating cause and effect in time and place; cumulative, indirect, synergistic environmental effects making it exceedingly difficult to claim or assign blame; more distant and nontransparent supply chains; excessive temporal and spatial discounting; exploitation of common property or open-access resources; ill-defined, insecure, or nonexistent property rights; absence of consumer, investor, and regulator concern for environmental and social side-effects; and the ease of garnering perverse subsidies, tax breaks, and deregulation from governments.

In the presence of significant negative externalities, prices generated within free markets will obviously fail to reflect ecological and social truth. The absence of correct signals regarding resource scarcity and damage will distort private cost-benefit calculations, resulting in overexploitation, mis-pricing of risk, and underinvestment in the conservation, protection, and regeneration of ecosystem services. The big question is how significant are negative externalities in today's capitalist economy? Neoclassical economists have generally assumed them to be very low and thus safely dismissed. Research efforts aimed at calculating the hidden costs of driving, flying, computing, electrifying, consuming meat, etc., however, show otherwise. The US National Research Council (2009), for example, conservatively estimated the hidden costs of fossil energy production and use in the US in 2005 at more than $120 billion. When the full range of externalized life-cycle costs (e.g. environmental damages, climate change-induced effects, governmental subsidies, economic costs, military and security costs, infrastructure costs, etc.) are added in, the total external costs of petroleum use in the US jump by some estimates to over $1,000 billion per year, implying that a fuel tax to internalize these costs would be in the 3 to 4 dollar range per gallon (see Victoria Transport Policy Institute 2010).

Contention 3: capitalism commands political and regulatory capture

Gus Speth warns that progress toward sustainability in the US is stymied by a massive political crisis: "the government in Washington is hobbled, corrupted by money, and typically at the service of economic interests, focused on the short-term horizons of election cycles, and poorly guided by an anemic environmental politics, a poorly informed public, and a pathetic level of public discourse on the environment" (2008: 62–63). While the erosion of democratic governance in the US and elsewhere has many explanations, direct and indirect corporate capture of politics and regulation stands at the forefront. The motivations and mechanisms of capture are now well understood: "regulatory capture occurs because groups or individuals with a high-stakes interest in the outcome of policy or regulatory decisions can be expected to focus their resources and energies in attempting to gain the policy outcomes they prefer, while members of the public, each with only a tiny individual stake in the outcome, will ignore it all together" (Laffont & Tirole 1991).

Business interests spent $2.8 billion to lobby policymakers and regulators in Washington in 2008 (representing 86 percent of total federal lobbying dollars) (Assadourian 2010: 14). Total spending to lobby Congress rose from $1.44 billion in 1998 to $3.49 billion in 2009, with nearly 14,000 officially registered lobbyists working the halls of the federal government. Informal estimates of the total number of lobbyists range up to 35,000, implying 38 lobbyists for each and every congressperson (Speth 2008: 162). These lobbyists work to secure favorable tax treatment and credits, procurement contracts, loan guarantees, subsidies, regulatory cutbacks, imposition of tariffs on foreign imports, and many other forms of "corporate welfare." They also work to impede new or stronger laws which have become "tortuously difficult to enact and invariably studded with purposeful loopholes designed to delay effective enforcement for years, even decades" (Greider 2003: 32).

In 2008 corporate interests spent $3.9 billion on donations to candidates for US federal political office, representing 71 percent of total political contributions (Assadourian 2010: 13–14). A growing body of research shows that corporate political contributions, lobbying efforts and political connections have significantly affected the allocation of government resources and added positive value for corporate shareholders (see e.g. Cooper et al. 2010). Beyond lobbying and campaign contributions, the insidious "revolving door" of moving executives across legislative, regulatory, lobbyist, consultancy, and private-sector positions has also lead to "ideological and social capture" of senior policy-makers and regulators (Davidoff 2010).

Capture of government by capitalism is buttressed by corporate capacities to control and manipulate the mental dispositions of all actors in society towards perpetual growth, rampant consumerism, and deregulation. Perhaps the greatest concern in this realm lies with growing consolidation of media ownership into the hands of just a few media conglomerates which control over half of the information networks in the world. Critics argue that concentrated corporate domination of what citizens watch, hear, or read on any day has slanted media toward pro-business ideology, far-right politics, sensationalism instead of critical journalism, reliance on PR and press releases as news, and hyper-commercialism serving the desires of advertisers, and away from unbiased, independent journalism (see McChesney 2008). Additional mechanisms of deep capture subverting truth, independence and accountability include the growing infiltration of industry into academia and large donations to charities, professional societies and research institutes aimed at silencing criticism and gaining "innocence by association."

Contention 4: capitalism commands degenerative globalization

While globalization involves a wide variety of cultural, political, legal, technological, and military dimensions, the focus here is on economic globalization in the form of cross-border trade, foreign direct investment and flows of financial capital. While the world has witnessed previous waves of economic globalization, the current one "is characterized by a combination of magnitude, spatial reach, and pace that has no counterpart in the history of the planet" (Young et al. 2006: 30). The International Monetary Fund estimates that the value of trade as a percentage of world GDP (gross domestic product) rose from 42 percent in 1980 to 62 percent in 2007; the ratio of foreign investment to world GDP increased from 6.5 percent in 1980 to 32 percent in 2006, and the stock of international bank loans and other financial claims as a percentage of world GDP soared from about 10 percent in 1980 to 48 percent in 2006 (IMF 2008). These increases greatly exceed the growth rate of overall world output in recent decades. Most of this rapid growth is accounted for by multinational firms interconnecting both high-income markets and a relatively small number of "emerging" middle-income markets.

Marxists suggested long ago that the imperatives of capital accumulation would necessitate spatial and "imperialist" extension of capitalism (see Harvey 2007). The consequences of this extension for environmental sustainability remain highly contested despite a massive surge of scholarly interest in the topic (see Christmann & Taylor [Chapter 3] this volume). This is due to the extraordinary complexity of the phenomenon along with ideological dogmatism and paradigmatic differences which conspire to create a "dialog of the deaf" between the critics and supporters of globalization. There are literally hundreds of direct and indirect pathways by which economic globalization might impact the environment, both negatively and positively.

Arguments in support of negative impact are diverse and interact with all of the other commandments of capitalism. This author (Gladwin 1998) has argued that globalization: results in enhanced economic efficiency arising from specialization and interdependence through international exchange leading to lower prices, output expansion and faster rates of economic growth; provides access to the world's remaining stocks of unexploited or underutilized natural capital, inevitably accelerating their depletion; makes it possible for high-income countries to live beyond their means by appropriating the biocapacity from other parts of the world, contributing to overshoot; promotes resource-intensive lifestyles through advertising exalting materialistic values and behaviors, as well as commercializing the lives of the world's children; boosts the generation and displacement of environmental externalities; facilitates biological invasions via international freight transport; displaces small-scale farming with materially intensive, large-scale, mono-cultural, export-oriented industrial farming systems; physically separates production from consumption, diffusing responsibility and accountability for environmental costs; and induces an environmental and social "race to the bottom" through standards-lowering competition, limiting the ability of individual governments to regulate firm behavior, redistribute income, finance social programs and impose tougher environmental standards. How these negative impacts balance out with the positive impacts of globalization may never be known.

Contention 5: capitalism commands financial myopia

Financialization, as a secular tendency in modern capitalism, refers broadly to the "increasing role of financial motives, financial markets, financial actors and financial institutions in the operations of the domestic and international economies" (Epstein 2005: 3). The three central characteristics of contemporary financialized capitalism, according to Bresser-Pereira, are "first, a huge increase in the total value of financial assets circulating around the world as a consequence of the multiplication of financial instruments facilitated by securitization and by derivatives; second, the decoupling of the real economy and the financial economy with the wild creation of fictitious financial wealth benefiting capitalist rentiers; and third, a major increase in the profit rate of financial institutions and principally in their capacity to pay large bonuses to financial traders for their ability to increase capitalist rents" (2010: 8–9).

The ascendancy of finance in contemporary capitalism is variously attributed to the stagflation and falling profit rates in the real sector during the 1970s, financial deregulation of the early 1980s, worldwide liberalization of capital movements, adoption of investment banking practices by commercial banks, and technological revolutions in information and telecommunications. As a result, the total value of the world's financial assets—including equities, private and public debt, and bank deposits—climbed from US $12 trillion in 1980 (equal to 120 percent of global GDP) to $196 trillion in 2007 (equal to 359 percent of global GDP or "real" wealth) (McKinsey Global Institute 2008). With "socially responsible investments" standing at only about $4 trillion worldwide (Social Investment Forum Foundation 2010), this implies that only about 2 percent of the world's total financial assets were being invested according to positive or negative screens based on social environmental and governance criteria.

The spectacular growth of financialization is indicated by a variety of other statistics (see Epstein 2005). Trading in US equities grew from $136 billion in 1970 to $14.2 trillion in 2000. Direct ownership of these stocks by US households dropped from 92 percent in 1950 to 24 percent in 2008, with control shifting into the hands of giant pension, mutual fund, and other financial institutions. As a result, long-term investing based on intrinsic value shifted to short-term speculation based on stock prices (turnover of stocks ranging from 20 to 30 percent in the 1950–60s grew to an estimated 300 percent in 2008). US credit market debt rose from 1.6 times the nation's GDP in 1973 to over 3.5 times GDP by 2007. The annual ratio of global foreign-exchange trading to world trade rose from 2:1 in 1973 to 90:1 in 2004. The share of US GDP accounted for by the financial sector grew from 11 percent in 1950 to 20 percent in 2005. The pre-tax profits of financial corporations in the US rose from an average of 14 percent of all corporate profits in the 1960s to 37 percent of all corporate profits during 2000–2006.

Korten believes that the financialization of capitalism has served to produce "an out-of-control and out-of-touch financial system devoted to speculation, inflating asset bubbles, stripping corporate assets, and predatory lending…we have a morally bankrupt money system accountable only to itself, detached from reality, and driven by unadulterated individualistic greed" (2009: 43 and 137). At the macro-level, financialization is blamed for a variety of sins, including greater insecurity, misdirection of talent, erosion of trust, concentration of wealth, global financial instability, concentration of political power, and the corruption of democracy, all inimical to sustainability (see Johnson & Kwak 2010).

At the firm level, financial values become leading institutional and organizational design criteria (Froud & Williams 2000). The "manic logic" of finance capital, impatiently searching for ever-higher and quicker market returns, is credited for the ascendancy of shareholder wealth maximization (especially in regard to insider and institutional owners) and short-termism in contemporary non-financial corporate decision-making (see Dore 2008), which has shifted managerial incentives toward raising the price of their company's stock and price to earnings ratios, rather than increasing the company's intrinsic value (see Bogle 2005). The growing transfer of non-financial corporate earnings to financial markets in the form of interest payments, dividend payments, and stock buybacks, along with the growth of income of non-financial firms derived from their own investments in short-term liquid financial assets and financial subsidiaries (Krippner 2005) is theorized to have resulted in decreased fixed investment rates, R&D spending and non-financial innovation, all working against long-term investments in sustainability.

Contention 6: capitalism commands freedom from regulation

Karl Polanyi, in his book *The Great Transformation*, warned that "to allow the market mechanism to be the sole director of the fate of human beings and the natural environment…would result in the demolition of society" (1944: 73). It is clear that all of the commandments of capitalism reinforce each other, but the bedrock foundation of them all is the poltical-economic philosophy of neo-liberalism. As captured by George Monbiot, "neo-liberalism claims that we are best served by maximum market freedom and minimum intervention by the state. The role of government should be confined to creating and defending markets, protecting private property, and defending the realm. All other functions are better discharged by private enterprise, which will be prompted by the profit motive to supply essential services. By this means, enterprise is liberated, rational decisions are made and citizens are freed from the dehumanizing hand of the state" (Monbiot 2007: 1). Confronted with stagflation in the 1970s, the return to pre-WWI economic liberalism became a project of both industrial and, especially, financial capitalists "to reestablish the conditions for capitalist accumulation and to restore the power of economic elites" (Harvey 2005: 19). The re-ascendance of market fundamentalism was advanced by the rise of conservative "Thatcherism" in Britain and "Reaganomics" in the US during the 1980s.

Neo-liberalism became the ideological foundation of the "Washington Consensus" forged between the IMF, World Bank, and US Treasury on what constituted the set of policies that would best promote development. It emphasized the downsizing of government, deregulation, privatization of state-owned resources, elimination of trade barriers, reorientation of economies toward exports to earn foreign exchange for debt repayments, capital market liberalization, competitive exchange rates, tight money supply control, and constraints on wage growth (see Williamson 1990). These conditions were widely imposed on developing nations as the price of securing loan extensions as part of structural adjustment programs during the 1980–90s. The Consensus was dedicated to economic efficiency and according to Stiglitz: "paid too little attention to issues of equity, employment and competition…it focused too much on just an increase in GDP, not on other things that affect living standards, and focused too little on sustainability—on whether growth could be sustained economically, socially, politically or environmentally" (2006: 17).

Despite frayed confidence in the Consensus, neo-liberalism in general remains the dominant ideology shaping our world today. Critic Susan George traces its power to the brilliance of its proponents, making neo-liberalism "seem as if it were the natural and normal condition of humankind...the only possible economic and social order available to us...the major world religion with its dogmatic doctrine, its priesthood, its law-giving institutions and perhaps most important of all, its hell for heathen and sinners who dare to contest the revealed truth" (1999: 2–3).

Assessing the effects of this secular religion is quite difficult, given its multidimensional character, tight interactions with other capitalist propensities, and complex mix of direct and indirect, as well as local, regional and global consequences. A careful review of the impacts of neo-liberalism on the environment in Latin America by Liverman and Vilas discovered little evidence that the environment was better protected under neo-liberal policies and that its effects were highly "contingent on history and place" (2006: 331 and 356). Friends of the Earth International (2000: 7) more boldly asserts that neo-liberalism "encourages the pursuit of profit regardless of social and environment costs. It is associated with increasing levels of inequality, both between and within countries; the concentration of resources and power in fewer and fewer hands resulting in an erosion of democracy; economic, social, political and economic exclusion; economic instability; spiraling rates of natural resource exploitation; and a loss of biological and cultural diversity. It prevents the maintenance and development of locally-appropriate and sustainable systems of commerce."

Deep controversy surrounds the benefits and costs of neo-liberalism-induced devolution of regulatory responsibilities to local levels; privatization and commodification of un-owned, state-owned, and common property resources such as forest, freshwater and biodiversity; and the shift from command-and-control regulation to free-market environmentalism. There is much less debate as to the consequences of neo-liberalist deep cuts to national fiscal and administrative resources for environmental protection. John Judis (2010: 1–4) reports that all three neo-liberal Republican predecessors to President Obama in the US worked to weaken or destroy the nation's environmental regulatory apparatus by heading the involved agencies with business executives, corporate lawyers, and lobbyists; slashing the budgets of the regulatory agencies; and promoting cost-benefit analysis as an instrument of deregulation by stressing costs rather than benefits. Robert F. Kennedy, Jr. (2004) reports that the George W. Bush administration launched over 300 major rollbacks of US environmental laws; removed protection from millions of acres of public lands, wetlands, and water-bodies; muzzled, purged, and punished governmental environmental scientists; and manipulated, suppressed, and misrepresented all science at odds with corporate profits in an unprecedented manner.

THE MUTUAL REINFORCEMENT
OF CAPITALIST COMMANDMENTS

The operating codes or instructions of modern capitalism, which firms must comply with to survive, severely constrain the possibilities of bringing business into deep harmony with the full community of life. The mainstream B&NE field, as revealed in this Handbook, has largely, and perhaps dangerously, ignored these constraints. It is vital in moving forward to understand that the commandments of capitalism causally interact to create a powerful self-reinforcing system. All of the imperatives feed off each other to variously reduce restraints against, or increase possibilities for, the expansion and continued domination of capitalism. For example, the consuming passion for growth and accumulation through profits drives globalization, commodification, consumerism, and reward systems through-out society based on expansionist metrics. Corporate dominance of politics ensures the liberalized deregulation of commerce, and resultant freedom from responsibility and accountability, thereby magnifying possibilities for cost externalization, especially through global supply chains. This shifting lowers costs and prices, thus feeding elite consumption growth and faster liquidation of natural capital. Financialization fuels growth through credit and exorbitant demands for faster and higher profits, as well as concentratrating wealth and power, which in turn, increases elite political access and influence, thereby ensuring more privatization of profits and socialization of losses, ad infinitum.

The intensity and extensity of reinforcing loops within the current capitalist system suggest that partial or superficial interventions aimed at changing the system will encounter considerable "policy resistance" (e.g. likelihood of being delayed, diluted or defeated by the system's defensive responses to such attempted interventions). The behaviors within, and the conditions generated by, capitalism derive largely from more elemental and powerful mental programing. This suggests that interventions focusing only on changing behaviors (e.g. we'll solve this through more enlightened leaders or reduced advertising), or on ameliorating conditions (e.g. we'll solve this though greater redistribu-tion or more environmental restoration), are likely to have only limited impact. Even intervening to change institutions (e.g. we'll solve this by substituting sustainability for growth metrics or by raising fuel taxes) may also be of limited value if the addiction to growth as the answer to all problems remains intact. Unless we fundamentally change minds, we are unlikely to significantly change much of anything else about unsustainable capitalism. Finally, we should expect, because of the powerful mutually reinforcing nature of the system, that substantive change is unlikely to emerge from within the system and will have to be imposed from the outside. Mander (1991: 137) advises that we "must aban don the idea that corporations can reform themselves. To ask corporate executives to behave in a morally sensible manner is absurd. Corporations, and the people within them, are following a system of logic that leads inexorably toward dominant behaviors. To ask corporations to behave otherwise is like asking an army to adopt pacifism."

REFORMATION OF CAPITALISM AND THE B&NE FIELD

John Maynard Keynes declared after WWI that "the decadent international but individ-ualistic capitalism, in the hands of which we have found ourselves...is not a success. It is not intelligent, it is not beautiful, it is not just, it is not virtuous—and it doesn't deliver the goods. In short, we dislike it, and we are beginning to despise it. But when we wonder what to put in its place, we are extremely perplexed (1933: 239).

Assessments as to whether capitalism can be reformed to make it truly work for a sustainable future run the gamut from absolutely not, to hopefully so. Pessimists claim that power imbalances, addictions, idolatries, apathies, momentums, malignancies, inertias, lock-ins, rationalizations, and denials within and surrounding modern capitalism are too deep to expect any real change. Capitalism, in this view, is fundamentally irreparable, and will continue to devour nature until it destroys the ultimate basis of its own existence and sets off an eco-socialist revolution (see Magdoff & Foster 2010).

Many others reject this dark fate and believe that capitalism can indeed be reinvented to deliver a sustainable future. There is no shortage of visions for life after contemporary capitalism. Passionate, creative, and uplifting images have been painted for possible eco, whole earth, deep, steady state, localized, restorative, common good, and participatory economies of the future (see Speth 2008 for a review of these visions). The radically different foundational values underlying these economies (e.g. equity, diversity, solidarity, interdependence, responsibility, caring, etc.) make it possible to envision truly democratic, natural, commons-protecting, and moral varieties of capitalism that could work as if the world matters (see Porritt 2005 for a survey). These inspirational visions are all long on diagnoses of the environmental and social ills of modern capitalism and principles for future sustainable economies, but short on the pragmatic strategies and mechanisms needed to bring about the profound shifts of human consciousness and power alterations needed to make these sustainable systems possible.

"We have entered a period of danger...and consequences" warned Winston Churchill in 1936 as the Nazis were amassing and deploying their powers (see his quote at the start of this chapter). The same warning applies to the B&NE field today as the evidence of global environmental devastation and disruption mounts. The Earth needs a new operating system that massively reduces the destructive throughput growth, cost externalization, political capture, global degeneration, financial myopia, and regulatory minimization fomented by our current capitalism. Is the field willing to take on this grand challenge as its core purpose? How would the field need to evolve if it was to genuinely and resolutely pursue what eco-theologian Thomas Berry (2000) called "The Great Work" of fostering mutually enhancing human–Earth relations? Where would it go, and what would it do, to discover, construct, and ensure adoption of a new sustainable operating system? The answer, I believe, lies in grounding the work of the field more deeply in the bio-physical, socio-political, and moral-spiritual realms.

Many of the operating instructions for a sustainable economic system are derivable through "bio-mimicry," using nature as a model, measure, and mentor, based on billions of years of evolutionary wisdom. "The conscious emulation of life's genius," according to biologist Janine Benyus (1997: 2) suggests principles such as reliance on current solar income rather than fossilized energy, complete recycling rather than waste, regeneration rather than liquidation, local self-reliance rather than globalization, sufficiency rather than excess, resilience rather than efficiency, and qualitative improvement rather than quantitative expansion. The B&NE field needs to become proficient at analyzing the impacts of business according to the laws of biology, ecology, and thermodynamics which really matter, rather than the capitalist growth, profitability, market share, and competitive advantage metrics that contribute to ecological destruction.

The B&NE field must also rise up to the profound question posed by Jack Harich: "Why, despite over 30 years of prodigious effort, has the human system failed to solve the environmental sustainability problem?" (2010: 1). Harich argues that the forces resisting change have overwhelmed the forces favoring change and the underlying motivation to solve the problem. Paying greater attention to systemic change resistance would push the field more deeply into the realms of sociology and political science focusing on cultural transformation, power structures, civil society, perversion of democracy, social traps, and all of the "deep capture" imperatives of capitalism as reviewed above. At the organizational level, a vastly expanded focus on transformational change would require increased attention to change leadership, coalition-building, partnerships and alliances, open-sourcing, safe-to-fail experiments, intra-organizational entrepreneurship, the role of crises, intensity of exit and entry barriers, etc.

At the core, B&NE scholars must begin to raise profound moral questions about the wanton destruction of the life-support systems of the planet. They must address what business morally owes future human generations, the currently deprived and vulnerable, and the billions of other species that inhabit this planet. The field must offer judgments of what is right versus wrong and good versus evil. It must also assign duties and moral obligations, demand sacrifices, and normatively focus on what should be. Without reverence for life, care for creation and compassion for suffering, the field risks losing its heart and soul. It must lead to fundamental change. Niccolo Machiavelli in his *The Prince* back in 1532 warned that "there is nothing more difficult to take in hand, more perilous to conduct, or more uncertain in its success, than to take the lead in the introduction of a new order of things." Is the B&NE field up to this challenge?

References

Assadourian, E. (2010). "The Rise and Fall of Consumer Cultures," in L. Starke and L. Mastny (eds.), *2010 State of the World: Transforming Cultures*. New York: W.W. Norton, 3–20.

Bakan, J. (2004). *The Corporation: The Pathological Pursuit of Profit and Power*. New York: Free Press.

Baumol, W. (2002). *The Free Market Innovation Machine: Analyzing the Growth Miracle of Capitalism*. Princeton, N. J.: Princeton University Press.

Benyus, J. M. (1997). *Biomimicry: Innovation Inspired by Nature*. New York: William Morrow and Company.

Berry, T. (2000). *The Great Work: Our Way into the Future*. New York: Harmony Books.

Bogle, J. C. (2005). *The Battle for the Soul of Capitalism*. New Haven: Yale University Press.

Bookchin, M. (1980). *Toward an Ecological Society*. Montreal: Black Rose Books.

—— (1990). *Remaking Society: Pathways to a Green Future*. Montreal: Black Rose Books.

Bresser-pereira, L. (2010). "The Global Financial Crisis and a New Capitalism." Levy Economics Institute Working Paper 592, May 2010, viewed 17, November, 2010, <http://www.levy.org>

Carson, R. (1962). *Silent Spring*. Boston: Houghton Mifflin Co.

Cooper, M., H. Gulen, & A. Ovtchinnikov (2010). "Corporate Political Contributions and Stock Returns," *The Journal of Finance*, 65(2): 687–724.

Daly, H. E. & Farley, J. (2004). *Ecological Economics: Principles and Applications*. Washington, D.C.: Island Press.

Davidoff, S. M. (2010). "The Government's Elite and Regulatory Capture," *The New York Times*, June 11, 2010, viewed 17, November, 2010, <http://dealbook.blogs.nytimes.com/2010/06/11the-governments-elite-and-regulatory-capture/>

Dore, R. (2008). "Financialization of the Global Economy," *Industrial and Corporate Change*, 17(6): 1097–1112.

Epstein, G. (ed.) (2005). *Financialization and the World Economy*. Northhampton, MA: Edward Elgar Publishers.

Foster, J. B. (1999). *The Vulnerable Planet: A Short History of the Environment*. New York: Monthly Review Press.

Friends Of The Earth International. (2000). *Towards Sustainable Economies: Challenging Neoliberal Economic Globalization*. December 2000, viewed 17, November, 2010, <http://www.foei.org/en/resource/trade/archive/1_Dec_Summm_full.html/>

Froud, J. & Williams, K. (2000). "Shareholder Value and Financialization: Consultancy Promises and Management Motives," *Economy and Society*, 29(1): 80–110.

George, S. (1999). *A Short History of Neoliberalism: Twenty Years of Elite Economics and Emerging Opportunities for Structural Change*, viewed 17, November, 2010, <http://www.globalexchange.org/campaigns/econ101/neo-liberalism.html>

Gladwin, T. N. (1998). "Economic Globalization and Ecological Sustainability: Searching for Truth and Reconciliation," in N. Roome (ed.) *Sustainability Strategies for Industry*, Washington, D.C.: Island Press.

Grieder, W. (2003). *The Soul of Capitalism*. New York: Simon and Schuster.

Hawken, P. (2007). *Blessed Unrest*. New York: Viking Penquin.

—— (2009). *University of Portland Commencement Address to the Class of 2009*, viewed 17, November, 2010, <http://www.up.edu/commencemnet/default.aspx?cid=9456&pid=3144>

—— Lovins, A., & Lovins, L. H. (1999). *Natural Capitalism: Creating the Next Industrial Revolution*. Boston: Little, Brown and Company.

Harich, J. (2010). "Change Resistance as the Crux of the Environmental Sustainability Problem," *Systems Dynamics Review*, 26(1): 35–72.

Harvey, D. (2005). *A Brief History of Neoliberalism*. Oxford: Oxford University Press.

—— (2007). *The Limits to Capital*. London: Verso Books.

International Monetary Fund Staff. (2008). *Globalization: A Brief Overview*, viewed 17, November, 2010, <http://www.imf.org/external/np/exr/ib/2008/053008.htm>

Jackson, T. (2009). *Prosperity Without Growth: The Transition to a Sustainable Economy*. London: U.K. Sustainable Development Commission.

Johnson, S. & Kwak, J. (2010). *13 Bankers: The Wall Street Takeover and the Next Financial Meltdown*. New York: Random House.

Judis, J. B. (2010). "The Quiet Revolution," *The New Republic*, February 1, 2010, viewed 17, November, 2010, <http://www.tnr.com/print/article/politics//the-quiet-revolution/>

Kapp, K. W. (1950). *The Social Costs of Private Enterprise*. Cambridge, MA.: Harvard University Press.

Kennedy Jr., R. F. (2004). *Crimes Against Nature*. New York: HarperCollins.

Keynes, J. M. (1933). "National Self-Sufficiency," *The Yale Review*, June 1933, 21/4: Section 3/III.

Korten, D. C. (2009). *Agenda for a New Economy: From Phantom Wealth to Real Wealth*. San Francisco: Berret-Koehler.

Kovel, J. (2002). *The Enemy of Nature: The End of Capitalism or the End of the World*. London: Zed Books.

Krippner, G. (2005). "The Financialization of the American Economy," *Socio-Economic Review*, 3(2): 173–208.

Laffont, J. J. & Tirole, J. (1991). "The politics of government decision making. A theory of regulatory capture," *Quarterly Journal of Economics* 106(4): 1089–1127.

Liverman, D. & Vilas, S. (2006). "Neoliberalism and the Environment in Latin America," *Annual Review of Environmental Resources*, 31: 327–363.

McChesney, R. (2008). *The Political Economy of Media*. New York: Monthly Review Press.

McKinsey Global Institute. (2008). *Mapping Global Capital Markets: Fifth Annual Report*. San Francisco: McKinsey and Company.

Magdoff, F. & Foster, J. B. (2010). "What Every Environmentalist Needs to Know About Capitalism," *Monthly Review*, March 2010: 1–18, viewed 17, November, 2010, <http://monthlyreview.org/10030/magdoff-foster.php>

Mander, J. (1991). *In the Absence of the Sacred*. San Francisco: Sierra Club Books.

—— (1996). "The Rules of Corporate Behavior," in J. Mander and E. Goldsmith (eds.), *The Case Against the Global Economy*, San Francisco: Sierra Club Books, 309–322.

Millenium Ecosystem Assessment (2005). *Ecosystems and Human Well-Being: Synthesis*. Washington, D.C.: Island Press.

Monbiot, G. (2007). "How Did We Get Into This Mess," *The Guardian*, 28 August 2007, viewed 17, November, 2010, <http://www.monbiot.com/archives/2007/08/28/how-did-we-get-into-this-mess/>

Polanyi, K. (1944). *The Great Transformation*. Boston: Beacon.

Porritt, J. (2005). *Capitalism As If The World Matters*. London: Earthscan.

Rockstom, J. et al (2009). "A Safe Operating Space for Humanity," *Nature*, 461(24): 472–475.

Social Investment Forum Foundation (2010). *Report on Socially Responsible Investing: Trends in the United States*. Washington, D. C.: Social Investment Forum.

Speth, J. G. (2008). *The Bridge at the Edge of the World: Capitalism, the Environment, and Crossing from Crisis to Sustainability*. New Haven: Yale University Press.

Stiglitz, J. E. (2006). *Making Globalization Work*. New York: W. W. Norton.

United Nations Environment Programme (2007). *The Global Environment Outlook: Environment for Development [GEO-4]*. Nairobi: UNEP.

US National Research Council (2009). *Hidden Costs of Energy: Unpriced Consequences of Energy Production and Use*. Washington, D.C.: National Acadamies Press.

Victoria Transport Policy Institute (2010). *Resource Consumption External Costs*. (June 30, 2010), viewed 17, November, 2010, <<www.vtpi.org/tca/tca0512.pdf>

White, C. (2009). "The Barbaric Heart: Capitalism and the Crisis of Nature," *Orion Magazine* (May–June 2009), viewed 17, November, 2010, <http://orionmagazine.org./index.php/articles/article/4680/>

Wilber, K. (1995). *Sex, Ecology and Spirituality: The Spirit of Evolution*. Boston: Shambhala Publications.

Willamson, J. (1990). *Latin American Adjustment: How Much has Happened?* Washington, D.C.: Institute for International Economics.

World Wildlife Fund For Nature (2010). *Living Planet Report 2010: Biodiversity, Biocapacity and Development*. Gland, Switzerland: WWF.

Young, O. Berkhout, F., Gallopin, G., Janssen, M., Ostrom, E., & Vanderleeuw, S. (2006). "The Globalization of Socio-Ecological Systems: An Agenda for Scientific Research," Global Environmental Change, 16(3): 304–316.

INDEX

profit-seeking 462, 463–4, 466–8, 469
values-driven 462, 463, 464–6, 469
see also environmental performance
Investor Responsibility Research Center 84
investor returns 471–6
iron triangle theory 214
ISEA 3000 416
ISEAL Alliance 115
ISO standards 142
  ISO 2009 318
  ISO 9000 107, 108, 116, 236
  ISO 14001 32–3, 41, 42–3, 60, 61, 107, 108,
    110, 116, 217, 230, 231, 239, 281, 285, 328,
    562, 621
  ISO 26000 107, 528
  pressures to adopt 229–47
isomorphism 223
issue framing 254–5

jargon 202
Jevons, Stanley 484
Johnson, Eric 166
Jones Lang LaSalle 643
Judis, John 668
jurisdictional competition 147
just-in-time deliveries 274

Kahneman, Daniel 161
Kelly, Florence 543
Kennedy, Robert (CEO Union Carbide) 112
Kennedy, Robert F. Jr. 668
Kepone 547
Keynes, John Maynard 669
Killer Coke campaign 8
Kimberly-Clark 257
Kinder, Lydenberg, & Domini (KLD)
  assessment 38
knowledge-sharing 328
KPMG International 456
Krieger, Lou 640
Kyoto Protocol 222

labelling of green products 368, 369
Larrick, Richard 167

lawsuits 256
lead 329
leadership 34
  actions of 198
  in environmental action 198
  organizational 627
  in sustainability 198
lean systems 270
learning organizations with operational
    performance excellence 300
legacies 186–8
  see also intergenerational beneficence
legal issues 140–57
  compliance 147–9
  delay of wise policies 169–71
  design of 144–6
  domestic law 141, 142
  as driver for reuse 303–4
  enforcement 114–15, 129–30, 146–7
  formulation of 143–4
  future research 152–3
  global aspects 150–1
  impacts of 149–50
  informal law 141, 142–3
  international law 141
  Martin v. Wadell 543
  *Santa Clara County v. Southern Pacific
      Railway Company* 650
  soft laws 141, 142–3
  sources of 140–3
  see also individual laws
legislation
  as constraint to commercial use 540
  as driver for reuse 303–4
  Superfund 452, 454
  take-back 303
  see also legal issues; and individual laws
      and Acts
legitimacy theory 112, 450–1
Leopold, Aldo, *Sand County Almanac* 546
Levitt, Steven D., *Freakonomics* 164
LexisNexis 84
licensing 148–9
life cycle 293
  analysis 4, 274, 278–80, 311, 438, 582, 604
  costing 321, 435
  management 317